BANKRUPTCY PRACTICE SERIES

BANKRUPTCY DESK REFERENCE

Integrated Code and Rules

Jacqueline Varma
Law Offices of Jacqueline Varma
Adjunct Professor, Southern Methodist University,
Cox Business School
Dallas, Texas

SHEPARD'S/McGRAW-HILL, INC.
P.O. Box 35300
Colorado Springs, Colorado 80935-3530

THE *McGRAW•HILL* COMPANIES

New York • St. Louis • San Francisco • Auckland • Bogota • Caracas
Colorado Springs • Hamburg • Lisbon • London • Madrid • Mexico
Milan • Montreal • New Delhi • Panama • Paris • San Juan • Sao Paulo
Singapore • Sydney • Tokyo • Toronto

Library of Congress Cataloging-in-Publication Data

Varma, Jacqueline.
Bankruptcy desk reference : integrated code and rules / Jacqueline Varma.
p. cm. — (Bankruptcy practice series)
Includes index.
ISBN 0-07-172473-7
1. Bankruptcy—United States. I. Title. II. Series.
KF1524.V37 1993
346.73; 078—dc20
[347.30678]

93-16965
CIP

ISBN 0-07-172745-0
8381

The Sponsoring Editors for this book were Jon H. Starr and Kyle B. Usrey. The Legal Editor was Cathy McIntyre.

Shepard's Bankruptcy Practice Series

Bankruptcy Practice for the General Practitioner, Second Edition
Chapter 11 Reorganizations
Chapter 13 Practice and Procedure
Chapter 12 Farm Reorganizations
Creditors' Rights in Bankruptcy, Second Edition
Guide to Effective Bankruptcy Litigation

Shepard's Bankruptcy Practice Series

Bankruptcy Practice for the General Practitioner, Second Edition
Chapter 11 Reorganizations
Chapter 13 Practice and Procedure
Chapter 12 Farm Reorganizations
Creditors' Rights in Bankruptcy, Second Edition
Guide to Effective Bankruptcy Litigation

Dedicated To:

Professor Harvey Wingo
Philip I. Palmer, Jr., Esq.

With deepest respect,

Jacqueline Varma

Acknowledgment

To the many colleagues, members of the bankruptcy bar, and clerks of the court who gave their time so generously and unconditionally to make this book possible.

To Pam Barry who took my words and worked her computer "wizardry" to turn them into a book.

To Shepard's/McGraw-Hill, who made it all a reality.

My sincere appreciation,

Preface

Several years ago, while I was "matching up" requirements of the Bankruptcy Code in one book with requirements of the federal Bankruptcy Rules from another book, I realized how much simpler it would be if everything were explained in one place, or at least in one book.

Bankruptcy Desk Reference is that synthesis—the merger of related Bankruptcy Code sections with federal Bankruptcy Rules. *Bankruptcy Desk Reference* is not a replacement for the Code, Rules, or treatises. It is intended to be a "first stop," the launching pad to determine quickly "what's required, when it's required, how it's required," and "who gets notice of it" under bankruptcy law.

In any bankruptcy case, you need to know the bottom line quickly. That's what I aimed for with this book—a complete bottom line.

Contents

Summary

Detailed

II. Bankruptcy Code—General

I. Historical Development

I. Historical Development

A. Overview of Bankruptcy Law—Title 11, United States Code

Article 1, §8, clause 4 of the United States Constitution grants Congress the power "to establish . . . uniform laws on the subject of bankruptcies throughout the United States." Congress is not required to enact a bankruptcy law, only authorized and empowered to do so. Nevertheless, since 1898, federal bankruptcy law has been a constant factor in the debtor-creditor relationship in the United States.

1. Bankruptcy Act of 1898

The first major federal bankruptcy legislation was the Bankruptcy Act of 1898. Forty years later, the Bankruptcy Act was significantly amended by the Chandler Act of 1938. It took another 40 years for a major overhaul of the bankruptcy system to occur. On November 6, 1978, after years of study, hearings, and debates, the Bankruptcy Reform Act of 1978 was passed by Congress. *30 Stat 544 (1898); 52 Stat 541 (1938); Pub L No 95-598, 92 Stat 2549 (1978); HR Rep No 595, 95th Cong, 1st Sess (1977); S Rep No 989, 95th Cong, 2d Sess (1978); 11 USC §101 et seq.*

2. Bankruptcy Code of 1978

Effective October 1, 1979, the Bankruptcy Reform Act of 1978 [Bankruptcy Code] repealed the former Bankruptcy Act of 1898 and enacted a new Title 11, United States Code. One of the significant changes of the 1978 Bankruptcy Code and related legislation was creation of the office of the U.S. trustee. Originally, the U.S. trustee was established as a five-year pilot program in 18 federal judicial districts. The program was to end on April 1, 1984. The U.S. trustee, appointed by the Attorney General of the United States, performed certain administrative and advisory functions. One primary function was to establish, maintain, and supervise a panel of private trustees to serve under Chapter 7 liquidation cases. Additionally, the U.S. trustee was required to supervise the administration of cases and trustees in Chapter 7, 11, and 13 cases. In 1986, the U.S. trustee pilot program was made permanent. *Pub L No 95-598, 92 Stat 2549 (1978); Pub L No 99-554, 100 Stat 3097 (1986); 28 USC §§581-587.*

3. 1984 Amendments—The Bankruptcy Amendments and Federal Judgeship Act of 1984

Under former §1471 of Title 28, United States Code, bankruptcy judges were granted jurisdiction or authority to hear all Chapter 7, 9, 11, or 13 bankruptcy cases and all types of lawsuits that were related to or occurred in such bankruptcy cases. Bankruptcy judges are appointed under Article I, §8 of the United States Constitution. Article I bankruptcy judges are chosen by the respective federal circuit court of appeals to serve 14-year terms, with eligibility for reappointment, and their salaries may be reduced by Congress. Article III federal district judges are nominated by the President, confirmed by the United States Senate, have life tenure, and their salaries may be increased but not decreased by Congress. Yet prior to 1982, Article I bankruptcy judges had greater jurisdiction to hear more types of lawsuits than Article III federal district courts. In June of 1982, this changed.

The jurisdiction of bankruptcy courts under former §1471 of Title 28 was challenged as unconstitutional in the case of *Northern Pipeline Construction Co v Marathon Pipe Line Co,* 458 US 50 (1982). The issue presented to the Supreme Court was whether former §1471 granted too much power and authority to Article I bankruptcy judges, in violation of Article III of the United States Constitution. The Supreme Court determined that the broad grant of jurisdiction given to bankruptcy courts under former §1471 of Title 28 was unconstitutional, but stayed (delayed) its judgment until October 4, 1982, to afford Congress time to reform the bankruptcy courts or amend former §1471. This stay was later extended to December 24, 1982. On December 24, 1982, Congress had passed no new legislation.

To alleviate the situation, the Administrative Office of the United States Courts prepared and transmitted a SampleOrder and Emergency Rule (Emergency Rule) to the United States courts of appeals, district courts, and bankruptcy courts. The Emergency Rule authorized federal district courts to refer bankruptcy cases under Title 11 to bankruptcy judges during the period of October 1, 1979, to June 27, 1984, the transition period from the repealed 1898 Bankruptcy Act to the new 1978 Bankruptcy Code. *Administrative Office of US Courts, Sample Order and Emergency Rule (1982).*

By June 27, 1984, Congress still had not enacted new legislation. The Executive Committee of the Judicial Conference then adopted the *Resolution of June 28, 1984,* to govern the operation of bankruptcy cases and related matters. This resolution directed that all bankruptcy cases be filed with the federal district court. The bankruptcy court was deemed a separate administrative unit of the federal district court. Bankruptcy cases could then be referred to magistrates (bankruptcy judges) by the federal district judge. *Judicial Conference of US, Resolution of June 28, 1984.*

Finally, on June 29, 1984, Congress passed the Bankruptcy Amendments and Federal Judgeship Act of 1984, Pub L No 98-353, 98 Stat 333. The Act was signed by the President on July 10, 1984, the enactment date. The effective date of the 1984 Amendments was October 7, 1984, with certain exceptions. The Bankruptcy Amendments Act of 1984 basically retained the system established under the Resolution of June 28, 1984. The bankruptcy court was a "unit" of the federal district court. Federal district judges could "refer" all bankruptcy cases to the bankruptcy judges in their judicial district. Today, bankruptcy judges are "judicial officers" of the federal district courts under this referral system. *Pub L No 98-353, 98 Stat 333 (1984); 28 USC §151 et seq.*

4. 1986 Amendments—The Bankruptcy Judges, U.S. Trustees, and Family Farmer Bankruptcy Act of 1986

On October 3, 1986, Congress passed the Bankruptcy Judges, U.S. Trustees, and Family Farmer Bankruptcy Act of 1986, Pub L No 99-554, 100 Stat 3097. The 1986 Bankruptcy Act was signed by the President on October 27, 1986, and generally became effective on November 26, 1986.

The 1986 Amendments provided for three major changes to the Bankruptcy Code. First, the 1986 Act authorized appointment of an additional 52 bankruptcy judges. Second, the Act made the U.S. trustee system permanent and nearly nationwide, under the authority of the Attorney General of the United States, and repealed Chapter 15 of the Code which had dealt with the U.S. trustee system as a pilot program. Third, the 1986 Amendments included a new Chapter 12 dealing with the debt adjustment of family farmers. The family farmer provisions became effective on November 26, 1986, but did not affect any cases filed before such date. However, cases pending on November 26, 1986, could be converted to Chapter 12. Chapter 12, as presently enacted, is automatically repealed on October 1, 1993. All Chapter 12 cases and related matters pending on October 1, 1993, may be completed as if Chapter 12 were not repealed. *Pub L No 99-554, 100 Stat 3097 (1986), repealed Chapter 12 on Oct 1, 1993 by Pub L No 99-554, tit III, §302(f).*

5. 1988 Amendments: The Retiree Benefits Bankruptcy Protection Act of 1988

The 100th Congress passed the Retiree Benefits Bankruptcy Protection Act of 1988, effective June 16, 1988, the date of enactment. Under the 1988 Amendments, a Chapter 11 debtor may modify retiree benefits only after good-faith negotiations with the retirees' authorized representative fail. Retiree benefits may be reduced but not eliminated completely. *Pub L No 100-334, 102 Stat 610, effective June 16, 1988; 11 USC §§1114, 1129(a)(13).*

6. 1990 Amendments

In 1990, Congress passed the following statutes which amended the Bankruptcy Code:

a. Pub L No 101-311

Swap agreements and forward contracts are instruments used by corporations and financial institutions to hedge their bets and prevent losses resulting from fluctuations in interest and currency-exchange rates. Under this 1990 Act, swap agreements and forward contracts are not subject to the Bankruptcy Code's automatic stay provisions. *Pub L No 101-311, 104 Stat 267 (1990); 11 USC §362(b)(6), (7), (14).*

b. Pub L No 101-508 [Omnibus Budget Reconciliation Act of 1990]

This 1990 Act amended the Bankruptcy Code to prevent debtors who are educational institutions from losing accreditation and licensing when they file a bankruptcy petition. The act also amended the discharge provisions of the Code. Certain student loans are now nondischargeable debts under all bankruptcy cases, including Chapter 13 cases. *Pub L No 101-508 (1990); 11 USC §§103(a)(h), 523(a)(8), 541(b)(3), 1328(a)(2).*

c. Pub L No 101-509 [Treasury, Postal Service and General Government Appropriations Act of 1990]

This Act increased the compensation of Chapters 12 and 13 standing trustees. Standing trustees will additionally receive the cash value of employment benefits paid to other comparable federal employees. *Pub L No 101-509 (1990); 28 USC §586(e)(1).*

d. Pub L No 101-581 [Criminal Victims Protection Act of 1990-Mothers Against Drunk Drivers (MADD) Law]

This Act made obligations resulting from the death or personal injury caused by a debtor operating a motor vehicle while under the influence of a drug, alcohol, or other substance a nondischargeable debt of any individual (natural person) bankruptcy debtor, including Chapter 13 debtors. *Pub L No 101-581, 104 Stat 2865 (1990); 11 USC §§103(a), 523(a)(9), 1141(d)(2), 1228(a)(2), 1328(a)(2).*

e. Pub L No 101-647 [Crime Control Act of 1990]

This Act made obligations under any final judgment or decree arising from a debtor's fraud or defalcation while acting as a fiduciary to a financial institution nondischargeable debts, except under Chapters 9 and 13. The Act further made obligations resulting from a debtor's malicious or reckless failure to maintain the capital of a federal depository institution under a written commitment nondischargeable debts, except under Chapters 9 and 13. *Pub L No 101-647, 104 Stat 4867 (1990); 11 USC §§103(a), (e), 523(a)(11), (12), 901, 1141(d)(2), 1228(a)(2), 1328(a)(2).*

f. Pub L No 101-650 [Judicial Improvements Act of 1990]

This Act extended until October 1, 2002, the bankruptcy administrator program, effective only in Alabama and North Carolina as a substitute for the U.S. trustee system. The Act also extended the 14-year term of a bankruptcy judge an additional 180 days until a successor is appointed; and allowed bankruptcy judges to issue final appealable orders to abstain from hearing, or to remand a proceeding to another court. *Pub L No 101-650 (1990); 28 USC §§152(a)(1), 1334(c)(2), 1452(b).*

7. 1991 Amendments

In 1991, Congress passed only two bills amending bankruptcy law.

a. Pub L No 102-198 [Act to Make Certain Technical Corrections in the Judicial Improvements Act of 1990]

This technical amendment modified §305(c) of the Code by inserting the words "title 28" for "this title" (Title 11). Section 305(c) allows a bankruptcy court order to abstain or not abstain from hearing a bankruptcy case to be appealed only to the federal district court. Pub L No 102-198 (1991); 11 USC §305(c).

b. Pub L No 102-140 [Appropriations for the Departments of Justice and State, the Judiciary, and Related Agencies for Fiscal Year September 30, 1992]

This Act amended Title 28, §1930(a), United States Code, as follows:

(1) Filing fees for Chapter 11 nonrailroad debtors increased from \$500 to \$600. *28 USC §1930(a)(3), effective Dec 27, 1991;*

(2) Quarterly fees in Chapter 11 cases increased for all disbursements. *28 USC §1930(a)(6), effective Dec 27, 1991;* and

(3) Certain percentages of filing and quarterly fees collected under Chapter 11 cases were allocated to the U.S. trustee system. *28 USC §§589a(f), 1930(a)(3), (4), (6), effective Dec 27, 1991.*

8. 1992 Amendments

In 1992, four bankruptcy bills were passed by Congress.

a. Pub L No 102-361 [Bankruptcy Judgeship Act of 1992]

This 1992 Act was passed in response to the significant increase in bankruptcy filings, from 613,606 cases in 1988 to 943,987 cases filed in 1991. This 1992 Act amended Title 28, United States Code, to provide for an additional 35 bankruptcy judges: 25 permanent and 10 temporary bankruptcy judges. *Pub L No 102-361 (1992); Administrative Office of the US Courts; HR 5688; HR Rep No 825, 102d Cong, 2d Sess (1992); 138 Cong Rec (1992); 28 USC §152(a), (b).*

b. Pub L No 102-365 [Rail Safety Enforcement and Review Act of 1992]

This Act amended §365 of Title 11 by limiting the right of a trustee or debtor-air-carrier to assume, assign, or reject an unexpired lease of an airport terminal or gate. If a "termination event" occurs, the trustee or debtor who is an affected air-carrier-lessee may not assign an unexpired lease of an aircraft terminal or gate; and may be "deemed" to have rejected such lease unless it has been assumed by the fifth day after the termination event. A *termination event* occurs if a voluntary Chapter 7 petition is filed by a debtor who is an "affected" air-carrier-lessee, as defined under Pub L No 102-365, 106 Stat 972 and the Federal Aviation Act of 1958, 49 United States Code; if such debtor's bankruptcy case is converted to Chapter 7; or if the automatic stay is lifted with regard to certain essential aircraft or its equipment or parts needed for the debtor's effective reorganization. As presently enacted, these amendments to §365 of the Code are effective for the 12-month period beginning September 3, 1992, and apply to all debtor-air-carrier bankruptcy proceedings pending during this 12-month period. Congress will determine whether the amendments should continue to apply after such period. *Pub L No 102-365, 106 Stat 972 (1982), HR 2607; 11 USC §365(c)(4), (d)(5)-(9), (f)(1), as amended.*

c. Pub L No 102-395 [Appropriations for Departments of Commerce, Justice, and State, the Judiciary, and Related Agencies for Fiscal Year 1993]

Effective for fiscal year January 1, 1993, this Act provides for Environmental Cost Index (EST) increases of bankruptcy judges' salaries by 3.2% annually. *Pub L No 102-395, effective Oct 1, 1992.*

d. Pub L No 102-486 [Comprehensive National Energy Policy Act of 1992]

This Act amended §101 of Title 11 by adding new §101(21A) defining "farmout agreement." The act also amended §541 of Title 11 by adding new Subsection 541(b)(4) which excludes from property of the bankruptcy estate the debtor's interest in certain liquid or gaseous hydrocarbons which the debtor transferred or assigned under a farmout agreement. However, the consideration that the debtor retains or is entitled to receive under such transfer is part of the estate. *Pub L No. 102-486, amending and adding 11 USC §§101(21A), 541(b)(4), Oct 24, 1992.*

9. 1994 Amendments

In 1994, Congress passed two Acts that amended Title 11. The later Act made sweeping changes to the practice of bankruptcy law:

a. Pub L No 103-322 [Violent Crime Control and Law Enforcement Act of 1994]

This Act amended §523(a) of the Bankruptcy Code and added a thirteenth exception to discharge. A debt for payment of any restitution order issued under Title 18, United States Code, is nondischargeable under Chapters 7, 11, 12, and Chapter 13. *Pub L No. 103-322, 108 Stat 1796 (1994); 11 USC §§103(a), 523(a), 1141(d)(2), 1228(a)(2), 1328(a)(3).*

b. Pub L No 103-394 [Bankruptcy Reform Act of 1994]

This Act made substantial changes to the Bankruptcy Code and significantly increased the rights of creditors and debtors in bankruptcy cases. Some of the most important amendments include:

(1) Requiring that a final hearing on motions to lift the automatic stay be concluded no later than the thirtieth day after the preliminary hearing ends, unless the court extends the time upon consent of the parties-in-interest or for compelling circumstances;

(2) Doubling the amount of federal bankruptcy exemptions allowed to an individual debtor under §522(d) of the Bankruptcy Code;

(3) Increasing the total amount of debt permitted to file a Chapter 13 petition to $1 million for an individual debtor, or individual debtor and his spouse if a joint petition is filed;

(4) Expanding the role of the U.S. Trustee's Office in Chapter 7 cases and with regard to fee applications generally;

(5) Increasing the exceptions to the automatic stay for governmental authorities; paternity suits; and spouses, ex-spouses, and children of bankruptcy debtors;

(6) Curbing the trustee's super-avoidance powers and setting a maximum three-year statute of limitations period for the trustee to file a super-avoidance action;

(7) Protecting post-petition security interests on rents and hotel and public lodging revenues;

(8) Providing small business debtors a faster track through Chapter 11 reorganization cases;

(9) Providing that the judicial council of the federal circuits may establish a three-judge bankruptcy appellate panel service (BAPS) to hear appeals of bankruptcy cases upon consent of the appellant and appellee and authorization of the majority of the district judges for the federal judicial district where the bankruptcy case is pending. In the absence of such a BAPS or the requisite consent of the parties, the district courts will continue to hear appeals under 28 USC §158(a);

(10) Setting an 89-day post-petition grace period for Chapter 11 single asset real estate debtors. By the 90th day post-petition, such debtor must either file a Chapter 11 plan of reorganization that has a reasonable possibility of confirmation or commence fair market interest rate payments to mortgagees, or risk the bankruptcy court's lifting the automatic stay; and

(11) Expanding the role of bankruptcy courts to expedite all bankruptcy proceedings and consolidate Chapter 11 hearings on the disclosure statement and confirmation of the plan of reorganization. *Pub L No 103-394.*

B. Federal Rules of Bankruptcy Procedure

1. Overview

The Federal Rules of Bankruptcy Procedure (FRBP or Federal Bankruptcy Rules), like the Federal Rules of Civil Procedure, govern the procedural aspects of bankruptcy cases and hearings (trials and contested matters) to implement the provisions of the Bankruptcy Code. As Congress amends the Bankruptcy Code, amendments to the Bankruptcy Rules also become necessary.

2. Bankruptcy Rules Amendments

Section 2075, Title 28, United States Code, empowers the United States Supreme Court "to prescribe by general rules, . . . the forms . . . practice and procedure in cases under Title 11" (cases under Chapters 7, 9, 11, 12, and 13 of the Bankruptcy Code). Section 331 of Title 28 permits the Judicial Conference Committee on Rules of Practice and Procedure to submit new rules, amendments, and forms to the Supreme Court for its approval. The Chief Justice of the Supreme Court must then send all approved changes to Congress. The Bankruptcy Rules and Forms may be changed but may not reduce, enlarge, or modify the substantive provisions of the Bankruptcy Code. The Chief Justice must submit the new rules to Congress no later than May 1st of the year in which such rules are prescribed. The rules become effective on December 1st of the same year unless Congress acts on the rules or if otherwise provided by law. *Pub L No 103-394, §104(f), effective October 22, 1994, amending 28 USC §2075. Judicial Improvements and Access to Justice Act, Pub L No 100-702 (1988); 28 USC §§331, 2071, 2075.*

C. Local Bankruptcy Rules

Federal Bankruptcy Rule 9029 permits each federal district court, by action of a majority of its judges, to adopt local bankruptcy rules governing bankruptcy cases and proceedings within its judicial district. The federal district court may also authorize bankruptcy judges of the district to adopt local bankruptcy rules to govern practices before their court. Local bankruptcy rules may not be inconsistent with the FRBP and may neither prohibit nor limit the use of Official Bankruptcy Forms. *FRBP 9029; FRCP 83.*

D. Official Bankruptcy Forms

The Judicial Conference of the United States prescribes Official Bankruptcy Forms (Official Forms). The Director of the Administrative Office of the United States may issue additional bankruptcy forms. The Official Forms must be used where appropriate. However, only substantial compliance is required. The Official Forms may be combined or their content altered to facilitate their use, but the Official Forms must be consistent with the substantive provisions of the Bankruptcy Code and the FRBP. *FRBP 9009, advisory committee's note.*

Research Guide

Drake, *Bankruptcy Practice for the General Practitioner* chs 1, 2 (Shepard's/McGraw-Hill 2d ed 1990)

Drake & Morris, *Chapter 13: Practice and Procedure* ch 1 (Shepard's/McGraw-Hill 1983)

Murphy, *Creditor's Rights in Bankruptcy* ch 1 (Shepard's/McGraw-Hill 2d ed 1988)

Pollard & Burton, *Guide to Effective Bankruptcy Litigation* ch 1 (Shepard's/McGraw-Hill 1988)

II. Bankruptcy Code—General Overview

II. Bankruptcy Code—General Overview

A. Organization and Structure of the Bankruptcy Code
   11 USC §103
   1. Chapter 1: General Provisions
   2. Chapter 3: Case Administration
   3. Chapter 5: Creditors, Debtor, and the Estate
   4. Chapter 7: Liquidation
   5. Chapter 9: Adjustment of Debts of a Municipality
   6. Chapter 11: Reorganization
   7. Chapter 12: Adjustment of Debts of a Family Farmer with Regular Annual Income
   8. Chapter 13: Adjustment of Debts of an Individual with Regular Income

B. Key Bankruptcy Terms
   11 USC §§101, 902, 1101
   FRBP 9001-9002

C. Who May Be a Debtor
   1. Generally
      11 USC §109(a), (g)
   2. Chapter 7
      11 USC §109(b)
   3. Chapter 9
      11 USC §§101(40), 109(c)
   4. Chapter 11
      11 USC §109(b), (d)
   5. Chapter 12
      11 USC §§101(18)-(19), 109(f)
   6. Chapter 13
      11 USC §109(e)

D. Filing Fees
28 USC §1930(a), (b), Judicial Conference Schedule of Fees (8)
FRBP 1006
1. Prescribed Fees
2. Installment Fees

E. How a Bankruptcy Case Is Commenced
1. Voluntary Cases
11 USC §§301, 342
FRBP 1002, 1005-1009
2. Joint Cases
11 USC §§302, 342
FRBP 1002, 1004-1009, 1015
3. Involuntary Cases
11 USC §§303, 342
FRBP 1003-1004, 1010-1011, 1018

F. Nine Stages of Every Voluntary Bankruptcy Case
1. Stage One—File Petition
11 USC §§301-302, 342
FRBP 1002, 1004-1005, 1008-1009, 2002
2. Stage Two—Automatic Stay Invoked
11 USC §§361-362
28 USC §1930(b), Judicial Conference Schedule of Fees (21)
FRBP 4001, 9013-9014
a. Generally
b. Actions the Automatic Stay Does Not Stop
c. Relief from the Stay
(1) Court Lifts the Stay
(a) Motion for Relief
(b) Service of Motion
(c) Answer May Be Required
(d) Grounds for Lifting the Stay
(e) Hearing Before 30th Day
(f) Final Hearing
(g) Violation of Automatic Stay
(2) Trustee Abandons Property
(3) Automatic Stay Ends
3. Stage Three—Creation of a Bankruptcy Estate
11 USC §541
a. What Property Is in the Estate
b. What Property Is Not in the Estate
c. Who Owns the Estate

4. Stage Four—Turn Over Property to the Estate
   11 USC §§542-543
   FRBP 6002, 7001(1) et seq
   a. Generally
   b. Complaint for Turnover Order
   c. Exceptions
   d. Custodian
5. Stage Five—Exemptions Claimed by the Debtor
   11 USC §§521(1), 522(b), (d), (l)
   FRBP 1007(b), 4003
   a. What Is Exempt Property
   b. Purpose for Exemptions
   c. Who Claims Exemptions
   d. How and When to Claim Exemptions
   e. Exemption Law(s)
   f. Objections to Exemptions
   g. Amended List of Exemptions
   h. Waiver of Exemptions
6. Stage Six—Meeting of Creditors
   11 USC §§103(a), 341, 343
   FRBP 2003
   a. What It Is
   b. When It Is Held
   c. Where It Is Held
   d. Who Attends
   e. Who Presides
   f. Special Examination of Chapter 7 Debtors
7. Stage Seven—Distribution of the Estate
   11 USC §§323, 503, 507, 541, 554, 724-726, 901, 944, 1129, 1225, 1226(c), 1325, 1326(c)
   FRBP 3009-3011
   a. Generally
   b. Priority Claims
      11 USC §§503, 507
      FRBP 3001-3008
   (1) What They Are
   (2) Rules of Distribution
   (3) Nine Categories of Priority Claims
      (a) First Priority Claims
      (b) Second Priority Claims
      (c) Third Priority Claims
      (d) Fourth Priority Claims
      (e) Fifth Priority Claims

(f) Sixth Priority Claims
(g) Seventh Priority Claims
(h) Eighth Priority Claims
(i) Ninth Priority Claims
(4) Procedures for Allowance of Priority Claims
(a) Allowance of Claims Generally
(b) Allowance of Second through Eighth Priority Claims
(c) Allowance of First Priority Claims
(d) Notice and Hearing on First Priority Claims

8. Stage Eight—Discharge of the Debtor
11 USC §§727, 944, 1141, 1228, 1328
FRBP 2002(f)(4)-(5), 4002, 4004-4007, 7001(4), (6) et seq
   a. Generally
   b. What It Is
   c. Legal Effects
   d. Who Receives the Discharge
   e. When Is a Discharge Granted
   f. Waiver of Discharge
9. Stage Nine—Closing the Case
11 USC §350
FRBP 5009
   a. Chapters 7, 12, and 13 Cases
   b. Chapter 11 Cases
   c. Chapter 9 Cases
   d. Reopening a Case

G. Requirements of Debtor's Attorney
11 USC §§327-331
FRBP 2002(a)(7), 2014, 2016-2017
1. Required Court Documents
   a. Statement of Compensation
   b. Application for Compensation
2. Denial or Return of Compensation
   a. Procedures for Denial or Return of Compensation
   b. Grounds for Denial or Return of Compensation

Research Guide

II. Bankruptcy Code—General Overview

A. Organization and Structure of The Bankruptcy Code

The Bankruptcy Code (Title 11) contains eight chapters:

1. Chapter 1: General Provisions
2. Chapter 3: Case Administration
3. Chapter 5: Creditors, Debtor, and the Estate
4. Chapter 7: Liquidation

5. Chapter 9: Adjustment of Debts of a Municipality
6. Chapter 11: Reorganization
7. Chapter 12: Adjustment of Debts of a Family Farmer with Regular Annual Income
8. Chapter 13: Adjustment of Debts of an Individual with Regular Income

Chapters 1 (general provisions), 3 (case administration), and 5 (creditors, debtor, and the bankruptcy estate) are comprehensive chapters that apply to Chapter 7, 11, 12, and 13 bankruptcy cases, and to a limited degree to Chapter 9 cases involving a municipality. Chapters 7, 9, 11, 12, and 13 are the operative chapters of the Bankruptcy Code. A bankruptcy petition must be filed under either Chapter 7, 9, 11, 12, or 13. *11 USC §103; HR Rep No 595, 95th Cong, 1st Sess 316 (1977).*

In a Chapter 7 liquidation case, a trustee is appointed to take possession of all the debtor's nonexempt property. The Chapter 7 trustee will eventually liquidate (sell) such property and distribute the proceeds to creditors. A secured creditor with a valid lien on property will receive the lesser of the collateral (or its value) or the amount of the secured creditors's claim allowed by the bankruptcy court. The Chapter 7 trustee will distribute remaining proceeds pro rata to unsecured creditors. *See "Stage Five—Exemptions Claimed by the Debtor" and "Stage Seven—Distribution of the Estate," discussed below; Chapter III; 11 USC §§103(a), 323, 724-726.*

In all other bankruptcy cases (Chapters 11, 12, and 13), the debtor retains possession of exempt and nonexempt property. The debtor is afforded this right by paying unsecured creditors at least the value of the nonexempt property and paying secured creditors the lesser of the value of their collateral or the allowed amount of their claim under a plan. *See Chapters III-VII; 11 USC §§103(a)(3), 901, 944, 1129, 1225, 1325.*

B. Key Bankruptcy Terms

The following terms are frequently used in bankruptcy cases.

1. **Adversary Complaint:** lawsuit filed in a Chapter 7, 9, 11, 12, or 13 bankruptcy case. *FRBP 7001 et seq.*

2. **Allowed Claim:** claim of a creditor allowed by the bankruptcy court for sharing in distribution of the bankruptcy estate. *11 USC §§501-502; FRBP 3001, 3002(a), 3003-3008.*

3. **Bankruptcy Code (Code):** Title 11, United States Code.

4. **Case:** bankruptcy proceeding commenced by filing a bankruptcy petition under Chapter 7, 9, 11, 12, or 13 of the Bankruptcy Code. *11 USC §§301-304.*

5. **Claim:** any right to payment, or equitable remedy for breach of performance that creates a right to payment. *11 USC §101(5).*

6. **Clerk:** bankruptcy clerk (court officer for receiving bankruptcy records) if one has been appointed in a federal judicial district; otherwise, the clerk of the federal district court. *FRBP 9001-9002.*
7. **Consumer Debt:** debt incurred primarily for personal, family, or household purposes. *11 USC §101(8).*
8. **Court:** bankruptcy or federal district court or judge (the judicial officer) before whom a bankruptcy case or proceeding is pending. *FRBP 9001-9002.*
9. **Creditor:** entity that holds a claim against the bankruptcy debtor. *11 USC §101(10).*
10. **Debtor:** entity against whom a claim is held; bankruptcy debtor, including a person under Chapter 7, 11, 12, or 13, or municipality under Chapter 9 of the Bankruptcy Code. *11 USC §§101(13), 109.*
11. **Debtor-In-Possession (DIP):** Chapter 11 or 12 bankruptcy debtor. *11 USC §§1101(1), 1203.*
12. **Entity:** includes a person, estate, trust, governmental unit, and U.S. trustee. *11 USC §101(15).*
13. **Equity Security Holder:** person who holds an equity security (stock, corporate share, limited partner's interest in a limited partnership, warrant to buy or sell a corporate share or limited partnership interest) of a bankruptcy debtor. *11 USC §101(16)-(17).*
14. **Estate:** bankruptcy estate created by filing a Chapter 7, 11, 12, or 13 petition, consisting of all the debtor's interests in property, wherever such property may be located. *11 USC §541.*
15. **Exempt Property:** property claimed by an individual debtor that is not subject to the claims of unsecured creditors. However, exempt property is generally subject to the claim of any secured creditor with a valid lien against such property under applicable nonbankruptcy law. *11 USC §522(b)-(d).*
16. **Individual:** natural person; not a partnership or corporation.
17. **Insider:** includes a relative or general partner of an individual debtor; director, officer, or person in control of a corporate debtor; general partner or relative of a general partner of a partnership debtor; and partnership of a debtor who is a general partner. *11 USC §101(31).*
18. **Meeting of Creditors:** meeting between the debtor and creditors in a Chapter 7, 11, 12, or 13 case, at which the U.S. trustee presides and the debtor is examined under oath about the administration of the bankruptcy case and the bankruptcy estate. *11 USC §§341, 343.*
19. **Notice:** includes service by mail, personal delivery, or any other manner allowed under the Federal Rules of Civil Procedure for service of motions or process in federal district court. Notice to the debtor, trustee, or any committee in a bankruptcy case includes notice to any attorney representing such entity in a bankruptcy case.

20. **Order for Relief:** filing of a voluntary bankruptcy petition; or the order adjudicating a debtor to be a bankruptcy debtor after an involuntary bankruptcy petition is filed. *11 USC §§301-303.*

21. **Party-In-Interest:** a debtor, creditor, trustee, U.S. trustee, or person who has an interest in property of the debtor or the estate or the administration of a bankruptcy case.

22. **Person:** includes an individual, partnership, and corporation, but does not include a governmental entity unless such entity acquired an asset from a person under a loan guarantee agreement or as a receiver or liquidating agent of a person. *11 USC §101(41).*

23. **Personal Property:** movable goods.

24. **Petition:** bankruptcy petition filed to commence a Chapter 7, 9, 11, 12, or 13 case. *11 USC §§301-304.*

25. **Post-Petition:** period after a bankruptcy petition is filed. *11 USC §§301-304.*

26. **Pre-Petition:** period before a bankruptcy petition is filed. *11 USC §§301-304.*

27. **Priority Claims:** unsecured claims entitled to payment from the bankruptcy estate before general unsecured creditors are paid. *11 USC §§503, 507, 726.*

28. **Proceeding:** bankruptcy case; hearing before the bankruptcy or federal district court concerning a contested or uncontested issue in a bankruptcy case. *FRBP 9013-9014.*

29. **Pro-Rata Payment:** the same percentage of payment to each member of the same class of creditors or equity security holders. *11 USC §§103(a), (e), 503, 507, 726(b), 901, 1123(a)(4), 1222(a)(3), 1322(a)(3).*

30. **Real Property:** land or real estate, together with all improvements thereon that cannot be removed without damaging the land.

31. **Request:** motion for relief sought in a bankruptcy case, which may be contested or uncontested. *FRBP 9013-9014.*

32. **Secured Claim:** claim secured by a lien or charge against property of the debtor or estate to secure payment of a debt or performance of an obligation; amount of a creditor's debt owed to the debtor subject to a setoff against a creditor's claim held against the debtor. *11 USC §§101(37), (50)-(51), 506(a).*

33. **Secured Creditor:** creditor whose claim is subject to a setoff or is secured by a lien on property of the debtor or estate. A creditor's claim is secured for the lesser of the allowed amount of the claim or the value of collateral or amount subject to a setoff. A creditor's claim may be both secured (for the value of the collateral or amount subject to a setoff) and unsecured (for the difference between the allowed amount of the claim and the value of the collateral or amount subject to a

setoff). Thus, if a creditor has a $100 claim allowed by the court and the collateral is worth $20, the creditor is undersecured, with a secured claim of $20 and an unsecured (deficiency) claim of $80. If the creditor's allowed claim is $100 and $30 is owed by the creditor to the debtor and subject to a setoff, the creditor's secured claim is $30 and unsecured claim is $70. A creditor whose allowed claim is less than the value of collateral is oversecured. *11 USC §§101(5), (10), (37), (50)-(51), 362(b)(7), 506(a), 553. See "Avoidable Setoffs," Chapter XII.*

34. **Setoff:** procedure by which a creditor may offset a claim against the debtor against an obligation owed to the debtor. Thus, a creditor with a $100 allowed claim against the debtor and who owes the debtor $25 may be allowed to setoff the two amounts for net allowed claim of $75. *See "Avoidable Setoffs," Chapter XII. 11 USC §§362(a)(7), 506(a), 553.*

35. **Standing Trustee:** individual appointed by the U.S. trustee under 28 USC §586(b), subject to approval of the United States Attorney General, to serve as a trustee under Chapter 12 or 13 cases. *28 USC §586(b).*

36. **Trustee:** includes a Chapter 9 debtor and a Chapter 11 or 12 debtor-in-possession; individual appointed by the U.S. trustee pursuant to court order in Chapter 11 cases; individual selected from a panel of private trustees established and maintained by the U.S. trustee for Chapter 7 cases; and individual appointed by the court to file an action to recover an avoidable preferential, fraudulent, or unauthorized post-petition transfer of property if the Chapter 9 debtor refuses to file such actions. *11 USC §§322, 701, 902(5), 926, 1104, 1202, 1302; 28 USC §586(a).*

37. **Unsecured Claim:** claim that is not secured by a lien. *11 USC §101(5), (37), (50)-(51).*

38. **U.S. Trustee:** individual appointed by the Attorney General to serve as U.S. trustee under bankruptcy cases for a term of five years and thereafter until a successor is appointed and qualifies; includes an assistant U.S. trustee and any designee of a U.S. trustee. *28 USC §§581-582; FRBP 9001(11).*

C. Who May Be a Debtor

1. Generally

To be eligible to be a debtor under the Bankruptcy Code, the debtor must be a person (individual, partnership, or corporation) who resides or has a domicile, place of business, or property in the United States or must be a municipality. However, an individual (natural person) or family farmer may not be a bankruptcy debtor until 181 days after the court dismissed a previous bankruptcy case, if the prior case was dismissed because:

a. The debtor willfully failed to obey a court order or appear before the court to prosecute (continue) the previous case; or

b. The debtor requested and received a voluntary dismissal of the previous case after a motion for relief from the automatic stay was filed. *11 USC §§101(27), (41), 109(a), (g); see Chapter II; "Stage Two—Automatic Stay Invoked," discussed below, and Chapter XIV.*

The debtor must file his bankruptcy petition with the clerk of the bankruptcy court. If the debtor is an individual with primarily consumer debts (incurred for personal, family, or household purposes), the clerk must first give the debtor written notice about each Chapter (7, 11, 12, or 13) under which such debtor could file a bankruptcy petition. The clerk must then mail notice of the debtor's bankruptcy petition (the order for relief) to the debtor, any trustee, the U.S. trustee, all creditors, all committee(s), the SEC in Washington, DC, and local District Director of the IRS in a Chapter 11 case, all indenture trustees, and to any other entity required by court order or local bankruptcy rules. *11 USC §§109, 301-302, 342(a)-(b); FRBP 2002(f)(1), (k), 5005(a), 9001(3)-(4), 9002(3)-(4).*

2. Chapter 7

A person may be a debtor under Chapter 7. However, a railroad, insurance company, bank, industrial bank, savings and loan association, homestead association, small business investment company licensed by the Small Business Administration under §301(c) or (d) of the 1958 Small Business Investment Act, or credit union may not be a debtor under Chapter 7. *11 USC §109(b).*

3. Chapter 9

Only a municipality specifically authorized by state law to be a bankruptcy debtor may file a bankruptcy petition under Chapter 9. *11 USC §109(c).*

4. Chapter 11

Only a person who may be a Chapter 7 debtor may file a petition under Chapter 11, with two exceptions. First, a stockbroker (person who deals in securities), commodity broker (futures commission or leverage transaction merchant, or commodity options dealer) may file a bankruptcy petition under Chapter 7 but not under Chapter 11. Only Chapter 7 contains special rules for treatment of customer accounts that form the substance of stockbroker and commodity broker liquidations. Second, a railroad may file a petition under Chapter 11, but not under Chapter 7. *11 USC §§101(7), (54), 109(b), (d); HR Rep No 595, 95th Cong, 1st Sess 318-20 (1977); S Rep No 989, 95th Cong, 2d Sess 31 (1978).*

A Chapter 11 debtor does not have to be a business debtor. Individual debtors who are not engaged in business may file for protection under Chapter 11 if such debtors could also be Chapter 7 debtors. *Toibb v Radloff, 501 US 157, 111 S Ct 2197 (1991); 11 USC §109(b), (d).*

5. Chapter 12

A Chapter 12 debtor must be a family farmer with regular annual income sufficiently stable to make payments under a Chapter 12 plan. A family farmer may be an individual, partnership, or corporation.

a. Individual Chapter 12 Debtor

On the date the petition is filed, the debtor (alone or with his spouse) must be engaged in farming operations and have aggregate debts that do not exceed $1.5 million. The debtor must also have at least 80 per cent of his aggregate, noncontingent, liquidated debts arise from farming operation(s) (tillage of the soil, farming, ranching) which the debtor owns or operates. However, a debt for the principal residence of such individual, or individual and his spouse, is excluded unless the debt arises out of farming operation(s). And the debtor's farming operations must have produced more than 50 per cent of the debtor's gross income for the preceding taxable year before the Chapter 12 petition is filed.

b. Corporate or Partnership Chapter 12 Debtor

The corporate or partnership debtor must be owned by one family (including relatives of such family) which conducts the farming operation(s). The debtor's aggregate debts must not exceed $1.5 million on the date the petition is filed and more than 80 per cent of the value of its assets must relate to farming operation(s). A debt for a dwelling owned by the corporation or partnership and used by a shareholder or partner as a principal residence is excluded unless such debt arises out of farming operation(s). Finally, if the debtor issues stock, it must not be publicly traded. *11 USC §§101(18), (21), 109(f).*

6. Chapter 13

A Chapter 13 debtor must be an individual with regular income that owes, on the date the bankruptcy petition is filed, less than $250,000 noncontingent, liquidated, unsecured debts; and less than $750,000 noncontingent, liquidated, secured debts. An individual and his spouse with the same aggregate debt structure may file a joint petition under Chapter 13. However, a stockbroker or commodity broker may not file a petition under Chapter 13. *11 USC §109(e).*

D. Filing Fees

Title 28, United States Code, governs the respective filing fee required for each bankruptcy case.

1. Prescribed Fees

The prescribed filing fee must be paid to the bankruptcy clerk when the bankruptcy petition is filed, unless installment fee payments are allowed by the court.

a. Chapter 7 case: $160 ($130 filing fee plus $30 administrative fee);

b. Chapter 9 case: $300;

c. **Chapter 11 case:** $800 if the debtor is not a railroad/$1,000 for a railroad;

d. **Chapter 12 case:** $200; and

e. **Chapter 13 case:** $160 ($130 filing fee plus $30 administrative fee). *28 USC §1930(a)(1)-(5)(b), Judicial Conference Schedule of Fees (8); FRBP 1006(a).*

2. **Installment Fees**

An individual debtor may file a single petition or joint voluntary petition with his spouse without paying the required filing fee if the petition is accompanied by a signed application to pay such fee in installments. The debtor's application must state three matters:

a. **The debtor is unable to pay the filing fee except in installments.**

b. **The proposed terms for installment payments.**

The number of installments may not exceed four and the final installment payment must not be later than the 120th day after the petition is filed. The court may extend the date(s) for installment payments if cause is shown. However, the court may not extend the final payment later than the 180th day after the petition is filed.

c. **The debtor has neither paid money nor transferred property to an attorney for services related to the bankruptcy case.**

The court must rule on the debtor's application before the meeting of creditors (*see "Stage Six—Meeting of Creditors," discussed below*). The court may order the debtor to pay the clerk the full filing fee or to make installment payments. The court order must set the number and respective amounts and dates of installment payments, subject to the above rules. Neither the debtor's attorney nor any other person who renders services to the debtor under the bankruptcy case may be paid until the filing fee has been fully paid. *28 USC §1930(a); FRBP 1006(b); Official Bankr Form 3.*

E. How a Bankruptcy Case is Commenced

1. Voluntary Cases

A voluntary bankruptcy case begins by the debtor filing a bankruptcy petition under Title 11 with the bankruptcy clerk. The debtor must sign an acknowledged bankruptcy petition, pay the requisite filing fee (in full or installments) established for each bankruptcy case, and comply with federal and local bankruptcy rules. The bankruptcy petition must also be signed by any attorney representing the debtor. Upon filing the petition, a bankruptcy order for relief is automatically issued in a voluntary Chapter 7, 11, 12, or 13 case without a hearing before the bankruptcy court. *11 USC §301; FRBP 1002, 1006, 1008, 5005(a), 9001(3), 9002(3); Official Bankr Forms 1, 2.*

The Code also requires the debtor to file a list of creditors (mailing matrix) or schedules of assets and liabilities with the petition. Additionally, the debtor must file a schedule of current income and expenditures, statement of financial affairs, and statement of executory contracts, unless the court orders otherwise. However, the debtor may commence a bankruptcy case by filing a bankruptcy petition with a list of creditors, paying the filing fee at the bankruptcy clerk's office or submitting an application to pay such fee in installments, and thereafter filing the required schedules and statements before the 15th day after the voluntary petition is filed. *11 USC §521; FRBP 1007; Official Bankr Forms 1, 2, 6, 7; see "Procedure Two—Debtor's Duties," Chapters III-V.*

2. Joint Cases

Under Title 11, a husband and wife may file a joint case by filing a joint bankruptcy petition with the bankruptcy clerk under Chapters 7, 11, 12, or 13. However, both the husband and wife must be eligible to be debtors under the particular chapter in which the petition is filed. Only a husband and wife may file a joint case, not an individual and his business. A bankruptcy order for relief is automatically issued upon filing a voluntary joint petition without a hearing before the bankruptcy court. The court will then determine the extent to which the debtors' estates should be consolidated. *11 USC §§301-302; FRBP 1015.*

3. Involuntary Case

a. Generally

An involuntary petition may only be filed under Chapters 7 and 11 and only against a person who is eligible to be a debtor under the respective chapters. Chapters 9, 12, and 13 are totally voluntary. An involuntary petition may not be filed under such chapters.

An involuntary petition may not be filed against a farmer, family farmer, or a charitable or eleemosynary institution (church, school, charitable organization or foundation) under any chapter. *11 USC §303(a); Official Bankr Form 5.*

b. Who May File an Involuntary Petition

(1) Twelve or More Creditors

If the debtor has twelve or more creditors, then at least three creditors must join as petitioning creditors to file the involuntary petition. Each creditor must have a claim against the debtor that is not contingent (dependent upon a future event) as to liability and that is not the subject of a bona fide dispute by the debtor. The claims of all (three or more) petitioning creditors must total at least $10,000 more than the value of any lien on the debtor's property held by any of the petitioning creditors. *11 USC §303(b)(1).*

Generally, petitioning creditors are unsecured creditors whose claims must total at least $10,000. However, a secured creditor may be one of the petitioning creditors. Thus, if there are four petitioning creditors—Creditor A with an unsecured claim of $3,000, Creditor B with an unsecured claim of $3,000, Creditor C with a fully secured claim of $1,000 (the collateral is worth the amount of the claim), and Creditor D with an unsecured claim of $5,000—the $10,000-aggregate-claims requirement has been met. The aggregate claims ($11,000) of Creditors A, B, and D total at least $10,000 more than the $1,000 value of the lien held by one of such creditors (Creditor C). *See Paradise Hotel Corp v Bank of Nova Scotia, 18 CBC2d 838 (3d Cir 1988).*

(2) Fewer Than Twelve Creditors

If the debtor has fewer than twelve creditors, only one creditor with a claim of at least $10,000 is required to file the involuntary petition. Employees, insiders of the debtor, and recipients of avoidable transfers under bankruptcy law are not counted in the total number of creditors. Also, a creditor who received a voidable preference or fraudulent transfer of property from the debtor is not counted in the total number of creditors. *See Chapter XII. 11 USC §303(b)(2).*

(3) Partnership Debtor

If the debtor is a partnership, an involuntary petition may be filed against the partnership:

(a) By less than all the general partners; or

(b) If all the general partners are bankruptcy debtors, then by any general partner or creditor of the partnership or by a bankruptcy trustee of one of the general partners. *11 USC §303(b)(3); FRBP 1004(b).*

c. Grounds for Filing an Involuntary Petition

There are only two grounds for filing an involuntary petition. The petitioning creditor(s) have the burden of proving at least one of the two grounds:

(1) The debtor is generally not paying his debts as they mature and become due.

Debts subject to a bona fide dispute by the debtor are not counted; or

(2) A custodian was appointed and took possession of substantially all of the debtor's property during the 120 days immediately before the involuntary petition was filed.

A trustee, receiver, or agent appointed under a security agreement is not counted if such entity was appointed to enforce a lien by taking possession of less than substantially all of the debtor's property. *11 USC §303(h).*

d. Procedures in an Involuntary Bankruptcy Case

(1) File Petition and Pay Fee

The petitioning creditors must file the involuntary petition with the bankruptcy clerk and pay the respective filing fee. *See "Filing Fees," discussed above; 28 USC §1930(a); FRBP 1006; Official Bankr Form 5.*

(2) Serve Petition

Filing an involuntary petition commences an adversary proceeding (lawsuit). The bankruptcy clerk must immediately issue a summons after the involuntary petition is filed. The petitioning creditors must serve a copy of the involuntary petition with the summons on the debtor by first-class mail or any other manner provided for service of a summons and complaint in federal district court. *FRBP 1010, 7004(a)-(b); Official Bankr Form 5; Procedural Bankr Form B 250E.*

When an involuntary petition is filed against a partnership, the clerk must immediately issue a summons to be served on each general partner who is not a petitioner. The petitioners must then serve a copy of the involuntary petition with a summons on each nonpetitioning general partner in any manner allowed for service of process in federal district court. *FRBP 1004(b), 1010, 7004(a)-(b), (f); Procedural Bankr Form B 250E.*

(3) Debtor's Answer

The debtor has the right to contest the involuntary petition. If he wishes to oppose the petition, the debtor must file an answer with the court and serve it on the petitioning creditors before the 20th day after the summons is served on the debtor. However, the time for the debtor to file and serve an answer is extended if the debtor files a motion to dismiss the involuntary petition within such 20-day period for: (a) lack of subject matter or personal jurisdiction of the court; (b) improper venue; (c) insufficiency of process or service of process; (d) failure to state a claim upon which relief may be granted; or (e) failure to join an indispensable person. The debtor must then file and serve an answer before the 10th day after notice of the court's ruling denying or postponing disposition of the motion to dismiss until trial on the merits; or before the 10th day after service of a more definite statement if the court grants a motion for more definite statement. If the debtor does not timely file and serve an answer, the court must enter an order for relief on the next day or as soon as practical, adjudicating the debtor to be a bankruptcy debtor. *FRBP 1011(b)-(c), 1013(b)-(c); FRCP 12(a)-(b); Procedural Bankr Form B 253.*

If the debtor does timely file and serve an answer, the court must set a trial date at the earliest possible time. The debtor may only assert a counterclaim against the petitioners to defeat the grounds or allegations stated in the involuntary petition. If the debtor alleges in the answer to an involuntary petition with fewer than three petitioning creditors that he has twelve or more creditors, the debtor must file a list of creditors with the answer. The list of creditors must include the name, address, amount, and brief statement of the nature of the claim held by each creditor. If it appears that there are in fact twelve or more creditors, the court must allow other creditors a reasonable time to join in the petition before the hearing (trial) on the petition is held. *FRBP 1003(b), 1011(d).*

If the involuntary petition is filed against a partnership, an answer may be filed by either a nonpetitioning general partner or person denying an allegation that such person is a general partner. The answer must be filed with the court and served on the petitioners before the 20th day after service of the summons or an order for relief adjudicating the debtor a bankruptcy debtor will be entered by default. *FRBP 1011, 1013.*

(4) Additional Petitioning Creditors

After the involuntary petition is filed, any other unsecured creditor whose claim is not contingent may join in the petition as a petitioning creditor. However, the unsecured creditor who wishes to join as an additional petitioning creditor must do so before the court issues an order for relief or order dismissing the involuntary petition. *11 USC §303(c).*

(5) Operation of Debtor's Business

After an involuntary petition is filed, a business debtor may continue business operations, including using, acquiring, or disposing of property, until the court issues an order for relief or other order directing otherwise. Creditors' claims allowed by the court which arise in the ordinary course of the debtor's business or financial affairs between the date that the involuntary petition is filed and the earlier date of the order for relief or appointment of a trustee are treated as second priority claims for purposes of distribution of the estate. *See "Priority Claims," discussed below; "File Proof of Claim," Chapter XIV; 11 USC §§303(f), 502(f), 507(a)(2).*

(6) Court's Ruling

After the trial on the involuntary petition, the Court must either enter an order for relief adjudicating the debtor a bankruptcy debtor, dismiss the petition, or enter any other order(s) that the court deems appropriate. If the court dismisses the petition and the debtor does not waive his right to judgment, the court may award the debtor costs and reasonable attorneys' fees against the petitioning creditors plus compensatory and punitive damages against any petitioning creditor who filed the involuntary petition in bad faith. *11 USC §§105(a), 303(i); FRBP 1013.*

F. Nine Stages of Every Voluntary Bankruptcy Case

There are nine stages common to voluntary bankruptcy cases, regardless of whether the bankruptcy petition is filed under Chapter 7, 11, 12, or 13.

1. Stage One—File Petition

Filing a bankruptcy petition immediately sets in process four events. First, filing the bankruptcy petition commences or begins the bankruptcy case. Second, at the moment the petition is filed, an automatic stay is invoked, barring any act by a creditor or any other entity against the bankruptcy debtor, his property, or property of the estate, with certain exceptions, discussed below. Third, filing the petition creates a bankruptcy estate, consisting of all the debtor's interests and rights to all his property, wherever located. Fourth, filing a voluntary bankruptcy petition constitutes an order for relief under bankruptcy law, immediately affording the debtor protections under Title 11. *11 USC §§301, 362, 541; see "Stage Two—Automatic Stay Invoked" and "Stage Three—Creation of a Bankruptcy Estate" discussed below.*

2. Stage Two—Automatic Stay Invoked

a. Generally

Filing a voluntary (or involuntary) bankruptcy petition operates as an automatic stay (temporary injunction) prohibiting all creditors and other entities from attempting to collect a debt or obligation owed by the debtor, generally before the petition was filed. This automatic stay or injunction includes a bar against:

(1) Commencing or continuing any lawsuit or action against the debtor to collect or enforce a pre-petition claim;

(2) Attempting to repossess any property of the debtor;

(3) Contacting the debtor to collect or enforce a pre-petition debt owed by the debtor;

(4) Enforcing any pre-petition judgment against the debtor or property of the estate (all the debtor's property and interests in property that are not claimed as exempt. *See discussion below*);

(5) Taking any act to obtain possession or exercise control over property of the estate, whether the claim arose pre- or post-petition;

(6) Taking any act to create, perfect, or enforce any lien against property of the estate;

(7) Attempting to setoff any debt owed by a creditor to the debtor against a claim held by the creditor against the debtor; and

(8) Commencing or continuing any proceeding before the United States Tax Court involving the debtor, whether the tax claim arose pre- or post-petition. *11 USC §362(a)(1)-(8).*

b. Actions the Automatic Stay Does Not Stop

The automatic stay does not enjoin numerous actions by secured creditors, government, regulatory, and other entities to enforce certain powers, including:

(1) Maintaining or continuing perfection of a pre-petition security interest by giving timely notice to the trustee and filing a continuation statement or taking any other action required by applicable law;

(2) Commencing or continuing a criminal action against the debtor;

(3) Commencing or continuing an action or proceeding to establish paternity;

(4) Commencing or continuing an action to establish or modify a court order for alimony, maintenance, or support payments;

(5) Collecting alimony, maintenance, or support payments from property that is not property of the bankruptcy estate (the individual debtor's wages or salary earned after filing a Chapter 7 or 11 petition);

(6) Commencing or continuing an action or proceeding by a governmental unit to enforce its police or regulatory powers. Administrative proceedings brought by the Federal Reserve Board against an insured bank fall within the parameters of a "governmental unit's police or regulatory power." *See Board of Governors of the Federal Reserve System v MCorp Financial, Inc, 502 US 32, 112 S Ct 459 (1991);*

(7) An audit to determine the debtor's tax liability by a governmental unit;

(8) The demand for tax returns by a governmental unit;

(9) Making an assessment for any tax and issuing a notice and demand for payment of the tax assessment. However, no post-petition tax lien will result from such an assessment unless: (a) the tax debt is otherwise nondischargeable in the debtor's bankruptcy case under 11 USC §§507(a)(2)(8) and 523(a)(1); and (b) the property or its proceeds to which the tax lien would attach under applicable nonbankruptcy law is either exempted by the debtor under 11 USC §522(b)(d), abandoned to the debtor by the trustee under 11 USC §554 or

§725, or revested in the debtor under a confirmed plan or under 11 USC §1141(b), §1227(b), or §1327(b);

(10) Issuing notice of a tax deficiency to the debtor by a governmental unit;

(11) Creating or perfecting a statutory lien for an ad valorem property tax imposed by a municipality or political subdivision of a state or by the District of Columbia. However, the underlying property tax must mature or otherwise become due postpetition for the automatic stay exception to apply;

(12) Enforcing a nonmonetary judgment obtained by a governmental unit to enforce its police or regulatory powers;

(13) Presenting a negotiable instrument issued by the debtor and giving notice and protesting dishonor of such instrument;

(14) The setoff by a swap participant under a swap agreement of a claim for payment owed by the debtor against any payment owed to the debtor or against any cash, securities, or other property of the debtor owed by the swap participant to guarantee, secure, or settle the swap agreement;

(15) The setoff by a repo participant under a repurchase agreement of a claim for a margin or settlement payment owed by the debtor against cash, securities, or other property of the debtor owed by the repo participant to margin, guarantee, secure, or settle the repurchase agreement;

(16) The setoff by a commodity broker, forward contract merchant, stockbroker, financial institution, or securities clearing agency under a commodity, forward, or securities contract, of a claim for a margin or settlement payment owed by the debtor against cash, securities, or other property of the debtor owed by such broker, merchant, institution, or agency, to margin, guarantee, secure, or settle such contract;

(17) An act by a lessor to obtain possession of nonresidential real estate (commercial land) under a lease that terminated by the expiration of the stated term of the lease either pre- or postpetition;

(18) An action by an accrediting agency concerning the accreditation status of an educational institution debtor;

(19) An action by a state licensing body concerning the licensure of an educational institution debtor;

(20) An action by the Secretary of Housing and Urban Development to foreclose a mortgage or deed of trust held by the Secretary and insured, or formerly insured, under the National Housing Act, involving five or more living units of property; or

(21) An action by the Secretary of Education or a guaranty agency as defined under the 1965 Higher Education Act, *20 USC §1001 et seq.*, concerning the debtor's eligibility to participate in programs authorized by the Higher Education Act. *11 USC §§362(b), 541(a)(6), 1207, 1306.*

c. Relief from the Stay

A party-in-interest (creditor, co-owner of property) may obtain relief from the automatic stay in basically three ways: the court may lift the stay; the trustee or Chapter 11 or 12 DIP may abandon the property at issue; or the automatic stay may terminate under bankruptcy law without necessity of a court order lifting the stay.

(1) Court Lifts the Stay

(a) Motion for Relief

The bankruptcy court may lift the automatic stay with regard to a particular creditor or other party-in-interest. The party-in-interest must file a motion for relief from the stay and pay a $60 filing fee. The party-in-interest must serve a copy of the motion for relief on the debtor and prove grounds for the court to lift the stay. (*See "Grounds for Lifting the Stay," discussed below*). *11 USC §362(d); 28 USC §1930(b), Judicial Conference Schedule Of Fees (21); FRBP 4001, 9014.*

(b) Service of Motion

A motion for relief from the stay does not commence an adversary proceeding. But the motion must be served on the debtor by first-class mail, personal delivery by a disinterested person at least 18 years old, or by any other manner provided for service of process in federal district court. A copy of the motion for relief should also be served on any trustee and committee appointed in the debtor's case. *FRBP 4001, 7004, 9013-9014.*

(c) Answer May Be Required

The motion for relief is not an adversary complaint. The debtor does not have to file an answer or response unless the court or local bankruptcy rules direct otherwise. No default judgment or lifting of the stay will be obtained for failure to file an answer or response unless an answer is required by court order or local Bankruptcy Rules. *FRBP 9014; see Local Bankr Rules.*

(d) Grounds for Lifting the Stay

There are essentially three grounds for lifting the automatic stay:

(i) For cause, including lack of adequate protection of the co-owner's or creditor's interest in property (collateral). The debtor has the burden of proof on the issue of adequate protection. The debtor must prove there is adequate protection. The creditor or co-owner does not have to prove the absence of adequate protection to prevail, although such party-in-interest will generally allege facts supporting this ground if asserted in the motion and will present evidence on the issue at the hearing; or

(ii) Lack of equity in the property protected by the automatic stay and such property is not necessary for the debtor's effective reorganization (rehabilitation under Title 11). The creditor or party filing the motion for relief has the burden of proving lack of equity. But the debtor or trustee or party opposing the motion has the burden of proving that the property is necessary for the debtor's successful rehabilitation under his bankruptcy case. This burden requires the debtor or trustee or party opposing the motion to prove to the court that there is "a reasonable possibility" that the debtor will successfully reorganize (rehabilitate) under Title 11 "within a reasonable time." *United Savings Association v Timbers of Inwood Forest Associates, 484 US 365 (1988); 11 USC §362(g);* or

(iii) The debtor is a single asset real estate debtor (usually a Chapter 11 debtor) and, by the end of the 90th day after the order for relief is entered, the debtor has either: (a) failed to file a plan of reorganization that reflects a reasonable possibility of confirmation by the court within a reasonable time; or (b) failed to begin making monthly payments to *each* secured creditor with a lien against the real estate equal to the current fair market rate of interest on the value of each creditor's lienhold interest in the land. Creditors with a judgment lien (obtained by judgment, levy, sequestration, or other legal or equitable process) or an unmatured statutory lien on the real estate are excluded from the 90-day mandates and remain subject to the automatic stay of the Bankruptcy Code. The bankruptcy court may extend the 90-day period for cause, but a motion and court order must be entered before the end of the 90-day period. *HR 5116, Pub L No 103-394, §218, amending and adding 11 USC §§101(51)(B) and 362(d)(3)(A)(B).*

Single asset real estate is a legal term of art defined by the Bankruptcy Code as any real property (except residential realty with fewer than four residential units) that: (a) constitutes a single property or project; (b) generates substantially all the debtor's gross income; (c) provides no other substantial business conducted by the debtor except the business of operating the realty and activities incidental to such business operations; and (d) has a maximum of $4 million noncontingent, liquidated secured debt(s). *HR 5116, Pub L No 103-394, §218(a), amending and adding 11 USC §101(51)(B).*

(e) Hearing Before 30th Day

The debtor or trustee or other party-in-interest (any creditors' committee) must obtain at least a preliminary hearing on the motion for relief before the 30th day after the motion is filed or the automatic stay will terminate by operation of bankruptcy law, without necessity of a court order lifting the stay. If the stay terminates or is lifted by the court, the creditor may proceed against the debtor and/or collateral under applicable nonbankruptcy law, depending on the relief sought under the creditor's motion. However, the bankruptcy court does have the equitable and legal power to issue an order reinstating the automatic stay. *11 USC §§105(a), 362(e); FRBP 4001; see "Motion for Relief from Automatic Stay," Chapter XIV.*

(f) Final Hearing

If the initial hearing is only a preliminary hearing, the court must find that there is a "reasonable likelihood" the debtor will prevail at the final hearing to order the stay continued. The final hearing then must conclude no later than the 30th day after the preliminary hearing ends, or the automatic stay terminates without necessity of a court order. However, the 30-day period may be extended by: (i) consent of all the parties-in-interest; or (ii) the bankruptcy court, *for a specific time*, if the court finds compelling circumstances exist for the extension of time. *11 USC §§105(a), 362(e), FRBP 4001, see "Motion for Relief from Automatic Stay," Chapter XIV.*

The party opposing the motion for relief should obtain a court order extending the 30-day period *before* such period expires. *11 USC §362(e).*

Thus, the journey of the debtor and a creditor who files a motion for relief from the automatic stay is as follows:

Day 1:	**Motion for relief from automatic stay filed;**
Day __ (See Local Bankr. Rules) after motion for relief filed:	**Local bankruptcy rules may require timely answer by debtor or other party-in-interest trustee upon penalty of stay being lifted;**
Day 30 after motion filed:	**Stay automatically terminates unless hearing (preliminary or final) held and order issued continuing the stay;**
Day 30 after preliminary hearing ends:	**Final hearing must conclude if initial hearing was preliminary hearing or stay terminates.** ***11 USC §362(d)-(e); FRBP 4001; see Local Bankruptcy Rules.***

(g) Violation of Automatic Stay

(i) Generally:

With limited exceptions, an action taken by any entity which violates the automatic stay is void *ab initio* (from the beginning) and has no legal effect. In the eyes of the law, such action is a legal nullity. A Chapter 9, 11, or 12 debtor or a trustee in any other case may file an adversary complaint to recover any property of the debtor or estate seized by the creditor post-petition. No filing fee will be required if a Chapter 9 debtor (municipality) files the adversary complaint. A $120 filing fee will be required if a Chapter 11 or 12 debtor-in-possession or a trustee files the complaint. However, such filing fee is payable only from any estate which may exist. If there is no estate (all property is claimed as exempt by the debtor or abandoned by the trustee; or no nonexempt property is recovered by the debtor or trustee), no filing fee is collected. *28 USC §1930(b), Judicial Conference Schedule of Fees (6). See In re Frosdick, 5 CBC2d 1123 (Bankr ND Ohio 1981); In re Grover, 3 CBC2d 257 (Bankr D Colo 1980); and In re Hawaii Mini-Storage Systems, 1 CBC2d 616 (D Haw 1980).*

The debtor or trustee must serve a copy of the adversary complaint with a summons on the defendant-creditor by first-class mail, personal delivery by a disinterested person at least 18 years old, or any other manner allowed for service of process in federal district court. If the creditor has not seized property but has taken some other action, the debtor or trustee may file an adversary complaint to enforce the automatic stay (injunction), to impose sanctions against the creditor, or for other equitable relief. *11 USC §362; FRBP 7001(1), (7), 7004 et seq; Official Bankr Forms B 250A, B, C.*

If the trustee or an individual debtor can prove injury caused by the creditor's willful violation of the automatic stay, such creditor must pay the actual damages, including the costs and attorneys' fees, incurred by the trustee or individual debtor in filing and prosecuting the adversary complaint. In appropriate circumstances, the creditor must also pay punitive damages for the creditor's willful violation of the stay. A willful violation may occur if the creditor takes any action against the debtor, his property, or property of the estate after receiving a telephone call from the debtor or his attorney notifying the creditor that a petition has been filed. A telephone call from the debtor or his attorney before the petition is filed notifying the creditor that a petition will be filed may be sufficient notice to constitute a "willful violation" if the creditor takes any unauthorized post-petition action against the debtor, his property, or property of the estate. *11 USC §362(a), (h).*

(ii) Protected Post-Petition Transfers

Two particular post-petition transfers of property of the estate are protected even though they technically violate the stay:

a) Involuntary Gap Transfer for New Value

A post-petition transfer of the estate's property made during the *involuntary gap period* (between the dates of filing an involuntary petition and the order for relief) is protected to the extent the transferee gives new post-petition value. Value includes post-petition services rendered to the debtor or estate. But value does not include the transferee's paying or securing a pre-petition debt owed to the debtor. If new post-petition value is given by the transferee, neither the debtor nor trustee may recover the property transferred in the exchange, even if the transferee knew that an involuntary petition had been filed. The transferee is also protected to the extent of new post-petition value given. *11 USC §549(b);*

b) Post-Petition Transfer of Real Property to Good-Faith Purchaser

Real property transferred post-petition to a good faith purchaser is protected if the purchaser-transferee meets five conditions:

i) The purchaser must have acted in good faith;

ii) The good-faith purchaser must have given present fair equivalent value for the land;

iii) The good-faith purchaser must not have knowledge that a bankruptcy petition was filed;

iv) No copy or notice of the bankruptcy petition must have been filed in the mortgage deed or real estate records in the county where the land is located before the purchaser perfected his interest in the land under applicable nonbankruptcy law; and

v) No hypothetical bona fide purchaser of the land must be able to obtain an interest under applicable nonbankruptcy law that is superior to that of the actual purchaser. *11 USC §549(c).*

If all five of the above requirements are met, the purchaser-transferee and the transferred property are protected. Neither a debtor nor a trustee may recover the real estate or seek sanctions against the purchaser.

If the purchaser fails to meet any one of the five requirements, a debtor or trustee may recover the real estate by filing an adversary complaint and serving a copy of the complaint with a summons on the purchaser in any manner provided for service of process in federal district court. No filing fee is required if a debtor files the adversary complaint. A $120 filing fee is required if a Chapter 11 or 12 DIP or a trustee files the complaint, but such fee is payable only from any bankruptcy estate that may exist. *11 USC §§522(h), 549(c), 550-551; 28 USC §1930(b), Judicial Conference Schedule Of Fees (6); FRBP 7001, 7004; see Chapters XII & XIII.*

If the transferred real estate is recovered, the purchaser will have a lien on the land to the extent of present value given in the exchange, if the purchaser proves four requirements:

i) The amount of present value given;

ii) The purchaser acted in good faith;

iii) The purchaser had no knowledge that a bankruptcy petition was filed; and

iv) No copy or notice of the bankruptcy petition was filed before the purchaser perfected his interest in the land under applicable non-bankruptcy law. *11 USC §549(c).*

The purchaser must file a timely proof of claim in the debtor's bankruptcy case asserting a lien on the land and include the original or copy of all real estate documents. *See "File a Proof of Claim," Chapter XIV; 11 USC §§501, 502(h), 549(c); FRBP 3001(c), 3002-3003.*

(2) Trustee Abandons Property

A second form of relief from the automatic stay is for a trustee or Chapter 11 or 12 DIP to *abandon property* (disavow interests and rights to property) of the estate. Abandoned property is no longer part of the estate. A trustee or DIP may abandon property of the estate if it is burdensome (too costly) and of inconsequential value and benefit to the estate (no equity for unsecured creditors). The trustee or DIP may voluntarily abandon property of the estate or a party-in-interest may file a motion or request seeking a court order compelling abandonment. If property is voluntarily abandoned, the trustee or DIP must give at least 15 days' prior notice, unless the court reduces the time. Notice must be mailed to the U.S. trustee, all creditors, committee(s) appointed in the debtor's bankruptcy case, indenture trustees, and to such other entities required by court order or local bankruptcy rules. Such parties-in-interest must then file any objection to abandonment before the 15th day after the notice was mailed, unless the court orders otherwise. *11 USC §554; FRBP 6007; see "Compelled Abandonment of Property," Chapter XIV;* and

(3) Automatic Stay Ends

A third way relief from the stay occurs is when the automatic stay terminates by operation of bankruptcy law, without necessity of a court order lifting the stay.

(a) Debtor and His Property

The automatic stay protecting the debtor and his property ends without a court order lifting the stay on the earliest date that the debtor's bankruptcy case is closed or dismissed, or the debtor receives or is denied a discharge. *11 USC §362(c)(2)(A)-(C);*

(b) Property of the Estate

The automatic stay protecting property of the estate ends without a court order lifting the stay if a party-in-interest files a motion for relief from the stay and the debtor, trustee, or other party-in-interest (creditors' committee):

(i) Fails to obtain at least a preliminary hearing before the 30th day after the motion is filed; or

(ii) Fails to obtain a court order before such 30th day continuing the stay pending a final hearing. The court may continue the stay only if the debtor or trustee proves there is a "reasonable likelihood" he will win at the final hearing; or

(iii) Fails to conclude a final hearing no later than the 30th day after any preliminary hearing ends, unless such 30-day period is extended by consent of all parties-in-interest or by the court for a specific time based upon compelling circumstances; or

(iv) Fails to file a timely answer or response to the motion for relief if required by court order or local bankruptcy rules. *11 USC §362(c), (e); see Local Bankruptcy Rules; Chapter XIV.*

The automatic stay protecting property of the estate also ends without a court order lifting the stay if the debtor's bankruptcy case is dismissed. Unless the court, for cause, orders otherwise, dismissing a case revests property of the estate in the debtor or its pre-petition owner and lifts the automatic stay protecting the debtor and his property. *11 USC §§349(b), 362(c).*

3. Stage Three—Creation of a Bankruptcy Estate

Filing a voluntary (or involuntary) bankruptcy petition commences the bankruptcy case and creates a bankruptcy estate.

a. What Property Is in the Estate

(1) Generally

The bankruptcy estate consists of all legal or equitable interests of the debtor in property, wherever such property may be located and regardless of who may have possession of such property on the date the petition is filed. Generally, all community property of the debtor and the nonbankruptcy spouse is included in the bankruptcy estate unless such community property is subject to the sole management and control of the nonbankruptcy spouse and the property is not liable for a claim against either the debtor or the debtor and his spouse under applicable nonbankruptcy law. *11 USC §541(a)(1)-(2); see United States v Nordic Village, Inc, 503 US 30, 112 S Ct 1011 (1992).*

(2) Chapters 7 and 11

Under Chapters 7 and 11, the bankruptcy estate includes all pre-petition property of the debtor and property that the debtor acquires, or becomes entitled to acquire, before the 180th day after filing the bankruptcy petition; (a) by a will or other inheritance; (b) by a property settlement agreement with the debtor's spouse or under any divorce decree; or (c) as a beneficiary of a life insurance or other death benefit plan. *11 USC §541(a)(5).*

(3) Chapters 12 and 13

Under Chapters 12 and 13, all pre-petition and post-petition property of the debtor becomes part of the estate until confirmation and all payments required by a confirmed (court approved) plan have been paid. *11 USC §§1207(a), 1306(a).*

(4) Chapter 9:

There is no bankruptcy estate under a Chapter 9 case. *See Chapter VII. 11 USC §§103(a), (e), 541(a), 901(a).*

b. What Property Is Not in the Estate

The bankruptcy estate does not consist of the following:

(1) Powers over property if the debtor may exercise such powers solely as an executor, trustee, guardian, or other fiduciary for the benefit of another entity;

(2) Post-petition earnings or wages earned by an individual debtor under Chapters 7 and 11. *See In re Fitzsimmons, 725 F2d 1208 (9th Cir 1984); and In re Haynes, 679 F2d 718 (7th Cir 1982), cert denied, 459 US 970.*

(3) The debtor's eligibility to participate in authorized programs under the Higher Education Act of 1965, *20 USC §1001 et seq, 42 USC §2751 et seq;*

(4) Any accreditation status of the debtor as an educational institution;

(5) Any state licensure of the debtor as an educational institution;

(6) Any interest of a debtor-lessee in nonresidential (commercial) real estate under a lease that terminated at the end of the stated term of the lease either pre- or post-petition;

(7) Any interest of the debtor as beneficiary of property held in trust and subject to a "spendthrift clause" (restriction on the transfer of a beneficial interest of the debtor in a trust) that is enforceable under applicable nonbankruptcy law. *See Patterson v Shumate, 504 US 753, 112 S Ct 2242 (1992).*

(8) Any interest of the debtor in liquid or gaseous hydrocarbons that the debtor has transferred or agreed to transfer under a farmout agreement or any written agreement directly related to a farmout agreement, if such interest would otherwise be part of the estate only as: (a) an executory contract; or (b) by the trustee's exercise of his strong-arm powers as a hypothetical bona fide purchaser of real estate, other than fixtures, who has perfected his interest under applicable nonbankruptcy law on the date the debtor's petition is filed (*see "Other Avoidable Unperfected Interests—Trustee's Strong-Arm Powers," Chapter XII, and "Assumption or Rejection of Executory Contracts and Unexpired Leases," Chapter XIV*). However, any consideration which the debtor retains, receives, or is entitled to receive under such farmout agreement does become part of the estate. *Pub L No 102-486 (1992), amending and adding 11 USC §541(b)(4), effective Oct 24, 1992;*

(9) Any interest of the debtor in liquid or gaseous hydrocarbons that constitutes a term overriding royalty (production payment) that the debtor sold pre-petition under a written production payment agreement if such debtor's interest could only be included in the estate by virtue of 11 USC §542 (turnover order);

(10) Any interest of the debtor in cash or cash equivalents constituting proceeds of a money order if: (a) the debtor sold the money order no later than the 14th day pre-petition under an agreement with the money order issuer that prohibited commingling such proceeds with other property of the debtor; and (b) the money order issuer actually took action pre-petition to prohibit the commingling. Such money order proceeds are then excluded from the estate *even if* the debtor *did* commingle the proceeds with other property; and

(11) Property that has been removed from the estate through abandonment by the trustee, exemptions claimed by the debtor, or the automatic stay terminating by court order or bankruptcy law. *11 USC §§103, 362, 522, 541, 554, 901, 1207,*

1306; see "Stage Five—Exemptions Claimed by the Debtor," discussed below.

c. Who Owns the Estate

The bankruptcy estate is held in trust by the trustee or Chapter 11 or 12 debtor-in-possession for the ultimate beneficiaries or owners, the unsecured creditors. The debtor no longer owns the property once the bankruptcy estate is created. The debtor may remove property from the estate if he claims property as exempt under applicable exemption laws (*see "Stage Five—Exemptions Claimed by the Debtor," discussed below*). Secured creditors with a valid lien on the estate's property will receive the lesser amount of either their allowed claim, or their respective collateral (or its value) by the end of the bankruptcy case. It is then unsecured creditors who own the remaining nonexempt property and the equity, if any, in nonexempt secured property of the estate. Any surplus property remaining in the estate after all allowed unsecured claims have been paid will revert to the debtor. *11 USC §§323(a), 506(a), 541(a), 726(a)(6).*

4. Stage Four—Turn Over Property to the Estate

a. Generally

Subject to exceptions listed below, any entity who has possession, custody, or control over property of the estate that the trustee may use, sell, or lease, or that the debtor may exempt, must deliver such property to the trustee or Chapter 11, 12, or 13 debtor. Such entity must also file an accounting with the court for the property or its value from the date of receipt of possession, custody, or control until delivery to the trustee or debtor. A copy of the accounting should also be mailed or delivered to the debtor, any trustee, the U.S. trustee, and all committee(s) appointed in the debtor's case. *11 USC §§103(a),(e)-(f), 363, 522, 541-543, 901, 1101(1), 1107, 1203, 1207, 1303-1304, 1306; FRBP 9034; see United States v Whiting Pools, 462 US 198 (1983) and United States v Nordic Village, Inc, 503 US 30, 112 S Ct 1021 (1992).*

b. Complaint for Turnover Order

An appointed trustee or Chapter 11, 12, or 13 debtor may file an adversary complaint for a turnover order directing any entity in possession, custody, or control of property of the debtor or estate to deliver and account for such property. If the trustee or Chapter 11 or 12 debtor-in-possession files such complaint, a $120 filing fee is required only from any estate that may exist. If a Chapter 13 debtor files the complaint, no filing fee is required. A copy of the complaint with the summons must be served on such entity by first-class mail, personal delivery by a disinterested person at least 18 years old, or by any other method allowed for service of process in federal district court. A copy of the complaint should also be mailed to the debtor if filed by the trustee, any appointed trustee if filed by the debtor, the U.S. trustee, all committee(s), and any other entity required by court order or local bankruptcy rules. *11 USC §§103(a), (e), (f), 363, 522, 541-543, 901, 1101(1), 1107, 1203, 1207, 1303-1304, 1306; 28 USC §1930(b), Judicial Conference Schedule of Fees (6); FRBP 7001(l), 7004 et seq, 9034; see Local Bankruptcy Rules.*

c. Exceptions

The following seven exceptions apply to the turnover and accounting requirements in a bankruptcy case:

(1) Property that is of inconsequential value and benefit to the estate does not have to be turned over or accounted for. *11 USC §§102(5), 542(a);*

(2) An entity that owes an unmatured debt to the debtor or estate or a debt that is not payable on order or demand does not have to pay such debt to the trustee or debtor. *11 USC §542(b);*

(3) A debt that is subject to a setoff under applicable bankruptcy and nonbankruptcy law does not have to be turned over. However, the automatic stay prohibits a creditor's unilateral setoff of such debt without first filing a motion for relief from the stay and obtaining a court order authorizing the setoff. *11 USC §§103(a)(1), 362(a)(7), (d)-(e), 542(b), 553; see "Avoidable Setoffs," Chapter XII, and "Nine Stages of Every Voluntary Bankruptcy Case—Stage Two—Automatic Stay Invoked," discussed above, and "Motion for Relief from Automatic Stay," Chapter XIV;*

(4) An entity who transfers property of the debtor or estate post-petition but in good faith and without actual notice or actual knowledge of the debtor's bankruptcy case need not turn over such property to the trustee or debtor. However, an appointed trustee or Chapter 11 or 12 debtor-in-possession may file a complaint against the transferee to avoid the post-petition transfer and recover such property. *11 USC §§103(a), 542(c), 549(a)(1)-(2)(A), 550(a)(1)-(2), 1107, 1203; FRBP 7001(1) et seq; see "Avoidable Unauthorized Post-Petition Transfers," Chapter XII;*

(5) A life insurance company may transfer property of the debtor or estate to such company if:

(a) The transfer is made in good faith;

(b) The transfer is to pay a premium to the insurance company or to enforce a nonforfeiture insurance option;

(c) The transfer is required to be made automatically under a prepetition insurance contract between the debtor and such insurance company; and

(d) The insurance contract is property of the estate. *11 USC §542(d);*

(6) The property, or information contained in such property, is determined to be subject to a privilege under applicable nonbankruptcy law by the bankruptcy court, after a hearing is held with notice to the entity in possession, debtor, any appointed trustee, the U.S. trustee, all committee(s), and any other entity required by court order or local bankruptcy rules. *11 USC §§102(1)(A)-(B), 542(e); FRBP 9034; see Commodity Futures Trading Commission v Weintraub, 471 US 343 (1985)*; or

(7) The entity in possession, custody, or control of property of the debtor or estate is a custodian excepted from compliance. *See discussion below; 11 USC §§542(a), 543(c)(3),(d).*

d. Custodian

(1) Who Is a Custodian

A *custodian* is:

(a) A receiver or trustee of the debtor's property appointed under a nonbankruptcy legal proceeding or case;

(b) An assignee under a general assignment for the benefit of the debtor's creditors; or

(c) A trustee, receiver, or agent appointed under a contract or applicable law who is authorized to take charge of the debtor's property to enforce a lien or administer the property for the debtor's creditors. *11 USC §§101(11), 103(a), 543.*

(2) Requirements of the Custodian

Subject to exceptions listed below, a custodian who has knowledge of the filing of a voluntary or involuntary petition in the debtor's case must comply with the following three requirements:

(a) Cease administering or making any disbursements of property of the debtor or estate except as necessary to preserve the property. Such property includes all proceeds, product, offspring, rents, or profits obtained from the property. *11 USC §543(a);*

(b) Deliver the property to the trustee or Chapter 11, 12, or 13 debtor. *11 USC §§103(a), 363, 522, 541, 543, 1101(1), 1107, 1203, 1207, 1303-1304, 1306;* and

(c) Promptly file with the court an accounting of the property and its value from the date such property came into the possession, custody, or control of the custodian until the date of delivery. The custodian must also immediately mail or deliver a copy of the accounting to the U.S. trustee and any other entity required by court order or local bankruptcy rule. *11 USC §543(b)(2); FRBP 6002(a), 9034.*

(3) Court Examination

The bankruptcy court must:

(a) Examine and hold a hearing on the custodian's accounting and prior administration of property, as the court deems appropriate under the facts and circumstances of the case. The clerk or other court–appointed person must mail notice of the hearing date to the custodian, debtor, any appointed trustee, the U.S. trustee, all committee(s), creditors, to the SEC in Washington, D.C., and the applicable District Director of the IRS in a Chapter 11 case, and to all other entities as required court order or local bankruptcy rules. If the hearing involves an application for compensation for services rendered or reimbursement of expenses incurred by the custodian for more than $500, at least 20 days' prior notice of the hearing date must be provided, unless the court or local bankruptcy rules provide otherwise. *11 USC §§102(1)(A)-(B), 543(c); FRBP 2002(a)(7), (i)-(j), 6002, 9007, 9034(e), (k); see "Application for Compensation," discussed below, and Chapter IV;*

(b) Issue any order(s) necessary to protect all entities to whom the custodian became obligated with regard to property of the debtor or Estate, including proceeds, product, offspring, rents, or profits from such property. *11 USC §§105(a), 543(c)(1);*

(c) Provide reasonable compensation to the custodian for services rendered and costs and expenses incurred, which may be first priority claims. *11 USC §§503(b)(3)(E), 543(c)(2); FRBP 2002(a)(7); see "Application for Compensation", discussed below, and Chapter IV;* and

(d) Charge the custodian for any improper or excessive disbursements that were not made in compliance with applicable law or approved by a nonbankruptcy court of competent jurisdiction pre-petition after notice to the debtor and all affected parties and a hearing. *11 USC §543(c)(3).*

(4) Exceptions

After notice and a hearing, the bankruptcy court may excuse a custodian from compliance if:

(a) The interests of creditors, and equity security holders of solvent debtor, would be better served by allowing the custodian to remain in possession, custody, or control of the property without filing an accounting or any further intervention by the bankruptcy court; or

(b) The custodian is an assignee under an assignment for the benefit of creditors where: (i) the custodian was appointed or took possession of the debtor's property more than 120 days before the voluntary or involuntary petition was filed in the debtor's case; and (ii) delivery of the property is not required to prevent fraud or injustice. However, the custodian must file an accounting and the bankruptcy court may issue any order necessary to protect all entities to whom the custodian became obligated concerning the debtor's property, including proceeds, product, offspring, rents, or profits, from such property. *11 USC §§103(a), 105(a), 543(c)(3), (d)(2); FRBP 6002.*

5. Stage Five—Exemptions Claimed by the Debtor

a. What Is Exempt Property

Exempt property is generally property that is not subject to the claims of unsecured creditors. Secured creditor(s) with a valid, lawful lien on the debtor's property retain their lien even after the property is claimed as exempt.

b. Purpose for Exemptions

The purpose of Title 11 is to rehabilitate the bankruptcy debtor and to give him and his dependents a fresh start. Under the Code, all property of the debtor becomes property of the bankruptcy estate once the petition is filed. The debtor is permitted to exempt certain property needed for his fresh start and to keep him and his dependents off welfare. Once property is claimed as exempt, it is removed from the bankruptcy estate and the claims of unsecured creditors. But a secured creditor with a valid lien on the exempted property retains such lien. *11 USC §§506(a), 522(b)(2); HR Rep No 595, 95th Cong, 1st Sess 360-61 (1977).*

c. Who Claims Exemptions

Only an individual debtor or his dependent(s) are permitted to claim exemptions. Corporations, partnerships, and other businesses and associations are not allowed exemptions. If property could be exempted by the debtor or his dependent(s) but is not claimed as exempt, such property remains part of the estate subject to the claims of unsecured creditors and secured creditors with a valid lien. *11 USC §§521(l), 522(b); Official Bankr Form 6, Schedule C; FRBP 1007, 4003.*

d. How and When to Claim Exemptions

(1) Debtor

Exemptions are determined as of the date the petition is filed. The bankruptcy debtor must claim property as exempt on Schedule C of the schedules of assets and liabilities. These schedules must be filed with the petition or before the 15th day thereafter, unless the court extends the time for cause. *11 USC §521(1); FRBP 1007(b)-(c); Official Bankr Form 6, Schedule C.*

(2) Dependent of the Debtor

If the debtor fails to claim allowed exemptions timely (*see, discussion above*), a dependent of the debtor may file the list of exemptions (Schedule C) of the schedules of assets and liabilities before the 30th day after expiration of the debtor's time to file (generally, before the 44th day after the petition is filed). *11 USC §522(1); FRBP 1007(c), 4003(a); Official Bankr Form 6, Schedule C.*

e. Exemption Law(s)

There are basically three types of exemption laws available to a debtor: federal Bankruptcy Code exemption law; federal nonbankruptcy exemption laws; and state or local exemption laws. An individual debtor, or debtor and his spouse in a joint case, must select between Bankruptcy Code or nonbankruptcy exemption laws. The debtor (or debtor and spouse) may exempt certain unsecured property and the equity in certain secured property under federal Bankruptcy Code exemption law (§522(d) of the Code), unless prohibited from using the Bankruptcy Code's exemption provisions by state law where the debtor has permanently resided for the greater part of the immediate 180-day period before the petition was filed. Alternatively, instead of federal Bankruptcy Code exemption law, the debtor (or debtor and spouse) may exempt property under federal nonbankruptcy exemption law(s) and state and local exemption laws in effect where the debtor has had a place of domicile for the greater part of such 180-day pre-petition period. *11 USC §522(b), (d).*

A debtor may not claim property exempt under both federal Bankruptcy Code exemption law (11 USC §522(d)) and a state, local, or federal nonbankruptcy exemption law. Similarly, in a joint case, both spouses must exempt property under either federal Bankruptcy Code exemption law; or alternatively, one spouse may exempt property under applicable state and local exemption laws and the other spouse may exempt property under federal nonbankruptcy exemption law(s). But one spouse may not claim exemptions under federal Bankruptcy Code exemption law and the other spouse under state, local, or federal nonbankruptcy exemption laws. If both spouses cannot agree on which type of exemption laws to select (bankruptcy or nonbankruptcy exemptions), they are deemed to have elected federal Bankruptcy Code exemptions if permitted by applicable state law. *11 USC §§102(5), 522(b), (d).*

Examples of federal nonbankruptcy exemption laws include federal laws exempting social security payments, 42 USC §407; injury or death compensation payments from war risk hazards, 42 USC §1717; civil service retirement benefits, 5 USC §§729, 2265; certain federal homestead lands on debts contracted before issuance of the patent, 43 USC §175; and veterans benefits, 45 USC §352(E). Thus, the debtor (or debtor and spouse) may exempt social security payments under Title 42, United States Code, and exempt property under the debtor's applicable state exemption laws. *HR Rep No 595, 95th Cong, 1st Sess 360-61 (1977); 11 USC §522(b), (d); Official Bankr Form 6, Schedule C.*

f. Objections to Exemptions

The trustee or any creditor may file an objection to the debtor's (or his dependent's) list of exemptions. An objection to exemptions must be filed with the court before the 30th day after: (1) the conclusion of the first meeting of creditors, or (2) any amended list of exemptions is filed in the case, unless the court extends the time. However, a motion to extend time to file objections must be filed before such 30th day. The party filing the motion to extend time or the objection to exemptions must serve a copy by first-class mail on the debtor (and his dependent if such individual filed the list of exemptions) and his attorney, on any trustee in the case, and on any other entity required by court order or local bankruptcy rules. *FRCP 4003, 9014; Official Bankr Form 6, Schedule C; see Taylor v Freeland & Kronz, 503 US 638, 112 S Ct 1644 (1992).*

g. Amended List of Exemptions

As a matter of right, the debtor may amend exemptions claimed under Schedule C of the schedule of assets and liabilities at any time before the case is closed. The debtor must mail or personally deliver notice of the amendment to any trustee and creditor affected by the amendment, and to such other entities required by court order or local bankruptcy rules. *FRBP 1009(a).*

A dependent of the debtor, a creditor, or any other party-in-interest (trustee, co-owner of property) may file a motion seeking a court order directing the debtor to amend his schedule of exemptions. The party-in-interest must serve a copy of the motion by first-class mail, or personal delivery by a disinterested person at least 18 years old, on the debtor, trustee, and any other entity directed by court order or local bankruptcy rules. The court must hold a hearing on any motion to compel the debtor to amend his schedule of exemptions, unless local bankruptcy rules provide otherwise. The party-in-interest filing the motion, clerk of the court, or other court-authorized person must mail notice of the hearing date to the same entities required to receive a copy of the motion. The clerk must mail notice of any amendment of the schedule of exemptions to the U.S. Trustee and the parties designated by the court. *11 USC §§102(1)(A)-(B), 521(1), 522(b), (d)(1); FRBP 1009(a), 9007, 9014; Official Bankr Form 6, Schedule C.*

h. Waiver of Exemptions

Any waiver of exemptions signed by the debtor in favor of an unsecured creditor is unenforceable under bankruptcy law. Exempt property protects the debtor's fresh start. The right to claim exemptions is closely guarded. *11 USC §522(e).*

6. Stage Six—Meeting of Creditors

a. What It Is

A meeting of creditors is an examination of the debtor under oath, on penalty of perjury, on any matter that may affect the debtor's bankruptcy case, administration of the estate, the debtor's assets and liabilities, or the debtor's discharge. Perjury committed during a meeting of creditors is a bankruptcy crime, punishable by a fine of as much as $5,000 and/or imprisonment for as long as five years. *See "Meeting of Creditors" and "Bankruptcy Crimes and Penalties," Chapter XIV; 11 USC §§341, 343; 18 USC §152.*

In a Chapter 7 case, a trustee or an unsecured creditors' committee may be elected at the meeting of creditors. *11 USC §§341, 343; FRBP 2003(b);*

b. When It Is Held

The meeting of creditors under Chapter 7, 11, or 13 generally must be held not less than 20 days or more than 40 days after the order for relief or a voluntary petition is filed. The Chapter 12 meeting of creditors generally must be held not less than 20 or more than 35 days after the petition is filed. No meeting of creditors is held under Chapter 9. *11 USC §§103(e), 901; FRBP 2003(a);*

c. Where It Is Held

The meeting of creditors may be held in any building where court is regularly held; or at any other place designated by the U.S. trustee that is within the federal judicial district and convenient for the parties-in-interest. If the designated place is not regularly staffed by the U.S. trustee, the meeting of creditors may be held not more than 60 days after the order for relief. *FRBP 2003(a);*

d. Who Attends

A creditor or party-in-interest may attend the meeting of creditors and examine (question) the debtor under oath on any matter that may affect the administration of the debtor's estate, case, assets and liabilities, or discharge. The debtor must appear and submit to the examination under oath. The bankruptcy judge does not preside at and may not attend any meeting of creditors. *11 USC §§341, 343; FRBP 2003;*

e. Who Presides

The U.S. trustee or his delegate presides at the meeting of creditors and administers the oath to the debtor. *FRBP 2003(b); see "Meeting of Creditors," Chapter XIV.*

In Alabama and North Carolina, which are not part of the U.S. trustee system, a bankruptcy administrator or his designee may preside at the meeting of creditors and administer the oath to the debtor. *Pub L No 103-394, §105 (1994).*

f. Special Examination of Chapter 7 Debtors

During the meeting of creditors in a Chapter 7 case, the trustee, U.S. trustee, or his delegate must additionally examine the debtor to ensure that he (the debtor) is aware of:

(1) His ability and possible right to file a bankruptcy petition under Chapter 11, 12, or 13;

(2) The potential consequences of receiving a bankruptcy discharge, including the legal effect of such discharge upon the debtor's credit history. Under the Fair Credit Reporting Act, 15 USC §1681 et. seq., consumer reporting services must delete any bankruptcy more than 10 years old from an individual's credit report, unless such credit report is used in connection with: (a) a credit transaction of at least $50,000; (b) an insurance policy of at least $50,000; or (c) an employment application for a job with a salary of at least $20,000;

(3) The legal effect of receiving a bankruptcy discharge; and

(4) The legal effect of reaffirming a debt that would otherwise be dischargeable under bankruptcy law. *11 USC §341(d); FRBP 2003(b); see "Procedure Seven-ÚDischarge of the Debtor" and "Reaffirmation of Debt," Chapter III.*

7. Stage Seven—Distribution of the Estate

a. Generally

The debtor's bankruptcy estate eventually will consist of all property which was not abandoned by the trustee, claimed as exempt by the debtor or a dependent, and for which the automatic stay was not terminated or lifted by court order. Secured creditors with a valid lien against property of the estate will receive the lesser of their allowed claim or their collateral (or its value) at least by the end of the debtor's case. The remaining nonexempt, unsecured property, plus any equity in nonexempt, secured property of the estate, belongs to unsecured creditors. The trustee, as the representative of the estate and its beneficiaries, must distribute the estate, or the proceeds from sale of property of the estate, pro rata (same percent) to unsecured creditors whose claims are allowed by the court. The first unsecured creditors to receive payment from the estate must be unsecured creditors with allowed priority claims. If there is any money or property remaining in the estate after all priority claims have been fully paid, then general unsecured creditors with allowed claims may receive payment. *11 USC §§323(a), 362, 503, 507, 554, 726; see "File Proof of Claim," Chapter XIV.*

b. Priority Claims

(1) What They Are

Priority claims are claims generally held by unsecured creditors entitled to first payment from the debtor's bankruptcy estate. There are eight categories of priority claims, numbered in order of their priority and payment status.

(2) Rules of Distribution

Four general rules govern distribution of the bankruptcy estate to creditors:

(a) First, all members of the same priority claim category or group must receive full payment of their allowed claims before any member of a lower priority claim category may be paid anything. An allowed claim is one for which a proof of claim has been filed (or is deemed filed under Chapters 9 and 11) and for which no objection has been filed and sustained by the court. *See "File Proof of Claim," Chapter XIV;*

(b) Second, all eight priority claim categories must be paid in full before any payment may be made to general unsecured creditors;

(c) Third, if there is not enough money or property in the bankruptcy estate to pay all members of the same priority claim category in full, then each member of the same category must be paid pro rata (same percentage of payment). If a priority claim category is paid pro rata, the lower order priority claim categories and general unsecured creditors must receive nothing; and

(d) Fourth, a secured creditor with an allowed claim secured by a valid lien against property of the estate must receive the lesser of his allowed claim or his collateral (or its value) by the end of the case. If there is any equity left in the secured property after the secured creditor has been paid, such equity will be distributed to unsecured creditors according to the first three rules for distribution outlined above. If any equity or property of the estate remains after all unsecured creditors are paid, such property will revert to the debtor. *11 USC §§501-503, 507, 724, 726(a)(6), 925, 1111(a); FRBP 3001-3003, 3007.*

(3) Nine Categories of Priority Claims

(a) First Priority Claims

These are administrative claims and expenses allowed by

the court and incurred after the bankruptcy petition is filed but before the earlier date that the debtor is discharged or a plan is confirmed. Administrative claims are not claims for "administrative" work but represent the actual, necessary costs and expenses of preserving the estate. First priority administrative claims include unsecured claims for:

(i) Wages, salaries, or commissions for services rendered to the debtor, any committee, or to the estate after the petition is filed, and which helped to preserve the estate;

(ii) Post-petition taxes incurred by the estate that are not seventh priority claims. These include taxes the trustee incurs in administering the estate;

(iii) Tax refunds received by the estate and attributable to an excessive allowance of a tentative carryback adjustment, whether the taxable period occurred pre- or post-petition;

(iv) Reasonable compensation allowed to an attorney, accountant, or other professional hired by the debtor, trustee, or committee in the debtor's case;

(v) Trustee's costs and expenses incurred in rendering services to the estate;

(vi) Actual, necessary expenses incurred by a petitioning creditor who files and prosecutes an involuntary petition against the debtor;

(vii) Reasonable compensation for professional services rendered to a petitioning creditor by an attorney or accountant in connection with filing and prosecuting an involuntary petition;

(viii) Any unpaid filers fees, charges, or mileage required by Chapter 119 or 123, Title 28, United States Code; and

(ix) Actual, necessary expenses of a member of a Chapter 11 unsecured creditors' committee incurred in the performance of official duties as a committee member. *11 USC §§503, 507; HR Rep No 595, 95th Cong, 1st Sess 355 (1977).*

The creditor who seeks the status of a first priority claimholder must file a request for payment of administrative expenses and file a timely proof of claim indicating that the claim is filed as a first priority administrative claim (*see "Allowance of First Priority Claims," discussed below*). However, any professional person, whether an attorney, accountant, or other professional, who is to render services to a debtor, trustee, or committee must first obtain a court order authorizing his representation. Unless such court order is obtained prior to employment, the professional should not be paid from the estate and his proof of claim as an administrative claim should be disallowed. *11 USC §§327-330, 1103, 1114; FRBP 2014, 3002(a); Official Bankr Form 10; see "Procedures for Allowance of Priority Claims," discussed below;*

(b) Second Priority Claims

These are allowed unsecured claims incurred after an involuntary bankruptcy petition is filed but before the earlier date that a trustee is appointed or an order for relief is entered in the debtor's bankruptcy case. *11 USC §507(a)(2).*

(c) Third Priority Claims

These are allowed unsecured claims of individuals and corporations held against the debtor for wages, salaries, commissions, including vacation, severance, and sick-leave pay, earned within 90 days before the earlier date that the debtor ceased business or the bankruptcy petition (voluntary or involuntary) was filed, but only to the extent of $4,000 per individual or corporation. Sales commissions of independent contractors (individuals or corporations) with only one employer, earned during the relevant 90-day pre-petition period are third priority claims only if the independent contractor earned at least 75 percent of his income from selling the debtor's goods or services during the immediate 12 months before the earlier date that the debtor ceased business or the bankruptcy petition was filed. *11 USC §507(a)(3).*

(d) Fourth Priority Claims

These are allowed unsecured claims of individuals held against the debtor for contributions to employee benefit plans as the result of services rendered to the debtor within 180 days before the earlier date that the debtor ceased business or the bankruptcy petition (voluntary or involuntary) was filed, but only to the extent of the number of employees covered by such plan multiplied by $2,000, less the total amounts paid to such employees as third priority claimholders and to any other employee benefit plan on behalf of such employees. *11 USC §507(a)(4).*

(e) Fifth Priority Claims

These are allowed unsecured claims of individuals engaged in producing or raising grain that are filed against a debtor who owns or operates a grain storage facility and the unsecured claims of United States fisherman filed against a debtor who bought fish or fish produce from such United States fisherman and who operates a fish produce storage or processing facility, but only to the extent of $2,000 per individual. *11 USC §507(a)(5).*

(f) Sixth Priority Claims

These are allowed unsecured claims of individuals who deposited money with the debtor before the petition was filed for the purchase or rental of consumer property or services (for personal, family, or household use) that were not provided, but only to the extent of $900 per individual. *11 USC §507(a)(6).*

(g) Seventh Priority Claims

These are allowed unsecured or secured claims for a debt owed to the debtor's spouse, ex-spouse, or child for bona fide alimony, maintenance, or support payments that arose in connection with a separation agreement, property settlement agreement, divorce decree, or other court order of record determined under state or territorial law. However, such claims lose their priority status if they are assigned either voluntarily or involuntarily (by operation of law) to another entity. *11 USC §507(a)(7).*

(h) Eighth Priority Claims

These are allowed unsecured claims for certain taxes owed by the debtor, generally before the petition was filed:

(i) Income taxes for which a tax return was last due within three years before the petition was filed (income taxes owed by the debtor within the three-year pre-petition period);

(ii) Income taxes assessed against the debtor within the 240-day pre-petition period, plus any additional time that an offer in compromise was made during such 240-day period;

(iii) Income taxes which were incurred pre-petition but which may still be assessed against the debtor post-petition under applicable tax law or an agreement with the debtor;

(iv) Property taxes assessed pre-petition and which were last due within one year before the petition was filed;

(v) Employment taxes on wages, salaries, or commissions earned by an employee of the debtor prepetition for which a tax return was last due within three years before the petition was filed;

(vi) Excise taxes for which a return was last due within three years before the petition was filed;

(vii) Customs duty for importing merchandise generally due within one year before the petition was filed;

(viii) Taxes which the debtor or trustee was required to collect or withhold and for which such debtor or trustee may be liable in any capacity. This category includes "trust fund" taxes such as income taxes or the employee's share of social security taxes which an employer or responsible officer is required to withhold from an employee's pay under §6672 of Title 26 (Internal Revenue Code) or other applicable tax law. It does not matter whether the tax year to which such taxes relate occurred pre- or post-petition;

(ix) Tax penalties for an actual pecuniary loss relating to one of the above priority tax claims. *11 USC §507(a)(7); S Rep No 989, 95th Cong, 2d Sess 68-73 (1978).*

(i) Ninth Priority Claims

Allowed unsecured claims arising from any commitment made by the debtor to maintain the capital of an insured depository institution. The debtor's commitment must have been made to the federal depository institutions regulatory agency or any predecessor of such agency. *11 USC §507(a)(8).*

(4) Procedures for Allowance of Priority Claims

(a) Allowance of Claims Generally

Any claim against the estate must be allowed by the court before payment may be made by the trustee or debtor. Under Chapters 9 and 11, a proof of claim is deemed filed and allowed by the debtor filing a list of creditors (Chapter 9) or schedules of liabilities (Chapter 11), unless the debtor: (a) failed to list the creditor's claim, or (b) listed the claim as disputed, contingent, or unliquidated. In such cases, the creditor must file a timely proof of claim to share in distribution of the estate or payment under a plan. Under Chapters 7, 12, and 13, a creditor must file a timely proof of claim (before the 90th day after the first date set for the meeting of creditors) to receive payment from the Chapter 7 trustee or under a Chapter 12 or 13 plan. Unless an objection is filed by a trustee, debtor, creditor, or other party-in-interest, a properly and timely filed proof of claim is deemed allowed by the court when it is filed. *11 USC §§501, 502(a); FRBP 3001-3008; see "File Proof of Claim—When to File," Chapter XIV.*

(b) Allowance of Second Through Eighth Priority Claims

A creditor who wants payment of a second through eighth priority claim must file a proof of claim timely and properly, and indicate on the proof of claim his priority claim status. Facts contained in the proof of claim should support the creditor's assertion of a priority status. An original or copy of all documents supporting the priority claim must be attached to the claim. (Official Bankruptcy Form 10 presently does not reflect eighth priority claims. However, the basis for the priority claim, date the debt was incurred by the debtor, and amount of the unsecured eighth priority claim may be stated under Numbers 1, 2, 4, and 5 of Form 10 and checked under boxes indicated "other"). *11 USC §§501, 502(a), 507(a); FRBP 3001(c), 3002(a), 3003-3008; Official Bankr Forms 10, 11A; see "File Proof of Claim," Chapter XIV.*

(c) Allowance of First Priority Claims

An entity who wishes to assert and receive payment for a first priority administrative claim must strictly comply with the following procedures:

(i) Keep careful records documenting the goods and/or services provided to the debtor, trustee, any committee, or estate post-petition; *FRBP 3001(c);*

(ii) File a timely request for payment of administrative expenses. First priority administrative claims should be paid by the debtor or trustee timely according to the requirements of the creditor. Any creditor who does not receive timely payment for post-petition goods and/or services rendered to the debtor, trustee, committee, or estate may file a request for payment of first priority administrative expenses. The request should state specific facts showing the grounds for asserting a first priority claim (*see "First Priority Claims," discussed above*). The original or copies of all documents supporting the claim should be attached to the request. A copy of the request must be served by first-class mail on the debtor, any trustee, all committee(s), the U.S. trustee, and on any other entity required by court order or local bankruptcy rules. The request does not commence an adversary proceeding and no filing fee is required. The request must be filed no later than the date set by the court or local bankruptcy rules, unless the court permits a late filing for cause shown. However, a creditor may file a request at any time before such court-fixed date. *11 USC §§503(a)-(b), 507(a)(1); FRBP 9013-9014.*

Any person who provides professional services for the debtor, trustee, committee, or the estate must first obtain a court order authorizing such professional services, and then file a fee application as part of the request for payment of first priority administrative expenses. The debtor's attorney must additionally file a statement of compensation paid or agreed to be paid by the debtor. Copies of such documents must be mailed or personally delivered to the debtor, any trustee, the U.S. trustee, all committee(s), and to any other entity required by court order or local bankruptcy rules. *See "Requirements of Debtor's Attorney," discussed below; 11 USC §§327-331; FRBP 2014, 2016-2017, 9013-9014.*

(iii) File a timely proof of claim. The creditor asserting a first priority claim should also file a timely proof of claim (*see* "File Proof of Claim—When to File," Chapter XIV). Official Bankruptcy Form 10 does not presently reflect first priority claims. However, the basis for the claim, date(s) the claim was incurred, and amount of the claim may be indicated under Numbers 1, 2, 4, and 5 of Form 10 and checked under boxes indicated "other." The original or copies of all documents supporting the first priority claim status should be attached to the proof of claim. *11 USC §§501, 502(a), 503, 507(a)(1); FRBP 2002(f)(3), 3001(c), 3002(a), 3003(c)(3); see "File Proof of Claim—When to File," Chapter XIV.*

(d) Notice and Hearing on First Priority Claims

The court must hold a hearing on any request for payment of first priority administrative expenses, unless local bankruptcy rules provide otherwise. The clerk of the court or other court-authorized person must mail notice of the hearing date to the creditor filing the request, the debtor, any trustee, the U.S. trustee, all committee(s), and to any other entity required by court order or local bankruptcy rules. A copy of any order allowing a first priority administrative claim should be attached to the creditor's proof of claim, if possible. *11 USC §§102(1)(A)-(B), 503(a); FRBP 9007, 9013-9014.*

8. Stage Eight—Discharge of the Debtor

a. Generally

If the debtor complies with the requirements of the Code, including federal and local bankruptcy rules, the debtor may receive a discharge from the bankruptcy court.

b. What It Is

A discharge is a court order relieving the debtor of personal liability for most pre-petition debts under Chapters 7 and 12; most pre- and post-petition debts that arose before the date of confirmation of a plan under Chapters 9 and 11; and most pre-petition debts and certain necessary post-petition consumer debts which arose before the date of confirmation of a plan under Chapter 13, where prior approval of the standing trustee was practical and was obtained. *11 USC §§524, 727, 944(b), 1141(d), 1228, 1305(a)(2), 1328; see Chapters III-VII.*

c. Legal Effects

The debtor's discharge has four legal effects, even if the debtor waived discharge of the particular debt:

(1) Relieves the debtor of personal liability for all debts discharged by the court;

(2) Voids pre- or post-petition judgments, decrees, and orders against the debtor to the extent of any personal liability of the debtor, if the underlying debt was discharged in the debtor's bankruptcy case;

(3) Permanently enjoins all entities from taking any action, act, or conduct to collect a discharged debt from: (a) the debtor personally; (b) the debtor's unsecured exempt property; and (c) property the debtor acquires post-petition. This injunction extends to protect community property that the debtor acquires post-petition unless the underlying community claim would be excepted from discharge. *See "Exceptions to Discharge," Chapter III;* and

(4) Lifts the automatic stay regarding the debtor's exempt secured property. A secured creditor with a lawful, valid lien against exempt property of the debtor may now foreclose upon the collateral or follow any other procedures allowed under the pre-petition security agreement and applicable nonbankruptcy law. However, in the event of a deficiency, the secured creditor may not take any action against the debtor personally to collect such creditor's deficiency claim. The creditor is unsecured with regard to its deficiency claim. And

an unsecured creditor is permanently enjoined from taking any act against either the debtor or his property to collect a discharged pre-petition debt. *11 USC §§362(c), 524; see "Relief from the Stay," discussed above; Johnson v Home State Bank, 501 US 78, 111 S Ct 2150, remanded, 940 F2d 609 (10th Cir), cert denied, 501 US 1217, 111 S Ct 2824 (1991).*

The debtor's discharge does not affect the bankruptcy estate. The automatic stay still applies to protect property of the estate. *11 USC §§362(c)(1), 524.*

d. Who Receives the Discharge

Only the bankruptcy debtor receives a discharge under the Bankruptcy Code. A codebtor, guarantor, surety, or nonbankruptcy debtor who might be liable with the bankruptcy debtor on a pre-petition debt does not receive a discharge. Thus, a spouse or ex-spouse who did not file a bankruptcy petition does not receive a discharge and remains personally liable for community debts even if a divorce decree states otherwise under applicable nonbankruptcy law. *11 USC §524(e).*

e. When Is a Discharge Granted

(1) Chapter 7

The Chapter 7 debtor receives a discharge as soon as possible after the 60th day following the first date set for the meeting of creditors if no objection to discharge has been filed. A discharge hearing may be required by the court even if there is no objection to the debtor's discharge. *See Chapter III; 11 USC §§524(d), 727; FRBP 4004; Local Bankruptcy Rules.*

(2) Chapter 9

The municipal debtor receives a discharge when the Chapter 9 plan is confirmed (approved) by the court and the debtor deposits legally binding, sufficient consideration with a court-appointed disbursing agent for distribution under the plan. *11 USC §944; see Chapter VII.*

(3) Chapter 11

The Chapter 11 debtor generally receives a discharge when the plan of reorganization is confirmed by the court. *11 USC §1141; see Chapter IV.*

(4) Chapters 12 and 13

The Chapter 12 or 13 debtor receives a discharge after making all payments required by a confirmed plan or on the date the court grants a hardship discharge. *11 USC §§1228, 1328; see Chapters V & VI.*

f. Waiver of Discharge

A debtor may sign a written waiver of discharge of all debts. Such waiver of discharge in toto must be signed after the petition is filed and must be approved by the court. *11 USC §§524, 727(a)(10), 1141(d)(4), 1228(a), 1328(a); HR Rep No 595, 95th Cong, 1st Sess 365-66 (1977).*

9. Stage Nine—Closing the Case

After the bankruptcy estate has been fully administered, the court will terminate the services of any trustee and close the case.

a. Chapters 7, 12, and 13 Cases

The Chapter 7 trustee and Chapter 12 and 13 standing trustee must file a final report and account of the administration of the bankruptcy estate. The U.S. trustee or other party-in-interest (creditor, debtor) must file any objection to the trustee's final report before the 30th day after the final report is filed. If there are no objections, the court will presume the estate has been fully administered, discharge the trustee, and close the case. *11 USC §§350(a), 704(9), 1202(b)(1), 1302(b)(1); FRBP 5009.*

b. Chapter 11 Cases

After the bankruptcy estate has been fully administered by a debtor-in-possession or trustee in a Chapter 11 case, the court must enter a final decree closing the case unless the confirmed Chapter 11 plan specifies a different date. The court may close the case on its own motion or on motion of a party-in-interest (trustee, creditor, debtor). A final decree closing the Chapter 11 case may be entered even though payments under a Chapter 11 plan have not been completed. The court still retains jurisdiction to enforce its orders, and the bankruptcy case may be reopened to administer assets, afford relief to the debtor, or for any other cause to further the interests of justice. *11 USC §§350(a)-(b), 1142; FRBP 3022, 5010; see Local Bankruptcy Rules; Procedural Bankr Forms B 270-271.*

c. Chapter 9 Cases

The court must close a Chapter 9 case after the municipality has fully administered the case. No estate is created in a Chapter 9 case. The court retains jurisdiction over the Chapter 9 case as long as necessary for the Chapter 9 plan to be successfully implemented. *11 USC §§901, 945(a)-(b); see Chapter VII.*

d. Reopening a Case

Any bankruptcy case may be reopened in the bankruptcy court in which the case was originally closed. The debtor or any other party-in-interest (U.S. trustee, creditor, former trustee) may file a motion to reopen the case for cause, including the need to administer assets or to afford relief to the debtor. The motion to reopen a closed case does not commence an adversary proceeding. However, the clerk of the court must collect the same filing fee then in effect for filing a bankruptcy petition under that case, unless the case is reopened merely to correct an administrative error or for actions related to the debtor's discharge. The motion to reopen the case must be served on any entity required by the court or local bankruptcy rules, by first-class mail or any other manner allowed for service of motions in federal district court. *11 USC §350(b); 28 USC §1930(a), Language To Clarify Reopened Bankr Code Cases; FRBP 5010, 7005, 9013-9014; see Local Bankruptcy Rules.*

G. Requirements of Debtor's Attorney

Once the debtor files the bankruptcy petition, all property of the debtor, wherever located, becomes property of the bankruptcy estate. The debtor may claim certain property as exempt, thereby removing it from the estate. But unless the debtor's attorney is to be paid from the debtor's exempt property, the attorney will receive compensation for services rendered in the bankruptcy case from the bankruptcy estate. Every debtor's attorney must strictly comply with the requirements of bankruptcy law to continue legal representation of the debtor post-petition and to receive any compensation for such legal services from the estate. *11 USC §§327-331; FRBP 2016-2017.*

1. Required Court Documents

a. Statement of Compensation

Every attorney who represents a bankruptcy debtor must file a statement of compensation either paid by the debtor during the immediate one year pre-petition or agreed to be paid post-petition. This statement of compensation must be filed and a copy delivered to the U.S. trustee before the 15th day after filing a voluntary petition or the order for relief in an involuntary bankruptcy case. The court or local bankruptcy rules may extend such time. The statement must be filed even if the debtor's case is handled pro bono or no compensation will be sought from the estate. *11 USC §329; FRBP 2016(b).*

The statement of compensation must include the terms and provisions for payment, including the terms of any fee-sharing agreement between the debtor's attorney and any nonmembers or nonregular associate of the attorney's law firm. The debtor's attorney must also file a supplemental statement of compensation before the 15th day after receiving any payment or reaching any agreement for compensation which was not disclosed in the original statement of compensation. *11 USC §329; FRBP 2016(b).*

b. Application for Compensation

A debtor's counsel who seeks compensation for services rendered in the bankruptcy case must also file an application for compensation. This application may be filed for interim and, thereafter, final compensation.

(1) Application for Interim Compensation

Debtor's counsel may file an application for interim compensation for payment from the estate once every 120 days after the voluntary petition is filed or after the order for relief in an involuntary case. The court or local bankruptcy rules may reduce such time to permit more frequent filings. *11 USC §331; FRBP 2016(a); see Local Bankruptcy Rules.*

(2) Application for Final Compensation

The debtor's attorney may elect to wait until all services in the debtor's bankruptcy case have been rendered and file an application for final compensation. *FRBP 2016(a).* However, if the bankruptcy court has previously awarded interim fees to the debtor's attorney, the court must reduce the amount of final compensation to be awarded by the total amount of interim compensation paid. If the interim compensation paid to the debtor's attorney exceeds the total allowed compensation, the court may issue a disgorgement order requiring the debtor to remit the excess to the bankruptcy estate for unsecured creditors. *11 USC §330(a)(5).*

(3) Procedures

(a) Requirements of Application for Compensation

The application for interim or final compensation must contain the following relevant factors:

(i) Services rendered in the debtor's case and time expended for such services;

(ii) Whether such services were necessary to the administration of the debtor's case or beneficial to the completion of the bankruptcy case;

(iii) Whether the debtor's attorney performed such services within a reasonable time given the complexity, importance, and nature of the problems or issues addressed in the bankruptcy case. Compensation awarded for preparation of a fee application must be based on the level and skill reasonably required for such preparation;

(iv) Costs and expenses incurred by the attorney in rendering services to the debtor;

(v) Rates charged by the attorney for each service provided to the debtor or to complete the bankruptcy case;

(vi) Whether the compensation requested is reasonable compared to the compensation customarily charged

by comparably skilled attorneys in nonbankruptcy cases;

(vii) Payments previously made or promised by the debtor for services in the bankruptcy case;

(viii) Source of all payments made or promised by the debtor for services in the bankruptcy case;

(ix) The existence and terms of any fee-sharing arrangement between the debtor's attorney and any nonmember or nonregular associate of the attorney's law firm; and

(x) Any other provision required by local bankruptcy rules. *11 USC §330(a)(1)-(3); FRBP 2016(a).*

(b) Service of Application

An application for compensation does not commence an adversary proceeding. No filing fee is required. The debtor's attorney must serve a copy of the application on the U.S. trustee except in Chapter 9 cases, and on the debtor, all committee(s) appointed in the case, the trustee, and any other entity required by court order or local bankruptcy rules. The application may be served by first-class mail or personal delivery. *FRBP 2016, 9013, 9034; see Local Bankruptcy Rules.*

(c) Notice and Hearing

The court must hold a hearing on any application for compensation, unless local bankruptcy rules provide otherwise. The clerk of the court must give at least 20 days' notice of any hearing on an application for compensation for more than $500. Such notice must be mailed to the debtor, U.S. trustee, any trustee, all committee(s), creditors, equity security holders and indenture trustees; and to the SEC in Washington, DC, and District Director of the IRS for the district in which a Chapter 11 case is pending. *11 USC §§330(a), 331; FRBP 2002(a)(7), (i)-(k), 2016, 9034.*

(d) Review by U.S. Trustee

When the U.S. trustee deems it appropriate, or when required by local bankruptcy rules, the U.S. trustee must:

(i) Review all applications for compensation filed under 11 USC §330 according to procedural guidelines adopted by the executive office of the U.S. trustee. Such guidelines must be uniformly applied to all fee applications unless the U.S. trustee finds that circumstances warrant different treatment;

(ii) File written comments with the court about each §330 fee application for final compensation reviewed; and

(iii) Object to a fee application when the U.S. trustee believes an objection is appropriate. *28 USC §586(a)(3)(A).*

2. Denial or Return of Compensation

The court may deny, cancel, or order the return of any payment made by the debtor or estate to the debtor's attorney, if the amount of compensation paid exceeds the reasonable value of the attorney's services rendered in the case. *11 USC §329(b); FRBP 2017.*

a. Procedures for Denial or Return of Compensation

(1) Motion

A party-in-interest (debtor, trustee, U.S. trustee, creditor) may file a motion for denial of compensation sought or return of compensation paid by the debtor to his attorney pre- or post-petition. Additionally, the court on its own motion may deny compensation sought or order the return of compensation paid pre-or post-petition. A motion filed by a party-in-interest does not commence an adversary proceeding. No filing fee is required. The movant should serve a copy of the motion on the debtor, trustee, all committee(s) appointed in the debtor's case, the U.S. trustee, and any other entity required by court order or local bankruptcy rules. Service of the motion may be obtained by first-class mail, personal delivery by a disinterested person at least 18 years old, or by any other method allowed for service of process in federal district court. *11 USC §§327, 329(b); FRBP 2017, 7001(1), 7004, 9013-9014; see Local Bankruptcy Rules.*

(2) Notice and Hearing

The court must hold a hearing on any motion for denial or return of compensation. The clerk or other court-appointed person must mail notice of such hearing to parties required by the court or local bankruptcy rules. *11 USC §§102(1)(A)-(B), 329(b); FRBP 2017, 9007; see Local Bankruptcy Rules.*

b. Grounds for Denial or Return of Compensation

The court may deny compensation to the debtor's attorney, or order the attorney to return any compensation previously received (pre- or post-petition) if such compensation: (1) is excessive; (2) reflects an unnecessary duplication of services; or (3) indicates that services were not necessary to the administration of the bankruptcy case or reasonably likely to benefit the bankruptcy estate. Compensation may be excessive either to the estate, the debtor,

or both, with regard to the amount or quality of legal services rendered in any way during the bankruptcy case. *11 USC §§329(b), 330; FRBP 2017.*

Research Guide

Anderson, *Chapter 11: Reorganizations* chs 1, 3, 11 (Shepard's/McGraw-Hill 1983)

Anderson & Morris, *Chapter 12: Farm Reorganizations* chs 1, 2, 7, 8 (Shepard's/McGraw-Hill 1987)

Drake, *Bankruptcy Practice for the General Practitioner* chs 3, 5 (Shepard's/McGraw-Hill 2d ed 1990)

Drake & Morris, *Chapter 13: Practice and Procedure* chs 3-5 (Shepard's/McGraw-Hill 1983)

Jaroslavsky, *Practical Bankruptcy Procedure* chs 1, 2, 5, 6 (Shepard's/McGraw-Hill 1993)

Murphy, *Creditor's Rights in Bankruptcy* chs 1, 3 (Shepard's/McGraw-Hill 2d ed 1988)

Pollard & Burton, *Guide to Effective Bankruptcy Litigation* ch 1 (Shepard's/McGraw-Hill 1988)

III. Chapter 7—Liquidation

III. Chapter 7—Liquidation
- A. General Overview
- B. Preparing the Client
- C. Stages of a Chapter 7 Case
- D. Procedures Under a Chapter 7 Case
  1. Procedure One—The Debtor
     11 USC §109(a)-(b), (g)
  2. Procedure Two—Debtor's Duties
     11 USC §§301-302, 341, 521, 541-542
     28 USC §1930(a)(1), (b), Judicial Conference Schedule of Fees (8)
     FRBP 1006-1008, 2003, 4002-4003
     - a. File Petition and List of Creditors
     - b. File Schedules and Statements
     - c. File Statement of Intention
     - d. Attend Meeting of Creditors
     - e. Cooperate with Chapter 7 Trustee
     - f. File Statement of Any Address Change
     - g. Attend Discharge Hearing
  3. Procedure Three—Chapter 7 Trustee
     11 USC §§321-323, 326, 330, 503, 507, 701-705
     28 USC §§586a, 1930(a)(1)
     FRBP 2008, 2010, 2015, 6009
     - a. Appointment
     - b. Selection of Trustee
     - c. Electing a Trustee
     - d. Eligibility and Qualification of Trustee
       - (1) Eligibility
       - (2) Qualification

e. Trustee's Duties
f. Trustee's Fees
4. Procedure Four—Exempt Property
11 USC §522(b), (d)
FRBP 1007-1008, 4003
5. Procedure Five—Conversion
11 USC §706
FRBP 1017, 1019, 2002(a)(5), (f)(2), (i), (k), 9034
a. By the Debtor
b. By Another Entity
c. Hearing
d. Notice of Hearing
e. Court's Ruling and Notice
f. Conversion Fee
6. Procedure Six—Dismissal
11 USC §707
FRBP 1017, 2002(a)(5), (f)(2), (i), (k), 9034
a. Request by Debtor
b. Request by Party-In-Interest
c. Request by U.S. Trustee Only
d. Service of Request
e. Notice of Hearing
f. Notice of Court Order
g. Legal Effect of Dismissal Order
7. Procedure Seven—Discharge of the Debtor
11 USC §524
FRBP 2002(f)(4)-(5)
a. Discharge Granted
(1) Redemption of Property
11 USC §722
FRBP 6008
(2) Reaffirmation of Debt
11 USC §524(c)-(f)
FRBP 4008
b. Discharge Denied
(1) Denial of Discharge
11 USC §727
FRBP 2002(f)(4), 4002, 4004-4006, 7001(4) et seq, 9034
(2) Exceptions to Discharge (Nondischargeability of Pre-Petition Debt)
11 USC §523
FRBP 2002(f)(5), 4007, 7001(6) et seq

III. Chapter 7—Liquidation

A. General Overview

Chapter 7 is one of the most frequently used bankruptcy chapters. Chapter 7 is a *straight liquidation proceeding*. The debtor's nonexempt assets are sold by a Chapter 7 trustee and the proceeds from such sale are distributed pro rata (same percentage of payment), first to creditors with priority claims, then to general unsecured creditors of the Chapter 7 debtor. Secured creditors with a valid lien receive the lesser of their respective collateral (or its value), or the amount of their allowed claim. *11 USC §§724-726.*

B. Preparing the Client

The prospective bankruptcy debtor should be required to bring the following information and documents to the initial attorney-client interview:

1. Complete list of all creditors, in alphabetical order, giving each creditor's name; mailing address; telephone number; amount of claim; whether secured (creditor holds a lien against some property of the

debtor) or unsecured (general trade creditors, charge-card creditors, etc.);

2. Tax returns filed by the debtor for the immediately preceding four-year period;
3. List of all property owned or claimed by the debtor, including personal and real property;
4. List of written questions to ask the attorney, legal assistant, or legal secretary;
5. Copies of all contracts signed by the debtor which represent obligations of the debtor, including: credit-charge agreements; deeds; leases; loan agreements; security agreements; Uniform Commercial Code financing statements; trust agreements; partnership agreements; or any other contract(s) reflecting a debt;
6. Copies of all financial statements prepared for or submitted by the debtor to any creditor or financial institution during the immediately preceding four-year period;
7. Copies of all inventories of the debtor's property prepared during the immediately preceding three-year period;
8. List of tax obligations for the immediately preceding four years for which a tax return was due;
9. List of all credit charge cards issued to the debtor or debtor and his spouse by a savings and loan, credit union, bank, or other financial institution; the respective credit card numbers; and the amounts owed on each credit card;
10. List of all checking account and savings account numbers, including respective amounts in each account and the respective financial institution in which each account is located; and
11. Current monthly budget, including all gross income received and expenses or obligations paid during the average month.

C. Stages of a Chapter 7 Case

The Nine Stages common to all voluntary bankruptcy cases govern a Chapter 7 case. *See "Nine Stages of Every Voluntary Bankruptcy Case," Chapter II.*

D. Procedures Under a Chapter 7 Case

There are seven procedures in a Chapter 7 case. Procedures one through four and seven occur in all successful Chapter 7 cases. Procedures five and six may occur in an unsuccessful Chapter 7 case.

1. Procedure One—The Debtor

A person (individual, partnership, or corporation) may be a debtor under Chapter 7. However, a railroad, insurance company, bank, savings and loan association, homestead association, small business investment company licensed by the Small Business Administration under §301(c) or (d) of the 1958 Small Business Investment Act, or credit union may not be a Chapter 7 debtor. *11 USC §109(b).*

2. Procedure Two—Debtor's Duties

The Chapter 7 debtor must perform seven duties to obtain a discharge:

a. The debtor must file a Chapter 7 petition with a list of creditors (mailing matrix) and pay the $150 filing fee at the bankruptcy clerk's office, unless installment payments are sought. *See "Installment Fees," Chapter II; 28 USC §1930(a)(1), (b), Judicial Conference Schedule of Fees (8); 11 USC §§301-302; FRBP 1002, 1005-1006, 5005; Official Bankr Forms 1, 2, 3;*

However, if the debtor is an individual with primarily consumer debts, the clerk must give the debtor written notice of each chapter under which the debtor could file a petition before a petition is filed. The clerk must then give notice of the debtor's Chapter 7 petition before the 20th day after it is filed. Such notice must be mailed to the debtor, any trustee, the U.S. trustee, all creditors, committee(s), indenture trustees, and to any other entity required by court order or local bankruptcy rules. *11 USC §§103(a), 109, 301-302, 342(a)-(b); FRBP 2002(f)(1), (i)-(k), (o), 5005; Official Bankr Form 9;*

b. The debtor must file the schedules of assets and liabilities, statement of financial affairs, schedule of current income and expenditures, and statement of executory contracts.

These schedules and statements must be filed with the bankruptcy petition or before the 15th day thereafter, unless the court extends such time, for cause. *11 USC §521(1); FRBP 1007;*

c. The individual debtor must file a statement of intention concerning property of the estate that secures a consumer debt, stating whether the debtor wishes to surrender or retain such property.

If the debtor wishes to keep the secured consumer property, the debtor must first claim the property as exempt on Schedule C of Official Bankruptcy Form 6. The debtor must then either redeem the property if it is secured, consumer, personal property (pay the secured creditor cash for the market value of the property) or reaffirm the underlying pre-petition debt. *See "Redemption of Property" and "Reaffirmation of Debt" discussed below.* The debtor must file the statement of intention by the earlier date of the first meeting of creditors or before the 30th day after the Chapter 7 petition is filed, unless the court extends the time, for cause, within such period. The debtor must also mail or personally deliver a copy of the statement of intention to the Chapter 7 trustee and all creditors identified in the statement. Finally, the debtor must perform according to the statement of intention before the 45th day after the statement is filed, unless the court extends the time, for cause, within the 45-

day period. *11 USC §§521(2), 524(c)-(d), 722; FRBP 1007(b)(2); Official Bankr Forms 6-8;*

d. The debtor must attend the meeting of creditors and any other examination of the debtor ordered by the court. *11 USC §§341, 343; FRBP 2003, 4002. See "Stage Six—Meeting of Creditors," Chapter II and "Meeting of Creditors," Chapter XIV; "Rule 2004 Examination," Chapter XIV;*

e. The debtor must cooperate with the Chapter 7 trustee or he may be denied a discharge of his otherwise dischargeable pre-petition debts.

Such cooperation includes:

(1) Providing the trustee with written notice of the location of any real property of the debtor and the name and address of every person holding money or property subject to the debtor's withdrawal or control. However, such notice is not required if the debtor has filed his schedules of assets and liabilities; and

(2) Assisting the trustee with the preparation of any inventory of property, the examination of proofs of claims, and the administration of the case. *11 USC §521(3); FRBP 3001-3008, 4002;*

f. The debtor must file a statement indicating any change of address. *FRBP 4002;* and

g. The debtor must attend the discharge hearing, unless such hearing or the debtor's attendance is not required by the court or local bankruptcy rules. *11 USC §§524(c)-(d), 727; FRBP 4002, 4004.*

3. Procedure Three—Chapter 7 Trustee

a. Appointment

After the Chapter 7 bankruptcy petition is filed, the U.S. trustee must promptly appoint an interim trustee from the panel of disinterested persons established by the U.S. trustee to serve in Chapter 7 cases. If no member of the panel is willing to serve as interim trustee, the U.S. trustee may serve as trustee. The services of the interim trustee end if a Chapter 7 trustee is elected during the first meeting of creditors. If no trustee is elected, the interim trustee remains the Chapter 7 trustee in the debtor's case. *11 USC §§321-322, 701-702; FRBP 2003(b)(3).*

b. Selection of Chapter 7 Trustee

During the first meeting of creditors, certain unsecured creditors may vote to elect a trustee to replace the interim trustee and serve as Chapter 7 trustee. To be a member of this voting group, the unsecured creditor must have filed a proof of claim or a written statement showing a right to vote no later than the first date set for the meeting of creditors. The proof of claim or written statement must not be objected to for voting purposes and must state that the creditor:

(1) **Is not an insider (relative, control person, director, shareholder) of the debtor;**

(2) **Does not have any interest materially adverse to other unsecured creditors; and**

(3) **Does have a voting claim.** A *voting claim* is an unsecured, undisputed, pre-petition, fixed, liquidated claim that is not a priority claim, and that may be satisfied from property of the bankruptcy estate. *11 USC §702(a); FRBP 2003(b)(3), 3001-3002; see "File Proof of Claims," Chapter XIV; Official Bankr Form 10.*

c. Procedures to Elect a Trustee

Once the voting group of unsecured creditors is determined at the first meeting of creditors, the election of a Chapter 7 trustee becomes a three-step process:

(1) Request Election

Unsecured creditors who hold at least 20 per cent in dollar amount of the total voting claims must request election of a trustee;

(2) Voting Claims Must Actually Vote

Unsecured creditors holding at least 20 per cent in dollar amount of the voting claims must actually vote to elect a trustee at the meeting of creditors; and

(3) Majority Vote for the Winner

The winning candidate for Chapter 7 trustee must receive a majority in dollar amount of the voting claims from votes cast at the election. *11 USC §§701, 702; S Rep No 989, 95th Cong, 2d Sess 92-93 (1978); HR Rep No 595, 95th Cong, 1st Sess 378-79 (1978); FRBP 2003(b).*

d. Eligibility and Qualification of Trustee

(1) Eligibility

(a) Individual

An individual who has not served as examiner in the case is eligible to serve as a Chapter 7 trustee if:

(i) The individual resides or has an office in the federal judicial district where the bankruptcy case is pending, or in any adjacent federal judicial district; and

(ii) The individual is competent to perform the duties of a trustee (see "Trustee's Duties" discussed below). *11 USC §§321, 704; FRBP 2015.*

(b) Corporation

A corporation that has not served as examiner in the case is eligible to serve as trustee if:

(i) The corporation has an office in the federal judicial district where the case is pending, or in an adjacent district; and

(ii) The corporation's charter or bylaws authorize it to act as trustee. *11 USC §§321, 704.*

(c) U.S. trustee

If necessary, the U.S. trustee for the federal judicial district where the debtor's bankruptcy case is pending is eligible to serve as Chapter 7 trustee. *11 USC §321(c).*

(2) Qualification

A person qualifies as a Chapter 7 trustee if he timely files a bond in favor of the United States conditioned on the faithful performance of his official duties. Such bond must be filed before the fifth day after the person is selected as trustee and before beginning his official duties. The U.S. trustee will immediately notify the person of his selection as trustee and the amount of the trustee's bond.

The U.S. trustee may authorize a blanket bond in favor of the United States conditioned on the faithful performance of official duties of one trustee who qualifies in a number of bankruptcy cases or of several trustees who qualify in different cases. *11 USC §322; FRBP 2008, 2010.*

A person selected as Chapter 7 trustee must file a written notice of acceptance with the court and U.S. trustee before the fifth day after receiving the U.S. trustee's notice of selection, or such person is deemed to have rejected the position. If a person has filed a blanket bond and been selected trustee in a Chapter 7, 12, or 13 case, such person must file a written notice of rejection with the court and U.S. trustee before the fifth day after receiving the U.S. trustee's notice of selection, or such person is deemed to have accepted the position. *11 USC §322; FRBP 2008.*

Any party-in-interest may file a proceeding in the name of the United States on the trustee's bond for the use of an entity injured by the breach of the trustee's official fiduciary duties. Such proceeding must be filed no later than two years after the date the trustee is discharged by the court (*see* "Closing the Chapter 7 Case," discussed below). However, a trustee is neither liable personally nor on his bond for any penalty or forfeiture incurred by the debtor in the case. *11 USC §§322(c)-(d), 350; FRBP 2010(b), 5009.*

e. Trustee's Duties

The Chapter 7 trustee must perform the following 14 duties:

(1) As soon as possible after the petition is filed, mail notice of the Chapter 7 case to every entity known to hold money or property subject to the debtor's control or withdrawal, unless such entity has knowledge or has already been notified of the bankruptcy case. Such entities include every bank, savings or building and loan association, public utility company, landlord who holds a deposit of the debtor, and every insurance company who issued a policy with a cash surrender value payable to the debtor;

(2) Collect and account for all property of the estate;

(3) Reduce property of the estate to money;

(4) Represent the estate, including filing any necessary action or defending an action on behalf of the estate and appearing and defending the estate in any pending action by or against the debtor. *See Chapter XIV;*

(5) Before the 30th day after qualifying as trustee, file a complete inventory of the debtor's property with the court and U.S. trustee, unless such inventory has already been filed;

(6) Keep a record of receipts and disposition of all money and property received;

(7) Ensure that the individual debtor performs as indicated under the debtor's statement of intention (*see* "Procedure Two—Debtor's Duties," discussed above);

(8) Investigate the financial affairs of the debtor;

(9) Examine proofs of claims and object to allowance of any claim that appears improper, if advisable;

(10) Oppose the debtor's discharge, if advisable;

(11) Furnish information about the estate and its administration if requested by a party-in-interest, unless the court orders otherwise;

(12) File periodic reports and summaries of the debtor's business operations if the court authorizes the trustee to operate the debtor's business for the benefit and orderly liquidation of the estate. Such reports and summaries must be filed with the court, the U.S. trustee, and any government unit responsible for collecting or determining any tax arising out of the operation of the debtor's business. The reports and summaries must include: (a) a statement of all receipts and disburse-

ments; (b) the amounts of deductions for all taxes required to be withheld or paid for employees and where such amounts are deposited; and (c) any other information required by the court or U.S. trustee;

(13) File a final report and account of the administration of the estate with the court and U.S. trustee; and

(14) Perform any other duty required by court order or local bankruptcy rules. *11 USC §§323, 704, 721; FRBP 2015, 6009.*

f. Trustee's Fees

(1) Generally

Subject to court approval, the Chapter 7 trustee may receive from the estate:

(a) Reasonable compensation for services rendered in the case. Such compensation may not exceed the following cumulative amounts based upon the amount of disbursements made by the trustee to parties-in-interest except the debtor:

Maximum Allowed Compensation:		Disbursements To Parties Other Than The Debtor:
25%	of	$0 through $5,000; plus
10%	of	$5,000.01 through $50,000; plus
5%	of	$50,000.01 through $1 million; plus
3%	of	Amounts over $1 million

(b) Compensation for actual legal or accounting services provided for the estate, if the court has authorized the trustee to represent the estate as an attorney or accountant as well as trustee;

(c) Reimbursement for actual, necessary expenses;

(d) Forty-five dollars from the Chapter 7 filing fee paid by the debtor; and

(e) Any additional fees prescribed by the Judicial Conference of the United States including fees as prescribed under 28 USC §1914(b), including notice of appearance fees and fees charged against distributions made in bankruptcy cases. Beginning October 22, 1995, another $15 may be paid to Chapter 7 trustees in addition to the $45 fee paid from the filing fee. *11 USC §§103(a), 326(a), 330.*

The trustee's compensation is paid after his services have been rendered in the case.

If the U.S. trustee is serving as Chapter 7 trustee, all compensation awarded by the court must be paid to the clerk. The clerk will then deposit the money into the U.S. trustee system fund. *11 USC §§326(a), 330(a)-(b), 503(b)(2), 507(a)(1); 28 USC §§586a, 1930(a)(1);*

(2) Procedures

(a) File Request for Compensation

The trustee's compensation and expenses allowed by the court are payable as a first priority claim. The trustee must file an application for compensation and reimbursement of expenses in the same manner required by the debtor's attorney (*see "Requirements of Debtor's Attorney—Application for Compensation," Chapter II*). A copy of the application should be served by first-class mail or personal delivery on the debtor, the U.S. trustee, any official creditors' committee elected at the meeting of creditors, and any other entity required by court order or local bankruptcy rules. If there are not sufficient funds in the estate to pay all allowed first priority claims in full, then the Chapter 7 trustee must share the funds pro rata (same percentage) with other first priority claimholders. No other priority claim category and no general unsecured creditors will receive any distribution of the estate's funds. *11 USC §§326, 330, 341, 343, 503(a)-(b), 507(a)(1), 702, 705; FRBP 2003(a)-(b)(1), (3), 2016(a), 9013, 9034; see "Stage Six—Meeting of Creditors," "Stage Seven—Distribution of the Estate," and "Requirements of Debtor's Attorney," Chapter II;*

(b) Notice of Hearing

The clerk of the court must give at least 20 days' notice of the hearing date on the trustee's application for compensation and reimbursement of expenses if the total amount requested by the trustee is more than $500. The notice must be mailed to the debtor, the trustee, the U.S. trustee, all creditors, indenture trustees, any committee elected in the case, and to any other party required by court order or local bankruptcy rules. *11 USC §§326, 330-331; FRBP 2002(a)(7)(i), 2016(a), 9034.*

(c) When Paid

The trustee's allowed compensation and expenses may be paid at the end of the Chapter 7 case; or as interim compensation awarded every 120 days after a voluntary petition is filed or the order for relief in an involuntary case, unless the court allows otherwise. However, the trustee may only be paid for services rendered. The trustee, as the representative of the estate, will make such payments as ordered by the court. *11 USC §§323(a), 326(a), 330-331, 503(b), 507(a)(1).*

4. Procedure Four—Exempt Property

The Chapter 7 debtor who is an individual is entitled to claim exemptions under federal bankruptcy exemption law, §522(b), (d) of the Code; or under federal, state, and/or local nonbankruptcy exemption law(s). Property which may be claimed as exempt but is not exempted remains property of the bankruptcy estate. *11 USC §§521(l), 522, 541; FRBP 1007, 4003; Official Bankr Form 6, Schedule C; see "Stage Five Exemptions Claimed by the Debtor," Chapter II.*

5. Procedure Five—Conversion

a. By the Debtor

Under bankruptcy law, the Chapter 7 debtor has the absolute right to convert his Chapter 7 case at any time to Chapter 11 (Reorganization), Chapter 12 (Family Farmer Debt Adjustment), or Chapter 13 (Individual Debt Adjustment), unless the debtor's present case was converted to Chapter 7 from Chapter 11, 12, or 13; or the debtor is not eligible to be a debtor under such other chapter. The debtor must file a motion to convert and serve a copy of the motion by first-class mail or personal delivery on the trustee, the U.S. trustee, any committee, and any other entity required by court order or local bankruptcy rules. The right of conversion may not be waived by the debtor. If the Chapter 7 case is a converted case, the debtor's right to convert is conditional and depends upon court approval. *11 USC §§109, 706(a), (d); FRBP 1017(d), 7005, 9013, 9034;*

b. By Another Entity

The court may convert a Chapter 7 case to Chapter 11 at any time if a party-in-interest files a request or motion to convert. The party-in-interest filing the motion to convert must serve a copy of the motion on the debtor by first-class mail, personal delivery by a disinterested third person at least 18 years old, or any other method allowed for service of process under the Federal Rules of Civil Procedure. The party-in-interest should also serve a copy of the motion on the Chapter 7 trustee, U.S. trustee, any committee appointed in the debtor's case, and on any other entity required by court order or local bankruptcy rules. The motion does not commence an adversary proceeding and no filing fee is required. No response is required by the debtor to the motion to convert unless the court or local bankruptcy rules direct otherwise. *11 USC §706(b); FRBP 1017, 7004-7005, 9013-9014, 9034;*

c. Hearing

The court must hold a hearing on the debtor's motion to convert if the present Chapter 7 case is a converted case, unless local bankruptcy rules direct otherwise. The court must always hold a hearing on a motion to convert filed by a party-in-interest if the debtor timely contests the motion. The party who filed the motion has the burden of proving:

(1) That the debtor is eligible to be a debtor under the particular chapter to which conversion is sought;

(2) That the debtor has sufficient regular income to fund and make all payments required by a plan under the chapter to which conversion is sought; and

(3) If the motion is to convert to Chapter 12 or 13, the debtor must have filed the motion to convert or voluntarily consented to conversion to such chapter. Chapters 12 and 13 are totally voluntary. *11 USC §§109, 706(a)-(d); FRBP 1017(b), (d), 9013-9014;*

d. Notice of Hearing

The clerk or other court-appointed person must give at least 20 days' notice by mail of the hearing on a motion to convert the debtor's Chapter 7 case. The notice must be sent to the debtor, the U.S. trustee, the Chapter 7 trustee, any committee in the debtor's case, all creditors, equity security holders, indenture trustees, and any other entity required by court order or local Bankruptcy Rules. *FRBP 2002(a)(5), (i), (k), 9034;*

e. Court's Ruling and Notice

If the debtor is eligible to be a debtor under the chapter to which conversion is sought and cause is proven for the conversion, the court will enter an order of conversion. The clerk or other court-authorized person must mail notice of the conversion order to the debtor, the U.S. trustee, the Chapter 7 trustee, any committee, all creditors, equity security holders, indenture trustees, and parties-in-interest in the debtor's case. *FRBP 2002(f)(2), (i), (k), 9034;*

f. Conversion Fee

If the debtor requests conversion from Chapter 7 (or 13) to Chapter 11, the debtor must pay a $400 conversion fee. No other fee is required from the debtor even though an original Chapter 11 petition requires a $600 filing fee. No fee is required to convert from Chapter 7 to Chapter 13 because the filing fees are the same ($150). *28 USC §1930(a)(1), (3), (b), Judicial Conference Schedule of Fees (8); FRBP 1017, 2002(a)(5), (f)(3), 9013-9014.*

6. Procedure Six—Dismissal

a. Request by Debtor

The debtor may file a motion to dismiss his Chapter 7 case. The court must hold a hearing on such motion after proper notice to the U.S. trustee, Chapter 7 trustee, creditors, and other parties-in-

interest as required by court order or local bankruptcy rules. *See discussion, below; 11 USC §§102(1)(A)-(B), 707; FRBP 1017(a), 2002(a)(5), (k), 9034.*

b. Request by Party-In-Interest

The debtor's Chapter 7 case may be dismissed upon request or motion filed by a party-in-interest (creditor, U.S. trustee, Chapter 7 trustee). The party-in-interest must file the motion and prove grounds for the dismissal, including:

(1) Unreasonable delay by the debtor that prejudices creditors' rights; or

(2) The debtor failed to pay any required filing fees or other fees. *11 USC §707(a); 28 USC §1930(a)-(b); FRBP 1006.*

c. Request by U.S. Trustee Only

Two grounds for dismissal of a Chapter 7 case may only be asserted by the U.S. trustee. The U.S. trustee is the only party-in-interest who may file a motion to dismiss the debtor's Chapter 7 case on grounds that:

(1) The debtor failed to file his required schedules and statements with the petition or before the 15th day thereafter, or by any later date set by the court; or

(2) In a Chapter 7 case involving an individual debtor with primarily *consumer debts* (debts incurred for personal, family, or household use), granting the debtor a discharge under Chapter 7 would be a substantial abuse of the provisions of Chapter 7.

The court may also sua sponte dismiss an individual debtor's case for substantial abuse. An example of a substantial abuse of the provisions of Chapter 7 is the debtor who intentionally and willfully incurs significant debts knowing that he will soon file a Chapter 7 petition to avoid paying such debts. However, there is a presumption under bankruptcy law in favor of the debtor and granting the debtor a discharge. *11 USC §§521(1), 707(a)(3), (b); FRBP 1007, 1017(e).*

The U.S. trustee must file a motion to dismiss for substantial abuse no later than 60 days after the first date set for the meeting of creditors, unless the court extends the time for cause. The motion must inform the debtor of all matters which will be presented to the court for determination. *11 USC §707(b); FRBP 1017(e).*

d. Service of Request

A motion or request to dismiss does not commence an adversary proceeding. No filing fee is required. The party-in-interest filing the motion must serve a copy on the debtor by first-class mail, personal delivery by a disinterested person at least 18 years old, or any other method allowed for service of a summons and complaint in federal district court. The party-in-interest should also mail or personally deliver a copy of the Motion to Dismiss to the U.S. trustee and the Chapter 7 trustee (unless such entity is the movant), and to all other parties directed by the court or local bankruptcy rules. The debtor does not have to file an answer or response, unless required by local bankruptcy rules. No default judgment can be obtained against the debtor for failure to answer a motion to dismiss unless the court or local bankruptcy rules direct otherwise. *FRBP 1017(d)-(e), 9013-9014.*

e. Notice of Hearing

(1) Generally

The court must hold a hearing on a motion to dismiss filed by the debtor or party-in-interest, unless local bankruptcy rules provide otherwise. The clerk or other court-authorized person must give at least 20 days' notice of the date of the hearing by mail to the debtor, the U.S. trustee, the Chapter 7 trustee, any committee, all creditors, indenture trustees, and any other entity required by court order or local bankruptcy rules. The clerk obtains the names and addresses of creditors from the list of creditors (mailing matrix) which the debtor must file with the petition or by the date set by the court. *11 USC §§521, 707; FRBP 1007, 2002(a)(5), (i), (k), 9034.*

(2) Court's Sua Sponte Motion to Dismiss for Substantial Abuse

If the hearing is on the court's own motion to dismiss the individual debtor's Chapter 7 case for substantial abuse, the clerk or other court-authorized person must mail notice of the hearing date to the debtor no later than the 60th day after the first date set for the meeting of creditors. The notice must inform the debtor about all matters which the court will consider at the hearing. *11 USC §507(b); FRBP 1017(e), 9014.*

f. Notice of Court Order

The clerk or other court-authorized person must also mail notice if the court orders dismissal of the Chapter 7 case. Such notice must be given to the debtor, the U.S. trustee, the Chapter 7 trustee, any committee, all creditors, indenture trustees, and any other entity required by court order or local bankruptcy rules. *FRBP 2002(f)(2), (i), (k), 9034.*

g. Legal Effect of Dismissal Order

(1) Dismissal with prejudice bars a debtor from refiling a Chapter 7 petition at any time and at any place. Rarely does a court issue an order dismissing a case with prejudice;

(2) Dismissal without prejudice does not bar a debtor from filing another Chapter 7 petition. The debtor may refile a petition. In fact, the debtor may refile a petition the same day the case is dismissed unless the court's order or local bankruptcy rules state otherwise. However, if the Chapter 7 case was dismissed because the debtor willfully failed to obey a court order or appear before the court to prosecute the case, or if the debtor requested dismissal after a motion for relief from the automatic stay was filed, the individual debtor must wait 181 days to refile any bankruptcy petition. *11 USC §109(g); see Local Bankruptcy Rules;*

(3) Status Quo Reinstated

Unless the court orders otherwise, dismissal of the debtor's case will reinstate the debtor, his creditors, and all parties-in-interest to their respective legal positions and status that existed immediately before the debtor filed the petition. Dismissal revests property of the estate in the debtor or other entity as existed pre-petition. Further, the automatic stay protecting the debtor, his property, and property of the estate terminates upon dismissal of a bankruptcy case, unless the court orders otherwise. Thus, a lawsuit which had been pending against the debtor in a nonbankruptcy court and enjoined by the automatic stay may now continue. *11 USC §§349, 362(c), 707.*

7. Procedure Seven—Discharge of the Debtor

The Chapter 7 debtor who is an individual will be granted a discharge as soon as possible after the 60th day after the first date set for the meeting of creditors. Corporate, partnership, or other debtors who are not natural persons do not receive a discharge under Chapter 7. Unless required by court order or local bankruptcy rules, the court does not have to hold a discharge hearing if there are no reaffirmation agreements or objections either to the debtor's general discharge or to the dischargeability of a particular pre-petition debt. If a discharge hearing is held, the clerk of the court will generally give at least 30 days' notice by mail of the date set for a discharge hearing to the debtor, the U.S. trustee, the Chapter 7 trustee, all creditors, equity security holders, indenture trustees, and any other entity required by court order or local bankruptcy rules. However, notice of the date of the discharge hearing may be combined with notice of the order for relief and first date set for the meeting of creditors. The debtor must attend the discharge hearing if a reaffirmation agreement has been made or an objection to discharge or dischargeability of a debt is filed. *11 USC §§102(1)(A)-(B), 524(d); FRBP 2002(a)(1), (f)(1), (4)-(5), (k), 4002, 4008, 9007, 9013-9014, 9034.*

At the discharge hearing, the debtor will either be granted a discharge of all pre-petition debts, or denied a discharge of one or more of such debts.

a. Discharge Granted

The clerk of the court must promptly mail a copy of the final discharge order to the debtor, trustee, U.S. trustee, all creditors, equity security holders, indenture trustees, and any other entity required by court order or local bankruptcy rules. Discharge of the individual Chapter 7 debtor relieves the debtor of personal liability for all pre-petition debts that are not excepted from discharge (*see "Exceptions to Discharge," discussed below*). If the debtor claimed certain property as exempt, such (exempt) property was removed from the bankruptcy estate and thus from the reach of the trustee and unsecured creditors. Exempt property cannot be used by the trustee to satisfy claims of unsecured creditors. However, exempt property with a lawful lien against it remains collateral of the secured creditor. The secured creditor may not enforce a pre-petition claim against the debtor personally after his discharge. But the secured creditor may foreclose on collateral that is exempt property using applicable nonbankruptcy law after the debtor has received a discharge. The automatic stay terminates with regard to the debtor and his exempt property on the date the debtor is discharged. *11 USC §§362(c), 506(a), 727; FRBP 2002(f), (k), 4004(g); Official Bankr Form 18; see Johnson v Home State Bank, 501 US 78, 111 S Ct 2150, remanded, 940 F2d 609 (10th Cir), cert denied, 501 US 1216, 111 S Ct 2824 (1991).*

Thus, if the Chapter 7 debtor wishes to retain secured exempt property after his discharge, he must use at least one of two procedures. The debtor must either *redeem* (buy back) the collateral from the secured creditor, or reaffirm the pre-petition debt with the creditor and court approval. In the case of a consumer debtor (one whose debts are primarily consumer debts), the Chapter 7 statement of intention previously filed by the debtor should indicate which of these procedures the debtor will use. *See "Procedure Two—Debtor's Duties," discussed above; 11 USC §521(2); FRBP 1007; Official Bankruptcy Form 8.*

(1) Redemption of Property

Only a Chapter 7 debtor who is an individual may redeem tangible, personal, consumer property securing a dischargeable consumer debt (debt incurred for personal, family, or household purposes). The debtor may not redeem real property. The debtor redeems property by paying cash in lump sum to the secured creditor for the *value* of the lien, which is the lesser of the fair market value of the property (collateral) or the amount of the secured creditor's claim allowed by the court.

Installment payments are not allowed. The property that the debtor wishes to redeem or buy back must either be property the debtor has claimed as exempt or property the trustee has abandoned from the estate. But the debtor may redeem the entire property, not just any equity in the property, even if the debtor claimed exemptions under §522(d) of the Bankruptcy Code, which permits the debtor to exempt only his (equity) interest in property. Thus, if the debtor exempted a motor vehicle under §522(d) valued at $3,000 and the amount of the secured creditor's allowed claim against the property was $2,000, the debtor may redeem the entire property for $2,000 (lesser of the value of the collateral or amount of the secured claim), even though the debtor's exemptible interest was just $1,000 under §522(d)(2). *11 USC §§522(d)(2), 722; HR Rep No 595, 95th Cong, 1st Sess 380-81 (1977); see Ford Motor Credit Co v Polk, 17 CBC2d 684 (9th Cir 1987); In re Edwards, 901 F2d 1383 (7th Cir 1990).*

The trustee, on behalf of the estate, may also redeem property from a lien or from a sale to enforce a secured creditor's lien. The debtor or trustee seeking to redeem property must file a motion to redeem and serve a copy of it on the secured creditor, the trustee (or debtor if the trustee is the movant), all committee(s) appointed under the debtor's case, and all other entities directed by the court or local bankruptcy rules. Service may be obtained by first-class mail, personal delivery by a disinterested person at least 18 years old, or by any manner permitted for service of process in federal district court. A hearing on the motion to redeem will be held before the court, unless local bankruptcy rules provide otherwise. Such hearing may be combined with the discharge hearing. *11 USC §§102(1)(A)-(B), 722; FRBP 4004(c), 6008, 7004, 9013-9014.*

(2) Reaffirmation of Debt

(a) Generally

A Chapter 7, (11, 12, or 13) debtor may reaffirm a pre-petition debt that is otherwise dischargeable under the Code. The Chapter 7 debtor who cannot redeem secured property must reaffirm the underlying debt to keep such property. Reaffirmation by the debtor affects his fresh start because the debtor agrees to remain personally liable for the pre-petition debt that would otherwise be discharged. Reaffirmation, therefore, is closely scrutinized by the court to assure strict compliance with bankruptcy law by the debtor, the debtor's attorney (if one), and the respective creditor. *11 USC §§103(a), 524(c)-(d); FRBP 4008.*

(b) Procedures

The debtor must observe the following procedures to reaffirm a pre-petition debt:

(i) File a Reaffirmation Agreement

The debtor and creditor must enter into the reaffirmation agreement before the debtor receives a discharge. The reaffirmation agreement must generally be filed with the court by the 30th day after the date the discharge order is entered, unless the court or local bankruptcy rules allow otherwise. As a practical matter, a reaffirmation agreement is generally filed by the date set by the court for the discharge hearing. *11 USC §524(c)-(d); FRBP 4008;*

(ii) File a Motion for Approval of Reaffirmation Agreement

The debtor must also file a motion for approval of reaffirmation agreement. The motion may be filed either before or at the hearing set by the court on the reaffirmation agreement. A copy of the motion must be served on the respective creditor, trustee, and all other entities as directed by court order or local bankruptcy rules. *11 USC §524(c)-(d); FRBP 4008, 9013-9014; see Local Bankruptcy Rules;*

(iii) Hearing

The court must hold a hearing on the reaffirmation agreement if the debtor was not represented by an attorney during the negotiations of the agreement or if the court or local bankruptcy rules so require. Hearing on the debtor's reaffirmation agreement must be held no later than the 30th day after the discharge order is entered. However, the hearing on the motion and the discharge hearing are frequently combined. The clerk of the court must give at least ten days' notice by mail to the debtor, Chapter 7 trustee, and all other entities directed by the court or local bankruptcy rules if the hearing on the debtor's motion is held after the discharge hearing. *11 USC §524(d); FRBP 4008; see Local Bankruptcy Rules.*

(c) Requirements for Court Approval

The reaffirmation agreement must be based on a debt that is dischargeable under bankruptcy law and must meet six requirements for court approval:

(i) The reaffirmation agreement must be made before the debtor is granted a discharge;

(ii) The reaffirmation agreement must contain a clear, conspicuous statement advising the debtor that he may rescind the agreement any time before the later date that the debtor is discharged or before the 60th day after the reaffirmation agreement is filed with the bankruptcy court. The debtor may rescind by merely giving notice of rescission to the creditor and the court;

(iii) The reaffirmation agreement must contain a clear, conspicuous statement advising the debtor that a reaffirmation agreement is not required under either bankruptcy or nonbankruptcy law or under any reaffirmation agreement that does not comply with the provisions of 11 USC §524(c).

(iv) The reaffirmation agreement must be filed with the bankruptcy court before or at the hearing on the motion for approval of reaffirmation agreement;

(v) The reaffirmation agreement must be accompanied by a declaration or affidavit of any attorney that represented the debtor during negotiations of the agreement, stating that:

(a) the agreement constitutes a fully informed and voluntary agreement by the debtor;

(b) the agreement does not impose an undue hardship on the debtor; and

(c) the attorney fully advised the debtor about the legal effect and consequences of a reaffirmation agreement and any default that might occur under the agreement;

(vi) The debtor must not rescind the reaffirmation agreement before the later date that he receives his discharge or the 60th day after the agreement is filed with the court; and

(vii) If a consumer debt is being reaffirmed and the debtor was not represented by an attorney during negotiations for the reaffirmation agreement, the bankruptcy court must find that the agreement does not impose an undue hardship on the debtor or a dependent and that the agreement is in the best interests of the debtor, unless the debtor is reaffirming a consumer debt secured by his real property. *11 USC §524(c)-(d); FRBP 4008.*

(d) Court's Obligations

If the court holds a hearing on the debtor's motion for approval of reaffirmation agreement, the court must inform the debtor that:

(i) A reaffirmation agreement is not required under either bankruptcy or nonbankruptcy law;

(ii) The debt reaffirmed will not be discharged under the debtor's bankruptcy case;

(iii) The debtor will remain personally liable for the reaffirmed debt and must continue to pay the creditor according to terms of the reaffirmation agreement or risk a judgment against him or foreclosure against any collateral securing the debt or both; and

(iv) The debtor may not receive another discharge under Chapter 7 for at least six years after the date the present bankruptcy petition was filed. However, the debtor may receive a discharge under Chapter 12 or 13 without waiting six years. Thus, the debtor may use a *Chapter 20 procedure* by first receiving a discharge under Chapter 7 and thereafter filing a Chapter 13 petition to reschedule a secured claim from which the debtor had been personally discharged under the Chapter 7 case. *See Johnson v Home State Bank, 501 US 78, 111 S Ct 2150, remanded, 940 F2d 609 (10th Cir), cert denied, 501 US 1216, 111 S Ct 2824 (1991). 11 USC §§524, 727; FRBP 4008; Chapter V.*

b. Discharge Denied

If a discharge is not granted, the Chapter 7 debtor will either be denied a discharge of all pre-petition debts (denial of discharge) or he will be denied a discharge of particular pre-petition debt(s) (exception to discharge). The debtor remains personally liable for each pre-petition debt that is not discharged under Chapter 7:

(1) Denial of Discharge

Denial of discharge under Chapter 7 is a debt death sentence. The debtor will almost always be personally liable for all such pre-petition debts. There are basically eleven grounds for denial of discharge of a Chapter 7 debtor. Four grounds require automatic denial of discharge without the necessity of a creditor or trustee filing an objection to discharge. Seven grounds must be asserted by a creditor or trustee filing an objection:

(a) No Objection Required

The court must deny a Chapter 7 debtor a discharge of all pre-petition debts if any of the following four conditions exist. No objection need be filed with the court but one may be filed by a creditor, trustee, or U.S. trustee:

(i) The debtor is not an individual. Corporations, partnerships, and other non-natural persons are not entitled to a Chapter 7 discharge;

(ii) The debtor has been granted a discharge under Chapter 7 or 11 within the immediate six years before the date of filing the present Chapter 7 petition;

(iii) The debtor was granted a discharge under Chapter 12 or 13 within the immediate six years before filing the present Chapter 7 petition. However, the debtor may still be granted a Chapter 7 discharge if: a) the debtor paid either 100 per cent of all unsecured claims, or 70 per cent of such unsecured claims under the prior Chapter 12 or 13 case; b) this 70 per cent was the debtor's best efforts; and c) the Chapter 12 or 13 plan was filed in good faith; or

(iv) The court has approved a written waiver of discharge of all pre-petition debts filed by the debtor post-petition. *11 USC §727(a)(1), (8)-(10).*

(b) Objection Required

The trustee, a creditor, or the U.S. trustee must file a timely objection to the discharge of the debtor if based on one or more of the following seven grounds, or the debtor will be granted a discharge:

(i) The debtor destroyed, transferred, or concealed his property within one year before filing the Chapter 7 petition or property of the bankruptcy estate after filing the petition, and the debtor engaged in such conduct with the intent to hinder, delay, or defraud a creditor or officer (trustee) of the bankruptcy estate. Such conduct may also be a bankruptcy crime punishable by fine and/or imprisonment. *See "Bankruptcy Crimes and Penalties," Chapter XIV; 11 USC §727(a)(2); 18 USC §152;*

(ii) The debtor destroyed, transferred, concealed, falsified, or failed to keep documents or books concerning the debtor's business transactions or financial condition, unless such conduct was justified under all the circumstances of the debtor's case. This conduct may also be a bankruptcy crime, punishable by fine and/or imprisonment. *See "Bankruptcy Crimes and Penalties," Chapter XIV. 11 USC §727(a)(3); 18 USC §152;*

(iii) The debtor has failed to explain satisfactorily any loss or deficiency of assets to pay the debtor's present liabilities. *11 USC §727(a)(5);*

(iv) The debtor refused to obey a court order, or testify or respond to a material question even after the debtor was granted immunity regarding such question. *11 USC §727(a)(6);*

(v) The debtor knowingly and fraudulently made a false oath or account or presented or used a false claim at any time during his Chapter 7 case. A false oath or claim could occur on the debtor's Chapter 7 petition, at the meeting of creditors, at any hearing, on the debtor's statement of financial affairs or schedules of assets and liabilities, or on a proof of claim. But the falsity must have been knowingly and fraudulently committed by the debtor. Such conduct may also be a bankruptcy crime, punishable by fine and/or imprisonment. *See "File Proof of Claim" and "Bankruptcy Crimes and Penalties," Chapter XIV; 11 USC §727(a)(4); 18 USC §§152, 3571; 28 USC §1746; FRBP 1007-1008;*

(vi) The debtor knowingly and fraudulently made a deal with a creditor or other entity after filing the petition, unless such agreement is approved by the bankruptcy court. This conduct may also be a bankruptcy crime. *See "Bankruptcy Crimes and Penalties," Chapter XIV; 11 USC §727(a)(4)(C); 18 USC §152;* or

(vii) The debtor knowingly and fraudulently withheld any information, books, documents, papers, or records concerning his property or financial affairs from an officer (trustee) of the bankruptcy estate. This conduct, too, may be a bankruptcy crime. *See "Bankruptcy Crimes and Penalties," Chapter XIV: 11 USC §727(a)(4)(D); 18 USC §152.*

(c) Procedures to Deny Discharge

(i) Notice of when to File Objection to Discharge

The clerk of the court or other court-authorized person must give at least 25 days' notice of the date set by the court to file an objection to discharge of the debtor. Unless the court extends the time, the objection must not be filed later than the 60th day after the first date set for the meeting of creditors. The notice must be sent to the debtor, the U.S. trustee, the Chapter 7 trustee, all creditors, committee(s), indenture trustees, and parties-in-interest required by court order or local bankruptcy rules, either by mail or publication if notice by mail is impractical. *FRBP 2002(f)(4), (i), (k)-(l), 4004(a)-(b), 9034;*

(ii) Objection

The creditor, Chapter 7 trustee, or U.S. trustee must file an Objection to Discharge asserting one or more of the seven grounds for denial of discharge stated above. An Objection to Discharge is an adversary complaint. The creditor, Chapter 7 trustee, or U.S. trustee if acting as a Chapter 7 trustee, must pay a $120 filing fee and serve a copy of the objection with a summons on the debtor by first-class mail, personal delivery by a disinterested person at least 18 years old, or by any other manner allowed for service of process under the Federal Rules of Civil Procedure. However, if the Chapter 7 trustee or U.S. trustee acting as Chapter 7 trustee files the objection, the $120 filing fee is only payable from the estate, if any materializes. A copy of the objection should also be served by mail or personal delivery on any committee and other entity required by court order or local bankruptcy rules. *FRBP 4005, 7001(4), 7004 et seq; 28 USC §§1914(a)-(b), 1930(b), Judicial Conference Schedule Of Fees (6);*

(iii) Hearing and Notice of Court's Ruling

The court must hold a trial on an objection to discharge. If the court rules in favor of the debtor and grants a discharge, the clerk of the court must immediately mail a copy of the court's final discharge order to the debtor, the U.S. trustee, the Chapter 7 trustee, and all creditors. If the court rules against the debtor and denies a discharge, the clerk must promptly mail a copy of the final order denying discharge to the debtor, the U.S. trustee, the Chapter 7 trustee, and all creditors. *11 USC §727; FRBP 2002(f)(4), (6), (k), 4004, 4006, 9034.*

(2) Exceptions to Discharge (Nondischargeability of Pre-Petition Debt)

Exception to discharge or nondischargeability of a debt is an adversary procedure by which the debtor is denied a discharge of a particular pre-petition debt. This procedure applies to all bankruptcy cases, except Chapter 9 cases, and to a limited extent only under Chapter 13 cases. *11 USC §§103(a), (e), 901, 523(a), 901; see Chapters VII & V, respectively.*

(a) No Objection Required

Twenty-five pre-petition debts are deemed nondischargeable under bankruptcy law. No objection or adversary complaint need be filed for such debts to be nondischargeable. However, a complaint to determine dischargeability may be filed by a creditor or trustee to protect such entity's rights:

- (i) Taxes entitled to second or eighth priority status. *See "Priority Claims," Chapter II;*
- (ii) Taxes for which the debtor failed to file a required tax return;
- (iii) Taxes for which the debtor filed a late return within two years before filing the petition;
- (iv) Taxes for which the debtor filed a fraudulent return or which the debtor willfully attempted, by any manner, to evade or defeat;
- (v) Any debt known to the debtor which he failed to list under his schedules of liabilities (Offl. Bankr. Form 6, Schs. D-G) in time to permit the respective creditor to file a timely proof of claim or complaint to determine dischargeability, unless such creditor had sufficient notice or actual knowledge of the debtor's bankruptcy case;
- (vi) Alimony, maintenance, or support payments owed by the debtor to his spouse, ex-spouse, or child under a divorce decree or settlement agreement, unless such debt was assigned to another entity that is not a federal or state government or political subdivision of a state;
- (vii) An educational benefit overpayment, loan, scholarship, or stipend which was insured or guaranteed by a government unit or nonprofit institution, unless such debt matured more than seven years before the debtor filed the petition, (excluding any applicable suspension of debt repayment period), or nondischargeability of the debt would cause an undue hardship to the debtor and his dependents;

(viii) A debt for death or personal injury caused by the debtor operating a motor vehicle while intoxicated from use of alcohol, a drug, or other substance;

(ix) Any fine or penalty relating to a nondischargeable tax. The fine or penalty must in fact be penal in nature;

(x) A debt which the debtor listed or could have listed on his schedules of liabilities in a prior bankruptcy case for which either the court denied or the debtor waived discharge;

(xi) A debt represented by a final order, decree, or judgment of a federal or state court, if the debt was issued by a federal depository institution's regulatory agency or contained in a settlement agreement and was based upon the debtor's fraud or defalcation as a fiduciary to a federal depository institution or insured credit union. However, if a regulatory agency of a federal depository institution, acting as a conservator, receiver, or liquidating agent of an insured depository institution, is appointed in time to reasonably comply with the bar date to object to dischargeability, then the regulatory agency must file a timely objection to dischargeability of such debt. *See "Procedures to Determine Dischargeability of a Debt," discussed below; 11 USC §523(c)(2);*

(xii) A debt for the debtor's malicious or reckless failure to fulfill a commitment to a federal depository institution's regulatory agency to maintain the capital of an insured depository institution. However, if the debtor's commitment to maintain capital would be terminated because of the regulatory agency's conduct, the debt is dischargeable;

(xiii) A debt for payment of a criminal restitution order under Title 18, United States Code. *Pub L No 103-322, "The Violent Crime Control and Law Enforcement Act of 1994" (Sept 13, 1994), amending and adding 11 USC §523(a)(13);*

(xiv) A debt incurred by the debtor to pay a federal tax that would be nondischargeable under 11 USC §523(a)(1) (taxes entitled to second or eighth priority status; taxes for which the debtor failed to file a required tax return or filed a fraudulent return; or taxes for which the debtor filed a late return within the two-year pre-petition period); or

(xv) A debt for a post-petition fee or assessment owed to a membership association arising out of the debtor's ownership interest in a condominium or share of a cooperative housing project for a period in which the debtor actually occupied such premises or rented the premises and received the payments. However, a pre-petition membership fee or assessment *is* dischargeable in the debtor's present or subsequent bankruptcy case. *11 USC §523(a)(1), (3), (5), (7), (12), (13), (14), (16).*

Debts for taxes (*Paragraphs (i)-(iv) above*), debts which the debtor failed to list on his schedules of liabilities (Paragraph (v) above), or debts for educational loans or overpayments (Paragraph (vii) above) may be discharged in a subsequent Chapter 7 case of the debtor even if such debts are held nondischargeable under the present (Chapter 7) case. Most other debts nondischargeable under Chapter 7 will pose difficulties for the debtor under any case except Chapter 13. *See Chapter V; 11 USC §§103(a), 523(b), 1141(d)(2), 1228(a)(2), 1328(a)-(b); Official Bankr Form 6, Schedules D-H.*

(b) Objection Required

A creditor must timely file an adversary complaint to determine dischargeability of five types of pre-petition debts, or such debts will be discharged. *See "Procedures to Determine Dischargeability of a Debt," discussed below*:

(i) A debt incurred by the debtor through misrepresentation or actual fraud. Two types of consumer debts carry a presumption that the debtor acted under false pretenses or fraudulently and that the debts are nondischargeable. First are consumer debts for luxury good or services, totalling more than $1,000, owed to a single creditor, and incurred by an individual debtor 60 days or less before the Chapter 7 petition was filed. Luxury goods and services are not goods or services reasonably acquired for the support or maintenance of the debtor or his dependent. The second type of consumer debt that carries a presumption of false pretenses or fraud and nondischargeability is cash advances, extended under an open-end credit plan as defined by the Consumer Credit Protection Act (15 USC §1601 *et seq*), for more than $1,000, obtained by an individual debtor 60 days or less before filing the Chapter 7 petition. *11 USC §523(a)(2);*

(ii) A debt for fraud or defalcation while the debtor was acting in a fiduciary capacity. *11 USC §523(a)(4);*

(iii) A debt for embezzlement or larceny. *11 USC §523(a)(4);*

(iv) Tort debts representing the debtor's willful and malicious injury to another entity or such entity's property but that do not involve the operation of a motor vehicle while under the influence of alcohol, a drug, or other substance. *11 USC §523(a)(6), (c)(1);* and

(v) A debt arising under a divorce or separation, separation agreement, divorce decree, or similar court order issued according to state or territorial law that is not alimony, maintenance, or support payments to the debtor's spouse, ex-spouse, or child. Hold harmless agreements, property settlement obligations, and obligations to pay attorney's fees of a spouse or ex-spouse are examples of such a nondischargeable debt. However, these separation—or divorce—related debts will also be dischargeable if:

  (a) the debtor does not have the ability to pay such debts from income or property that is not reasonably necessary for the support or maintenance of the debtor, his dependent, or the debtor's business; or

  (b) the debtor's benefit from receiving a discharge of such debt outweighs any detrimental consequences that would result to the debtor's spouse, ex-spouse, or child.

There are two situations in which the creditor does not have to file a timely objection to dischargeability involving one of the above five types of debts. **First,** a regulatory agency of a federal depository institution does not have to file a complaint to determine dischargeability of these four types of debts if the regulatory agency is acting as a receiver or liquidating agent for an insured depository institution and the debtor is an affiliated party of a federal depository institution, unless the regulatory agency was appointed receiver or liquidating agent in time to file a complaint by the date set by the court. **Second,** if the debtor failed to list the creditor on the debtor's schedules of liabilities in time to permit the creditor to comply with the bar date to file a proof of claim and to object to dischargeability, then no objection to dischargeability of such debt is required unless the creditor had notice or actual knowledge of the bankruptcy case to file a timely claim and objection. *See "Procedures to Determine Dischargeability of a Debt," discussed below. 11 USC §523(a)(3), (c)(2).*

(c) Procedures to Determine Dischargeability of a Debt

(i) Notice of when to File a Complaint

The clerk or other court-authorized person must give notice by mail to all creditors of the last date to file a complaint to determine dischargeability of a pre-petition debt. A complaint to determine the dischargeability of a debt based on the debtor's alleged fraud, embezzlement, larceny, or willful and malicious tort that does not involve the operation of a motor vehicle while under the influence of a drug, alcohol, or other substance must be filed by the 60th day after the first date set for the meeting of creditors, unless the court extends the time for cause, within such period. The clerk must give creditors, the debtor, the U.S. trustee, and Chapter 7 trustee at least 30 days' prior notice of the last date to file such a complaint. *FRBP 2002(f)(5), (i), 4007(b)-(c), 9034.*

A complaint to determine dischargeability of any other debt may be filed at any time, even after the bankruptcy case is closed, unless the court or local bankruptcy rules state otherwise. The clerk of the court must give notice of any date fixed by the court or local bankruptcy rules to file such complaint. Notice must be mailed to the debtor, creditors, U.S. trustee, and Chapter 7 trustee. *FRBP 2002(f)(5), (i), 4007, 9034; see "Reopening a Case," Chapter II; Brown v Felsen, 442 US 127 (1979);*

(ii) File the Complaint

A complaint to determine dischargeability of a debt is an adversary proceeding. The creditor must pay a $120 filing fee and serve the complaint with a summons on the debtor by first-class mail, personal delivery by a disinterested party at least 18 years old, or by any other method allowed for service of process in federal district court. A copy of the complaint should also be served on the trustee. The creditor has the burden of proving one or more of the above grounds for nondischargeability. *See Grogan v Garner, 498 US 279, 111 S Ct 654 (1991); 11 USC §523, 28 USC §§1914(b), 1930(b), Judicial Conference*

Schedule Of Fees (6); FRBP 4007, 7001, 7004 et seq; Procedural Bankr Forms B 250A, B, C.

(iii) Caveat

A complaint to determine dischargeability of a debtor's consumer debt for alleged fraud or misrepresentation can be a double-edged sword. If the court rules that the consumer debt is dischargeable, the court must grant judgment for the debtor and award the debtor his costs, including reasonable attorneys' fees, incurred in defending such complaint, unless the court finds that the creditor's position was substantially justified or that special circumstances exist which would make award of the debtor's costs and fees unjust. *11 USC §523(d).*

c. Discharge Revoked

(1) Who May File to Revoke Discharge

A trustee, U.S. trustee, or creditor may file an adversary complaint to revoke discharge. *11 USC §727(d); FRBP 7001(4) et seq.*

(2) Grounds to Revoke Discharge

Revocation of discharge must be based upon one or more of three grounds:

(a) The debtor obtained his discharge through fraud and the trustee or creditor had no knowledge of such fraud until after the discharge was granted;

(b) The debtor acquired or had the legal right to acquire property of the bankruptcy estate and the debtor knowingly and fraudulently failed to report, deliver, or surrender such property to the trustee; or

(c) The debtor refused to obey a court order or testify after immunity had been granted to the debtor. *11 USC §727(d).*

(3) Procedures to Revoke Discharge

(a) File Complaint

The creditor, trustee, or U.S. trustee must file an adversary complaint to revoke discharge of the debtor. The creditor must pay a $120 filing fee. If the trustee files the complaint, the $120 filing fee is payable only from the estate, if any materializes. No filing fee is required from the U.S. trustee unless he is acting as a Chapter 7 trustee. The party filing the complaint to revoke discharge must serve a copy of the complaint with a summons on the debtor by first-class mail, personal delivery by a disinterested person at least 18 years old, or by any manner allowed for service of process of a civil suit in federal district court. A copy of the complaint should also be mailed or delivered to the U.S. trustee and Chapter 7 trustee unless he filed the complaint. *11 USC §727(d)-(e); 28 USC §1930(b), Judicial Conference Schedule Of Fees (6); FRBP 4006, 7001(4) et seq.*

(b) When a Complaint Must Be Filed

A complaint to revoke discharge based upon the debtor's alleged fraud must be filed before one year after the date the debtor's discharge is granted. A complaint to revoke discharge based upon either of the other two grounds (the debtor failed to deliver or report property of the estate or the debtor refused to obey a court order or testify after immunity was granted) must be filed before the date that the case is closed or one year after the debtor is granted a discharge, whichever is later. *11 USC §727(e);*

(c) Notice and Hearing

The court must hold a trial on a complaint to revoke discharge. The clerk or other court-ordered person must mail notice of the trial date to the debtor, the party filing the complaint, the U.S. trustee, the Chapter 7 trustee, and all other parties-in-interest required by the court or local bankruptcy rules. The party filing the complaint has the burden of proving at least one of the three grounds for revocation of discharge (*see* "Grounds to Revoke Discharge," discussed above);

(d) Notice of Court's Decision

If the court rules against the debtor and revokes the discharge, the clerk must promptly mail notice of the revocation of discharge to the debtor, the U.S. trustee, the Chapter 7 trustee, all creditors, committee(s), and to all other parties-in-interest directed by court order or local bankruptcy rules. *11 USC §727(d); FRBP 2002(f)(6), (i), (k), 4006, 9034.*

(4) Life After Revocation of Discharge

If the court revokes the debtor's discharge, the debtor could be denied a discharge or his case could be dismissed or converted to Chapter 11, 12, or 13, at the court's discretion. Whether the court dismisses the case or allows conversion to another chapter will depend upon the ground for revocation. However, only Chapter 13 would afford the debtor a discharge from many debts which are otherwise nondischargeable under Chapter 7, 11, and 12. *See Chapter V; 11 USC §§706, 707, 727(a)(4)(A)-(B).*

(a) Dismissal

If the ground for revocation was the debtor's fraud in obtaining his discharge, the court will probably deny any motion to convert and dismiss the debtor's case, after notice to creditors and hearing. The clerk of the court must mail notice of the court's order denying discharge and dismissing the case, either with the notice of revocation of discharge or separately, to the debtor, U.S. trustee, Chapter 7 trustee, and all creditors. Such notice is essential to protect creditors' rights. Under bankruptcy law, the statute of limitations to file an action in a nonbankruptcy court is tolled by the debtor's filing his petition. Tolling of this statute of limitations ends on the later of 30 days after the debtor is denied or loses his right to a discharge and the case is dismissed or the end of the limitations period under applicable nonbankruptcy law. If creditors do not receive notice of the revocation or denial of discharge and dismissal of the case and the statute of limitations period expires, the debtor will then obtain essentially the same benefits from his Chapter 7 case as a debtor whose discharge is not revoked. Dismissal of the debtor's case should return the debtor and his creditors to their pre-petition positions. Notice of revocation of discharge and dismissal implements this process. *11 USC §§108(c), 349, 362(c)(2), 727(d)-(e); FRBP 2002(f)(6), 4006, advisory committee's note; see "Procedure Six—Dismissal," discussed above.*

(b) Conversion

If the debtor requests and is permitted to convert his case to Chapter 11, the debtor must pay a $400 conversion fee. No other fee is required of the debtor even though an original Chapter 7 petition would require a $600 filing fee. If the debtor is permitted to convert to Chapter 13, no additional fee is required. The debtor must comply with all requirements for conversion previously discussed. *See "Procedure Five—Conversion," discussed above; 11 USC §706; 28 USC §1930(a)(1), (3), (b), Judicial Conference Schedule of Fees (8).*

(c) File New Petition

If the debtor's case is dismissed without prejudice after revocation of discharge, he may file a new petition. Since the grounds for revocation of discharge involve the debtor's fraud, refusal to obey a court order or testify after grant of immunity, or fraudulent failure to report or deliver property of the estate, the debtor may have to wait

181 days after dismissal to file a new petition. *11 USC §§109(g), 727(d); see "Who May Be a Debtor," Chapter II.*

If the debtor's Chapter 7 case is dismissed with prejudice, the debtor may never file another Chapter 7 petition in any bankruptcy court anywhere. *11 USC §§109(g), 727(d)-(e).*

E. Distribution of the Chapter 7 Estate

1. Who Distributes

The Chapter 7 trustee, as representative of the bankruptcy estate, will sell or otherwise liquidate (reduce to cash) property in the estate to satisfy allowed unsecured claims on a pro rata basis. A creditor must file a timely proof of claim to receive distribution under Chapter 7. A claim is deemed allowed if a proof of claim is timely filed without objection. Any party-in-interest (debtor, creditor, trustee) may object to a proof of claim. *See "File Proof of Claim," Chapter XIV; 11 USC §§323, 501, 502; FRBP 3002, 3008-3009.*

2. When Distribution Occurs

The trustee will make dividend payments to creditors as soon as practical given the facts of the particular Chapter 7 case. Disbursements will be made in amounts and on dates ordered by the court. Dividend disbursements to unsecured creditors are paid pro rata. All creditors who belong to the same category or group of creditors under bankruptcy law will receive the same percentage of payment of their allowed prepetition claims. *See "Priority Claims," Chapter II; "File Proof of Claim," Chapter XIV; 11 USC §726; FRBP 3002, 3008-3009.*

3. Abandonment of Property

The trustee may abandon property of the estate that he determines is burdensome and of inconsequential value and benefit to the estate. The trustee may abandon such property to any party-in-interest who has a possessory or security interest in the property or to the debtor. The trustee must serve notice of the proposed abandonment by first-class mail on the debtor, U.S. trustee, any committee elected in the case, all creditors, indenture trustees, and all other parties required by court order or local bankruptcy rules. A party-in-interest must file and serve on the trustee any objection to the notice of proposed abandonment before the 15th day after the notice is mailed, unless the court orders otherwise. If a timely objection is filed and served, the court must hold a hearing on the notice. *11 USC §§554, 725; FRBP 6007, 9013-9014; HR Rep No 595, 95th Cong, 1st Sess, 377 (1977); S Rep No 989, 95th Cong, 2d Sess 92 (1978).*

Any property scheduled on the debtor's schedule of assets and liabilities that is not otherwise administered (disbursed or abandoned) by the trustee at the time the Chapter 7 case is closed is deemed abandoned to the debtor and fully administered for all purposes. *11 USC*

§§350, 554(b); Official Bankr Form 6, Schedules A-G; see "Compelled Abandonment of Property," Chapter XIV.

4. Order of Disbursements

The trustee must segregate any community from noncommunity property, including their proceeds. The trustee will then disburse property or proceeds of the estate in the following order:

a. Secured Property

(1) Generally

A secured creditor with a valid lien against property of the estate that is neither avoidable nor subordinated under bankruptcy law will receive the lesser of the allowed amount of his claim or the collateral or proceeds from its liquidation. The trustee may recover from such collateral or its proceeds the reasonable, necessary costs and expenses which the trustee incurred to preserve or dispose of the collateral, but only to the extent the secured creditor benefited from the trustee's actions. Such costs and expenses are considered first priority claims. *See "Priority Claims," Chapter II.* If there is any remaining *equity* in the collateral (excess value after all claims against the property are paid, including the trustee's reasonable costs and expenses), the secured creditor may recover interest, reasonable costs, charges, and attorneys' fees provided for under the pre-petition contract between the debtor and creditor. Thus, the oversecured creditor may receive interest that accrues post-petition but at the pre-petition contract rate. However, the creditor's interest, costs, and fees are permitted only to the extent of the remaining equity. If any further equity exists after the trustee and secured creditor recover their respective amounts, such equity and all remaining property of the estate will belong to unsecured creditors with allowed claims. *11 USC §§323, 503(b), 506(a)-(c), 507(a)(1), 724-726.*

(2) Avoidable Liens for Fines, Penalties, Forfeitures

The trustee may avoid a lien securing a true fine, penalty, forfeiture, or multiple, exemplary, or punitive damages. The trustee must file an adversary complaint and pay a $120 filing fee only from the estate, if any is realized. A copy of the complaint with a summons must be served on the secured creditor by first-class mail, personal delivery by a disinterested person at least 18 years old, or by any other manner allowed for service of process in federal district court. A copy of the complaint should also be mailed or delivered to the debtor, any committee, and all other entities required by court order or local bankruptcy rules. The respective creditor will then have an unsecured claim for such fine, penalty, or damages if the trustee prevails. *11 USC §§724(a), 726(a)(4); FRBP 7001(2) et seq; Procedural Bankr Forms B 250A, B, C.*

(3) Subordinated Tax Liens

Valid tax liens that are not otherwise avoidable may nevertheless be subordinated under Chapter 7. The trustee must distribute property of the estate securing a valid tax lien, or proceeds received from such property, in the following order:

(a) First, to secured creditors whose liens are senior to the tax liens, if such creditors' claims are allowed by the court;

(b) Second, to unsecured creditors with first through sixth priority claims allowed by the court, but only to the extent of the allowed amount of the secured tax claim. In other words, such priority claimholders step into the shoes of the tax collector. The secured tax claim is thus subordinated to unsecured priority claims (first through sixth) with a higher priority status than seventh priority unsecured tax claims (*see* "Priority Claims," Chapter II);

(c) Third, to the tax collector, but only to the extent that the allowed secured tax claim is greater than the total amount of first through sixth priority claims paid by the trustee;

(d) Fourth, to secured creditors whose liens are junior to the tax lien, if such creditors' claims are allowed by the court;

(e) Fifth, to the tax collector to satisfy any remaining unpaid, allowed secured claim; and

(f) Sixth, any remaining value or equity goes to the estate for distribution to general unsecured creditors. *11 USC §§502, 506(a), 724; HR Rep No 595, 95th Cong, 1st Sess 382 (1977); see "File Proof of Claim," Chapter XIV; Chapter XII.*

If there is more than one creditor in any of the above six distribution groups, all members of the same group must receive a pro rata share (same percentage) of the property or proceeds of the estate allocated to their group. *11 USC §724(c).*

(4) Subordinated Statutory Liens

A statutory lien that is not otherwise avoidable under bankruptcy law and whose priority is determined like tax liens under the 1954 Internal Revenue Code, 26 USC §6323, must be subordinated and treated like tax liens as outlined above for purposes of distribution of the estate. An example of such a statutory lien is the Employee Retirement Income Security Act (ERISA) lien. *11 USC §§724(d), 725; HR Rep No 595, 95th Cong, 1st Sess 382 (1977); S Rep No 989, 95th Cong, 2d Sess 96 (1978); see Chapter XII.*

b. No Community Property (Normal Liquidation Rules)

After the trustee has satisfied allowed secured claims, if there is no community property, he must distribute the remaining estate according to normal liquidation rules, in the following manner:

(1) To priority claimholders in the order of their priority status under 11 USC §507. The §507 priority claimholders must have either filed a *timely* proof of claim (before the 90th day after the first date set for the meeting of creditors) or filed a *late* proof of claim *before* the date that the trustee begins to distribute the estate. *11 USC §§501, 726; FRBP 3002(c); see "File Proof of Claim," Chapter XIV.*

However, first priority administrative claims incurred under a converted Chapter 7 case (debtor originally filed a petition under a different chapter and converted to Chapter 7) have priority over and must be paid before first priority administrative claims incurred under the original, superseded case. If there are sufficient funds in the estate to pay 100 per cent of all eight priority claim groups, then the trustee will pay the next group (unsecured creditors for whom a proof of claim was timely filed), discussed below. If there are insufficient funds to pay all eight priority claim groups, first priority claims must be paid before second priority claims; second priority claims must be paid before third priority claims; and on down the priority ladder (*see* "Priority Claims," Chapter II). Members of the same priority group must share existing funds pro rata (same percentage of payment). *11 USC §§503(a), 507(a)(1)-(8), 726(b).*

Thus, if the estate has $8,000 of proceeds and there are $4,000 allowed first priority administrative claims and $6,000 allowed third priority claims, the first priority administrative claims will be fully paid; the third priority claims will be paid pro rata. Each third priority claimholder will receive two-thirds of his allowed pre-petition claim up to a maximum amount of $2,000 per individual. ($4,000 funds in the estate after paying first priority claims to be disbursed among $6,000 aggregate allowed third priority claims ($4,000/$6,000)). No other priority claimholders or unsecured creditors will be paid. *See "Priority Claims," Chapter II; 11 USC §§503(b), 507(a), 726(b).*

Under the above scenario, if the estate had $13,000 with only the two priority groups, first priority administrative claims and third priority claims would be paid 100 per cent of their allowed claims, without interest. Unsecured creditors historically do not receive interest on their pre-petition claims, unless sufficient funds are available in the estate to pay all creditors. After payment of all priority claims, the trustee would then disburse the remaining $3,000 of the estate to general unsecured creditors as indicated, below;

(2) To nonpriority unsecured creditors whose proof of claim was timely filed.

This group includes four types of unsecured creditors:

(a) Unsecured Creditors Who Timely Filed a Proof of Claim

Under Chapter 7, a proof of claim must be filed before the 90th day after the first date set for the meeting of creditors, unless the court extends the time. *FRBP 3002(c);*

(b) Unsecured Creditors Whose Proof of Claim Was Filed Timely by the Debtor or Trustee

If the unsecured creditor fails to file a proof of claim by the first date set for the meeting of creditors, the debtor or trustee may file a claim before the 30th day after such creditor's maximum time to file expires (generally before the 119th day after the first date set for the meeting of creditors). *11 USC §§501(c), 726(a)(2); FRBP 3004;*

(c) Unsecured Creditors Whose Proof of Claim Was Filed Timely by a Co-Debtor, Guarantor, or Surety

If the unsecured creditor fails to file a proof of claim before the 90th day after the first date set for the meeting of creditors, any co-debtor, guarantor, or surety of the debtor may file a claim before the 30th day after the date the creditor's time to file expires. *11 USC §§501(b), 726(a)(2); FRBP 3005;* and

(d) Unsecured Creditors Without Knowledge of the Case Who Filed a Proof of Claim in Time for Distribution

If the unsecured creditor filed a proof of claim 90 or more days after the first date set for the meeting of creditors, he may still receive dividend payments if two conditions are met. First, the unsecured creditor must file a proof of claim at least in time for the trustee to make a dividend payment. Second, the creditor must not have had notice or actual knowledge of the debtor's bankruptcy case in time to file a proof of claim timely (*see* "File a Proof of Claim—When to File," Chapter XIV);

All four types of unsecured creditors may share pro rata in the estate's funds after the trustee has paid priority claims. *11 USC §§501, 502, 726(a); FRBP 3002(c), 3004-3005;*

(3) To unsecured creditors who filed a proof of claim late and had knowledge or notice of the debtor's Chapter 7 case in time to file a timely claim;

(4) To any creditor (secured or unsecured) whose claim is for a true fine, penalty, or forfeiture and is not compensation for actual monetary loss (the claim is not for compensatory damages);

(5) Post-petition interest payments to the above creditors computed at the legal rate of interest in the judicial district from the date the Chapter 7 petition was filed; and

(6) Any remaining funds or property in the estate will revert to the debtor. *11 USC §726(a)(1)-(6).*

c. Community and Noncommunity Property

If the estate consists of community property (subject to the debtor's sole, joint, or equal management or liable for a claim against the debtor or debtor and his spouse) and noncommunity property, the trustee must first segregate the two types of property and then make disbursements according to the following rules:

(1) First priority administrative claims must be paid pro rata from either community or non-community property or proceeds as the interests of justice require.

The court will weigh the interests of justice and decide by considering three factors:

(a) The amount of each type of property in the estate (community and noncommunity);

(b) The cost to preserve and liquidate each type of property; and

(c) Whether a particular administrative expense is attributable to the community or noncommunity property. *11 USC §726(c); S Rep No 989, 95th Cong, 2d Sess 97-98 (1978); HR Rep No 595, 95th Cong, 1st Sess 383-84 (1977);*

(2) All other allowed unsecured claims must be paid according to the normal liquidation rules stated above, but subject to four additional rules:

(a) First, community claims against either the debtor or his spouse must be paid from the estate's community property unless such property is solely liable for the debtor's debts under applicable nonbankruptcy law;

(b) Second, if there are remaining unpaid community claims against the debtor, such claims must be paid from community property that is solely liable for the debtor's debts;

(c) Third, if there are any remaining claims of any nature against the debtor (community or noncommunity), all such claims must be paid from the estate's noncommunity property; and

(d) Fourth, any remaining unpaid community claims against either the debtor or his spouse must be paid from all property left in the estate.

The above special rules might occur if the amount of community claims against the debtor's spouse are large while most of the estate's property is solely liable for the debtor's debts under applicable nonbankruptcy law. *11 USC §726(c); S Rep No 989, 95th Cong, 2d Sess 97-98 (1978); HR Rep No 595, 95th Cong, 1st Sess 383-84 (1977).*

5. Small Dividends

The Chapter 7 trustee may not make any dividend payment of less than $5, unless the court or local bankruptcy rules state otherwise. Such undistributed dividends are treated as unclaimed funds of the estate. Unclaimed funds are deposited with the court. The clerk of the court must hold such funds for five years. The unclaimed funds then escheat to the United States Treasury. *11 USC §347; HR Rep No 595, 95th Cong, 1st Sess 337 (1977); S Rep No 989, 95th Cong, 2d Sess 47-48 (1978); FRBP 3010.*

6. No Dividend

If the debtor's schedules of assets indicate that there are no assets in the estate (the debtor claimed all property as exempt), the notice of the meeting of creditors may also state that:

a. **There are no assets of the estate from which dividends may be paid;**

b. **It is not necessary to file a proof of claim; and**

c. **Further notice will be given if sufficient assets for dividend payments become available.**

The clerk of the court must give at least 20 days' notice by mail of the meeting of creditors to the debtor, trustee, all creditors, indenture trustees, and to the U.S. trustee. *FRBP 2002(a)(1), (e), (k); Official Bankr Form 6, Schedule C.*

7. Unclaimed Funds

The trustee must stop payment of any check remaining unpaid 90 days after the final distribution of the estate. The trustee must file a list of known names and addresses of persons entitled to receive such dividends. These unclaimed funds and all remaining unclaimed property of the estate are paid into the court. The clerk of the court must then hold the funds for their owner for five years. After five years, the unclaimed funds escheat to the United States Treasury. *11 USC §347(a); 28 USC §2041 et seq; FRBP 3011; S Rep No 989, 95th Cong, 2d Sess 47-48 (1978).*

F. Closing the Chapter 7 Case

1. When Closed

The trustee must file a final report and account and certify that the estate has been fully administered. If the net proceeds of the estate exceed $1,500, the clerk of the court must mail notice of a summary of the trustee's final report and account to the debtor, U.S. trustee, all creditors, committee(s), indenture trustees and to any other entity required by court order or local bankruptcy rules. If no objection is filed by a party-in-interest or U.S. trustee before the 30th day after the trustee's final report is filed, it is presumed that the estate has been fully administered. The court must then discharge the trustee and close the case. *11 USC §350(a); FRBP 2002(f)(8), (i), (k), 5009.*

2. Reopening a Case

A bankruptcy case may be reopened in the bankruptcy court in which the case was closed. The case may be reopened to administer assets, provide additional relief to the debtor, or for other cause. The debtor or party-in-interest must file a motion to reopen and serve a copy of the motion by first-class mail on such entities as directed by the court or local bankruptcy rules. A $120 filing fee is required with the motion unless the case is being reopened to correct an administrative error or for actions related to the debtor's discharge. The U.S. trustee will not have to appoint (or reappoint) a Chapter 7 trustee unless the court rules that one is necessary to protect the interests of creditors and the debtor or to insure the efficient administration of the case. *11 USC §350(b); 28 USC §1930(a)(1), see "Language to Clarify Reopened Cases"; FRBP 5010, 9013-9014.*

Research Guide

Drake, *Bankruptcy Practice for the General Practitioner* ch 11 (Shepard's/McGraw-Hill 2d ed 1990)

Jaroslavsky, *Practical Bankruptcy Procedure* chs 2, 5, 11, 13, 15-16 (Shepard's/McGraw-Hill 1993)

Murphy, *Creditor's Rights in Bankruptcy* ch 18 (Shepard's/McGraw-Hill 2d ed 1988)

IV. Chapter 11—Reorganization

IV. Chapter 11—Reorganization
- A. General Overview
- B. Preparing the Client
- C. Stages of a Chapter 11 Case
- D. Procedures Under a Chapter 11 Case
  1. Procedure One—The Debtor
     11 USC §109(a), (d), (g)
  2. Procedure Two—Debtor's Duties
     11 USC §§301, 341, 343, 521, 541, 1102, 1121, 1125, 1128, 1141
     28 USC §1930(a)(3), (6)
     FRBP 1007-1008, 2015, 3016-3017, 3019-3020, 4002-4003
     - a. Duties as Chapter 11 Debtor
       - (1) First Duty as Debtor—File the Chapter 11 Petition
       - (2) Second Duty as Debtor—File the List of 20 Largest Unsecured Creditors
       - (3) Third Duty as Debtor—File Application to Employ Counsel
       - (4) Fourth Duty as Debtor—File List of Equity Security Holders, Schedules of Assets and Liabilities, Statement of Financial Affairs, Schedule of Current Income and Expenditures, and Statement of Executory Contracts
       - (5) Fifth Duty as Debtor—Pay Quarterly Fees
       - (6) Sixth Duty as Debtor—Attend the Meeting of Creditors and Any Examination Ordered by the Court
       - (7) Seventh Duty as Debtor—Cooperate with the Unsecured Creditors' Committee

- (8) Eighth Duty as Debtor—Timely File a Plan of Reorganization
- (9) Ninth Duty as Debtor—Have the Plan Confirmed Timely
- (10) Tenth Duty as Debtor—File and Obtain Approval of Disclosure Statement
  - (a) When Disclosure Statement Is Required
  - (b) Notice of Hearing on Disclosure Statement
  - (c) Requirements for Court Approval of Disclosure Statement
  - (d) Notice of Approval of Disclosure Statement
  - (e) When Disclosure Statement Is Not Required
- (11) Eleventh Duty as Debtor—Attend the Confirmation Hearing
- (12) Twelfth Duty as Debtor—Attend Hearing on Complaint Objecting to Discharge
- (13) Thirteenth Duty as Debtor—Complete Payments Required by a Confirmed Plan
- (14) Fourteenth Duty as Debtor—File Statement of Change of Address
- (15) Fifteenth Duty as Debtor—Cooperate with Any Appointed Trustee or Examiner

b. The Small Business Debtor

c. Duties as DIP (Trustee)

3. Procedure Three—Selection of Unsecured Creditors' Committee
   11 USC §§1102-1103, 1009(b)
   FRBP 2007, 2014, 2016, 2018
   - a. Selection Post-Petition
   - b. Selection Pre-Petition
   - c. Committee Chairman, Attorney, and Other Professionals
     - (1) Chairman
     - (2) Professional Persons
     - (3) Procedures for Employment of Professional Persons
   - d. Duties of the Committee
   - e. Right to Immediate Meeting with DIP or Trustee
   - f. Right to Receive All Notices
4. Procedure Four—Appointment of Other Committees
   11 USC §1102(b)
5. Procedure Five—Appointment of Trustee or Examiner
   11 USC §§322, 323, 1104-1106
   FRBP 2007.1, 2008, 2010-2011, 2015, 5002, 6009

a. Trustee
b. Examiner
c. Notice and Hearing
d. Selection and Qualification
   (1) Selection of Chapter 11 Trustee
   (2) Qualifications of Chapter 11 Trustee
e. Duties of Trustee
f. Duties of Examiner
g. Legal Effect of Trustee or Examiner
   (1) Trustee
   (2) Examiner
h. Termination of Trustee or Examiner

6. Procedure Six—Compensation for Professional Persons Hired by the DIP or Committee
   11 USC §§327-331, 503(b), 507(a), 1129
   FRBP 2014, 2016-2017
   a. Requirements for Payment of Professional Persons
   b. Problems with Interim Compensation
   c. Disallowance of Claims of Professional Persons
7. Procedure Seven—Confirmation of a Plan of Reorganization
   a. Requirements for Confirmation of a Chapter 11 Plan
      11 USC §§1122-1125, 1128-1129
      FRBP 2002(b), 3013-3014, 3016-3018, 3020
   b. Optional Provisions Allowed in a Chapter 11 Plan
      11 USC §1123
      FRBP 3013
   c. Notice of Confirmation Hearing on a Plan of Reorganization
      11 USC §1128
      FRBP 2002(b), 3017(d), 9034
   d. Objections
      11 USC §§1126, 1128
      FRBP 3020, 9034
   e. Voting
      11 USC §§501-502, 1111, 1124, 1126
      FRBP 3017(d), 3018
      (1) Who May Vote
      (2) When to Vote
      (3) How to Vote
      (4) Number of Affirmative Votes Required for Confirmation
         (a) Impaired Classes of Creditors
         (b) Impaired Classes of Equity Security Holders

(c) Unimpaired Classes
(d) Disallowed Votes

f. Modification of a Plan of Reorganization
11 USC §1127
FRBP 3019, 9034

g. Confirmation Hearing
11 USC §§1128-1129
FRBP 2002(b), (i)-(k), 3020, 9034

h. Order Confirming Plan of Reorganization
11 USC §§1129, 1142
FRBP 2002(f)(7), (i)-(k), 3020(c), 9034

i. Appeal of Confirmation Order
28 USC §§158, 1930(c)
FRBP 8001 et seq

j. Legal Effects of Confirmation
11 USC §§1141-1142
FRBP 2002(f)(7), 4004-4008, 7001(4), (6) et seq

k. Post-Confirmation Orders
11 USC §§1142-1143
FRBP 3020(d)

1. Revocation of Confirmation and Discharge
11 USC §1144
28 USC §1930(b), Judicial Conference Schedule of Fees (6)
FRBP 4006, 7001(4)-(5) et seq

8. Procedure Eight—Conversion
11 USC §1112
FRBP 1017, 1019, 2002(a)(5), (f)(2), (i)-(k), 9034

a. Debtor's Absolute Right to Convert
b. Request to Convert Filed by Another Entity (Involuntary Conversion)
c. Request to Convert Filed by the U.S. Trustee
d. Procedures for Conversion
e. Notice of Conversion Order
f. Procedures After Conversion
(1) Debtor's Duties in the Converted Case
(2) Turn Over Property in the Converted Case
(3) New Time Periods in the Converted Case
(4) Priority of Administrative Claims in the Converted Case

9. Procedure Nine—Dismissal
11 USC §1112
FRBP 1017, 2002(a)(5), (f)(2), (i)-(k)(2), 9034

IV. Chapter 11—Reorganization

A. General Overview

Chapter 11 is generally used for corporations, partnerships, or individuals with larger debts ($250,000 or more unsecured debt; $750,000 or more secured debt). A Chapter 11 case is much more expensive and time consuming than either a Chapter 7, 12, or 13 case. The Chapter 11 debtor is able to reorganize his business or finances and extend payments to creditors under a confirmed (court approved) Chapter 11 plan of reorganization. The Chapter 11 debtor, as debtor-in-possession (DIP), functions as both debtor and trustee, with all the extraordinary powers of a bankruptcy trustee under the Code. The Chapter 11 debtor retains possession of his exempt and nonexempt property. The Chapter 11 debtor does not have to be a business debtor. *See Toibb v Radloff, 501 US 157, 111 S Ct 2197, 2202 (1991); 11 USC §§1101(1), 1107.*

B. Preparing the Client

The prospective Chapter 11 debtor should be requested to bring the same documents and information to the initial attorney-client interview as the Chapter 7 debtor. *See "Preparing the Client," Chapter III.*

C. Stages of a Chapter 11 Case:

The nine stages common to all voluntary bankruptcy cases apply to a Chapter 11 case. *See "Nine Stages of Every Voluntary Bankruptcy Case," Chapter II.*

D. Procedures under a Chapter 11 Case

There are eleven procedures in a Chapter 11 case. Procedures one, two, six, seven, ten, and eleven occur in all successful Chapter 11 cases (debtor's Chapter 11 Plan is confirmed by the Court). Procedures three, four, five, eight, and nine may occur in any Chapter 11 case.

1. Procedure One—The Debtor

A person who is eligible to file under Chapter 7 is eligible to file under Chapter 11, with two exceptions. First, stockbrokers and commodity brokers may file under Chapter 7 but may not file under Chapter 11. Chapter 7 is the only chapter geared to deal with liquidation of customer accounts. Second, railroads are excluded from Chapter 7 but may file under Chapter 11. The Chapter 11 debtor is known as a debtor-in-possession (DIP) and has all the powers of a trustee under the Bankruptcy Code. The debtor does not have to be engaged in business to file for protection under Chapter 11. *Toibb v Radloff, 501 US 157, 111 S Ct 2197 (1991); 11 USC §§103(a)-(d), 109(b), (d), 1101, 1107; HR Rep No 595, 95th Cong, 1st Sess 404 (1977); S Rep No 989, 95th Cong, 2d Sess 116 (1978).*

2. Procedure Two—Debtor's Duties

The DIP has 15 duties in his capacity as a debtor. Additionally, the court may order the DIP to perform 7 other duties in his capacity as trustee.

a. Duties as Chapter 11 Debtor—Generally

(1) First Duty as Debtor—File the Chapter 11 Petition

The debtor must file a signed, verified petition with a filing fee and mailing matrix (list of creditors). The filing fee is $800 if the debtor is not a railroad; $1,000 for a railroad. The filing fee may be paid in installments by an individual debtor (*see "Installment Fees," Chapter II.*) The debtor must also comply with applicable local bankruptcy rules for filing a petition. A joint petition may be filed under Chapter 11 by the debtor and his spouse. Rules and procedures governing a Chapter 11 case apply with equal force to a joint Chapter 11 case. Before the clerk accepts the Chapter 11 petition for filing, if the debtor is an individual with primarily consumer debts, the clerk must give such debtor written notice of each chapter of the Bankruptcy Code under which the debtor could file a petition. The clerk must also mail notice of the filing of the Chapter 11 petition (order for relief) to the debtor, U.S. trustee, all creditors, committee(s), indenture trustees, to the SEC in Washington, D.C. or to any other location designated by the SEC in a notice of appearance or written request filed with the court, and the District Director of the IRS where the debtor's case is pending. For an individual debtor with primarily consumer debts, such notice must be mailed before the 20th day after the Chapter 11 petition is filed. *11 USC §§109, 301, 302, 342(a)-(b); 28 USC §1930(a); FBRP 1002-1008, 2002(f)(1), (i)-(k), (o), 5005; Official Bankr Forms 1, 2, 3, 9.*

(2) Second Duty as Debtor—File the List of 20 Largest Unsecured Creditors

In addition to the Mailing Matrix, the debtor must file with the voluntary petition a list of the 20 largest unsecured creditors, which includes the names, addresses, and respective amounts of the 20 unsecured creditors with the largest claims against the debtor. Insiders (relatives, officers, directors, or controlling persons) of the debtor must be excluded from the list. In an involuntary case, this list must be filed before the second day after the order for relief (adjudicating the debtor a bankruptcy debtor) is entered. The members of the unsecured creditors' committee will be appointed by the U.S. trustee from this list (*see "Procedure Three—Selection of Unsecured Creditors' Committee," discussed below*). *11 USC §1102 (a), (b)(1); FRBP 1007(d); Official Bankr Form 4.*

(3) Third Duty as Debtor—File Application to Employ Counsel

(a) Debtor's Requirements

The debtor may retain an attorney before filing the petition to represent the debtor in his Chapter 11 case. But immediately after filing the petition, the debtor must file an application to employ counsel with the court. The attorney must be a disinterested person who does not hold or represent an adverse interest to the estate. A copy of the application must be served by first-class mail or personal delivery on the U.S. trustee and any committee appointed in the case. The application must include:

(i) Specific facts showing why counsel is needed to represent the debtor under Chapter 11;

(ii) Name of the attorney;

(iii) Reasons why the attorney in question was selected by the debtor;

(iv) Statement that the attorney is a disinterested person who does not hold or represent an adverse interest to the estate;

(v) Professional services to be rendered by the attorney under the debtor's Chapter 11 case;

(vi) Any proposed fee arrangement;

(vii) All known connections between the attorney and any party-in-interest (debtor, creditor, U.S. trustee) or any party-in-interest's attorney(s) or accountant(s); and

(viii) Verified statement of the attorney stating such attorney's connections with any party-in-interest (debtor, creditor, U.S. trustee) or any party-in-interest's attorney(s) or accountant(s). *11 USC §§327-330; FRBP 2014(a).*

Unless the debtor files and the court approves such application, the debtor's attorney may not be paid from the bankruptcy estate. Since all property of the debtor, wherever located, becomes part of the estate when the petition is filed, any pre-petition fee retainer the debtor may have given to his attorney will generally become part of the estate. Thus, the attorney may not use a pre-petition retainer after the petition is filed unless the debtor's application to employ counsel is approved by the court. If the application to employ counsel lists a law partnership, corporation, or named individual as the debtor's attorney, any partner, member, or regular associate of such entity may act as the debtor's attorney, without need for further application or court order. *11 USC §§327-331, 541; FRBP 2014, 9034;*

(b) Attorney's Requirements

After the debtor files the application to employ counsel, his attorney must comply with the following requirements:

(i) File Statement of Compensation Paid

The debtor's attorney must file with the court a statement of compensation paid or agreed to be paid by the debtor for the bankruptcy case within one year before the petition was filed. The attorney must file the statement of compensation before the 15th day after a voluntary petition is filed or the order for relief in an involuntary case, unless the court extends the time for cause within such period. A copy of the statement must be served by first-class mail on the U.S. trustee, any committee, and all other entities required by court order or local bankruptcy rules. This statement must be filed even if the attorney will not seek compensation for services rendered in the debtor's case. *11 USC §329; FRBP 2016(b), 9034.*

(ii) File Application for Compensation

If the debtor's attorney wishes to be paid for services rendered in the Chapter 11 case, he must file an application for interim or final compensation. The application must state:

a) Services rendered for the debtor under the Chapter 11 case and the time extended for such services;

b) Costs and expenses incurred for providing legal representation to the debtor;

c) Total amounts requested;

d) Previous payments made or promised for legal services in the Chapter 11 case;

e) Source of any previous payments made or promised for legal services in the Chapter 11 case;

f) Whether any payment previously made was shared and with whom. Bankruptcy law prohibits fee splitting (sharing compensation) by a debtor's attorney, a trustee, or a professional person hired by a trustee, debtor-in-possession, or Chapter 11 unsecured creditors' committee if such person seeks compensation as a first priority claim (*see "Priority Claims," Chapter II*), with two exceptions. First, partners, members, and regular associates of the same professional organization (association, partnership, corporation) may share compensation and reimbursement. Second, an attorney for a petitioning creditor who files an involuntary petition may share compensation and reimbursement with another attorney who contributes services or expenses to the petitioning creditor's attorney;

g) The terms of any fee-sharing agreement between the debtor's attorney and any nonmember or nonassociate of such attorney or such attorney's firm; and

h) Any other provision required by local bankruptcy rules or court order. *11 USC §§327, 330(a), 503(b)(2), 504, 507(a)(1); FRBP 2016(a); HR Rep No 595, 95th Cong, 1st Sess 356 (1977); S Rep No 989, 95th Cong, 2d Sess 67 (1978).*

A copy of the application must be served on the debtor, U.S. trustee, any Chapter 11 trustee, all committee(s) appointed in the debtor's case, and any other entity required by court order or local bankruptcy rules. The application may be served by first-class mail or any other method for service of process in federal district court. The court must hold a hearing on any application for compensation, unless local bankruptcy rules provide otherwise. The clerk of the court must give at least 20 days' notice of the hearing on all applications for compensation which exceed $500. Notice of the hearing must be mailed to the debtor, U.S. trustee, trustee, all committee(s), creditors, equity security holders, and indenture trustees, the SEC in Washington, D.C., or to any other location designated by the SEC in a notice of appearance or written request filed with the court, the District Director of the IRS where the debtor's case is pending, and to any other entity required by court order or local bankruptcy rules. *11 USC §§330-331; FRBP 2002(a)(7), (i), (k), 2016, 9013-9014.*

Interim compensation may only be applied for once every 120 days after a voluntary petition is filed or order for relief in an involuntary case, unless the court or local bankruptcy rules permit otherwise. *11 USC §331.*

When deemed appropriate, the U.S. trustee must: (i) review all applications for final compensation filed under 11 USC §330 to assure compliance with procedural guidelines adopted by the Executive Office of the U.S. trustee; (ii) file comments concerning the fee application with the court; and (iii) object to the fee application when appropriate. Official procedural guidelines must be uniformly applied to all fee applications, unless the U.S. trustee believes circumstances exist to warrant different treatment. *28 USC §586(a)(3)(A).*

(4) Fourth Duty as Debtor—File List of Equity Security Holders, Schedules of Assets and Liabilities, Statement of Financial Affairs, Schedule of Current Income and Expenditures, and Statement of Executory Contracts

The list of equity security holders and schedules and statements must be filed with the petition or before the 15th day after the petition is filed, unless the court extends the time for cause, within such period. In an involuntary Chapter 11 case, these documents must be filed before the 15th day after entry of the order for relief, unless the court extends the time. The list of equity security holders must include the name of each of the debtor's equity security holders, the respective number and kind of interests registered in each holder's name, and the last known address or place of business of each equity security holder. Schedules and statements previously filed under an original Chapter 7 or 13 case are deemed filed if the case is converted to Chapter 11. The clerk of the court must mail or deliver a copy of the schedules and statements to the U.S. trustee. The debtor should mail or deliver a copy of such documents to the attorney or chairman for the unsecured creditors' committee. *See "Procedure Three—Selection of Unsecured Creditors' Committee," discussed below; 11 USC §§103(a), 521; FRBP 1007(a)(3), (b)-(c), 1009, 9006(b); Official Bankr Forms 6-7.*

(5) Fifth Duty as Debtor—Pay Quarterly Fees

The Chapter 11 debtor must pay quarterly fees based upon the amount of disbursements made by the debtor during each calendar quarter or fraction thereof from the date of filing the petition until the earlier date that a Chapter 11 plan is confirmed or the case is converted or dismissed. The quarterly fees are paid to the U.S. trustee for deposit in the Treasury. The minimum quarterly fee is $250, even if no disbursements are made. The fees then increase on an incremental basis based upon the amount of disbursements made by the debtor during each calendar quarter.

Quartery Disbursements:	Quarterly Fees:
$0 up to $15,000 per quarter	$ 250
$15,000 up to $150,000 per quarter	$ 500
$150,000 up to $300,000 per quarter	$1,250
$300,000 up to $3 million per quarter	$3,750
$3 million or more per quarter	$5,000

The quarterly fee is due the last day of the calendar month after the calendar quarter for which the fee is owed. *28 USC §1930(a)(6).*

(6) Sixth Duty as Debtor—Attend the Meeting of Creditors and Any Examination Ordered by the Court

The debtor must attend the meeting of creditors just like the Chapter 7, 12, and 13 debtor. The debtor must also submit to any other examination ordered by the court. *11 USC §§341, 343; FRBP 2003, 4002; see "Stage Six—Meeting of Creditors," Chapter II; "Rule 2004 Examination," Chapter XIV.*

(7) Seventh Duty as Debtor—Cooperate with the Unsecured Creditors' Committee

The Code requires the U.S. trustee to attempt to appoint an unsecured creditors' committee and empowers the committee with the right to meet with the debtor, investigate the business or financial affairs of the debtor, and help formulate (write) a plan of reorganization. *See "Procedure Three—Selection of Unsecured Creditors' Committee," discussed below.* Failure to cooperate with the committee could result in the appointment of an examiner or trustee or in dismissal or conversion of the debtor's Chapter 11 case. Appointment of a trustee results in the Chapter 11 debtor losing his debtor-in-possession status and losing the exclusive right to file and have confirmed a Chapter 11 plan during the first 180 days after the petition is filed. *11 USC §§1103, 1104, 1121(b), (c); see "Procedure Five—Appointment of Trustee or Examiner" and "Procedure Seven—Confirmation of a Plan of Reorganization," discussed below.*

(8) Eighth Duty as Debtor—File a Plan of Reorganization Timely

Unless the debtor qualifies and elects to be a *small business debtor (see, "Small Business Debtor," discussed below)*, a debtor has a 180-day period of exclusivity in which only the Chapter 11 debtor may file and have confirmed his plan of reorganization. This period of exclusivity begins the day after the petition is filed (or order for relief in an involuntary case) and is divided into two time periods. The first time period is the 120 days immediately after the petition is filed (or order for relief in an involuntary Chapter 11 case). To retain the period of exclusivity, the debtor must file his plan either with the petition or no later than the 120th day after the petition is filed or order for relief in an involuntary case. The court may extend (or reduce) the 120-day period, for cause. But the debtor must file a motion for extension before the 120-day period expires. Unless a trustee has been appointed or the court reduces the time, only the debtor may file a plan during the first 120 days. The second time period is the next immediate 60 days. The debtor must have his plan confirmed by the court before the 60th day after the first 120-day time period expires, unless the court extends such time for cause during the 180-day period (the debtor must have his plan confirmed before 180 days after the Chapter 11 petition is filed or order for relief in an involuntary case). An order extending (or reducing) the first 120-day or the entire 180-day period of exclusivity is interlocutory but may be appealed as a matter of right to the federal district court or to any bankruptcy appellate panel service established in the federal judicial circuit where the debtor's case is pending. If the debtor fails to observe either of the two time periods during the 180-day period of exclusivity, any party-in-interest (creditor, trustee, committee), except the U.S. trustee, may file a plan for confirmation by the court. Thus, after the debtor's period of exclusivity has expired, there could be several competing plans filed in a Chapter 11 case. However, a party-in-interest may not file a Chapter 11 plan after the court has entered an order approving any disclosure statement, unless: (a) the court denies confirmation of the plan relating to such disclosure statement; or (b) the court or local bankruptcy rules allow a plan to be filed at a later date. *11 USC §§307, 1121(a)-(d); 28 USC §158(a)(2), (b)-(c); FRBP 3016(a); see Local Bankruptcy Rules; "Tenth Duty as Debtor—File and Obtain Approval of Disclosure Statement" and "Procedure Seven—Confirmation of a Plan of Reorganization," discussed below.*

(9) Ninth Duty as Debtor—Have the Plan Confirmed Timely

If the DIP filed a plan by the 120th day after the petition was filed or order for relief in an involuntary Chapter 11 case, he must have his plan confirmed by the court before 180 days after the order for relief to retain the period of exclusivity, unless the court extends the time. But the DIP must seek an extension of time before the 180 days expire. An order extending (or reducing) the DIP's 180-day period of exclusivity, though interlocutory, may be appealed as a matter of right to the federal district court or to any bankruptcy appellate panel service established in the federal judicial circuit where the debtor's case is pending. If the 180 days expire without confirmation of the DIP's plan or a court order extending the 180-period of exclusivity, any entity (including a creditor, creditors' committee, any trustee except the U.S. trustee, or examiner) may file a plan. There could be multiple plans filed by different entities competing for creditors' votes and court confirmation after the DIP loses his period of exclusivity. *11 USC §§307, 1121(c)-(d); 28 USC §158(a)(2), (b)-(c); FRBP 301(b).*

The bankruptcy court may hold a status conference and order a combined hearing on confirmation of a plan and approval of any required disclosure statement *(see "Disclosure Statement," discussed below)* to assure that the Chapter 11 case is handled economically and expeditiously. The court may act *sua sponte* or on motion of a party-in-interest. A combined disclosure statement-confirmation hearing would eliminate at least one 25-day notice period normally required in a Chapter 11 case. *See, "Notice of Hearing on Disclosure Statement" and "Notice of Approval of Disclosure Statement" discussed below; 11 USC §§103(a), 105(d)(2)(B)(vi), 1125, 1126, 1128, 1129; FRBP 2002(b), 3016, 3017, 3018.*

(10) Tenth Duty as Debtor—File and Obtain Approval of Disclosure Statement

(a) When Disclosure Statement Is Required

Unless the debtor qualifies and elects to be a *small business debtor (see "Small Business Debtor," discussed below)*, a debtor or any proponent of a Chapter 11 plan who intends to solicit votes of acceptance for the plan must file and obtain court approval of a disclosure statement before soliciting votes. The disclosure statement may be filed with the plan or by any other date set by the court. *11 USC §1125(b), (f); FRBP 3016(c);*

(b) Notice of Hearing On Disclosure Statement

The Court must hold a hearing when a disclosure statement is required of a debtor or other proponent of a plan who intends to solicit votes. The clerk or other court-authorized person must give at least 25 days' notice by mail of the date set by the court for the hearing and date to file objections to the disclosure statement. Such notice must be sent to the debtor, the U.S. trustee, any Chapter 11 trustee, committee(s), creditors, indenture trustees, equity security holders, the SEC in Washington, D.C., or to any other location designated by the SEC in a notice of appearance or written request filed with the court, the District Director of the IRS for the district where the Chapter 11 case is pending, and any other party required by court order or local bankruptcy rules. *11 USC §1125(b); FRBP 2002(b), (i)-(k), 3017(a), 9034; Official Bankr Form 12.*

The court may fix the scope and format of the notice on the hearing to approve a disclosure statement. The notice will be sent to the debtor, U.S. trustee, any Chapter 11 trustee, committee, SEC, and any party-in-interest who files a written request must include a copy of the plan and disclosure statement. All other creditors and equity security holders receive only the notice of hearing date and date to file objections to the disclosure statement. No plan or disclosure statement is included with such notices. It is the responsibility of the creditor or equity security holder to go to the clerk's office to review the disclosure statement or to file a written request asking the clerk to mail a copy of the disclosure statement or plan before the hearing on the disclosure statement is held. *11 USC §105(d)(2)(B)(v); FRBP 2002(b), 3016(c), 3017(a), 9014; see Local Bankruptcy Rules.*

The court may act *sua sponte* or on motion of a party-in-interest to hold a status conference and order a combined hearing on the disclosure statement and confirmation of the plan. A combined hearing would require only one 25-day notice period to creditors and parties-in-interest. *11 USC §§103(a), 105(d)(2)(B)(vi), 1125, 1126, 1128, 1129; FRBP, 2002(b), 3017, 3018.*

Objections to the disclosure statement must be timely filed and served on the debtor, any trustee, the U.S.

trustee, committee(s), and any other party required by court order or local bankruptcy rules. Objections may be served by first-class mail, but must be filed and served by the date set by the court as indicated in the clerk's notice. *11 USC §1125(b); FRBP 2002(b), 3017(d), 9014, 9034.*

(c) Requirements for Court Approval of Disclosure Statement

If a disclosure statement is required, it must contain adequate information sufficient to enable a hypothetical reasonable investor, typical of the class of creditors or equity security holders who will be voting, to make an informed decision about the plan. Thus, the disclosure statement must include enough information to allow a creditor or equity security holder to determine if the Plan is beneficial or detrimental to his interests. The court decides whether the disclosure statement contains adequate information based upon bankruptcy law. The court may consider, but is not governed by, any nonbankruptcy law, rule, or regulation. An agency or official who enforces any nonbankruptcy law, rule, or regulation governing nonbankruptcy disclosure statements, including the SEC, may appear and be heard at the hearing on the disclosure statement, but may not appeal a bankruptcy court order approving the disclosure statement. *11 USC §§1109(a), 1125(d).*

A person who solicits votes or who participates in the offer, issuance, sale, or purchase of a security under a Chapter 11 plan will be protected from legal and equitable liability for the violation of any (securities or other) laws, rules, or regulations if two conditions are met. Such person must:

(i) Act in good-faith reliance on a court-approved disclosure statement; and

(ii) Comply with all applicable requirements of the Code. *11 USC §1125(d)-(e); HR Rep No 595, 95th Cong, 1st Sess 408 (1977); S Rep No 989, 95th Cong, 2d Sess 120, 122 (1978).*

(d) Notice of Approval of Disclosure Statement

Once the disclosure statement is approved by the court, the clerk, debtor, or other court-authorized person must give at least 25 days' notice by mail of such approval. The notice must be sent to the debtor, U.S. trustee, any Chapter 11 trustee, all committee(s), all creditors, equity security holders, indenture trustees, the SEC in Washington, DC, and the District Director of the IRS where the case is pending. The notice must contain the following documents and information:

(i) Copy of the plan of reorganization or court-approved summary of the plan;

(ii) Copy of the court-approved disclosure statement. However, the same disclosure statement does not have to go to every class of creditors or equity security holders listed in a plan (*see "Classifying Claims," discussed below*). Different disclosure statements (as to amounts, details, other information) may be sent to different classes of creditors or equity security holders as long as each member of the same class receives the same version of the disclosure statement;

(iii) The date set by the court for the confirmation hearing on the plan;

(iv) The date set by the court to file votes to accept or reject the plan;

(v) The date set by the court to file objections to the plan;

(vi) Copy of the court order approving the disclosure statement;

(vii) Copies of all other orders relating to the disclosure statement or plan;

(viii) Ballot for voting to accept or reject the plan; and

(ix) Any other information required by the court or local bankruptcy rules. *11 USC §§1125(c), 1128(a); FRBP 2002(b), (i)-(k), 3017(d), 9034; Official Bankr Forms 13, 14.*

(e) When Disclosure Statement Is Not Required

If the DIP or other proponent of the plan does not intend to solicit votes of acceptance for the plan, then a disclosure statement is not necessary. A DIP or other proponent of a plan may choose not to solicit votes if there are no impaired classes of creditors or if the debtor is certain that at least one class of impaired creditors will vote to accept the plan even without solicitation. A class of creditors is not impaired if the Chapter 11 plan:

(i) Does not alter the legal, equitable, and contractual rights of the creditor as such rights existed pre-petition; or

(ii) Restores the creditor to his original contractual position by: a) curing any pre- or post-petition default of the debtor (other than the debtor's insolvency or filing the petition); b) reinstating the original pre-default maturity date; c) compensating the creditor for damages incurred as a result of the debtor's default (other than filing the petition); and d) leaving unaltered all other rights of the creditor under the pre-petition agreement; or

(iii) Provides that the creditor will receive cash for the amount of such creditor's allowed claim on the effective date of the plan (*see "Procedure Seven—Confirmation of a Plan of Reorganization," discussed below*). *11 USC §§1124-1125; FRPB 3017(a)-(d).*

(11) Eleventh Duty as Debtor—Attend the Confirmation Hearing

The Bankruptcy Code requires a hearing on confirmation of a plan of reorganization. Neither the Code nor the FRBP require the DIP to attend the confirmation hearing. However, local bankruptcy rules or the court may require the debtor's attendance. In most Chapter 11 cases, this is one hearing the debtor will not choose to miss. *11 USC §1128; FRBP 3020(b)(2).*

(12) Twelfth Duty as Debtor—Attend Hearing on Complaint Objecting to Discharge

The debtor must attend a hearing on any complaint objecting to discharge or dischargeability of a debt and testify if called as a witness. *11 USC §§523, 1141(d)(1); FRBP 4002, 4004, 4007; see "Procedure Ten—Discharge," discussed below.*

(13) Thirteenth Duty as Debtor—Complete Payments Required by a Confirmed Plan

The DIP will generally receive a discharge when the plan of reorganization is confirmed, unless an objection to discharge or dischargeability of a debt has been filed. The debtor must complete all payments required by the confirmed plan to retain the discharge. Failure to make such payments could also result in dismissal or conversion of the debtor's Chapter 11 case. *11 USC §§1112, 1141(d)(1); see "Procedure Ten—Discharge," discussed below.*

(14) Fourteenth Duty as Debtor—File Statement of Change of Address

The debtor must file a written statement with the clerk giving any change of address. *FRBP 4002(5).*

(15) Fifteenth Duty as Debtor—Cooperate with Any Appointed Trustee or Examiner

In the event a trustee or examiner is appointed in a Chapter

11 case, the debtor must cooperate fully, including assisting in the preparation of any required inventories; examining proofs of claims; and aiding in the administration of the estate. *FRBP 4002(4).*

b. The Small Business Debtor

(1) Who Qualifies as a Small Business Debtor

A *small business* (debtor) is a bankruptcy term of art defined as a person (individual, partnership, or corporation) engaged in commercial or business activities whose aggregate noncontingent, liquidated, secured and unsecured debt is no greater than $2M. However, the Bankruptcy Code specifically excludes from the definition of *small business* any person whose primary business activity is owning or operating real property and incidental activities, regardless of the amount of such person's aggregate debt. *HR 5116, Pub L No 103-394, §217 amending and adding 11 USC §101(51C).*

(2) Advantages of a Small Business Debtor

The Bankruptcy Code provides three principal consequences to the *small business* debtor: the unsecured creditors' committee may be eliminated *(see "Procedure Three—Selection of Unsecured Creditors' Committee," discussed below);* there is a reduced time for all bankruptcy plans to be filed; and there may be an expedited confirmation of a plan.

(a) Elimination of the Unsecured Creditors' Committee

The unsecured creditors' committee is appointed by the U.S. trustee to represent all unsecured creditors in a Chapter 11 case. The committee generally consists of the seven unsecured creditors who hold the largest unsecured claims against the debtor and who have no interests materially adverse to the bankruptcy estate or to other unsecured creditors. *11 USC §1102; see "Procedure Three—Selection of Unsecured Creditors' Committee," discussed below.*

The Bankruptcy Code allows the court to order that an unsecured creditors' committee not be appointed in the small business debtor's Chapter 11 case. A motion must be filed by a party-in-interest (debtor, creditor, trustee) and the court must find that cause exists to eliminate the committee. Such committee functions as the fiduciary for all unsecured creditors in a Chapter 11 case and may investigate the debtor's financial condition, consult frequently with the debtor, help formulate a Chapter 11 plan of reorganization, and seek appointment of a trustee when necessary. However, an unsecured creditors' committee and any attorney, accountant, or other professional employed by such committee (with court order) also increases the amount of first priority administrative claims against the bankruptcy estate. First priority claims against the estate reduce the amount of funds available to pay general unsecured creditors. *11 USC §§503(a), 507(a)(1), 1102, 1103; HR 5116, Pub L No 103-394, §110, amending and adding 11 USC §§503(b)(3)(F) and 217(b), amending and adding 11 USC §1102(a)(3); see "Stage Seven—Distribution of the Estate," "Priority Claims," Chapter 11.*

(b) Reduced Time for Filing Any Plan

Under the 1994 Bankruptcy Act, a small business debtor who elects to be considered as a small business has a reduced 100-day period of exclusivity after the order for relief to file a plan of reorganization, rather than the 120-day period of exclusivity generally afforded a Chapter 11 debtor-in-possession. Further, all Chapter 11 plans must be filed before the 160th day after the order for relief if the debtor elects to be considered a small business. *HR 5116, Pub L No 103-394, §217(d) amending and adding 11 USC §1121(e).*

The Court may *reduce* the 100-day and/or 160-day period(s) for cause if: (i) a party-in-interest (debtor, creditor, trustee) files a timely motion to reduce time before the 100-day or 160-day period expires; (ii) cause is shown for the reduction in time; and (iii) notice and hearing are provided to all parties-in-interest required by the Bankruptcy Code, federal and local bankruptcy rules, or court order. *HR 5116, Pub L No 103-394, §217(d) amending and adding 11 USC §1121(e); 11 USC §§102(1)(A)(B), 105, 307, 323(a); FRBP 9007, 9013-9014, 9029.*

The court may *increase* the debtor's 100-day period of exclusivity for cause if: (i) a party-in-interest files a timely motion to increase time before the 100 days expire; (ii) cause is shown for the extension of time; (iii) notice and hearing are provided to all parties-in-interest required by the Bankruptcy Code, federal and local bankruptcy rules, or court order; and (iv) the debtor shows the court that the need for increased time was caused by circumstances for which the debtor should not be held accountable. *HR 5116, Pub L No 103-394, §217(d) amending and adding 11 USC §1112(e); 11 USC §§102(1)(A)(B); FRBP 3017, 9007, 9013-9014, 9017, 9029.*

(c) Expedited Confirmation of Chapter 11 Plan

The Bankruptcy Code generally prohibits the solicitation of votes for any Chapter 11 plan unless the author (proponent) has obtained court approval of the disclosure statement and transmits the disclosure statement with the plan or its summary to creditors whose votes are solicited. *See "Procedure Two—Debtor's Duties," "Tenth Duty as Debtor—File and Obtain Approval of Disclosure Statement," discussed above; 11 USC §1125(b), 1126; FRBP 3017, 3018.*

However, the debtor who qualifies and elects to be considered a small business debtor may solicit votes for its plan before final court approval of the disclosure statement and may obtain a combined hearing on confirmation of the plan with hearing on final approval of the disclosure statement. *HR 5116, Pub L No 103-394, §217(e) amending and adding 11 USC §1125(f).*

To use the expedited confirmation procedures, the Chapter 11 debtor must:

(i) elect to be considered a small business;

(ii) seek conditional court approval of its disclosure statement;

(iii) provide adequate information to each creditor and party-in-interest whose vote is solicited based upon the conditionally approved disclosure statement;

(iv) at least 10 days before the confirmation hearing, mail a copy of the conditionally approved disclosure statement to each party whose vote has been solicited and to any other party-in-interest required by court order and federal or local bankruptcy rules;

(v) obtain a hearing on final approval of the disclosure statement, which may be combined with the confirmation hearing;

(vi) provide notice of the hearing on final approval of the disclosure statement to all creditors and parties-in-interest required by court order and federal and local bankruptcy rules; and

(vii) elect whether to obtain a separate or combined hearing on the disclosure statement and confirmation of the plan. *HR 5116, Pub L No 103-394, §217, amending and adding 11 USC §101(51C), 1102(a)(3), 1121(e), 1125(f); FRBP 3016-3018, 3020.*

A combined hearing on the disclosure statement and confirmation of the plan saves the debtor time and money. Generally, the proponent (author) of a Chapter 11 plan must give at least 25 days' prior notice of the hearing on the disclosure statement and 25 days' prior notice of the confirmation hearing to all creditors and parties-in-interest (creditors' committee(s), SEC, IRS, trustee, U.S. trustee) as required by court order and federal and local bankruptcy rules. The small business debtor may eliminate one 25-day notice period by seeking conditional court approval of its disclosure statement and obtaining the combined disclosure statement-plan confirmation hearing. *HR 5116, Pub L No 103-394, §217(e) amending and adding 11 USC §1125(f); FRBP 2002(b)(i)(k), 3017(a), 9034.*

c. Duties as DIP (Trustee)

The debtor as DIP possesses not only the powers, but also the following seven responsibilities and duties of a trustee:

(1) First Duty as DIP (Trustee)—File a complete inventory of property of the DIP before the 30th day after the petition is filed, unless such inventory has already been filed;

(2) Second Duty as DIP (Trustee)—Keep a record of receipts and disbursements of money and other property;

(3) Third Duty as DIP (Trustee)—File periodic reports and summaries of business operations.

Include amounts of all withholding and other taxes, the place where such taxes are deposited, and a statement of receipts and disbursements made by the DIP during each reporting period. These reports and summaries must be filed with the court, the U.S. trustee, and all applicable government entities, as required by court order or local bankruptcy rules. *See Local Bankruptcy Rules;*

(4) Fourth Duty as DIP (Trustee)—Give Notice as soon as possible of the Chapter 11 petition to all entities who the DIP knows are holding money or property which the DIP could withdraw or have withdrawn.

Such entities include banks, savings or building and loan associations, utility companies, any landlord who holds a deposit of the debtor, and every insurance company that issued a policy with a cash surrender value payable to the debtor. If such entities have knowledge of the petition or previously received notice of the Chapter 11 case, the DIP does not have to give additional notice;

(5) Fifth Duty as DIP (Trustee)—File a statement of disbursements and quarterly fees paid for each calendar quarter.

These statements must be filed no later than the last day of the month following each calendar quarter, beginning the first quarter (or fraction thereof) after the petition is filed and continuing until the earlier date that the debtor's Chapter 11 plan is confirmed or the Chapter 11 case is converted or dismissed. The debtor must serve a copy of such statements on the U.S. trustee by first-class mail or personal delivery;

(6) **Sixth Duty as DIP (Trustee)—Represent the estate.**

This includes filing any necessary actions or defending the estate; and appearing or defending on behalf of the estate in any pending action previously filed by or against the debtor. *11 USC §§323, 1101(1), 1107; 28 USC §1930(a)(6); FRBP 6009; see Chapter XII.*

The DIP is not, however, entitled to receive compensation or fees as trustee for services rendered on behalf of the estate. *11 USC §1107(a);* and

(7) **Seventh Duty as DIP (Trustee)—Comply with any other duty required by court order or local bankruptcy rules.** *11 USC §1107(a); FRBP 2015; see Local Bankruptcy Rules.*

3. Procedure Three—Selection of Unsecured Creditors' Committee

a. Selection Post-Petition

The U.S. trustee must attempt to appoint members of an unsecured creditors' committee as soon as practical after the Chapter 11 petition is filed, unless the debtor is a small business debtor *(see "The Small Business Debtor," discussed above).* The U.S. trustee chooses the members from the list of 20 largest unsecured creditors that the debtor-in-possession must file with the petition. *See "Second Duty of Debtor—File the List of 20 Largest Unsecured Creditors," discussed above.* The unsecured creditors' committee generally consists of seven creditors who have the largest unsecured claims against the debtor and who are willing to serve on the committee. The size of the committee may be increased by the U.S. trustee. The committee acts as a fiduciary and represents all unsecured creditors. If requested by a party-in-interest (stockholder, secured creditor), the court may order the U.S. trustee to appoint other committees. The members of a committee should have similar claims against the debtor but no adverse interests to each other or the entities they represent. *11 USC §1102; see "Procedure Four—Appointment of Other Committees," discussed below.*

b. Selection Pre-Petition

The unsecured creditors' committee may be organized by unsecured creditors before the petition is filed, as long as the members are "fairly chosen" and actually represent the interests of all of the debtor's unsecured creditors. The DIP or a member of the committee selected pre-petition should then file an application for court order approving the pre-petition committee. The application must state that:

(1) The members were fairly chosen by a majority in number and dollar amount of unsecured creditors who were present or represented at the selection meeting, who are not insiders of the debtor, and who hold allowed, undisputed, liquidated general unsecured claims that are not materially adverse to the interests of other unsecured creditors;

(2) At least five days' prior written notice of the selection meeting was given to the 100 unsecured creditors with the largest claims or to all unsecured creditors with claims over $1,000;

(3) Written minutes of the meeting were kept and are available, showing the names of unsecured creditors who were present or represented and voted, the respective amounts of their claims, and how they voted;

(4) The committee was selected by unsecured creditors whose claims are allowed by the court and who do not hold mutually adverse interests to general unsecured creditors; and

(5) The organization of the committee was fair and proper in all respects. *11 USC §1102(b); FRBP 2007(b); see "File Proof of Claim," Chapter XIV.*

c. Committee Chairman, Attorney, and Other Professionals

(1) Chairman

The unsecured creditors' committee may select a chairman or co-chairmen to represent the committee and facilitate its work.

(2) Professional Persons

The committee may also hire one or more attorneys, accountants, or other professional persons to work for the committee. The attorney, accountant, or other professional person must not hold any adverse interest(s) to the committee or bankruptcy estate. Such professional person may represent the Committee and one or more members of the committee or unsecured creditors as long as the professional can represent the committee fairly and without reservation. *11 USC §1103(a)-(b).*

(3) Procedures for Employment of Professional Persons

The chairman of the committee, or committee itself, must file an application for court order approving the professional person (attorney, accountant). A copy of the application must be mailed or personally delivered to the debtor, U.S. trustee, and any other person required by court order or local bankruptcy rules. The application must state:

(a) The name of the person to be employed;

(b) Specific facts showing the court why employment of the professional person is necessary and why such person was selected by the committee;

(c) The professional services to be rendered;

(d) Any proposed arrangement for compensation to the professional person;

(e) Statement that the professional person does not represent any other entity who holds an adverse interest to the committee or the estate;

(f) All known connections between the professional person and the court, the debtor, the U.S. trustee or anyone employed in his office, any creditor, and any attorney or accountant of such parties-in-interest. The court may not approve the appointment of a professional person who is a relative of the court (judge) approving the appointment. The court may approve the appointment of a professional person who is a relative of the U.S. trustee for the region where the case is pending, unless the court determines that such relationship would render the employment improper under the circumstances of the case; and

(g) Verified statement of the professional person setting forth such person's connections with the debtor, U.S. trustee, creditors, other parties-in-interest, or their respective attorneys and accountants.

If a partnership or corporation or named individual is appointed as attorney or accountant for the committee, any partner, member, or associate of the professional person may act as the committee's attorney or accountant without further court order. *11 USC §§328, 1103(a); FRBP 2014(a), 5002, 9034.*

d. Duties of the Committee

The unsecured creditors' committee has the legal right to perform eight duties:

(1) Consult with the DIP or any appointed Chapter 11 trustee about the administration of the Chapter 11 case;

(2) Investigate the DIP's acts, conduct, assets, liabilities, financial condition, and business operations;

(3) Investigate the desirability of continuing the DIP's business and any other matter relevant to the Chapter 11 case or to formulating (writing) the plan of reorganization;

(4) Participate with the DIP in formulating a plan;

(5) Advise all unsecured creditors of the committee's recommendation to support or object to any plan formulated;

(6) Collect votes for or against the plan and file such votes with the court, debtor, or any other entity required by the court or local bankruptcy rules;

(7) Request court appointment of a Chapter 11 trustee or examiner as the committee believes necessary. (*See "Appointment of Trustee or Examiner," discussed below*); and

(8) Perform all other services which the committee believes are in the best interests of unsecured creditors. *11 USC §1103(c).*

e. Right to Immediate Meeting with DIP or Trustee

The unsecured creditors' committee has the legal right to meet with the DIP or any trustee appointed in the debtor's case immediately after the committee is appointed by the U.S. trustee. The purpose of such meeting is to discuss any matters relevant to the committee's official duties as representative of unsecured creditors (*see "Duties of the Committee," discussed above*). *11 USC §1103(d).*

f. Right to Receive All Notices

The clerk of the court must serve copies of all notices mailed by its office to the unsecured creditors' committee and any other committee appointed by the U.S. trustee. *FRBP 2002(i).*

4. Procedure Four—Appointment of Other Committee(s)

Any party-in-interest may apply for a court order directing the U.S. trustee to appoint additional committees consisting of unsecured or secured creditors or equity security holders (stockholders) who do not hold adverse interests to each other. A committee of equity security holders should generally consist of seven persons who hold the largest amount of equity securities (stock, shares) of the debtor and who are willing to serve on the committee. This number may be increased by the U.S. trustee. *11 USC §1102(a)(2), (b)(2).*

5. Procedure Five—Appointment of Trustee or Examiner

The U.S. trustee, a creditor, committee, or any other party-in-interest may file a request for appointment of a trustee or examiner at any time in the debtor's Chapter 11 case before confirmation of a plan. The request must be filed after the petition is filed but before confirmation (court approval) of a plan. The request does not commence an adversary proceeding and no filing fee is required. The request must be served on the debtor, the U.S. trustee, all committee(s), and any other party directed by the court or local bankruptcy rules. Service of the request may be obtained by first-class mail, personal delivery by a disinterested person at least 18 years old, or by any other method allowed for service of process in federal district court. *11 USC §§307, 1104(a)-(b), 1109(b); FRBP 2007.1, 9013-9014, 9034.*

a. Trustee

Grounds for appointment of a trustee are numerous, but the amount of assets and liabilities and number of equity security holders of the debtor are not grounds and should not be considered by the court. The most common grounds for appointment of a trustee, which may exist pre- or post-petition, include:

(1) Fraud;

(2) Dishonesty by the debtor;

(3) Incompetence of the debtor;

(4) Gross mismanagement by the debtor's current management;

(5) Such appointment would be in the best interests of the estate, creditors, and any equity security holders; or

(6) Any other cause warranting appointment of a trustee. *11 USC §1104(a).*

If a trustee is appointed in the debtor's case, the trustee is automatically substituted for the debtor-in-possession as a party-in-interest in any pending or subsequent matter. *FRBP 2012(a).*

b. Examiner

If the court does not appoint a trustee, an examiner may be appointed. Grounds for appointment of an examiner include:

(1) The best interests of the estate, creditors, and any equity security holders would be served; or

(2) The debtor's fixed, liquidated, unsecured debts exceed $5 million, excluding debts owed to an insider and debts for goods, services, or taxes. *11 USC §1104(b).*

c. Notice and Hearing

The court must hold a hearing on any request for appointment of a trustee or examiner. The clerk, party-in-interest filing the request, or other court-authorized person must give notice of the hearing date to the debtor, U.S. trustee, all creditors, committee(s), and any other person as directed by the court or local bankruptcy rules. The party filing the request has the burden of proving one or more ground(s) discussed, above, for appointment of a trustee or examiner. *11 USC §§102(1)(A)-(B), 1104(a)-(b); FRBP 2012, 9013-9014, 9034.*

d. Selection and Qualification

(1) Selection of Chapter 11 Trustee

If a party-in-interest (creditor) files a request for election of a trustee no later than the 30th day after the bankruptcy court orders the appointment of a Chapter 11 trustee, the U.S. trustee must call a special meeting of creditors to elect the trustee. During this meeting of creditors, certain unsecured creditors may vote to elect one disinterested person to serve as the Chapter 11 trustee. To be a member of this voting group, the unsecured creditor should file a proof of claim or a written statement showing a right to vote by the first date set for the meeting of creditors. The proof of claim or written statement must not be objected to for voting purposes and must state that the creditor:

(a) Is not an insider (relative, control person, director, shareholder) of the debtor;

(b) Does not have any interest materially adverse to other unsecured creditors; and

(c) Does have a voting claim. A *voting claim* is an unsecured, undisputed, pre-petition, fixed, liquidated claim that is not a priority claim, and that may be satisfied from property of the bankruptcy estate. *11 USC §702(a); FRBP 2003(b)(3), 3001-3002; see "File Proof of Claims," Chapter XIV; Official Bankr Form 10.*

Once the voting group of unsecured creditors is determined at the meeting of creditors, the election of a Chapter 11 trustee becomes a three-step process:

(i) Request Election

Unsecured creditors who hold at least 20 per cent in dollar amount of the total voting claims must request election of a trustee;

(ii) Voting Claims Must Actually Vote

Unsecured creditors holding at least 20 per cent in dollar amount of the voting claims must actually vote to elect a trustee at the meeting of creditors; and

(iii) Majority Vote for the Winner

The winning candidate for Chapter 11 trustee must receive a majority in dollar amount of the voting claims from votes cast at the election. *11 USC §§701, 702, 1121(b); S Rep No 989, 95th Cong, 2d Sess 92-93 (1978); HR Rep No 595, 95th Cong, 1st Sess 378-79 (1978); FRBP 2003(b).*

If there is no timely request for election of a Chapter 11 trustee or if the court orders appointment of an examiner, the U.S. trustee will appoint a trustee or examiner. The U.S. trustee must consult with various parties-in-interest (committee(s), creditors, the debtor) before selecting a trustee or examiner. The U.S. trustee is not bound to select a Chapter

11 trustee from the panel of private trustees established for Chapter 7 cases. *11 USC §1104(c); HR Rep No 595, 95th Cong, 1st Sess 402 (1977).*

(2) **Qualifications of Chapter 11 Trustee**

An individual or corporation authorized by its charter or bylaws may qualify as trustee or examiner. However, a person who has served as examiner may not serve as trustee in the same case. *11 USC §321(a)-(b).*

The court may not approve the appointment of an individual as trustee or examiner if such individual is a relative of the court (judge) approving the appointment or of the U.S. trustee for the region where the case is pending. The court may not approve the appointment of a trustee or examiner who is or has been so connected with the court or U.S. trustee that the appointment would be improper. *11 USC §1104; FRBP 5002.*

If a person, other than the U.S. trustee, is ordered by the court to serve as Chapter 11 trustee, such person must file a bond with the court before the 5th day after selection by the U.S. trustee and before starting his official duties. The bond is issued in favor of the United States and conditioned upon the trustee's faithful performance of his official duties. The U.S. trustee determines the amount of the bond and the sufficiency of the surety on such bond. However, a trustee is not liable either personally or on his bond for any penalty or forfeiture incurred by the debtor. Any hearing on the bond must be commenced before two years after the date the Chapter 11 trustee is discharged from the bankruptcy case by the court. *11 USC §§322(a)-(b)(2), (c)-(d), 350(a); FRBP 2010, 3022, 5009; see "Procedure Eleven—Closing the Chapter 11 Case," discussed below.*

e. Duties of Trustee

The trustee must perform the following duties, unless the court or local bankruptcy rules direct otherwise:

(1) Operate the debtor's business;

(2) Investigate the acts, conduct, assets, liabilities, and financial condition of the debtor;

(3) Investigate the debtor's business operations and the desirability of continuing such business;

(4) File a report of all investigations made, including any facts relating to the debtor's fraud, dishonesty, incompetence, misconduct, mismanagement, or irregularity in managing his finances; and the existence of any cause of action (lawsuits) for the estate. All reports should be filed as soon as practical;

(5) File periodic reports and summaries of the debtor's business operations, including a statement of all receipts and disbursements. These reports and summaries must be filed with the court, U.S. trustee, and any relevant government taxing authority. The statement of disbursements must include all disbursements and quarterly fees paid during each calendar quarter. The statement of disbursements must be filed no later than the last day of the month after each calendar quarter until a plan is confirmed or the Chapter 11 case is converted or dismissed;

(6) File a list of creditors and the schedules of assets and liabilities, statement of financial affairs, schedule of current income and expenditures, and statement of executory contracts if the debtor failed to do so;

(7) As soon as practical, file a plan or report why no plan will be filed; or recommend conversion or dismissal of the debtor's case;

(8) If the debtor failed to file a tax return, furnish information for such taxable year to any government unit requiring a return. The information may be obtained from the debtor's books, records, and other available information. The trustee will incur no personal liability for furnishing such information;

(9) Account for all property received by the trustee;

(10) Examine proofs of claims and object to the allowance of any claim that appears improper;

(11) Furnish information about the estate and its administration if requested by a party-in-interest, unless the court orders otherwise;

(12) After confirmation of the plan, file any other necessary or court-ordered reports, including a final report and account of the administration of the estate; and

(13) Serve copies of all reports or summaries on the U.S. trustee, all committee(s) appointed in the debtor's case, and on any other entity required by court order or local bankruptcy rules. Service may be obtained by first-class mail. *11 USC §§704(2),(5),(7)-(9), 1106(a), 1108; 28 USC §1930(a)(6); FRBP 2015.*

f. Duties of Examiner

An examiner appointed by the U.S. trustee must perform the specific duties required of a trustee outlined under Paragraphs (2-5, 13), above, unless the court orders otherwise. The examiner must also serve copies of all reports and summaries on the U.S. trustee, all committee(s), and any other entity directed by court order or local bankruptcy rules, and perform any other duty required by the court or local bankruptcy rules. *11 USC §1106(b).*

g. Legal Effect of Trustee or Examiner

(1) Trustee

The appointment of a trustee terminates the debtor's: (a) status as a debtor-in-possession; (b) rights and powers to act as a trustee; and (c) 180-day period of exclusivity to file and have only the debtor's plan of reorganization confirmed by the court. Any entity, including one or more creditors, the trustee, debtor, and any other party-in-interest may file competing plans for confirmation (approval) by the court once a trustee is appointed. However, the U.S. trustee may not file a plan. Each proponent of a plan must also file and obtain court approval of a disclosure statement before soliciting votes for confirmation of any plan. *11 USC §§307, 1107-1108, 1121(b), (c)(1); FRBP 2012; see "Tenth Duty as Debtor—File and Obtain Approval of Disclosure Statement," discussed above.*

(2) Examiner

Appointment of a examiner does not terminate the debtor's DIP status with its concomitant rights and powers. The DIP retains his dual roles as debtor and trustee, his 180-day period of exclusivity to file and have only his plan confirmed, and all rights and super-avoiding powers of a trustee. *See 11 USC §§1101(1), 1106-1107, 1121; Chapter XII.*

The DIP would prefer appointment of an examiner to a trustee if any court-ordered appointment appears likely. A trustee would generally not be needed in any case where protections afforded by a trustee could be equally provided by an examiner. A trustee also would not be appropriate where the costs and expenses of the trustee would be disproportionately greater than the value of services and protections which the trustee would provide to the estate (*see "Trustee's Fees," Chapter III*). The possibility of appointing an examiner thus gives the court, debtor, creditors, and equity security holders greater flexibility and enables the court to select the best remedy for the particular case. *11 USC §§102(a), 322, 326, 1104; HR Rep No 595, 95th Cong, 1st Sess 402 (1977); S Rep No 989, 95th Cong, 2d Sess 115 (1978).*

h. Termination of Trustee or Examiner

The court may remove a trustee or examiner at any time before confirmation of a plan if requested by the U.S. trustee or a party-in-interest (creditor, committee, trustee, or examiner). Such request does not commence an adversary proceeding. No filing fee is required. The party filing the request must serve a copy on the debtor, the U.S. trustee, any trustee, all Committee(s), and any other entity required by court order or local bankruptcy rules. Service may be obtained by first-class mail or any other manner allowed for service of process in federal district court. A hearing must then be held, unless local bankruptcy rules state otherwise. If the court grants the request and terminates the trustee, the debtor may be restored to DIP status, management of property of the estate, and operation of the debtor's business. *11 USC §§102(1)(A)-(B), 1105; FRBP 9013-9014, 9034.*

6. Procedure Six—Compensation for Professional Persons Hired by the DIP, Trustee, or Committee

a. Requirements for Payment of Professional Persons

(1) How and When Paid

The DIP, trustee, and unsecured creditors' committee may employ professional persons (attorney, accountant) who are disinterested and have no adverse interests to the estate. Such professional persons may be employed on any reasonable terms approved by the court, including a retainer, hourly rate, or contingency fee basis. As a rule, the committee itself has no funds and the DIP personally has insufficient funds (post-petition wages, salary, commissions of an individual debtor) to pay the professional. Compensation must then be paid from the bankruptcy estate. Since such fees are generally first priority administrative expenses, they are paid either upon confirmation of the plan or as interim compensation. *11 USC §§327-331, 503(a), (b)(1), 507(a)(1), 541(a)(6), 1129(a)(9)(A); see "Priority Claims," Chapter II.*

The professional person may choose one or both of the following methods for payment, which may be carefully reviewed by the U.S. trustee in accordance with procedural guidelines adopted by the Executive Office of the U.S. trustee:

(a) Compensation upon Confirmation of Plan

If the professional person waits until confirmation of the plan, he must be paid in cash on the effective date of the plan for the full amount of his administrative claim allowed by the court, including reasonable costs and expenses incurred for his services, unless the professional person agrees otherwise. The proponent of a confirmed plan (DIP, committee, creditor, trustee) is responsible for paying all allowed first priority administrative expenses. The professional person may elect to receive deferred cash or other payments under the plan. But the decision of full cash or deferred payments lies with the professional person. *11 USC §§330, 1129(a)(9)(A); 28 USC*

§586(a)(3)(A); see "Procedure Seven Confirmation of a Plan of Reorganization," discussed below;

(b) Interim Compensation

The professional person may choose to file an application for interim compensation for services rendered during the case, including reasonable and necessary costs and expenses. If there is money available in the estate and the court so approves, interim compensation may be paid to the professional person once every 120 days after the voluntary petition is filed or order for relief in an involuntary case. The court or local bankruptcy rules may allow payment of interim compensation more frequently. The professional may receive interim compensation one or more times during the case and agree to full payment of his remaining first priority administrative claims in cash or deferred payments under a confirmed plan. *11 USC §§330-331, 1103, 1129(a)(9)(A).*

(2) File Application for Compensation

Any professional person who seeks compensation for services rendered under a Chapter 11 case must file an application for interim or final compensation. The application must include the following 12 matters:

a) Services rendered for the debtor, trustee, or committee under the Chapter 11 case and the time expended for such services;

(b) Rates charged for each service performed;

(c) Whether the services were necessary or beneficial to the administration of the case at the time such services were performed;

(d) Whether the services were performed within a reasonable amount of time given the complexity, importance, and nature of the issues or problems addressed in the case;

(e) Whether the requested compensation is reasonable based upon compensation customarily charged by comparably skilled practitioners in nonbankruptcy cases;

f) Costs and expenses incurred for providing representation to the debtor, trustee, or committee;

g) Total amounts requested;

h) Previous payments made or promised for services in the Chapter 11 case;

i) Source of any previous payments made or promised for services in the Chapter 11 case;

j) Whether any payment previously made was shared and with whom;

k) The terms of any fee-sharing agreement between the applicant and any non-member or non-associate of such applicant or such applicant's firm; and

l) Any other provision required by local bankruptcy rules or court order. *11 USC §§330-331; FRBP 2016(a).*

A copy of the application for compensation must be served on the debtor, U.S. trustee, any Chapter 11 trustee, all committee(s) appointed in the debtor's case, and any other entity directed by court order or local bankruptcy rules. The application may be served by first-class mail or any other method for service of motions in federal district court. The court must hold a hearing on any application for compensation. The clerk of the court must give at least 20 days' notice of the hearing on all applications for compensation which exceed $500. Such notice must be mailed to the debtor, U.S. trustee, trustee, all committee(s), creditors, equity security holders, indenture trustees, and any other entity required by court order or local bankruptcy rules. *11 USC §§330-331; 28 USC §586(a)(3)(A); FRBP 2002(a)(7), (i), (k), 2016, 7005, 9013-9014, 9034.*

(3) Review by U.S. Trustee

Any application for final compensation filed under §330 of the Bankruptcy Code may be reviewed by the U.S. trustee in accordance with procedural guidelines adopted by the Executive Office of the U.S. trustee. The guidelines must be uniformly applied to all fee applications reviewed, unless the U.S. trustee believes circumstances warrant different treatment. The U.S. trustee must additionally file written comments with the court about fee applications reviewed and may object to any fee application. *28 USC §586(a)(3)(A); 11 USC §330; FRBP 2016.*

(4) Court Determination

The court, acting *sua sponte* or on motion of any party-in-interest (creditor, trustee, U.S. trustee), may award less compensation than requested. The court may not allow compensation for unnecessary duplicative services or for services that were not reasonably likely to benefit the estate or necessary to the administration of the case. Although compensation may be awarded for preparing the fee application, it must be based upon the level and skill reasonably required to prepare the application. The court must reduce the amount of final compensation to be awarded by the total amount of any interim fees previously paid. *28 USC §330(a).*

Any fee application for more than $500 requires a hearing. The clerk, applicant, or other entity required by court order or local bankruptcy rules must give at least 20 days' notice of the hearing to the debtor, all creditors, all creditors' committees, the U.S. trustee, any Chapter 11 trustee, the SEC in Washington, D.C., or any other location designated by the SEC in a notice of appearance or written request filed with the court, the District Director of the IRS where the debtor's case is pending, and to any other entity required by court order or local bankruptcy rules. *FRBP 2002(a)(i)(2).*

b. Problems with Interim Compensation

Two inherent problems exist with payment of interim compensation in a Chapter 11 case if no plan is confirmed or the case is eventually converted to Chapter 7:

(1) Violation of Pro Rata Rule

Under bankruptcy law, all first priority administrative expenses allowed by the court should be paid pro rata (same percentage). Further, under Chapter 11, all allowed administrative expenses (attorneys, accountants, trade creditors) must finally be paid 100 per cent in cash on the effective date of a confirmed plan, unless such priority claimholders agree otherwise. If no Chapter 11 plan is confirmed and the case is converted to Chapter 7, professional persons who received interim compensation during the case may receive more payment of their Chapter 11 administrative claims than other professional persons and trade creditors who chose to wait until confirmation of a plan for payment. This violates the pro rata rule. *See "Priority Claims," Chapter II;*

(2) Violation of the Chapter 7 Priority Administrative Expense Payment Rule

The problem is then compounded by other bankruptcy law. First priority administrative expenses incurred under a case converted to Chapter 7 have priority over and must be paid before administrative expenses incurred under the superseded Chapter 11 (12 or 13) case. But if, by the time the case is converted, there is insufficient or no bankruptcy estate left to pay Chapter 7 administrative expenses, those creditors who received interim payment of their Chapter 11 administrative expenses technically violated the "Chapter 7 priority administrative expense payment" rule. *11 USC §§330-331, 503(a), (b)(1), 507(a)(1), 726(b), 1129(a)(9)(A).*

c. Disallowance of Claims of Professional Persons

The court may limit the amount of compensation or deny compensation of administrative expenses requested by any professional person. A claim will be limited or disallowed if:

(1) the amount sought is unreasonable in light of unforeseen developments in the case;

(2) the professional is not a disinterested person or holds an adverse interest to the estate; or

(3) the services rendered by the professional person do not justify the amount requested.

The court may also order a professional person, including the attorney for the debtor, trustee, or committee, to return some or all of any compensation previously paid. *11 USC §§105(a), 328(a), 329; FRBP 2017.*

7. Procedure Seven—Confirmation of a Plan of Reorganization

A Chapter 11 plan of reorganization can be the most complex and creative of all bankruptcy plans. There are 21 basic requirements for confirmation of a Chapter 11 plan. Additionally, there are several optional (permissive) provisions which a Chapter 11 plan may contain:

a. Requirements for Confirmation of a Chapter 11 Plan

The court must confirm a Chapter 11 plan if it meets the following 21 requirements:

(1) Classifies Claims and Interests

(a) How to Classify

The Chapter 11 Plan must classify creditors' claims and equity security (stockholder) interests. The debtor or other proponent of a plan may create as many classes of claims or interests as he wishes as long as each member of a particular class is substantially similar to other members of the same class. "Substantially similar" is a legal term of art. It means the legal rights or interests of all members of a class should be substantially the same. Thus, general unsecured creditors would usually be placed in one class, because their legal interests and rights are substantially similar, even though the amount of their claims may vary. Similarly, co-debtors, guarantors, and sureties of the debtor's obligations may be placed in a different class. Each secured creditor is generally placed in a separate class consisting of one member only—that secured creditor. The legal basis for such classification is that each secured creditor generally has a lien on different collateral. If two or more secured creditors have a lien on the same collateral, then such secured creditors may be included in the same class of creditors or placed in different classes based on their respective lienhold positions (first lien, second lien). The same legal principle governs classification of equity security interests. The members of a particular class of equity security interests should have the same type of stock or other security of a debtor and the same rights and interests with regard to such security. A Chapter 11 plan may also designate a class of unsecured creditors with relatively small pre-petition claims which are reduced for administrative convenience under the plan. *11 USC §§1122(a)(b), 1123(a)(1); FRBP 3013.*

(b) How to Designate Classes:

Classes should be numbered consecutively. First, second, and eighth priority claims (administrative expenses, unsecured gap creditors, certain unsecured tax claims) are not classified or designated as classes. These priority claims are simply identified by their priority status (first priority claims, second priority claims, eighth priority claims). *11 USC §1123(a)(1); see "Priority Claims," Chapter II.*

(c) Objection to Classes:

A party-in-interest (creditor, stockholder) may file a motion objecting to a plan's classification of claims or interests. A copy of the motion must be served by first-class mail on the debtor, proponent of the plan if not the debtor, any trustee, the U.S. trustee, all committee(s), and on such other entities required by court order or local bankruptcy rules. Such motion does not commence an adversary proceeding and no filing fee is required. The court will then hold a hearing on the motion to determine the proper classification, which may be combined with the confirmation hearing. Notice of the hearing date should be mailed to the debtor, any trustee, the proponent of the plan if other than the debtor, the U.S. trustee, all committee(s), and any other entity as directed by the court or local bankruptcy rules. *FRBP 3013, 9013-9014, 9034.*

(2) Designates any class of claims or interests that is not impaired by the terms of the plan.

An unimpaired class and each member of such class is conclusively presumed to have accepted the plan without voting. A claim or equity security interest is unimpaired if the plan:

(a) Does not modify the pre-petition rights of the creditor or equity security holder; or

(b) Cures any default that occurred pre- or post-petition (except a default that occurred by the debtor's insolvency or filing a petition), reinstates the pre-default maturity date of the claim or equity security interest, and compensates such entity for any damages suffered as a result of the debtor's default. *11 USC §§1124, 1126(f).*

Creditors who, on the effective date of the plan, will receive a cash payment equal to the allowed amount of their claims are nevertheless impaired claims under the Bankruptcy Code. Similarly, equity security holders who are to receive cash on the effective date of the plan equal to the greater of any fixed liquidation preference or fixed redemption price are impaired interests. Such creditors and equity security holders may constitute voting classes of claims or interests under a plan. *See "Dissenting Unsecured Creditors," discussed below; 11 USC §§1124, 1126 (c)(d)(f), 1129(a)(b).*

The "effective date of the plan" is a bankruptcy term of art which may vary from plan to plan. Such date could be designated as the date of confirmation of the plan; the date the confirmation order is entered by the court; or the date the confirmation order becomes final. An order becomes final if there are no appeals or the order is affirmed on appeal. *See "Appeal of Bankruptcy Court Order," Chapter IX; Local Bankruptcy Rules;*

(3) Describes the terms, conditions, and amounts of payment of any claims or interests that are impaired by the plan;

(4) Provides the same terms, conditions, and amounts of payment for all members of the same class (pro rata payments);

(5) Provides adequate means for implementing the plan. Adequate means may include any combination of the following:

(a) Sale of property of the debtor or estate;

(b) Merger of the debtor with one or more entities;

(c) Transfer of property to another entity (third party funder) who will then make all payments required by the plan;

(d) Issue of new securities of the debtor or third party funder in payment of any claim or interest;

(e) Curing any default. The amount necessary to cure a default under a plan of reorganization must be determined according to the terms of any underlying agreement entered into after October 22, 1994, and applicable nonbankruptcy law. However, with regard to agreements entered into before October 22, 1994, an oversecured creditor under a long-term promissory note is entitled to pre-confirmation interest under 11 USC §506(b) and post-confirmation interest under 11 USC §1129(a)(7)(b)(2)(A) on arrearages cured under the plan. *11 USC §§506(b), 1123(d), Pub L 103-394, Title VII, §702; Rake v. Wade, 113 S Ct 2187, 124 L Ed 2d 424, 28 CBC 2d 983 (1993);*

(f) Retention of property by the debtor; or

(g) Any other provision approved by the court;

(6) Provides that the charter of any corporate debtor, merger, or third party funder will contain provisions to:

(a) Prohibit issuance of nonvoting securities;

(b) Provide for appropriate division of powers among all voting classes of securities; and

(c) Protect the rights of any preferred class of securities, including adequate provisions for electing directors in the event of any default in dividend payments to such preferred security holders;

(7) Includes provisions that protect the interests of creditors, security holders, and public policy by the manner officers, directors, trustees, or their successors are selected under the plan;

(8) Complies with all requirements of the Bankruptcy Code;

(9) States that the plan has been proposed in good faith and not by any means forbidden by law;

(10) States that any payment to be made under the plan for services, costs, or expenses relating to the plan or Chapter 11 case has been or will be approved as reasonable by the court;

(11) Discloses the identity and affiliation of any individual who will serve as post-confirmation director, officer, or voting trustee of the debtor, affiliate, or successor to the debtor and states that the services of such director, officer, or voting trustee are consistent with the interests of creditors, equity security holders, and public policy;

(12) Discloses the identity and amount of compensation of any insider employed or retained by the reorganized debtor;

(13) Provides, where applicable, that any governmental regulatory commission with post-confirmation jurisdiction over rates charged by the debtor has approved any rate changes proposed by the plan or that the rate changes will be subject to approval of such regulatory commission;

(14) Provides that each creditor or equity security holder who is impaired by the plan has accepted the plan; or that by the effective date of the plan, such creditor or equity security holder will receive at least the amount he would receive if the debtor were liquidated under Chapter 7.

This *floor* or minimum payment is an adaption of the "best interest of creditors" test. A creditor or equity security holder is assured of receiving at least the amount that would be received under Chapter 7 if he does not accept the plan. *11*

USC §1129(a)(7)(A); HR Rep No 595, 95th Cong, 1st Sess 412 (1977);

(15) Provides that if a class of impaired secured creditors elects to be fully secured, such class will receive property (not necessarily cash) on the effective date of the plan, equal to the full amount of the members' allowed claims.

Under Chapter 11, the general rule is that a secured claim is treated as if the creditor had recourse against the debtor, even if the secured claim was nonrecourse under the pre-petition loan agreement or applicable nonbankruptcy law. But the preferred recourse status for nonrecourse secured claims ends under bankruptcy law if: (a) the collateral is sold in the bankruptcy proceeding; (b) a Chapter 11 plan proposes that the collateral be sold; or (c) the class of creditors of which the secured creditor is a member elects to be fully secured. *11 USC §§363, 1111(b)(1)(A); 124 Cong Rec H11,103 (daily ed Sept 28, 1978), S17,420 (daily ed Oct 6, 1978).*

Normally, a creditor is secured to the lesser of the value of its collateral or amount of its claim. However, under Chapter 11, certain secured creditors may elect, as a class, to be fully secured for the total amount of their allowed claims. A class of secured creditors *elects* to be fully secured if at least two-thirds in dollar amount and more than 50 per cent in number of the allowed claims of such class so choose. Since a class of secured creditors will frequently have only one member, such election becomes relatively simple. However, the class may not elect to be fully secured if: (i) the value of collateral securing the claims of the class is "inconsequential"; or (ii) any member of the class has recourse against the debtor and the collateral is sold under the bankruptcy case or is to be sold under the plan. The secured creditor may, however, bid in the full amount of his claim at any sale, unless the court orders otherwise for cause. *See Chapter VIII; 11 USC §§363(k), 506(a), 1111(b), 1129(a)(7).*

A class of secured creditors may elect to be fully secured at any time before the conclusion of the hearing on the disclosure statement or by any later date set by the court or local bankruptcy rules (*see "Tenth Duty as Debtor—File and Obtain Approval of Disclosure Statement," discussed above*). Unless the election is made at the hearing on the disclosure statement, the elective must be in writing and signed by each class member election to be fully secured. If at least two-thirds in dollar amount and more than 50 per cent in number of a class of secured creditors elects to be fully secured, the election is binding on all members of the class with regard to the plan. *11 USC §1111(b)(1)-(2); FRBP 3014.*

If a class elects to be fully secured, the plan must provide that each member of such class will have the entire allowed amount of his claim secured by a lien on his respective collateral, even if the value of the collateral is less than the amount of the allowed claim. Further, the plan must provide that each member of such class of fully secured creditors receive payments of a principal face amount equal to the full allowed amount of the claim and of a present value equal to the value of the collateral. Payments may be present or deferred payments under the plan. *11 USC §§1111(b), 1129(a)(7)(B); 124 Cong Rec H11,103 (daily ed Sept 28, 1978), S17,420 (daily ed Oct 6, 1978).*

Thus, if a fully secured creditor has an allowed claim of $10,000 secured by collateral valued at $7,000 for purposes of distribution under Chapter 11, the plan must propose that: (a) the creditor will retain his lien on the collateral to secure the full $10,000 allowed claim; (b) the creditor will receive present or deferred payments of a principal face amount of at least $10,000 under the plan; and (c) the present value of the payments will not be less than $7,000, the value of the collateral, even if payments are deferred under the plan. Valuation of the collateral must occur on the effective date of the plan, thereby taking into account the present value of money by discounting the value of any deferred payments under the plan. If payments to the creditor are deferred, the plan must propose a sufficient interest rate to give the creditor his present value of money. *HR Rep No 595, 95th Cong, 1st Sess 413-18 (1977); 124 Cong Rec H11,103 (daily ed Sept 28, 1978), S17,420 (daily ed Oct 6, 1978);*

(16) States that if there are any impaired classes of claims, at least one class of impaired creditors has voted to accept the plan, without counting the votes of any insider. A class of claims that is to receive cash on the effective date of the plan equal to the allowed amount of such claims is an impaired class under the Bankruptcy Code. Such class may constitute the one class of impaired claims that votes to accept the plan. However, if the plan does not propose to make interest payments to such impaired claimholders to compensate for the delayed use of money, the class may withhold its vote or vote against the plan. *See "Dissenting Unsecured Creditors" and "Number of Affirmative Votes Required for Confirmation," discussed below; 11 USC §1124;*

(17) Provides that priority claims will be paid as follows, unless the respective claimholder agrees otherwise:

(a) First and second priority claims allowed by the court will be paid cash in full on the effective date of the plan (*see "Priority Claims," Chapter II*);

(b) Classes consisting of third through seventh priority claims that accept the plan will receive deferred cash payments equal in value to the amount of the respective priority claim allowed by the court. The court will determine all values as of the effective date of the plan, allowing for the present value of money;

(c) Classes of third through seventh priority claims that reject the plan will receive cash for the allowed amount of the respective priority claim, unless the particular claimholder agrees otherwise. Such cash-on-the barrel payments must be made on the effective date of the plan;

(d) Eighth priority claims will receive deferred cash payments over no more than six years after the date the (tax) claim was assessed, unless the taxing authority agrees otherwise. Payments must be equal in value to the allowed amount of the priority tax claim. The value of deferred cash payments must also be determined as of the effective date of the plan; and

(e) Under the amendments to the Code, ninth priority claims are not statutorily required to be specially paid under a Chapter 11 plan. However, such priority claims may be nondischargeable debts of an individual debtor. Local bankruptcy rules, court order, or prudence should mandate particular provisions for payment of such priority claims. *11 USC §§507(a)(8), 523(a)(12), 1129 (a)(9), 1141(d)(2); see "Priority Claims," Chapter II, "Legal Effects of Confirmation," below.*

(18) States that it is not likely the debtor will be liquidated or further reorganized after confirmation of the plan; or specifically provides for such liquidation or further reorganization.

The court must make a determination about the feasibility of the proposed plan;

(19) States that all fees required by Title 28, §1930, United States Code, either have been or will be paid by the effective date of the plan.

Such fees include the filing fee, quarterly fees, and any required fees for filing an adversary complaint;

(20) **Provides for continued payment of all retiree benefits after the effective date of the plan, in amounts and for the duration agreed to by the debtor or established by the court before confirmation.** *See "Retiree Benefits," Chapter XIV;*

(21) **Does not discriminate unfairly and is fair and equitable with regard to each class of impaired claims or interests that has not accepted the plan.** This is the *cram down* provision of Chapter 11. A plan may be crammed down a dissenting class of impaired creditors or equity security holders if the plan meets certain standards of fairness to the dissenting, impaired classes. A plan is "fair and equitable" if impaired, dissenting secured creditors, unsecured creditors, and equity security holders will receive the following treatment:

(a) **Dissenting secured creditors with impaired claims must either:**

(i) Retain their liens on collateral and receive deferred cash payments equal to the lesser of the value of their collateral or allowed amount of their claim, plus interest, over the term of the plan. Value is determined by the court as of the effective date of the plan; or

(ii) Retain their liens on proceeds received from the sale of collateral, and either receive such proceeds in deferred cash payments with interest over the term of the plan or receive the indubitable equivalent of such proceeds; or

(iii) Receive the indubitable equivalent of their allowed secured claims valued by the court as of the effective date of the plan. *Indubitable equivalent* is another bankruptcy term of art. The term essentially means comparable value. It is the bankruptcy court which determines what constitutes the indubitable equivalent or comparable value of a creditor's allowed secured claim. Indubitable equivalent could be the receipt of stock or equity in the reorganized debtor or a successor to the debtor under the plan. Value is determined as of the effective date of the plan to allow for the present value of money. *11 USC §1129(a), (b)(1)-(2)(A); 124 Cong Rec H11,103 (daily ed Sept 28, 1978), S17,420 (daily ed Oct 6, 1978); HR Rep No 595, 95th Cong, 1st Sess 413 (1977);*

(b) **Dissenting unsecured creditors must receive property (cash or otherwise) equal in value to the full amount of their allowed unsecured claims, or no creditor or equity security holder whose legal rights and interests are junior to such unsecured creditors may receive anything under the plan.**

This cram down provision incorporates the absolute priority rule starting with the dissenting class on down. The dissenting class must be paid in full before any junior classes may receive payment. The provision requires either that all dissenting unsecured creditors (not just priority claims) be paid the full amount of their allowed prepetition claims, or that unsecured creditors who do not receive full payment under the Plan must own the debtor's business or non-exempt property. Claims of insiders, equity security holders (stockholders), and the debtor are junior and thus subordinated in ranking and legal rights to the unpaid claims of unsecured creditors under bankruptcy law. The value of property received by unsecured creditors must again be determined by the court as of the effective date of the plan. *11 USC §§510(b)-(c), 1129(b)(1)-(2)(B); 124 Cong Rec H11,103 (daily ed Sept 28, 1978), S17,420 (daily ed Oct 6, 1978); HR Rep No 595, 95th Cong, 1st Sess 413-18 (1977);* and

(c) Dissenting equity security holders (stockholders, bondholders) must either receive property (cash or otherwise) equal in value to the greatest of any:

(i) fixed liquidation value,

(ii) fixed redemption price, or

(iii) the value of such equity security (stock, bond) to which the holder is entitled; or any stockholder or bondholder with junior shares must receive nothing (lose their holdings) under the plan.

Value of property received under the plan is again determined by the court as of the effective date of the plan. *11 USC §1129(b)(1)-(2)(C).*

b. Optional provisions allowed in a Chapter 11 plan

As long as a Chapter 11 Plan meets the 21 requirements outlined above, it may contain any other provision allowed by bankruptcy or nonbankruptcy law and approved by the court. Such permissive provisions may include:

(1) The assumption or rejection of executory contracts, subject to protections afforded collective bargaining agreements and retiree benefits under bankruptcy law (*see "Assumption or Rejection of Executory Contracts and Unexpired Leases," "Collective Bargaining Agreements" and "Retiree Benefits," Chapter XIV*);

(2) The enforcement, settlement, or adjustment of any claim held by the debtor or estate against another entity;

(3) Modifying the rights of secured or unsecured creditors, including the interest rate to be provided to creditors for

deferred payments under a plan. However, the plan may not modify any pre-petition contract rights of a homestead mortgagee with a lien only on the debtor's principal residence. The entire debt of such homestead mortgagee is treated as secured and may not be bifurcated into a secured and unsecured claim under §506(a) of the Bankruptcy Code. *11 USC §1123(b)(5); see Nobelman v American Savings Bank, 113 S Ct 2106, 124 L Ed 2d 228, 28 CBC 2d 977 (1993).*

(4) The sale of all or substantially all of the debtor's property and distribution of the proceeds received from such sale among creditors.

If the proponent of a plan in an individual debtor's case is not the debtor, the plan may not provide for the use, sale, or lease of the debtor's exempt property unless the debtor consents;

(5) Retention of the jurisdiction of the bankruptcy court, post-confirmation, to hear and determine all matters relating, directly or indirectly, to full implementation of the confirmed plan;

(6) The effective date of the plan. This provision should be specifically included in every plan; or

(7) Any other provision which does not violate the requirements of the bankruptcy code. *11 USC §§522(b), (d), 1123(b)-(c), 1142(b).*

c. Notice of Confirmation Hearing on a Plan of Reorganization

The clerk, debtor, proponent of the plan, or other court-authorized person must give at least 25 days' notice by mail of the date of the confirmation hearing and date for filing objections to the plan. Such notice should be included with the information and documents sent with notice of approval of the disclosure statement to the debtor, U.S. trustee, any Chapter 11 trustee, all committee(s), creditors, equity security holders, indenture trustees, the SEC in Washington, D.C., the District Director of the IRS where the case is pending, and any other entity required by court order or local bankruptcy rules. *See "Notice of Approval of Disclosure Statement," discussed above; 11 USC §1128; FRBP 2002(b), (i)-(k), 3017(d), 3020(b)(2), 9034; Official Bankr Forms 13, 14.*

d. Objections

Any party-in-interest (creditor, trustee, U.S. trustee, stockholder) may file an objection to confirmation of the plan. The party-in-interest must file an objection by the date indicated in the notice of confirmation hearing. An objection does not commence an adversary proceeding and no filing fee is required. The party-in-interest must state the grounds for objection and serve a copy of the objection by first-class mail or personal delivery by a disinterested person at least 18 years old on the debtor, U.S. trustee, any Chapter 11 trustee, all committee(s), the proponent of the plan if not the debtor, and any entity as required by the court or local bankruptcy rules. The right to object is exclusive of and in addition to the right to vote against a plan. An objection may be filed without a vote cast. The objection will be considered at the confirmation or other hearing designated by the court or local bankruptcy rules. *11 USC §§102(1)(A), 1126, 1128(b); FRBP 3020(b)(1)-(2), 7004, 9014.*

e. Voting

(1) Who May Vote

A plan may be accepted or rejected by a creditor with an impaired claim that has been allowed by the court and by an equity security holder whose impaired interest has been allowed. If the United States is a creditor, the Secretary of the Treasury may vote to accept or reject a plan. A claim or interest is deemed allowed when a proof of claim is properly and timely filed. In a Chapter 11 case, the proof of claim is generally considered filed for the amount listed in the debtor's schedules of liabilities. However, if the creditor or equity security holder objects to the amount listed in the schedules or if the debtor has either failed to list or listed such a claim or interest as disputed, contingent, or unliquidated, then the creditor or security holder must file a proof of claim by the date fixed by the court. *11 USC §§501-502, 1111(a), 1126(a); FRBP 3003(c), 3018; see "File Proof of Claim," Chapter XIV.*

The notice of approval of the disclosure statement will generally include the dates set by the court for filing votes, objections to confirmation, proofs of claims, and for the hearing on confirmation of the plan. The notice should also state where to file the ballots (votes) and proofs of claims. Generally, ballots for voting are served on the debtor or unsecured creditors' committee, unless the court or local bankruptcy rules indicate otherwise. The debtor or committee will then file the votes with the court. Proofs of claims are filed with the clerk of the court. If a proof of claim is required but not timely filed, such creditor or equity security holder is excluded from voting and distribution under a plan (no payment). *11 USC §§501, 1111(a), 1126(a), 1129(b); FRBP 3002(a), 3003(c)(2)-(3), 3017(d), 3018(a), 5005; see "File Proof of Claim," Chapter XIV.*

(2) When to Vote

Voting may occur before or after the petition is filed. If the debtor wrote a plan and solicited votes pre-petition, the votes for or against the plan may be filed with the court post-petition by the creditor or equity security holder. Pre-petition votes will be counted if:

(a) The debtor or proponent of the plan solicited votes after disclosing adequate information required under any applicable nonbankruptcy law, rule, or regulation;

(b) There is no required nonbankruptcy law, rule, or regulation for disclosing adequate information but the debtor solicited votes pre-petition after disclosing adequate information required for a bankruptcy disclosure statement;

(c) A creditor or equity security holder whose claim is based on a security of record was in fact the record holder of such security on the date votes were solicited pre-petition;

(d) The pre-petition plan was sent to substantially all impaired creditors and equity security holders of the same class; and

(e) The debtor did not require an unreasonably short time for voting for or against the pre-petition plan. *11 USC §1126(b); FRBP 3018(b).*

A creditor or equity security holder may withdraw or change a vote cast pre- or post-petition if the court permits. The creditor or equity security holder must file a request to change votes, showing cause for the withdrawal or change. This request must be filed by the date set by the court for voting indicated in the notice of court approval of the disclosure statement. A copy of the request must be served upon the debtor, any trustee, the U.S. trustee, all committee(s), creditors, and equity security holders, and any other entity required by court order or local bankruptcy rules. Service may be by first-class mail, personal delivery by a disinterested person at least 18 years old, or by any other manner for service of a summons and complaint in federal district court. The request does not commence an adversary proceeding and no filing fee is required. *FRBP 3017, 3018(a), 9013-9014, 9034; Official Bankr Forms 13, 14.*

Pre- and post-petition votes must be received by the clerk, debtor, or other court-appointed person by the date fixed by the court. Notice of such date must be included in the notice of order approving the disclosure statement. *FRBP 3017(c)-(d); Official Bankr Forms 13, 14; see "Tenth Duty as Debtor—File and Obtain Approval of Disclosure Statement," discussed above.*

(3) How to Vote

Votes accepting or rejecting a plan must be written; identify the plan; signed by the creditor, equity security holder, or authorized agent of such entity; and conform essentially to Official Bankruptcy Form 14. If more than one plan is submitted for votes, a creditor or equity security holder may file a vote with the court for each plan and may indicate preference(s) among competing plans. The court may confirm only one plan. However, the court must consider the preferences of creditors and equity security holders in determining which among competing plans to confirm. The plan must meet all 21 requirements for confirmation outlined above. *See "Requirements for Confirmation of a Chapter 11 Plan," discussed above; 11 USC §1129(c); FRBP 3018(c); Official Bankr Forms 11A, 11B, 14, 15;*

(4) Number of Affirmative Votes Required for Confirmation

(a) Impaired Classes of Creditors

The Code requires that if there are any classes of impaired claims under a plan, then at least one class of creditors with impaired claims must vote to accept the plan, excluding acceptance(s) of any insider. A class of creditors that is to receive cash on the effective date of the plan equal to the allowed amount of the pre-petition unsecured claims of its members is an impaired class under bankruptcy law and may vote for or against the plan. An impaired class of creditors is considered to have accepted a plan by counting only the voting members of the class. At least two-thirds in dollar amount and more than one-half in number of the voting creditors must vote to accept for the plan to be considered accepted by the impaired class. For example, if an impaired class of creditors has 150 members with claims totaling $2,000, but only 100 members with claims of $1,000 vote, it is these 100 voting members with aggregate claims of $1,000 who are considered in determining whether the class accepts or rejects the plan. Under bankruptcy law, 51 members of this hypothetical class with claims totaling at least $666.67 must vote to accept the plan. If 51 members vote to accept but their claims total $665, the impaired class has not accepted the plan. Similarly, if 50 members vote with claims of $666.67, the class has not voted to accept the plan. The court must disallow any votes solicited or cast in bad faith. *11 USC §§1124, 1126(a), (e), 1129(a)(10).*

(b) Impaired Classes of Equity Security Holders

An impaired class of equity security holders votes to accept a plan if, of the members who actually vote, holders of at least two-thirds in dollar amount of the outstanding equity securities of the debtor vote to accept the plan. A class of equity security holders that is to receive cash on the effective date of the plan equal to the greater amount of any liquidation preference or redemption price fixed under the terms of the security is impaired and may vote for or against the plan. The court must disallow votes solicited or cast in bad faith. And even if all impaired classes of equity security holders vote to accept the plan, if there are any impaired classes of creditors under a plan, at least one class of such impaired class of creditors must vote to accept the plan without counting acceptance(s) of any insiders. *11 USC §§1126(d)-(e), 1129(a)(10); see "Requirements for Confirmation of a Chapter 11 Plan," discussed above;*

(c) Unimpaired Classes

If a class of creditors or equity security holders is not impaired, such class is conclusively deemed to have accepted the plan. The members of such class may not vote to reject the plan and no ballot need be sent to them. But, as stated, if there is a class of impaired creditors, at least one of such classes must vote to accept the plan or the plan may not be confirmed by the court. If a plan proposes that a certain class of creditors or equity security holders will receive nothing, then such class is deemed to have rejected the plan without necessity of voting. *11 USC §§1126(f)-(g), 1129(a)(10).*

(d) Disallowed Votes

The court may disallow or refuse to count votes solicited or cast in bad faith. A party-in-interest must file a request for disallowance or designation of votes that were not cast in good faith or properly obtained. The request must identify the entity whose vote is to be rejected and assert that such entity's vote was either: (1) not cast in good faith; (2) not solicited in good faith; or (3) not obtained properly (the proponent of the plan failed to obtain court approval of a disclosure statement; improper notice of confirmation hearing or improper ballots for votes were sent to parties-in-interest). The party who files the request must serve a copy by first-class mail or any other manner allowed for service of process in federal district court, on the debtor, any trustee, all committee(s), the U.S. trustee, and any other entity required by the court or local bankruptcy rules. The court must thereafter hold a hearing on the request. *11 USC §§102(1)(A)-(B), 1126(e); FRBP 7004, 9013-9014, 9034.*

f. Modification of a Plan of Reorganization

(1) Generally

The debtor or other proponent of a plan may modify the plan at any time before confirmation and even after confirmation if cause exists and there has not been "substantial consummation" of the plan. *Substantial consummation* exists when three events concur:

(a) Distribution has begun under the plan;

(b) All or substantially all of the property to be transferred under the plan has been so transferred; and

(c) The business or management of all or substantially all of the property dealt with by the plan has been assumed by the debtor or his successor under the plan. *11 USC §§1101(2), 1127(a)-(b).*

A modified plan must meet all 21 requirements outlined above for confirmation of an original plan. If votes are to be solicited, the proponent of a modified plan must obtain court approval of a disclosure statement which provides adequate information to permit a creditor or equity security holder to make an informed decision about the modified plan. *11 USC §§1125, 1127(a)-(c); see "Requirements for Confirmation of a Chapter 11 Plan" and "Tenth Duty as Debtor—File and Obtain Approval of Disclosure Statement," discussed above.*

(2) Modification before Confirmation:

A plan modified before confirmation automatically becomes the plan to be considered for confirmation. Unless the court or local bankruptcy rules state otherwise, the clerk or other court-authorized person must give at least 25 days' notice of the date set by the court to accept or reject the (modified) plan. Notice must be sent by mail to the debtor, any trustee, the U.S. trustee, all committee(s), creditors, equity security holders, indenture trustees, the SEC in Washington, D.C., and to the District Director of the IRS where the case is pending. *11 USC §1127(a)-(b); FRBP 2002(b), (i)-(k), 9006(c), 9034.*

(3) Modification Before Confirmation but After Notice

A plan may be modified after notice of the confirmation hearing has been mailed but before the date to cast votes. The clerk or other court-authorized person must give at least 20 days' notice by mail of the date set by the court to accept or reject such modified plan, unless local bankruptcy rules require otherwise. Notice must be sent to the debtor, any trustee, the U.S. trustee, all committee(s), creditors, equity security holders, indenture trustees, the SEC in Washington, D.C., and to the District Director of the IRS where the case is pending. However, the modified plan need only be sent to creditors or equity security holders whose interests are adversely affected by the modifications, unless the court or local bankruptcy rules provide otherwise. *11 USC §1127; FRBP 2002(a)(6), (i)-(j), 3019, advisory committee's note, 9034.*

A plan may also be modified after notice of its confirmation hearing and after votes have been cast. The court must hold a hearing to determine whether the modifications adversely affect the interests of any creditor or equity security holder who previously voted. Notice of the hearing date must be mailed to the debtor, any trustee, the U.S. trustee, all committee(s), and any other entity as required by the court or local bankruptcy rules. Such hearing on the effect of the modifications may occur at the scheduled confirmation hearing. If the court determines that the modifications do not adversely affect the interests of a creditor or equity security holder who previously voted, such party-in-interest may not change his vote because the plan was modified. A modification that does not change the rights of a creditor or equity security holder from rights provided in the pre-modified plan does not adversely affect such interests. However, if the court determines that the modifications do adversely affect the rights of any creditor or equity security holder, such entity should have 20 days to consider whether to accept or reject the modified plan, unless the court or local bankruptcy rules direct otherwise. *11 USC §§102(1)(A)-(B), 1127(d); FRBP 2002(a)(6), (i), 3019, advisory committee's note, 9006(c), 9007, 9034.*

(4) Modification Post-Confirmation

A plan of reorganization may even be modified after confirmation by the court if substantial consummation of the plan has not yet occurred and the modified plan meets all 21 requirements for confirmation of an original plan (*see "Requirements for Confirmation of a Chapter 11 Plan" and "Substantial Consummation," discussed above*).

The proponent of the modified plan must obtain approval of a new disclosure statement if additional information is needed to enable a creditor or equity security holder to make an informed decision about the post-confirmation modifications and if the proponent intends to solicit votes for the modified plan. At least 25 days' notice must be given prior to any hearing date on a new disclosure statement, unless the court or local bankruptcy rules require otherwise.

The court must then hold a confirmation hearing on the post-confirmation modified plan. The clerk should give at least 25 days' notice by mail of the dates set by the court for voting, filing objections, and the confirmation hearing, unless the court reduces such time. All notices must be mailed to the debtor, U.S. trustee, any Chapter 11 trustee, all committee(s), creditors, equity security holders, indenture trustees, the SEC in Washington, D.C., and the District Director of the IRS where the case is pending. The proponent of the modified plan must show the court that circumstances justify the post-confirmation modification and that the modified plan meets all requirements for confirmation of an original plan. Creditors and equity security holders who previously voted under the original plan may change their votes if their interests are adversely affected by the modifications. *11 USC §1127(b), (d); FRBP 2002(b), (i)-(k), 9006, 9034; see "Tenth Duty as Debtor—File and Obtain Approval of Disclosure Statement" and "Requirements for Confirmation of a Chapter 11 Plan," discussed above.*

g. Confirmation Hearing

The court must hold a confirmation hearing after 25 days' notice has been mailed to all required parties-in-interest. The Code does not require the debtor's presence, although few debtors choose to ignore this hearing. Only one plan may be confirmed by the court, regardless of the number of competing plans filed. The court must consider the preferences of creditors and equity security holders in determining which competing plan to confirm. *11 USC §§1128, 1129(c).*

h. Order Confirming Plan of Reorganization

The clerk or other court-directed person must promptly mail a copy of the order confirming (approving) a plan of reorganization to the debtor, the U.S. trustee, any Chapter 11 trustee, all committee(s), creditors, equity security holders, indenture trustees, the SEC in Washington, D.C., the District Director of the IRS where the case is pending, and to such other parties-in-interest required by court order or local bankruptcy rules. *FRBP 2002(f)(7), (i)-(k), 3020(c), 9034; Official Bankr Form 15.*

i. Appeal of Confirmation Order

A confirmation order may be appealed to a district court in the federal judicial district where the case is pending; or to a three-judge bankruptcy appellate panel within the district if there is consent of all parties to appeal to the panel and if the district judges for the district where the case is pending by majority vote permit appeal to the panel. The appellant must file a notice of appeal with the bankruptcy clerk before the tenth day after the confirmation order is entered by the bankruptcy court. The notice of appeal must include:

(1) The names of the debtor, any trustee, all committee(s), and any other named party to the appealed confirmation order

(objecting creditor, equity security holder, or other party-in-interest);

(2) The respective attorney's name, address, and telephone number for the debtor, any trustee, all committee(s), and other named party to the appeal; and

(3) A $5 filing fee.

The appellant must file a sufficient number of copies of the notice of appeal to enable the bankruptcy clerk to mail such copies to all named parties to the appeal. The appellant must comply with all other requirements to perfect an appeal. *See Chapter IX; 28 USC §§158(a)-(b), 1930(c); FRBP 8001-8002, 8004; Official Bankr Form 17.*

j. Legal Effects of Confirmation

Confirmation of a Chapter 11 plan has four legal effects:

(1) The confirmed plan binds the debtor, any entity issuing securities or acquiring property of the debtor under the plan, and all creditors, equity security holders and general partners of the debtor, even if the plan impairs the interests of such entities or such entities voted to reject the plan;

(2) Confirmation vests all property of the bankruptcy estate in the debtor free and clear of the claims of creditors or equity security holders, unless stated otherwise in the plan or confirmation order;

(3) Confirmation generally discharges the debtor from personal liability for all debts incurred before confirmation of the plan. Thus, confirmation of any Chapter 11 plan generally discharges the debtor from pre- and post-petition debts incurred before confirmation even if the debtor was not the proponent of the confirmed plan. However, there are three exceptions to the general rule:

(a) First, an individual debtor will not receive a discharge from any pre-petition debt that would be nondischargeable or excepted from discharge under Chapter 7 (*see "Exceptions to Discharge," Chapter III*);

(b) Second, a Chapter 11 debtor will be denied a discharge of all debts if: (i) the confirmed plan provides that all or substantially all of the estate's property will be liquidated (sold or transferred for value), and (ii) the debtor does not thereafter engage in business, and (iii) the debtor would be denied a discharge under Chapter 7 (the debtor is not a natural person or there would be grounds for denial of discharge if the individual debtor had filed under Chapter 7. *See "Denial of Discharge," Chapter III*); and

(c) Third, the debtor will be denied a discharge of all debts if the court approves a written waiver of discharge signed by the debtor post-petition; and

(4) Confirmation terminates all rights and interests of the debtor's equity security holders and general partners as provided for in the plan or confirmation order. *11 USC §1141(a)-(d); see "Procedure Ten—Discharge," discussed below.*

k. Post-Confirmation Orders

The court retains jurisdiction or power to enter all orders necessary to administer the estate and implement the plan after confirmation. *11 USC §§1142-1143; FRBP 3020(d).*

The district or bankruptcy court may issue a supplemental injunction post-confirmation in a Chapter 11 case involving a debtor named as a defendant in an asbestos-related action at the time the voluntary petition was filed or order for relief was entered in an involuntary case. Prior notice and hearing must be given to all parties-in-interest. The supplemental injunction may only be issued if:

(1) An order confirming the plan has been entered;

(2) The plan provides for a trust that will assume the asbestos-related claims of the debtor; and

(3) The trust will be funded, in whole or part, by the securities of one or more debtor(s) involved in the plan and by such debtor(s)' obligations to make future dividend and other payments to the trust.

The injunction must require that all present and future asbestos-related claims be pursued against the trust rather than the debtor or any successor-in-interest or transferee of the debtor. *11 USC §§524(g), 1142.*

l. Revocation of Confirmation and Discharge

The confirmation order may be revoked by the court. Because confirmation of a plan also discharges the debtor, revocation of confirmation also revokes the debtor's discharge. A party-in-interest (creditor, equity security holder, trustee) must file an adversary complaint seeking revocation of confirmation and discharge and pay a $120 filing fee. However, if a trustee files the complaint, the $120 filing fee is collected only from any estate which may eventually exist. A copy of the complaint with summons must be served on the debtor and any Chapter 11 trustee by first-class mail, personal delivery by a disinterested person at least 18 years old, or by any other manner provided for service of a summons and complaint in federal district court. A copy of the complaint should also be mailed or personally delivered to the U.S. trustee and all committee(s) in the debtor's case. The only ground for revocation of confirmation is that the debtor obtained confirmation through fraud on the court and that the party-in-interest seeking revocation was not aware of such fraud before the confirmation hearing. The adversary complaint must be filed before the 180th day after the date the court entered the confirmation order. *11 USC §§1141(d)(1), 1144; 28 USC §1930(b), Judicial Conference Schedule of Fees (6); FRBP 2002(f)(6), (k), 7001(4), 7004 et seq; Procedural Bankr Forms B 250A, B, C.*

An order revoking confirmation of a Chapter 11 plan must include sufficient provisions to protect any entity who acquired rights under the plan in good-faith reliance upon the confirmation order. The order must also expressly revoke the debtor's discharge. The clerk of the court must promptly mail notice of the revocation order after it becomes final. Such notice must be sent to the debtor, the U.S. trustee, any Chapter 11 trustee, all committee(s), creditors, equity security holders, indenture trustees, the SEC in Washington, DC, the District Director of the IRS where the case is pending, and any other entity required by court order or local bankruptcy rules. *11 USC §1144; FRBP 2002(f)(6), (i)-(k), 4006, 9034.*

8. Procedure Eight—Conversion

a. Debtor's Absolute Right to Convert

The debtor has the absolute right to convert his case to Chapter 7 if the following conditions are met: (1) the debtor is a DIP; (2) the debtor originally could have filed a Chapter 7 petition; (3) the present Chapter 11 case was not filed involuntarily; and (4) the present Chapter 11 case was not converted (to Chapter 11) at the request of another entity. The debtor must file a motion to convert and serve it on any Chapter 11 trustee, the U.S. trustee, all committee(s), and any other entity required by court order or local bankruptcy rules. Service may be obtained by first-class mail, personal delivery, or any manner allowed for service of motions in federal district court. No hearing is required if the above four conditions are supported by the debtor's motion and record of the case. *11 USC §§109, 1112(a), (f); FRBP 1017(d), 7005, 9013, 9034.*

The debtor also has the right to convert to Chapter 12 or 13 if: (1) the debtor originally could have filed a petition under such chapter; (2) the debtor has not received a discharge (a Chapter 11 plan has not been confirmed); and (3) the debtor requests conversion to Chapter 12, such conversion must be equitable to the debtor, estate, and creditors. The debtor must file a motion to convert and serve a copy of the motion as outlined above. *11 USC §§109, 1112(d), (f); FRBP 1017(d), 7005, 9013, 9034.*

If the above requirements are not met, the debtor may, at the court's discretion, convert his case to a chapter in which he may properly be a debtor. But he does not have the absolute right to convert. *11 USC §§109, 1112(a), (d), (f).*

b. Request to Convert Filed by Another Entity (Involuntary Conversion)

A party-in-interest (creditor, equity security holder, Chapter 11 trustee, bankruptcy administrator in Alabama or North Carolina, or U.S. trustee) may file a motion to convert the debtor's Chapter 11 case. Many grounds exist for conversion. The Code includes ten grounds for an (involuntary) conversion:

(1) There has been a continuing loss or diminution (reduction) to the bankruptcy estate and there is not a reasonable likelihood that the debtor will be able to rehabilitate (reorganize);

(2) The debtor has shown an inability to effectuate (file, have confirmed, and/or implement) a plan;

(3) The debtor has caused unreasonable delay that is prejudicial to creditors;

(4) The debtor has failed to file a plan timely, including any extension of time allowed by the court;

(5) The court has denied confirmation of every plan filed by the debtor and the court has denied the debtor's request for additional time to file a new or modified plan;

(6) The court revoked its confirmation order and denied confirmation of new or modified plan;

(7) The debtor has been unable to substantially consummate a confirmed plan. Substantial consummation occurs when:

(a) all or substantially all of the debtor's property has been transferred; (b) the debtor or a successor to the debtor named under the plan has assumed the business or management of substantially all property dealt with by the plan; and (c) distribution has begun under the plan;

(8) The debtor has materially defaulted in performance under a confirmed plan;

(9) The plan terminated by the occurrence of an event or condition stated in the plan; or

(10) The debtor failed to pay any required fees or charges (filing fee, quarterly fees, fees for filing an adversary complaint). *11 USC §§1101(2), 1112(b); 28 USC §1930(a)-(b).*

The court cannot involuntarily convert a Chapter 11 case to Chapter 7 if the debtor is a farmer, nonprofit corporation, or an eleemosynary institution, unless the debtor eventually requests or consents to such conversion. The court may not involuntarily convert the debtor's case to Chapter 12 or 13, because such chapters are entirely voluntary. And the court may not involuntarily convert a Chapter 11 case to any chapter in which the debtor may not properly be a debtor. *11 USC §§109, 303(a)-(b), 1112(c)-(d), (f).*

c. Request to Convert Filed by the U.S. Trustee

Only the U.S. trustee may file a motion to convert the debtor's Chapter 11 case to Chapter 7 if based on two grounds:

(1) The debtor failed to file the required Chapter 11 schedules and statements with the voluntary petition or before the 15th day thereafter or by any later date set by the court. *See "Fourth Duty As Debtor," discussed above;* or

(2) The debtor failed to file a list of 20 largest unsecured creditors or a list of all unsecured creditors if there are less than 20, either with the voluntary petition or before the 15th day thereafter, or by the date set by the court extending such time. *11 USC §§521(1), 1112(e); FRBP 1007(c)-(d); see "Second Duty as Debtor—File the List of 20 Largest Unsecured Creditors," discussed above.*

d. Procedures for Conversion

(1) By the Debtor

The debtor must file a motion to convert stating that he has the absolute right to convert and the requirements outlined above; or, if the conversion is discretionary with the court, the debtor's motion must state the reasons for such conversion and that the debtor may properly be a debtor under such other chapter. The motion does not commence an adversary proceeding and no filing fee is required. The debtor must serve the motion on any trustee, the U.S. trustee, all committee(s), and any other entity required by court order or local bankruptcy rules, by first-class mail or any manner provided for service of a summons and complaint in federal district court. *11 USC §1112; FRBP 1017(d), 9013-9014, 9034;*

(2) Involuntary Conversion

A party-in-interest, other than the debtor, who files a motion to convert must state the ground(s) thereunder and serve a copy of the motion on the debtor, the U.S. trustee, any Chapter 11 trustee, all committee(s), and any other entity required by court order or local bankruptcy rules. The motion may be served by first-class mail, personal delivery by a disinterested person at least 18 years old, or by any other manner allowed for service of process in federal district court. The motion does not commence an adversary proceeding and no filing fee is required. No response or answer need be filed to the motion to convert unless the court or local bankruptcy rules direct otherwise. *11 USC §1112(b)-(f); FRBP 1017(d), 7004, 9014, 9034; see Local Bankruptcy Rules;*

(3) Notice and Hearing

The court must hold a hearing on any motion to involuntarily convert a Chapter 11 case and on any motion to convert filed by a debtor who does not have the absolute right to convert, unless local bankruptcy rules direct otherwise. The clerk or other court-authorized person must give at least 20 days' notice by mail of the hearing on a motion to convert. Such notice must be sent to the debtor, the U.S. trustee, any Chapter 11 trustee, all committee(s), creditors, equity security holders, indenture trustees, the SEC in Washington, D.C., the District Director of the IRS where the case is pending, and any other entity required by court order or local bankruptcy rules. *FRBP 1017(d), 2002(a)(5), (i)-(k), 9034.*

e. Notice of Conversion Order

When a case is converted from Chapter 11 to Chapter 7, 12, or 13, the clerk or other court-authorized person must mail a notice of the conversion order. Such notice should include the date the conversion order was entered and the new dates for a meeting of creditors, for filing complaints to deny discharge or determine the dischargeability of a debt, and for filing any required proofs of claims in the converted Chapter 7, 12, or 13 case. This notice must be sent to the debtor, the U.S. trustee, any Chapter 11 trustee, all committee(s), creditors, indenture trustees, the SEC in Washington, D.C., and District Director of the IRS where the case is pending. *11 USC §§342, 348(c), 1112; FRBP 1019(2), 2002(f)(2), (i)-(k), 9034; Bankr Forms B 221A, B; see "Denial of Discharge" and "Exceptions to Discharge," Chapter III.*

f. Procedures After Conversion

(1) Debtor's Duties in the Converted Case

The debtor whose case has been converted from Chapter 11 to Chapter 7 or 13 should observe the following:

(a) No Filing Fee

The Chapter 11 filing fee is greater than the Chapter 7 or 13 fee ($800 vs $150). No new filing fee is required but no rebate is provided, either. *28 USC §1930(a)(1), (3), (b), Judicial Conference Schedule of Fees (8);*

(b) File Mailing Matrix, Schedules, and Statements

Documents filed in the superseded Chapter 11 case are deemed filed in the converted case, unless the court or local bankruptcy rules direct otherwise. If the debtor has not previously filed the mailing matrix, schedule of assets and liabilities, statement of financial affairs, schedule of current income and expenditures, and statement of executory contracts, these documents must be filed before the 15th day after entry of the conversion order. *11 USC §348; FRBP 1007, 1019(1)(A);*

(c) File Statement of Intention

If a statement of intention is required (the individual debtor's debts are primarily consumer debts secured by property of the estate), but has not been filed in a converted Chapter 7 case, the debtor must file a statement of intention before the earlier of the first date set for the meeting of creditors under the converted Chapter 7 case or before the 30th day after entry of the conversion order, unless the court extends the time for cause within such period. The debtor must perform under the statement of intent before the 45th day after the statement is filed. *11 USC §§348, 521(2); FRBP 1019(1)(B);*

(d) File Schedule of Unpaid Debts

In a converted Chapter 7 case, the debtor or any Chapter 11 trustee must file a schedule of unpaid debts incurred after the Chapter 11 petition was filed. This schedule must include the name and address of each post-petition creditor. The schedule must be filed before the 15th day after entry of the conversion order unless the court or local bankruptcy rules direct otherwise. A debt, other than a first priority administrative claim, that arises after the debtor filed his Chapter 11 petition but before entry of the conversion order is treated like a pre-petition claim. The clerk of the court must send the U.S. trustee a copy of all schedules filed by the debtor under the converted Chapter 7 case. *11 USC §348(d); FRBP 1019(5);* and

(e) File Final Report and Account

The debtor or any Chapter 11 trustee must file a final report and account with the court and serve a copy on the U.S. trustee before the 30th day after entry of the conversion order, unless the court or local bankruptcy rules direct otherwise. The final report and account should include a schedule of all the debtor's property, including executory contracts and unexpired leases and any other property acquired between the dates of filing the Chapter 11 petition and entry of the conversion order. *FRBP 1019(5).*

(2) Turn Over Property in the Converted Case

The debtor or any Chapter 11 trustee must turn over all property of the bankruptcy estate, including books and records in his possession or control, to the Chapter 7 trustee. *11 USC §§348(e), 542-543; FRBP 1019(4).*

(3) New Time Periods in the Converted Case

The date of entry of the conversion order commences new time periods for a meeting of creditors, filing proof of claims, and filing adversary complaints objecting to discharge of the debtor or dischargeability of a debt under the converted Chapter 7 case.

(a) Meeting of Creditors

A new meeting of creditors under the converted Chapter 7 (or 13) case must generally be held not less than 20 days or more than 40 days after entry of the conversion order, unless the court or local bankruptcy rules order otherwise. The clerk must give at least 20 days' notice by mail of the conversion order and date for the new meeting of creditors. Such notice must be sent to the debtor, the U.S. trustee, any other trustee, all committee(s), creditors, equity security holders, indenture trustees, and other parties-in-interest directed by the court or local bankruptcy rules. *11 USC §§342, 348(c); FRBP 2002(a)(1), (5), (k), 2003(a), 9034; see "Meeting of Creditors," Chapter XIV;*

(b) Filing Proofs of Claims in a Converted Case

A proof of claim filed by a creditor in the superseded Chapter 11 case is deemed filed in the converted Chapter 7 case. A proof of claim was deemed filed in the Chapter 11 case for any creditor whose claim was listed in the Chapter 11 schedules of liabilities, unless listed as disputed, contingent, or unliquidated. Nevertheless, a creditor who did not actually file a proof of claim in the superseded Chapter 11 case should file a proof of claim in the converted Chapter 7 case to protect his rights, regardless of how his claim was listed in the debtor's Chapter 11 schedules of liabilities. All proofs of claims must be filed in the converted Chapter 7 case before the 90th day after the first date set for the new meeting of creditors under the converted case. A proof of claim timely filed supersedes a claim listed on the debtor's schedules of liabilities. A creditor who is required to file a proof of claim and who fails to file one will not share in any distribution of the estate made by the Chapter 7 trustee. *11 USC §§502, 726, 1111(a); FRBP 1019(3), (6), 3002, 3003(b)(1), (c)(4); see "Distribution of the Chapter 7 Estate," Chapter III;*

(c) Complaints to Deny Discharge or to Determine Dischargeability in a Converted Chapter 7 Case

(i) Denial of Discharge

An adversary complaint objecting to discharge (or denial of discharge) of the debtor must be filed no later than the 60th day after the first date set for the new meeting of creditors in the converted Chapter 7 case, unless the court extends the time. The clerk must give the debtor, the U.S. trustee, the Chapter 7 trustee, and all creditors and parties-in-interest at least 25 days' notice by mail of the last date to file such adversary complaint. *11 USC §§340(a), 727(a); FRBP 1019(2), 4004(a), 7001 et seq; see "Denial of Discharge," Chapter III.*

(ii) Nondischargeable Debts

An adversary complaint to determine the dischargeability of a particular pre-petition debt (exception to discharge) may be filed at any time under the converted Chapter 7 case unless the ground(s) for such complaint are the debtor's alleged fraud or misrepresentation; fraud or defalcation while acting as a fiduciary; embezzlement or larceny; or willful and malicious torts that do not involve the operation of a motor vehicle while under the influence of alcohol, drugs, or other substance. A complaint based on these grounds must be filed no later than the 60th day after the first date set for the new meeting of creditors in the converted Chapter 7 case, unless the court extends the time. The clerk must give the debtor, the U.S. trustee, the Chapter 7 trustee, all creditors and parties-in-interest at least 30 days' notice of the last date to file an adversary complaint to determine dischargeability of a debt based on ground(s) of fraud; defalcation; embezzlement; or non-vehicular, non-drug-related willful and malicious torts. For all other complaints to determine dischargeability of a debt, the clerk must give such notice as the court or local bankruptcy rules require. *11 USC §523(a)(2), (4), (6), (c); FRBP 1019(2), 2002(f)(5), (k), 4007(b)-(c); see Local Bankruptcy Rules; "Exceptions to Discharge," Chapter III.*

(4) Priority of Administrative Claims in the Converted Case

An allowed first priority claim for administrative expenses incurred in a converted Chapter 7 case has priority over all administrative claims incurred in the superseded Chapter 11 case. The Chapter 7 trustee must pay the Chapter 7 administrative claims in full before he pays administrative claims incurred under the superseded Chapter 11 case. If there are not sufficient funds or property in the estate to pay all administrative claims, the Chapter 7 administrative claims must be paid pro rata and the administrative claims incurred in the superseded Chapter 11 case and all other unsecured creditors will not be paid. *11 USC §§503, 507, 726(b); see "Priority Claims," Chapter II.*

9. Procedure Nine—Dismissal

a. By the Debtor

The debtor may file a motion to dismiss his Chapter 11 case. The court must hold a hearing on such motion, unless local bankruptcy rules direct otherwise. *11 USC §1112(b); FRBP 1017(a); see Local Bankruptcy Rules.*

b. By Another Entity

Any other party-in-interest may file a motion to dismiss the debtor's Chapter 11 case. Many grounds exist for dismissal. The Code includes the same ten grounds for dismissal as those for conversion of a debtor's Chapter 11 case. The court must hold a hearing on such motion and determine whether dismissal or conversion of the Chapter 11 case is in the best interests of the estate and creditors. *See "Procedure Eight—Conversion," discussed above; 11 USC §1112(b)-(c); FRBP 1017(a).*

c. Service, Notice, and Hearing

The court must hold a hearing on any motion to dismiss and determine whether conversion or dismissal is in the best interests of the estate and creditors. The party filing the motion to dismiss must serve a copy of the motion by first-class mail, personal delivery by a disinterested person at least 18 years old, or any other method allowed for service of process in federal district court, on the debtor, any trustee, the U.S. trustee, all committee(s), and any other entity required by court order or local bankruptcy rules. The motion does not commence an adversary proceeding and no filing fee is required. The clerk or other court-authorized person must give at least 20 days' notice by mail of the hearing date to the debtor, the U.S. trustee, any Chapter 11 trustee, all committee(s), creditors, equity security holders, indenture trustees, the SEC in Washington, D.C., the District Director of the IRS where the case is pending, and any other entity required by court order or local bankruptcy rules. *11 USC §1112(b); FRBP 1017(a), 2002(a)(5), (i)-(k), 7004, 9013-9014.*

d. Legal Effect of Dismissal

Unless the court orders otherwise, dismissal of a Chapter 11 case: (1) revests property of the estate in the debtor, (2) lifts the automatic stay; and (3) has the same legal effect as if no petition had been filed. Creditors may proceed to collect their claims from the debtor or his property under nonbankruptcy law. Dismissal does not prevent the debtor from filing another bankruptcy petition, unless the Chapter 11 case was dismissed "with prejudice." However, if the Chapter 11 case was dismissed for the debtor's willful failure to obey a court order or prosecute his case (failure of the debtor to file required schedules and statements, unreasonable delay that was prejudicial to creditors), or because the debtor requested dismissal after a motion for relief from the automatic stay was filed, the debtor must wait 181 days to refile any petition. But dismissal of the Chapter 11 case does not necessarily affect the debtor's right to discharge in a subsequent bankruptcy case. *11 USC §§109(g), 349, 362(c).*

e. Notice of Dismissal

The clerk of the court must mail notice of the dismissal of the debtor's Chapter 11 case. Such notice must be given to the debtor, U.S. trustee, any Chapter 11 trustee, all committee(s), creditors, equity security holders, indenture trustees, the SEC in Washington, D.C., the District Director of the IRS where the case is pending, and any other entity required by court order or local bankruptcy rules. *FRBP 2002(f)(2), (i)-(k), 9034.*

10. Procedure Ten—Discharge

a. Generally

The debtor will receive a discharge under Chapter 11 on the date a plan is confirmed. The discharge includes all debts that arose before confirmation, with three exceptions:

(1) A particular nondischargeable debt under Chapter 7 is also nondischargeable under an individual Chapter 11 case.

Thus, the individual Chapter 11 debtor may not be discharged from personal liability for debts incurred through fraud, misrepresentation, tortious conduct, or any debt otherwise nondischargeable under a Chapter 7 case. The same rules and procedures govern nondischargeability of a debt under Chapters 7 and 11 of an individual debtor's case. *See "Exceptions to Discharge," Chapter III; "Objections to Discharge or Dischargeability of a Debt," discussed below;*

(2) A debtor is denied a discharge of all debts if:

(a) the plan provides for liquidation (sale or transfer for value) of all or substantially all property of the estate;

(b) the debtor does not engage in business after the plan is consummated; and

(c) the debtor would be denied a discharge under Chapter 7.

A corporate or partnership Chapter 11 debtor whose confirmed plan provides for the sale or transfer for value of (substantially) all property and cessation of business by the debtor is denied a discharge; **and**

(3) The Chapter 11 debtor is denied a discharge of all debts if the court approves a written waiver of discharge signed by the debtor post-petition. *11 USC §1141(d).*

The clerk must promptly give notice if the debtor is granted or denied a discharge. Such notice must be mailed to the debtor, the U.S. trustee, Chapter 11 trustee, all committee(s), equity security holders, creditors, indenture trustees, the SEC in Washington, D.C., the District Director of the IRS where the Chapter 11 case is pending, and any other entity required by court order or local bankruptcy rules. *11 USC §1141(d)(2); FRBP 2002(f)(6)-(7), (i)-(k), 4004(g), 4006, 9036.*

b. Objections to Discharge or Dischargeability of a Debt

(1) Discharge

An objection to discharge of all debts of a Chapter 11 debtor must be filed no later than the first date set for the confirmation hearing, unless the court or local bankruptcy rules allow otherwise. The clerk must give at least 25 days' notice of such date for filing objections. Notice must be mailed to the debtor, U.S. trustee, any Chapter 11 trustee and his attorney, all creditors, committee(s), and any other entity required by court order or local bankruptcy rules. Such notice is generally included in the notice of approval of the disclosure statement. *FRBP 2002(b), (f), (i), (k), 3017(d), 4004(a), 9034; see "Tenth Duty as Debtor—File and Obtain Approval of Disclosure Statement," discussed above.*

An objection to discharge may be filed by any party-in-interest (creditor, U.S. trustee, trustee, committee). The objection commences an adversary proceeding. A $120 filing fee is required, unless the U.S. trustee who is not acting as a Chapter 11 trustee files the objection. However, if the Chapter 11 trustee files an objection, the filing fee is only payable from any estate that may eventually exist. A copy of the objection to discharge must be served with a summons on the debtor by first-class mail, personal delivery by a disinterested person at least 18 years old, or by any other manner allowed for service of process in federal district court. A copy of the objection should also be mailed or personally delivered to any trustee (if the objection is filed by another party-in-interest), all committee(s), and to any other entity required by court order or local bankruptcy rules. The objection must state the grounds for denying the debtor a discharge (the plan provides for liquidation of all or substantially all the estate's property; the debtor will not engage in business after consummation of a plan; and the debtor would be denied a discharge under Chapter 7). *11 USC §§321(c), 727, 1141(d)(3); 28 USC §1930(b), Judicial Conference Schedule of Fees (6); FRBP 4004(a), 7001(4) et seq; see "Denial of Discharge," Chapter III; Procedural Bankr Forms B 250A, B, C.*

(2) Dischargeability

An objection to dischargeability of a particular pre-petition debt may generally be filed at any time unless the court or local bankruptcy rules state otherwise. However, an objection to dischargeability of a debt involving the debtor's alleged fraud or misrepresentation; defalcation while a fiduciary; embezzlement; larceny; or nonvehicular, nondrug-related willful and malicious tort must be filed no later than the 60th day after the first date set for the meeting of creditors, unless the court extends the time for cause, within such period. The clerk or other court-authorized person must give at least 30 days' notice of this date by mail to the debtor, all creditors, any trustee, the U.S. trustee, all committee(s), the SEC in Washington, D.C., the District Director of the IRS where the case is pending, all indenture trustees, and to any other entity required by court order or local bankruptcy rules. *11 USC §§523(a), 1141(d)(2); FRBP 2002(f)(5), (i), (j), 4007(a)-(c).*

An objection to dischargeability of a particular pre-petition debt must be filed by a creditor. This objection also commences an adversary proceeding and requires a $120 filing fee and service of process in the same manner and according to the same procedures governing objections to discharge of all debts, discussed above. *11 USC §§523, 1141(d)(2); 28 USC §1930(b), Judicial Conference Schedule of Fees (6); FRBP 4007, 7001(6), 7004 et seq; see "Exceptions to Discharge," Chapter III; Procedural Bankr Forms B 250A, B, C.*

c. Revocation of Discharge

The only ground for revocation of discharge is that the debtor obtained his discharge through fraud on the court and the party seeking revocation had no knowledge of the fraud before the confirmation hearing. Revocation of discharge also revokes confirmation of the debtor's plan. A party-in-interest (creditor, trustee, committee) must file an adversary complaint before 180 days after the date the confirmation order is entered by the court and pay a $120 filing fee. The same adversary procedures governing revocation of confirmation, discussed above, also govern revocation of discharge. If the debtor's discharge is revoked, the clerk of the court must promptly mail notice of the final order revoking the discharge to the debtor, the U.S. trustee, any trustee, all creditors, the SEC in Washington, D.C., the District Director of the IRS where the case is pending, all committee(s), indenture trustees, and to any other entity required by court order or local bankruptcy rules. The debtor's Chapter 11 case should then be dismissed or converted to another Chapter. *11 USC §§1112(b), 1144; 28 USC §1930(b), Judicial Conference Schedule Of Fees (6); FRBP 2002(f)(6), (i)-(k), 4008, 7001(4), 9034.*

11. Procedure Eleven—Closing the Chapter 11 Case

The court must enter a final order closing the Chapter 11 case after the case has been fully administered. The court may close a case on its own motion or on a motion of any party-in-interest (debtor, creditor, equity security holder, U.S. trustee). The court should not delay closing the case because payments under a confirmed Chapter 11 plan have not been completed. The court may consider several factors in determining whether to close the case:

a. Whether the confirmation order has become final;

b. Whether any deposits required by a confirmed plan have been made;

c. Whether property required to be transferred under a confirmed plan has been transferred;

d. Whether the business or property has been assumed by the debtor or his successor-in-interest under the confirmed plan;

e. Whether payments have commenced under the confirmed plan; and

f. Whether there has been a final resolution of all motions, contested matters, or adversary complaints in the Chapter 11 case.

A final order closing the case does not deprive the court of jurisdiction or prevent reopening the Chapter 11 case to administer assets, accord relief to the debtor, or further other equitable interests. *11 USC §350; FRBP 3022, advisory committee's note, 5010; HR Rep No 595, 95th Cong, 1st Sess 338 (1977); S Rep No 989, 95th Cong, 2d Sess 49 (1978).*

Research Guide

Anderson, *Chapter 11: Reorganizations* (Shepard's/McGraw-Hill 1983)

Drake, *Bankruptcy Practice for the General Practitioner* ch 12 (Shepard's/McGraw-Hill 2d ed 1990)

Jaroslavsky, *Practical Bankruptcy Procedure* chs 2, 5, 11-13, 15, 16 (Shepard's/McGraw-Hill 1993)

Murphy, *Creditor's Rights in Bankruptcy* chs 15-17 (Shepard's/McGraw-Hill 2d ed 1988)

Pollard & Burton, *Guide to Effective Bankruptcy Litigation* ch 17 (Shepard's/McGraw-Hill 1988)

V. Chapter 13—Individual Debt Adjustment

V. Chapter 13—Individual Debt Adjustment
- A. General Overview
- B. Preparing the Client
- C. Stages Modified in a Chapter 13 Case
  1. Automatic Plus Codebtor Stay
     11 USC §1301
     FRBP 9013-9014
  2. Bankruptcy Estate
     11 USC §§541, 1306
  3. No Turnover of Property to Trustee
     11 USC §§542-543, 1303, 1306(b)
  4. Discharge
     11 USC §1328
     a. Liberal Discharge
     b. Hardship Discharge
- D. Procedures Under Chapter 13
  1. Procedure One—The Debtor
     11 USC §109(a), (e), (g), 301-303
  2. Procedure Two—Debtor's Duties
     11 USC §§301, 341, 521, 1321, 1326
     28 USC §1930(a)(1), (b), Judicial Conference Schedule of Fees (8)
     FRBP 1002, 1006-1008, 2015(c), 3015, 4002-4003
  3. Procedure Three—Standing Trustee
     11 USC §§103(a), 321, 323, 347, 1302
     28 USC §586(b), (e)
     FRBP 2002, 2015, 3010-3011, 5009, 6009
     a. Generally

b. Duties of Chapter 13 or Standing Trustee

4. Procedure Four—Confirmation of Chapter 13 Plan
   a. Requirements for Confirmation
      11 USC §§1322, 1325
      FRBP 2002(b), 3015, 3020
   b. Optional Provisions of a Plan
   c. Notice of Confirmation Hearing and Date to File Objections
      11 USC §1324
      FRBP 2002(a)(6), (b), 3015, 3020, 9034
   d. Confirmation Hearing
      11 USC §1324
      FRBP 3020
   e. No Voting
      11 USC §1324
      FRBP 3020
   f. Debtor's Disposable Income
      11 USC §1325(b)
   g. Legal Effects of Confirmation
      11 USC §1327
      FRBP 2002(f), (k), 3020(c), 9034
   h. Post-Confirmation
      11 USC §§1325(c), 1329-1330
      FRBP 3020(d)
5. Procedure Five—Conversion from Chapter 13
   11 USC §1307
   FRBP 1017, 1019, 2002(a)(5), (f)(2), (k), 9034
   a. By the Debtor (Voluntary Conversion)
   b. By Another Entity (Involuntary Conversion)
   c. Procedures After Conversion
   d. Priority of Administrative Claims
6. Procedure Six—Dismissal
   11 USC §1307
   FRBP 1017, 2002(a)(5), (f)(2), (k), 9034
   a. By the Debtor (Voluntary Dismissal)
   b. By Another Entity (Involuntary Dismissal)
   c. Legal Effect of Dismissal
7. Procedure Seven—Discharge of the Debtor
   11 USC §§103(a), 523-524, 1328
   28 USC §1930(b), Judicial Conference Schedule of Fees (6)
   FRBP 2002(f)(4)-(6), 4004-4008, 7001(4), (6) et seq, 9034
   a. When
   b. Hearing

c. Debts Discharged
   (1) Liberal Discharge
   (2) Hardship Discharge
   (3) Complaint to Determine Dischargeability
d. Notice of Court Order

8. Procedure Eight—Closing the Case
11 USC §§347, 350, 704(9), 1302(b)
FRBP 5009-5010
   a. Small Dividends
   b. Unclaimed Dividends
   c. Final Report and Account

E. Advantages to Chapter 13
   1. Chapter 13 Versus Chapter 7
      a. First—Leverage Over Creditors
      11 USC §§103(a), 521(1)-(2), 523-524, 542-543, 722, 726-727, 1303-1304, 1306(b), 1322, 1325, 1328
      FRBP 3015-3020, 4004-4008, 6006, 6008
   b. Second—Liberal Discharge
   11 USC §§727, 1328
   FRBP 4004-4008, 7001(4), (6) et seq
   c. Third—Retention of Property
   11 USC §§103(a), 541-543, 726, 1306(b), 1325
   FRBP 4008, 6008
   d. Fourth—Use, Sale, or Lease of Property
   11 USC §§103(a), 363, 1303-1304
   FRBP 2002(a)(2), (c), 4001, 6004, 9013-9014, 9034
   e. Fifth—Entirely Voluntary
   11 USC §§103(a), 301-303, 1321
   FRBP 1003, 1010-1013
   f. Sixth—Absolute Right of Conversion
   11 USC §§103(a), 706(a), 1307(a)
   FRBP 1004, 1017, 1019, 2002(f)(2), (k), 9034
   g. Seventh—Codebtor Stay
   11 USC §§103(a), 362(a), 1301
   FRBP 9013-9014
   h. Eighth—Improved Credit
2. Chapter 13 Versus Chapter 11
   a. Cheaper
   28 USC §1930(a)(1), (3), (6), (b), Judicial Conference Schedule of Fees (8)
   b. Quicker
   11 USC §§1125-1126, 1129, 1321, 1325

FRBP 2002(b), 3015-3020

c. Liberal Discharge
11 USC §§1141, 1328
FRBP 2002(f)(4)-(5), 4004-4008, 7001(4), (6) et seq

d. Easier
11 USC §§1125-1126, 1129, 1324-1325
FRBP 2002(b), 3015-3020

e. Voluntary
11 USC §109(b), (d)-(e), 301-303, 1121, 1321
FRBP 1003-1004, 1010-1013

f. Codebtor Stay
11 USC §§103(a), 362(a), 1301
FRBP 9013-9014

g. No Creditors' Committee(s)
11 USC §§1102-1103, 1302
FRBP 2007, 2018

F. Disadvantages to Chapter 13

1. Generally

a. Larger Bankruptcy Estate
11 USC §§541, 1306(a)

b. Standing Trustee's Surcharge
28 USC §586(e)(1)-(2)

c. Super-Garnishment Order
11 USC §§1142(b), 1325(c)
FRBP 3020(d)

2. Chapter 13 Versus Chapter 11

a. More Limited Powers
11 USC §§103(a), 323, 363, 522(f)-(k), 547-551, 1107, 1122-1123, 1129, 1302-1304, 1322, 1325
FRBP 3015

b. Later Discharge
11 USC §§1141(d), 1328(a)

c. Fewer Post-Petition Debts Discharged
11 USC §§523, 1141(d), 1305, 1328

d. Less Leverage with Homestead Mortgagee and Other Creditors
11 USC §§1123(a)(5)(E), (G)-(H), 1129(b), 1322(b)(2), (5), (c), 1325

Research Guide

V. Chapter 13—Individual Debt Adjustment

A. General Overview

Chapter 13 of the Bankruptcy Code allows an individual (natural person) with regular income to restructure his debts over a period of three to five years. The Chapter 13 debtor retains both exempt and nonexempt property. The debtor must pay the value of nonexempt property to unsecured creditors through the Chapter 13 plan of adjustment. A Chapter 13 trustee, usually a standing trustee, is appointed by the U.S. trustee. The Chapter 13 or standing trustee administers the Chapter 13 case, presides at the meeting of creditors, receives payments from the debtor under the Chapter 13 plan, and distributes such payments to creditors as provided by the plan. *11 USC §§109(e), 1302, 1322(c), 1326; 28 USC §586(b); see "Procedure Three—Standing Trustee," discussed below.*

B. Preparing the Client

The same preparation for the initial attorney-client meeting should be made under Chapter 13 as indicated for the Chapter 7 debtor. *See "Preparing the Client," Chapter III.*

C. Stages Modified in a Chapter 13 Case

The same nine stages common to all voluntary bankruptcy cases govern a Chapter 13 case (*see "Nine Stages of Every Voluntary Bankruptcy Case," Chapter II*). However, four of these stages are modified under Chapter 13.

1. Automatic Plus Codebtor Stay

Filing the Chapter 13 petition invokes the automatic stay to protect the bankruptcy debtor and a codebtor stay to protect certain individual nonbankruptcy debtors. Six requirements must be met for a nonbankruptcy debtor to be protected by the codebtor stay. *11 USC §1301.*

a. Requirements for Codebtor Stay

The six requirements for continuing the Chapter 13 codebtor stay are:

(1) The nonbankruptcy debtor must be an individual (natural person);

(2) This individual must be a *codebtor*

A codebtor is liable with the Chapter 13 debtor for a consumer debt as someone who has secured a consumer debt owed by the Chapter 13 debtor (someone who has cosigned or given collateral to secure the bankruptcy debtor's consumer debt);

(3) The nonbankruptcy codebtor must not be in the business of guarantying debts (must not be a professional surety);

(4) The Chapter 13 debtor must have received the legal consideration or benefit (property or services) that is the basis for the consumer debt;

(5) The Chapter 13 plan must propose to pay the consumer debt in full under the plan, including pre-petition interest contractually agreed to; and

(6) Continuation of the codebtor stay must not cause irreparable harm to the interests of the creditor.

The codebtor stay lasts until the earlier date the Chapter 13 case is closed, dismissed, converted to Chapter 7 or 11, or the codebtor stay is lifted. *11 USC §1301; FRBP 9013-9014.*

b. Relief from Codebtor Stay

(1) File Request for Relief

The creditor must file a request for relief from the codebtor stay and prove that at least one of the six requirements for such stay has not been met. A request for relief does not commence an adversary proceeding and no filing fee is required.

(2) Serve the Request

The creditor must serve the request on the Chapter 13 debtor and nonbankruptcy codebtor by first-class mail, personal delivery by a disinterested person at least 18 years old, or by any other manner that a summons and complaint may be served in federal district court. A copy of the request should also be mailed or personally delivered to the Chapter 13 or standing trustee and to any other entity required by court order or local bankruptcy rules. *11 USC §1301; FRBP 9013-9014.*

(3) Response to Request for Relief

Unless local bankruptcy rules or the court directs otherwise, no response or answer need be filed to a request for relief from the codebtor stay, with one exception. The Code requires that the Chapter 13 debtor or codebtor file and serve an objection to termination of the codebtor stay on the creditor filing the request for relief, if the request alleges that the Chapter 13 plan does not propose full payment of the consumer debt with the pre-petition interest rate. This objection must be filed and served before the 20th day after the creditor filed the request for relief. Service may be obtained by first-class mail or personal delivery. If a timely objection is not filed, the codebtor stay will automatically terminate, without necessity of court order, on the 20th day after the creditor filed his request. If a timely objection is filed, a hearing will be set before the court. A copy of the objection to the request for relief from the codebtor stay should also be mailed or delivered to the codebtor (or debtor if the codebtor filed the objection), to the Chapter 13 or standing trustee, and to any other entity required by the court or local bankruptcy rules. *11 USC §1301(d); FRBP 7004-7005, 9013-9014.*

2. Bankruptcy Estate

The bankruptcy estate under Chapter 13 is greatly expanded. The Chapter 13 estate includes not only all of the debtor's present interests in all types of property, wherever located, on the date the petition filed, but also all property acquired by the Chapter 13 debtor after the petition is filed until all payments have been made under the plan or the Chapter 13 case is closed, dismissed, or converted to Chapter 7 or 11. Thus, post-petition earnings and wages of the debtor become part of the bankruptcy estate in a Chapter 13 case. *11 USC §§541, 1306.*

3. No Turnover of Property to Trustee

After filing the petition, the Chapter 13 debtor remains in possession of all property of the bankruptcy estate, including exempt and nonexempt property. Any third party in possession of property that would be part of the debtor's bankruptcy estate must turn over such property to the Chapter 13 debtor. The debtor must account for all nonexempt and exempt property under his schedules of assets and pay the value of such nonexempt property to unsecured creditors under the plan. *11 USC §§541-543, 1306(b); Official Bankr Form 6, Schedules A-C, G, I, J; see "Procedure Four—Confirmation of Chapter 13 Plan," discussed below.*

4. Discharge

Chapter 13 provides for two types of discharges: a liberal discharge for the debtor who completes all payments required by a Chapter 13 plan confirmed (approved) by the Court; or a hardship discharge for the debtor who is unable either to make all payments under the confirmed plan or to modify the plan post-confirmation.

a. Liberal Discharge

A Chapter 13 debtor must receive a discharge as soon as practical after the debtor has completed all payments required by the confirmed plan. The debtor will be discharged from liability for all but seven types of debts.

(1) Maintenance, alimony, or support payments owed by the debtor to the debtor's spouse, ex-spouse, or child are not discharged under Chapter 13, unless such debt has been assigned to an entity other than the federal government or a state or political subdivision of a state.

(2) Long-term debts, consisting of secured or unsecured claims which the debtor could pay off under a pre-petition contract after the maximum five years allowed for payments under a Chapter 13 plan, are not discharged (mortgage or other payments where, on the date the petition is filed, the pre-petition

contract allowed the debtor more than five years to pay the debt).

(3) Priority tax claims must be fully paid under the Chapter 13 plan, unless the government entity agrees otherwise. The Code requires that a Chapter 13 plan propose full payment of all priority claims as a condition to confirmation by the court. If the debtor fails to make payments required by a confirmed plan, the debtor may apply for a hardship discharge under Chapter 13 or his case may be dismissed or converted to Chapter 7 or 11. But seventh priority tax claims are not dischargeable under either a Chapter 13 hardship discharge or Chapter 7 or 11 discharge. *See "Priority Claims," Chapter II; "Hardship Discharge," discussed below.*

(4) Post-petition consumer debts for property or services necessary for the debtor's performance under the Chapter 13 plan are not discharged if the creditor timely filed a proof of claim allowed by the court and the debtor could have obtained the standing trustee's approval before incurring the consumer debt but failed to do so, without the creditor's knowledge. *See "File Proof of Claim," Chapter XIV.*

(5) A debt for educational money loaned, insured, or guaranteed by a governmental unit or nonprofit organization is not discharged, unless the debt was first due more than seven years (excluding any applicable suspension of repayment period) before the Chapter 13 petition was filed or nondischargeability of this debt would cause an undue hardship on the debtor and his dependents.

(6) A debt for death or personal injury caused by the debtor unlawfully operating a motor vehicle while under the influence of a drug, alcohol, or other substance is not discharged.

(7) A debt for restitution owed to a crime victim or a criminal fine is not discharged if part of the debtor's sentence for conviction of a crime. *11 USC §§507(a)(7), 523(a)(5), (8)-(9), 1305(a)(2), 1322(b)(5), 1328(a)(1)-(3), (d).*

b. Hardship Discharge

The debtor who is unable to make all payments required by a confirmed Chapter 13 plan may receive a hardship discharge if three requirements are met.

(1) Requirements and Procedures

The Chapter 13 debtor must file a motion for hardship discharge and prove the following:

(a) Circumstances causing the debtor to default in payments under the confirmed Chapter 13 plan were not the debtor's fault;

(b) Unsecured creditors with allowed claims have already received as much money or property as they would receive under Chapter 7 (unsecured creditors have received the value of nonexempt property in the bankruptcy estate); and

(c) It is not practical for the debtor to modify his Chapter 13 plan further after confirmation. *11 USC §1328(b).*

The debtor should serve a copy of the motion by first-class mail or personal delivery on the standing trustee, the U.S. trustee, and on any other entity required by court order or local bankruptcy rules. The motion does not commence an adversary proceeding and no filing fee is required. The court will hold a hearing on the motion with notice to the debtor, standing trustee, creditors, and such other entities as required by court order or local bankruptcy rules. *11 USC §§102(1)(A), (B), 1328(b); FRBP 9007, 9013, 9034; see Local Bankruptcy Rules.*

(2) Limitations of Hardship Discharge

A hardship discharge has its limitations. The Chapter 13 debtor no longer receives a liberal discharge. All pre-petition debts which could be excepted from discharge or determined to be nondischargeable under Chapter 7 may now be determined nondischargeable under Chapter 13. The same adversary procedures govern nondischargeability of a pre-petition debt under a Chapter 7 discharge and a Chapter 13 hardship discharge. *See "Exceptions to Discharge," Chapter III.*

After the Chapter 13 debtor files a motion for hardship discharge, the court must set a hearing on the motion and a date by which adversary complaints to determine the dischargeability of pre-petition debts must be filed based on the debtor's alleged fraud or misrepresentation; fraud while acting as a fiduciary; embezzlement; larceny; or nonvehicular, nondrug-related intentional, willful tort. The clerk of the court must give the debtor, standing trustee, all creditors, and indenture trustees at least 30 days' notice by mail of this date fixed by the court. The court may extend both the date to file such complaints and time for the clerk's notice, for cause, within such period. All other complaints to determine dischargeability of a pre-petition debt based on any other ground may be filed at any time, even after the Chapter 13 case is closed, unless the court or local bankruptcy rules direct otherwise. *See "Exceptions to Discharge," Chapter III; 11 USC §§523, 1328(b); FRBP 2002(f)(5), 4007(a)-(d), 7001 et seq.*

(3) Nondischargeable Debts Under Hardship Discharge

The Chapter 13 debtor who receives a hardship discharge will remain personally liable for four types of debts:

(a) All nondischargeable pre-petition debts under §523(a) of the Code applicable to a Chapter 7 or 11 debtor (*See "Exceptions to Discharge," Chapter III*);

(b) Long-term debts;

(c) Unpaid priority tax claims; and

(d) Post-petition consumer debts which were necessary for the debtor's performance under the plan if based on an allowed claim and prior approval of the standing trustee could practically have been obtained but was not obtained by the debtor. *11 USC §§103(a), 523(a), 1305(a)(2), (b), 1328(b)-(d); see "File Proof of Claim," Chapter XIV.*

(4) When Granted

The bankruptcy court may grant the debtor a hardship discharge at any time after confirmation of the Chapter 13 plan if the debtor proves the three requirements for such discharge outlined above. The clerk must mail a copy of the final discharge order to the debtor, the U.S. trustee, standing trustee, all creditors, indenture trustees, and to any other entity required by court order or local bankruptcy rules. *11 USC §§102(1)(A), 523(a), (c), 524, 1305(a)(2), 1328(b)-(d); FRBP 4004(g), 9007, 9034.*

D. Procedures under Chapter 13

There are eight procedures in a Chapter 13 case. Procedures one, two, three, four, seven, and eight occur in all successful Chapter 13 cases. Procedures five and six occur in those Chapter 13 cases that are not successfully completed.

1. Procedure One—The Debtor

Only an individual (natural person) or individual and his spouse may be Chapter 13 debtor(s). On the date of filing the petition, the debtor (single petition) or debtor and spouse (joint petition) must owe less than $250,000 aggregate noncontingent, liquidated, unsecured debts and less than $750,000 aggregate noncontingent, liquidated, secured debts. Only voluntary petitions may be filed under Chapter 13. *11 USC §§109(a), (e), (g), 301-303.*

2. Procedure Two—Debtor's Duties

The Chapter 13 debtor, whether under a single or joint petition, has ten duties. The debtor must:

a. File a signed, verified Chapter 13 petition together with a $160 filing fee ($130 filing fee plus $30 administrative fee) and mailing matrix (list of creditors).

The debtor may apply for payment of the filing fee in installments (*see "Installment Fees," Chapter II*). *11 USC §§301-302; FRBP 1002, 1006-1008; 28 USC §1930(a)(1), (b), Judicial Conference Schedule of Fees (8); Official Bankr Forms 1, 3;*

b. File verified schedules of assets and liabilities, statement of financial affairs, and schedule of current income and expenditures.

These Chapter 13 schedules and statements must be filed either with the petition or before the 15th day thereafter if a mailing matrix was filed with the petition. The court may extend the date for filing if the debtor files a motion showing cause before the required time period expires. *FRBP 1007(b), 1008; Official Bankr Forms 6, 7;*

c. File the Chapter 13 plan of adjustment either with the petition or before the 15th day thereafter, unless the court extends the time upon a motion of the debtor filed within such period and showing of cause.

The debtor may modify the plan at any time before or after confirmation. However, only the debtor may file a Chapter 13 plan. *11 USC §§1321, 1323, 1329; FRBP 3015(b);*

d. Begin making payments proposed by the plan before the 30th day after the plan is filed, unless the court allows otherwise.

These payments are made directly to the Chapter 13 or standing trustee, even if the debtor's Chapter 13 plan has not been confirmed by the court. If the plan is confirmed, the standing trustee will disburse these payments to creditors as indicated by the plan. If the plan is not confirmed, the standing trustee will return such payments to the debtor after deducting administrative expenses allowed by the court. *11 USC §1326(a);*

e. Attend the meeting of creditors and any other examination ordered by the court. *11 USC §§341(a), 343; FRBP 2003, 4002. See "Stage Six—Meeting of Creditors," Chapter II, & "Meeting of Creditors," Chapter XIV; "Rule 2004 Examination," Chapter XIV;*

f. Cooperate with the standing trustee.

Failure to cooperate with the Chapter 13 or standing trustee could result in dismissal or conversion of the debtor's Chapter 13 case to Chapter 7 (*see Procedures Five & Six, below*). *FRBP 4002;*

g. File a statement of change of address, if the debtor changes his address post-petition.

A copy of this statement should be served by first-class mail or personal delivery on the Chapter 13 or standing trustee and any other entity required by court order or local bankruptcy rules. *FRBP 4002; see Local Bankruptcy Rules;*

h. If the debtor is *engaged in business* (the debtor is self-employed and incurs trade credit from such employment), he must:

(1) Before the 30th day after filing the petition, file and deliver to the U.S. trustee a complete inventory of the debtor's property;

(2) Keep a record of receipts and disbursements of money and property received;

(3) File periodic reports and summaries of the operation of the debtor's business, including a statement of:

(a) the amount of deductions for all employee withholding or other employee taxes, and

(b) the place where such amounts are deposited.

The reports and summaries must be filed with the court, the U.S. trustee, and the appropriate governmental unit charged with responsibility for determining or collecting any tax arising from the debtor's business operations; and

(4) As soon as possible after filing the Chapter 13 petition, give notice of the Chapter 13 case to every entity who is known to hold money or property subject to the debtor's withdrawal or control if such entity does not have previous knowledge or notice of the case.

Such entities includes a bank, savings or building and loan association, public utility company, landlord holding a deposit of the debtor, and any insurance company who has issued a policy with a cash surrender value payable to the debtor.

A copy of all reports and summaries should also be served on the Chapter 13 or standing trustee by first-class mail or personal delivery. *11 USC §§704(8), 1304(a); FRBP 2015(a), (c), 7005;*

i. Attend the confirmation hearing.

The Bankruptcy Code does not require the debtor's personal attendance at the confirmation hearing. However, local bankruptcy rules, which vary from district to district, may require his attendance. *11 USC §1324; see Local Bankruptcy Rules;* and

j. Complete payments provided under a confirmed plan to obtain the liberal discharge. *11 USC §1328; see "Procedure Seven—Discharge of the Debtor," discussed below.*

3. Procedure Three—Standing Trustee

a. Generally

The U.S. trustee, charged with supervision of cases under Chapters 7, 11, 12, and 13, may appoint one or more individuals to serve as standing trustee over all Chapter 12 and Chapter 13 cases filed in judicial districts with large numbers of such cases. This appointment is subject to the approval of the Attorney General and continued supervision of the U.S. trustee. If no standing trustee is appointed, the U.S. trustee may appoint a disinterested person as trustee for each Chapter 12 or 13 case or the U.S. trustee may serve as such trustee. *11 USC §§321-323, 1302(a); 28 USC §586(b).*

b. Duties of Chapter 13 or Standing Trustee

The Chapter 13 or standing trustee has ten general duties common to all bankruptcy trustees and five specific duties under Chapter 13.

(1) General Duties Common to All Trustees

A Chapter 13 or standing trustee must:

(a) Account and keep a record of all property received and the disposition of money and property received;

(b) Examine proofs of claims and object to improper claims of creditors if such action would benefit the bankruptcy estate;

(c) Oppose the debtor's discharge when warranted;

(d) Furnish information about the administration of the bankruptcy estate when requested by a party-in-interest, unless the court orders otherwise;

(e) Investigate the financial affairs or business of the debtor;

(f) Represent the estate, including filing any action on behalf of the estate or entering an appearance and defending any pending action by or against the debtor;

(g) If the debtor is engaged in business, file a report of any investigation of such business and mail or deliver a copy of the report to any entity required by the court or local bankruptcy rules;

(h) File a final report and account of the administration of the bankruptcy estate with the court and U.S. trustee;

(i) File a list of known names, addresses, and respective amounts owed to all entities to whom the standing trustee issued a check which remained unpaid 90 days after the final distribution under the debtor's confirmed plan.

The trustee must stop payment on such checks. The unclaimed funds and any other property of the estate are then paid into the court. The clerk must hold such funds for their owners for five years. After such time, the unclaimed funds escheat to the United States Treasury; and

(j) Perform any other duty required by the court or local bankruptcy rules. *11 USC §§323, 347(a), 704(2)-(7), (9), 1302(b)(1), (c); 28 USC §2041 et seq; FRBP 2015(c)(2), 3011, 6009.*

The Chapter 13 or standing trustee should file and deliver a copy of all required reports and lists to the U.S. trustee as required by the court or local bankruptcy rules. *FRBP 2015, 6009; see Local Bankruptcy Rules. See Chapter XII.*

(2) Five Specific Duties of the Chapter 13 or Standing Trustee

A Chapter 13 or standing trustee must perform the following five duties specifically for Chapter 13 cases:

(a) Preside at the meeting of creditors if the U.S. trustee so requests;

(b) Advise, except on legal matters, and assist the debtor in performance under the Chapter 13 plan;

(c) Ensure that the debtor begins making timely payments under the Chapter 13 plan.

The first payment must be received by the standing trustee before the 30th day after the plan is filed, unless the court orders otherwise;

(d) As soon as practicable, disburse payments to creditors as provided by a confirmed plan or court order; and

(e) Appear and be heard at three hearings:

(i) any valuation hearing involving the value of a lien securing property of the estate;

(ii) the confirmation hearing to confirm a Chapter 13 plan; and

(iii) any post-confirmation hearing to consider further modification of a plan confirmed by the court.

11 USC §§1323-1324, 1329; 28 USC §586(a)(3); FRBP 2003; see "Valuation of Collateral," Chapter XIV.

4. Procedure Four—Confirmation of Chapter 13 Plan

a. Requirements for Confirmation

The bankruptcy court must confirm (approve) a Chapter 13 plan if 10 requirements are met.

(1) The plan must provide for submission to the standing trustee of sufficient future income to make all payments under the plan.

(2) The plan must provide for full payment of all allowed priority claims.

The payments may be made in deferred cash payments over the term of the plan. *See "Priority Claims," Chapter II.*

(3) The plan must provide for the same treatment (amounts) for all creditors within the same class of creditors.

A *Class* is a designated group of creditors whose members have essentially the same nonbankruptcy legal rights and interests against the debtor. Generally, all unsecured creditors are placed in the same class and each secured creditor with different collateral is placed in a separate class. However, the debtor may place a creditor who has an unsecured consumer claim against a nonbankruptcy codebtor in a separate class from other unsecured creditors.

(4) The plan must have been proposed and filed by the debtor in good faith.

(5) The plan must provide that each secured creditor will either receive its collateral or retain its lien on the collateral and receive property (money or otherwise) on the effective date of the plan equal to the lesser of the value of the collateral or the amount of the creditor's allowed claim, over a maximum of five years.

Value of property distributed under a Chapter 13 plan is determined as of the effective date of the plan to allow for the present value of money. Thus, the plan must provide for some interest rate during the term of payments under the plan. The interest rate will depend on what the court or local bankruptcy rules require.

(6) The plan must provide that unsecured creditors receive property (money or otherwise) on the effective date of the plan at least equal in value to the amount that they would receive under Chapter 7.

Thus, unsecured creditors must receive the value of the debtor's bankruptcy estate (nonexempt property) over a maximum of five years. The value of property to be distributed under the plan is determined as of the effective date of the plan to allow for the present value of money. However, unsecured creditors generally do not receive interest for the deferred use of such property.

(7) The term of the plan must not exceed five years from the date of the first payment made under the plan.

The first payment must start before the 30th day after the plan is filed, unless the court extends the time. However, the term of a plan may be less than five years.

(8) All fees and charges required under the Chapter 13 case must have been paid.

(9) **The debtor will be able to make all payments and to comply with all provisions required by the plan (feasibility test).**

(10) **The plan itself complies with all requirements of the Code.** *11 USC §§1322, 1325; FRBP 3013, 3015, 3020.*

If the plan fails to meet one or more of the 10 requirements, the debtor may file a modified plan, even at the hearing, to obtain court approval. The modified plan then becomes the Chapter 13 plan. *11 USC §§1322-1323, 1325; 28 USC §1930(a); FRBP 3013, 3019; Official Bankr Form 6, Schedules A-H.*

b. Optional Provisions of a Plan

A Chapter 13 plan may also include provisions to:

(1) **Assume or reject executory contracts.** *See "Assumption or Rejection of Executory Contracts and Unexpired Leases," Chapter XIV;*

(2) **Pay all or part of any post-petition consumer debt which was necessary for the debtor's performance under the plan;**

(3) **Cure any pre- or post-petition default(s) in long-term mortgage payments within a reasonable time under the plan while maintaining current mortgage payments to the mortgagee.**

The debtor may submit payments to the Chapter 13 or standing trustee to cure pre- or post-petition mortgage default(s) within a reasonable time under the plan while the debtor submits current mortgage payments directly to the mortgagee. What is a "reasonable time" to cure default(s) will depend on the facts and circumstances of each case. A pre- or post-petition default in homestead mortgage payments may be cured under a Chapter 13 plan until the date that the debtor's homestead is sold at a foreclosure sale conducted according to applicable nonbankruptcy law. *11 USC §1322(c)(1).*

The amount necessary to cure a default in a mortgage agreement entered into *after* October 22, 1994, must be determined by the terms of the underlying agreement and applicable nonbankruptcy law. However, the amount necessary to cure a mortgage default in an agreement entered into *before* October 22, 1994, is determined by applicable bankruptcy law, including §§506(b) and 1325(a)(5) of the Bankruptcy Code. Thus, the Chapter 13 plan must provide that an oversecured creditor (value of the collateral exceeds the claim) receive both preconfirmation, post-petition interest on the arrearages cured under the plan *and* post-confirmation interest on such arrearages as required by 11 USC §§506(b), 1325(a)(5). *Rake v Wade, 113 S Ct 2187, 124 L Ed 2d 424 (1993); Pub L No 103-394,*

§§305(c) and 702(b)(2)(D), amending 11 USC §1322(e); 11 USC §§103(a), 506(b), 1325(a)(5).

Finally, in a case where the last homestead mortgage payment under the original payment schedule will become due before expiration of the three-to- five-year term of the Chapter 13 plan, the debtor may stretch out such mortgage payments under the full term of his plan. *11 USC §1322(c)(2)*;

(4) Modify the pre-petition contract rights of secured creditors by paying such creditors property equal to the lesser of the value of their collateral or amount of their allowed claim, plus some rate of interest.

The value of all property to be distributed under the plan must be determined by the court as of the effective date of the plan (*see "Requirements for Confirmation," discussed above*). However, the pre-petition secured claim of a creditor with a lien only on the debtor's real estate used as a principal residence may not be modified by the plan except to cure long-term mortgage arrearages under the plan while maintaining current payments to the mortgagee. The entire debt must be treated as secured. *See In re Nobleman, 113 S Ct 2106, 124 L Ed 228, 28 CBC 2d 977 (1993)*;

(5) Modify the pre-petition rights of any unsecured creditor;

(6) Cure or waive any other default;

(7) Pay all or part of any claim from property of the estate or exempt property of the debtor;

(8) Vest property of the estate in the debtor or another entity on or after confirmation of the plan;

(9) Pay one class of creditors before another class, as long as no class receives payments more than five years after the date the first payment was due under the plan.

The first payment is generally due before the 30th day after the plan is filed and the plan must be filed before the 15th day after the petition is filed, unless the court extends such times); and

(10) Perform any other act which is not inconsistent with the requirements of the Code. *11 USC §§1321, 1322(b)-(c), 1326(a)-(b), 1329(c); FRBP 2002(b), 3013, 3015, 3020, 6006.*

c. Notice of Confirmation Hearing and Date to File Objections:

(1) Generally

The clerk or other court-authorized person must give at least 25 days' notice by mail of the date set by the court to file objections to confirmation of the debtor's plan and the date set for the confirmation hearing. The notice must include a copy or summary of the plan. The notice must be sent to the debtor, the U.S. trustee, the Chapter 13 or standing trustee, all creditors, indenture trustees, and all other entities required by court order or local bankruptcy rules. All objections must be timely filed. An objection is not an adversary complaint and no filing fee is required. A copy of the objection must be served on the debtor by first-class mail, personal delivery by a disinterested person at least 18 years old, or by any other method allowed for service of process in federal district court. A copy of the objection should also be mailed to the Chapter 13 or standing trustee and to any other entity required by court order or local bankruptcy rules. *FRBP 2002(a)(6), (b), 3015, 3019-3020, 7004, 9014, 9034; see Local Bankruptcy Rules.*

(2) Modification

The debtor may modify his plan even after notice of the initial confirmation date has been mailed to creditors and parties-in-interest. The modified plan then becomes the plan to be considered for confirmation by the court. The debtor must serve a copy of the (modified) plan by first-class mail or personal delivery on the Chapter 13 or standing trustee. The debtor must also serve a copy of the (modified) plan on any creditor whose interests are adversely affected by the modifications. If there are creditors adversely affected by the modifications, the court may reset the confirmation hearing date to allow such creditors at least 20 days to consider whether to object to the modifications. The clerk or other court-authorized person must mail notice of any new date for confirmation and for filing objections by creditors adversely affected by the (modified) plan. Such notice must be sent to the debtor, the U.S. trustee, the Chapter 13 or standing trustee, all creditors, indenture trustees, and any other entity as required by court order or local bankruptcy rules. *11 USC §§102(1)(A)-(B), 1323; FRBP 2002(a)(6), 7005, 9013-9014.*

d. Confirmation Hearing

The bankruptcy court must hold a confirmation hearing on the debtor's Chapter 13 plan, unless local bankruptcy rules direct otherwise. The debtor's attendance at the hearing is not required by the Code, but may be required by court order or local bankruptcy rules. *11 USC §1324; FRBP 2002(b), 3015, 3020; see Local Bankruptcy Rules.*

e. No Voting

Chapter 13 does not allow for voting by ballots. A creditor who agrees to the debtor's plan simply takes no action. The Chapter 13 or standing trustee or creditor who objects to confirmation of the plan must file a written objection by the date set by the court, stating the grounds for objection allowed under the Code (*see "Requirements for Confirmation," discussed above*). Hearing on any objection may be held on the date set for the confirmation hearing. *11 USC §1324; FRBP 3020, 9014.*

f. Debtor's Disposable Income

If the Chapter 13 or standing trustee or an unsecured creditor files an objection to confirmation, the court may confirm the debtor's plan only if it provides for one of two options on the effective date of the plan. The first option is that the debtor's plan must provide for payment of the total amount of the objecting creditor's allowed unsecured claim(s) over the term of the plan. The second option is that the plan must provide that all the debtor's projected disposable income for the next three years will be applied to payments under the plan. *Disposable income* is "net—net" income. It is derived by deducting from the debtor's gross income: (1) all required taxes and withholdings; (2) all necessary expenses for the maintenance and support of the debtor or the debtor's dependent(s); and (3) all necessary business expenses if the debtor is engaged in business. The three-year period for paying disposable income begins on the date the first payment is due under the plan. This first payment is due before the 30th day after the plan is filed, unless the court extends such time. *11 USC §1325(b), 1326(a).*

The result of each option is significant. Under the first option, all general unsecured creditors should receive 100 per cent of their allowed pre-petition claims, because each member of the same class of creditors must be treated alike. Thus, if the plan proposes full payment to the objecting unsecured creditor who is in a class with general unsecured creditors, all unsecured creditors in the same class must receive full payment of their allowed pre-petition claims. *11 USC §§1322(a)(3), 1325(b).*

Under the second option, the debtor's projected disposable income must be applied to make payments, but not necessarily to the objecting or any other unsecured creditor. Thus, an objection filed by an unsecured creditor or the Chapter 13 or standing trustee (who represents the estate and ultimately unsecured creditors) may in fact benefit a secured creditor. The Code does not direct a specific class of creditors which must receive the debtor's projected disposable income. *11 USC §§322-323, 1302, 1325(b).*

g. Legal Effects of Confirmation

Unless otherwise stated in the plan or confirmation order, confirmation of the debtor's Chapter 13 plan has three legal effects.

(1) A confirmed plan binds the debtor and all creditors to its stated terms and conditions, even if a creditor objected to the plan or will receive nothing under the plan.

(2) Confirmation of the plan revests all property of the bankruptcy estate (nonexempt property) in the debtor.

The debtor, not unsecured creditors, now has ownership (and possession) of nonexempt property. But the value of property, determined as of the effective date of the plan, to be distributed to unsecured creditors under the plan will be at least the amount such creditors would receive under Chapter 7.

(3) Except as stated in the plan or confirmation order, nonexempt property is free and clear of all interests of any creditor whose claim is provided for by the plan. *11 USC §§1325, 1327; Official Bankr Form 15.*

h. Post-Confirmation

Four events could occur after confirmation of a Chapter 13 plan: a bankruptcy super-garnishment order could be issued by the court; the debtor could modify his plan; the debtor could receive a hardship discharge or convert or dismiss his case; or confirmation of the plan could be revoked and the debtor's case could be dismissed or converted to another Chapter.

(1) Super-Garnishment Order

The bankruptcy court may order any entity from whom the debtor receives income to pay all or part of such income to the Chapter 13 or standing trustee for distribution under the plan. Thus, the court may order the debtor's employer, accounts receivable customers, or a government unit to pay nonexempt money owed to the debtor to the Chapter 13 or standing trustee instead. *11 USC §1325(c).*

(2) Post-Confirmation Modification of a Plan

(a) Generally

The debtor may voluntarily modify his Chapter 13 plan even after confirmation by filing a motion with the court. This modification must occur before completion of payments proposed by the confirmed plan. The debtor must serve a copy of the motion and modified plan on the Chapter 13 or standing trustee by first-class mail or personal delivery.

Only the debtor may file a modified plan. But the Chapter 13 or standing trustee or any creditor may also file a motion for the court to order the debtor to modify his plan post-confirmation or risk dismissal or conversion of his case. Such motion does not commence an adversary proceeding and no filing fee is required. A copy of the motion to compel modification must be served on the debtor by first-class mail, personal delivery by a disinterested person at least 18 years old, or by any manner allowed for service of process in federal district court. A copy of the motion should also be mailed or personally delivered to the Chapter 13 or standing trustee if the movant is not the trustee.

A modified plan may increase or reduce the amount of payments, or extend or reduce the time for payments. However, the term of any plan, including one modified post-confirmation, may not be more than five years from the date the first payment is due under the original plan. The first payment is due before the 30th day after the date the plan is filed, unless the court extends the time; and the plan must be filed before the 15th day after the petition is filed, unless the court orders otherwise. *11 USC §§1321, 1326, 1329; FRBP 3015, 3020, 9013-9014.*

(b) Procedures

The modified plan becomes the plan if approved by the court. Generally, only those creditors whose claims are adversely affected by the modified plan must receive notice of the modifications. The clerk must give such creditors and the Chapter 13 or standing trustee at least 20 days' notice by mail of the date set by the court to file an objection to the modified plan. A hearing will then be held if an objection to the modified plan is timely filed. If a creditor's objection is sustained: (i) the debtor may be allowed by the court to modify his plan further; (ii) the debtor may seek a hardship discharge; or (iii) the debtor's Chapter 13 case may be dismissed or converted to Chapter 7 or 11. *11 USC §§1307, 1329; FRBP 2002(a)-(b), 9014; see Local Bankruptcy Rules.*

(3) Hardship Discharge

If the debtor is unable to make all payments proposed by a confirmed plan and unsecured creditors have received what they would under Chapter 7, the debtor may file a request for a hardship discharge or his case may be dismissed or converted to another chapter. *See "Stages Modified in a Chapter 13 Case—Hardship Discharge," discussed above; "Procedure Five—Conversion from Chapter 13" and "Procedure Six—Dismissal," discussed below; 11 USC §§1307, 1328(b)-(c); FRBP 1019, 2002(a), (f)(2), (k), 9013-9014.*

(4) Revocation of Confirmation, Conversion, or Dismissal

The order confirming a Chapter 13 plan may be revoked by the court post-confirmation. A creditor, Chapter 13 or standing trustee, or other party-in-interest must file a request to revoke confirmation before the 180th day after the confirmation order is entered. A request to revoke a confirmation order commences an adversary proceeding and requires a $120 filing fee and trial. However, if the Chapter 13 or standing trustee files the request to revoke discharge, the filing fee is only payable from any estate that may exist. A copy of the request with summons must be served on the debtor by first-class mail, personal delivery by a disinterested person at least 18 years old, or by any other method allowed for service of a summons and complaint in federal district court. A copy of the request should also be served by mail or personal delivery on the Chapter 13 or standing trustee, if another party filed the request, and the U.S. trustee. The only legal ground for revocation of confirmation is that the debtor obtained confirmation of his Chapter 13 plan through fraud and the creditor was not aware of such fraud before the plan was confirmed. *11 USC §1330; 28 USC §1930(b), Judicial Conference Schedule of Fees (6); FRBP 7001(5), 7004 et seq, 9034; Procedural Bankr Forms B 250A, B, C.*

If the court revokes the confirmation order, the debtor may be allowed to modify his plan and seek confirmation of another plan by a date set by the court or the debtor's Chapter 13 case may be dismissed or converted to Chapter 7 or 11, at the court's discretion. The clerk must give the debtor, the U.S. Trustee, the standing trustee, all creditors, indenture trustees, and all other entities required by court order or local bankruptcy rules, notice by mail of the court's final order revoking discharge and decision to dismiss or convert the debtor's case. *11 USC §§1307, 1330; FRBP 1017, 1019, 2002(f)(2), (6), (k), 4006, 9034.*

5. Procedure Five—Conversion from Chapter 13

a. By the Debtor (Voluntary Conversion)

Because Chapter 13 is entirely voluntary, the debtor has the absolute right to convert his case to Chapter 7, as long as the debtor originally could have filed a petition under such chapter. The debtor must file a notice of conversion. No hearing or court order is required, but the debtor must serve a copy of the notice by mail or personal delivery on the standing trustee, the U.S. trustee, and any other entity directed by court order or local bankruptcy rules. The date of the debtor's notice is the date of the order for relief in the converted case. If the debtor wishes to convert to Chapter 11, he must pay a $400 conversion fee (even though an original filing fee for Chapter 11 is $600). If the debtor seeks to convert to Chapter 7, no additional fee is required. The clerk of the court must mail notice of the conversion to the standing trustee, U.S. trustee, all creditors, indenture trustees, and to any other entity required by court order or local bankruptcy rules. *11 USC*

§§102(1), 1307(a); 28 USC §1930(a)(1), (3); FRBP 1017, 2002(f)(2), (k), 9007, 9013, 9034.

b. By Another Entity (Involuntary Conversion)

Unless the debtor is a farmer, the debtor's Chapter 13 case may be involuntarily converted to another chapter in which the debtor may properly be a debtor upon motion of the Chapter 13 or standing trustee, U.S. trustee, creditor, or other party-in-interest. Many grounds for conversion exist. The Code expressly includes ten grounds.

(1) Grounds for Conversion

(a) The debtor's unreasonable delay during the course of his Chapter 13 case is prejudicial to creditors.

(b) The debtor failed to pay filing fees or other charges required under Chapter 123 of Title 28, United States Code.

(c) The debtor failed to file a Chapter 13 plan timely (with the petition or before the 15th day thereafter or by any court-extended date).

(d) The debtor failed to begin making payments timely (before the 30th day after the plan is filed or by any court-extended date).

(e) The court denied confirmation of the debtor's Chapter 13 plan and denied the debtor any additional time to file another plan or modify his plan.

(f) The debtor committed a material default with regard to a requirement of a confirmed plan.

(g) The court revoked its confirmation order and denied confirmation of a plan modified post-confirmation.

(h) The confirmed plan terminated by its own terms other than completion of payments.

(i) The debtor failed to file his schedules and statements timely (with the petition or before the 15th day thereafter or by any court-extended date).

This ground is available only to the U.S. trustee.

(j) The debtor failed to timely file the information contained in a Chapter 7 debtor's statement of intention, indicating whether the debtor will surrender or how he will retain property of the estate securing a dischargeable consumer debt.

In Chapter 13, the debtor must include such information in his Chapter 13 plan, which must be filed with the petition or before the 15th day thereafter, unless the court extends the time or local bankruptcy rules require otherwise. However, a motion to convert based on this ground is also available only to the U.S. trustee. *11 USC §§307, 521(a)(2), 1307(c)(1)-(10), (f); FRBP 1017, 3015; see Local Bankruptcy Rules; "File Statement of Intention," Chapter III, Chapter II.*

(2) When a Motion to Convert Must Be Filed

A motion to convert the debtor's case to Chapter 11 or 12 must be filed by a party-in-interest (creditor, U.S. trustee, Chapter 13 or standing trustee) before the debtor's plan is confirmed by the court. A motion to convert to Chapter 7 may be filed by a party-in-interest at any time. *11 USC §1307(a), (d), FRBP 1017, 9013-9014, 9034.*

(3) Procedures

A motion to convert a Chapter 13 case is not an adversary complaint. No filing fee is required. The Chapter 13 or standing trustee, U.S. trustee, or creditor must file the motion and serve a copy on the debtor by first-class mail, personal delivery by a disinterested person at least 18 years old, or by any other manner provided for service of process in federal district court. If a creditor files the motion, a copy should also be mailed or personally delivered to the Chapter 13 or standing trustee and U.S. trustee. The clerk or other court-authorized person must give the debtor, U.S. trustee, Chapter 13 or standing trustee, all creditors, and indenture trustees notice by mail of the hearing date on the motion to convert. *11 USC §§102(1)(A)-(B), 1307; FRBP 2002, 9007, 9014, 9034.*

(4) Notice of Conversion

If the debtor's Chapter 13 case is converted by the court, the clerk must mail notice of the conversion order to the debtor, the U.S. trustee, the standing trustee, all creditors, and indenture trustees. *FRBP 2002(f)(2), (k), 9034; Procedural Bankr Form B 223A, B.*

c. Procedures After Conversion

(1) Debtor's Duties

The debtor whose case has been converted from Chapter 13 (superseded case) to Chapter 7 or 11 (converted case) has the same duties as an original Chapter 7 or 11 debtor. *See "Procedure Two—Debtor's Duties," Chapter III & IV.*

(a) Fees

The debtor who seeks conversion from Chapter 13 to Chapter 7 will not pay an additional filing fee. The filing fee for Chapters 7 and 13 is $150. The debtor who seeks a voluntary conversion from Chapter 13 to Chapter 11 must pay only a $400 conversion fee. *28 USC §1930(a)(1), (3), (b), Judicial Conference Schedule of Fees (8).*

(b) File Mailing Matrix, Schedules and Statements

The list of creditors (mailing matrix), bankruptcy schedules and statements previously filed in the superseded Chapter 13 case are deemed filed in the converted Chapter 7 or 11 case, unless the court orders otherwise. If the debtor has not filed such documents by the date the conversion order is entered, he must file the mailing matrix, schedules of assets and liabilities, and statement of financial affairs before the 15th day after entry of the conversion order. If the case is converted to Chapter 7, the (individual) debtor whose debts are primarily consumer debts secured by property of the estate must file his statement of intention by the earlier of the first date set for the meeting of creditors under the converted Chapter 7 case or before the 30th day after entry of the conversion order. The debtor must perform under the statement of intention before the 45th day after the statement of intention is filed. *11 USC §521(1)-(2); FRBP 1007, 1019(1).*

The debtor under a converted Chapter 7 case must also file a schedule of unpaid debts representing debts incurred after the Chapter 13 petition was filed but before the conversion order was entered. If a Chapter 13 plan was confirmed before the conversion order was entered, the debtor must additionally file a schedule of property and schedule of executory contracts and unexpired leases, representing property and executory contracts acquired after filing the original Chapter 13 petition but before entry of the conversion order. These schedules must also be filed in the converted case before the 15th day after entry of the conversion order. *FRBP 1019(5).*

(2) Turn Over Property

After a trustee is selected under the converted Chapter 7 case, the debtor, Chapter 13 or standing trustee, and all other parties must turn over to the Chapter 7 trustee all property and records of the bankruptcy estate (nonexempt property, documents, and records). If the Chapter 13 case is converted to Chapter 11, the debtor as DIP is also the trustee. An entity with property of the debtor or estate in the superseded Chapter 13 case must turn over such property to the DIP. *11 USC §§348(e), 542-543, 1101, 1107; FRBP 1019(4)-(5).*

If the debtor converted the Chapter 13 case to Chapter 7 or 11 *in good faith*, the bankruptcy estate in the converted case will consist of all property in the debtor's possession on the date of conversion that would have been property of the estate on the date the original Chapter 13 petition was filed. Property that the debtor acquired post-petition under the Chapter 13 case will not be included in the estate of the converted Chapter 7 or 11 case. Bankruptcy schedules, including exemptions claimed on Schedule C, filed in the Chapter 13 case will be deemed filed in the converted case, unless the bankruptcy court orders otherwise. However, the debtor may amend any bankruptcy schedule previously filed until the case is closed. If bankruptcy schedules were not filed in the superseeded Chapter 13 case, the debtor must file his schedules before the 15th day after entry of the conversion order, unless the court or local bankruptcy rules require otherwise. *11 USC §§103(a), 348(f)(1), 1306, 1307; FRBP 1009, 1019.*

If the debtor converted his Chapter 13 case *in bad faith,* the bankruptcy estate in the converted Chapter 7 or 11 case will consist of all property of the estate *on the date of conversion.* Thus, property acquired by the debtor post-petition under the Chapter 13 case will be included in the bankruptcy estate of the converted case. *11 USC §§103(a), 348(f)(2), 1306, 1307.*

Valuations of property and secured claims made under the superseded Chapter 13 case will apply in the converted case. Allowed secured claims under the converted case will be reduced commensurately with the amount of any payments made to secured creditors under the Chapter 13 plan. *11 USC §§103(a), 348(f)(1)(B), 1325(a)(5).*

(3) New Time Periods

The date of entry of the order converting the debtor's Chapter 13 case to Chapter 7 or 11 commences new time periods for holding a meeting of creditors and for filing proofs of claims and complaints objecting to discharge of the debtor or dischargeability of a debt under the converted Chapter 7 or 11 case.

(a) Meeting of Creditors

The date of entry of the conversion order is considered the date of the order for relief for purposes of holding a meeting of creditors under the converted case. The meeting of creditors must generally be held not less than 20 or more than 40 days after entry of the conversion order. As in other bankruptcy cases, the clerk or other court-authorized person must give the debtor, the trustee, all creditors, indenture trustees, and any committee in the converted case at least 20 days' prior notice by mail of the new date for the meeting of creditors under the converted case. *11 USC §§341, 343, 348(c); FRBP 2002(a)(1)(i), 2003(a); see "Stage Six—Meeting of Creditors," Chapter II and "Meeting of Creditors" Chapter XIV.*

(b) Proofs of Claims

All proofs of claims actually filed by a creditor in the superseded Chapter 13 case are deemed filed in the converted Chapter 7 or 11 case. If a creditor did not file a claim in the superseded (Chapter 13) case or wishes to file a new claim, such proof of claim must be filed before the 90th day after the first date set for the new meeting of creditors under the converted Chapter 7 case and by the date fixed by the court in a converted Chapter 11 case. The clerk or other court-authorized person must give notice by mail of the date for timely filing proofs of claims in the converted case. Such notice must be sent to the debtor, trustee, all creditors, indenture trustees, and any committee in the converted case. *11 USC §§342, 348(c); FRBP 1019(2)-(3), 2002(a)(8), (f)(3), 3002-3003; see "File Proof of Claim," Chapter XIV.*

(c) Complaints to Deny Discharge and Determine Dischargeability

(i) Denial of Discharge

An adversary complaint objecting to discharge of all debts of the debtor must be filed no later than the 60th day after the first date set for the new meeting of creditors under the converted Chapter 7 case, and no later than the first date for the confirmation hearing set by the court under a converted Chapter 11 case, unless the court extends the time for cause, within such period. The clerk must give creditors, the debtor, any trustee, committee, and the U.S. trustee at least 25 days' notice by mail of the last date to file such complaint. *11 USC §§348, 727, 1141(d)(3); FRBP 2002(f)(4)-(5), (k), 4004(a)-(b), 9034; see "Denial of Discharge," Chapter III.*

(ii) Exceptions to Discharge

A complaint to determine dischargeability of a particular pre-petition debt may generally be filed at any time under the converted case, unless the court or local bankruptcy rules direct otherwise. However, complaints to determine dischargeability of particular debts based upon the debtor's alleged fraud; misrepresentation; fraud while acting as a fiduciary; embezzlement; larceny; or nonvehicular, nondrug-related willful and malicious tort claims must be filed by the 60th day after the first date set for the new meeting of creditors under the converted Chapter 7 or 11 case. The clerk must give at least 30 days' notice by mail of the last date to file a complaint based upon such grounds to all creditors, the debtor, trustee, any committee, indenture trustees, and, in a Chapter 11 case, the SEC in Washington, DC, and District Director of the IRS where the case is pending. *11 USC §523; FRBP 2002(f)(5), (i)-(j), 4007(b)-(c).*

d. Priority of Administrative Claims

Allowed first priority administrative claims incurred under a converted Chapter 7 case have priority over all administrative claims incurred under the debtor's superseded Chapter 13 case. Thus, Chapter 7 administrative claims must be paid in full before the Chapter 13 administrative claims may be paid by the Chapter 7 trustee. Administrative claims under a converted Chapter 11 case do not have priority over such claims incurred in the superseded Chapter 13 case. All administrative claims incurred post-petition share pro rata status under a converted Chapter 11 case. *11 USC §§503(a)-(b), 507(a)(1), 726(b); see "Priority Claims," Chapter II.*

6. Procedure Six—Dismissal

a. By the Debtor (Voluntary Dismissal)

If the debtor's case is an original Chapter 13 case (the debtor originally filed a petition under Chapter 13), the debtor has the absolute right to dismiss at any time by filing a motion to dismiss. Any waiver of this absolute right is unenforceable. No hearing or court order is required. The court must honor the debtor's motion. The motion does not commence an adversary proceeding and no filing fee is required. The debtor must serve a copy of the motion by mail or personal delivery on the Chapter 13 or standing trustee, the U.S. trustee, and any other entity directed by court order or local bankruptcy rules. The clerk or other court-appointed person must mail notice of the dismissal to the U.S. trustee, the Chapter 13 or standing trustee, debtor, all creditors, and indenture trustees. *11 USC §1307(b); FRBP 1017, 2002(f)(2), (k), 9013, 9034.*

If the debtor's present case is a converted Chapter 13 case (the debtor originally filed under a different chapter and converted to Chapter 13), the bankruptcy court has the discretion whether to grant the debtor's motion to dismiss. Unless local bankruptcy rules provide otherwise, the court must hold a hearing on the debtor's motion to consider what is in the best interests of creditors and the estate. The clerk or other court-authorized person must give notice by mail of the debtor's motion and hearing date to the U.S. trustee, the Chapter 13 or standing trustee, all creditors, and any other entity directed by court order or local bankruptcy rules. The required notice will be mailed to creditors listed on the debtor's list of creditors (mailing matrix) filed with the debtor's petition. If the court grants the debtor's motion, the clerk or other court-authorized person must also mail notice of the order dismissing the debtor's case to the U.S. trustee, the Chapter 13 or standing trustee, the debtor, all creditors, and indenture trustees. If the debtor's motion to dismiss is denied, the court should allow the debtor to convert his case. Chapter 13 is totally voluntary and the debtor should not be forced to remain a Chapter 13 debtor involuntarily. *11 USC §§109, 303, 1307(b); S Rep No 595, 95th Cong, 1st Sess 428 (1977); FRBP 1017(a), (d), 2002(f)(2), (k), 9013-9014, 9034.*

b. By Another Entity (Involuntary Dismissal)

The debtor's Chapter 13 case may be involuntarily dismissed upon motion filed by the Chapter 13 or standing trustee, U.S. trustee, a creditor, or other party-in-interest. *11 USC §1307(c); FRBP 1017.*

(1) Grounds for Involuntary Dismissal

The Code expressly lists ten grounds for dismissal of the debtor's Chapter 13 case on motion of the trustee or a creditor. These are the same grounds as those for involuntary conversion of the debtor's Chapter 13 case. *See "By Another Entity (Involuntary Conversion)," discussed above.*

(2) Procedures for Involuntary Dismissal

(a) File Motion

The Chapter 13 or standing trustee, U.S. trustee, creditor, or other party-in-interest must file a motion to dismiss showing ground(s) for dismissal. A copy of the motion must be served on the debtor by first-class mail, personal delivery by a disinterested person at least 18 years old, or by any other method provided for service of a summons and complaint in federal district court. A copy of the motion should also be mailed or personally delivered to the Chapter 13 or standing trustee, if another party filed the motion, and to the U.S. trustee. The motion does not commence an adversary proceeding. No filing fee is required. The debtor does not have to file a response, unless the court or local bankruptcy rules require otherwise. *11 USC §1307(c); FRBP 1017, 9013-9014, 9034; see Local Bankruptcy Rules.*

(b) Notice and Hearing

The court must hold a hearing on the trustee's or creditor's motion to dismiss. The trustee or creditor has the burden of proving ground(s) for dismissal. The clerk or other court-authorized person must mail notice of the motion and hearing date to the debtor, Chapter 13 or standing trustee, U.S. trustee, all creditors and to any other entity required by court order or local bankruptcy rules. If the court grants the motion, the clerk must also mail notice of the dismissal order to the debtor, U.S. trustee, Chapter 13 or standing trustee, the debtor, all creditors, and indenture trustees. *11 USC §1307(c); FRBP 1017, 2002(f)(2), (k), 9014, 9034; see Local Bankruptcy Rules.*

c. Legal Effect of Dismissal

Dismissal of any bankruptcy case has the same legal effect upon creditors and the debtor as if no petition had been filed, unless the court orders otherwise. Property of the estate revests in the debtor. The automatic stay is lifted and creditors may proceed against the debtor and his property under applicable nonbankruptcy law. Unless the debtor's case is dismissed with prejudice, the debtor may refile a petition under any chapter of the Code in which he may properly be a debtor. However, the debtor may have to wait 181 days to refile a bankruptcy petition if the Chapter 13 case was dismissed involuntary for the debtor's willful failure to obey a court order or appear and prosecute his case (the debtor failed to timely file required schedules, statements, or a plan) or if the debtor's case was dismissed voluntarily after a creditor filed a motion for relief from the automatic stay. *11 USC §§109(a)-(g), 349(a)-(b), 362(c)(1)-(2).*

7. Procedure Seven—Discharge Of the Debtor

Chapter 13 provides for a liberal discharge if the debtor completes all payments required by a confirmed plan or a hardship discharge if the debtor's default under his plan was not his fault, unsecured creditors received at least as much as they would under Chapter 7, and post-confirmation modification of the plan is not practical. *See "Stages Modified in a Chapter 13 Case," discussed above; 11 USC §1328(a)-(b).*

a. When

The debtor will receive a discharge as soon as practical after he completes all payments required by a confirmed plan, or the court grants the debtor a hardship discharge. *11 USC §1328(a)-(b).*

b. Hearing

No hearing is required for the court to grant the debtor a liberal discharge, unless the court or local bankruptcy rules direct otherwise. A hearing may be required under the debtor's motion for hardship discharge as directed by the court or local bankruptcy rules. The motion does not commence an adversary proceeding and no filing fee is required. The debtor must serve a copy of the motion on the U.S. trustee and Chapter 13 or standing trustee by first-class mail or any other manner provided for service of process in federal district court, with notice to creditors as directed by the court or local bankruptcy rules. *11 USC §§102(1)(A)-(B), 1328(a)-(b); FRBP 9007, 9013-9014, 9034.*

c. Debts Discharged

(1) Liberal Discharge

Under a liberal discharge, the debtor will receive a discharge of all but seven types of debts.

(a) Maintenance, alimony, or support payments owed by the debtor to the debtor's spouse, ex-spouse, or child are not discharged, unless such debt was assigned to a nongovernment entity other than under §402(a)(26) of the Social Security Act, 42 United States Code.

(b) Long-term debts, consisting of secured or unsecured claims which the debtor could pay off under a pre-petition contract after the maximum five years allowed for payments under a Chapter 13 plan (mortgage or other payments where, on the date the petition is filed, the pre-petition contract allowed the debtor more than five years to pay the debt), are not discharged.

(c) Priority tax claims must be fully paid under the Chapter 13 plan, unless the government entity agrees otherwise. The Code requires that a Chapter 13 plan propose full payment of all priority claims as a condition to confirmation by the court. If the debtor fails to make payments required by a confirmed plan, the debtor may apply for a hardship discharge under Chapter 13 or his case may be dismissed or converted to Chapter 7 or 11. But seventh priority tax claims are not dischargeable under either a Chapter 13 hardship discharge or Chapter 7 or 11 discharge. *See "Priority Claims," Chapter II.*

(d) Post-petition consumer debts for property or services necessary for the debtor's performance under the Chapter 13 plan are not discharged if the creditor timely filed a proof of claim allowed by the court and the creditor did not know that the debtor could practically have obtained the standing trustee's approval before incurring the consumer debt but failed to do so. *See "File Proof of Claim," Chapter XIV.*

(e) A debt for educational money loaned, insured, or guaranteed by a governmental unit or nonprofit organization is not discharged, unless the debt was first due more than seven years (excluding any applicable suspension of repayment period) before the Chapter 13 petition was filed or nondischargeability of this debt would cause an undue hardship on the debtor and his dependents.

(f) A debt for death or personal injury caused by the debtor unlawfully operating a motor vehicle while under the influence of a drug, alcohol, or other substance is not discharged.

(g) A debt for restitution owed to a crime victim or a criminal fine included in the debtor's sentence upon conviction of a crime is not discharged if restitution was part of the debtor's sentence for conviction of a crime. *11 USC §§507(a)(7), 523(a)(5), (8)-(9), 1305(a)(2), 1322(b)(5), 1328(a)(1)-(3), (d).*

(2) Hardship Discharge

Under a Chapter 13 hardship discharge, all pre-petition debts which could be excepted from discharge under Chapter 7 may now be nondischargeable under Chapter 13. *See "Exceptions to Discharge," Chapter III; 11 USC §1328(b)-(c).*

(3) Complaint to Determine Dischargeability

(a) Liberal Discharge

A creditor may file a complaint at any time to determine the dischargeability of one of the seven types of nondischargeable debts under a liberal discharge (*see "Liberal Discharge," discussed above*), unless the court or local bankruptcy rules direct otherwise. Such complaint may even be filed after the Chapter 13 case is closed, in which case the court must reopen the case. The creditor must pay a $120 filing fee. The complaint with summons must be served on the debtor by first-class mail, personal delivery by a disinterested person at least 18 years old, or by any other method allowed for service of process in federal district court. A copy should also be served by mail or personal delivery on the Chapter 13 or standing trustee. No additional fee is required to reopen a case for actions relating to the debtor's discharge. *11 USC §§350(b), 523, 1328(a)(1)-(3); 28 USC §1930(a)-(b), Judicial Conference Schedule of Fees (6); Language to Clarify Reopened Cases; FRBP 4007(a)-(b), 7001(6), 7004 et seq; Procedural Bankr Forms B 250A, B, C.*

(b) Hardship Discharge

A complaint to determine the dischargeability of a debt under a hardship discharge may be filed at any time unless the court or local bankruptcy rules state otherwise; or the ground(s) are the debtor's alleged fraud or misrepresentation; fraud while acting in a fiduciary capacity; embezzlement; larceny; or a nonvehicular, nondrug-related willful and malicious tort. The court must set a date to file a complaint based on such grounds after the debtor files a motion for hardship discharge. The clerk of the court must give creditors at least 30 days' notice by mail of the date so fixed by the court. The creditor must pay a $120 filing fee and serve a copy of the complaint with summons on the debtor in any manner allowed for service of process in federal district court. A copy of the complaint should also be served by first-class mail or personal delivery on the Chapter 13 or standing trustee. *11 USC §§103(a), 523, 1328(b)-(c); 28 USC §1930(b), Judicial Conference Schedule of Fees (6); FRBP 2002(f)(5), 4007, 7001(6), 7004 et seq; see Local Bankruptcy Rules; Procedural Bankr Forms B 250A, B, C.*

d. Notice of Court Order

The clerk must promptly give notice by mail to the debtor, the U.S. trustee, the Chapter 13 or standing trustee, all creditors, and indenture trustees of the court's order granting or denying the Chapter 13 debtor a discharge. *FRBP 2002(f)(6), (k), 4004(g), 4006; Official Bankr Form 18.*

8. Procedure Eight—Closing the Case

a. Small Dividends

The Chapter 13 or standing trustee may not disburse a dividend payment of less than $15 to any creditor, unless directed otherwise by court order or local bankruptcy rules. The trustee will allow undisbursed small dividends to accumulate and, at the latest, disburse such remaining funds with the final dividend payment. *11 USC §1326(c); FRBP 3010.*

b. Unclaimed Dividends

The Chapter 13 or standing trustee must stop payment on any dividend check that is not claimed by the 90th day after the final distribution of payments under the plan. The trustee must pay the remaining unclaimed funds into the court and file a list of known names, addresses, and respective amounts owed to creditors entitled to such funds. The clerk of the court will hold the funds for five years for their owners. After such time, any unclaimed property will escheat to the United States Treasury. *11 USC §§103(a), 347(a), 1326(c); 28 USC §2041 et seq; FRBP 3011.*

c. Final Report and Account

The Chapter 13 or standing trustee must file a final report and account of the administration of the estate with the court. The trustee must send a copy of such report and account to the U.S.

trustee. After the estate has been fully administered, the court must close the Chapter 13 case. *11 USC §§350(a), 704(9), 1302(b)(1).*

E. Advantages to Chapter 13

1. Chapter 13 Versus Chapter 7

The Chapter 13 debtor's rights and powers are inherently greater than those of the Chapter 7 debtor in eight respects.

a. First—Leverage Over Creditors

The Chapter 13 debtor has tremendous leverage over creditors which the Chapter 7 debtor does not have. The Chapter 13 debtor may keep all his property; cure homestead mortgage arrearages; and defer priority tax claims. *See "Requirements for Confirmation" and "Optional Provisions of a Plan," discussed above.*

(1) Chapter 13 Debtor Keeps All Property

The Chapter 13 debtor may retain possession of all property, exempt and nonexempt. The debtor keeps his nonexempt property (the bankruptcy estate) by paying the value of such property to the standing trustee for distribution to unsecured creditors over the term of the Chapter 13 plan. The debtor keeps secured property (whether exempt or nonexempt) by providing that the secured creditor retain its lien and by paying the lesser of the value of the collateral or the amount of the secured creditor's allowed claim, plus interest, over the term of the plan. The debtor makes all payments to the standing trustee who disburses them to creditors, unless otherwise stated in the plan or confirmation order. Values of all property distributed under the plan are determined as of the effective date of the plan. *11 USC §§1306, 1325-1326; see "Procedure Four—Confirmation of Chapter 13 Plan," discussed above.*

The Chapter 7 debtor must surrender all nonexempt property to the Chapter 7 trustee who then liquidates (sells) the estate and disburses the proceeds. Secured creditors will receive either their collateral or the lesser amount of the value of their collateral or the allowed amount of their claim. The Chapter 7 trustee will disburse funds remaining in the estate pro rata, first to priority claimholders and then to general unsecured creditors. The Chapter 7 debtor may only retain exempt secured property if he reaffirms the debt or redeems the property. If the secured creditor does not consent or the court does not approve the reaffirmation agreement, the Chapter 7 debtor loses his secured property unless he can redeem the collateral. If the property is real estate or other nonredeemable property or the debtor cannot obtain sufficient cash to redeem and buy back the collateral, he again loses his secured property. *11 USC §§524, 722, 725-726; FRBP 4008, 6008; see "Reaffirmation of Debt" and "Redemption of Property," Chapter III.*

(2) Chapter 13 Debtor May Cure Mortgage Arrearages

The Chapter 13 debtor may cure pre- and post-petition arrearages in homestead or other long-term (mortgage) payments under a Chapter 13 plan, while maintaining current (mortgage) payments directly to the secured creditor under the plan. Thus, Chapter 13 provides the debtor a means to retain his homestead even if he has defaulted in payments pre- and/or post-petition and even if the secured creditor does not consent to the plan. *11 USC §1322(b)(5).*

The Chapter 7 debtor is at the mercy of the secured creditor-mortgagee if he has defaulted in payments on his homestead. A debtor may not redeem real property under Chapter 7. If the secured creditor (mortgagee) does not consent to payments under a reaffirmation agreement, the Chapter 7 debtor will lose his homestead if he has defaulted in mortgage payments. *11 USC §§524, 722; FRBP 4008, 6008; see "Reaffirmation of Debt" and "Redemption of Property," Chapter III.*

(3) Chapter 13 Debtor May Defer Priority Tax Claims Over Five Years

The Chapter 13 debtor may defer payments of seventh priority tax claims by making cash payments to the Chapter 13 or standing trustee over the term of the Chapter 13 plan. This term may be as long as five years from the date the first payment was due under the plan. The Chapter 13 or standing trustee must generally receive the first payment before the 30th day after the debtor files the plan, unless the court extends the time. The debtor must file his plan before the 15th day after the petition is filed, unless the court allows otherwise. The Chapter 13 or standing trustee will then disburse payments to the IRS as provided by the confirmed plan. *11 USC §§1322(a)(2), 1325(c), 1326(a)(1), 1329(c); FRBP 3015.*

The Chapter 7 debtor may not defer payments of his priority tax debt unless the IRS consents to an extension of payments under a reaffirmation agreement which the court must approve. If no extension of payments is agreed to, the Chapter 7 debtor remains personally liable for immediate payment of his priority tax debts, which could result in a tax judgment, lien against the debtor's property, and foreclosure. *See "Priority Claims," Chapter II; 11 USC §§507(a)(7), 523(a)(1), 524(c)-(d).*

b. Second—Liberal Discharge

Chapter 13 provides the debtor with a liberal discharge if he makes all payments required by a confirmed plan. The Chapter 13 debtor will receive a discharge of debts incurred through the debtor's fraud, failure to list creditors on his schedules of liabilities, and intentional, willful tortious conduct that does not involve the unlawful operation of a motor vehicle while intoxicated from use of drugs, alcohol, or other substance. The Chapter 7 debtor may be denied a discharge of these and other particular pre-petition debts. *See "Exceptions to Discharge," Chapter III. 11 USC §§103(a), 523(a), 1328(a), (d).*

c. Third—Retention of Property

As stated, the Chapter 13 debtor retains all property, both exempt and nonexempt property of the bankruptcy estate. The Chapter 7 debtor must turn over all nonexempt property to the Chapter 7 trustee for liquidation and distribution of proceeds to creditors. The Chapter 13 debtor will pay at least the value of nonexempt property to unsecured creditors under his Chapter 13 plan. *11 USC §§541-543, 726, 1306(b), 1325(a)(4).*

d. Fourth—Use, Sale, or Lease of Property

The Chapter 13 debtor may use, sell, or lease nonexempt property, exclusive of the standing trustee, as long as the debtor complies with applicable bankruptcy law for such use, unsecured creditors receive at least the value of such property (bankruptcy estate) over the term of the plan, and secured creditors retain their liens and receive the lesser of the value of their collateral or amount of their allowed claims with interest under the plan. *11 USC §§103(a), 363, 1303-1304, 1325; FRBP 2002(a)(2), (c), 4001, 6004, 9013-9014, 9034; see "Requirements for Confirmation," discussed above; Chapter VIII.*

The Chapter 7 debtor must surrender all nonexempt property to the Chapter 7 trustee for liquidation and distribution, unless he redeems the property or reaffirms the underlying debt. It is the Chapter 7 trustee who may use, sell, or lease property of the estate. *11 USC §§103(a), 323, 363, 524, 541, 722; see Chapter VIII.*

e. Fifth—Entirely Voluntary

Chapter 13 is entirely voluntary. Only the debtor may file a Chapter 13 petition. Only the debtor may file a Chapter 13 plan or modify such plan (although the trustee or a creditor may file a motion for the court to order the debtor to file a modification). An involuntary petition may be filed against a Chapter 7 debtor who is not a farmer, family farmer, or eleemosynary institution (church, school, charitable organization). *11 USC §§303, 1321, 1323, 1329; FRBP 1003-1004, 1010-1011, 1013, 3015, 3019-3020.*

f. Sixth—Absolute Right of Conversion

The Chapter 13 debtor has the absolute right to convert his Chapter 13 case to Chapter 7, even if his present Chapter 13 case is a converted case (debtor originally filed under another chapter and converted to Chapter 13). The Chapter 7 debtor has the absolute right to convert his case only if he originally filed under Chapter

7 and has not previously converted his case. If the debtor's Chapter 7 case is a converted case, the debtor may convert to another chapter in which he may properly be a debtor only if the court approves, after notice to creditors and hearing. *11 USC §§109, 706(a), (d), 1307(a), (f); FRBP 1017.*

g. Seventh—Codebtor Stay

Chapter 13 protects the bankruptcy debtor and certain individual (natural person) codebtors from attempts of creditors to collect a pre-petition consumer debt. Chapter 7 provides no protection to an individual codebtor who is liable with the bankruptcy debtor on a consumer debt or who provided collateral to secure a consumer debt of the bankruptcy debtor. *11 USC §1301; see "Automatic Plus Codebtor Stay," discussed above.*

h. Eight—Improved Credit

Payment of debts under a Chapter 13 plan may improve a debtor's post-petition credit rating.

2. Chapter 13 Versus Chapter 11

Chapter 13 has seven distinct advantages over a Chapter 11 case.

a. Cheaper

Chapter 13 is much cheaper than Chapter 11. The filing fee for Chapter 13 is $150. The filing fee for an individual Chapter 11 debtor is $600, plus quarterly fees required to maintain a Chapter 11 case until confirmation of a Chapter 11 plan of reorganization. Furthermore, attorneys' fees for Chapter 13 are generally a fraction of the cost of attorneys' and other fees for Chapter 11. *28 USC §1930(a)(1), (3), (6), (b), Judicial Conference Schedule of Fees (8); see "Duties as Chapter 11 Debtor," Chapter IV.*

b. Quicker

A Chapter 13 case is generally much quicker to complete than a Chapter 11 case. The actual time from date of commencement to confirmation varies by debtor and district, but the average Chapter 13 case takes approximately two to three months from the date of filing the Chapter 13 petition until confirmation of a plan by the court, compared to six months to two years or more for confirmation of a Chapter 11 plan.

c. Liberal Discharge

Only Chapter 13 affords a debtor a liberal discharge, including debts incurred through fraud; embezzlement; intentional and willful torts that do not involve the unlawful operation of a motor vehicle while intoxicated from drugs, alcohol, or other substance. Such fraud and tort debts may be nondischargeable under Chapters 7, 11, and 12. *11 USC §§103(a), 523(a), 1141(d)(2), 1228(a)(2),*

1328(a)(2); see "Exceptions to Discharge," Chapter III; "Liberal Discharge," discussed above.

d. Easier

Chapter 13 does not require or permit actual voting as a condition for confirmation of a plan. Chapter 11 requires the debtor to obtain a minimum number and dollar amount of affirmative votes as a condition for confirmation. Chapter 11 also requires the debtor to file and obtain court approval of a disclosure statement prior to soliciting votes for confirmation of a plan. Chapter 13 does not require a disclosure statement. Finally, payment and other terms of a Chapter 13 plan are usually far simpler than those of Chapter 11 plan. *11 USC §§1125-1126, 1129, 1322, 1325; see "Procedure Seven—Confirmation of a Plan of Reorganization," Chapter IV.*

e. Voluntary

No involuntary petition may be filed under Chapter 13. An involuntary petition may be filed against a debtor under Chapter 11, unless he is a farmer or eleemosynary institution. Moreover, under certain conditions in Chapter 11, an entity other than the debtor may file and have confirmed a Chapter 11 plan of reorganization. The debtor is the only entity who may file and have confirmed a Chapter 13 plan of adjustment. *11 USC §§303(a), 1121(c), 1321; FRBP 1003-1004, 1010-1011, 3015-3016; see "Procedure Seven—Confirmation of a Plan of Reorganization," Chapter IV.*

f. Codebtor Stay

Chapter 13 provides a stay against collection of a pre-petition consumer debt for certain individuals who are liable with or who secured a consumer debt for the bankruptcy debtor. Chapter 11 generally does not allow for protection of codebtors. *11 USC §1301; see "Automatic Plus Codebtor Stay," discussed above.*

g. No Creditors' Committee(s)

There are no creditors' committees under Chapter 13. An unsecured creditors' committee is an active participant under Chapter 11. This committee executes some duties performed by the standing trustee, including investigating the financial conditions of the debtor. But the unsecured creditors' committee also has the legal right under Chapter 11 to meet frequently with the debtor, to participate in writing a Chapter 11 plan, and to collect and file votes for a plan. Furthermore, it is not uncommon for a Chapter 11 case to have the unsecured creditors' committee, an examiner or trustee, and the Chapter 11 debtor as key players vying for dominance of their respective interests and for confirmation of a plan. *11 USC §§1102-1103, 1105-1106, 1121(c), 1302; FRBP 2007, 2018; see "Procedure Three—Selection of Unsecured Creditors' Committee," Chapter IV.*

F. Disadvantages to Chapter 13

1. Generally

There are three general disadvantages to a Chapter 13 case which do not exist under either Chapter 7 or 11.

a. Larger Bankruptcy Estate

The bankruptcy estate under Chapter 13 is larger than under Chapter 7 or 11. The Chapter 13 estate includes all pre- and post-petition property acquired by the debtor until the earlier date that the Chapter 13 case is closed, dismissed, converted, or the debtor has completed all required payments under a confirmed Chapter 13 plan. The estate under Chapter 7 and 11 consists of all property presently owned by the debtor on the date of filing the petition and only limited future property acquired by the debtor before 180 days after the petition is filed by will or inheritance; property settlement agreement with the debtor's spouse, ex-spouse, or under a divorce decree; or as a beneficiary under a life insurance or other death-benefit plan. *11 USC §§103(a), 541(a)(5), 1306; see "Stage Three—Creation of a Bankruptcy Estate," Chapter II.*

b. Standing Trustee's Surcharge

Title 28, United States Code, permits the standing trustee to impose upon each Chapter 13 debtor a *surcharge* or percentage fee of up to 10 per cent of the total payments received by the trustee under each Chapter 13 plan. This surcharge is the standing trustee's fee for the actual, necessary expenses incurred in administering Chapter 13 cases, and is usually in addition to such trustee's annual compensation. However, if the maximum amount allowed for the percentage fee exceeds the trustee's adjusted compensation plus actual, necessary, allowed expenses, the standing trustee must remit the difference to the U.S. trustee for deposit in the U.S. trustee System Fund. *28 USC §586(e)(1)-(2).*

c. Super-Garnishment Order

Chapter 13 expressly provides for the court to order an entity from whom the debtor receives any nonexempt income, including the debtor's employer, to pay all or part of such income to the Chapter 13 or standing trustee for disbursement to creditors under the Chapter 13 plan. Chapter 7 has no such provision. Chapter 11 contains a less express provision for the court to order a party (including an employer) to perform any act necessary for consummation of a Chapter 11 plan. *11 USC §§1142(b), 1325(c); FRBP 3020(d).*

2. Chapter 13 Versus Chapter 11

There are four additional disadvantages of Chapter 13 compared to Chapter 11

a. More Limited Powers

The rights and powers of the Chapter 13 debtor are far more limited than the broad powers of the Chapter 11 DIP. The Chapter 13 debtor has the right to sell, use, or lease property of the bankruptcy estate (nonexempt property) exclusive of the standing trustee, as long as the interests of creditors in such property are adequately protected. The Chapter 13 debtor who is self-employed and incurs trade credit may also operate his business exclusive of the standing trustee post-petition, provided that the interests of affected creditors are adequately protected. But the Chapter 11 DIP has these rights and many more. Unless a trustee is appointed in a Chapter 11 case, the DIP performs as two entities. He is the debtor and trustee. The DIP thus has all rights and powers of a trustee, including the right to recover preferential and fraudulent transfers and to avoid certain liens and setoffs. The Chapter 13 debtor generally does not have such super powers, unless his exemptible property is at issue. *11 USC §§103, 323, 363, 522(f)-(k), 547-551, 1107, 1122-1123, 1129, 1302-1304, 1322, 1325; see Chapters VIII, XII, XIII.*

b. Later Discharge

The Chapter 13 debtor receives his discharge after completing all payments required by a confirmed plan. The Chapter 11 debtor receives his discharge on the date his plan is confirmed, even before payments may have begun under the Chapter 11 plan. *11 USC §§1141(d)(1)(A), 1328(a).*

c. Fewer Post-Petition Debts Discharged

The Chapter 13 debtor may receive a discharge of only certain post-petition taxes and post-petition consumer debts necessary to the debtor's performance under the plan if prior approval of the trustee for such consumer debts either was obtained or could not practically have been obtained, even if such post-petition creditors receive little or nothing under the confirmed plan. But the individual Chapter 11 debtor receives a discharge of all post-petition debts that arise before confirmation of a plan, unless such debts are otherwise nondischargeable under bankruptcy law. *See "Exceptions to Discharge," Chapter III; "Procedure Seven—Confirmation of a Plan of Reorganization," Chapter IV; 11 USC §§523, 1141(d)(1)-(2), 1305(a)(1)-(2), 1328.*

d. Less Leverage with Homestead Mortgagee and Other Creditors

The Chapter 13 debtor may cure pre- and post-petition arrearages in home mortgage payments under his Chapter 13 plan. But the Chapter 13 debtor may not extend payments beyond a maximum five-year term under his Chapter 13 plan, beginning the date the first payment was due under the Chapter 13 plan (before the 30th day after the plan was filed). As long as the Chapter 11 plan is "fair and equitable" and "does not discriminate unfairly," the Chapter 11 debtor may defer payments over a term that may well exceed five years, if necessary to enable the debtor to reorganize. *11 USC §§1123(a)(5)(E), (G)-(H), 1129(b), 1322(b)(2), (5), (c), 1325; see "Requirements for Confirmation of a Chapter 11 Plan," Chapter IV, "Procedure Four—Confirmation of Chapter 13 Plan," discussed above.*

Research Guide

Drake, *Bankruptcy Practice for the General Practitioner* ch 13 (Shepard's/McGraw-Hill 2d ed 1990)

Drake & Morris, *Chapter 13: Practice and Procedure* (Shepard's/McGraw-Hill 1983)

Jaroslavsky, *Practical Bankruptcy Procedure* chs 2, 5, 11-13, 15, 16 (Shepard's/McGraw-Hill 1993)

Murphy, *Creditor's Rights in Bankruptcy* ch 20 (Shepard's/McGraw-Hill 2d 1988)

Pollard & Burton, *Guide to Effective Bankruptcy Litigation* ch 18 (Shepard's/McGraw-Hill 1988)

VI. Chapter 12—Adjustment of Debts of a Family Farmer with Regular Annual Income

VI. Chapter 12—Adjustment of Debts of a Family Farmer With Regular Annual Income

A. General Overview

Chapter 12 is a hybrid of Chapters 13 and 11. The procedures of Chapter 12 more closely resemble Chapter 13; but the Chapter 12 debtor, as a debtor-in-possesion (DIP), has the broad powers of a Chapter 11 trustee or DIP. Chapter 12 provides the means by which a family farmer may restructure his debts over a period of three to five years. The family farmer provisions of Chapter 12 do not affect cases filed before November 26, 1986. However, cases that were pending before a bankruptcy court prior to November 26, 1986, could be converted to Chapter 12. The 1986 Amendments to the Bankruptcy Code which enacted Chapter 12 also contained a sunset provision repealing Chapter 12 on October 1, 1993. But all Chapter 12 cases and related matters pending before the court on such date may continue to be heard and determined as if Chapter 12 were not repealed. *Pub L No 99-554, tit III, §302(f), 100 Stat 3124 (1986); 132 Cong Rec H8999 (daily ed Oct 2, 1986); 11 USC §1203.*

B. The Debtor

Chapter 12 is reserved exclusively for a family farmer, a term of art defined under the Code (*see discussion below*). The family farmer, whether an individual, partnership, or corporation, is a farmer with relatively small debt structure who receives an annual income sufficiently stable to make payments under a Chapter 12 plan of adjustment. *11 USC §§101(18), 109(f), 1201 et seq.*

1. Individual Debtor

If the Chapter 12 debtor is an individual (natural person), he must meet four requirements on the date the petition is filed to be a family farmer eligible for Chapter 12.

a. The debtor, or debtor and his spouse if a joint petition is filed, must be engaged in *farming operation(s)*.

Farming is tillage of the soil; ranching; production or raising of crops, poultry, livestock, or any of such products in an unmanufactured state).

b. The debtor, individually or with his spouse, must have aggregate debts of $1.5 million or less.

c. **The debtor, alone or with his spouse, must have incurred at least 80 per cent of the aggregate, noncontingent, liquidated debts from farming operations owned by the debtor or debtor and his spouse.**

A debt for the principal place of residence of the debtor or debtor and spouse is not counted unless such principal-residence debt arose out of farming operation(s).

d. **The debtor, or debtor and spouse, must receive more than 50 per cent of gross income from such farming operation(s) for the taxable year immediately preceding the taxable year in which the Chapter 12 petition is filed.** *11 USC §§101(18), (21), 109(f).*

2. Corporate Debtor

If the Chapter 12 debtor is a corporation, the debtor must meet six requirements on the date the petition is filed to be a family farmer.

a. **The debtor must have more than 50 per cent of the outstanding stock or equity ownership held by one family or by one family and its relatives.**

b. **Such family or its relatives must own or operate the farming operation(s).**

c. **More than 80 per cent of the value of the debtor's assets must be related to farming operation(s).**

d. **The debtor's aggregate debts must not exceed $1.5 million.**

e. **The debtor must have incurred at least 80 per cent of its aggregate, noncontingent, liquidated debts from farming operation(s).**

A debt for a dwelling owned by the corporation and maintained by a shareholder or owner as his principal residence is excluded from the debt requirements, unless the principal-residence debt arose out of the farming operation(s).

f. **Any stock issued by the corporation must not be publicly traded.** *11 USC §§101(18), (21), 109(f).*

3. Partnership Debtor

If the Chapter 12 debtor is a partnership, the debtor must meet only the first five requirements listed above for the corporate Chapter 12 debtor. *11 USC §§101(18)-(19), (21), 109(f).*

C. Stages and Procedures under Chapter 12 Cases

The nine stages common to all voluntary bankruptcy cases also govern a Chapter 12 case. Chapter 12 is really an offspring of Chapters 11 and 13. The procedures for Chapter 13 apply to Chapter 12, with certain distinctions. *See "Procedures Under Chapter 13," Chapter V.*

D. Distinctions Between Chapter 12 and Chapter 13

There are ten principal distinctions between the provisions of Chapters 12 and 13.

1. The Chapter 12 Debtor is a DIP

The Chapter 12 debtor has greater powers than the Chapter 13 debtor. A Chapter 12 debtor is a DIP with all the rights and powers of a trustee or Chapter 11 DIP, including the power to avoid certain preferential and fraudulent transfers, setoffs, and certain unperfected statutory liens. *See Chapter XII.*

The Chapter 12 debtor may have his DIP status removed for cause, including the debtor's pre- or post-petition fraud, dishonesty, incompetence, or gross mismanagement of its affairs. A party-in-interest (creditor, standing trustee, U.S. trustee) must file a motion or request to remove the debtor's DIP status. The party-in-interest must serve a copy of the motion on the debtor, the standing trustee, all creditors, and parties-in-interest directed by the court or local bankruptcy rules. The motion may be served by first-class mail or any other manner allowed for service of process in a federal district court. The motion does not commence an adversary proceeding and no filing fee is required. The court must hold a hearing on the motion, unless local bankruptcy rules provide otherwise. The date of the hearing should be included with service of the motion or by such other notice as required by court order or local bankruptcy rules. The party-in-interest filing the motion has the burden of proving ground(s) for removal of the debtor's DIP status. If the debtor's DIP status is removed, the standing trustee or other court-appointed person will operate the debtor's farm and assume the DIP's super-avoiding powers. *11 USC §§102(1)(A)-(B), 1107, 1202-1203, 1204(a)-(b); FRBP 7004, 9007, 9014; see Chapter XII.*

The court may reinstate a Chapter 12 debtor's DIP status if a party-in-interest (debtor, creditor, standing trustee) files a motion to reinstate. The same procedures discussed above govern removal and reinstatement of a DIP status. *11 USC §1204; FRBP 9007, 9013-9014.*

2. Debt Structure

The $1.5 million debt structure of the Chapter 12 debtor is more liberal in dollar amount but the requirements are more numerous than those of the Chapter 13 debtor. *11 USC §§101(18), 109(e)-(f); see "Who May Be a Debtor," Chapter II, and "Procedure One—The Debtor," Chapter V.*

3. Standing Trustee

The standing trustee's powers and involvement differ in five respects under Chapter 12.

a. The Chapter 12 standing trustee does not investigate the financial affairs of the Chapter 12 debtor, unless ordered to do so by the court after a party-in-interest (creditor), standing trustee, or U.S. trustee files a motion and shows cause for such investigation.

b. The Chapter 12 standing trustee does not advise and assist the debtor in performance under a Chapter 12 plan.

c. The standing trustee or other appointed trustee must make and file any required state or local income tax return for the estate of an individual Chapter 12 debtor for each post-petition tax period until the case is closed. The taxable period of an individual debtor is divided into two periods for purposes of any required state or local income tax. The pre-petition period ends on the date the petition is filed; the post-petition period commences on such date. *11 USC §1231(a)-(b).*

d. The services of the standing trustee must be terminated by the court after the debtor is granted a discharge under Chapter 12. *11 USC §1228.*

e. The Chapter 12 debtor, as a DIP, also represents the estate and has the power to file adversary complaints to avoid preferential and fraudulent transfers, certain setoffs, and unperfected and statutory liens. *11 USC §§323, 1202(b), 1203, 1228(e), 1231(a)-(b); see Chapter XII.*

4. Meeting of Creditors

Under Chapter 12, the U.S. trustee must generally hold a meeting of creditors not less than 20 or more than 35 days after the petition is filed. This latest date to hold a meeting of creditors is reduced in Chapter 12 from 40 to 35 days to comply with the expedited procedures for confirmation of a Chapter 12 plan and administration of the Chapter 12 case. *11 USC §§1221, 1224; FRBP 2003.*

5. Adequate Protection to Continue the Automatic Stay

If a secured creditor files a motion for relief from the automatic stay for lack of adequate protection for the creditor's collateral, Chapter 12 provides four express statutory methods for the debtor to adequately protect the collateral or an entity's ownership interest in property and have the stay continued.

a. The debtor may make periodic cash payments to the secured creditor equal to any reduction in value to the collateral or an entity's ownership interest in property which may occur if the stay is continued.

b. The debtor may provide an additional or replacement lien to compensate for any reduction in value to collateral or an entity's ownership interest in property from continuation of the stay.

c. The debtor may provide any other means allowed by the court to adequately protect the value of property securing a creditor's claim or subject to an entity's ownership interest. However, the court may not grant a first priority administrative claim as adequate protection against any reduction in value to property.

d. The Chapter 12 debtor may pay the secured creditor or entity with an ownership interest the reasonable rent for use of farmland customary in the debtor's farming community, based upon the rental value, net income, and earning capacity of the property at issue. *11 USC §1205; see "Stage Two—Automatic Stay Invoked," Chapter II; "Motion for Relief from Automatic Stay," Chapter XIV.*

6. Expedited Notice of Confirmation Hearing

The clerk or other court-authorized person must give at least 20 days notice of dates set by the court for filing objections to the Chapter 12 plan and for the confirmation hearing. Under Chapters 9, 11, and 13, the clerk must give at least 25 days' notice of such dates. The notice must be mailed to the debtor, the U.S. trustee, the standing trustee, all creditors, and indenture trustees. *11 USC §§1221, 1224-1225; FRBP 2002(a)(9), (k), 9034.*

7. Chapter 12 Plan of Adjustment

The requirements for filing and confirmation of a Chapter 12 plan differ from those of Chapter 13 in four main respects.

a. The Chapter 12 plan must be filed by the debtor not later than the 90th day after the petition is filed, unless the court extends the time for cause, within such period. The debtor must file any motion to extend time no later than the 90th day, showing substantial justification for any extension of time, and serve a copy of the motion on the standing trustee and any other entity required by court order or local bankruptcy rules. Service may be obtained by first-class mail or any method for service of process in federal district court. If the motion to extend time is opposed, the court must hold a hearing. *11 USC §§102(1)(A)-(B), 1221; FRBP 9007, 9013-9014.*

b. The Chapter 12 plan must be confirmed by the court not later than the 45th day after the plan is filed, unless the court extends the time for cause. *11 USC §1224.*

c. The Chapter 12 plan may modify the rights of secured creditors whose allowed claims are secured only by a lien on the debtor's principal residence. However, as under Chapter 13, the maximum term for payments under a Chapter 12 plan is five years from the date the first payment is due under a confirmed plan. *11 USC §§1222(b)(2), 1229(c).*

d. Under Chapter 12, the debtor is not required to begin making payments before the plan is confirmed by the court, unless the court or local bankruptcy rules direct otherwise. *11 USC §1226; Stahn v Haeckel, 920 F2d 555 (8th Cir 1990).*

8. **Chapter 12 Discharge Less Liberal**

Both Chapter 12 and 13 debtors may receive a discharge after completing all payments required by a confirmed plan; or a hardship discharge if the debtor's failure to complete payments was not his fault, unsecured creditors received at least what they would under Chapter 7, and further modification of a plan after confirmation is not practical. *11 USC §§1228, 1328.*

However, the Chapter 12 debtor does not receive the liberal discharge afforded the Chapter 13 debtor even if he makes all payments required by a confirmed plan. Specifically, all particular pre-petition debts which are nondischargeable (excepted from discharge) under Chapters 7 and 11 are also nondischargeable under Chapter 12. The family farmer, therefore, has just as much concern as the Chapter 7 or 11 debtor about pre-petition debts involving fraud; misrepresentation; embezzlement; willful and malicious injury to another entity or property; and debts not scheduled on the debtor's schedules of liabilities to permit a creditor without knowledge or notice of the petition to file a timely proof of claim. Unlike Chapter 13, there is very little difference between a regular and a hardship discharge to a Chapter 12 debtor. *11 USC §§103(a), 523, 1228, 1328; see "Exceptions to Discharge," Chapter III; Official Bankr Form 6 Schedules D-H.*

9. **Self-Terminating**

As presently enacted, Chapter 12 is repealed on October 1, 1998. However, all Chapter 12 cases and related proceedings pending on October 1, 1998, may be continued after October 1, 1998, as if Chapter 12 had not been repealed. *Pub L No 99-554, tit III, §302(f), 100 Stat 3124 (1986).*

10. **Standing Trustee's Greater Percentage Fee**

Under Chapter 12, the standing trustee may receove a surcharge or percentage fee greater than the amount received under Chapter 13. Under each Chapter 12 plan, the Chapter 12 standing trustee may collect a surcharge no greater than 10 per cent of payments received totalling $450,000 or less; and no more than 3 per cent of payments received totalling more than $450,000. The Chapter 12 (and 13) standing trustee may voluntarily seek less than the maximum amounts allowed for the percentage fee. However, if the maximum amount allowed for the percentage fee under Chapter 12 (or 13) exceeds the maximum annual salary and actual necessary expenses allowed for the standing trustee, he must remit the difference to the U.S. trustee. All amounts so remitted must be deposited by the U.S. trustee into the U.S. Trustee System Fund. *28 USC §586(e)(1)-(2).*

Research Guide

Anderson & Morris, *Chapter 12: Farm Reorganizations* (Shepard's/McGraw-Hill 1987)

Drake, *Bankruptcy Practice for the General Practitioner* ch 14 (Shepard's/McGraw-Hill 2d ed 1990)

Jaroslavsky, *Practical Bankruptcy Procedure* chs 2, 5, 11-13, 15, 16 (Shepard's/McGraw-Hill 1993)

Murphy, *Creditor's Rights in Bankruptcy* ch 19 (Shepard's/McGraw-Hill 2d ed 1988)

Pollard & Burton, *Guide to Effective Bankruptcy Litigation* ch 13 (Shepard's/McGraw-Hill 1988)

VII. Chapter 9—Adjustment of Debts of a Municipality

d. Fourth Duty—File List of Certain Title Holders to Real Property Subject to Special Assessments or Taxes
e. Fifth Duty—File Plan of Adjustment
f. Sixth Duty—File Disclosure Statement
g. Seventh Duty—Obtain Confirmation of Plan to Obtain Discharge

3. Procedure Three—Unsecured Creditors' Committee
11 USC §§103(e)-(f), 901, 1102-1103
4. Procedure Four—Appointment of Trustee
11 USC §§901-902, 926
FRBP 9013-9014
5. Procedure Five—Confirmation of Plan of Adjustment
11 USC §§103(e)-(f), 901, 924, 941, 943-944, 1123, 1129, 1144
FRBP 3016-3020, 9034
   a. Requirements for Confirmation
   b. Notice and Hearing on Confirmation of Plan
   c. Objection to Plan
   d. Voting on the Plan
   e. Notice of Confirmation Order
   f. Legal Effects of Confirmation
   g. Debts Not Discharged
   h. Court Retains Jurisdiction After Confirmation
   i. Appeal
   j. Revocation of Confirmation
6. Procedure Six—Dismissal
11 USC §§103(e)-(f), 109(c), 921(c), 923, 930
FRBP 1007(a), (e), 2002(f)(2), (k), 9034
   a. Mandatory Dismissal
   b. Permissive Dismissal
   c. Notice and Hearing on Motion to Dismiss
   d. Notice of Dismissal
7. Procedure Seven—Discharge
11 USC §944
FRBP 7001(4) et seq
8. Procedure Eight—Closing the Case
11 USC §§350(b), 901, 945(b)
FRBP 5010, 9013-9014

Research Guide

VII. Chapter 9—Adjustment of Debts of a Municipality

A. General Overview

Chapter 9 permits a municipality to restructure its debts over the term of a plan of adjustment. Under Chapter 9, the municipality possesses broad powers of a trustee to incur post-petition debt and to avoid certain preferential and fraudulent transfers, as well as certain liens. In several respects, Chapter 9 is a modification of a Chapter 11 reorganization. Many provisions of Chapter 11 also govern Chapter 9. However, the jurisdiction and power of the bankruptcy court is more restricted under Chapter 9. The bankruptcy court may not interfere with either the state's control over the municipality or the Chapter 9 municipal debtor's political and governmental powers or use of its property and revenues. *11 USC §§103(e)-(f), 109(c), 901, 902(5), 903-904, 926; 28 USC §§151, 157, 1334(a), (d).*

B. Preparing the Client

In addition to the general preparation required of all prospective bankruptcy debtors (*see "Preparing the Client," Chapter III*), a client who seeks to file a Chapter 9 petition should also bring the following information to the initial attorney-client interview:

1. **List, preferably in alphabetical order, of names, addresses, and respective amounts of all bond and note holders of the municipality;**
2. **Copy of the municipal charter and bylaws, if any;**
3. **Copy of any other state authorization for the municipality's existence;**
4. **List, preferably in alphabetical order, of names and addresses of all record title owners or holders of real estate against which the municipality has levied a special assessment or special tax to pay the cost of improving such real estate.**

   A special assessment or special tax is not a general property tax;
5. **List by legal description, including city, county, and state, of all real property against which the municipality has levied a special assessment or special tax to pay the cost of improving such property;**
6. **List and respective amounts of all sources of revenue for the municipality for the preceding two years; and**
7. **List of all systems or projects of the municipality primarily used or intended to be used for transportation, utility, or other services.**

C. Stages Modified Under Chapter 9

The stages common to all voluntary bankruptcy proceedings generally apply to a Chapter 9 case (*see "Nine Stages of Every Voluntary Bankruptcy Case,"*

Chapter 11). However, five of those stages are modified significantly under Chapter 9.

1. Modified Stage One—The Petition

a. Voluntary

Only a voluntary petition may be filed under Chapter 9 and only by a municipality. A municipality is a political subdivision or public agency or instrumentality of a state. Involuntary cases are not permitted under Chapter 9 for two principal reasons. First, the Tenth Amendment of the United States Constitution protects against any invasion of a state's sovereignty. Second, to permit an involuntary Chapter 9 petition would constitute an inappropriate public policy of permitting a small number of the municipality's creditors to determine the fate of the municipality whose public officials are elected to represent all the people. *11 USC §§101(40), 109(c), 303(a); S Rep No 989, 95th Cong, 2d Sess 33 (1978); Official Bankr Form 1, as modified (see "Procedure One—The Debtor," discussed below).*

A municipality may be an unincorporated tax or special assessment district that does not have its own officers or officials. In such cases, the Chapter 9 petition may be filed by any governing authority, board, or body with authority to levy taxes or assessments for the municipality. *11 USC §§101(40), 109(c), 921(a).*

b. Notice, Hearing, and Assignment of Judge

Filing a Chapter 9 petition is unlike other voluntary bankruptcy petitions in five respects.

(1) The petition does not automatically constitute an order for relief;

(2) The chief judge of the federal circuit court of appeals for the judicial district where the petition is filed, not the federal district judge, assigns the Chapter 9 case to a bankruptcy judge.

(3) Notice of the filed petition must be given to creditors and parties-in-interest, including bond and note holders, before an order for relief may be issued by the court.

(4) The bankruptcy court must hold a hearing before issuing an order for relief if any objection to the Chapter 9 petition is filed by a party-in-interest.

(5) The clerk or other court-authorized person must publish notice of the Chapter 9 petition and order for relief once each week for three consecutive weeks in at least one newspaper of general circulation in the federal judicial district where the petition is filed; and in such other newspaper with a general circulation among the municipality's bond dealers and bondholders as the court or local bankruptcy rules may require.

11 USC §§103(e), 901, 921, 923; 28 USC §157(a); FRBP 2002(f); see Local Bankruptcy Rules.

A municipality may file a Chapter 9 petition in any federal judicial district where it is located. Once a Chapter 9 petition is filed, it is referred to the chief judge of the federal circuit court of appeals for the judicial district where the petition was filed. The chief judge of the circuit court of appeals then designates a bankruptcy judge to conduct the case. *11 USC §921(b); HR Rep No 595, 95th Cong, 1st Sess 398 (1977).*

The debtor or clerk, as directed by the court, must give notice by mail of the Chapter 9 petition to all creditors, bond and note holders obtained from the mailing matrix (list of creditors) which the debtor must file by a date fixed by the court. The debtor or clerk must also publish such notice at least once each week for three consecutive weeks in at least one newspaper or other publication of general circulation published in the district where the case is pending and in such other newspaper which has a general circulation among the municipality's bond dealers and bondholders as the court or local bankruptcy rules may require. *11 USC §§923-924; FRBP 1007(a), (e); see Local Bankruptcy Rules.*

The bankruptcy court must then hold a hearing on the petition if a party-in-interest files an objection to the Chapter 9 petition. The objection does not commence an adversary proceeding and no filing fee is required. The court may, at its discretion, dismiss the petition if the court finds that the municipality did not file the petition in good faith or finds that the petition was otherwise improperly filed. *See "Procedure One—The Debtor," discussed below; 11 USC §§109(c), 921(c)-(d).*

If the bankruptcy court does not dismiss the Chapter 9 petition, the court must then issue an order for relief. The clerk or other person directed by the court must give notice of the order for relief to the debtor, U.S. trustee, all creditors and indenture trustees. Names and addresses of creditors are obtained from the debtor's mailing matrix (list of creditors) filed with the petition or by the date set by the court. Notice of the order for relief must also be published at least once a week for three consecutive weeks in at least one newspaper of general circulation in the district where the case is pending and in such other newspaper which has a general circulation among the municipality's bond dealers and bondholders as required by court order or local bankruptcy rules. *11 USC §§901, 921(d), 923-924; FRBP 1007(a), (e), 2002(f)(1).*

c. Jurisdiction of the Court

The bankruptcy court's jurisdiction is more limited in a Chapter 9 case. In all other bankruptcy cases, once the petition is filed, the bankruptcy court has exclusive jurisdiction and power over all the debtor's property and interests in property wherever such property may be located. But in a Chapter 9 case, the bankruptcy court may not interfere either with the state's authority over the municipality or with the municipality's political and governmental powers, choice of services and benefits it will provide to its inhabitants, or use and enjoyment of its income-producing property, unless the municipality consents or the Chapter 9 plan provides otherwise. However, municipal debt composition plans prescribed by state law and any judgment entered under such state law are not binding on any creditor who does not consent to such debt composition. The municipality's debt repayment is ultimately governed by a confirmed (court approved) plan of adjustment. *28 USC §§151, 1334(d); 11 USC §§903-904.*

2. Modified Stage Two—Automatic Stay

Filing a Chapter 9 petition not only operates as an automatic stay against all entities seeking to collect a pre-petition debt from the municipality or its property, but also operates as an automatic stay to protect certain officers and inhabitants of the municipality. The automatic stay of Chapter 9 prohibits all entities from engaging in two additional types of activities:

a. Commencing or continuing any type of action or proceeding against an officer or inhabitant of the municipality that seeks to enforce a claim against the debtor.

This protects the municipality by preventing a creditor from filing a lawsuit against an officer or inhabitant of the municipality to collect taxes due to the municipality; and

b. Enforcing a lien on taxes or other assessments owed to the municipality.

This protects the revenues and cash flow of the municipality. *11 USC §§103(e), 362, 901, 922; HR Rep No 595, 95th Cong, 1st Sess 398 (1977); see "Stage Two—Automatic Stay Invoked," Chapter II; "Motion for Relief from Automatic Stay," Chapter XIV.*

The automatic stay under Chapter 9 does not prohibit payment to creditors who have a lien on special or pledged revenues of the municipality. Thus, revenue bond holders whose claims are payable solely from special revenues of the municipality may continue to receive such revenues post-petition. However, creditors whose claims are solely payable from such special or pledged revenues are treated as having no recourse against the municipality. Special revenues include: (1) receipts from the ownership or operation of the debtor's projects or systems primarily used to provide transportation, utility, or other services; (2) special excise taxes imposed on particular activities or transactions; (3) incremental tax receipts from the benefited area in tax-increment financing; and (4) other revenues, receipts, and taxes levied specifically to finance the debtor's projects or systems other than general property, sales, or income taxes that are not tax-increment financing. Thus, a tax levied by the municipality to finance construction of a stadium; receipts from the municipality's operation of water, sewage, waste, or electric systems; and the municipality's regulatory fees and stamp taxes are all examples of special revenues. *11 USC §§103(e)-(f), 362, 901, 902(2), 922(d), 927; HR Rep No 1011, 100th Cong, 2d Sess 6-13 (1988); S Rep No 506, 100th Cong, 2d Sess 21 (1988).*

3. Modified Stage Three—No Bankruptcy Estate

Under other bankruptcy cases, filing a petition immediately creates a bankruptcy estate consisting of all presently owned property of the debtor wherever located and generally certain future property of the debtor. The debtor, if an individual, may remove property from the estate by claiming exemptions under federal bankruptcy exemption law; or under federal nonbankruptcy and state and local exemption laws. The remaining property comprises the bankruptcy estate. The trustee is the representative or fiduciary of the estate and of unsecured creditors who will eventually own the estate after secured creditors receive their collateral or the lesser of the value of their collateral or their allowed claim. *11 USC §§102(5), 323(a), 522(b), (d); see "Stage Three—Creation of a Bankruptcy Estate," Chapter II.*

The traditional concept of a bankruptcy estate really has little application under Chapter 9. The municipality which files a Chapter 9 petition operates as a bankruptcy trustee. Under nonbankruptcy law, the municipality and its property exist to serve the public, not the municipality. Under Chapter 9, such property remains property of the municipal debtor even after the petition is filed. But if the municipality abuses its fiduciary duty to creditors (its public) as a Chapter 9 debtor, creditors may object to the petition, file a motion to dismiss, or vote to reject the plan, including any modified plan. If the debtor has insufficient votes for confirmation of its plan, even if modified, the court must then deny confirmation and dismiss the Chapter 9 case. *11 USC §§103(e), 901, 902(1), (5), 921, 930(a)(2), (5), (b), 941-942, 1126(a), (c), 1128(b), 1129(a)(10), (b)(1)-(2); see "Procedure Seven—Confirmation of a Plan of Reorganization," Chapter IV; "Procedure Five—Confirmation of a Plan of Adjustment," discussed below.*

4. Modified Stage Four—No Meeting of Creditors

Under Chapter 9, no Meeting of Creditors is required by the Code. However, under FRBP 2004, if a party-in-interest files a motion for Rule 2004 examination, the court may order the examination of any entity, including examination of the municipality through an officer or other public official. The motion for Rule 2004 examination must be served on the appropriate officer or agent of the municipality, all committee(s), and any trustee in the same manner provided for services of a summons and complaint in federal district court. The motion does not commence an adversary complaint and no filing fee is required. *11 USC §§103(e)-(f), 901; FRBP 2003-2004, 9013-9014; see "Meeting of Creditors" and "Rule 2004 Examination," Chapter XIV.*

5. Modified Stage Five—Discharge

The municipality receives a discharge of pre-petition debts when the Chapter 9 plan is confirmed by the court and the municipality deposits sufficient legal consideration or security with a court-appointed disbursing agent sufficient to make all payments required by the plan. The municipality will be discharged of all pre-petition debts unless: (a) the plan or court order excepts a debt from discharge; or (b) an entity who is owed a pre-petition debt did not have notice or actual knowledge of the Chapter 9 case before the plan was confirmed. *11 USC §944(b)-(c); FRBP 3020; Official Bankr Forms 15, 18.*

D. Procedures Under Chapter 9

There are eight procedures in a Chapter 9 case. Procedures one through three, five, seven, and eight occur in all successful Chapter 9 cases. Procedures four and six may occur in a Chapter 9 case that is not successfully completed.

1. Procedure One—The Debtor

Only a municipality which files a petition properly and in good faith may be a Chapter 9 debtor.

a. Requirements to File Chapter 9

To file a Chapter 9 petition, a municipality must sign a verified petition with a statement which alleges that the municipality meets four specific requirements to be a Chapter 9 debtor. The petition and statement must assert that:

(1) **The municipality is specifically authorized to file a Chapter 9 petition by state law or by a governmental officer or organization empowered by state law to authorize the municipality to file a petition. The municipality must be so authorized by name or in its capacity as a municipality.**

Copies of all official empowering documents should be attached to the petition;

(2) **The municipality is insolvent and thus not paying its undisputed debts as they become due or is unable to pay such debts as they become due;**

(3) **The municipality wishes to effect (file and implement) a plan of adjustment to restructure its debts; and**

(4) **At least one of the following:**

(a) The municipality obtained an agreement from creditors who hold at least a majority in dollar amount of the claims of each class which the municipality intends to impair under a plan. Thus, the municipality must have negotiated with creditors and worked out a pre-petition agreement to file the Chapter 9 petition and the plan. Creditors from each impaired class under the plan who hold at least a majority in amount of the claims of such class must have consented to this agreement. The municipality also must have disclosed adequate information to such creditors to enable them to make an informed judgment whether the proposed plan will be beneficial or detrimental to their interests; or

(b) The municipality could not obtain the agreement described above, but it negotiated in good faith with its creditors and tried but failed to obtain the required agreement from such creditors with impaired claims; or

(c) The municipality was unable to negotiate with creditors as described, above, because the municipality in good faith believed negotiations would have been impractical. The municipality should state sufficient facts showing why such negotiations were impractical; or

(d) The municipality reasonably believes a creditor will attempt to obtain a preferential transfer that would be avoidable under bankruptcy law. *11 USC §§101(32), 109(c), 901(a), 1125; Official Bankr Form 1; see "Avoidable Preferential Transfers," Chapter XII.*

The municipality may file a petition in any federal judicial district in which the municipality is located. But filing a Chapter 9 petition does not automatically constitute an order for relief. After notice of the petition is published in a newspaper of general circulation, any party-in-interest (creditor, U.S. trustee, bondholder) may file an objection. The objection does not commence an adversary proceeding and no filing fee is required. A copy of the objection must be served on the municipality by first-class mail or any other method allowed for service of a summons and complaint on a municipality in federal district court. The court must then hold a hearing on the objection. Notice of the hearing date must be published or otherwise given to creditors and bondholders as directed by court order or local bankruptcy rules. The court may dismiss the petition if it determines that the municipality did not file the petition in good faith or that the debtor otherwise failed to meet the above requirements for filing under Chapter 9. If the court finds that the petition was filed in good faith and meets the requirements of the Bankruptcy Code, the court must enter an order for relief adjudicating the municipality to be a Chapter 9 debtor. *See "Modified Stage One—The Petition," discussed above.*

Appeal of a bankruptcy court order for relief will not affect continuation of the Chapter 9 case. The court may neither delay nor order a stay of any proceeding in the case. Reversal of the bankruptcy court's order on appeal will not affect any court-authorized post-petition debt of the municipality secured by a lien on the debtor's property or a post-petition claim granted a super priority administrative claim status. *See Chapter VIII; 11 USC §§103(e)-(f), 109(c), 921(e), 923; FRBP 2002(f)(1), 9007, 9014.*

b. Powers of the Chapter 9 Debtor

The Chapter 9 debtor, like the Chapter 11 DIP, functions as both debtor and trustee representing the interests of the municipality and creditors. The municipality thus possesses the super-avoiding powers of a trustee to avoid certain fraudulent and preferential transfers, setoffs, and liens. *11 USC §§103(e)-(f), 544-550, 901, 902(1)(5), 926; see Chapter XII.*

If the municipality refuses to file an action to recover a preferential or fraudulent transfer of property, or to avoid certain setoffs or statutory or unperfected liens avoidable under bankruptcy law, a creditor may file a motion for appointment of a trustee to file such adversary complaints in the bankruptcy court. However, under Chapter 9, a transfer of property by the municipality to or for the benefit of a bond or note holder in payment of such bond or note is not an avoidable preferential transfer, even if the transfer meets all the requirements of an otherwise avoidable preferential transfer under bankruptcy law. The incidence of preferential treatment to these creditors by a municipality is not likely to be great. However, if the municipality pays such bond or note holders with an actual intent to delay, hinder, or defraud other creditors, the payments may be recovered as fraudulent transfers by a court-appointed trustee. *11 USC §926(a)-(b), S Rep No 506, 100th Cong, 2d Sess 22 (1988); see "Avoidable Preferential Transfers," and "Avoidable Fraudulent Transfers or Obligations," Chapter XII.*

2. Procedure Two—Debtor's Duties

The municipality must perform the following seven duties under Chapter 9.

a. First Duty—File Petition and Pay Filing Fee

The municipality must file a Chapter 9 petition properly and in good faith and pay a $300 filing fee. *See "Procedure One—The Debtor," discussed, above; 11 USC §§109(c), 921(c); 28 USC §1930(a)(2); see "Requirements to File Chapter 9," discussed above.*

b. Second Duty—File List of Creditors and Special Tax Papers

(1) When to File and Contents

A Chapter 9 debtor does not have to file the schedules of assets and liabilities, statement of financial affairs, and other documents usually filed by debtors in other bankruptcy cases. However, the municipality must file a list of creditors (mailing matrix) containing the names, preferably in alphabetical order, addresses, and respective claims of each creditor. The list or mailing matrix must be filed by the date fixed by the court. It is from the list of creditors that the required notices to creditors of the Chapter 9 petition and order for relief may properly be sent. *11 USC §§901, 923-924; FRBP 1007(a)-(b), (e).*

(2) Effect of Filing List of Creditors

A creditor whose name and claim appears on the list of creditors (mailing matrix) does not have to file a proof of claim under Chapter 9 with three exceptions. First, if the claim is listed under the mailing matrix as disputed, contingent, or unliquidated, the creditor must file a timely proof of claim. Second, if the creditor disputes the amount of its claim listed under the list of creditors, the creditor should file a proof of claim timely or it is bound by the amount indicated under the list of creditors. Third, if the creditor is not included under the debtor's list of creditors, such creditor must file a timely proof of claim. *11 USC §§501, 901, 924-925; see "File Proof of Claim," Chapter XIV.*

As in Chapter 11 cases, any required proof of claim must be filed in a Chapter 9 case by the date set by the court. Such date should be included in the notice of order for relief mailed to creditors by the debtor or clerk of the court. If a proof of claim is required but not timely filed, the creditor will not be allowed to vote on the Chapter 9 plan and will not share in any distribution under the plan (no payment of its claims), even though the creditor's claim may be discharged. *11 USC §§103(e)-(f), 501-502, 901, 923, 925, 944(a), (c)(2); FRBP 3003(c)(2)-(3).*

If a required proof of claim is timely filed, the amount listed under the proof of claim controls and supersedes any amount listed by the municipality under the list of creditors. The municipality must then file an objection to allowance of claim if it wishes to dispute the creditor's claim. The municipality must serve a copy of the objection on the creditor with notice of the hearing date set by the court at least 30 days before such hearing. The objection and notice may be served by first-class mail or personally delivered to the creditor by a disinterested person at least 18 years old in the same manner provided for service of a summons and complaint in federal district court. The objection does not commence an adversary complaint and no filing fee is required. *FRBP 3003(c)(4), 3007, 7004, 9014; see "File Proof of Claim," Chapter XIV.*

c. Third Duty—File List of 20 Largest Unsecured Creditors

In addition to the list of creditors, the municipality, like the Chapter 11 debtor, must file a list containing the names, preferably in alphabetical order, addresses, and respective claims of the 20 unsecured creditors who hold the largest amount of unsecured claims against the municipality. Insiders (elected officials or their relatives) of the debtor are excluded from the list. This list of 20 largest unsecured creditors must be filed with the Chapter 9 petition, unless the court or local bankruptcy rules permit otherwise. *11 USC §101(31); FRBP 1007(d); Official Bankr Form 4.*

d. Fourth Duty—File List of Certain Title Holders to Real Property Subject to Special Assessments or Taxes

If the Chapter 9 plan requires a revision of assessments that adversely changes the proportion of special assessments or special taxes to be assessed against real property from the proportion in effect on the date the petition was filed, the municipality must also file a list of record title holders. This list must include the names, preferably in alphabetical order, and addresses of each legal or equitable title holder to real property adversely affected by the proposed assessments or taxes. These special tax payers, together with other parties-in-interest, have the right to object to confirmation of a Chapter 9 plan. The list of record title holders also provides the means for mailing required notices under Chapter 9. *11 USC §§901, 902(4), 923, 943(a), 1128; FRBP 1007(e); see "Procedure Five—Confirmation of Plan of Adjustment," discussed below.*

e. Fifth Duty—File Plan of Adjustment

The municipality must file a Chapter 9 plan of adjustment. The plan must be filed with the petition or by the date fixed by the court. The municipality may modify its plan at any time before it is confirmed by the court. The modified plan then becomes the Chapter 9 plan which must meet all requirements of Chapter 9 for confirmation. *11 USC §§941-943; see "Procedure Five—Confirmation of Plan of Adjustment," discussed below.*

f. Sixth Duty—File Disclosure Statement

The Chapter 9 debtor must file a disclosure statement and obtain court approval of the statement before the municipality may solicit post-petition votes for its plan. If the municipality does not intend to solicit votes of acceptance for the plan post-petition, a disclosure statement is not required. *11 USC §§901, 1125(a)-(b), 1126(a)-(c), (e)-(g).*

The same rules and regulations governing the filing, notice of hearing, adequate information, and notice of approval of a Chapter 11 disclosure statement apply equally to a Chapter 9 disclosure statement. *See "Tenth Duty as Debtor—File and Obtain Approval of Disclosure Statement," Chapter IV, 11 USC §§901, 1125, 1126(a)-(c), (e)-(g); FRBP 3016, 3017(a)-(d).*

g. Seventh Duty—Obtain Confirmation of Plan to Obtain Discharge

Confirmation of a Chapter 9 plan and deposit of sufficient, binding, legal consideration or security with a court-appointed disbursing agent to make payments under the plan will also discharge the municipality of pre-petition debts unless: (1) the plan or confirmation order excepts a debt from discharge; or (2) an entity to whom a pre-petition debt is owed did not have notice or actual knowledge of the Chapter 9 case before the court confirmed the plan. The same rules and procedures governing confirmation of a Chapter 11 plan apply to confirmation of a Chapter 9 plan, unless modified by court order or local bankruptcy rules. *See "Procedure Seven—Confirmation of a Plan of Reorganization," Chapter IV; 11 USC §§524(a)(1)-(2), 901, 944(b)-(c); FRBP 3017-3020.*

3. Procedure Three—Unsecured Creditors' Committee

Chapter 9 also provides for appointment by the U.S. trustee of an unsecured creditors' committee consisting generally of seven unsecured creditors who hold the largest unsecured claims against the municipality and who are willing to serve on the committee. The same rules and regulations governing the appointment and duties of a Chapter 11 unsecured creditors' committee apply equally to a Chapter 9 unsecured creditors' committee. *See "Procedure Three—Selection of Unsecured Creditors' Committee," Chapter IV. 11 USC §§901, 1102-1103; FRBP 2007.*

4. Procedure Four—Appointment of Trustee:

a. Grounds for Appointment of a Trustee

The only ground for appointment of a trustee in a Chapter 9 case is the debtor's failure to exercise its super-avoiding powers. A Chapter 9 debtor is empowered to avoid preferential and fraudulent transfers, unauthorized post-petition transfers, and certain setoffs and statutory and unperfected liens avoidable under bankruptcy law. If the municipality fails to exercise any of such powers, a creditor or the committee may file a motion for appointment of a trustee. The creditor or committee must serve a copy of the motion on the debtor by first-class mail or any other manner for service of a summons and complaint in federal district court. The motion does not commence an adversary complaint and no filing fee is required. *11 USC §§901, 902(5), 926; FRBP 9013-9014; see Chapter XII.*

b. Function and Effect of Appointment of a Trustee

The sole function of a Chapter 9 trustee is to file any available adversary complaints which the municipality failed or refused to file to avoid and recover preferential or fraudulent transfers, unauthorized post-petition transfers, or certain setoffs or unperfected or statutory liens. Appointment of a Chapter 9 trustee does not affect the municipality's exclusive right to file a Chapter 9 plan for confirmation by the court. *11 USC §§901, 926, 941; FRBP 7001(1); see Chapter XII.*

5. Procedure Five—Confirmation of Plan of Adjustment

Only the municipality may file a Chapter 9 plan of adjustment, even if a trustee is appointed. *11 USC §§901, 926, 941; HR Rep No 595, 95th Cong, 1st Sess 399 (1977).*

a. Requirements for Confirmation

Many requirements for confirmation of a Chapter 11 plan must also be met by the municipality. In addition, the municipality must meet specific requirements unique to Chapter 9.

(1) Common Provisions Required of Chapter 9 and 11 Plans

The court must confirm a Chapter 9 plan that meets the following twelve requirements also required of a Chapter 11 plan.

(a) The plan designates classes of claims where all members of a class have common legal rights and interests. First priority (administrative) claims are not classified as a class of creditors. Instead, they are designated as first priority claims and paid cash in full on the effective date of the plan, unless the claimholder agrees otherwise. First priority administrative expenses are the only priority claims allowed under Chapter 9. *See "Requirements for Confirmation of a Chapter 11 Plan," Chapter IV; 11 USC §§103(e), 503, 507(a)(1), 901, 943(a)(5).*

(b) The plan designates which classes of creditors are not impaired.

(c) The plan describes the treatment of any class of impaired creditors under the plan.

(d) The plan provides for the same treatment (percentage of payment) for each member of the same class of creditors, unless the particular class member agrees to less favorable treatment.

(e) The plan provides adequate means for its implementation. This may include provision(s) that the municipality retain, transfer, or sell some or all of its property; distribute some or all of its property in satisfaction of any lien;

extend the maturity date of a debt; change (reduce) the interest rate of a debt; amend the debtor's charter; or issue bonds or other notes in payment of a debt to the extent allowed under applicable nonbankruptcy law or by its charter.

(f) The municipality has complied with all applicable provisions of the Bankruptcy Code relevant to filing the petition, performing its duties as a debtor, and proposing the plan.

(g) The plan has been proposed in good faith and not by any means forbidden by law, including applicable bankruptcy and nonbankruptcy law.

(h) The plan states, in good faith, that any rate change proposed by the plan for the debtor's services has been approved by, or is conditioned upon obtaining approval of, any governmental (federal or state) regulatory commission with power to regulate such rates after the plan is confirmed.

(i) The plan provides that each holder of a first priority administrative claim will receive, on the effective date of the plan, cash for the amount of his claim allowed by the court, unless such creditor agrees otherwise.

(j) The plan states that all amounts to be paid by the debtor or any other person for services or expenses incurred in the case or related to the plan have been disclosed and are reasonable.

(k) The plan states that if there are any impaired classes under the plan, at least one class of impaired creditors has voted to accept the Plan.

(l) The plan states that it does not discriminate unfairly and is "fair and equitable" to each class of impaired creditors who rejected the plan. *11 USC §§901, 943(b)(1)-(6), 1123(a)(1)-(5), 1129(a)(2)-(3), (6), (8), (10), (b)(1)-(2)(A)-(B); see "Requirements for Confirmation of a Chapter 11 Plan," Chapter IV.*

(i) Fair and Equitable to Secured Creditors

The term "fair and equitable" requires that the plan provide that each member of a class of impaired, secured creditors who rejected the plan receive property (cash or otherwise) equal to the allowed amount of his secured claim (lesser of the value of collateral or amount subject to a setoff and the allowed amount of the claim), determined as of the effective date of the plan. This date may be the confirmation date, the date the confirmation order is entered or becomes final, or any other date stated in the plan and allowed by the court or local bankruptcy rules. The "effective date of the plan" valuation recognizes the time value or deferred use of money and contemplates a "present value analysis." The court should discount the value of any property to be distributed under the plan in the future (face future value) to allow for inflation and deferred use and enjoyment of such property. This discounted value is the present value of property. The discounted valuation may be avoided if the plan proposes a sufficient interest rate for deferred distribution of property. *11 USC §§901, 1129(b)(1)-(2)(A); HR Rep No 595, 95th Cong, 1st Sess 413-18 (1977).*

The secured creditor may receive the present value of the allowed amount of his secured claim in one of three ways. First, the plan may propose that the creditor retain its lien on the collateral and receive deferred cash payments equal to the value of the collateral over the term of the plan, plus sufficient rate of interest. Second, and alternatively, the plan may propose for sale of the collateral free and clear of liens with such liens attaching to the proceeds. The plan may then propose payment of the proceeds at once or in deferred cash payments with sufficient interest to give the creditor his present-value equivalent and compensate him for any deferred right to the use and benefit of the property. Or third, the plan may propose to give the secured creditor the "indubitable equivalent" of his allowed secured claim by receipt of notes, bonds, or other property. This latter method will almost always require a valuation of the municipality's cash flow, revenues, and asset structure. *11 USC §1129(b); S Rep No 989, 95th Cong, 2d Sess 127-28 (1978).*

(ii) Fair and Equitable to Unsecured Creditors

The term "fair and equitable" also requires the plan to provide that each member of a class of impaired, unsecured creditors who rejected the plan either receive property equal to the full amount of his unsecured claim allowed by the court or receive at least the amount such unsecured creditor would receive under Chapter 7, but then no class of creditors whose legal rights are junior to such unsecured creditor may receive or retain any property under the plan. Property to be distributed to unsecured creditors under the plan must also be valued as of the effective date of the plan (present value) and may be cash or otherwise distributed in deferred payments over the term of the plan. Thus, if unsecured creditors will not be paid the full amount of their allowed unsecured claims, the plan may be crammed down such dissenting creditors, but junior classes should not receive or retain any property under the plan. This is known as the absolute priority rule embodied in the fair-and-equitable requirement for confirmation. *11 USC §§901, 1129(b)(1)-(2)(B); 124 Cong Rec H11,103 (daily ed Sept 28, 1978), S 17,420 (daily ed Oct 6, 1978).*

(2) Required Provisions of Chapter 9 Plan Only

In addition to the twelve common requirements for confirmation of Chapter 9 and 11 plans, the Chapter 9 plan must meet three requirements unique to a municipal debtor. The plan must:

(a) Meet all requirements of Chapter 9;

(b) Provide that any regulatory or electoral approval required under nonbankruptcy law to implement any provision of the plan has been obtained; or that such provision is conditioned upon the municipality obtaining the necessary approval; and

(c) Be in the best interests of creditors and be feasible. The *best interests of creditors test* does not mean liquidation value. The test is intended to provide more of a return to creditors than liquidation value even if the municipality's assets could be liquidated like a Chapter 11 debtor. Under a Chapter 9 plan, creditors should be provided the "going concern value" of their claims. This value generally requires a comparison of the municipality's revenues and expenditures. In addition, the municipality's taxing power and the extent to which any tax increases may be necessary and feasible should also be considered. *11 USC §943(b)(2), (6)-(7); S Rep No 989, 95th Cong, 1st Sess 399-400 (1977).*

(3) Common Provisions Permitted Under Chapter 9 and 11 Plans

As under Chapter 11, a Chapter 9 plan may include any other provision which is not prohibited by law, including: (a) impairing claims; (b) settlement or adjustment of claims; (c) sale of all or substantially all of the municipality's property;

or (d) the assumption, rejection, or assignment by the municipality of any executory contract or unexpired lease which has not previously been rejected. However, a lease to a municipality which may be terminated if the municipality fails to appropriate rent is not, solely by such terms, regarded as an executory contract or unexpired lease for purposes of assumption, rejection, or assignment under bankruptcy law. *11 USC §§103(e)-(f), 365, 901, 929, 1123(b); see "Assumption or Rejection of Executory Contracts and Unexpired Leases," Chapter XIV.*

b. Notice and Hearing on Confirmation of Plan

The court must hold a hearing on confirmation of a Chapter 9 plan after the municipality has obtained court approval of a disclosure statement, and all parties-in-interest have received notice of the confirmation hearing and had an opportunity to vote and to object to the plan. The debtor, clerk, or other court-authorized person must give such notice at least 25 days before the confirmation hearing, by mail or publication, to the debtor, any Chapter 9 trustee, all committee(s), indenture trustees, creditors, bond and note holders, and special tax payers. The notice must include: (1) the date fixed by the court to file objections; (2) the date fixed by the court to file votes on the plan; (3) a ballot for voting and the entity authorized by the court to receive, tally, and file the votes; (4) the date set for the confirmation hearing; (5) copies of the disclosure statement and Chapter 9 plan or court-approved summary of the plan; (6) copies of all orders relating to the disclosure statement and plan; and (7) all other matters contained under such notice in a Chapter 11 case. *See "Notice of Approval of Disclosure Statement," Chapter IV. 11 USC §§103(e)-(f), 901, 943, 1124-1125, 1128; FRBP 2002(b), (i), (l), 3017(d), 3020(b)(2).*

c. Objection to Plan

Any party-in-interest, including a special tax payer, may file an objection to confirmation of the Chapter 9 plan by the date set by the court indicated in the notice of confirmation hearing. A *special tax payer* is a record title holder to real property against which a special assessment or special tax has been levied. Proceeds from these special assessments or taxes constitute the sole source for payment of a bond, note, or other obligation issued by the municipality to pay the costs of improving such real property. The objecting party must file an objection, stating the grounds, and serve a copy of the objection by first-class mail or personal delivery by a disinterested person at least 18 years old on the municipality's officer authorized by state law to receive service of process. A copy of the objection should be mailed to any trustee, all committee(s), and to any other entity required by court order or local bankruptcy rules. An objection does not commence an adversary complaint and no filing fee is required. The court must hold a hearing on any objection which may be combined with the confirmation hearing. *11 USC §§102(1)(A)-(B), 103(e)-(f), 901, 902(3)(4), 943(a), 1129; FRBP 2002(b), 3020(b), 9014.*

d. Voting on the Plan

(1) Who May Vote

As in Chapter 11, any creditor with an allowed claim against the debtor may vote to accept or reject the plan. Ballots for voting should be included with the notice of confirmation hearing. A creditor who voted pre-petition to accept or reject the plan is bound by his vote unless: (a) the municipality failed to disclose adequate information to such creditor in violation of any governing nonbankruptcy law or the disclosure statement requirements of bankruptcy law; (b) the Chapter 9 plan was not transmitted to substantially all creditors of the same class; or (c) creditors were provided an unreasonably short time to vote pre-petition. The creditor who wishes to change his pre-petition vote must file a motion to change vote by the original date set by the court to vote indicated in the notice of confirmation hearing. The creditor must state the grounds for such motion and serve a copy of the motion on the debtor, any trustee, and all committee(s) by first-class mail or any other manner allowed for service of process allowed under the Federal Rules of Civil Procedure. A hearing will then be held, unless local bankruptcy rules permit otherwise. The motion does not commence an adversary complaint and no filing fee is required. *11 USC §§103(e)-(f), 102(1)(A)-(B), 901, 1125-1126; FRBP 3017(d), 3018, 9013-9014; Official Bankr Form 14; see "Tenth Duty as Debtor—File and Obtain Approval of Disclosure Statement," Chapter IV.*

(2) Who May Not Vote

The rules governing which classes of creditors are deemed to have accepted or rejected a plan without voting are the same for Chapters 9 and 11. A class of creditors whose pre-petition legal rights are unchanged or whose allowed pre- and post-petition claims are paid in full on the effective date of the plan are unimpaired and conclusively deemed to have accepted the plan. A class of creditors who will not receive anything under the plan in payment of pre-petition claims is deemed to have rejected the plan. Neither of these classes should receive a ballot. *11 USC §§901, 1124, 1126(f)-(g); see "Procedure Seven—Confirmation of a Plan of Reorganization," and "Impaired Classes of Creditors," and "Impaired Classes of Equity Security Holders," Chapter IV; Official Bankr Form 14.*

(3) Modification of a Plan After Votes Are Cast

The municipality may modify its plan before confirmation even after creditors have voted. The modified plan becomes the plan if the municipality has met all requirements for confirmation, including disclosure of adequate information about the modified plan. The same rules governing modification of a Chapter 11 plan apply to modification of a Chapter 9 plan. The municipality must serve a copy of the modified plan on any trustee and all committee(s). But unless the court orders otherwise, the municipality does not have to submit the modified plan to creditors who voted before the modification if their claims are not adversely affected by the modifications. Such creditors are bound by their original votes unless the court allows them to change their votes. *11 USC §§901, 942, 1125, 1127(d); FRBP 3018(a), 3019; see "Modification of a Plan of Reorganization," Chapter IV.*

(4) Special Tax Payers

Special tax payers are not formally allowed to vote on a Chapter 9 plan. The Code allows Chapter 9 creditors whose claims are allowed by the court to vote. A special tax payer does not have a pre-petition claim (right to payment) against the municipality simply because he is a special tax payer. Even a special tax payer adversely affected by a proposed increase in special assessments or taxes under a plan does not have a post-petition claim against the debtor solely because of the proposed increases. Thus, such entity is not regarded as creditor with an allowed claim under bankruptcy law and is not allowed to vote for or against a plan. However, a special tax payer may clearly file an objection to confirmation of a Chapter 9 plan. And an objection, by its nature, is a "vote" to reject the plan. The objection may be heard by the court at the confirmation or other hearing. *11 USC §§101(5), (10), 103(e), 901, 902(2), (4), 943(a), 1126(a).*

e. Notice of Confirmation Order

The clerk or other court-authorized person must promptly mail notice of the confirmation order to the debtor, any Chapter 9 trustee, all committee(s), creditors, bond and note holders, and special tax payers. The court may order notice by publication if notice by mail is impractical or insufficient. *FRBP 1007(e), 2002(f)(7), (i), (l), 3020(c), 9007-9008; Official Bankr Forms 15, 18; see Local Bankr Rules.*

f. Legal Effects of Confirmation

A confirmed Chapter 9 plan has two legal effects.

It binds the municipality and all creditors to its terms; and it enables the municipality to receive a discharge.

(1) Binding Effect

Confirmation of a Chapter 9 plan binds the debtor and all creditors to the terms of the plan. It does not matter whether a creditor accepted or rejected the plan, filed a proof of claim, or had its claim allowed or disallowed by the court. The provisions of a confirmed plan control even if a creditor is to receive nothing under the plan. *11 USC §944(a).*

(2) Discharge of Debtor

The municipality is discharged of all pre-petition debts when three events concur:

(a) The Chapter 9 plan is confirmed by the court;

(b) The municipality has deposited any legal consideration to be distributed under the plan with a court-appointed disbursing agent. This legal consideration can be cash, bonds, or notes issued by the debtor, or any other property which the court approves; and

(c) The court has determined that such legal consideration is a valid, binding obligation of the municipality with valid provisions for its payment. *11 USC §944(b).*

g. Debts Not Discharged

The municipality will not receive a discharge of two types of debts.

(1) Any debt excepted from discharge by the confirmed plan or confirmation order.

(2) Any debt owed to any entity who had neither notice nor actual knowledge of the Chapter 9 case before the court confirmed the plan.

This exception to discharge may be avoided if the municipality files a complete list of creditors by the date fixed by the court. *11 USC §944(c); FRBP 1007(a), (e); Official Bankr Form 18.*

h. Court Retains Jurisdiction After Confirmation

The bankruptcy court retains jurisdiction over a Chapter 9 case after confirmation until the plan has been successfully implemented, unless the confirmation order indicates otherwise. The court may issue any order required for consummation of the plan, including an order directing the debtor or any other entity to deliver necessary property or documents or to perform any other act. If an entity receives such post-confirmation order and does not perform as directed, the court may prohibit the disobeying party from receiving any distribution under the plan or impose other sanctions. *11 USC §§103(e)-(f), 105(a), 901, 945, 1142(b), 1143; FRBP 3020(d).*

i. Appeal

An order confirming a Chapter 9 plan may be appealed by a party-in-interest, including a special tax payer. The rules governing notice of appeal of other bankruptcy court orders also govern appeal of an order confirming a Chapter 9 plan. *See "Appeal of Bankruptcy Court Order," Chapter IX; 11 USC §§901, 943(a), 1126(a), 1128; 28 USC §158(a)-(b); FRBP 2002(b), (i), (l), 3017(d), 8001 et seq; Official Bankr Form 17.*

j. Revocation of Confirmation

(1) Who May Seek Revocation

Any party-in-interest (creditor, trustee, special tax paper) may file an adversary complaint to revoke an order confirming a Chapter 9 plan. Revocation of the confirmation order necessarily revokes the debtor's discharge. The rules and regulations governing revocation of a Chapter 11 confirmation order apply to a Chapter 9 case. *See "Revocation of Confirmation and Discharge," Chapter IV; 11 USC §§901, 1144; FRBP 7001(4)-(5) et seq.*

(2) When Revocation Must Occur

A party-in-interest seeking revocation must file an adversary complaint before 180 days after the date the confirmation order is entered and pay a $120 filing fee. If a trustee files the complaint, the $120 fee is only payable from any bankruptcy estate that may exist. The only ground for revocation is that the municipality used fraud to obtain the confirmation order and the plaintiff had no knowledge of the alleged fraud until after the plan was confirmed. The plaintiff must serve a copy of the adversary complaint with a summons on the municipality by first-class mail, personal delivery by a disinterested person at least 18 years old, or by any other manner allowed for service of process in federal district court, by serving any officer or agent of the debtor authorized by applicable nonbankruptcy law to receive service of process. The plaintiff should also mail or personally deliver a copy of the adversary complaint to any trustee and to all committee(s). *11 USC §§901, 1144; FRBP 7001(4)-(5), 7004 et seq; Official Bankr Form 16C; Procedural Bankr Form B 250A, B, C.*

(3) Notice and Hearing

The court must hold a trial (hearing) on the adversary complaint to revoke a confirmation order. The clerk, debtor, or other court-authorized person must give notice of the hearing date by first-class mail or publication to all parties-in-interest required by the court or local bankruptcy rules. If the plaintiff prevails and proves fraud, the court must then: (a) revoke the confirmation order, (b) revoke the municipality's discharge, and (c) issue any other order necessary to protect any entity who acquired rights in good-faith reliance on the confirmation order. After the revocation order becomes final, the clerk must promptly give notice of the court's revocation of the confirmation order and debtor's discharge. Such notice must be given by mail or publication to the debtor, committee(s), all creditors, bondholders, indenture trustees, and all other parties-in-interest required by the court or local bankruptcy rules. *11 USC §§102(1), 103(e)-(f), 901, 1144; FRBP 2002(f)(6), (i), (l), 4006, 9007-9008.*

6. Procedure Six—Dismissal

A Chapter 9 case cannot be converted to another chapter, because Chapter 9 is the only chapter dealing with adjustment of a municipality's debts. However, a Chapter 9 case can be dismissed. Any party-in-interest, including a creditor, any trustee, the unsecured creditors' committee, the U.S. trustee, the debtor, and presumably a special tax payer affected by the plan, may file a motion to dismiss. A copy of the motion must be served on the debtor, any trustee, all committee(s), and on any other entity required by court order or local bankruptcy rules. Service may be obtained by first-class mail, personal delivery by a disinterested person at least 18 years old, or by any other method allowed for service of process in federal district court. The motion does not commence an adversary proceeding and no filing fee is required. *11 USC §§103(e)-(f), 109(c), 901, 930; FRBP 1017(d), 7004, 9013-9014.*

a. Mandatory Dismissal

The court must dismiss a Chapter 9 case if it refuses to confirm all plan(s) proposed by the municipality, including any modified plan(s). The Code does not expressly provide for (mandatory) dismissal if the municipality files a motion to dismiss. However, Chapter 9 is entirely voluntary. The municipality may be a debtor only under Chapter 9, and only the municipality may file a Chapter 9 plan. It is unlikely, therefore, that the court would refuse a municipality's motion to dismiss, thereby forcing it to remain in Chapter 9 involuntarily. *11 USC §§103(e)-(f), 109, 901, 930(b), 941-942.*

b. Permissive Dismissal

The court may, in its discretion, dismiss a Chapter 9 case if the party seeking dismissal proves one or more of the following eight grounds:

(1) **The municipality failed to file its petition in good faith;**

(2) **The Chapter 9 petition failed to comply with the requirements of the Code** (*see* "Procedure One—The Debtor," discussed above);

(3) **The municipality failed to prosecute its Chapter 9 case.** *Want of prosecution* may include the debtor's failure to file a list of creditors or other documents by the date fixed by the court, failure to propose a plan in good faith, or failure to cooperate or to provide sufficient information to the unsecured creditors' committee to enable the committee to perform its duties or to enable a trustee to recover a preferential or fraudulent transfer;

(4) **The municipality has caused unreasonable delay that is prejudicial to creditors.**

This delay could take many forms: the municipality's refusal to provide a list of creditors or other documents, refusal to cooperate with any appointed committee, or refusal to propose a plan in good faith;

(5) **The municipality failed to propose and file a plan by the date set by the court, including any extension(s) of time allowed by the court.**

Only the debtor may file a Chapter 9 plan. The Code does not provide a time limit for the debtor to file its plan, but the court or local bankruptcy rules may set a date for filing;

(6) **The Chapter 9 plan has not been accepted by the date fixed by the court, including any extension(s) of time allowed by the court;**

(7) **The court denied confirmation of the municipality's Chapter 9 plan because it failed to meet the requirements of Chapter 9, and the court denied any additional time for the municipality to modify its plan or to file another plan; or**

(8) **The court retained jurisdiction over the case after the plan was confirmed and the municipality committed a material default of a term in the confirmed plan or a condition specified in the confirmed plan occurred requiring termination of the plan.** *11 USC §§921(c), 930(a), 941-942; FRBP 2002(b), 3016-3017.*

c. Notice and Hearing on Motion to Dismiss

The court must hold a hearing on any motion to dismiss a Chapter 9 case. The clerk or other court-authorized person must give notice of the hearing date. Such notice must be given by mail or publication to the debtor, any trustee, all committee(s), creditors, bond and note holders, indenture trustees, and special tax payers. The clerk obtains the names and addresses of such entities from the debtor's list of creditors and list of record title holders filed with the court. *11 USC §§102(1)(A)-(B), 103(e)-(f), 924, 930, 943(a); FRBP 1007(a), (d)-(e), 1017(a), 9007-9008.*

d. Notice of Dismissal

If the court dismisses the Chapter 9 case, the clerk, debtor, or other court-appointed person must give notice of the dismissal order. Such notice must be promptly mailed to the debtor, any Chapter 9 trustee, all committee(s), creditors, bond and note holders, and special tax payers whose names and addresses have been filed with the clerk. Notice must also be published by the clerk, debtor, or other court-authorized person at least once a week for three successive weeks in at least one newspaper of general circulation in the district where the Chapter 9 petition was filed and in such other newspaper of general circulation among the debtor's bond dealers and bondholders as required by the court or local bankruptcy rules. *11 USC §§923-924; FRBP 1007(a), (e), 2002(f)(2), (i), (l).*

7. Procedure Seven—Discharge

As stated, the municipality receives a discharge of its pre-petition debts when a plan is confirmed and the municipality deposits valid, binding security or legal consideration to be distributed under the plan with a disbursing agent appointed by the court. The legal consideration must be sufficient to implement the plan. *11 USC §944(b)-(c).*

The municipality does not receive a discharge of any debt excepted from discharge by the confirmed plan or the confirmation order or of any debt owed to a creditor who did not have notice or actual knowledge of the Chapter 9 case before the plan was confirmed. *11 USC §944(c).*

The clerk or other court-authorized person must promptly give notice of entry of the confirmation order and debtor's discharge by mail or publication to the debtor, any trustee, all committee(s), creditors, bond holders, special taxpayers, and any other entity required by court order or local bankruptcy rules. *FRBP 2002(f)(7), (i), (l), 3020(c); Official Bankr Form 18.*

8. Procedure Eight—Closing the Case

The court must close a Chapter 9 case after administration of the case has been completed. However, the court may retain any jurisdiction necessary for the municipality to implement its plan successfully. The case may be reopened to administer assets, afford relief to the debtor, or for other cause. The debtor or party-in-interest seeking to reopen a case must file motion to reopen and pay a $300 filing fee, unless the ground for the motion is to correct an administrative error or to file an action related to the debtor's discharge. *11 USC §103(e)-(f), 350(b), 901, 945(a)-(b); 28 USC §1930(a)(2), see Judicial Conference of the United States, Language to Clarify Reopened Bankruptcy Code Cases; FRBP 5010, 9013-9014.*

Research Guide

Drake, *Bankruptcy Practice for the General Practitioner* ch 12 (Shepard's/McGraw-Hill 2d ed 1990)

VIII. Business Aspects of Bankruptcy

VIII. Business Aspects of Bankruptcy
- A. General Overview
  11 USC §§103(a), 363-364, 1107, 1203, 1303-1304
- B. Use, Sale, or Lease of Estate's Property
  11 USC §§362(d)-(f), 363, 552
  FRBP 2002(a)(2), (c), 4001(b), (d), 6004, 9013-9014, 9034
  1. Types of Property
     - a. Cash Collateral
     - b. Noncash Collateral
  2. Use of Property
     - a. General Rule—Ordinary Course of Business Use
     - b. Cash Collateral Exception
     - c. Nonordinary Course of Business Use
  3. Procedures to Use, Sell, or Lease Property of the Estate
     - a. Ordinary Course of Business Use
     - b. Cash Collateral Use
     - c. Noncash Collateral Used Other Than in Ordinary Course of Business
       - (1) File Motion for Authority to Use, Sell, or Lease Property Other Than in the Ordinary Course of Business
       - (2) Service of Motion or Complaint
       - (3) Notice of Motion or Complaint
       - (4) Hearing
       - (5) File Itemized Statement of Property Sold
       - (6) Execute Necessary Instruments
     - d. Sale of Property Under $2,500
  4. Requirements to Sell Property Free and Clear of Third Party's Interests

VIII. Business Aspects of Bankruptcy

A. General Overview

The Code authorizes the trustee to use, sell, or lease property of the bankruptcy estate and to obtain post-petition credit subject to certain limitations. Post-petition credit provisions apply to all bankruptcy cases but with fewer restrictions under Chapter 9, where the municipal debtor is allowed the use of its property without many of the limitations imposed in other cases. Provisions governing the use, sale, or lease of property of the estate apply to all cases except Chapter 9. There is no estate under Chapter 9 and the court may not interfere with the Chapter 9 municipal debtor's use or enjoyment of its property, unless such debtor consents directly or under its plan. *See Chapter VII. 11 USC §§103(a), (e), 363-364, 541, 901, 904; FRBP 4001(a)-(d), 6004, 9014.*

The Chapter 11 or 12 debtor, as debtor-in-possession (DIP), walks in the shoes of a trustee and represents the bankruptcy estate. The DIP is given the general rights and powers of a bankruptcy trustee and the specific right to continue operating his business without special court order. Use, sale, or lease of the estate's property and obtaining post-petition credit are often crucial to the successful reorganization of a Chapter 11 or 12 debtor. *11 USC §§103(a), (e), 363-364, 901, 1107-1108, 1203; S Rep No 989, 95th Cong 2d Sess 116 (1978).*

But it is not just the trustee and Chapter 11 or 12 DIP who are given business tools with which to rehabilitate under a bankruptcy case. The Chapter 9 debtor (municipality) may use its revenues and income-producing property without interference by the bankruptcy court, unless the municipality consents or provides otherwise in a Chapter 9 plan. Subject to adequate protection and other limitations, the Chapter 13 debtor may use, sell, or lease exempt and nonexempt property exclusive of the standing trustee and may use cash collateral and obtain post-petition credit if he is engaged in business (self-employed and incurs trade credit related to such employment). *11 USC §§103(a), (e)-(f), (h)-(i), 363-364, 901, 904, 1107-1108, 1203, 1303-1304; FRBP 4001, 6004, 9014.*

The ability of any trustee or debtor to use, sell, or lease property and obtain credit post-petition is balanced by restrictions imposed by bankruptcy law to protect creditors and the estate. But the trustee and debtor are afforded broad measures to restructure financial or business affairs, maximize the bankruptcy estate, and (ideally) to increase debt repayment to creditors. *11 USC §§103(a), (e)-(f), (h)-(i), 363(d)-(e), 364(d), 901, 904, 1107-1108, 1203, 1303-1304; FRBP 4001, 6004, 9014.*

B. Use, Sale, or Lease of Estate's Property

The Chapter 11, 12, and 13 debtor or an appointed trustee may use, sell, or lease property of the estate even if a pre-petition contract or applicable nonbankruptcy law contains an "ipso facto" or "bankruptcy" clause which attempts to limit or terminate the debtor's interest in property because of the debtor's insolvency or bankruptcy petition. Such ipso facto or forfeiture clauses are not enforceable under the Code. But the latitude given to the trustee or debtor to use, sell, or lease property of the estate depends on the type and use of the property at issue.

1. Type of Property

Bankruptcy law divides property of the estate which the trustee or Chapter 11, 12, or 13 debtor may use, sell, or lease into two basic categories—cash collateral and noncash collateral.

a. Cash Collateral

"Cash collateral" is a bankruptcy term of art. There are three requirements for property to be considered cash collateral.

(1) First, the property must be either cash, negotiable instruments, documents of title, securities, deposit accounts, or

other cash equivalents; or proceeds, profits, rents, or products of secured property (collateral) covered by a pre-petition security agreement, including the rental fees, charges, accounts, and other payments for the use or occupancy of public rooms and facilities (hotels, motels, lodging properties). Such property maybe acquired pre- or post-petition. A mortgage lender holding a valid pre-petition assignment of rents is entitled to have its post-petition rents treated as cash collateral and to adequate protection by the debtor or trustee, even if the lender failed to invoke state law mortgage remedies pre-petition. *HR 5116, Pub L No 103-394 §214, amending 11 USC §363(a).*

(2) Second, the property must be property of the bankruptcy estate, whether acquired by the debtor pre- or post-petition.

(3) Third, a third party, other than the bankruptcy debtor or estate, must have an interest in the property. This interest may be a security interest, co-ownership interest (tenancy in common, joint tenancy, tenancy by the entirety), or dower or curtesy interest. *11 USC §§363(a)-(b), (e), (h), (j)-(k), 552(b).*

b. Noncash Collateral

This category includes all other property of the estate that is not cash collateral. Such property may be secured or unsecured or subject to an ownership or other property interest of a third party. *11 USC §363(a).*

2. Use of Property

Post-petition use of the estate's property determines the ease with which it may be sold, leased, or otherwise used by the debtor or trustee.

a. General Rule—Ordinary Course of Business Use

With the exception of cash collateral, the debtor or trustee authorized to operate the debtor's business may use, sell, or lease the estate's property in the ordinary course of the debtor's business without any notice, hearing, or court order. The debtor or trustee may also enter into necessary transactions related to the sale, lease, or use of property in the ordinary course of business without notice or hearing, unless the court or local bankruptcy rules direct otherwise. This gives a debtor or trustee the opportunity to generate cash and other property with which to formulate and implement a plan or to increase the value of the estate for distribution to creditors. The debtor may continue his business-as-usual transactions even if a pre-petition agreement contains an "ipso facto" or "bankruptcy" clause purporting to terminate, forfeit, or modify the debtor's interest in property in the event of the debtor's insolvency or bankruptcy. The Code, in effect, nullifies such ipso facto clauses. *11 USC §363(c)(1), (l), 721, 901, 904, 1107-1108, 1203, 1303-1304;*

HR Rep No 959, 95th Cong, 1st Sess 344 (1978); S Rep No 989, 95th Cong, 2d Sess 55 (1978).

b. Cash Collateral Exception

Use of cash collateral is the exception to the general ordinary-course-of-business rule. The debtor or trustee may only use, sell, or lease cash collateral if the secured creditor or other third party (co-owner, spouse) consents or if the court so authorizes after notice and hearing. The debtor or trustee must at all times segregate and account for cash collateral in his possession, custody, or control, unless the third party consents otherwise. This cash collateral exception applies even if the use of cash collateral is in the ordinary course of the debtor's business operations. *11 USC §§363(c)(2), (4); FRBP 2002(a)(2), 4001(b), (d), 9014.*

c. Nonordinary Course of Business Use

The debtor or trustee may only use, sell, or lease property that is not in the ordinary course of business after notice and hearing. *See "No Consent of Third Party—Notice and Hearing," discussed below; 11 USC §102(1)(A)-(B), 363(b)(1); FRBP 2002(a)(2), (c), 6004, 9014.*

3. Procedures to Use, Sell, or Lease Property of the Estate

a. Ordinary Course of Business Use

There are no special procedures or court order required for the debtor or trustee to use, sell, or lease noncash collateral or other property in the ordinary course of the debtor's business operations, unless the court or local bankruptcy rules direct otherwise or a party-in-interest files a motion for adequate protection. *11 USC §363(c)(1), (d)-(e), (l); FRBP 4001, 9014.*

b. Cash Collateral Use

The debtor or trustee must strictly observe the following procedures before using cash collateral for any post-petition use.

(1) Consent of Third Party

The fastest method for the debtor or trustee to use cash collateral post-petition is to obtain the consent of each third party who has an interest in the cash collateral. The debtor or trustee should then proceed as follows:

(a) Segregate or otherwise carefully account for all cash collateral, whether obtained pre- or post-petition;

(b) Obtain a signed written agreement of each third party (secured creditor, co-owner, spouse) who has an interest in the cash collateral permitting the post-petition use of cash collateral. This written agreement may be obtained pre- or post-petition;

(c) File a motion for approval of agreement to use cash collateral. The motion does not commence an adversary proceeding and no filing fee is required. The motion should include:

(i) Facts showing the need to use cash collateral;

(ii) Facts showing how use of cash collateral will generate funds with which to implement a plan or liquidate the debtor's business;

(iii) Facts showing how the debtor or trustee will provide adequate protection of each third party's interests in the cash collateral (by replacement or additional lien and/or periodic cash payments); and

(iv) Attached copy of the agreement between the debtor or trustee and third party to the motion. *11 USC §§361, 363(c)(2)(A), (e); FRBP 4001(d)(1)(D);*

(d) Serve a copy of the motion and agreement on the U.S. trustee, the third party with an interest in the cash collateral, trustee or standing trustee, committee(s), and any other entity required by court order or local bankruptcy rules. If there is no committee appointed in a Chapter 11 case, a copy of the motion and agreement should be served on the 20 unsecured creditors with the largest claims against the debtor. Service may be obtained by first-class mail or personal delivery. *11 USC §363(c)(2)(A); FRBP 4001(d)(1), 9013-9014;*

(e) Serve notice of date to file objections to the motion if the court or local bankruptcy rules so require. The notice must be mailed to the U.S. trustee and unsecured creditors' committee or to the 20 largest unsecured creditors if no committee has been appointed in a Chapter 11 case. Unless the court or local rules specify otherwise, the last date to file objections to a motion for approval of cash collateral agreement must be before the 15th day after the notice is mailed. A copy of any objections must be served by first-class mail or any other manner allowed for service of process in federal district court on the debtor or trustee, and to any other entity required by court order or local bankruptcy rules. *FRBP 4001(d)(2), 9014, 9034.*

The court, in its discretion, may not require additional service of a notice of the date to file objections if it determines that service of copies of the motion with agreement provided sufficient notice and opportunity for hearing for all affected parties-in-interest. *11 USC §§102(1)(A)-(B), 363(c)(2)(A); FRBP 4001(d)(4), 7004-7005, 9007, 9013-9014, 9034;*

(f) Hearing

The court may enter an order approving the motion and agreement to use cash collateral without a hearing if no objection is timely filed. If an objection is filed timely, the court must hold a hearing. At least five days' prior notice of the hearing date must be given to the objecting party, the debtor, any trustee, the U.S. trustee, each third party with an interest in the cash collateral, the unsecured creditors' committee or 20 largest unsecured creditors if there is no Chapter 11 committee, and to any other entity required by court order or local bankruptcy rules. *11 USC §363(c)(2)(A); FRBP 4001(d)(3), 9013-9014, 9034.*

(2) No Consent of Third Party

If the debtor or trustee is not able to obtain the third party's consent to use cash collateral post-petition, the following procedures must be strictly observed:

(a) Segregate and account for the cash collateral (whether obtained pre- or post-petition);

(b) File motion for authorization to use cash collateral.

The motion should state facts showing:

(i) the need to use cash collateral;

(ii) how use of cash collateral will enable the debtor to reorganize or the trustee to liquidate the debtor's business; and

(iii) the means for providing adequate protection of the third party's interest in the cash collateral (replacement or additional lien or periodic payments). The motion does not commence an adversary proceeding and no filing fee is required;

(c) Serve the motion on the third party by first-class mail or any other manner allowed for service of process in federal district court.

A copy of the motion must also be mailed to the U.S. trustee, any trustee or standing trustee, the unsecured creditors' committee or 20 largest unsecured creditors if no Chapter 11 committee has been appointed, and on any other entity required by court order or local bankruptcy rules. No answer or response is required to the motion unless the court or local bankruptcy rules direct otherwise;

(d) Notice and Hearing

The Court must hold a hearing on a contested motion to use cash collateral. The court may set a final hearing or preliminary hearing. A final hearing may not be scheduled before the 15th day after the motion was served. However, the debtor's (or trustee's) motion may request a preliminary hearing before such time. The court must schedule all hearings according to the debtor's (or trustee's) needs. At the preliminary hearing, if the court finds there is a reasonable likelihood the debtor or trustee will prevail at a final hearing, it may authorize the interim use of cash collateral in amounts necessary to prevent immediate, irreparable harm to the estate. *11 USC §102(1)(A)-(B), 363(c)(2)(B), (3), (e); FRBP 4001(b), 9014, 9034.*

Notice of all hearings must be mailed by the clerk or other court-authorized person to the debtor, any trustee or standing trustee, each third party with an interest in the cash collateral, the U.S. trustee, the unsecured creditors' committee or 20 largest unsecured creditors if no Chapter 11 committee exists, and to any other entity as required by court order or local bankruptcy rules. The court may direct that service of the contested motion and notice of all hearings be combined. *11 USC §102(1)(A)-(B), 363(c)(3); FRBP 4001(b), 9007, 9014, 9034; see Local Bankruptcy Rules.*

c. Noncash Collateral Used Other Than in Ordinary Course of Business

The debtor or trustee who wants to use, sell, or lease property that is not cash collateral other than in the ordinary course of business must observe the following six procedures.

(1) File motion for authority to use, sell, or lease property (noncash collateral) other than in the ordinary course of business.

The motion must include:

(a) General description of the property to be used, sold, or leased;

(b) Facts showing the need to use, sell, or lease the property other than in the ordinary course of the debtor's business;

(c) The time and place of any public sale or lease or the terms and conditions of a private sale or lease;

(d) The means for providing any required adequate protection to each third party with an interest in the property (replacement or additional lien or periodic cash payments); and

(e) Copy of any agreement regarding the proposed use, sale, or lease of property should be attached to the motion. *11 USC §§361-362, 363(b)(2); FRBP 2002(a)(2), (c), 6004; see Local Bankruptcy Rules.*

If the motion is to sell property free and clear of the liens of a secured creditor, such motion does not commence an adversary proceeding and no filing fee is required. However, if the motion is to sell property free and clear of a co-owner's (spousal or tenancy) interests, it is a complaint which does commence an adversary proceeding. If the motion commences an adversary proceeding, a $120 filing fee is required of a Chapter 11 or 12 DIP or trustee but only from any bankruptcy estate that may exist. *11 USC §363(b), (f), (h); FRBP 6004, 7001(3), 9013-9014; 28 USC §1930(b), Judicial Conference Schedule of Fees (6).*

(2) Service of Motion or Complaint

The debtor or trustee must serve a copy of the motion to use, sell, or lease property (including sale of property free and clear of liens) other than in the ordinary course of business by first-class mail or personal delivery by any disinterested person at least 18 years old on each third party with an interest in the property. A copy of the motion should also be served by first-class mail on the U.S. trustee, any trustee, committee(s), and on any other entity required by court order or local bankruptcy rules. No answer or response is required to the motion unless directed otherwise by court order or local bankruptcy rules. The debtor or trustee must serve a copy of a complaint to sell property free and clear of a co-owner's interests with a summons by first-class mail or any other method allowed for service of process in federal district court. A timely answer or response is required to this complaint before the 30th day after the date of issuance of the summons, unless the court orders otherwise. *11 USC §363(b), (f), (h); FRBP 6004, 7001(3), 7004, 7012, 9014, 9034; see Local Bankruptcy Rules; Procedural Bankr Forms B 250A, B, C.*

(3) Notice of Motion or Complaint

The clerk of the court, debtor, trustee, or other court-appointed person must give at least 20 days' notice of the proposed use, sale, or lease of property other than in the ordinary course of business, unless the court reduces the time for such notice. The notice must be mailed to the debtor, each third party with an interest in the property, any trustee or standing trustee, the U.S. trustee, all committee(s), creditors, equity security holders, indenture trustees; and to the SEC in Washington, D.C., and local District Director of the IRS in Chapter 11 cases. The notice must include:

(a) General description of the subject property;

(b) Time and place of a any public sale or terms and conditions of any private sale;

(c) Date of any hearing set by the court on the proposed use, sale, or lease of property other than in the ordinary course of business (*see "Hearing," discussed below*); and

(d) Date by which objections to the proposed use, sale, or lease must be filed with the court and served on the debtor or trustee and U.S. trustee. Objections must generally be filed and served no later than the fifth day before the proposed sale, lease, or use of the property, unless the court or local bankruptcy rules direct otherwise. An objection does not commence an adversary proceeding and no filing fee is required. An objection may be served by first-class mail or any other method for service of a summons and complaint in federal district court. *11 USC §363(b); FRBP 2002(a)(2), (c), (i)-(k), 6004(a)-(b), 9013-9014, 9034.*

The court may order that service of the motion and notice of proposed use, sale, or lease of property be combined. *11 USC §§102(1)(A)-(B), 105(a), 363(b); FRBP 9007, 9014; see Local Bankruptcy Rules.*

(4) Hearing

If a party-in-interest (creditor, third party with interest in the property, trustee or standing trustee, or U.S. trustee) files a timely objection, the court must hold a hearing. If there are no objections, the court may enter an order granting the motion to use, sale, or lease property without a hearing. *11 USC §§102(1)(A)-(B), 363(b); FRBP 6004(e), 9007.*

(5) File Itemized Statement of Property Sold

Unless it is impractical, after the sale is completed, the debtor or trustee must file an itemized statement of all property sold, indicating the name of each purchaser and the price received for each item of property or for the property as a whole if sold in bulk. If an auctioneer sells the property, he must file the statement and serve a copy on the debtor or trustee. The debtor, trustee, or auctioneer must also serve a copy of the itemized statement on the U.S. trustee and any other entity required by court order or local bankruptcy rules. Service may be obtained by first-class mail or personal delivery. *FRBP 6004(f)(1), 9034.*

(6) Execute Necessary Instruments

The debtor or trustee must execute all documents ordered by the court which are necessary to complete the transfer of property. *11 USC §§105(a), 363(b); FRBP 6004(f)(2).*

d. Sale of Property Under $2,500

If the aggregate, gross value of all nonexempt property of the estate is less than $2,500, the debtor or trustee may give only a general notice of intent to sell such property other than in the ordinary course of business. Gross value is the total value of the property without regard to the amount of any claim secured by a lien on the property. It is not necessary to give a detailed notice specifying the time and place of sale of any particular property. However, the notice must:

(1) Generally describe the property of the estate and indicate that its gross value is less than $2,500;

(2) Indicate that the debtor or trustee intends to sell such property at a future date; and

(3) State the date to file objections to the notice.

Such date must be before the 15th day after the date the notice is mailed, unless the court or local bankruptcy rules indicate otherwise. An objection does not commence an adversary proceeding and no filing fee is required. A copy of the objection must be served by first-class mail or any other method allowed for service of process in federal district court on the debtor, any trustee, the U.S. trustee, all committee(s), and any other entity required by court order or local bankruptcy rules. *11 USC §§102(1)(A)-(B), 363(b); FRBP 6004(d); advisory committee's note 9014.*

The debtor or trustee must serve the notice of intent to sell property under $2,500 by first-class mail on all creditors, committee(s), indenture trustees, any trustee or standing trustee, the U.S. trustee, and on all entities directed by court order or local bankruptcy rules. If an objection is timely filed, the debtor or trustee, clerk, or other court-authorized person must mail notice of the hearing date to the objector, the debtor or trustee, the U.S. trustee, all committee(s), and to any other entity required by court order or local bankruptcy rules. *11 USC §§102(1)(A)-(B), 363(b); FRBP 6004(d)-(f), 7004-7005, 9007, 9013-9014, 9034.*

4. Requirements to Sell Property Free and Clear of Third Party's Interests

a. Dower and Curtesy Rights

The Chapter 11 or 12 debtor or an appointed trustee may sell property of the bankruptcy estate free and clear of any dower or curtesy rights. This rule applies whether such property is sold in the ordinary or nonordinary course of the debtor's business operations. However, the rule is limited if there are co-ownership (or tenancy) or other interests in the property. (*see "Community or Other Co-Owned Property," discussed below*).

The debtor or trustee must distribute to the widow (dower rights) or widower (curtesy rights) his or her proportionate ownership share of the proceeds after deducting the costs and expenses of the sale allowed by the court. *See "Rights of the Third Party," discussed below; 11 USC §363(b), (g), (j), 1101, 1107, 1203.*

b. Secured Property

The Chapter 11, 12, or 13 debtor or trustee may sell secured property of the estate free and clear of lien(s) if at least one of the following situations applies.

(1) Applicable nonbankruptcy law permits sale of the property free and clear of any security interest (lien).

The Uniform Commercial Code permits public or private sale of secured personal property after the debtor's default, with the lien attaching to the proceeds. State real estate laws similarly permit sale of encumbered real estate free and clear of the mortgage, with the lien attaching to the proceeds of sale. *See UCC §9-504; Local Real Estate Code.*

(2) The secured creditor could be compelled to accept money in satisfaction of his security interest by a legal or equitable proceeding.

(3) The price for which the secured property will be sold through the bankruptcy court is greater than the total amount of all liens against the property.

(4) The secured creditor consents to the sale.

(5) The security interest against the property is subject to a bona fide dispute by the debtor or trustee. *11 USC §363(f).*

If at least one of the above conditions is met, the property may be sold free and clear of all liens, but the liens will attach to the proceeds in order of their nonbankruptcy priority status, unless the court orders otherwise. The secured creditor has the right to bid for the property at the sale, unless the court directs otherwise. If the secured creditor is the highest bidder, he may offset the amount of his allowed secured claim held against the debtor or estate against the purchase price bid for the property. *11 USC §§323, 363(f), (k), 553(a), 1101, 1107, 1203, 1303; FRBP 6004.*

c. Community or Other Co-Owned Property

The Chapter 11 or 12 debtor or an appointed trustee may sell property of the estate free and clear of the interests of a third party co-owner (spouse, tenant-in-common, joint tenant, tenant-by-the-entirety), if all the following requirements are met.

(1) It is not practical to partition the property between the bankruptcy estate and third party co-owner and sell only the estate's undivided interest in the property.

(2) Sale of the entire property free and clear of the co-owner's interests will bring the estate significantly more money than sale of only the estate's undivided interest in property.

(3) **The benefit to the estate outweighs any detriment to the co-owner from sale of the property free and clear of the co-owner's interests.**

(4) **The property is not used in the production, transmission, or distribution for sale of electric energy or of natural or synthetic gas for heat, light, or power.**

A co-owner's interest in a public utility is protected where sale could disrupt services. *11 USC §§323, 363(h), 1101, 1107, 1203, 1303; FRBP 7001(3) et seq; S Rep No 589, 95th Cong, 2d Sess 56-57 (1978); HR Rep No 595, 95th Cong, 1st Sess 346 (1977).*

The Code further protects co-owners by giving a right of first refusal to the co-owner or spouse to purchase the property at the ultimate sales price brought through the bankruptcy court. If the co-owner does not purchase the property, the debtor or trustee must distribute to the co-owner (or spouse) his proportionate ownership share of the proceeds after deducting the reasonable costs and expenses attributable to the sale and allowed by the court. However, no compensation to the debtor or trustee may be deducted from the proceeds. The remaining proceeds belong to the estate. *11 USC §363(i)-(j); HR Rep No 595, 95th Cong, 1st Sess 346 (1977); S Rep No 989, 95th Cong, 2d Sess 57 (1978).*

5. Rights of the Third Party

The third party with interests in the estate's property proposed to be used, leased, or sold has five possible legal rights under bankruptcy law.

a. Right to File a Motion to Prohibit Use, Sale, or Lease of Property

(1) Generally

The third party with an interest in property of the estate may file a motion at any time during the bankruptcy case to prohibit or condition the use, sale, or lease of such property whether in the ordinary or nonordinary course of the debtor's business. The motion does not commence an adversary proceeding and no filing fee is required. The third party must serve a copy of the motion on the debtor and any trustee by first-class mail or any other manner allowed for service of process in federal district court. A copy of the motion should also be mailed to the U.S. trustee, all committee(s), and to any other entity required by court order or local bankruptcy rules. *11 USC §363(e); FRBP 4001(a), 7004, 9014, 9034.*

The court must prohibit or condition the use, sale, or lease of such property to the extent necessary to adequately protect the interests of the third party. The third party has the burden of proving the existence, validity, and extent of his interests (lien, ownership) in the estate's property under applicable nonbankruptcy law. The debtor or trustee has the burden of showing that there is adequate protection of the third party's interests in the property at issue. *11 USC §§362(g), 363(e), (o); FRBP 4001(a)(1), (d), 6004, 9014.*

(2) Ex Parte Relief

The court may afford ex parte relief and grant the third party's motion without a hearing. However, ex parte relief may only be granted if the motion to prohibit or condition the use, sale, or lease of property includes the following:

(a) Affidavit (or verified motion) stating specific facts which show immediate and irreparable injury, loss, or damage will result to the third party unless an ex parte injunction or order prohibiting or conditioning the use, sale, or lease of property is issued by the bankruptcy court; and

(b) Certificate of the third party's attorney stating specific facts which show the efforts to give notice of the motion to the debtor or trustee and why further efforts to give the debtor or trustee notice of the motion should not be required. *11 USC §§102(1)(A)-(B), 363(e); FRBP 4001(a)(2), 9014.*

If the court grants the motion ex parte, the third party must immediately give oral notice of the court's order and mail a copy of the order to the debtor or trustee and to any committee in the case. The debtor or trustee may then file a motion for reconsideration of the ex parte order and appear before the court with only two days' prior notice to the third party, unless the court reduces the time for such prior notice. The court must hold a hearing on the motion for reconsideration as quickly as possible under the facts of the case. *11 USC §§102(1)(A)-(B), 363(e); FRBP 4001(a)(2), 9007.*

b. Right to File Motion to Lift Automatic Stay

The third party (creditor, co-owner, spouse) may file a motion for relief asking the court to lift or condition the automatic stay to protect the interests of the third party in property proposed to be used, leased, or sold. Such motion does not commence an adversary proceeding but a $60 filing fee is required. A copy of the motion for relief must be served on the debtor and any appointed trustee by first-class mail or by any other method allowed for service of process in federal district court. A copy of the motion should also be mailed to all committee(s), and to any other entity required by court order or local bankruptcy rules. The debtor, trustee, or committee opposing the motion must obtain at least a preliminary hearing before the 30th day after the motion is filed or the stay is automatically lifted with regard to the relief sought by the third party under the motion. *See "Stage Two—Automatic Stay Invoked," Chapter II; "Mo-*

tion for Relief from Automatic Stay," Chapter XIV; 11 USC §§362(d)-(e), 363(d); FRBP 4001, 7004, 9014.

c. Right to Receive Proceeds of Sale

The third party is entitled to receive his pro tanto share of proceeds received from the sale of property of the estate to the extent of his allowed secured claim or his ownership interests in the property under applicable nonbankruptcy law. The debtor or trustee may deduct from proceeds owed to a spouse or co-owner the necessary costs and expenses incurred in the sale and allowed by the court. The debtor or trustee may deduct from proceeds owed to a secured creditor the reasonable, necessary costs and expenses of preserving and disposing of the collateral, but only to the extent such costs and expenses benefit the secured creditor and are allowed by the court. However, the trustee may not deduct from any proceeds his compensation allowed under bankruptcy law. The remaining proceeds will belong to the estate. *11 USC §§102(5), 326, 363(f), (j), 506(a), (c), 541.*

d. Right to Super First Priority Claim

The court may allow the use, sale, or lease of collateral conditioned upon the debtor's or trustee's providing adequate protection for the secured creditor's interests in the property. Adequate protection may be provided by giving the secured creditor an additional or replacement lien on property, periodic cash payments, or any other means allowed by the court, other than providing the secured creditor a first priority administrative claim. If, however, the secured creditor's interests in the collateral prove not to be adequately protected while the use, sale, or lease of collateral benefited or helped preserve the estate, such secured creditor is entitled to a super first priority claim against the estate. A super first priority claim must be paid from property of the estate before any other first priority claims are paid. The secured creditor must file a timely proof of claim asserting a super first priority claim and state sufficient facts to support such claim. The creditor should attach the original or copies of all documents establishing a valid lien under applicable nonbankruptcy law and a copy of the court's order conditioning the use, sale, or lease of the collateral. *See "File Proof of Claim," Chapter XIV; "Priority Claims," Chapter II. 11 USC §§362(d), 363(d)-(e), 503(b), 507(a)(1), (b); FRBP 3002-3007.*

e. Right to Purchase the Property

The spouse or co-owner has the right of first refusal to buy the property for the final price offered at a sale through the bankruptcy court. The secured creditor has the right to bid for the property at any sale in the bankruptcy court, unless cause exists for the court to order otherwise, and may offset his claim against the purchase price if he buys the property. *11 USC §§363(f)-(h), (j)-(k), 506(a), 553.*

6. Legal Effect of Appeal

Good-faith purchasers or lessees of property through the bankruptcy court are protected. If the court's order authorizing the sale or lease is reversed or modified on appeal, the rights of the good-faith purchaser or lessee are not affected even if the purchaser or lessee knew about the appeal, unless the bankruptcy court's order and the sale or lease are stayed pending the appeal. The appellant must file a timely notice of appeal and motion for stay of judgment. The notice must be filed with the bankruptcy clerk. The motion for stay of judgment is generally filed with the bankruptcy court first, but may be filed with the appellate court (federal district court or bankruptcy appellate panel) if the motion states facts showing why the stay was not sought from the bankruptcy court. *See "Appeal of Bankruptcy Court Order," Chapter IX;* *11 USC §363(m); FRBP 8001, 8005.*

7. Bad-Faith Sales

Collusive bidding (control of sales price by bidders) on property sold through the bankruptcy court is prohibited. The debtor or trustee may file an adversary complaint, jointly or severally, against each collusive bidder, seeking to:

a. **(1) Avoid the sale and recover the property; or (2) Recover from any collusive bidder damages in the amount of the difference between the value of the property sold and the (collusive) sales price received; plus**

b. **Recover reasonable costs and expenses, including attorney's fees, incurred in avoiding the sale or recovering damages for the estate; and**

c. **Recover punitive damages for the estate against any collusive bidder who willfully disregarded bankruptcy law governing the sale.** *11 USC §363(n).*

A Chapter 11 or 12 DIP or an appointed trustee must pay a $120 filing fee only from any bankruptcy estate that may exist. No filing fee is required if a Chapter 13 debtor files the complaint. The debtor or trustee must serve a copy of the complaint with summons on the collusive-bidder defendant by first-class mail or any other manner allowed for service of process in federal district court. *11 USC §§323, 363(n), 1101, 1107, 1203, 1303-1304; 28 USC §1930(b), Judicial Conference Schedule of Fees (6); FRBP 7001(1), 7004 et seq; Procedural Bankr Forms B 250A, B, C.*

C. Post-Petition Credit

The debtor or trustee who is authorized to operate the debtor's business frequently needs to obtain post-petition credit. Both the debt incurred to operate the debtor's business and the property generated post-petition will belong to the estate. Therefore, bankruptcy law establishes strict rules governing the estate's obtaining credit and incurring debt post-petition. Such rules apply equally to liquidating cases where the trustee must wind up the debtor's business and to operating cases where the debtor must generate funds to formulate and implement a plan. The Code permits three types of post-petition debt subject to specific rules and procedures. *11 USC §§103(a), (c), 323(a), 364, 721, 901, 904, 1101(1), 1107-1108, 1203, 1304; FRBP 4001(c)-(d), 9013-9014, 9034.*

1. Three Types of Post-Petition Credit

a. Unsecured Credit or Debt Incurred in the Ordinary Course of Business

The Chapter 11 or 12 debtor, the Chapter 13 debtor engaged in business, and an appointed trustee authorized to operate the debtor's business may incur unsecured credit or debt in the ordinary course of post-petition business operations. No motion, notice to parties-in-interest, or court order is required. However, the court may limit the amount of post-petition, ordinary course of business debt upon request filed by a party-in-interest (U.S. trustee or creditor). Ordinary course of business debt is usually an allowed first priority administrative expense against the estate. The post-petition unsecured creditor must file a timely proof of claim indicating his first priority claim status. *See "Priority Claims," Chapter II; "File Proof of Claim," Chapter XIV; 11 USC §§503(b)(1), 507(a)(1), 364(a), 721, 1101(1), 1107-1108, 1203, 1304; FRBP 3001-3003; Official Bankr Form 10.*

b. Unsecured Credit or Debt Incurred Not in the Ordinary Course of Business

The court may authorize the debtor or trustee to incur unsecured post-petition credit or debt other than in the ordinary course of business operations which will also be allowed as a first priority administrative expense. The debtor must file a motion and the court must require notice to creditors and parties-in-interest and a hearing (*see "Procedures," discussed below*). The creditor extending such post-petition credit other than in the ordinary course of the debtor's business should file a timely proof of claim with a copy of the court order indicating his first priority claim status. *See "File Proof of Claim," Chapter XIV; "Priority Claims," Chapter II; 11 USC §§364(b), 503(b)(1), 507(a)(1); FRBP 3001(b)-(c), 3005, 4001(c)-(d), 9013-9014; Official Bankr Form 10;* or

c. Special Priority Debt

If the Chapter 9, 11, 12, or 13 debtor or trustee authorized to operate the debtor's business is not able to obtain unsecured debt allowable as a first priority administrative expense either in the ordinary or nonordinary course of business, he may seek to obtain four types of special priority post-petition debt. Each type requires prior notice to parties-in-interest and hearing before the court (*see "Procedures," discussed below*).

(1) Super Priority Unsecured Debt

The court, after notice to parties-in-interest and hearing, may authorize the debtor or trustee to obtain post-petition unsecured debt that will be granted super priority claim status over all other priority claims. Thus, this unsecured creditor's claim will be paid from the estate even before any first priority administrative expense or any other unsecured claim against the estate may be paid. The creditor should file a timely proof of claim with a copy of the court order indicating a super priority claim status, and state sufficient facts in the claim to show such status. The creditor should attach the original or copies of all other relevant documents to the proof of claim showing the extension of post-petition credit. *See "Priority Claims," Chapter II; "File Proof of Claim, Chapter XIV; 11 USC §§103(a), (e), 364(c)(1), 503(a)-(b), 507(b), 901, 1107-1108, 1203, 1304; FRBP 3001(c)-(d), 3002(a), 3003, 4001(c)-(d); Official Bankr Form 10.*

(2) Secured Debt on Previously Unencumbered Property of the Estate

The court, after notice and hearing, may authorize the debtor or trustee to obtain secured debt by granting the creditor a post-petition lien on the estate's unsecured property. The debtor or trustee and creditor should execute all necessary documents to enable the creditor to perfect his post-petition lien under applicable nonbankruptcy law. The creditor should also file a timely proof of claim with a copy of the court order and all other relevant documents necessary to establish his security interest. *11 USC §364(c)(2); FRBP 3001(c)-(d), 3002(a), 3003, 4001(b), (d); see "File Proof of Claim," Chapter XIV; Official Bankr Form 10.*

(3) Debt Secured by Junior Lien on Secured Property of the Estate

After notice and hearing, the court may authorize the debtor or trustee to obtain secured post-petition debt by granting the creditor a junior (inferior) lien on certain of the estate's secured property. This property must have sufficient equity to adequately protect the interests of the pre-petition secured creditor(s) and the post-petition creditor who is granted the junior lien. The post-petition creditor and the debtor or trustee should execute all documents required for the creditor to perfect his post-petition lien under applicable nonbankruptcy law. This creditor should also file a timely proof of claim with the original or copies of all documents, including a copy of the court order establishing his junior lienhold status. *11 USC §364(c)(3); FRBP 3001(c)-(d), 3002(a), 3003, 4001(b), (d); see "File Proof of Claim," Chapter XIV; Official Bankr Form 10.*

(4) Priority Secured Debt (Senior or Co-Equal Lien)

The court, after notice and hearing, may authorize the debtor or trustee to obtain nonordinary course of business secured debt by granting the post-petition creditor a co-equal or priority (senior) lien on property of the estate that is already secured by a first lien. The debtor or trustee must prove three requirements before such debt may be allowed.

(a) First, such credit is necessary to continue the debtor's business and to enable the debtor to reorganize or the trustee to liquidate the business successfully.

(b) Second, the debtor or trustee can only obtain the needed credit by granting the lender a first or co-equal lien on certain of the estate's secured property.

(c) Third, the interests of existing lienholders are adequately protected. The debtor or trustee may prove adequate protection by: (i) establishing sufficient equity in the property; (ii) providing an additional or replacement lien to the existing lienholder(s); and/or (iii) providing periodic cash payments to the existing lienholder(s). If there is more than one existing pre-petition lienholder, the debtor or trustee must provide adequate protection for each pre-petition secured creditor's interests in the property. To the extent such existing secured interests are not adequately protected, the respective pre-petition secured creditor will have a super first priority claim against the estate payable before any first priority administrative expense may be paid in the debtor's case (but payable after payment of any unsecured creditor granted a super priority claim status. (*See "Super Priority Unsecured Debt," discussed above*). The pre-petition secured creditor whose interests are not adequately protected should file a timely proof of claim asserting a super first priority claim, state sufficient facts to support his super first priority claim, and attach all documents necessary to show a valid, perfected pre-petition lien and a copy of all relevant court order(s). The post-petition creditor granted a senior or co-equal lien and the debtor or trustee must execute all documents necessary to enable such creditor to perfect his post-petition lien under applicable nonbankruptcy law. This post-petition secured creditor should also file a timely proof of claim with a copy of all relevant court order(s) and other documents reflecting a perfected lien. *11 USC*

§§361, 364(d), 503(b)(1), 506(a), 507(a)(1), (b); FRBP 3001(c), 3002(a), 3003, 4001(c)-(d); see "File Proof of Claim," Chapter XIV; "Priority Claims," Chapter II; Official Bankr Form 10.

2. Procedures

The following procedures govern obtaining post-petition credit or debt.

a. Ordinary Course of Business Unsecured Debt

As stated, the debtor or trustee authorized to operate the debtor's business may obtain unsecured post-petition debt or credit in the ordinary course of business operations without notice, hearing, or court order. But the court may limit this right by a party-in-interest's (U.S. trustee, committee, or creditor) filing a motion to limit unsecured ordinary course of business debt which states sufficient grounds. Such motion does not commence an adversary proceeding and no filing fee is required. The party-in-interest must serve a copy of the motion on the debtor, any trustee or standing trustee, all committee(s), and all other entities directed by court order or local bankruptcy rules. A copy of the motion should also be served on the U.S. trustee, except under Chapter 9. Service may be obtained by first-class mail or any other method allowed for service of a summons and complaint in federal district court. An answer or response to the motion is not required unless the court or local bankruptcy rules direct otherwise. The court must hold a hearing on such motion, unless local bankruptcy rules state otherwise. *11 USC §§102(1)(A)-(B), 103(a), (e), 364(a), 721, 901, 904, 1101(1), 1107-1108, 1203, 1304; FRBP 9007, 9013-9014; see Local Bankruptcy Rules.*

b. NonOrdinary Course of Business Debt

(1) Generally

The debtor or trustee may only obtain unsecured or secured post-petition debt not in the ordinary course of business by complying with the following procedures.

(a) File Motion and Agreement

The debtor or trustee must file a motion for authority to obtain credit other than in the ordinary course of business. The motion should state:

(i) Facts showing the need to incur post-petition debt or credit other than in the ordinary course of business;

(ii) Amount and type of debt or credit to be incurred;

(iii) Name and address of the post-petition lender;

(iv) Terms and conditions of any post-petition credit agreement (whether the debt will be secured or unsecured, terms of payment);

(v) Name and address of each secured creditor with a pre-petition lien on any property that may be used to secure post-petition debt;

(vi) Description of any collateral and the respective lienhold positions of all secured creditors involved in the post-petition credit transaction;

(vii) Means for providing any required adequate protection of each secured creditor's interests in collateral that may be used to grant a senior, co-equal, or junior security interest to a post-petition creditor; and

(viii) Efforts of the debtor or trustee to obtain unsecured post-petition credit. *11 USC §364(b)-(d); FRBP 4001(c), advisory committee's note to 1987 Amendments.*

(b) Service of Motion

The debtor or trustee must serve a copy of the motion and post-petition agreement to obtain credit on the unsecured creditors' committee or 20 largest unsecured creditors if no committee has been appointed in a Chapter 9 or 11 case. Service may be obtained by first-class mail or any other manner allowed for service of process in federal district court. A copy of the motion and agreement should also be mailed to the U.S. trustee, any appointed trustee, and to any other entity required by court order or local bankruptcy rules. *FRBP 4001(c)(1), advisory committee's note to 1987 Amendments, 9014, 9034.*

(c) Notice and Hearing

The court must hold a hearing on any motion for authority to obtain credit other than in the ordinary course of business, unless local bankruptcy rules direct otherwise. Notice of the hearing date may be given with the motion by the debtor or trustee or any other person directed by court order or local bankruptcy rules. Notice of the hearing date must be mailed or delivered to all parties-in-interest who were required to be served a copy of the motion (*see* discussion above). The court may not begin a final hearing on the motion before the 15th day after service of the motion. However, the court may hold a preliminary hearing before the 15th day if requested in the motion. At the preliminary hearing, the court may authorize the debtor or trustee to obtain interim credit only to the extent necessary to prevent immediate and irreparable harm to the estate pending the final hearing. *11 USC §§102(1)(A)-(B), 364(b)-(d); FRBP 4001(c)(2), 9007, 9013-9014, 9034.*

(d) Burden of Proof

The debtor or trustee has the burden of proving adequate protection of the interests of any existing pre-petition secured creditors whose interests will be affected by the post-petition credit. This will require establishing: (i) the value of any collateral at issue; (ii) the amount of needed credit; (iii) the ability of the debtor or trustee to repay new post-petition debt; (iv) the likelihood of a successful reorganization; and (v) the ability of the debtor or trustee to provide a replacement lien, additional collateral, periodic cash payments, or other means to adequately protect the interests of existing pre-petition secured creditors. If the adequate protection proves insufficient, each pre-petition secured creditor whose interests are adversely affected will have a super first priority claim against the estate. *11 USC §§361, 364(d)(2), 503(a)-(b), 506(a), 507(b).*

(2) Consent of Existing Secured Creditor(s) to Co-Equal or Senior Lien

An existing secured creditor may consent to the debtor or trustee providing a co-extensive or senior (priority) lien on its collateral post-petition. This consent may be obtained before or after the motion for authority to obtain credit other than in the ordinary course of business has been filed. The debtor or trustee should comply with the following procedures.

(a) File Motion for Approval of Post-Petition Credit Agreement(s)

This motion should include the agreement between the debtor or trustee and the post-petition lender and the (settlement) agreement between the debtor or trustee and the pre-petition secured creditor who consents to the creation of a senior or co-equal lien in favor of the new lender. *FRBP 4001(d).*

(b) Serve Copy of the Motion and All Agreements

The debtor or trustee must serve a copy of the motion with all agreements on the unsecured creditors' committee or the 20 largest unsecured creditors if no committee has been appointed in a Chapter 9 or 11 case, the U.S. trustee any trustee or standing trustee, and on such other entities as directed by court order or local bankruptcy rules. Service may be obtained by first-class mail or personal delivery, unless local bankruptcy rules require otherwise. *FRBP 4001(d)(1), 7005, 9013-9014, 9034.*

(c) Serve Notice of Date to File Objections

The debtor, trustee, or other court-appointed person must serve notice of the date to file objections to the motion for approval of post-petition credit agreements. Such notice must be served by first-class mail on the unsecured creditors' committee or the 20 largest unsecured creditors if no committee has been appointed in a Chapter 9 or 11 case, the U.S. trustee, and on any other entity required by court order or local bankruptcy rules. Unless the court or local bankruptcy rules set a different date, all objections must be filed and served on the debtor or any appointed trustee before the 15th day after the notice was mailed. Objections may be served by first-class mail or any other method allowed for service of process in federal district court. A copy of the objection should also be mailed to the unsecured creditors' committee or 20 largest unsecured creditors if there is no committee, the U.S. trustee, and to any other entity required by court order or local bankruptcy rules. *FRBP 4001(d)(2), 7004, 9007, 9013-9014, 9034.*

(d) Hearing

The court may enter an order approving the motion and all agreement(s) without a hearing if no objections are timely filed. If an objection is timely filed or the court otherwise requires a hearing, at least five days' prior notice of the hearing date must be given to the debtor and any appointed trustee, the objecting party, the unsecured creditors' committee or 20 largest unsecured creditors if no Chapter 9 or 11 committee has been appointed, the U.S. trustee, and to such other entities as the court or local bankruptcy rules require. Notice of the hearing on objection(s) may be mailed by the clerk or other court-appointed person. *11 USC §§102(1)(A)-(B), 364(d); FRBP 4001(d)(3), 9007, 9034; see Local Bankruptcy Rules.*

The court may not require notices of the date to file objections and hearing date. The court may determine that service of the motion for authority to obtain post-petition credit afforded the required parties-in-interest sufficient notice of the terms of any agreement(s) and opportunity to object and request a hearing before the court. *11 USC §102(1)(A)-(B), 364(b)-(d); FRBP 4001(d)(4), 9007, 9013-9014; see Local Bankruptcy Rules.*

3. Protection of Good-Faith Lender on Appeal

Appeal of a bankruptcy financing order authorizing the debtor or trustee to obtain post-petition credit will not affect the interests of the good-faith lender even if he knows of the appeal and the bankruptcy court's order is reversed or modified on appeal, unless the order and incurring of post-petition debt are stayed pending the appeal. *11 USC §364(e); FRBP 8001 et seq; see "Appeal of Bankruptcy Court Order," Chapter IX.*

D. How Post-Petition Credit and the Use, Sale, or Lease of Estate's Property Affect General Unsecured Creditors

1. Theory

The purpose for allowing a debtor or trustee to use, sell, or lease property, or to obtain credit post-petition is to maximize and increase the size of the bankruptcy estate. Increasing the size of the estate should increase the amount of proceeds available to pay pre-petition debts. *11 USC §§363-364, 541(a)(6)-(7), 721, 1101(1), 1107-1108, 1203, 1206-1207, 1303-1304, 1306.*

2. Reality

Post-petition credit and use, sale, or lease of property has the potential to further diminish the bankruptcy estate and reduce the amount available to pay pre- and post-petition claims of unsecured creditors. The debtor or trustee is often forced to offer special priority status to creditors in exchange for necessary post-petition working capital. Any post-petition credit, whether obtained in the ordinary or nonordinary course of business, is at least afforded first priority claim status as an administrative expense, payable before general unsecured pre-petition creditors under bankruptcy law. And each additional super or special priority claimholder is also entitled to be paid in full, and before, general unsecured pre-petition creditors under the Bankruptcy Code laws of distribution. *11 USC §§361, 362(d), 363(d), 364(a)-(d), 503, 507(a)(1), (b), 726(a), 943(b)(5), 1229(a)(9)(A), 1222(a)(2), 1322(a)(2); see "Priority Claims," Chapter II.*

In the event the debtor's Chapter 11, 12, or 13 case is converted to Chapter 7, the following post-petition liens, special priority, and first priority claims must be paid in full and in the following order, before general unsecured pre-petition claims are paid.

Priority Status Given Post-Petition	How Incurred:
1. Post-Petition Senior (Priority), Co-Equal, And Junior LIENS—Payable before any unsecured claim(s), including super priority, super first priority, or first priority unsecured claims	Allowed to post-petition unsecured creditor(s) on previously unsecured or secured property of the estate, to enable the debtor or trustee to obtain necessary post-petition credit
2. Super Priority (Unsecured) Claim(s)—Payable from the estate before all other priority claims and before general unsecured creditors are paid	Allowed to post-petition unsecured creditor(s) to obtain necessary post-petition credit or working capital for the debtor or trustee
3. Super First Priority (Unsecured) Claim(s)—Payable after super priority claims but before all first priority claims and before general unsecured claims are paid	Allowed to each secured creditor whose post-petition interests in collateral were not adequately protected after the debtor or trustee obtained credit or used, sold, or leased collateral and attempted to provide adequate protection post-petition
4. First Priority (Unsecured) Claim(s)—Payable after super priority claims but before general unsecured claims are paid	Allowed to each post-petition unsecured creditor in the ordinary or nonordinary course of the debtor's business, unless the court rules otherwise *11 USC §§361, 362(d), 363(d)(e), 364(a)-(d), 503, 507(a)(1)(b), 726(1)*

Research Guide

Anderson, *Chapter 11: Reorganizations* ch 9 (Shepard's/McGraw-Hill 1983)

Anderson & Morris, *Chapter 12: Farm Reorganizations* ch 5 (Shepard's/McGraw-Hill 1987)

Drake, *Bankruptcy Practice for the General Practitioner* ch 9 (Shepard's/McGraw-Hill 2d ed 1990)

Drake & Morris, *Chapter 13: Practice and Procedure* chs 6, 7 (Shepard's/McGraw-Hill 1983)

Jaroslavsky, *Practical Bankruptcy Procedure* chs 7-9 (Shepard's/McGraw-Hill 1993)

Murphy, *Creditor's Rights in Bankruptcy* chs 7-9, 14 (Shepard's/McGraw-Hill 2d ed 1988)

Pollard & Burton, *Guide to Effective Bankruptcy Litigation* chs 8-11 (Shepard's/McGraw-Hill 1988)

IX. Jurisdiction of the Bankruptcy Court

(iii) Motion for Bankruptcy Court to Abstain from Proceeding
(iv) Motion to Abstain from Case
(v) Motion for Referral Order
(vi) Preliminary Hearing (Possible Mock-Trial) in the Bankruptcy Court
(4) Procedure Four—Parties Disagree Whether Core or Noncore

C. Jury Trials in Bankruptcy Cases
28 USC §§157, 1411

D. Appeal of Bankruptcy Court Order
28 USC §158(a)-(c)
FRBP 8001 et seq
1. To Federal District Court
2. To Bankruptcy Appellate Panel Service (BAPS)
a. Requirements for a BAPS Appeal
b. Composition of a BAPS
c. Reconsideration of the BAPS
3. Procedures on Appeal
FRBP 8001-8005, 8008-8010 et seq
a. Timely Appeal of Final Order
(1) What Is Required
(2) Where to File the Notice of Appeal
(3) When to File the Notice of Appeal
b. Timely Appeal of Interlocutory Order
c. Consent to Appeal to Bankruptcy Appellate Panel
d. Service of the Notice of Appeal
e. Appeal by Other Parties
f. Record on Appeal
g. Transmission of Record on Appeal
h. Appellate Court Clerk Dockets the Appeal
i. Briefs on Appeal
(1) When to File
(2) Where to File
(3) Length of Briefs
(4) How to File
(5) Form and Content of Briefs
(6) Number of Copies
(7) Proof of Service
j. Stay on Appeal
k. Disposition and Standard of Review on Appeal

E. Appeal of District Court Order
28 USC §§158(d), 1291-1292

Research Guide

IX. Jurisdiction of the Bankruptcy Court

A. Overview:

Jurisdiction is the power or authority which any court must have to hear a case or proceeding and render a valid judgment. If a court does not have jurisdiction, the court's order is void *ab initio* (of no legal force or effect from the beginning).

There are two types of jurisdiction which every court must have to lawfully hear any matter and issue a valid binding order or decree.

1. Subject Matter Jurisdiction

Subject matter jurisdiction is the power or authority of a court to hear a particular type of case or proceeding (bankruptcy, divorce, insurance, civil rights). Subject matter jurisdiction can never be conferred upon a court by the parties or litigants. Only a federal or state constitution or statute can give the power or authority to a court to hear a case. Thus, a debtor cannot go to a state court, file a bankruptcy petition, and thereby confer subject matter jurisdiction upon the state court to hear a bankruptcy case. The United States Constitution (art 1, §8, cl 4) and federal statute (28 USC §§151-152, 157, 1334) confer subject matter jurisdiction to hear bankruptcy cases and proceedings upon federal district and bankruptcy courts.

2. Personal Jurisdiction

Personal jurisdiction is the power or authority of a court to force a defendant or party to come into court, appear and defend himself, or suffer a default judgment. Personal jurisdiction generally can be conferred upon a court by the defendant appearing in court, even if the defendant does not know that his presence gives the court personal jurisdiction over him. A debtor or plaintiff always confers personal jurisdiction upon a bankruptcy court by filing the petition or adversary complaint.

The problem with personal jurisdiction is determining when it is lawful for a court to exercise personal jurisdiction and force an unwilling defendant or party-in-interest to come to court and defend on penalty of a default judgment. Federal and state courts have adopted due process requirements to resolve this problem. A defendant must have had "sufficient minimum contacts" with a state, so that maintaining an action and forcing a defendant to appear and defend or suffer a default judgment will not "offend traditional notions of fair play and substantial justice." *International Shoe Co v Washington, 326 US 310 (1945); Hanson v Deckla, 375 US 235 (1957).*

Federal law empowers the federal district court and bankruptcy court with exclusive subject matter jurisdiction to hear all Chapter 7, 9, 11, 12, and 13 cases. The debtor confers personal jurisdiction upon a bankruptcy court when he files a bankruptcy petition. A creditor confers personal jurisdiction when he files a proof of claim or otherwise appears before the bankruptcy court for purposes other than challenging the court's jurisdiction. The problem since 1982 is determining when bankruptcy courts have subject matter jurisdiction to hear and render a valid judgment in an adversary proceeding which is "related to" or "arises in or under" a bankruptcy case. *See Chapter I; Northern Pipeline Construction Co v Marathon Pipe Line Co, 458 US 50 (1982), Chapter I.*

B. Bankruptcy Cases, Hearings, Proceedings

1. Bankruptcy Cases (Chapters 7, 9, 11, 12, 13)

Jurisdiction of the bankruptcy courts is governed by Title 28, United States Code, not Title 11. Federal district courts have exclusive jurisdiction over bankruptcy cases (Chapter 7, 9, 11, 12, or 13 cases). With the exception of jurisdictional limitations under a Chapter 9 case, the federal district court in which the bankruptcy case is pending also has exclusive jurisdiction over all property of the debtor and the bankruptcy estate. It does not matter where property of the debtor or bankruptcy estate is located, or who has possession of such property, the federal district court has power and control over it. Sovereign immunity as to a governmental unit (the United States, a state, territory, district, municipality, or any agency or instrumentality of such entity) is generally abrogated under the Bankruptcy Code. *11 USC §§101(27), 103(a), 106, 541, 904; 28 USC §1334(a),(d), see United States v Nordic Village, Inc, 503 US 30, 112 S Ct 1011, 117 L Ed 2d 181 (1992), overruled in part by Pub L 103-394, §§113, 702, amending 11 USC §106, effective as to cases pending on Oct 22, 1994.*

Federal district courts are established under Article III of the United States Constitution. Federal district courts are divided into judicial districts or regions encompassing the 50 states, the District of Columbia, and Puerto Rico. In each judicial district are bankruptcy courts, established under Article I of the Constitution. Bankruptcy judges are appointed by the respective United States court of appeals for the judicial district and are judicial officers of the federal district courts. A bankruptcy judge is appointed for a term of 14 years. Upon expiration of the 14-year term and if the judicial council of the circuit so approves, the bankruptcy judge may continue to perform his judicial duties until the earlier of 180 days after expiration of his term or the date a successor is appointed. A bankruptcy judge may be removed only for incompetence, misconduct, neglect of duty, or physical or mental disability. A majority vote of the judges of the judicial council of the respective circuit in which the bankruptcy court is located is required to remove a bankruptcy judge from office. *28 USC §§151, 152(a), (e); see Chapter I.*

A bankruptcy judge must serve on a full-time basis and receives an annual salary of 92 per cent of the salary of a federal district judge.

A bankruptcy judge may not engage in the practice of law while on the bench. Further, a bankruptcy judge may not engage in any other practice, business, occupation, or employment which is inconsistent with or interferes with the performance of his judicial duties. *28 USC §§151, 152(a), (e), 153(a)-(b).*

Under the 1978 Bankruptcy Code, bankruptcy courts were courts of law, equity, and admiralty, with the concomitant broad powers and jurisdiction of such courts. Commencing with *Northern Pipeline Construction Co v Marathon Pipe Line Co,* 458 US 50 (1982), and the 1984 Amendments to the Code, the jurisdiction of the bankruptcy court changed drastically. The bankruptcy court is now a unit of the federal district court; bankruptcy judges are judicial officers of the federal district court. *28 USC §151; see Chapter I.*

Once a bankruptcy petition is filed, the federal district court in each judicial district may refer the Chapter 7, 11, 12, or 13 bankruptcy case to bankruptcy judges in the respective district. Federal district courts generally do refer bankruptcy cases to bankruptcy courts, usually by order of the chief judge of the district court for the judicial district. Bankruptcy judges have all the power, authority, and exclusive jurisdiction of federal district courts to hear any bankruptcy case referred by the federal district court. *28 USC §§151, 157(a), 1334(a).*

Once a Chapter 9 petition is filed, the chief judge of the United States court of appeals for the respective federal judicial district must designate the bankruptcy judge to hear the municipality's Chapter 9 case. The jurisdiction and power of the bankruptcy court are more limited in a Chapter 9 case than in other bankruptcy cases. *See Chapter VII; 11 USC §§103(e)-(f), 904, 921(b).*

2. Sovereign Immunity

The doctrine of sovereign immunity is generally abrogated under the Bankruptcy Code. The federal district or bankruptcy court has jurisdiction to hear a bankruptcy issue involving a governmental unit (United States, state, territory, commonwealth, district, municipality, or any agency or instrumentality of such entity). The court may issue an order, process, or judgment against the governmental unit under the Code or Federal Rules of Bankruptcy Procedure, including a monetary judgment. Enforcement of the order or judgment must be consistent with applicable nonbankruptcy law. Any monetary judgment issued by the bankruptcy court must be paid as if the judgment were rendered by the federal district court. *11 USC §§101(27), 103(a), 106; 28 USC §§1334(a),(d), 2412(d)(2)(A); see United States v Nordic Village, Inc, 503 US 30, 112 S Ct 1011, 117 L Ed 2d 181 (1992), overruled in part by Pub L No 103-394, §§113, 702, amending 11 USC §106, effective as to cases pending on Oct 22, 1994.*

A governmental unit that files a proof of claim in a bankruptcy case is deemed to have waived any existing sovereign immunity with regard to a mutual claim the estate might have against the government that arose out of the same transaction or occurrence as the government's claim. Any claim held by the estate against a governmental unit must be offset against the government's claim. *Pub L No 103-394, §§113, 702, amending 11 USC §106, effective as to cases pending on Oct 22, 1994, and overruling in part United States v Nodic Village, Inc, 503 US 30, 112 S Ct 1011, 117 L Ed 2d 181 (1992); see United States v Whiting Pools, 462 US 198 (1983); see "Setoffs," Chapter XII.*

3. Bankruptcy Proceedings and Hearings

a. General Overview

Once a bankruptcy petition is filed, difficulties occur in determining which proceedings and hearings (as opposed to the bankruptcy case) the bankruptcy court has jurisdiction to hear and resolve by a final order. The bankruptcy court derives its power from the jurisdiction of the federal district court. But the jurisdiction of Article I bankruptcy courts is neither as broad as nor equal to Article III federal district courts. The bankruptcy court does not have jurisdiction to hear and enter a final order in all proceedings that "arise in" or "under" or "relate to" a bankruptcy case. The federal district court generally does have such jurisdiction. *See Northern Pipeline Construction Co v Marathon Pipe Line Co, 458 US 50 (1982); 28 USC §§157(b), 1334(a)-(b).*

However, the federal district court does not have exclusive jurisdiction (the sole power) to hear all proceedings or hearings which could occur in a Chapter 7, 9, 11, 12, or 13 case. Federal district courts have original, but not exclusive, jurisdiction over proceedings and hearings that arise under the Code, or that arise in or relate to a Chapter 7, 9, 11, 12, or 13 bankruptcy case. A state court may have concurrent (shared) jurisdiction with the federal district court, depending upon the particular nonbankruptcy law(s) at issue in the proceeding. *28 USC §1334(b).*

b. Abstention of Federal District Court In a Bankruptcy Proceeding

(1) Permissive Abstention

If the interests of justice or *comity* (courtesy or respect) so warrant, a federal district court has the discretion to abstain from hearing a particular hearing or proceeding arising in or under or related to a bankruptcy case and to defer to the concurrent (shared) jurisdiction of a state court. A discretionary abstention decision of the federal district court is not reviewable on appeal. *28 USC §1334(b), (c)(1), (d)* .

(2) Mandatory Abstention

Unless the matter involves a personal injury tort or wrongful death claim, a federal district court must abstain from hearing a particular proceeding or hearing in a bankruptcy case and defer to the concurrent jurisdiction of a state court if five requirements are met.

(a) One of the litigants (parties) has filed a timely motion to abstain with the federal district court.

(b) The proceeding involves a claim or cause of action based on state law, not on a federal law, treaty, the United States Constitution, or on diversity of citizenship (28 USC §1332), and only relates to, but does not arise under, the Code or in the bankruptcy case. A proceeding *relates to* a bankruptcy case if it affects the size or administration of the bankruptcy estate, or has some "nexus" to the bankruptcy case, but does not directly invoke a substantive section of the Bankruptcy Code. A proceeding *arises under or in* a bankruptcy case if it invokes a substantive right of the Bankruptcy Code or if it could only arise in the context of a bankruptcy case. *See Robinson v Michigan Consolidated Gas Co, 918 F2d 579 (6th Cir 1990); In re Lemco Gypsym, Inc, 910 F2d 784 (11th Cir 1990); and In re Wood, 17 CBC2d 743 (5th Cir 1987), respectively.*

(c) The action or proceeding could not have been filed in any federal court if the bankruptcy petition had not been filed.

(d) An action or proceeding involving the same state law claim has been filed in a state court.

(e) The state law claim or cause of action can be timely *adjudicated* (tried and resolved) in a state court with appropriate jurisdiction over the subject matter. *28 USC §§1332, 1334(b)(2).*

All five requirements must be proven before the federal district court must abstain and defer to the state court. A mandatory abstention decision of the federal district court *to abstain* is not appealable. However, the court's decision *not to abstain* under 28 USC §1334(c)(2) is appealable. *28 USC §1334(d).*

The mandatory abstention provisions do not apply to personal injury tort or wrongful death claims. The federal district court may hear these claims or, in its discretion, abstain and allow another court with appropriate jurisdiction to determine such tort claims. *28 USC §§157(b)(2)(B), (4)-(5), 1334(b), (c)(1)-(2); In re Ben Cooper, Inc, 924 F2d 36 (2d Cir 1991), cert denied, 500 US 928, 111 S Ct 2041 (1991).*

(3) Referred Cases

Once a bankruptcy case is referred to a bankruptcy judge, the same permissive and mandatory abstention provisions discussed above generally apply, with three qualifications. First, personal injury tort and wrongful death claims may not be tried in the bankruptcy court. These claims must be tried in the federal district court, unless the district court abstains and defers to another court with appropriate jurisdiction. Second, the bankruptcy court may hear and enter a final order in core proceedings (directly affecting the administration of the estate), but may not always issue a final order in noncore proceedings (related to or having some connection with a bankruptcy case). A bankruptcy court may only issue a final appealable order in a noncore proceeding if the parties have consented and the federal district court has issued a referral order referring the noncore proceeding to the bankruptcy court. Otherwise, the bankruptcy court may only submit proposed findings of fact and conclusions of law to the federal district court, who then reviews the noncore proceeding *de novo* (possible new trial) and enters a final order. And third, if a timely motion to withdraw is filed by a party to the proceeding, the federal district court must withdraw a core or noncore proceeding from the bankruptcy court if the federal district court determines that resolution of the issues involves both bankruptcy law and other federal laws regulating organizations or activities affecting interstate commerce. *See "Core Proceedings" and "Noncore Proceedings," discussed below; 28 USC §§157(b)-(d), 1334(a)-(c); Citibank v White Motor Corp, 761 F2d 270 (6th Cir 1985).*

c. Basic Strategy

Since most federal district courts refer all bankruptcy (Chapter 7, 11, 12, or 13) cases to bankruptcy courts, four adversarial scenarios are possible in the bankruptcy court. First, a party-in-interest may wish to file a *lawsuit* (adversary complaint) against the debtor or trustee (estate). Second, the debtor or trustee may wish to file an adversary complaint against a party-in-interest. Third, a party may seek to remove an action pending in another court to the bankruptcy court. Or fourth, a party may seek to have the automatic stay lifted to permit continuation of an action pending in another court.

(1) Complaint Against the Debtor or Trustee

A party-in-interest who wishes to file an adversary complaint against the debtor or trustee (estate) must decide whether he believes the cause of action is core or noncore (*see "Core Proceedings" discussed below*). If he believes the proceeding is noncore, he must follow one of the three procedures outlined below regardless of whether the cause of action arose pre- or post-petition:

(a) File a motion for relief from the automatic stay to file a noncore cause of action in a state or other nonbankruptcy court. The motion should: (i) state the *grounds* (reasons) why the party believes the cause of action is noncore; and (ii) seek a bankruptcy court order lifting the stay to allow the cause of action to be filed in a state court. The *automatic stay* enjoins all acts against property of the estate and all actions against the debtor and his property to recover a pre-petition claim. If the cause of action arose pre-petition and involves determination of noncore matters, the bankruptcy court should lift the stay to permit the proceeding to be filed in a state or other court with appropriate jurisdiction, unless it appears that all the parties to the action will agree to the bankruptcy court's entering a final judgment or order in the proceeding. If the cause of action arose post-petition and the creditor will seek satisfaction of his claim from the estate, the bankruptcy court must lift the stay before the creditor may file the cause of action in a nonbankruptcy court and recover from the estate. The court should grant the motion and lift the stay to allow a state court to hear a post-petition claim that involves noncore matters. The purpose of the automatic stay is to allow for the orderly distribution of the debtor's assets and property of the estate to pay pre-petition claims. However, if the post-petition claim is a first priority administrative expense, the matter becomes a core proceeding and the court should deny the motion and direct the creditor to file a request for allowance of claim and a proof of claim asserting an administrative expense against the estate (*see "File Proof of claim," Chapter XIV*). The motion for relief from the automatic stay does not commence an adversary proceeding, but the creditor must pay a $60 filing fee. No filing fee is required to file a request for allowance of an administrative expense. A copy of the motion or request must be served on the debtor, any trustee, all committee(s), and on any other entity required by court order or local bankruptcy rules. Service may be obtained by first-class mail or by any other manner allowed for service of summons and complaint in federal district court. *See "Core Proceedings" & "Noncore Proceedings," discussed below; "Priority Claims," Chapter II; "File Proof of Claim" and "Motion for Relief from Automatic Stay," Chapter XIV; 11 USC §362(a)(1)-(4); 28 USC §§151, 157, 1930(b), Judicial Conference Schedule of Fees (21); FRBP 4001(a)(1), 9014; HR Rep No 595, 95th Cong, 1st Sess 343-44 (1977);* or

(b) File an adversary complaint in the bankruptcy court and a motion for withdrawal of the noncore adversary proceeding to the federal district court. The creditor may then continue the action in the federal district court or file a motion to abstain in the federal district court, seeking a federal district court order abstaining to allow the noncore proceeding to continue in a state or other court with concurrent jurisdiction. However, the federal district court has jurisdiction to hear noncore proceedings related to or arising in a bankruptcy case or under the Code. Unless mandatory abstention is required of the federal district court, the decision to abstain is discretionary. And if the cause of action involves either a personal injury tort or wrongful death claim, the federal district court must withdraw the proceeding from the bankruptcy court, but the mandatory abstention requirements do not apply. Similarly, if resolution of the action involves bankruptcy law and other federal laws regulating organizations or activities affecting interstate commerce, the federal district court must withdraw the proceeding from the bankruptcy court if a party to the action files a timely motion for withdrawal. *See "Abstention of Federal District Court in a Bankruptcy Proceeding" discussed above; "Motion for Withdrawal Order," discussed below; 28 USC §§151, 157(b)(1)-(2)(B), (4)-(5), (d), 1334(b), (c)(1)-(2); FRBP 7001(1) et seq;* or

(c) File an adversary complaint in the bankruptcy court, agree to have the action tried in the bankruptcy court, agree to entry of a final order by the bankruptcy court, and file a motion for referral order seeking a referral order from the federal district court for the noncore action to be determined by final order of the bankruptcy court. The motion for referral order, although filed with the bankruptcy clerk, will be heard by the federal district court. *See "Motion for Referral Order," discussed below; 28 USC §157(c)(1)-(2); FRBP 7001(1) et seq.*

(2) Complaint by Debtor or Trustee Against Party-In-Interest

If the debtor or trustee files an adversary complaint against a party-in-interest in the bankruptcy court, the defendant must decide if he believes the action is core or noncore and then file either a motion for withdrawal or motion for referral order according to procedures (b) or (c) outlined above. *28 USC §§157(b)-(d), 1334(b)-(c); FRBP 7001(1) et seq.*

(3) Remove Pending Action

An action pending in another court may be removed to the bankruptcy court. The nonbankruptcy party seeking removal must file a notice of removal in the bankruptcy court and pay a $120 filing fee. A copy of the notice with a summons must be served on all the parties to the removed action by first-class mail or any other method allowed for service of process in federal district court. The party seeking removal must indicate in the notice if the removed action is core or noncore and indicate whether such party consents to have the bankruptcy court enter a final judgment or order if the removed action is noncore. *See Chapter XI; 28 USC §§1452(a), 1930(b), Judicial Conference Schedule of Fees (6); FRBP 7001(1), (10) et seq, 9014, 9027.*

(4) File Motion for Relief to Permit Continuation of Pending Action

A nonbankruptcy party to a pre-petition action pending in another court may file a motion for relief from the automatic stay to permit continuation of the pre-petition action. The motion should state: (a) the grounds why the pending action is a noncore proceeding; and (b) seek a bankruptcy court order lifting the automatic stay to allow the pending action to be tried in another court. The motion for relief does not commence an adversary proceeding, but a $60 filing fee is required. A copy of the motion must be served by first-class mail or any other method allowed for service of process in federal district court on the debtor, any trustee, all committees, and any other entity required by court order or local bankruptcy rules. A copy of the motion should also be served on all parties to the pending action. *11 USC §362(d)(1); 28 USC §1930(b), Judicial Conference Schedule of Fees (21); FRBP 4001, 9014; see "Stage Two—Automatic Stay Invoked," Chapter II, and "Motion for Relief from Automatic Stay," Chapter XIV.*

Determining whether an action or proceeding is core or noncore thus becomes a crucial issue to making any basic strategy decision.

d. Core Proceedings

The bankruptcy court, as a "unit of" the federal district court, has exclusive jurisdiction to hear all Chapter 7, 9, 11, 12, and 13 bankruptcy cases. A bankruptcy judge also has authority to hear and enter a final order in all core proceedings that arise in or under a bankruptcy case. Core proceedings involve the administration of the bankruptcy estate, may be contested or uncontested, and include, but are not limited to, 16 types of proceedings:

(1) Matters related to the administration of the bankruptcy estate (determining the size, amount, or distribution of the estate);

(2) The bankruptcy court's allowance or disallowance of proofs of claims against the estate, including estimation of claims for distribution of the estate.

However, the federal district court, not the bankruptcy court, either must hear proceedings involving the liquidation or estimation of unliquidated, contingent, personal injury tort or wrongful death claims against a bankruptcy estate or may abstain and allow the tort action to be tried in a nonbankruptcy court with appropriate jurisdiction. *See Citibank v White Motor Corp, 761 F2d 270 (6th Cir 1985); 28 USC §§157(b)(2)(B)(4)-(5), 1334(b), (c)(1);*

(3) The bankruptcy court's allowance or disallowance of the debtor's exemptions claimed on Schedule C of the schedules of assets and liabilities.

Official Form 6, Schedule C;

(4) Counterclaims which a trustee (or Chapter 9, 11, or 12 debtor) files on behalf of the estate against a creditor who filed a proof of claim against the estate.

See "File Proof of Claim," Chapter XIV;

(5) Hearings and related orders to enable a trustee or debtor to obtain post-petition credit.

See Chapter VIII;

(6) Hearings to order an entity to turn over property to the trustee for the estate.

See "Stage Four—Turn Over Property to the Estate," Chapter II;

(7) Hearings to determine and avoid preferential transfers of property and to recover such property for the estate.

See Chapter XII;

(8) Hearings to lift, modify, or terminate the automatic stay.

See "Stage Two—Automatic Stay Invoked," Chapter II, and "Motion for Relief from Automatic Stay," Chapter XIV;

(9) Hearings to determine and avoid fraudulent transfers of property and to recover such property for the estate.

See Chapter XII;

(10) Hearings to determine the dischargeability of particular pre-petition debts.

See "Exceptions to Discharge," Chapter III;

(11) Hearings to object to the debtor's discharge (denial of discharge).

See "Procedure Seven—Discharge of the Debtor," Chapters III; "Procedure Ten—Discharge," Chapter IV; "Procedure Seven—Discharge of the Debtor," Chapter V; "Chapter 12 Discharge Less Liberal," Chapter VI; and "Procedure Seven—Discharge," Chapter VII;

(12) **Hearings to determine the validity, amount, or priority of any lien against any property involved in a bankruptcy case.**

See Chapter VIII; "Valuation of Collateral," Chapter XIV;

(13) **Confirmation hearings.**

See Chapters III-VII;

(14) **Hearings and related orders involving the trustee's or debtor's use or lease of any property involved in a bankruptcy case, including cash collateral.**

See Chapter VIII;

(15) **Hearings and related orders approving the sale of property involved in a bankruptcy case, other than property recovered by the trustee from third parties who have not filed a proof of claim in the bankruptcy case.**

See Chapter VIII; "File Proof of Claim," Chapter XIV; or

(16) **Any other proceeding which involves liquidation of property of the estate or the adjustment of the debtor-creditor or debtor-equity-security-holder status in a bankruptcy case.**

However, contingent or unliquidated, contested personal injury tort and wrongful death claims against the bankruptcy estate may not be tried in the bankruptcy court. The federal district court in the judicial district where the bankruptcy case is pending may, in its discretion, hear such personal injury or wrongful death action, or transfer the action to the federal district court in the judicial district where the claim arose, or abstain and allow the action to be tried in a state court with appropriate jurisdiction. *28 USC §157(b)(1)-(2), (4)-(5), 1334(b), (c)(1); see Citibank v White Motor Corp, 761 F2d 270 (6th Cir 1985).*

A proceeding may involve application of state law or a state law issue (contracts or breach of warranty) and still retain its core proceeding status. The bankruptcy judge determines if a proceeding is core or noncore, subject to appellate review by the federal district court or bankruptcy appellate panel. *28 USC §§157(b)(3), 158; see "Appeal of Bankruptcy Court Order," discussed below.*

e. Noncore Proceedings

A proceeding does not become noncore merely because it involves or is affected by state law. Title 28, United States Code, specifically requires that contested, unliquidated or contingent personal injury tort and wrongful death claims be tried in the federal district court or that such district court may, in its discretion, abstain and allow such claim(s) to be tried in a state court where an action was pending pre-petition. Title 28 also requires the federal district court to withdraw from the bankruptcy court any proceeding that involves resolution of bankruptcy law and other federal laws regulating organizations or activities affecting interstate commerce, if a party to such proceeding files a timely motion for withdrawal order. But many noncore issues may arise in or relate to a bankruptcy case and be heard by the bankruptcy court. *28 USC §157(b)(2)(B), (3)-(5), 1334(c)(1); see Citibank v White Motor Corp, 761 F2d 270 (6th Cir 1985).*

A bankruptcy court may hear a noncore proceeding, with two possible results. The first result is a hearing in the bankruptcy court and a subsequent *review de novo* (possible new trial) in the federal district court because the bankruptcy judge heard a noncore proceeding without the consent of all the parties to entry of a final order by the bankruptcy court and without a referral order from the federal district court. In the absence of such required consent and referral order, the bankruptcy court may only submit proposed findings of fact and conclusions of law to the federal district court. The federal district court must review the bankruptcy court's findings and conclusions de novo, which could mean a complete new trial in the federal district court. *De novo review* requires the district court to make an independent assessment of the issues and permits such court to take additional evidence. The federal district court will then enter a final order, subject to appeal to the respective federal circuit court of appeals for the judicial district. Thus, without the consent of all parties and the federal district court, any noncore proceeding held in the bankruptcy court could become a dress rehearsal or "mock trial." The real trial would be held thereafter in the federal district court. *28 USC §157(c)(1)-(2); see Home Insurance Co v Cooper & Cooper Ltd, 889 F2d 746 (7th Cir 1989); Moody & Jermoo's, Inc v Amoco Oil Co, 734 F2d 1200 (7th Cir 1984), cert denied, 469 US 982 (1984); and In re Lyon Capital Group, 13 CBC2d 355 (SDNY 1985).*

The alternative, second result is a real trial in the bankruptcy court with the bankruptcy judge issuing a final order subject to appeal like any other court order. No new trial is held in the federal district court. The federal district court merely reviews the final (or interlocutory order) of the bankruptcy court on appeal if such order is appealed. To obtain this second result and a real trial in the bankruptcy court with a final appealable order, consent to trial of the noncore proceeding in the bankruptcy court must be obtained from all the parties to the proceeding and a referral order must be obtained from the federal district court. *See "Procedures to Determine Core Versus Noncore Proceedings," discussed below; 28 USC §157(b)(3), (c)(1)-(2).*

f. Procedures to Determine Core Versus Noncore Proceedings

The initial issue when an adversary complaint or contested matter is filed in the bankruptcy court involving bankruptcy and nonbankruptcy (federal or state) law is whether the proceeding is core or noncore. Hearings on valuation of collateral, the automatic stay, an adversary complaint to avoid a preferential or fraudulent transfer of property or to object to the debtor's discharge are clearly core proceedings, because they invoke a substantive section of the Bankruptcy Code. But what about an adversary complaint filed by a trustee or debtor-in-possession to avoid a debtor's contract with a creditor and recover damages because of the creditor's alleged usury or deceptive trade practices? Such proceeding obviously affects the size and administration of the bankruptcy estate. Recovery of damages would increase the estate. But the lawsuit also involves questions of state and, perhaps, federal nonbankruptcy law. The bankruptcy judge will ultimately determine if the hearing is core or noncore after reviewing the pleadings of the parties. *11 USC §§502, 541; 28 USC §157(b)(2)-(3); FRBP 3007, 7001 et seq.*

(1) Procedure One—Plaintiff's Pleadings

In every adversary complaint filed with a bankruptcy court, the plaintiff (including counterclaim, cross-claim, or third-party plaintiff) must include: (a) the name, number, and chapter of the bankruptcy case; (b) a statement whether the proceeding is core or noncore; and (c) a statement whether the plaintiff consents to the bankruptcy court's hearing the proceeding and entering a final order if it is noncore. *FRBP 7008(a), 7014.*

(2) Procedure Two—Defendant's Answer

A defendant must serve an answer to an adversary complaint filed in the bankruptcy court before the 30th day after the date the summons is issued, unless the court orders a different time. A cross-claim, counterclaim, or third-party defendant must serve a reply before the 20th day after the counterclaim, cross-claim or third-party complaint is served. All answers or replies must contain: (a) an admission or denial that the proceeding is core or noncore; and (b) a statement whether such party consents to the bankruptcy court's hearing the proceeding and entering a final order if it is noncore. *FRBP 7012(a)-(b), 7014.*

(3) Procedure Three—All Parties Agree that the Proceeding Is Core or Noncore

(a) Core Proceeding

Even if all parties agree that the proceeding is a core proceeding, the bankruptcy court may, on its own, decide that the hearing is noncore and require a referral order from the federal district court to allow for trial and entry of a final, appealable order by the bankruptcy court. *28 USC §157(b)(3), (c)(2); see discussion below.*

(b) Noncore Proceeding

If the parties agree that the matter is a noncore proceeding, one of six procedures must be used.

(i) Sua Sponte Withdrawal by District Court

The federal district court may issue a withdrawal order withdrawing the entire bankruptcy case or just a proceeding from the bankruptcy court if cause exists (noncore proceeding). The district court may withdraw any bankruptcy case or proceeding on its own motion (sua sponte) or on timely motion of a party (*see* discussion below). *28 USC §157(d).*

(ii) Motion for Withdrawal Order

One of the parties may file a motion for withdrawal of the entire bankruptcy case or only the noncore proceeding by the federal district court. The motion must be timely filed with the bankruptcy clerk, state the grounds for withdrawal (noncore proceeding), and be served by first-class mail or any other method for service of process in federal district court on all parties to the proceeding, the debtor, any trustee, all committee(s), and any other entity required by the bankruptcy court or local bankruptcy rules. The motion does not commence an adversary proceeding, but a $60 filing fee is required if the motion is to withdraw reference of the entire bankruptcy case. Although the motion is filed with the bankruptcy clerk, it must be heard by the federal district court. If the motion is for withdrawal of the proceeding and the federal district court agrees that the proceeding is noncore, the district court should then issue a withdrawal order withdrawing the noncore proceeding to the district court. *28 USC §§157(d), 1930(b), Judicial Conference Schedule of Fees (21); FRBP 5011(a), 9013-9014.*

(iii) Motion for Bankruptcy Court to Abstain from Proceeding

One of the parties to the proceeding may file a motion to abstain with the bankruptcy clerk. The motion must state the grounds for the bankruptcy court's abstention from hearing the proceeding (noncore proceeding) and be served by first-class mail or any other method allowed for service of process in federal district court on all parties to the proceeding, the debtor, any trustee, all committee(s), and all other parties-in-interest required by court order or local bankruptcy rules. The bankruptcy court must abstain if the proceeding involves:

a) a personal injury tort or wrongful death claim. The federal district court, not the bankruptcy court, may hear such claims: *28 USC §157(b)(2)(B), (5);*

b) a state law claim or cause of action that could not have been filed in any federal court but for the bankruptcy petition, the action has been filed and may be timely adjudicated in a state court with appropriate jurisdiction, and the motion to abstain was timely filed. *28 USC §1334(c)(2);* or

c) a cause of action whose resolution requires consideration of both the bankruptcy code and other federal laws regulating organizations or activities affecting interstate commerce, and a timely motion for withdrawal order has also been filed. *28 USC §157(d); FRBP 5011(a); see "Motion for Withdrawal Order," discussed above.*

In all other situations, the bankruptcy court's decision whether to abstain is discretionary. A bankruptcy court order to abstain from hearing an action pending in the state court at the time the petition was filed and which does not involve a federal law, treaty, the United States Constitution, or diversity of citizenship may be appealed only to the federal district court. However, an order of the bankruptcy court not to abstain from hearing such an action pending in state court may be appealed to the federal district court, court of appeals, and Supreme Court. An abstention order will not affect the continuation of the automatic stay if the proceeding involves any action to obtain property of the estate. *11 USC §362(a)(3)-(4); 28 USC §§157(b)(2)(B), (4)-(5), 1332, 1334(c)(1)-(2); FRBP 5011; Advisory committee's note—1987 Amendment, 9013-9014; §309(b), Judicial Improvements Act of 1990; see "Stage Two—Automatic Stay Invoked," Chapter II, and "Motion for Relief from Automatic Stay" Chapter XIV.*

(iv) Motion to Abstain from Case

Except under Chapter 9, one party may file a motion to abstain asking the bankruptcy court to abstain from the entire bankruptcy (Chapter 7, 11, 12, or 13) case. The motion must be filed with the bankruptcy clerk and is heard by the bankruptcy court. The motion must state that the interests of creditors and the debtor would be better served by the bankruptcy court's abstention from the entire bankruptcy case. The motion must be served by first-class mail or any other method allowed for service of process in federal district court on all parties to the proceeding, the debtor, any trustee, all committee(s), and any other entity required by court order or local bankruptcy rules. Notice of the motion and hearing date must be mailed by the debtor, clerk, or other court-authorized person to all creditors, the debtor, parties to the proceeding, any trustee, all committee(s), and to such other entities as required by court order or local bankruptcy rules. An order of the bankruptcy court to abstain or not abstain from the entire bankruptcy case may only be appealed to the federal district court. No higher appellate court may review the order. *11 USC §§102(1)(A)-(B), 103(a), (e), 305, 901; FRBP 1017(c), 2002, 9007, 9013-9014.*

(v) Motion for Referral Order

All parties to the proceeding may consent to have the noncore proceeding heard before the bankruptcy court and to entry of a final order by the bankruptcy court that may be appealed to the federal district court or bankruptcy appellate panel. The parties should file a joint motion for referral order with the bankruptcy clerk. The motion should be served by first-class mail on the debtor, any trustee, all committee(s), and on all other parties-in-interest required by court order or local bankruptcy rules. The federal district court will hear the motion and may, in its discretion, then refer the noncore proceeding to the bankruptcy court for determination and entry of a final order. *28 USC §157(c)(2); FRBP 9007, 9013-9014.*

(vi) Preliminary Hearing (Possible Mock Trial) in the Bankruptcy Court

The parties may agree to allow the bankruptcy court to hear the noncore proceeding and issue only proposed findings of fact and conclusions of law subject to *review de novo* (possible new trial) in the federal district court. *28 USC §157(c)(1).*

(4) **Procedure Four—Parties Disagree Whether Core or Noncore**

If the parties cannot agree whether the hearing is core or noncore (one party claims it is noncore), the bankruptcy court will make the initial determination. Thereafter, one of the above six procedures must be used. If the proceeding is held to be noncore, there could be a review de novo in the federal district court unless a referral order is obtained from the federal district court to permit the bankruptcy court to hear a noncore proceeding and enter a final order. *See "Procedures to Determine Core Versus Noncore Proceedings," discussed above; 11 USC §305; 28 USC §§157(b)(2)-(3), (c)(1)-(2), (d), 1334; FRBP 1017(c), 5011, 9007, 9013-9014.*

C. Jury Trials in Bankruptcy Cases

Section 1411 of Title 28 permits an *individual* (natural person) a jury trial in bankruptcy cases where a right to jury trial would exist under nonbankruptcy law in actions involving personal inquiry and wrongful death tort claims. Personal injury or wrongful death tort claims in a bankruptcy case must be tried in the federal district court for the judicial district where the bankruptcy case is pending or where such claim arose or the federal district court may abstain and allow such tort claim to be tried in a (state) court if a lawsuit involving such claim was pending pre-petition. If the federal district court decides not to abstain, the federal district court where the bankruptcy case is pending will determine in which district the tort claim arose. *28 USC §§157(b)(4)-(5), 1334(c)(1)-(2), 1411; see Citibank v White Motor Corp, 761 F2d 270 (6th Cir 1985).*

The Bankruptcy Reform Act of 1994 amended Title 28 to permit jury trials by bankruptcy courts in cases filed after October 22, 1994, if three conditions exist. Section 157(e) of Title 28 requires that:

1. The right to a Seventh Amendment jury trial would apply in the proceeding before the bankruptcy court;
2. The district court in the federal judicial district where the bankruptcy case is pending has specially designated bankruptcy courts in its district to conduct jury trials; and
3. All parties to the proceeding expressly consent to a jury trial in the bankruptcy court. *Pub L No 103-394, §112 amending and adding 28 USC §157(e).*

The Supreme Court has ruled that a defendant who has not filed a proof of claim against the bankruptcy estate has a Seventh Amendment constitutional right to a jury trial when sued by a bankruptcy trustee to recover an alleged fraudulent transfer of money. However, a defendant who has filed a claim against the estate does not have a right to jury trial in a trustee's preference action. *See Granfinanciera, SA v Nordberg, 492 US 33 (1989); Langenkamp v Culp, 498 US 42, 111 S Ct 330 (1990); Katchen v Landy, 382 US 323 (1966).*

The federal circuit courts of appeals have been split on the issue of jury trials in the bankruptcy court on tort and nontort claims. Seven circuits considered the issue of jury trials in bankruptcy courts under the 1984 Bankruptcy Amendments and Federal Judgeship Act, before enactment of 28 USC §157(e) under the Bankruptcy Reform Act of 1994. The Second Circuit has held that jury trials may be held in the bankruptcy court. The Fourth, Fifth, Sixth, Seventh, Eighth, and Tenth Circuits have held that bankruptcy judges may not preside over jury trials. *Ben Cooper, Inc v The Insurance Co, 896 F2d 1394 (2d Cir), cert granted, 110 S Ct 3269, vacated & remanded, 111 S Ct 425 (1990), opinion reinstated on remand, 924 F2d 36 (2d Cir), cert denied, 111 S Ct 2041 (1991); Contra, Official Committee v Schwartzman (In re Stansbury Popular Place, Inc), 13 F3d 122 (4th Cir 1993), In re Clay, 35 F3d 190 (5th Cir 1994), Rafoth v National Union Fire Ins Co (In re Baker & Getty Financial Services, Inc), 954 F2d 1169 (6th Cir 1992), In re Grabell, 967 F2d 1152 (7th Cir 1992), In re United States Missouri Bank, 901 F2d 1449 (8th Cir 1990) and Kaiser Steel Corp v Frates, 911 F2d 380 (10th Cir 1990), respectively; 28 USC §1411.*

D. Appeal of Bankruptcy Court Order

1. To Federal District Court

Federal district courts have jurisdiction to hear appeals from final orders or decrees of a bankruptcy court within their respective judicial districts. Federal district courts also have jurisdiction to hear appeals from interlocutory orders issued by the bankruptcy court if a timely notice and proper motion for leave to appeal is filed with the bankruptcy clerk by the appellant. However, interlocutory orders issued by the bankruptcy court under 11 USC §112(d) increasing or reducing the Chapter 11 debtor's period of exclusivity to file and have a plan confirmed by the court are appealable by right to the federal district court. *28 USC §§157, 158(a); FRBP 8001, 8003.*

2. To Bankruptcy Appellate Panel Service (BAPS)

a. Requirements for a BAPS Appeal

The judicial council in each federal circuit must establish a Bankruptcy Appellate Panel Service (BAPS) to hear appeals, unless the council finds that insufficient judicial resources exist or that a BAPS would increase the delay or costs to the parties in a bankruptcy case. A BAPS may hear an appeal if:

(1) A majority of the district judges in the federal judicial district have authorized appeals to a BAPS; and

(2) All parties to the appeal consent to have the appeal heard by a BAPS. The parties will be deemed to have consented to a BAPS unless the appellant elects to have the appeal heard by the district court at the time the appeal is filed or the appellee elects to have a federal district court appeal no later than the 30th day after the notice of appeal is served. *28 USC §158(b)(1)(c).*

b. Composition of a BAPS

A BAPS will be composed of bankruptcy judges appointed by the judicial council from the judicial districts in each circuit. A three-judge panel of bankruptcy judges will hear an appeal. However, no bankruptcy judge may hear an appeal of a case that originated in his or her district. *28 USC §158(b)(1)(3)(5).*

Judicial councils of two or more federal circuits may establish a joint BAPS if authorized by the Judicial Conference of the United States. The joint BAPS will also be composed of bankruptcy judges from districts within the respective circuits. Consent of the parties to a joint BAPS appeal is required. The appellant must elect to have a federal district court hear the appeal when the appeal is filed and the appellee must make such election by the 30th day after the notice of appeal is served, or the required consent to a joint BAPS will be deemed given by the parties. *28 USC §158(b)(4)(c).*

c. Reconsideration of the BAPS

The judicial council must file a report with the Judicial Conference of the United States if the council finds that insufficient judicial resources exist in the circuit to establish a BAPS or that a BAPS would increase the costs or cause undue delay to the parties in a bankruptcy case. The judicial council must submit its report no later than the 90th day after making such a finding. The report must include a factual basis for the council's finding. The judicial council may reconsider its finding at any time. *28 USC §158(b)(1)(2)(A).*

At any time after one year after the date a BAPS is established, a majority of the district court judges in the circuit may file a request requiring the judicial council for the circuit to reconsider the BAPS. The judicial council must then redetermine whether sufficient funds exist to maintain a BAPS or whether the BAPS has resulted in increased costs or undue delay to the parties. *28 USC §158(b)(2)(B).*

The judicial council may make such a redetermination *sua sponte* at any time after three years after the date the BAPS is established. If the judicial council finds that either insufficient funds or increased cost or delay warrant discontinuation of the BAPS, the council may provide that pending appeals be heard by the BAPS before its orderly termination. *28 USC §158(b)(2)(C)(D). See "Procedure on Appeal" below; FRBP 8007(d), 8018; Local Appellate Rules; Local Bankruptcy and District Court Rules.*

3. Procedures on Appeal

Whether appeal of a bankruptcy court order is to the federal district court or a bankruptcy appellate panel, strict procedures must be observed.

a. Timely Appeal of Final Order

(1) What Is Required

Appeal of a final order of the bankruptcy court begins by filing a notice of appeal with the bankruptcy clerk. This notice must conform substantively to Official Bankruptcy Form 17. The notice must include the:

(a) Names of all parties to the order being appealed;

(b) Respective name, address, and telephone number of the attorney for each party to the appealed order;

(c) Five-dollar filing fee for the appeal; and

(d) Sufficient copies of the notice of appeal to enable the clerk of the bankruptcy court to mail a copy of the notice to the attorney of record for each party to the appealed order or to the party directly if he has no attorney of record. *28 USC §158(a)-(b), 1930(c); FRBP 8001, 8004; Official Bankr Form 17.*

(2) Where to File the Notice of Appeal

The notice of appeal must be filed with the bankruptcy clerk. If the notice is mistakenly filed with the clerk of the federal district court or the bankruptcy appellate panel, such clerk must: (a) note on the notice the date it was received; and (b) transmit the notice to the bankruptcy clerk. The notice is then deemed properly filed with the bankruptcy clerk on the date so noted. *FRBP 8002(a).*

(3) When to File the Notice of Appeal

The time to file a notice of appeal may be broken into two periods—a timely 10-day period or a dilatory 20-day period:

(a) Computing Time Generally

To compute the time in which any required action must be taken under the FRBP, the date of the event at issue is not counted. The next day begins the time period as day 1. The subsequent days are counted consecutively. The last day of the time period is counted unless the last day is a Saturday, Sunday, legal holiday, or other day the clerk's office is closed or inaccessible (inclement weather) for required filing of papers. In such cases, the last day of the time period is extended until the next working day for the clerk's office. Intervening Saturdays, Sundays, and legal holidays are included and counted during the computed time period unless the time period is less than eight days (seven days or less). In many cases, the required time will be extended by the court if a motion for extension of time is filed before the original time to act expires, and cause is shown for granting the extension of time. The time may also be extended by the court if a motion for extension of time is filed after the original time to act expires upon a showing of cause and excusable neglect for filing the motion untimely. *FRBP 9006(a)-(b).*

Thus, if an action must be filed within (before) 10 days after entry of a bankruptcy order and the order is entered on April 1st, the notice should be filed before April 11th, unless such date is a Saturday, Sunday, legal holiday, or day the clerk's office is otherwise closed, or the court extends the time. April 1st is the date of the event (order entered) and is not counted. April 2nd becomes day 1 of the time period. The subsequent days (April 2, 3, 4, 5. . . .) are counted consecutively. Intervening Saturdays, Sundays, and legal holidays are counted because the time period is greater than seven days. The 10th or last day is April 11th which is counted, but the time period to file is within (before) 10 days after the order is entered. *FRBP 8002, 9006(a).*

(b) Timely 10-Day Period for Notice of Appeal

The safest time to file a notice of appeal is before the 10th day after entry of the bankruptcy order being appealed. The time is shortened in bankruptcy cases (from 30) to 10 days to permit prompt appellate review which is often necessary to the administration of a bankruptcy case. A notice of appeal filed after the court has rendered its decision but before entry of the order is treated as filed on the date the order is entered. *FRBP 8002(a), advisory committee's note to Rule 8002.*

(c) Dilatory 20-Day Period

The bankruptcy court may, in its discretion, permit a notice of appeal to be filed no later than the 20th day after expiration of the (timely) 10-day period (on the 29th day after entry of the bankruptcy order). But a request to extend time to file the notice of appeal must be filed with the bankruptcy court. The safest time to file this request to extend time is before the 10th day after entry of the bankruptcy order (within the original timely 10-day period). However, the appellant may file a request to extend time with a notice of appeal no later than the 20th day after such 10-day period expires if he can show excusable neglect and if the bankruptcy order being appealed does not:

(i) Authorize the sale of any property;

(ii) Authorize the trustee or debtor to obtain credit or additional debt post-petition;

(iii) Approve a disclosure statement;

(iv) Confirm a plan;

(v) Dismiss a case; or

(vi) Convert a case to another chapter. *FRBP 8001(a), (c), 9006(b)(3).*

If a request to extend time is filed after the 20th day, no appeal may be taken. The bankruptcy court may not permit a notice of appeal to be filed after expiration of the 20-day period. *FRBP 8001, 8002(a), (c), 9006(b)(3).*

(d) Effect of Other Motions on the Time to Appeal

If any party files a timely motion for new trial, to amend or make additional findings of fact, or to alter or amend the judgment, the time period for filing a notice of appeal begins the date the bankruptcy court enters an order disposing of the last of such motions. A notice of appeal filed before disposition of such order has no legal effect until the order disposing of such motion is entered by the bankruptcy court. *FRBP 8002(b).*

b. Timely Appeal of Interlocutory Order

An interlocutory bankruptcy order (order which does not resolve all the issues raised in the adversary complaint or proceeding) may only be appealed with leave (permission) of the federal district court. *28 USC §158(a); FRBP 8003, advisory committee's note.*

(1) Requirements

Appeal from an interlocutory bankruptcy order requires filing a timely notice, motion, and proof of service.

(a) Timely notice of appeal must be filed with the bankruptcy clerk. *See "When To File the Notice of Appeal," discussed above;*

(b) Timely motion for leave to appeal must be filed with the notice of appeal or before the 10th day after entry of any order of the appellate court directing that a motion for leave to appeal be filed, unless such order states otherwise.

The motion for leave to appeal is filed with the federal bankruptcy clerk's office but is addressed to the appellate court (federal district court or bankruptcy appellate panel). The motion must include a:

(i) Statement of relevant facts necessary to understand the issues on appeal;

(ii) Statement of the issues and relief sought on appeal;

(iii) Statement of reasons why the motion for leave to appeal an interlocutory bankruptcy order should be granted; and

(iv) Copy of the interlocutory bankruptcy order being appealed and any opinion or memorandum of the bankruptcy court; and

(c) **Proof of service showing the date and manner of service of the motion for leave to appeal by the appellant and the name and address of each attorney of record for each party to the appeal, or each party if there is no attorney of record, so served. Service may be obtained by first-class mail.** *FRBP 8001(b), 8003(a), (c), advisory committee's note, 8008, 9013-9014.*

(2) If No Motion Filed

If the notice of appeal was timely filed but a motion for leave to appeal an interlocutory order is not filed timely, the appellate court may grant leave to appeal without the motion or issue an order directing the appellant to file the motion for leave to appeal. The motion must then be filed with the bankruptcy clerk before the 10th day after entry of the order of the appellate court, unless such order directs otherwise. *28 USC §158(a); FRBP 8001(a)-(b), 8003(a), (c).*

(3) Appellee's Response

The appellee may file an answer in opposition to the appellant's motion for leave to appeal. Any answer must be filed with the bankruptcy clerk before the 10th day after the motion for leave to appeal was served on the appellee. *FRBP 8003(a).*

(4) Transmission of Motion and Notice

The clerk of the bankruptcy court must transmit the notice of appeal, motion for leave to appeal, and any answer in opposition to the clerk of the appellate court. These papers must be transmitted as soon as all parties to the appeal have filed an answer or the time to file an answer has expired. *FRBP 8003(b).*

c. Consent to Appeal to Bankruptcy Appellate Panel

Unless local appellate rules direct otherwise, the parties must file a statement of consent to have the appeal heard by the bankruptcy appellate panel. The statement of consent may be filed separately or included in the notice of appeal. The statement must be filed with the bankruptcy clerk before the later date that the bankruptcy clerk transmits a copy of the record on appeal to the appellate court or the 30th day after the notice of appeal is filed. *28 USC §158(b); FRBP 8001(e), 8007(b), 8018; see "Transmission of Record on Appeal," discussed below.*

d. Service of the Notice of Appeal

After the appellant files a notice of appeal, the clerk of the bankruptcy court must mail a copy of the notice to each attorney of record for each party to the appealed order or directly to the party at his last known address if there is no attorney of record. The clerk must note the date the notice of appeal was filed on each copy of the notice sent to the parties or their attorneys and note on the docket the names of the parties and respective date(s) of mailing. The bankruptcy clerk must also mail or deliver a copy of the notice of appeal to the U.S. trustee. However, failure of the clerk to serve copies of the notice of appeal on the parties or the U.S. trustee does not affect the validity of the appeal. *FRBP 8004.*

e. Appeal by Other Parties

Once a timely notice of appeal has been filed, any other party to the appealed order may file a notice of appeal with the bankruptcy clerk. A notice of appeal filed by an appellee is called a cross-appeal. Notice of appeal filed by a nonappellee is a separate appeal. A cross-appeal or separate appeal must be filed before the 10th day after the first notice of appeal was filed by the original appellant. The bankruptcy court may, in its discretion, extend the time to file notice of a cross or separate appeal no more than 20 days after expiration of such 10-day period. But the cross or other appellant must file a request for extension of time within such 10-day period or no later than the 20th day after expiration of such period upon showing excusable neglect and that the appealed order does not involve: (1) the sale of property, (2) post-petition credit, (3) approval of a disclosure statement, (4) confirmation of a plan, or (5) dismissal or conversion of a bankruptcy case. The appellate court may consolidate the appeals. *FRBP 8002(a), (c), advisory committee's note.*

f. Record on Appeal

(1) Contents

The record on appeal consists of:

(a) All items timely designated by the parties;

(b) The notice of appeal;

(c) The order, judgment, or decree being appealed; and

(d) Any opinion or findings of fact and conclusions of law of the bankruptcy court. *FRBP 8006.*

(2) Required Papers and Time Periods

The parties to the appealed order must file the following papers timely.

(a) Appellant

The appellant must file a statement of designated items and a statement of issues to be included in the record on appeal. These statements must be filed with the bankruptcy clerk and served on the appellee before the 10th day after the appellant's notice of appeal is filed. If an interlocutory order is being appealed, the appellant must file and serve these statements before the 10th day after entry of the appellate court's order granting the motion for leave to appeal. Service may be obtained by first-class mail. *FRBP 8006, 9013-9014; see Local Bankruptcy Rules;*

(b) Appellee

The appellee may file with the bankruptcy clerk and serve on the appellant a statement of additional items to be included in the record on appeal. This statement of additional items must be filed and served before the 10th day after the date of service of the appellant's statement of designated items and statement of issues. If the appellee filed a notice of cross-appeal, he must also file and serve on the appellant a statement of designated items and statement of issues on cross-appeal before the 10th day after service of the appellant's statement of designated items and issues. Service may be obtained by first-class mail. *FRBP 8006, 9013-9014, see Local Bankruptcy Rules;*

(c) Appellant as Cross-Appellee

The appellant, as cross-appellee, may file and serve on the appellee-cross-appellant a statement of additional items to be included in the record on cross-appeal. This statement of the cross-appellee must be filed with the bankruptcy clerk and served on the cross-appellant before the 10th day after service of the appellee's (cross-appellant's) statement of designated items on cross-appeal. Service may be obtained by first-class mail. *FRBP 8006, 9013-9014, see Local Bankruptcy Rules;*

(d) Clerk's Copy of Designated Items

The appellant and appellee must provide the bankruptcy clerk with a copy of all items designated to be included in the record on appeal. The clerk will prepare a copy at the party's expense if the clerk's copy of designated items is omitted.

(3) Transcript

The appellant or cross-appellant must mail or personally deliver a written request for transcript to the court reporter. The reporter must then acknowledge on the request the date of receipt and the date of anticipated completion and deliver the endorsed request to the bankruptcy clerk. The reporter must complete the transcript before the 30th day after receipt of the request or seek an extension of time from the bankruptcy clerk who must then enter the extension of time on the docket and notify the parties to the appeal. The bankruptcy clerk must notify the bankruptcy judge if the reporter fails to complete the transcript within the extended time. *FRBP 8006, 8007(a).*

g. Transmission of Record on Appeal

Once the record on appeal is complete, the bankruptcy clerk must retain the original and promptly transmit a copy to the clerk of the appellate court (federal district court or bankruptcy appellate panel). *FRBP 8007(b).*

h. Appellate Court Clerk Dockets the Appeal

Once the record has been received, the clerk of the appellate court must enter the appeal on the appellate court docket and must promptly mail notice of the date the appeal was docketed to all parties to the appeal. *FRBP 8007(b).*

i. Briefs on Appeal

(1) When to File

The parties to the appeal must file briefs by the following dates, unless the appellate court specifies otherwise by local appellate rule or order:

(a) Appellant

The appellant must file a brief with the clerk of the appellate court and serve a copy on the appellee before the 15th day after the clerk of the appellate court entered the appeal on the docket. If the appeal is to a bankruptcy appellate panel, the appellant must file excerpts of the record as an appendix with the brief and serve both on the appellee within this same time period. The appendix must include nine items:

(i) The adversary complaint and answer;

(ii) Pretrial order, if any;

(iii) The appealed order, judgment, or decree;

(iv) All other relevant orders;

(v) The bankruptcy court's opinion or findings of fact or conclusions of law and citations of any published opinion of the bankruptcy court;

(vi) All motions and responses on which the bankruptcy court ruled;

(vii) The notice of appeal;

(viii) Relevant entries on the bankruptcy docket concerning the above items; and

(ix) The transcript or any portion that may be required by any rule of the bankruptcy appellate panel.

If the appellant omits any of the above nine items, the appellee may file an appendix with the omitted material and serve a copy of such appendix on the appellant by first-class mail or personal delivery. *FRBP 8007, 8008(a), (c), 8009(a)(1), (b), 8018.*

(b) Appellee

The appellee must file and serve a brief before the 15th day after the date of service of the appellant's brief. If the appellee has filed a cross-appeal, the brief must: (i) clearly indicate all issues and arguments relevant to the cross-appeal; and (ii) include a response to the appellant's brief. *FRBP 8009(a)(2).*

(c) Appellant

If the appellant wishes to file a reply brief, it must be filed and a copy served on the appellee before the 10th day after the date of service of the appellee's brief. *FRBP 8009(a)(3).*

(d) Appellee

If the appellee filed a cross-appeal, he may file a reply brief to the appellant's response to the issues on cross-appeal and serve it on the appellant before the 10th day after the date of service of the appellant's reply brief. No additional briefs are permitted unless allowed by the appellate court. *FRBP 8009.*

(2) Where to File

All briefs and appendixes are filed with the clerk of the appellate court. *FRBP 8007-8009.*

(3) Length of Briefs

Unless the appellate court indicates otherwise by local appellate rule or order, principal briefs (initial brief of appellant and appellee) must be 50 pages or less. Reply briefs of the appellant or cross-appellant must be 25 pages or less. Pages of the table of contents, tables of citations, and any addendum of relevant statutes, rules, or regulations are not counted. *FRBP 8010(c), 8018.*

(4) How to File:

Papers may be filed by first-class mail properly addressed to the clerk of the appellate court. Briefs are deemed filed when properly mailed (correctly addressed and stamped). All other papers which must be filed with the clerk of the appellate court are properly filed when received by such clerk within prescribed time limits. *FRBP 8008(a).*

(5) Form and Content of Briefs

Unless the appellate court indicates otherwise by local appellate rule or order, briefs must include the following contents and in the following order.

(a) Appellant's Brief

The appellant's brief must include:

(i) Table of contents, including page numbers;

(ii) Table of cases and statutes, alphabetized, with references to respective pages of the brief where cited;

(iii) Statement of the legal basis for jurisdiction of the appellate court (reference to 28 USC §158);

(iv) Statement of issues presented on appeal and the applicable standard of appellate review;

(v) Statement of the case, stating briefly the nature of the case, course of the proceeding in the bankruptcy court, disposition in the bankruptcy court, and statement of relevant facts to the issues raised on appeal, with appropriate references to the record;

(vi) Legal argument containing the appellant's contentions of the issues on appeal and the reasons for such contentions, with citations to authorities, statutes, and the record relied upon. A short summary may precede the legal argument; and

(vii) Short conclusion stating the exact relief sought. *FRBP 8010(a)(1), 8018.*

(b) Appellee's Brief

The appellee's brief must include the table of contents; alphabetized table of cases, statutes, and authorities, and legal argument as indicated above. The appellee's brief does not have to include statements of the legal basis of appellate jurisdiction, the issues, or the case, unless the appellee disagrees with the appellant's statements. Also, the appellee's brief does not have to include a conclusion. *FRBP 8010(a)(2), 8018.*

(6) Number of Copies

If an appeal is taken to the federal district court, the parties must file an original and one copy of all required papers. If an appeal is taken to the bankruptcy appellate panel, the parties must file an original and three copies of all required papers. However, the appellate court may, by local appellate rules or order, require additional copies. *FRBP 8008(a), 8018; see Local Appellate Rules.*

(7) Proof of Service

All papers filed with the clerk of the appellate court must include either an acknowledgment of service from the party served or proof of service from the party who made service. The proof of service must include a certified statement of the date and manner of service and the name and address of each person served. Service may be obtained by first-class mail or personal delivery. *FRBP 8008(c)-(d).*

j. Stay on Appeal

(1) Automatic 10-Day Stay

Enforcement of most bankruptcy court orders is subject to an automatic 10-day stay, without further court order. There can be no execution of judgment until the 11th day after entry of the judgment. However, the following bankruptcy orders are exempt from the automatic 10-day stay:

(a) Orders granting relief from the automatic or codebtor stay. *See "Stage Two—Automatic Stay Invoked," Chapter II; "Motion for Relief from Automatic Stay" Chapter XIV; and "Automatic Plus Codebtor Stay," Chapter V;*

(b) Orders affecting the use of cash collateral. *See Chapter VIII;* above;

(c) Orders dealing with the sale, lease, or use of property of the bankruptcy estate. *See Chapter VIII;*

(d) Orders authorizing the trustee or Chapter 9, 11, or 12 debtor to obtain post-petition credit. *See Chapter VIII;* and

(e) Orders authorizing the assumption or rejection of executory contracts or unexpired leases. *See "Assumption or Rejection of Executory Contracts and Unexpired Leases," Chapter XIV.*

Thus, postponing enforcement of the above orders and all other orders after the automatic 10-day stay period requires an order staying execution on appeal. *FRBP 7062, 8005.*

(2) Motion for Order Staying Execution on Appeal

The appellant or cross-appellant must file a motion for stay of judgment pending appeal. The motion generally must be presented to the bankruptcy judge but may be made to the appellate court if such motion states grounds why the stay was not obtained from the bankruptcy court. The bankruptcy court or appellate court may issue any appropriate order on terms necessary to protect the rights of all parties-in-interest during the appeal, including requiring a supersedeas bond. If the trustee or debtor-in-possession files an appeal, the bankruptcy court or appellate court may require a bond or other appropriate security; if the United States or an officer or agency or department of the government files the appeal, no bond or other security is required. Unless a stay pending appeal is issued, the reversal or modification on appeal does not affect a bankruptcy court order authorizing the sale or lease of property to a good-faith purchaser or lessee or post-petition secured or unsecured credit extended by a good-faith lender. *28 USC §§363(m), 364(e); FRBP 8005; see Chapter VIII.*

k. Disposition and Standard of Review on Appeal

The appellate court may affirm, modify, or reverse a bankruptcy court's order or remand with instructions for further proceedings. The findings of fact of the bankruptcy court will only be set aside if found clearly erroneous by the appellate court. *FRBP 8013.*

E. Appeal of District Court Order

Appeal of final order(s) of the federal district court sitting as an appellate court must be taken to the respective federal circuit court of appeals for the federal judicial district in which the bankruptcy case is pending. An interlocutory order issued by a federal district court sitting as an appellate court may also be appealed to the federal circuit court of appeals. *See Connecticut National Bank v Germain, 503 US 249, 112 S Ct 1146 (1992); 28 USC §§158(d), 1291-1292.*

Research Guide

Anderson, *Chapter 11: Reorganizations* ch 4 (Shepard's/McGraw-Hill 1983)

Anderson & Morris, *Chapter 12: Farm Reorganizations* ch 3 (Shepard's/McGraw-Hill 1987)

Drake, *Bankruptcy Practice for the General Practitioner* ch 4 (Shepard's/McGraw-Hill 2d ed 1990)

Drake & Morris, *Chapter 13: Practice and Procedure* ch 2 (Shepard's/McGraw-Hill 1983)

Jaroslavsky, *Practical Bankruptcy Procedure* ch 3 (Shepard's/McGraw-Hill 1993)

Murphy, *Creditor's Rights in Bankruptcy* ch 2 (Shepard's/McGraw-Hill 2d ed 1988)

Pollard & Burton, *Guide to Effective Bankruptcy Litigation* ch 1 (Shepard's/McGraw-Hill 1988)

X. Venue

X. Venue

A. Overview

Venue is the place or locality where an action may properly be tried. It is where a lawsuit or petition is filed and the case is heard. Venue is conferred by federal or state statute. However, the right to object to improper venue generally may be waived by any party and a court with proper jurisdiction may issue a valid, binding order even though the case was heard in the wrong place or venue. *See Chapter IX.*

B. Bankruptcy Cases and Proceedings

1. Where to File Cases

A Chapter 7, 9, 11, 12, or 13 petition should be filed in the federal judicial district of the United States where the debtor's residence, domicile, principal place of business, or principal assets in the United States have been located for the greater part of the immediate 180-day pre-petition period; or in the district where a bankruptcy case involving an affiliate, general partner, or partnership of the debtor has been filed. An *affiliate* is:

a. **An entity that directly or indirectly owns, controls, or has the power to vote at least 20 per cent of the issued voting securities (stock, notes, bonds, certificates of deposit, or debentures) of the debtor, unless such entity holds the debtor's securities as collateral and has not exercised his power to vote.**

   An entity that holds the debtor's securities in a fiduciary or agency capacity is an affiliate if such entity has the sole power to vote the securities;

b. **A corporation which the debtor directly or indirectly owns, controls, or has the power to vote at least 20 per cent of the issued voting securities or which an entity who directly or indirectly owns, controls, or has the power to vote at least 20 per cent of the issued voting securities of the debtor so owns, unless the entity holds such securities as collateral and has not exercised its power to vote.**

   An entity that holds such securities in a fiduciary or agency capacity is an affiliate if it has the sole power to vote the securities;

c. **A person whose business is operated by the debtor under a lease or operating agreement;**

d. **A person who has substantially all of his property operated under an operating agreement with the debtor; or**

e. **An entity that operates the debtor's business or substantially all of the debtor's property under a lease or operating agreement.** *11 USC §101(2); 28 USC §1408.*

Thus, if a debtor has always lived in Federal Judicial District 1 and had his only business in Federal Judicial District 2 for the immediately preceding seven months, the debtor may file his petition with a bankruptcy court in District 1 or 2. If the debtor has always lived in Judicial District 1 and had his only business in Judicial District 2 for five months, the debtor should file in District 1. If the same debtor's general partner has lived in Judicial District 3 for two years and filed a bankruptcy petition in such district, the debtor may file his petition in District 1 or 3. *28 USC §1408.*

2. Where to File Proceedings

a. General Rule

An adversary proceeding (adversary complaint) related to or arising in a bankruptcy case or under the Bankruptcy Code may be filed in the federal district court or bankruptcy court where the bankruptcy case is pending, unless one of the exceptions discussed, below, is applicable.

b. Exceptions to General Rule

(1) A trustee or debtor must file an adversary proceeding in the federal district court or bankruptcy court for the judicial district where the defendant resides if the proceeding arises in or relates to the bankruptcy case and is:

(a) to recover a money judgment or property worth less than $1,000; or

(b) to recover a consumer debt for less than $5,000. *28 USC §1409(b); 11 USC §§322-323, 522, (f)-(i), 901, 902(5), 1101(1), 1107, 1202, 1302.*

(2) A trustee or debtor may file an adversary proceeding in the federal district court or bankruptcy court where the bankruptcy case is pending or in the judicial district where the lawsuit could be filed under applicable nonbankruptcy venue law if such proceeding arises in or relates to the bankruptcy case and is:

(a) to recover any property for the estate valued at $1,000 or more ($5,000 or more if consumer debt); or

(b) to avoid any pre-petition transfer of the debtor's interest in property by the trustee or debtor exercising the rights of an actual unsecured creditor under applicable nonbankruptcy law. *See Chapter XII; 11 USC §§541, 544(b); 28 USC §1409(a), (c).*

(3) A trustee or debtor must file an adversary proceeding to recover a post-petition claim of the estate arising from the operation of the debtor's business in the federal district court or bankruptcy court for the judicial district where such lawsuit could be filed under applicable nonbankruptcy venue law. *28 USC §1408(d).*

(4) A plaintiff may file an adversary complaint against a trustee or Chapter 9, 11, or 12 debtor to recover a post-petition claim against the estate arising from the operation of the debtor's business in the federal district court or bankruptcy court for the judicial district where such lawsuit could be filed under applicable nonbankruptcy venue law or in the federal district court or bankruptcy court where the bankruptcy case is pending. *28 USC §1409(e).*

If the federal district court has referred bankruptcy cases to the bankruptcy judge, the above actions should be filed with the bankruptcy court in the appropriate judicial district. Whether any of the above proceedings may then be tried in the bankruptcy court depends upon the core or noncore status of the proceeding and the jurisdictional requirements of Title 28, United States Code. *See "Procedures to Determine Core Versus Noncore Proceedings," Chapter IX; 28 USC §§157, 1334, 1409(a)-(e).*

C. Change of Venue

1. Generally

A federal district court or bankruptcy court may transfer a bankruptcy case or adversary proceeding filed in a bankruptcy case to a federal district court or bankruptcy court in another judicial district if the interests of justice or convenience of the parties so warrants. *28 USC §1412; FRBP 1014.*

2. Transfer of Cases

a. Venue Proper

If a bankruptcy petition is filed in the proper judicial district, any party-in-interest (creditor, equity security holder, trustee) may timely file a motion to transfer the Chapter 7, 11, 12, or 13 case to another federal judicial district. The motion must be served by first-class mail or any other method allowed for service of process in federal district court on the debtor, the U.S. trustee, any trustee appointed in the case, all committee(s), and any other entity required by court order or local bankruptcy rules. The court must hold a hearing on the motion, unless local bankruptcy rules direct otherwise. Notice of the hearing date must be mailed or delivered to the debtor, the movant, the U.S. trustee, any trustee appointed in the case, all committees, and to any other entity as directed by court order or local bankruptcy rules. The motion does not commence an adversary proceeding and no filing fee is required.

The court, in its discretion, may transfer the bankruptcy case to another district in the interests of justice or for convenience of the parties. *28 USC §1412; FRBP 1014(a)(1), 9013-9014.*

b. Venue Improper

If the bankruptcy petition has been filed in the wrong federal judicial district, any party-in-interest (creditor, trustee, or U.S. trustee) may timely file a motion to transfer the bankruptcy case to the proper judicial district. The motion and notice of hearing date must be served in the same manner and on the same entities as a motion to transfer filed in a case of proper venue (*see discussion above*). The court may transfer the case to another district if the interests of justice or convenience of the parties so warrants. *28 USC §1412; FRBP 1014(a)(2), 9013-9014.*

c. Multiple Petitions Filed

If more than one voluntary or involuntary bankruptcy petition is filed in different federal judicial districts for the same debtor or related debtors (a partnership and one or more general partners, two or more general partners, or a debtor and an affiliate), a party-in-interest may file a motion to transfer in the court where the first bankruptcy petition was filed. The other courts must stay all proceedings on such other petitions until the court where the first petition was filed rules on the motion. The motion to transfer must be served by first-class mail or any other method allowed for service of process in federal district court on the debtor(s), any trustee(s), the U.S. trustees, all committee(s), and on such other entities as required by court order or local bankruptcy rules. The court where the first petition was filed must hold a hearing on the motion, unless local bankruptcy rules direct otherwise. Notice of the hearing must be mailed to the debtor(s), the movant, the U.S. trustee(s), all committee(s), and any other entity as directed by court order or local bankruptcy rules. The court where the first petition was filed may determine the judicial district or districts where the case(s) should continue in the interests of justice or convenience of the parties. The motion to transfer does not commence an adversary proceeding and no filing fee is required. *11 USC §102(1)(A)-(B); 28 USC §1412; FRBP 1014(b), 9013-9014.*

3. Transfer of Proceedings

A party-in-interest may file a motion to transfer all or part of an adversary proceeding to a federal district court or bankruptcy court in another judicial district, as the interests of justice, convenience of the parties, or bankruptcy venue provisions may require. The motion must be served by first-class mail or any other method allowed for service of process in federal district court on the debtor, any trustee, the U.S. trustee, all committee(s), and any other entity required by court order or local bankruptcy rules. The court must hold a hearing on the motion, unless local bankruptcy rules direct otherwise. Notice of the hearing should be mailed to entities as directed by the court or local bankruptcy rules. The motion does not commence an adversary proceeding and no filing fee is required. *11 USC §101(1)(A)-(B); 28 USC §§1409, 1412; FRBP 7004, 7087, 9007, 9013-9014.*

Research Guide

Anderson, *Chapter 11: Reorganizations* ch 4 (Shepard's/McGraw-Hill 1983)

Anderson & Morris, *Chapter 12: Farm Reorganizations* ch 3 (Shepard's/McGraw-Hill 1987)

Drake, *Bankruptcy Practice for the General Practitioner* ch 4 (Shepard's/McGraw-Hill 2d ed 1990)

Drake & Morris, *Chapter 13: Practice and Procedure* ch 2 (Shepard's/McGraw-Hill 1983)

Jaroslavsky, *Practical Bankruptcy Procedure* ch 4 (Shepard's/McGraw-Hill 1993)

Murphy, *Creditor's Rights in Bankruptcy* ch 2 (Shepard's/McGraw-Hill 2d ed 1988)

Pollard & Burton, *Guide to Effective Bankruptcy Litigation* ch 1 (Shepard's/McGraw-Hill 1988)

XI. Removal of Actions to Federal District Court or Bankruptcy Court

XI. Removal of Actions to Federal District Court or Bankruptcy Court
28 USC §§157, 1334, 1452
FRBP 7001(10) et seq, 9027

A. Removal of Civil Actions or Claims to the Bankruptcy Court
   1. General Rule
   2. Exceptions to General Rule
   3. When to Remove
      a. Pre-Petition Claim or Action
      b. Post-Petition Claim or Action

B. Procedures
   1. File Notice of Removal
   2. Contents of Notice
   3. File Copy of Notice of Removal in Nonbankruptcy Court
   4. After Removal
      a. Generally
      b. Service of Process
      c. Defendant Has Not Answered Before Removal
      d. Party Filed Pleading Before Removal
      e. Record
      f. Bonds, Security, Sequestration Before Removal

C. Remand and Abstention
   1. Remand
   2. Abstention

Research Guide

XI. Removal of Actions to Federal District Court or Bankruptcy Court

A. Removal of Civil Actions (Lawsuits) or Claims to the Bankruptcy Court

1. General Rule

A party to a civil lawsuit pending in a state or federal court and arising in or related to a bankruptcy case, or arising under the Bankruptcy Code, may remove all or part of the lawsuit to the federal district court or bankruptcy court in the judicial district and division where the lawsuit is pending. Whether the removed proceeding may be tried before the bankruptcy court or must be heard by the federal district court depends upon the core or noncore status of the removed action or claim and other jurisdictional requirements of Title 28, United States Code. *See "Procedures to Determine Core versus Noncore Proceedings," Chapter IX; 28 USC §§157, 1334(b)-(c), 1452(a); FRBP 9027.*

2. Exceptions to General Rule

Two types of civil claims or lawsuits may be removed to the federal district court or bankruptcy court:

a. **A proceeding before the United States tax court; or**

b. **A civil action by a governmental unit to enforce its police or regulatory powers.** *28 USC §1452(a).*

These actions are not subject to removal. However, the tax actions are stayed by the filing of the bankruptcy petition until the bankruptcy court lifts the automatic stay or the stay otherwise terminates. *11 USC §362; 28 USC §1452(a); see "Stage Two—Automatic Stay Invoked," Chapter II, and "Motion for Relief from Automatic Stay," Chapter XIV.*

3. When to Remove

a. Pre-Petition Claim or Action

A civil claim or action pending pre-petition in a state or federal court may only be removed to the federal district court or bankruptcy court by the latest of three dates:

(1) Before the 90th day after the debtor files a voluntary petition or after the order for relief in an involuntary bankruptcy case; or

(2) Before the 30th day after entry of an order lifting the automatic stay concerning the claim or action to be removed; or

(3) Before the 30th day after qualification of a Chapter 11 trustee, but no later than the 180th day after the debtor files a Chapter 11 petition or the order for relief in an involuntary Chapter 11 case if no trustee has yet qualified. A trustee *qualifies* if he files a bond with the bankruptcy court before the 5th day after

selection by the U.S. trustee and before beginning his official duties. The bond must be in favor of the United States and conditioned on faithful performance of the trustee's official duties. *11 USC §322(a); 28 USC §1452(a); FRBP 2008, 2010, 7001(10), 9027(a)(2); see "Procedure Five—Appointment of Trustee or Examiner," Chapter IV.*

b. Post-Petition Claim or Action

A claim or action filed post-petition and related to a bankruptcy case may only be removed to the federal district court or bankruptcy court by the earlier of two dates:

(1) Before the 30th after receipt of the initial pleading asserting the claim or action to be removed; or

(2) Before the 30th day after receipt of the summons if such initial pleading was not served with a summons. *FRBP 9027(a)(3).*

If the federal district court has referred bankruptcy cases to the bankruptcy court, the claim or action may be removed to the bankruptcy court in the federal judicial district and division where the removed claim or action was pending. Whether the removed claim or action may then be determined by final order of the bankruptcy court depends upon the core or noncore status of the removed proceeding and the jurisdictional requirements of Title 28, United States Code. *28 USC §§151-152, 157, 1334, 1452(a); FRBP 9027; see Chapter IX.*

B. Procedures

1. File Notice of Removal

The party seeking to remove a claim or action must file a notice of removal with the clerk of the federal district court. However, if the district court has referred bankruptcy cases to bankruptcy judges, the notice of removal must be filed with the clerk of the bankruptcy court. The notice commences an adversary proceeding. A nonbankruptcy party seeking removal must pay a $120 filing fee. If the debtor files the notice of removal, no filing fee is required. If the trustee or a Chapter 11 or 12 debtor-in-possession files the notice, the $120 filing fee is only payable from any bankruptcy estate that may exist. The notice of removal with a summons must be promptly served on all parties to the removed claim or action in any manner allowed for service of process in federal district court. *28 USC §§151, 157(a), 1452, 1930(b), Judicial Conference Schedule of Fees (6); FRBP 5005, 7001(10), 7004 et seq, 9027(a)(1), (b); Procedural Bankr Forms B 250A, B, C.*

2. Contents of Notice

The notice of removal must include the following:

a. Short, plain statement of the facts showing that the civil claim or action sought to be removed *arises under the Code* (invokes a substantive section of the Bankruptcy Code), or is *related to or arises in the bankruptcy case* (the claim or action could possibly affect the administration of the bankruptcy case or estate). *See Robinson v Michigan Consolidated Gas Co, 918 F2d 579 (6th Cir 1990); In re Lemco Gypsum, Inc, 910 F2d 784 (11th Cir 1990); 28 USC §§1334(b), 1452(a); FRBP 9027(a)(1);*

b. Statement whether the removed claim or action will be a core or noncore proceeding. *28 USC §157(b)(2)-(3); FRBP 9027(a)(1); see Chapter IX;*

c. Statement whether the party filing the notice of removal consents or opposes entry of final orders or judgments by the bankruptcy court if the removed claim or action is a noncore proceeding. *28 USC §157(c)(2); FRBP 9027(a)(1); see Chapter IX;*

d. Signature, office address, and telephone number of the attorney of record for the party filing the notice of removal or of the party if not represented by an attorney. *FRBP 9011, 9027(a)(1);* and

e. Copies of all process and pleadings relating to the removed claim or action. *FRBP 9027(a)(1).*

3. File Copy of Notice of Removal in Nonbankruptcy Court

The party filing the notice of removal must promptly file a copy of the notice of removal with the clerk of the state or federal court from which the claim or action was removed. The removal is effective when copy of the notice has been filed with the state or federal court clerk. Further proceedings may only be held in such state or federal court if the claim or action is remanded (*see "Remand and Abstention," discussed below*). *FRBP 9027(c).*

4. After Removal

a. Generally

The bankruptcy rules governing adversary proceedings also govern a removed claim or action. The federal district court or bankruptcy court may issue any orders and process necessary to bring all proper parties before such court, even if service of process was not issued in the state or federal court from which the claim or action was removed. *11 USC §105(a); 28 USC §§1334, 1452(a); FRBP 7001(10), 9027(c)(1), (g).*

b. Service of Process

If any defendant in the removed claim or action was not properly served with process before removal, service of process may be completed or new process may be issued after removal under the FRBP. Service of process on a defendant does not deprive him of his right to file a motion to remand the claim or action to the court from which it was removed (*see "Remand and Abstention," discussed below*). *FRBP 7001(10), 7004 et seq, 9027(f)-(g).*

c. Defendant Has Not Answered Before Removal

A defendant who has not filed an answer or pleading before removal must file an answer, defense, or objection under the FRBP by the latest of three dates:

(1) Before the 20th day after receipt of the initial pleading asserting the claim for relief on which the removed claim or action is based; or

(2) Before the 20th day after service of the summons on such initial pleading; or

(3) Before the 5th day after the notice of removal is filed.

The defendant's pleading must admit or deny that the removed claim or action is a core or noncore proceeding. The defendant's pleading must also include a statement whether the defendant consents or opposes entry of final orders or judgments by the bankruptcy court if the removed proceeding is noncore. *28 USC §157(b)-(c); FRBP 7012(b), 9027(f)-(g).*

d. Party Filed Pleading Before Removal

If any party to the removed action filed a pleading in the state or federal court before removal, repleading is not necessary unless the federal district court or bankruptcy court orders otherwise. However, all parties to the removed claim or action who did not file the notice of removal must file a statement in the federal district court or bankruptcy court admitting or denying that the removed proceeding is core or noncore and stating whether the party consents or opposes entry of final orders or judgments by the bankruptcy court if the removed proceeding is noncore. Such statement must be filed no later than the 10th day after the notice of removal was filed. The statement must contain the signature, address, and telephone number of the attorney of record for the party filing the statement, or of the party if not represented by an attorney. The party filing the statement must mail a copy of the statement to all other parties to the removed claim or action. *28 USC §157(b)-(c); FRBP 9011, 9027(c)(3), (g).*

e. Record

The federal district court or bankruptcy court may require the party filing the notice of removal to file certified copies of all documents and records relating to the removed claim or action previously filed in the state or federal court. If the clerk of the state or federal court refuses to deliver certified copies after proper demand or tender of all lawful fees by a party to the removed action, the party may file an affidavit with the federal district clerk or bankruptcy clerk asserting such facts. The federal district court or bankruptcy court may then order that the record be supplied by affidavit or otherwise. *11 USC §105(a); 28 USC §1334(d); FRBP 9027(e)(2), (h).*

f. Bonds, Security, Sequestration Before Removal

All bonds, security, injunctions, or orders obtained before removal remain in full force and effect until dissolved or modified by the federal district court or bankruptcy court. Any property attached or sequestered before removal must be held to answer for a final judgment or decree issued by the federal district court or bankruptcy court in the same manner such property would be held to answer a final judgment or decree from the state or federal court from which removal occurred. *FRBP 9027(i).*

C. Remand and Abstention

1. Remand

The federal district court or bankruptcy court may *remand* (return) any civil action or claim to the state or federal court from which such action or claim was removed. The party opposing a removed action or claim should file a motion to remand. The motion must be served on all parties to the removed claim or action, on the debtor, any trustee, all committee(s), and any other entity required by court order or local bankruptcy rules. Service may be obtained by first-class mail or any other manner allowed for service of process in federal district court. The motion does not commence an adversary proceeding and no filing fee is required. The court must hold a hearing on a motion to remand, unless local bankruptcy rules state otherwise. No answer or response to the motion is required, unless the court or local bankruptcy rules direct otherwise. The court's order to remand or to retain a removed action is not appealable to a federal circuit court of appeals or the Supreme Court. *11 USC §101(1)(A)-(B); 28 USC §1452(b); FRBP 7004, 9014, 9027(d).*

2. Abstention

The federal district court or bankruptcy court presiding over a bankruptcy case may abstain from hearing an adversary proceeding removed from another court. A motion to abstain must be filed with the federal district court or bankruptcy court. The motion must be served on all parties to the removed action, the debtor, any trustee, all committee(s), and any other entity required by court order or local bankruptcy rules. The motion may be served by first-class mail or in any other manner allowed for service of process in federal district court. The motion does not commence any adversary proceeding and no filing fee is required. No answer or response to the motion is required, unless the court or local bankruptcy rules direct otherwise. *28 USC §1334; FRBP 5021, 9013-9014; see Chapter IX.*

The federal district court or bankruptcy court must abstain from hearing a claim or action removed from a state court that can be timely adjudicated in such state court and that involves only state law claim(s) (neither a federal statute, the United States Constitution, nor diversity of citizenship is involved), if a party to the removed proceeding files a timely motion to abstain and the removed claim or action does not arise under the Code or in a bankruptcy case. However, personal injury tort and wrongful death claims filed against the estate are not subject to this mandatory abstention requirement in the federal district court. Such tort claims may be tried in the federal district court where the bankruptcy case is pending or the tort claim arose or the federal district court may abstain, in its discretion, and allow the action to be tried in a state court with appropriate jurisdiction. But such tort claims may not be tried in the bankruptcy court. A mandatory abstention order, like an order to remand, is not appealable to a federal circuit court of appeals or to the Supreme Court. *28 USC §§157(b)(2)(B), (4)-(5), 1334(b), (c)(1)-(2), 1452(a)-(b); FRBP 5011, 9014, 9027; see Citibank v White Motor Corp, 761 F2d 270 (6th Cir 1985); In re Ben Cooper, 924 F2d 36 (2d Cir 1991), cert denied, 111 S Ct 2041 (1991).*

Research Guide

Anderson, *Chapter 11: Reorganizations* ch 4 (Shepard's/McGraw-Hill 1983)

Anderson & Morris, *Chapter 12: Farm Reorganizations* ch 3 (Shepard's/McGraw-Hill 1987)

Drake, *Bankruptcy Practice for the General Practitioner* ch 4 (Shepard's/McGraw-Hill 2d 1990)

Jaroslavsky, *Practical Bankruptcy Procedure* ch 3 (Shepard's/McGraw-Hill 1993)

Murphy, *Creditor's Rights in Bankruptcy* ch 2 (Shepard's/McGraw-Hill 2d ed 1988)

Pollard & Burton, *Guide to Effective Bankruptcy Litigation* ch 20 (Shepard's/McGraw-Hill 1988)

XII. The Trustee's Super-Avoiding Powers

XII. The Trustee's Super-Avoiding Powers

A. Avoidable Preferential Transfers

11 USC §§101(54), 541, 547, 550-551

FRBP 7001(1) et seq

1. Definition
2. Purpose for Trustee's Power
3. Requirements to Avoid a Preferential Transfer
4. When a Preferential Transfer Occurs
5. Procedures to Avoid a Preferential Transfer
6. Defenses
   a. Contemporaneous Exchange
   b. Ordinary Course of Business Transaction
   c. Enabling Loan
   d. Net Result Rule
   e. Lien on Floating Mass (Improvement in Position Test)
   f. Valid Statutory Lien
   g. Bona Fide Alimony, Maintenance, or Support Paymenth. Minimal Value Transferred by Consumer Debtor

B. Avoidable Fraudulent Transfers or Obligations

11 USC §§101(54), 541, 544(b), 548, 550-551

FRBP 7001(1) et seq

1. Definition
2. Purpose for Power
3. Requirements to Avoid a Fraudulent Transfer
4. When a Transfer Occurs
5. Procedures
6. Defenses

C. Avoidable Unauthorized Post-Petition Transfers
11 USC §§101(54), 541, 549-551
FRBP 7001(1) et seq
1. Definition
2. Purpose for Trustee's Power
3. Requirements to Avoid a Post-Petition Transfer
4. Exceptions
5. Procedures

D. Avoidable Statutory Liens
11 USC §§101(53), 541, 545, 550-551
FRBP 7001(1) et seq
1. Definition
2. Purpose for Trustee's Power
3. Requirements to Avoid Statutory Lien
4. Procedures

E. Other Avoidable Unperfected Interests—Trustee's Strong-Arm Powers
11 USC §§541, 544(a), 550-551
FRBP 7001(1) et seq, 9013-9014
1. Definition
2. Purpose for Trustee's Strong-Arm Power
3. Requirements to Avoid an Unperfected Interest
4. Procedures to Avoid an Unperfected Lien

F. Avoidable Setoffs
11 USC §§553, 550-551
FRBP 7001(1) et seq, 9013-9014
1. Definition
2. Generally
3. Purpose for Trustee's Power
4. Requirements to Avoid a Pre-Petition Setoff
5. Requirements to Avoid a Post-Petition Setoff
6. Requirements to Prevent a Post-Petition Setoff (Disallowed Setoffs)
7. Procedures to Avoid a Setoff

G. Restrictions on Trustee's Super-Avoiding Powers
11 USC §§362(b)(3), (6)-(7), (14), 546, 548(c)-(d), 549(b)-(d), 550, 553(b)
1. Bankruptcy Statute of Limitations Restrictions
2. Limitations on Liability of Transferees
3. Nonbankruptcy Law Restrictions Recognized Under Bankruptcy Law
4. Chapter 11 Trustee's Right to Return Goods Limits Avoidance Powers of Subsequent Trustee(s)5. Protection of

Pre-Petition Margin, Settlement, and Swap Agreement Payments

Research Guide

XII. The Trustee's Super-Avoiding Powers

The Code generally grants a trustee, a Chapter 9 debtor, and a Chapter 11 or 12 debtor-in-possession (DIP) the power to avoid certain pre- and post-petition transfers of property and certain unperfected and statutory liens on property of the estate. Property involved in an avoidable transfer or lien may be recovered to increase the size of the bankruptcy estate and the distribution of property to unsecured creditors. The entity from whom the property is recovered will then have a claim against the bankruptcy estate for the amount of any value given to the debtor or any improvements made to the property before the transfer or lien is avoided. *11 USC §§502(d), (h), 544-551, 553(b), 901, 926, 1101(1), 1107, 1203; FRBP 3001-3007, 7001 et seq; see Chapter XIII.*

A. Avoidable Preferential Transfers

1. Definition

A *preferential transfer* is a transfer of the debtor's interest in property made pre-petition to favor one creditor or group of creditors over another. The preferred creditor(s) are typically trade suppliers of the debtor or a secured creditor threatening the debtor with foreclosure. *11 USC §547.*

A *transfer* of property may be by any mode. It includes every method by which the debtor disposed of, or parted with, his property or any interest in his property. The transfer may be direct or indirect, absolute or conditional, voluntary or involuntary. Thus, a foreclosure on property is an involuntary transfer of the debtor's property and his interest in such property. The debtor's execution of a security agreement may be a conditional transfer of property (the collateral). An entity's retention of title to the debtor's property as security is a transfer of the debtor's interest in such property. Similarly, transfer of possession, custody, or control of the debtor's property is a transfer, even if title to the property is not transferred. Thus, the concept of transfer under bankruptcy law is exceptionally broad because the purpose is to recover property, or its value, which will be added to increase the size of the bankruptcy estate. *11 USC §§101(54), 547, 550-551; S Rep No 989, 95th Cong, 2d Sess 26-27 (1978); HR Rep No 595, 95th Cong, 1st Sess 313-14 (1977).*

2. Purpose for Trustee's Power

The purpose of an adversary complaint to avoid a preferential transfer is to recover the property transferred, or its value, and thus increase the size and value of the bankruptcy estate for pro rata distribution to unsecured creditors whose claims are allowed by the court. The goal of bankruptcy law is the orderly distribution of the debtor's assets among all creditors, not a rushed distribution to the favored few. *S Rep No 989, 95th Cong, 2d Sess 26-27 (1978); 11 USC §§541, 547, 550-551; FRBP 7001(1) et seq.*

3. Requirements to Avoid a Preferential Transfer

The trustee, Chapter 9 debtor, or Chapter 11 or 12 DIP may avoid a preferential transfer if he proves five requirements.

a. The transfer was made to or for the benefit of a creditor.

Payments made by the debtor to a creditor who holds a guaranty are *double preferential transfers* if the other four requirements discussed below are met. The creditor received a preferential transfer (payments made to a creditor). The transfer was also for the benefit of a creditor (guarantor). The guarantor is a creditor with a contingent claim against the debtor. If the debtor defaults, the guarantor must pay the claim and generally becomes subrogated to the rights of the creditor. The trustee or appropriate debtor may file an adversary complaint in the bankruptcy court against the creditor and/or guarantor, jointly or severally, but only one recovery is allowed. *11 USC §§101(5), (12), (54), 509(a), 547(b)(1), 550-551; FRBP 7001(1)-(2) et seq.*

b. The transfer must be for or on account of an antecedent debt owed by the debtor before the transfer was made.

The transfer must have occurred pre-petition, and the debt must have been incurred and owed by the debtor before the transfer was made. However, estimated tax payments made by the debtor prepetition during the preference period are not recoverable preferences if the tax debt was not due when the debtor made the payments. The tax debt for which the payments were made was not an antecedent debt. *HR Rep No 595, 95th Cong, 1st Sess 372-73 (1977); 11 USC §§101(12), 547(b)(2).*

c. The transfer must have been made while the debtor was insolvent.

A debtor who is not a partnership or municipality is insolvent if his aggregate debts are greater than all his property at fair valuation, excluding exemptible property and property intentionally transferred, concealed, or removed to delay, hinder, or defraud creditors. In the case of a municipal debtor, the debtor is insolvent if it is unable to pay its debts as they become due or is generally just not paying its bona fide undisputed debts as such debts become due. A partnership debtor is insolvent if the sum of its partnership debts is greater than the total of: (1) all partnership property at fair valuation, excluding property intentionally transferred, concealed, or removed to delay, hinder, or defraud creditors; plus (2) the aggregate value at fair valuation of each general partner's nonpartnership property after all nonpartnership debts of such general partner have been paid. Exempt property and property of the general partner intentionally transferred or concealed to delay, hinder, or defraud creditors are again excluded from valuation. Under bankruptcy law, there is a presumption, which the creditor may rebut, that the debtor was insolvent 90 days or less before the bankruptcy petition was filed (on the 90th day to and including the date of filing the petition). *11 USC §§101(32), 547(b)(3), (f).*

d. The transfer must have been made during the 90 days immediately before the petition was filed (the 90th day is included in the preference period); or between the 90th day and one year before filing the petition if the creditor was an insider of the debtor when the transfer was made.

Effective for bankruptcy cases filed after October 22, 1994, a preferential transfer made for the benefit of an insider during the 90 days to one year pre-petition period may only be recovered from a transferee who was actually an insider on the date of the transfer. The Bankruptcy Reform Act of 1994 effectively overruled *In re VN Deprizio Construction Co (Levit v Ingersoll Rand Financial Corp), 874 F2d 1186 (7th Cir 1989)* and the line of cases that had authorized recapture of preference payments made a full year pre-petition from a non-insider creditor-transferee if an insider-guarantor benefited. *HR 5116, Pub L No 103-394, §202, amending and adding 11 USC §550(c).*

An *insider* includes a relative or general partner of an individual debtor; a corporation of which the debtor is a director, officer, or control person; a director, officer, control person, or general partner of a corporate debtor; and a general partner, control person, or relative of a general partner of a partnership debtor; or partnership if the debtor is a general partner of another partnership. *11 USC §§101(9), (12), (31), 547(b)(4).*

e. The transfer must enable the creditor to receive more than he would have received under a Chapter 7 liquidation proceeding had the transfer not occurred.

The bankruptcy court must focus upon the relative distribution among classes of creditors and the amount each member of the same class of creditors would receive under Chapter 7 to determine if the preferred creditor received too much. The court must also focus on the allowability of the claim (antecedent debt) for which the preferential transfer was made. If the creditor's claim would not have been allowed under bankruptcy law, then such creditor received more from the preferential transfer than he would have received under Chapter 7. If an undersecured creditor receives payment during the preference period, then such creditor may have received more than it would under Chapter 7. *11 USC §§547(b)(5), (g), 550-551; HR Rep No 595, 95th Cong, 1st Sess 372 (1977); S Rep No 989, 95th Cong 2d Sess 87 (1978).*

The trustee or debtor has the burden of proving each of the five requirements outlined above. *11 USC §547(b), (g).*

4. When a Preferential Transfer Occurs

The date a transfer occurs is crucial to determining if a preferential transfer is avoidable. Under bankruptcy law, the focus is upon when the transfer is so perfected that no entity may obtain an interest in the property under applicable nonbankruptcy law superior to that of the transferee.

A transfer cannot occur until the debtor has acquired rights in the transferred property. The rights may be ownership, option to purchase, leasing, or other legal or equitable rights. Once the debtor has acquired such rights and transferred the property, the date the preferred creditor perfects his interest and acquires a superior legal right to the property under applicable nonbankruptcy law determines the date the transfer occurred. If real property is at issue, a transfer is perfected when a bona fide purchaser from the debtor cannot obtain a superior interest in the property to that of the creditor-transferee. If personal property or fixtures are at issue, the transfer is perfected when a creditor on a simple contract cannot obtain a judicial lien on the same property superior to that of the transferee. If the transfer involves payment by ordinary check, a transfer occurs on the date of honor of the check. If a transfer of property is perfected on the date of the transfer or before the 10th day thereafter, the transfer is deemed to occur on the date the transfer was made. However, if the transfer creates a purchase money security interest perfected no later than the 20th day after the debtor receives possession of the collateral, the date the security interest is created is the date of the transfer. If the transfer is perfected 10 days or more after the exchange, the transfer occurs on the date of perfection. However, if the transfer was not perfected by the date the petition is filed, the transfer is deemed to occur immediately before the date the petition was filed. *11 USC §547(e)(1)(A)-(B), (2)(A)-(C), (3); HR Rep No 595, 95th Cong, 1st Sess 374-75 (1977); S Rep No 989, 95th Cong, 2d Sess 89 (1978); see Barnhill v Johnson, 503 US 393, 112 S Ct 1386 (1992).*

Many transfers do not require perfection by filing an instrument or document. Thus, if a creditor sells the debtor property on January 1, the debtor pays by check on August 15, the check is honored September 1, and the debtor files a petition on October 1, the date of the transfer of property was on September 1. *See 11 USC §547; Barnhill v Johnson, 503 US 393, 112 S Ct 1386 (1992); Durham v Smith Metal & Iron Co, 841 F2d 527 (4th Cir 1988).*

5. Procedures to Avoid a Preferential Transfer

Filing an action to avoid a preferential transfer commences an adversary proceeding. The trustee or appropriate debtor must file an adversary complaint and serve a copy of the complaint with a summons on the defendant-transferee by first-class mail or in any other manner allowed for service of process under the Federal Rules of Civil Procedure. If a trustee or debtor-in-possession files the complaint, a $120 filing fee is payable only from the bankruptcy estate, to the extent there is an estate. *28 USC §1930(b), Judicial Conference Schedule of Fees (6); FRBP 7001(1), 7004 et seq; Procedural Bankr Forms B 250A, B, C.*

6. Defenses

A transfer of property may meet all five requirements for a preference but is not avoidable because one or more exceptions or affirmative defenses exist. The defendant-transferee has the burden of proving at least one of the seven exception(s) exists. *11 USC §547(c), (g).*

a. Contemporaneous Exchange

If the debtor's transfer of property was intended by both the debtor and creditor (to or for whose benefit the transfer was made), and in fact was a substantially contemporaneous exchange of the debtor's property for new value given to the debtor by the creditor, the debtor's transfer is not an avoidable preference. The creditor may keep the property transferred by the debtor. Thus, if the creditor sells goods to the debtor on August 21, the debtor pays by check on September 1, the creditor ships the debtor new goods of comparable value on September 2, the check is presented for payment and honored by the bank on September 20, and the debtor files a bankruptcy petition on October 1, the transfer (check) was substantially contemporaneous and for new value (goods). A check transaction is intended to be a contemporaneous exchange and is *substantially contemporaneous* if the check is presented for payment before the 30th day after the date it was issued. *New value* may be money or an equivalent value in goods, services, or new credit. New value may also include the creditor's releasing property or its proceeds previously transferred by the debtor, as long as the initial transfer of such property cannot be avoided under any applicable law. However, the creditor's substitution (replacement) of a current obligation with another obligation is not new value. *11 USC §547(a)(2), (c)(1)(A); UCC §3-503; HR Rep No 595, 95th Cong, 1st Sess 373-74 (1977); see Barnhill v Johnson, 503 US 393, 112 S Ct 1386 (1992); Durham v Smith Metal & Iron Co, 841 F2d 527 (4th Cir 1988).*

b. Ordinary Course of Business Transaction

If the debtor's transfer of property to the creditor: (1) was made in the ordinary course of business or financial affairs of both parties and according to their ordinary business terms, and (2) paid a debt incurred in the ordinary course of business or financial affairs of both parties, no avoidable preference exists. This defense leaves normal business relations undisturbed. The term *financial affairs* thus includes nonbusiness activities of a consumer debtor, such as payment of utility bills. Further, payments on long-term as well as short-term debt may qualify as ordinary course of business payments and, thus, an exception to an avoidable preference. The policy of an avoidable preference is to discourage unusual actions by the creditor or debtor during his slide into bankruptcy, not to interfere with ordinary course of business payments or normal financial relations. *11 USC §547(c)(2); HR Rep No 595, 95th Cong, 1st Sess 373-74 (1977); see Union Bank v Wolas, 502 US 151, 112 S Ct 527 (1991).*

c. Enabling Loan

If the transfer was the creation of a purchase-money security interest where: (1) the debtor signed a security agreement, (2) the creditor then extended money or credit (new value) which the debtor used to buy the collateral described in the security agreement, and (3) the creditor perfected the security interest no later than the 20th day after the debtor received possession of the collateral, no avoidable preference exists. *11 USC §547(c)(3).*

d. Net Result Rule

If the debtor and creditor had several exchanges during the preference period (immediate 90 days pre-petition; or 90 days to one year pre-petition for an insider) and, after the last transfer by the debtor, the creditor extended new, unsecured value to the debtor, no avoidable preference exists to the extent of such new, unsecured value. *New value* again means the creditor gave the debtor money or its value in goods, services, or new credit or released property or its proceeds previously transferred to such creditor in a transfer that is not avoidable under any applicable law by the trustee or debtor. But, substituting a new obligation for an existing obligation is not new value. *11 USC §547(a)(2), (c)(4); HR Rep No 595, 95th Cong, 1st Sess 373 (1977).*

e. Lien on Floating Mass (Improvement in Position Test)

If the transfer involved payments to a creditor with a perfected security interest in a *floating mass* (inventory, accounts receivable, or their proceeds), such payments are not avoidable preferences except to the extent the payments improved the secured creditor's position by reducing a deficiency during the preference period to the prejudice of unsecured creditors. A two-point test is used. The amount of the secured creditor's claim must be determined on the date the petition is filed and on the 90th day (one year if the creditor is an insider) before the petition was filed. If the creditor first extended new value to the debtor less than 90 days before the petition was filed (or less than one year for an insider), the date new value was first given is substituted for the 90th day (one year for an insider). *11 USC §547(c)(5); HR Rep No 595, 95th Cong, 1st Sess 373 (1977); S Rep No 989, 95th Cong, 2d Sess 88 (1978).*

The improvement-in-position test thus requires a two-point measurement system. The secured creditor's claim must be determined on the 90th day (or one year for an insider) pre-petition and on the date the petition is filed. If the secured creditor is better off on the date the petition is filed than he was on the 90th day (one year for an insider) pre-petition, an avoidable preference occurred. However, *payments* (receivables or proceeds) made by the debtor during the preference period must have either reduced the creditor's deficiency (amount of claim less value of collateral), or converted the deficiency into a surplus. Unless a deficiency or undersecured claim existed on the *first date* (90th day or one year for an insider), no avoidable preference occurred. Intervening fluctuations in the secured creditor's claim between the first date and the date the petition was filed are not counted. *See 11 USC §547(c)(5); In re Clark Pipe & Supply Co, 20 CBC2d 1571 (5th Cir 1989); In re Missionary Baptist Foundation of America, Inc, 15 CBC2d 476 (5th Cir 1986).*

f. Valid Statutory Lien

If the transfer involves the fixing or creation of a statutory lien on any of the debtor's property and such lien is not otherwise avoidable under bankruptcy law, no avoidable preference exists. This exception protects transfers of the debtor's property in satisfaction of statutory liens that are not for payment of rent or triggered by the debtor's insolvency or bankruptcy petition. *11 USC §§545, 547(c)(6); see "Avoidable Statutory Liens," discussed below.*

g. Bona Fide Alimony, Maintenance, or Support Payment

Transfers by the debtor for alimony, maintenance, or support payments are protected during the full one year "insider" preference period if: (1) such transfers constitute bona fide payments of a debt to a spouse, former spouse, or the debtor's child; and (2) such transfers are made in connection with a separation agreement, divorce decree, court order of record, or determination by a governmental unit made pursuant to state or territorial law. *HR 1116, Pub L No 103-394, §304(f), amending and adding 11 USC §547(c)(7).*

However, alimony, maintenance, or support payments are not protected to the extent that they satisfy a debt that: (1) is assigned to another entity either voluntarily or involuntarily (by operation of law or otherwise); or (2) includes a liability that is not actually in the nature of alimony, maintenance, or support, regardless of how the debt is designated. *HR 1116, Pub L No 103-394, §304(f), amending and adding 11 USC §547(c)(7).*

What constitutes a bona fide alimony, maintenance, or support payment is a matter of federal bankruptcy law. The bankruptcy court must evaluate the parties' intent rather than their denomination of payments as "alimony, maintenance, or support." *See, In re Davidson, 947 F2d 1294 (5th Cir 1991).*

h. Minimal Value Transferred by Consumer Debtor

If the debtor is an *individual* (natural person) with primarily consumer debts and the aggregate value of all property transferred is less than $600, no avoidable preference exists. *11 USC §547(c)(7).*

B. Avoidable Fraudulent Transfers or Obligations

1. Definition

A *fraudulent transfer* of property or obligation occurs when the debtor intentionally conveys property or incurs a debt to delay, hinder, or defraud any creditor from receiving payment or when the debtor transfers too much and receives too little in return. A fraudulent transfer frequently occurs when the debtor transfers property as a gift to friends or relatives at a time when the debtor cannot pay his debts. *11 USC §548.*

2. Purpose for Power

The purpose for an adversary complaint to avoid a fraudulent transfer is to recover property (or its value) for the estate which the debtor removed to the deprivation of unsecured creditors. *11 USC §§548, 550-551; FRBP 7001(1) et seq.*

3. Requirements to Avoid a Fraudulent Transfer

Bankruptcy law gives the trustee or appropriate debtor (Chapter 9 debtor or Chapter 11 or 12 DIP) two methods to avoid a fraudulent transfer of property or obligation of the debtor. First, the trustee or appropriate debtor may exercise his own Bankruptcy Code fraudulent transfer powers to avoid the transfer of obligation. Second, the trustee or appropriate debtor may step into the shoes of an existing unsecured creditor whose claim is allowed by the bankruptcy court and exercise such creditor's rights under any applicable law. The trustee or debtor may use both methods if applicable under the facts of the case. *11 USC §§544(b), 548.*

a. Requirements to Exercise Trustee's Own Bankruptcy Code Fraudulent Transfer Powers

The trustee or Chapter 9, 11, or 12 debtor must prove two requirements to avoid a fraudulent transfer or obligation using bankruptcy law.

(1) The debtor transferred an interest in property or incurred a debt on or within one year before he filed the bankruptcy petition; and either

(2) (a) The debtor actually intended to defraud, hinder, or delay any entity (present or future) from receiving payment of a debt; or

(b) The debtor received less than reasonably equivalent value in exchange for the transfer and the debtor: (a) was insolvent or became insolvent as a result of the transfer or obligation, or (b) had unreasonably small capital left to engage in a present or future business or transaction as a result of the transfer or obligation, or (c) intended to incur or believed he would incur debts he would not be able to pay after the transfer or obligation; or

(c) The partnership debtor: (a) transferred property or incurred an obligation to a general partner and (b) the debtor was insolvent on such date or became insolvent as the result of such transfer or obligation. *11 USC §548(a)-(b).*

The reasonably equivalent value standard had been the subject of disagreement among the federal circuit courts. However, in *BFP v Resolution Trust Corporation, 114 S Ct 1757, 128 L Ed 2d 536 (1994),* the Supreme Court ruled that for purposes of avoiding a fraudulent transfer under 11 USC §548(d)(2), the reasonably equivalent value of foreclosed property is the price received at a properly conducted foreclosure sale. *See BFP v Resolution Trust Corp, 114 S Ct 1757, 128 L Ed 2d 556 (1994); overruling Durrett v Washington National Insurance Co, 621 F2d 201 (5th Cir 1980); In re Morris Communications NC, Inc, 914 F2d 458 (4th Cir 1990); Jacoway v Anderson, 835 F2d 342 (8th Cir 1988); Bundles v Baker, 856 F2d 815 (7th Cir 1988).*

If the trustee or debtor can prove a fraudulent transfer of an interest in property or obligation occurred, such transfer or debt will be avoided (nullified) under bankruptcy law. The property which was fraudulently transferred, or its value, may be recovered to increase the size of the bankruptcy estate. The recipient-transferee (creditor or purchaser) of the property who gave some (but not reasonably equivalent) value and acted in good faith will have a lien on the property recovered by the estate to secure the amount of value the transferee gave the debtor for the property. The good-faith purchaser will also have a lien on the recovered property to secure the lesser of the: (i) cost of any improvements (physical additions, changes, repairs, tax payments, or satisfaction of a senior or equal lien) made to the property after deducting any profits received, and (ii) any increase in value to the property as a result of such improvements. In the case of an obligation fraudulently incurred by the debtor, the creditor has a claim against the estate to the extent of any actual value (or credit) given to the debtor in the exchange. The good-faith transferee must file a timely proof of claim against the estate. *11 USC §§502(d), (h), 548(c), 550(d); FRBP 3001-3007, 7001 et seq; see "Limitations on Liability of Transferees," discussed below; "File Proof of Claim," Chapter XIV.*

Value for purposes of a fraudulent transfer means any property given by the transferee to the debtor or any payment or securing of a present or prior debt owed by the debtor. However, a transferee's unperformed promise to give support to the debtor or to the debtor's relative does not constitute value. *11 USC §548(d)(2)(A).*

b. Requirements to Step into the Shoes of an Unsecured Creditor

The trustee or Chapter 9, 11, or 12 debtor may avoid any transfer of an interest of the debtor in property or obligation of the debtor avoidable under any applicable law if he can step into the shoes of an unsecured creditor with an allowed claim who actually exists in the debtor's bankruptcy case. The trustee or debtor must prove that:

(1) There is at least one unsecured creditor whose claim is allowed in the debtor's bankruptcy case. This is frequently an easy task;

(2) There is applicable (nonbankruptcy) law that permits avoidance of the transfer or obligation by the unsecured creditor. The most frequently used statute is the Uniform Fraudulent Transfer Act. The provisions of this nonbankruptcy Fraudulent Transfer Act give creditors the power to avoid a debtor's fraudulent conveyance of property or obligation. The requirements of the Act and §548 of the Bankruptcy Code are similar in many respects, although the statute of limitations period is longer under the Uniform Fraudulent Transfer Act in certain situations. *See "Restrictions on Trustee's Super-Avoiding Powers," discussed below;* and

(3) The unsecured creditor would be able to avoid the transfer or obligation under such applicable law. This requires the trustee to prove the requirements of the applicable nonbankruptcy law, such as the Uniform Fraudulent Transfer Act, in the Bankruptcy Court. *11 USC §§502, 544(b); see Uniform Fraudulent Transfer Act.*

4. When a Transfer Occurs

a. Trustee's Own Bankruptcy Code Fraudulent Transfer Powers

A *fraudulent transfer* occurs under a §548 Bankruptcy Code action when the transferee has perfected his interest in the transferred property to such an extent that a bona fide purchaser from the debtor could not acquire a superior legal right to that of the transferee. If the transferee has not perfected his interest in the property before the bankruptcy petition was filed, the transfer is deemed to occur just before the date of filing the bankruptcy petition. In the case of a purchaser of real property, the transferee (creditor or purchaser) perfects his interest by obtaining and properly filing all necessary documents in the real estate or deed records as required by applicable nonbankruptcy law. If the property does not require perfection to obtain a superior legal right, then the transfer generally occurs on the date of the exchange. *11 USC §548d(1).*

b. Trustee Exercising Nonbankruptcy Powers of an Unsecured Creditor

The date of a fraudulent transfer or obligation under applicable nonbankruptcy law depends upon the particular statute. Under the Uniform Fraudulent Transfer Act, the date of the fraudulent transfer or obligation is determined in most respects like that of a preferential transfer under the Bankruptcy Code. *Compare 11 USC §§547(e), 548(d)(1), and Uniform Fraudulent Transfer Act—"When Transfer Is Made or Obligation Is Incurred."*

5. Procedures

The same procedures required for filing an adversary complaint to avoid a preferential transfer govern complaints to avoid a fraudulent transfer. *See "Procedures to Avoid a Preferential Transfer," discussed above. FRBP 7001(1) et seq; Procedural Bankr Forms B 250A, B, C.*

6. Defenses

Unlike an action to avoid a preferential transfer, the Bankruptcy Code does not offer specific affirmative defenses or exceptions to a fraudulent transfer action. To prevail, the defendant-transferee or creditor must disprove one or more of the requirements needed to prove the existence of a fraudulent transfer under applicable bankruptcy or nonbankruptcy law. However, to the extent the transferee or obligee (creditor) acted in good faith and gave value to the debtor, the transferee: (a) may retain any interest in property of the debtor so transferred; or (b) is deemed to have a lien on such property; or (c) may enforce an obligation incurred by the debtor. The good-faith transferee will also have a lien on property recovered by the trustee or debtor to secure the lesser of: (i) the cost of any improvements made to the property after the transfer, less any profits received or accrued from the property; and (ii) any increased value to the property resulting from such improvements. An *improvement* includes physical changes, repairs, or preservation of the property, or payment of any tax or superior or co-equal lien on the property. *11 USC §§548(a)-(c), 550(d).*

C. Avoidable Unauthorized Post-Petition Transfers

1. Definition

An avoidable post-petition transfer is one made by the debtor after the petition is filed that is not authorized by a bankruptcy court order or allowed by bankruptcy law. If the debtor's business is authorized to be operated, the trustee or Chapter 11, 12, or 13 debtor may operate the business as usual and incur post-petition debt that would otherwise occur in the normal course of such business. But the trustee or debtor needs a bankruptcy court order to incur unusual debt or to use, sell, or lease any property of the estate if such activities are not part of the debtor's usual business operations. A transferee of an avoidable post-petition transfer may also have violated the automatic stay and thus be subject to compensatory and/or punitive damages. *11 USC §§103,*

362(a)-(b), (h), 363(b)-(c), 364(a)-(b), 721, 1107-1108, 1203, 1303-1304; see Chapter VIII; "Stage Two—Automatic Stay Invoked," Chapter II, and "Motion for Relief from Automatic Stay" Chapter XIV.

2. Purpose for Trustee's Power

An unauthorized post-petition transfer of property deprives the estate of assets without the scrutiny of creditors and court approval to assure an appropriate reciprocal benefit for the estate. Recovery of property wrongfully transferred post-petition increases the value of the estate for distribution to unsecured creditors with allowed claims. *11 USC §§501-502, 541, 549-551; see "File Proof of Claims," Chapter XIV.*

3. Requirements to Avoid a Post-Petition Transfer

The trustee or debtor must prove two requirements to avoid and recover a post-petition transfer of property.

a. Property of the estate was transferred after the petition was filed; and

b. The transfer either:

(1) Was not authorized by the court or the Bankruptcy Code. *See "Stage Two—Automatic Stay Invoked," Chapter II, and "Motion for Relief from Automatic Stay," Chapter XIV; "Avoidable Setoff," discussed below; or*

(2) Occurred during the gap period between the dates of filing the involuntary petition and the order for relief, and the transferee did not give post-petition value to the estate (*see "Exceptions," discussed below*); or

(3) Was made by an entity in possession of property of the estate to someone other than the trustee or Chapter 9, 11, 12, or 13 debtor. *See "Exceptions," discussed below; 11 USC §§303(f), 542(c), 549(a);*

4. Exceptions

Four post-petition transfers may not be avoided and the property transferred may not be recovered.

a. Involuntary Gap Creditor Protected

A transfer of property by the debtor to a gap creditor or transferee after an involuntary petition is filed but before an order for relief is not avoidable to the extent of the value given by the transferee post-petition. It does not matter if the transferee had notice or knowledge of the bankruptcy case. He is protected to the extent of post-petition value given. *Value given* includes the performance of services for the debtor or his business but does not include paying or securing a debt owed pre-petition. *11 USC §§303(f), 549(b).*

b. Good-Faith Purchaser for Value Protected

A post-petition transfer of real property to a good-faith purchaser, who had no knowledge of the bankruptcy case and who gave present fair equivalent value, is not avoidable unless a copy or notice of the bankruptcy petition was properly filed or recorded under applicable nonbankruptcy law before the good-faith purchaser perfected his interests in the realty against a hypothetical bona fide purchaser. Thus, the debtor or trustee must file a copy or notice of the bankruptcy petition in the real estate or deed records of each county where the realty is located before the good-faith purchaser perfects and acquires a superior interest in the land under applicable nonbankruptcy law. If the good-faith purchaser had no knowledge of the bankruptcy case but gave less than present fair equivalent value, he will have a lien on the recovered real estate to the extent of any present value given, unless a copy or notice of the petition was properly recorded in the county records before the purchaser perfected his interests in the land under applicable nonbankruptcy law. If a copy or notice of the petition was properly recorded under applicable nonbankruptcy law before the purchaser perfected his interests, the purchaser will have only an unsecured claim against the estate for any value given to the debtor in the exchange. However, the good-faith purchaser who made improvements to the land after the transfer will have a lien on the land to secure the lesser of the cost of improvements to the land, after deducting any profits received from the property, and any appreciation in value to the land as a result of such improvements. *Improvements* include: (1) physical additions or changes, (2) repairs, (3) payment of real estate taxes, (4) satisfaction of any superior or equal lien(s) on the land, or (5) expenditures or efforts to preserve the land. *11 USC §§502(h), 549(c), 550(a), (d), 551; S Rep No 989, 95th Cong, 2d Sess 90 (1978); HR Rep No 595, 95th Cong, 1st Sess 375 (1977); see "File Proof of Claim," Chapter XIV.*

c. Transfer of Certain Life Insurance Premiums Protected

A life insurance company that acts in good faith may make a post-petition transfer of property of the debtor or estate to pay an insurance premium or nonforfeiture insurance option if the transfer is required to be automatically made under a pre-petition life insurance contract that is property of the estate. *11 USC §542(d);* and

d. Certain Setoffs Protected

The Code permits certain post-petition setoffs of the estate's property by a commodity broker, stockbroker, repo participant, swap participant, or a lessee or purchaser in possession of real property of the estate under a rejected executory contract. *11 USC §§362(b)(6)-(7),(14), 365(h)(2), (i)(2), 553; FRBP 4001, 6006; see "Avoidable Setoffs," discussed below; "Assumption or Rejection of Executory Contracts and Unexpired Leases," Chapter XIV.*

5. Procedures

An action to avoid a post-petition transfer of property is an adversary proceeding governed by the same rules that apply to adversary complaints to recover preferential and fraudulent transfers. *See "Procedures to Avoid a Preferential Transfer," discussed above; 11 USC §549; FRBP 7001(1) et seq; Procedural Bankr Forms B 250A, B, C.*

D. Avoidable Statutory Liens

1. Definition

Unlike a consensual lien which arises by agreement between the debtor and creditor, a statutory lien does not depend upon the consent of the debtor or creditor for its existence. A *statutory lien* is a lien created by federal or state statute or a lien for distress of rent, whether created by statute or otherwise. The power or authority of the legislature to enact a statutory lien may arise from the respective constitution. *11 USC §101(37), (53).*

Statutory liens do not include security interests or judicial liens (obtained by judgment, levy, or sequestration), even if such interests and liens are dependent upon or made fully effective by a statute. *11 USC §101(37), (53).*

2. Purpose for Trustee's Power

The purpose of avoiding a statutory lien is to remove the claims of statutory lienholders and free such property for the estate and unsecured creditors with allowed claims. The property, once subject to a statutory lien, now increases the value of the bankruptcy estate. *11 USC §§101(53), 545, 550-551.*

3. Requirements to Avoid a Statutory Lien

The trustee, Chapter 9 debtor, or Chapter 11 or 12 DIP may avoid three types of statutory liens

a. Liens Triggered by the Debtor's Insolvency

Statutory liens that first become effective when a bankruptcy or nonbankruptcy insolvency proceeding is filed involving the debtor are avoidable. This category includes liens first effective:

(1) At the occurrence of any type of insolvency proceeding (bankruptcy, receivership, or assignment for the benefit of creditors) against the debtor, filed by any entity (debtor, creditor, or trustee);

(2) When the debtor becomes insolvent;

(3) When the debtor's financial condition fails to meet a standard specified by statute; or

(4) At the time of levy of execution against the debtor's property by a sheriff, constable, or other entity who does not represent the statutory lienholder. *11 USC §545(1)(A)-(F).*

A debtor is *insolvent* if his aggregate debts are greater than the aggregate worth of all his property valued at fair valuation, excluding exempt property or property fraudulently transferred. Exempt property and property which the debtor fraudulently transferred or concealed with the intent of defrauding or delaying creditors are not valued. *11 USC §101(32);*

b. Unperfected Liens on Date of Petition

Statutory liens which are not perfected in the manner required by statute on the date the petition is filed are avoidable. A lien is not perfected if any bona fide purchaser of the debtor's property could obtain an interest in the property that is superior to that of the statutory lienholder. *11 USC §545(2);* and

c. Liens for Rent

Statutory liens for rent and (statutory or common law) liens for distress of rent (the debtor failed to pay the required rent) are avoidable. *11 USC §545(3)-(4); S Rep No 989, 95th Cong, 2d Sess 85-86 (1978).*

4. Procedures

The same procedures governing adversary complaints to avoid a preferential transfer apply to complaints to avoid a statutory lien. *See "Procedures to Avoid Preferential Transfers," discussed above; 11 USC §545; FRBP 7001(1) et seq; Procedural Bankr Forms B 250A, B, C.*

E. Other Avoidable Unperfected Interests—Trustee's Strong-Arm Powers

1. Definition

The Bankruptcy Code gives the trustee, Chapter 9 debtor, or Chapter 11 or 12 DIP the strong arm of three hypothetical entities whose liens or interests have been perfected by the date the bankruptcy petition is filed. These entities do not have to actually exist. The trustee or debtor is deemed to assume their superior status to avoid certain unperfected liens and interests. *11 USC §§541, 544(a), 550-551, 902(5), 926, 1101(1), 1107, 1203.*

2. Purpose for Trustee's Strong-Arm Powers

A creditor with an unperfected security interest and a purchaser who failed to timely or properly perfect his interests in real estate are really unsecured creditors. Their claims deserve no greater treatment than the claims of other unsecured creditors against the estate. Property of the debtor subject to such unperfected liens or interests is recovered to increase the value of the bankruptcy estate for pro rata distribution to all unsecured creditors with allowed claims. *11 USC §§541, 544(a), 550-551.*

3. Requirements to Avoid an Unperfected Interest

The trustee or Chapter 9, 11, or 12 debtor may avoid any security or ownership interest that was not perfected on the date the debtor's bankruptcy petition (voluntarily or involuntarily) was filed, if nonbankruptcy law requires perfection of such interest. The trustee or debtor avoids such liens or interests by assuming all rights and powers of three hypothetical entities:

a. **A creditor on a simple contract with a judicial lien on all the debtor's property on the date the bankruptcy petition is filed;**

b. **A creditor with a writ of execution against the debtor's property which was returned unsatisfied on the date the petition is filed; or**

c. **A bona fide purchaser of the debtor's real property who has perfected and has a superior interest in such property under applicable law on the date the petition is filed.** *11 USC §544(a)(1)-(3); S Rep No 989, 95th Cong, 2d Sess 85 (1978).*

The trustee's strong-arm powers do not require a creditor or transferee of the debtor's property to perfect if applicable nonbankruptcy law does not require perfection. *S Rep No 989, 95th Cong, 2d Sess 85 (1978).*

4. Procedures to Avoid an Unperfected Lien

Filing an action to avoid an unperfected lien or interest commences an adversary proceeding. The same procedures governing the trustee's other super-avoiding powers apply equally to this power. *See "Procedures to Avoid a Preferential Transfer," and "Avoidable Fraudulent Transfers or Obligations—Procedures," discussed above; 11 USC §544(a); FRBP 7001(1)-(2) et seq; Procedural Bankr Forms B 250A, B, C.*

F. Avoidable Setoffs

1. Definition

A *setoff* is a common law right of a creditor to net out what the debtor owes to the creditor against a mutual debt that the creditor owes to the debtor. The debtor usually owes more to the creditor than the creditor owes to the debtor. Therefore, the creditor offsets his claim by taking any property owed to the debtor in the creditor's possession to satisfy or reduce the amount of the claim. The typical example is a bank that loaned money ($50,000) to the debtor. The debtor has defaulted and not paid anything. But the debtor has a general savings account ($10,000) and general checking account fund ($15,000) with the bank. The funds in these two accounts represent a debt owed by the bank to the debtor. Even if the loan was not otherwise secured, the bank generally has a common law right to *offset* (take) the savings account and general checking account fund to reduce its claim against the debtor after the debtor defaults, if the savings and checking accounts are not special trust accounts. The setoff exists because the debtor owes the bank $50,000 and the bank owes the debtor $25,000 (savings and checking accounts). The balance of $25,000 owed by the debtor is known as an *insufficiency* under bankruptcy law, or the amount by which the creditor's claim against the debtor exceeds the creditor's debt owed to the debtor (creditor's claim minus creditor's debt equals insufficiency). *11 USC §553(b)(2); see Braniff Airways v Exxon Co, USA, 16 CBC2d 1447 (5th Cir 1987).*

The required *mutuality* exists for an allowable setoff if: (a) the debts are in the same right (both debts arose pre-petition); (b) the debts are between the same parties; and (c) the parties stand in the same capacity. Each party must own his own claim in his own right, with the right to collect the debt in his own name. *11 USC §553(a); see In re Bay State York Co, 26 CBC2d 1520 (Bankr D Mass 1992); In re Virginia Block Co, 5 CBC2d 317 (Bankr WD Va 1981).*

2. Generally

Bankruptcy law generally preserves the debtor's common law right of setoff if the creditor: (a) has an allowed pre-petition claim against the debtor; (b) owes a pre-petition debt to the debtor; and (c) mutuality exists. The Bankruptcy Code even gives the creditor with a right of setoff a lien or secured claim to the extent of the amount that may be subject to a setoff (creditor's debt owed to the debtor). But subject to certain authorized setoffs discussed below, the automatic stay prohibits the creditor's post-petition exercise of this right of setoff without first filing a motion for relief and obtaining lift of the stay. Bankruptcy law also allows the trustee or debtor to avoid a setoff made during the 90-day preference period before the debtor filed his petition, if the setoff improved the creditor's position by reducing the amount of the creditor's unsecured claim against the debtor. *See "Stage Two—Automatic Stay Invoked," Chapter II, and "Motion for Relief from Automatic Stay," Chapter XIV; 11 USC §§362(a)(7), (d), 553; see "Requirements to Avoid a Pre-Petition Setoff," and "Requirements to Avoid a Post-Petition Setoff," discussed below.*

3. Purpose for Trustee's Power

The amount of the setoff recovered from a creditor increases the value of the bankruptcy estate for distribution to all unsecured creditors with allowed claims. *11 USC §§541, 550-551, 553.*

4. Requirements to Avoid a Pre-Petition Setoff

a. The trustee, Chapter 9 debtor, or Chapter 11 or 12 DIP may avoid the amount the creditor improved his position by the setoff during the immediate 90-day pre-petition period by proving three requirements:

(1) The amount of the insufficiency on the date of the setoff. An *insufficiency* is determined by subtracting the amount the creditor owes to the debtor (example: \$25) from the amount of the creditor's claim against the debtor (example: \$70). The difference between the two amounts (creditor's claim minus creditor's mutual debt) is the amount of the insufficiency (\$70 − 25 = \$50 insufficiency). *11 USC §553(b)(2);*

(2) The amount of the insufficiency on the 90th day before the petition was filed; or if there was no insufficiency on the 90th day, then the amount of the insufficiency on the first day during the immediate 90-day pre-petition period when there was an insufficiency; and

(3) The amount by which the insufficiency on the date of the setoff was less than the amount of the insufficiency on the later of the 90th day pre-petition or the first day during such 90-day pre-petition period when there was an insufficiency. It is the amount of the difference between the two insufficiencies that determines the extent to which the amount of setoff may be avoided and recovered for the estate (amount of insufficiency on the 90th day pre-petition minus the amount of insufficiency on setoff date equals the maximum amount of the setoff amount that may be avoided and recovered; or, if there was no insufficiency on the 90th day, then the amount of the insufficiency which first existed during the 90-day pre-petition period minus the amount of insufficiency on the setoff date equals the maximum amount of the setoff amount that the trustee or debtor may avoid and recover). *11 USC §553(b).*

b. Example

On January 1, the debtor files a bankruptcy petition. On October 15 of the immediately preceding year, the debtor borrowed $400 from a Bank and deposited the $400 in a general checking account at that Bank. The debtor owes the Bank $400 and the Bank owes the debtor $400 on October 15—no insufficiency exists. On October 20, the debtor's checking account at the Bank first drops below $400 to $100, but the debtor still owes the Bank $400. There is a $300 insufficiency on October 20 ($400 claim against the debtor minus $100 mutual debt owed to the debtor by the Bank). On December 15, the debtor completely defaults in payments, his checking account at the Bank is $75, and he now owes the Bank $175. The Bank offsets the $75 on December 15. The insufficiency amount on December 15 is $100 ($175 claim against the debtor less $75 mutual debt owed to the debtor).

On October 20, the first date during the immediate 90-day pre-petition period on which an insufficiency existed, the insufficiency was $300. On December 15, the date of the setoff, the insufficiency was $100. The insufficiency on December 15 was $200 less than the insufficiency on October 20. The trustee or debtor may avoid no more than $200 of the setoff amount. Since the setoff amount was $75, the trustee or debtor may avoid and recover the full amount setoff during the 90-day pre-petition preference period. If the insufficiency on December 15 had been $250, then the trustee or debtor could only avoid $50 of the $75 setoff, because the difference between the insufficiency on October 20 and December 15 would be $50 ($300 insufficiency on October 20 minus $250 insufficiency on December 15 = $50). If the insufficiency on December 15 had been $350 while the insufficiency on October 20 was still $300, the trustee or debtor would not be able to avoid or recover any amount of the $75 setoff by the Bank. The creditor would not have improved his position by reducing his unsecured claim during the 90-day preference period. *11 USC §553(b); see Braniff Airways v Exxon Co USA, 16 CBC2d 1447 (5th Cir 1987).*

c. Exceptions

Five types of setoffs made 90 days or less pre-petition may not be avoided by the trustee or Chapter 9, 11, or 12 debtor, even if the creditor improved his unsecured position by such setoff:

(1) Margin or Settlement Payment Claims Under Certain Future Contracts

The trustee or Chapter 9, 11, or 12 debtor may not avoid a setoff of a mutual debt and claim made during the 90-day pre-petition period by a commodity broker or stockbroker, forward contract merchant, financial institution, or securities clearing agency, if the setoff involves:

(a) A claim for a margin or settlement payment held against the debtor; and

(b) The margin or settlement payment claim arose out of commodity, forward, or securities contracts; and

(c) The margin or settlement payment claim is offset against cash, securities, or property of the debtor held by or due from the broker, merchant, or financial institution to margin, guarantee, or settle such contracts. *11 USC §§362(b)(6), 553(b)(1); see Glossary;* or

(2) Margin or Settlement Payment Claims Under Certain Repurchase Agreements

A trustee or Chapter 9, 11, or 12 debtor may not avoid a setoff of a mutual debt and claim made during the 90-day pre-petition period by a repo participant, if the setoff involves:

(a) A claim for a margin or settlement payment held against the debtor; and

(b) The margin or settlement payment claim arose out of repurchase agreements; and

(c) The margin or settlement payment claim is offset against cash, securities, or other property of the debtor held by or due from the repo participant to margin, guarantee, secure, or settle the repurchase agreements. *11 USC §§362(b)(7), 553(b)(1); see Glossary;* or

(3) Settlement Payment Claims Under Certain Swap Agreements

The trustee or Chapter 9, 11, or 12 debtor may not avoid a setoff of a mutual debt and claim made during the 90-day pre-petition period by a swap participant, if the setoff involves:

(a) A claim for any payment held against the debtor in connection with any swap agreement; and

(b) The claim is offset against cash, securities, or other property of the debtor held by or due from the swap participant to guarantee, secure, or settle any swap agreement. *11 USC §§362(b)(14), 553(b)(1);* or

(4) Lessee's Claims Under Rejected Real Estate Lease

The trustee or debtor may not avoid a setoff of a mutual debt and claim made during the 90-day pre-petition period by a lessee in possession of the debtor's real estate, if the setoff involves:

(a) An unexpired lease of real property of the debtor in which the debtor is the lessor; and

(b) The debtor has rejected the unexpired lease; and

(c) The lessee is in possession and elects to remain in possession of the realty for the unexpired term of the lease, including any renewal or extension period available under the pre-petition terms of the lease; and

(d) The damages suffered by the lessee from the debtor's nonperformance after the date of rejection of the lease are offset against any rental payments owed to the debtor under the lease after the date of rejection. However, if the lessee elects to remain in possession and to continue to exercise the right of setoff post-petition, the lessee will have no further claim against the estate as the result of the rejected lease. *11 USC §§365(h)(2), 502(g), 553(b)(1); see "Assumption or Rejection of Executory Contracts and Unexpired Leases," Chapter XIV;* or

(5) Purchaser's Claims Under Rejected Executory Contract for Sale of Real Estate or Timeshare Interest

The trustee or Chapter 9, 11, or 12 debtor may not avoid a setoff of a mutual debt and claim made during the 90-day pre-petition period by a purchaser in possession of the debtor's real estate, if the setoff involves:

(a) An executory contract for the sale of real estate, or sale of a timeshare interest under a timeshare plan, under which the debtor is the seller; and

(b) The debtor has rejected the executory contract for sale of the realty or timeshare interest; and

(c) The purchaser is in possession and elects to remain in possession of the realty; and

(d) The damages suffered by the purchaser from the debtor's nonperformance of the contract of sale after the date of rejection are offset against any payments owed to the debtor under the contract after the rejection. If this right of setoff continues to be exercised post-petition, it will be the only legal right allowed the purchaser in possession of real estate under the debtor's bankruptcy case. The purchaser will have no further claim against the estate as the result of the rejected executory contract of sale. *11 USC §§365(h)(2), (i)(2), 502(g), 553(b)(1); see "Assumption or Rejection of Executory Contracts and Unexpired Leases," Chapter XIV.*

5. Requirements to Avoid a Post-Petition Setoff

a. Authorized Post-Petition Setoffs Excluded from the Automatic Stay

The automatic stay does not prohibit three types of protected post-petition setoffs. A motion for relief from the automatic stay is not required for these setoffs:

(1) A setoff by a commodity broker, forward contract merchant, stockbroker, financial institution, or securities clearing agency of a claim for a margin or settlement payment owed by the debtor under a commodity contract, forward contract, or securities contract, against a debt (cash, securities, or other property of the debtor) owed by the broker, merchant, institution, or agency under the contract to margin, guarantee, secure, or settle such contract;

(2) A setoff by a repo participant of a claim for a margin or settlement payment owed by the debtor under a repurchase agreement against a debt (cash, securities, or other property of the debtor) owed by the repo participant under the agreement to margin, guarantee, secure, or settle such repurchase agreement; or

(3) A setoff by a swap participant of a claim for payment owed by the debtor under any swap agreement against a debt (cash, securities, or other property of the debtor) owed by the swap participant under the agreement to guarantee, secure, or settle such swap agreement. *11 USC §§362(b)(6)-(7), (14), 553(a); see "Stage Two—Automatic Stay Invoked," Chapter II, and "Motion for Relief from Automatic Stay," Chapter XIV.*

b. Unauthorized Post-Petition Setoffs

Subject to the authorized setoffs listed above, a trustee or Chapter 9, 11, or 12 debtor may avoid a post-petition setoff by a creditor if the creditor violated the automatic stay by failing to first obtain a lift of the stay. A creditor who wishes to exercise his setoff rights post-petition should file any required proof of claim timely. He must also file a motion for relief from the automatic stay, pay a $60 filing fee, and serve a copy of the motion on the debtor, any trustee, and committee(s) by first-class mail or any other manner allowed for service of process under the Federal Rules of Civil Procedure. The debtor or trustee must then obtain a hearing before the court before the 30th day after the motion is filed or the automatic stay is automatically lifted under bankruptcy law and the creditor will be allowed to setoff without obtaining a court order. Additionally, local bankruptcy rules may require the debtor or trustee to file and serve a timely answer to the motion. If a hearing is timely held under the motion for relief, the court may authorize the setoff subject to any limitations imposed by bankruptcy law or which the court may impose in the interests of justice given the facts of the case. *See "Requirements to Prevent a Post-Petition Setoff," discussed below; 11 USC §§105(a), 362(a)-(b), (d)-(e), (h), 549(a), 553(a)-(b); 28 USC §1930(b), Judicial Conference Schedule of Fees (21); FRBP 4001, 9013-9014; "File Proof of Claims," Chapter XIV; "Stage Two—Automatic Stay Invoked," Chapter II, and "Motion for Relief from Automatic Stay," Chapter XIV; Local Bankruptcy Rules.*

If the creditor does offset property of the debtor or estate without first obtaining lift of the stay, the trustee or debtor must file an adversary complaint in order to avoid the unauthorized post-petition transfer of the property and recover the property as well as actual and perhaps punitive damages. If the creditor knew about the debtor's bankruptcy case and willfully setoff property of the debtor or estate post-petition without first obtaining relief from the stay, the individual debtor or trustee may recover the property setoff, or its value, and compensatory and punitive damages. *11 USC §§362(a)-(b), (d)-(e), (h), 553(a); FRBP 7001 et seq; see "Procedures to Avoid a Setoff," discussed below.*

6. Requirements to Prevent a Post-Petition Setoff (Disallowed Setoffs)

The court may not grant a creditor's motion for relief from the automatic stay to permit a post-petition setoff of a mutual pre-petition debt and claim of the creditor if the trustee or Chapter 9, 11, or 12 debtor proves at least one of four situations exists.

a. The creditor's claim is disallowed under bankruptcy law.

A proof of claim properly and timely filed by a creditor is allowed unless the court sustains an objection to the claim. Under Chapters 7, 12, and 13, a proof of claim must be filed with the court before the 90th day after the first date set for the meeting of creditors.

Under Chapters 9 and 11, a proof of claim is deemed filed if listed under the debtor's Chapter 9 list of creditors or Chapter 11 schedules of liabilities. However, if such claim is listed as disputed, contingent, or unliquidated by the Chapter 9 or 11 debtor, the creditor must file a timely proof of claim by the date set by the court. Failure to file a required proof of claim timely will bar the creditor from voting or receiving distribution of the estate from the trustee or under a plan. *11 USC §§103(a), (e)-(f), 501-502, 726, 901, 924-925, 1126(a), 1129, 1225, 1325; FRBP 1007, 3001-3007, 3017(d), 9014; see "File Proof of Claim," Chapter XIV; Official Bankr Form 6, Schedules D-H.*

For a proof of claim to be disallowed and thus precluded from a post-petition setoff, the trustee, debtor, or any other party-in-interest (creditor) must file an objection to claim and prove one or more of eight grounds for disallowance of claims under the Code. Such grounds include: the unenforceability of the creditor's claim; the claim exceeds the value of services provided; the claim is for an unmatured debt or unmatured interest; or the creditor failed to file a timely or proper proof of claim. However, tax claims disallowed by the court because they exceed the value of the estate's interest in the assessed property may be setoff against a mutual debt owed by the taxing authority. *11 USC §§102(1)(A)-(B), 502(b), 553(a)(1); FRBP 3007, 7001 et seq, 9014; see "File Proof of Claim," Chapter XIV; or*

b. **The creditor's claim against the debtor was transferred to the creditor post-petition by an entity other than the debtor; or**

c. **The creditor's claim against the debtor was transferred to the creditor by an entity other than the debtor, within the 90-day pre-petition period (89 days or less before the petition was filed), and while the debtor was insolvent; or**

d. **The creditor's debt owed to the debtor was incurred by the creditor:**

(1) Within the 90-day pre-petition period (89 days or less before the petition was filed); and

(2) The debtor was insolvent during this period; and

(3) The creditor incurred his claim against the debtor for the express purpose of obtaining a right to setoff. *11 USC §553(a)(1)-(3).*

As with a preferential transfer, there is a rebuttable presumption that the debtor was insolvent during the 90-day pre-petition period (90 days or less before the petition was filed). The creditor has the burden of rebutting the presumption. *11 USC §553(c).*

7. Procedures to Avoid a Setoff

The trustee or Chapter 9, 11, or 12 debtor must file an adversary complaint to avoid a pre-petition setoff that is not allowed under bankruptcy law and recover the property for the estate. Similarly, an adversary complaint must be filed to avoid a post-petition setoff that was not authorized by court order or bankruptcy law. The trustee or Chapter 11 or 12 DIP must pay a $120 filing fee only from the bankruptcy estate, if any exists. No fee is required from the Chapter 9 debtor. The trustee or debtor must serve a copy of the complaint with summons on the creditor by first-class mail or any other manner allowed for service of process in federal district court. *11 USC §§362, 549, 553; 28 USC §1930(b), Judicial Conference Schedule of Fees (6); FRBP 7001(1), (4) et seq; Procedural Bankr Forms B 250A, B, C.*

G. Restrictions on the Trustee's Super-Avoiding Powers

The super-avoiding powers of the trustee and Chapter 9, 11, or 12 debtors are broad but not unlimited. Both bankruptcy and nonbankruptcy laws impose restrictions.

1. Bankruptcy Statute of Limitations Restrictions

a. Actions to Avoid Preferences, Fraudulent Transfers, Statutory Liens, Unperfected Liens or Interests Under Trustee's Strong-Arm Power, and Setoffs

The trustee or Chapter 11 or 12 debtor must file an adversary complaint to avoid these transfers, liens, or interests by the earlier date that is: (1) the later of 2 years after *entry* of the order for relief or one year after appointment or election of the first trustee in a Chapter 11, 12, or 13 case *if* such trustee is appointed or elected no later than two years after the order for relief is entered; or (2) the date the bankruptcy case is closed or dismissed. *HR 1116, Pub L No 103-394, §216, amending 11 USC §546(a)(1); FRBP 7001 et seq.*

b. Actions to Avoid Unauthorized Post-Petition Transfers

The trustee or Chapter 9, 11, or 12 debtor must file an adversary complaint to avoid an unauthorized post-petition transfer by the earlier date of: (1) two years after the date of the unauthorized transfer; or (2) the date the case is closed or dismissed. *11 USC §§103(a), (e)-(f), 549(d), 901; FRBP 7001 et seq.*

c. Actions to Recover Property Under an Avoidable Transfer

The trustee or Chapter 9, 11, or 12 debtor may file a single adversary complaint to avoid a preferential, fraudulent, or unauthorized transfer of property, a setoff, or a statutory or unperfected lien, and to recover such property or its value for the estate. Alternatively, the trustee or debtor may file two separate adversary complaints: one complaint to avoid the transfer, lien, or interest and a second complaint to recover the property or its value for the estate. Any separate complaint to recover property or its value must be filed by the earlier date of: (1) one year after the date the transfer, lien, or interest was avoided by the court; or (2) the date the case is closed or dismissed. *11 USC §550(a), (e).*

2. Limitations on Liability of Transferees

a. Generally

A trustee or Chapter 9, 11, or 12 debtor may file an adversary complaint to recover property conveyed under an avoidable transfer against the initial (first) transferee or the entity for whose benefit the property was transferred and against an immediate or *mediate* (subsequent or secondary) transferee. But the trustee or debtor is allowed only one recovery. If the transfer occurred between 90 days and one year pre-petition, the trustee may recover from the transferee only if he or she was an insider on the date of the transfer. *11 USC §550(a), (c), (d).*

Any good-faith transferee (initial or subsequent transferee) of property under any avoidable transfer will have a lien on recovered property to secure the lesser of:

(1) The cost of *improvements* that the transferee made to the property after the avoidable transfer (physical changes, repairs, tax payments, debt payments to satisfy a senior or equal lien, or preservation of the property), after deducting any profits received or accrued to the transferee from the property; or

(2) Any appreciation in value to the property resulting from such improvements. *11 USC §550(e)(1).*

b. Fraudulent Pre-Petition Transfers

In addition to the above lien for costs or appreciation in value resulting from improvements, a good-faith initial transferee under an avoidable fraudulent transfer will have a lien on the transferred property to the extent of value given in the exchange to the debtor. *11 USC §548(c); see "Avoidable Fraudulent Transfers or Obligations," discussed above.*

c. Post-Petition Transfers

A good-faith purchaser under an avoidable post-petition transfer who had no knowledge of the bankruptcy petition and who gave less than present fair equivalent value will have a lien on the transferred property to the extent of any present value given in the transfer, unless the trustee or debtor properly filed a copy or notice of the petition in the real estate or deed records of each county where the land is located before the purchaser perfected his interests under applicable nonbankruptcy law. *11 USC §§549(c), 550(a), (b); see "Avoidable Unauthorized Post-Petition Transfers," discussed above.*

d. Protected Subsequent Transferees

The trustee or debtor may not recover property conveyed in an otherwise avoidable transfer from:

(1) A *secondary* (immediate or mediate) transferee who receives the property from an *initial* (first) transferee, if the secondary transferee:

(a) Acted in good faith;

(b) Acted without knowledge of the voidability of the transfer; and

(c) Gave value in the transfer. *Value* includes paying or securing a present or antecedent debt of the debtor. *11 USC §550(a)(2), (b)(1); HR Rep No 595, 95th Cong, 1st Sess 375-76 (1977);* or

(2) Any further good-faith subsequent transferee from a protected secondary transferee. *11 USC §550(a)(2), (b)(2); HR Rep No 595, 95th Cong, 1st Sess 375-76 (1977); S Rep No 989, 95th Cong, 2d Sess 90 (1978).*

Thus, the trustee's or debtor's right to recover property is limited with regard to good-faith subsequent transferees from the initial transferee. The good-faith requirement to protect a subsequent transferee is imposed to prevent a washing of recoverable property through an innocent transferee. An initial transferee may not insulate himself by transferring recoverable property to an innocent transferee and then receiving a retransfer of the property. To be excepted from liability, each subsequent transferee must have acted in good faith at all times. *HR Rep No 595, 95th Cong, 1st Sess 375-76 (1977); S Rep No 989, 95th Cong, 2d Sess 90 (1978).*

3. Nonbankruptcy Law Restrictions Recognized Under Bankruptcy Law

a. Relation Back Provisions

The Code limits the powers of the trustee or Chapter 9, 11, or 12 debtor to avoid an unperfected pre-petition lien or interest, statutory lien, post-petition transfer, and to exercise his strong-arm or successor-in-interest powers. If a transferee of such an avoidable lien or transfer still has time under generally applicable law to perfect his interest and acquire superior rights over intervening purchasers or lienholders, the transferee may do so even post-petition. Generally applicable law applies to bankruptcy proceedings and nonbankruptcy situations.

Applicable nonbankruptcy law frequently used is the relation-back provisions of §9.301(2) of the Uniform Commercial Code (UCC). A purchase-money security interest perfected before the 10th day after the debtor takes possession of the collateral (or 20th day under UCC §9.301(2) adopted by certain states) will relate back to the date the security interest attached to the collateral. The purchase-money lienholder will have a superior lien and priority over intervening creditors who perfected their liens between the date that the purchase-money creditor's security interest attached and the date the lien was perfected. Thus, using the 10-day relation-back provisions of many state UCC provisions, if the purchase-money security interest attached to the debtor's property on August 1, the debtor took possession of the collateral on August 5, and filed a bankruptcy petition on August 10, under generally applicable nonbankruptcy law, the creditor could still perfect his lien before August 15 and acquire a superior lien to creditors who perfected their liens between August 1 and August 14. The purchase-money secured creditor may exercise his existing right to perfect post-petition under bankruptcy law by giving proper notice to the trustee or Chapter 9, 11, or 12 debtor and following applicable nonbankruptcy law procedures to perfect before August 15. The notice should state: (1) the applicable nonbankruptcy law, (2) the date the creditor acquired his interest in property of the debtor, and (3) the manner and date by which the creditor may perfect his interest under applicable nonbankruptcy law. The notice should also include copies of all relevant documents. The automatic stay does not prohibit the creditor from giving the required notice to the trustee or debtor or from perfecting his security interest post-petition under applicable nonbankruptcy law. The purpose of allowing post-petition perfection is to protect persons whom state law protects, despite the fact that there was an intervening, and frequently unsuspected, bankruptcy petition. *11 USC §§362(b)(3), 546(b); UCC §9-301(2); HR Rep No 595, 95th Cong, 1st Sess, 371-72 (1977); S Rep No 989, 95th Cong, 2d Sess 86-87 (1978).*

b. Reclamation Restrictions

(1) Generally

Applicable nonbankruptcy statutory or common law allows a seller who sold goods to a debtor on credit in the ordinary course of the seller's business to reclaim the goods if the debtor received such goods while insolvent and the seller makes a timely demand to reclaim. The powers of the trustee or Chapter 9, 11, or 12 debtor to avoid a preferential transfer, post-petition transfer, unperfected pre-petition interest, or statutory lien are subject to this right of reclamation if the creditor complies with the following requirements. *See UCC §2-702:*

(a) Pre-Petition Reclamation

The creditor against whom an adversary complaint is filed to avoid a preferential transfer because of goods reclaimed during the 90-day preference period may assert as a defense the right of reclamation and prove that:

(i) The creditor sold the reclaimed goods to the debtor in the ordinary course of the creditor's business;

(ii) The debtor received such goods while insolvent; and

(iii) The creditor mailed or delivered to the debtor a written demand for reclamation of the goods before the tenth day after the debtor received the goods. *11 USC §§544(a)(1), 546(c)(1), 547; see "Avoidable Preferential Transfers," "Other Avoidable Unperfected Interests—Trustee's Strong-Arm Powers," and "Avoidable Statutory Liens," discussed above.*

(b) Post-Petition Reclamation

The creditor who wishes to reclaim goods post-petition must:

(i) File a motion for relief from the automatic stay to reclaim goods. The motion should include a written demand for reclamation and state that:

a) The creditor sold the goods to the debtor in the ordinary course of the creditor's business;

b) The debtor received such goods while insolvent;

c) The motion for relief with written demand has been served on the debtor and any appointed trustee before the 10th day after the debtor received the goods, or before the 20th day after the debtor's receipt of the goods if the 10-day period expires post-petition; and

d) The written demand is pursuant to §546(c) of the Code; and

(ii) Serve a copy of the motion for relief with written demand for reclamation on the debtor and any appointed trustee by first-class mail or any other manner allowed for service of process in federal district court. A copy of the motion with written demand for reclamation should also be mailed to all committee(s) and any other entity required by court order or local bankruptcy rules. *11 USC §§362(a)(3), (d)(1), 546(c); FRBP 4001, 9014; see "Stage Two—Automatic Stay Invoked," Chapter II, and "Motion for Relief from Automatic Stay," Chapter XIV.*

The court must either grant the creditor's motion for relief to allow the right of reclamation or deny the motion but grant the creditor a first priority administrative claim against the estate or lien on property of the estate to secure the allowed amount of the creditor's claim. *11 USC §§503(b), 507(a)(1), 546(c)(2)(A)-(B).*

(2) Sellers of Grain and United States Fishermen

The powers of the trustee or Chapter 9, 11, or 12 debtor to avoid preferential transfers, post-petition transfers, and statutory or unperfected pre-petition liens or interests are also subject to any statutory or common law right of reclamation of certain sellers of grain and United States fisherman. Sellers who are producers of grain sold to a grain storage facility, or United States fishermen who caught fish later sold to a fish processing facility owned or operated by the debtor may reclaim the grain or fish under certain conditions:

(a) The seller must have sold such goods in the ordinary course of his business;

(b) The debtor must have been insolvent when he received the goods; and

(c) The seller must mail a written demand to reclaim before the tenth day after the debtor receives the goods.

If the right of reclamation is sought post-petition, the written demand must be included in a motion for relief under procedures outlined above. *11 USC §§362(d)(1), 546(d); FRBP 4001, 9014.*

The court may only deny the right to reclaim if it grants the seller of grain or fish a lien on the property of the estate to secure the allowed amount of such creditor's claim. *11 USC §§362(a)(3), (d), 546(d).*

4. Chapter 11 Trustee's Right to Return Goods Limits Avoidance Powers of Subsequent Trustee(s):

The powers of the Chapter 11 trustee or debtor-in-possession (DIP) to exercise the strong-arm provisions of the Code or to avoid statutory liens, preferences, unauthorized post-petition transfers, or setoffs is limited under Chapter 11 cases filed after October 22, 1994.

A Chapter 11 trustee or DIP may return goods post-petition if the creditor consents and the return is in the estate's best interests. The creditor may then offset the purchase price of the goods against its *pre*-petition claim against the debtor. *HR 1116, Pub L No 103-395, §222, amending 11 USC §546 adding subsection (g)[h] and amending §553(b)(1).*

Subsection 546(h) of the Bankruptcy Code requires that:

(a) The Chapter 11 trustee or DIP file a motion to allow the post-petition return of goods no later than the 120th day after entry of the order for relief;

(b) **Notice and hearing be given to all parties-in-interest as required by federal and local bankruptcy rules;**

(c) **The creditor at issue shipped the goods to the debtor pre-petition;**

(d) **The creditor consents to the post-petition return of goods; and**

(e) **The bankruptcy court determines that the post-petition return of goods is in the "best interests of the estate."** *11 USC §102(1)(A-B); FRBP 6007, 9029; LRBP 9007; HR 1116, Pub L No 103-394, §222, amending and adding 11 USC §546(g)(h) and amending 11 USC §553(b)(1).*

If the above five conditions are met, the creditor *may* elect to offset the purchase price of the returned goods against his or her pre-petition claim against the debtor. Neither the DIP nor any subsequently appointed or elected trustee in the debtor's bankruptcy case may thereafter exercise the trustee's super-avoidance powers to recover either the returned goods, its value, or the amount offset by the creditor. *HR 1116, Pub L No 103-394, §222, amending and adding 11 USC §546(g)[h] and amending 11 USC §553(b)(1).*

5. **Protection of Pre-Petition Margin, Settlement, and Swap Agreement Payments**

The trustee or Chapter 9, 11, or 12 debtor may not avoid certain pre-petition margin, settlement, or swap agreement payments unless the debtor made such payments fraudulently, within one year of filing the petition, and with the intent of delaying, hindering, or defrauding any creditor. The following good-faith transfers are protected even though the payments received would otherwise be avoidable under one or more of the trustee's super-avoiding powers:

a. **Pre-petition transfer(s) of margin or settlement payments made by or to a commodity broker or stockbroker, forward contract merchant, financial institution, or securities clearing agency;**

b. **Pre-petition transfer(s) of margin or settlement payments made by or to a repo participant under a repurchase agreement; or**

c. **Pre-petition transfer(s) of swap agreement payments made by or to a swap participant under a swap agreement.** *11 USC §§362(b)(6), (7), (14), 546(e)-(g).*

Research Guide

Anderson, *Chapter 11: Reorganizations* ch 9 (Shepard's/McGraw-Hill 1983)

Anderson & Morris, *Chapter 12: Farm Reorganizations* ch 5 (Shepard's/McGraw-Hill 1987)

Drake, *Bankruptcy Practice for the General Practitioner* ch 5 (Shepard's/McGraw-Hill 2d ed 1990)

Drake & Morris, *Chapter 13: Practice and Procedure* ch 5 (Shepard's/McGraw-Hill 1983)

Jaroslavsky, *Practical Bankruptcy Procedure* ch 14 (Shepard's/McGraw-Hill 1993)

Murphy, *Creditor's Rights in Bankruptcy* chs 13, 14 (Shepard's/McGraw-Hill 2d ed 1988)

Pollard & Burton, *Guide to Effective Bankruptcy Litigation* chs 8, 12 (Shepard's/McGraw-Hill 1988)

XIII. The Debtor's Super-Avoiding Powers

XIII. The Debtor's Super-Avoiding Powers
11 USC §§522(b), (d), (f)-(l), 544-551
FRBP 4003(d), 7001(1) et seq, 9014

- A. Overview
- B. Which Debtors Have Super-Avoiding Powers
- C. Purpose for the Debtor's Super-Avoiding Powers
- D. What Super-Avoiding Powers May the Individual Debtor Exercise
  - 1. Debtor's Own Super-Avoiding Powers to Avoid Liens on Certain Exemptible Property
    - a. Generally
    - b. Limitations on the Debtor's Super-Avoiding Powers
  - 2. Debtor's Super-Avoiding Powers Derived from the Trustee's Failure to Exercise His Powers
  - 3. Debtor's Exemption Powers Over Property Recovered by Trustee
- E. Procedures to Exercise the Debtor's Super-Avoiding Powers
  - 1. Debtor's Own Super-Avoiding Powers
  - 2. Debtor's Derivative Super-Avoiding Powers
    - a. Request the Trustee to Exercise His Powers
    - b. File an Adversary Complaint
  - 3. Claim the Property Recovered as Exempt
    - a. How Property Is Exempted
    - b. Amended Schedules
- F. Restrictions on the Debtor's Super-Avoiding Powers
  - 1. Exemptible Property Restriction
  - 2. Statute of Limitations, Rights of Relation Back, and Reclamation Restrictions

3. Costs and Expenses of Recovering Property Restrictions
Research Guide

XIII. The Debtor's Super-Avoiding Powers

A. Overview

It is generally the trustee, Chapter 9 debtor, or Chapter 11 or 12 debtor-in-possession (DIP), as representative of the bankruptcy estate, who is given super-avoiding powers under the Bankruptcy Code. But the Code gives all *individual* (natural person) debtors certain super-avoiding powers to protect their right to claim exemptions and obtain a fresh start. *11 USC §522(b), (d), (f)-(k)(1).*

B. Which Debtors Have Super-Avoiding Powers

Only individual Chapter 7, 11, 12, or 13 debtors are given certain super-avoiding powers. And such powers may only be used to recover and preserve certain property that the debtor may claim as exempt under applicable nonbankruptcy or bankruptcy law. *11 USC §522(b), (d), (f)-(j)(1); Official Bankr Form 6, Schedule C; see "Stage Five—Exemptions Claimed by the Debtor," Chapter II.*

C. Purpose for the Debtor's Super-Avoiding Powers

The debtor may exercise certain super-avoiding powers to recover property that may be claimed as exempt under the Bankruptcy Code's exemption provisions (§522(d)); or under federal nonbankruptcy, and/or state or local exemption laws in effect on the date the petition is filed where the debtor has been domiciled for the greater part of the immediate 180-day pre-petition period. Exempt property protects the debtor and his dependents and fortifies their fresh start. *11 USC §§102(5), 522(b); see "Stage Five—Exemptions Claimed by the Debtor," Chapter II.*

D. What Super-Avoiding Powers May the Individual Debtor Exercise

1. Debtor's Own Super-Avoiding Powers to Avoid Liens on Certain Exemptible Property

a. Generally

Subject to limitations discussed below, a debtor who is an individual (natural person) may avoid a judicial lien or nonpossessory, nonpurchase-money lien on certain property to the extent such lien impairs an exemption that the debtor would have had if the lien had not existed. The debtor must be able to claim the property as exempt under §522(d) of the Bankruptcy Code or applicable nonbankruptcy exemption law(s) if the lien is avoided. *11 USC §522(f)(1); FRBP 4003(d), 7001 et seq, 9013-9014; see Owen v Owen, 500 US 305, 111 S Ct 133, 114 L Ed 2d 350 (1991).*

(1) Judicial Liens on Exemptible Property

These are liens obtained by a judgment against the debtor or by levy, sequestration, or other legal or equitable process against the debtor's property. *11 USC §§101(36), 522(b), (d), (f)(1).*

(2) Nonpossessory, Nonpurchase-Money Security Interests in Certain Exemptible Property

The individual debtor may avoid a nonpossessory, nonpurchase-money security interest in the following property:

(a) Consumer household goods or furnishings, wearing apparel, jewelry, appliances, musical instruments, books, animals and crops;

(b) Professional books, implements, or tools of the trade of a debtor or his dependent; and

(c) Professionally prescribed health aids for the debtor or his dependent. *11 USC §§522(b), (d), (f)(2)(A)-(C); see Owen v Owen, 500 US 305, 111 S Ct 1833, 114 L Ed 2d 350 (1991).*

b. Limitations on the Debtor's Super-Avoiding Powers

(1) Judicial Liens on Bona Fide Alimony, Maintenance, and Support Payments Protected

Effective for bankruptcy cases filed after October 22, 1994, a debtor may not avoid a judicial lien on exempt property to the extent that such lien secures a debt: (a) to a spouse, former spouse, or child of the debtor; (b) for bona fide alimony, maintenance, or support of such spouse or child, arising in connection with a separation or property settlement, divorce decree, or other court order of record made by a governmental unit according to state or territorial law; and (c) such debt is neither voluntarily nor involuntarily assigned (by operation of law) to another entity. *HR 5116, Pub L No 103-394, §304(d), amending 11 USC §522(f)(1).*

(2) Formula for Determining the Extent to Which a Judicial or Nonpossessory, Nonpurchase-Money Lien Impairs an Exemption

Prior to October 22, 1994, a debtor could avoid a judicial lien or nonpossessory, nonpurchase-money lien on property described above to the extent such lien impaired an exemption that the debtor would have had if the lien had not existed. The debtor could avoid such lien even if state law removed secured property from the scope of its exemption statute. If avoiding the judicial or nonpossessory, nonpurchase-money lien would entitle the debtor to an exemption under either §522(d) of the Bankruptcy Code or state law exemptions, then the lien could be *completely* avoided and the property recovered and exempted by the debtor. *Owen v Owen, 500 US 305, 111 S Ct 133, 114 L Ed 2d 350 (1991); 11 USC §522(f).*

The 1994 Bankruptcy Reform Act, effective October 22, 1994, overruled the Supreme Court's *Owen v Owen* decision in part and established a formula limiting the extent to which a judicial or nonpossessory, nonpurchase-money lien impairs a debtor's exemption. For bankruptcy cases filed after October 22, 1994, such lien may impair an exemption to the extent that:

(a) The sum of (i) the lien to be avoided, *plus* (ii) all other liens on the same property (excluding other liens already avoided), *plus* (iii) the dollar amount of the exemption that the debtor could claim if there were no liens;

(b) Exceeds the value of the debtor's interest in the exempt property if there were no liens.

For example, the debtor owns an automobile worth $6,000 subject to a $3,000 purchase money lien and a $2,000 nonpossessory, nonpurchase-money lien. The debtor elects to claim exemptions under the §522(d)(2) and may exempt only $2,400 of his interest (equity) in one automobile. The debtor, thus, may avoid only $1,400 of the $2,000 nonpossessory, nonpurchase-money lien, as follows:

(a) $7,400 (the sum of (i) $2,000, plus (ii) $3,000, plus (iii) $2,400)

(b) Exceeds $6,000 (the value of the debtor's interest in the automobile if there were no liens)

$1,400 = extent to which the avoidable lien impairs the debtor's exemption.

The 1994 Amendments to the Bankruptcy Code specifically excluded judgment liens arising out of a mortgage foreclosure from the limitations of the above formula. *HR 5116 Pub L No 103-394, §303, amending and adding 11 USC §522(f)(2)(C).*

(3) Nonpossessory, Nonpurchase-Money Liens on Tools of the Trade, Farm Animals, or Crops May Not Be Avoided to the Extent Their Value Exceeds $5,000

A debtor may not avoid a nonpossessory, nonpurchase-money lien on the debtor's or a dependent's otherwise exempt implements, professional books, tools of the trade, or farm animals or crops:

(a) to the extent the value of such exempt property exceeds $5,000;

(b) the debtor has chosen applicable state law exemptions under §522(b) of the Code, either voluntarily or by a state law requirement; and

(c) applicable state law either allows the debtor to claim an unlimited amount of exemptions or prohibits avoidance of a consensual lien (security interest) in exempt property. *HR 5116, Pub L No 103-394, §310, amending and adding 11 USC §522(f)(3).*

2. Debtor's Super-Avoiding Powers Derived from the Trustee's Failure to Exercise His Powers

If the trustee could have exercised, but failed to exercise, his super-avoiding powers to avoid an unperfected or statutory lien, a preferential or fraudulent transfer of property, or an unauthorized setoff or post-petition transfer of property, the debtor may then step into the shoes of the trustee to avoid such transfers and recover the property if five requirements are met:

a. The debtor may exempt the property at issue under bankruptcy or applicable nonbankruptcy exemption law(s);

b. The debtor transferred the property to the creditor involuntarily.

The debtor's satisfaction of a judgment lien obtained against the debtor against his wishes is an *involuntary transfer.* But enforcement of a consensual lien under a security agreement or deed of trust voluntarily entered into by the debtor may not constitute an involuntary transfer by the debtor. *In re Washkowiak, 15 CBC2d 206 (Bankr ND Ill 1986); see In re Smith, 5 CBC2d 1114 (Bankr ED Wis 1981);*

c. The trustee had the legal right under bankruptcy law to file an adversary complaint to avoid the transfer, lien, or setoff and recover the property;

d. The trustee did not file such an adversary complaint; and

e. The debtor did not try to conceal the property from the trustee, creditor(s), or the estate. *11 USC §522(b), (d), (g)(1), (h)(1)-(2), (i)(1)-(2).*

3. Debtor's Exemption Powers Over Property Recovered by Trustee

The trustee may avoid and recover property that was the subject of a preferential or fraudulent transfer, unperfected or statutory lien, unauthorized setoff, or post-petition transfer. The debtor may then claim such property exempt on Official Bankruptcy Form 6, Schedule C, if two requirements are met:

a. The property may be exempted under bankruptcy exemption law or under applicable federal, state and/or local exemption law(s); and

b. The debtor:

(1) Transferred the property involuntarily to the creditor (the underlying debt was incurred by the debtor involuntarily) and did not conceal such property; or

(2) Could have recovered the property independently of the trustee by avoiding a nonpossessory, nonpurchase-money security interest in exemptible consumer property; professional books, implements, or trade tools for the debtor or his dependent; or professionally prescribed health aids for the debtor or his dependent. *See "Debtor's Own Super-Avoiding Powers to Avoid Liens on Certain Exemptible Property," discussed above. 11 USC §§522(b), (d), (f)(2), (g); Chapter XII.*

E. Procedures to Exercise the Debtor's Super-Avoiding Powers

1. Debtor's Own Super-Avoiding Powers

The debtor may exercise his own super-avoiding powers to avoid a transfer of property by filing a motion to avoid the lien under §522(f). The motion must be served on the affected creditor by first-class mail or any other manner allowed for service of process in federal district court. The motion does not commence an adversary proceeding and no filing fee is required. The creditor does not have to file an answer or response, unless directed otherwise by court order or local bankruptcy rules. A copy of the motion should also be served by mail or personal delivery on any trustee or standing trustee, any committee(s), and on any other entity required by court order or local bankruptcy rules. *11 USC §522(f); FRBP 4003(d), 7004, 9013-9014.*

2. Debtor's Derivative Super-Avoiding Powers

The debtor who wishes to exercise super-avoiding powers derived from the trustee and avoid a transfer of exemptible property should follow the following procedures.

a. Request the Trustee to Exercise His Powers

If the exemptible property may be avoided and recovered by the trustee in the exercise of his super-avoiding powers, the debtor should first serve a written request to file the adversary complaint on the trustee by first-class mail or personal delivery. A copy of the written request may be filed with the court, unless the court or local bankruptcy rules direct otherwise. *11 USC §522(g)-(i); FRBP 7005, 9013.*

If the trustee does then file such an adversary complaint, the debtor should file a motion to intervene in the trustee's complaint to preserve the debtor's super-avoiding powers and his right to claim any property recovered as exempt. *11 USC §522(g)-(i); FRBP 7001 et seq, 7024.*

b. File an Adversary Complaint

If the trustee refuses to file an adversary complaint, the debtor must then file the adversary complaint. No filing fee should be required of the debtor even if the debtor is a Chapter 11 or 12 DIP. The debtor is not acting as a DIP (trustee) for the benefit of the estate but is filing the complaint to protect the debtor's exemption rights and his fresh start as an individual. *28 USC §1930(b), Judicial Conference Schedule of Fees (6); 11 USC §522(f), (h).*

The adversary complaint should seek at least two remedies. First, the complaint must seek to avoid the lien or transfer of property. Second, the complaint should seek to recover the property at issue or its value as exempt property. *11 USC §§522(f)-(i), 550-551.*

The debtor must serve a copy of the complaint with the summons on the defendant-creditor. Service of process may be by first-class mail or any other manner allowed under the Federal Rules of Civil Procedure. The debtor should also serve a copy of the complaint on any trustee or standing trustee by mail or personal delivery. *FRBP 7001, 7004 et seq.*

3. Claim the Property Recovered as Exempt

a. How Property Is Exempted

The debtor must claim property as exempt, whether recovered by exercise of the debtor's own super-avoiding powers or derivatively through exercise of the trustee's super-avoiding powers. Exemptions must be claimed on Schedule C, Official Bankruptcy Form 6 (schedules of assets and liabilities) and filed with the petition or before the 15th day after the petition is filed, unless the court extends such time. If the debtor fails to exempt property or its value so recovered, such property will remain part of the bankruptcy estate. *11 USC §§521, 522(f)-(i)(1), 541; FRBP 1007(b)-(c).*

b. Amended Schedules

If exemptible property is recovered by the debtor or trustee after the debtor has filed his schedule of assets and liabilities, the debtor may file an amendment to Schedule C at any time before the bankruptcy case is closed, unless the court or local bankruptcy rules direct otherwise. The debtor must serve a notice of the amended schedule by mail or personal delivery on the trustee or standing trustee, any creditor affected by the amendment, and on any other entity required by court order or local bankruptcy rules. The clerk must immediately deliver or mail a copy of the amended schedule to the U.S. trustee. No hearing is required unless a party-in-interest files an objection to the amended schedule of exemptions, or local bankruptcy rules state otherwise. Any objection must be filed before the 30th day after the debtor files the amended schedule, unless the court extends such time before the 30 days expire. *See Taylor v Freeland & Kronz, 503 US 638, 112 S Ct 1644 (1992); 11 USC §521(1); FRBP 1009(a), (e), advisory committee's note, 2002(f)(1), 4003(b), 9013.*

F. Restrictions on the Debtor's Super-Avoiding Powers

The debtor's super-avoiding powers are subject to three restrictions.

1. Exemptible Property Restriction

The debtor may recover only his exemptible interest in the property at issue. The extent of the debtor's exemptible interest depends upon which exemption law(s) the debtor selects. Bankruptcy Code exemption law permits the debtor to exempt the value of certain unsecured property and only the equity in certain secured property (*See §522(d), Title 11*). Some state and federal nonbankruptcy exemption laws allow the debtor to exempt the full market value of the property regardless of whether it is unsecured or secured property. But the debtor may only exercise a super-avoiding power to recover the value of his exemptible interest in the property, be it the full value or only the equity in such property. *11 USC §522(b), (d), (f)-(j); see State and Local Exemption Laws; "Stage Five—Exemptions Claimed by the Debtor," Chapter II; see Owen v Owen, 500 US 305, 111 S Ct 1833, 114 L Ed 2d 350 (1991).*

2. Statute of Limitations, Rights of Relation Back, and Reclamation Restrictions

The same statute of limitations and creditor's rights, including relation back of liens and reclamation of goods, that are imposed on the trustee's exercise of his super-avoiding powers apply to the debtor's super-avoiding powers. *See Chapter XII; 11 USC §§522(f)-(i), 546, 550;* and

3. Costs and Expenses of Recovering Property Restrictions

The debtor does not have to pay the usual $120 fee for filing an adversary complaint. However, the debtor must pay the following costs and expenses from any recovered, exempted property:

a. The debtor's aliquot share of costs and expenses incurred by the trustee in avoiding and recovering exemptible property.

The debtor's share of required payments is the ratio of the exemptible value to the total value of the recovered property. Thus, if the debtor exempts $1,000 of recovered property valued at $3,000, the debtor must pay the trustee one-third of the total costs and expenses incurred by the trustee in exercising his super-avoiding powers. If the debtor exempts the full value of such property, he must pay all administrative costs and expenses incurred by the trustee in exercising super-avoiding powers to recover exemptible property that will be of value only to the debtor, not to the estate or unsecured creditors. The trustee receives the debtor's aliquot share of administrative costs and expenses for the benefit of the estate and ultimate distribution to unsecured creditors. *11 USC §§323, 503, 507(a)(1), 522(k)(1);* and

b. All costs and expenses incurred by the debtor whether exercising his own super-avoiding powers or those of the trustee. *See*

"Procedures to Exercise the Debtor's Super-Avoiding Powers," discussed above. 11 USC §522(b), (d), (f)-(i), (k)(1)-(2).

Research Guide

Anderson, *Chapter 11: Reorganizations* ch 9 (Shepard's/McGraw-Hill 1983)

Anderson & Morris, *Chapter 12: Farm Reorganizations* ch 5 (Shepard's/McGraw-Hill 1987)

Drake, *Bankruptcy Practice for the General Practitioner* chs 5, 6 (Shepard's/McGraw-Hill 2d 1990)

Drake & Morris, *Chapter 13: Practice and Procedure* ch 6 (Shepard's/McGraw-Hill 1983)

Jaroslavsky, *Practical Bankruptcy Procedure* ch 14 (Shepard's/McGraw-Hill 1993) ch 14

Murphy, *Creditor's Rights in Bankruptcy* ch 14 (Shepard's/McGraw-Hill 2d 1988)

Pollard & Burton, *Guide to Effective Bankruptcy Litigation* ch 12 (Shepard's/McGraw-Hill 1988)

XIV. Creditor's Rights and Powers Under Bankruptcy Law

XIV. Creditor's Rights and Powers Under Bankruptcy Law
- A. File Proof of Claim
  - *11 USC §§501-502, 924-925, 1111(a)*
  - *FRBP 3001-3008*
  1. What Is a Proof of Claim
  2. Who May Sign the Proof of Claim
  3. Who May File a Proof of Claim
  4. Where to File
  5. When to File
     - a. Chapter 7, 12, and 13 Cases
     - b. Chapter 9 and 11 Cases
     - c. Notice of When to File a Proof of Claim
  6. Why File
  7. Legal Effect of Filing
  8. Contingent Claims
  9. Objection to Claims
     - a. Who May Object
     - b. How to Object
     - c. Grounds for Disallowance of Claim
     - d. Notice and Hearing
  10. Subordination of Claims
      - a. Generally
      - b. Subordinated Claims Under Bankruptcy Law
      - c. Equitable Subordination
  11. Reconsideration of Claims
  12. Allowance of Certain Post-Petition Claims
  13. Withdrawal of Claims

B. Motion for Relief from Automatic Stay
11 USC §§362, 1110, 1201, 1301
28 USC §1930(b), Judicial Conference Schedule of Fees (21)
FRBP 4001, 9013-9014
1. Generally
   a. Purpose for the Motion
   b. Grounds for Lifting or Modifying the Automatic Stay
   c. Adequate Protection Requirement
   d. Adequate Protection of Cash Collateral Requirement
   e. Procedures
   f. Notice and Hearing
   g. Ex Parte Relief
   h. Procedures for Settlement Agreement
   i. Creditor's Super First Priority Claim
2. Motion to Lift Codebtor Stay
3. Relief from Stay Against a Chapter 11 Air Carrier or Water Carrier Debtor

C. Compelled Abandonment of Property
11 USC §554
28 USC §1930(b), Judicial Conference Schedule of Fees (21)
FRBP 6007, 9013-9014
1. Generally
2. Motion to Compel Abandonment
3. Procedures
4. Abandonment to Debtor

D. Meeting of Creditors
11 USC §§341, 343
FRBP 2003
1. What It Is
2. When It Occurs
3. Where It Is Held
4. Notice of the Meeting
5. Who Attends
6. Who Presides
7. Final Meeting and Account

E. Rule 2004 Examination
FRBP 2004-2005, 9016, 9020
1. Who May Be Examined
2. Procedures
3. Scope of Examination
4. Where Held
5. Compelling Attendance at the Rule 2004 Examination

F. Valuation of Collateral
11 USC §506(a)

FRBP 3012, 9013-9014

1. Generally
2. When Valuation Occurs
3. Valuation Hearing

G. Right to Perfect a Security Interest or Reclaim Property Post-Petition
11 USC §§103(a), 362(b)(3), 546(b)-(c)
FRBP 4001, 9013-9014

H. Creditors' Committee(s)
11 USC §§103(e)-(f), 901, 1102-1103

I. Assumption or Rejection of Executory Contracts and Unexpired Leases
11 USC §§103(a), (e), 365, 502(g), 901
FRBP 6006, 9013-9014

1. Generally
2. Restrictions on Trustee's Powers—What Contracts and Leases Cannot Be Assumed or Assigned
3. When the Trustee or Debtor Must Assume or Reject
   a. Residential Real Estate and Personal Property
   b. Nonresidential (Commercial) Real Property
   c. Nonresidential Real Property Involving Airport Leases
   d. FDIC/RTC and Other Government Commitments of Chapter 11 Debtor
4. Requirements to Assume or Assign
5. Procedures to Assume, Assign, or Reject an Executory Contract or Unexpired Lease
6. Rights of the Nonbankruptcy Party After Rejection
   a. Generally
   b. Rejection of an Unexpired Lease of Land by Debtor-Lessor
   c. Rejection of Executory Contract for Sale of Land or Timeshare Interest by Debtor-Seller
   d. Claims of Nonbankruptcy Lessor Under Rejected Lease
   e. Rights to Intellectual Property of Licensee Under Rejected License Agreement
7. Legal Effect of Assumption, Assignment, or Rejection

J. Assumption or Rejection of Collective Bargaining Agreements and Assumption or Modification of Retiree Benefits Under Chapter 11

1. Collective Bargaining Agreements
   11 USC §1113
   FRBP 6006, 9013-9014
   a. General Overview

b. Requirements to Modify or Reject a Collective Bargaining Agreement
   (1) Submit Written Proposal
   (2) Provide Relevant Information
   (3) Good-Faith Negotiations
   (4) If Negotiations Fail, File Application to Modify or Reject Collective Bargaining Agreement
   (5) Obtain Court Approval
c. Procedures After Proposal Submitted
   (1) File Application to Reject
   (2) Hearing
   (3) Notice of Hearing
   (4) Court's Decision
   (5) Interim Measures
      (a) Protective Orders
      (b) Interim Changes in Collective Bargaining Agreement
      (c) Procedures to Obtain Interim Measures
d. Rights of Rejected Employees
e. Chapter 11 Plan and Continuing Jurisdiction of the Court

2. Retiree Benefits
   11 USC §1114
   FRBP 6006, 9013-9014
   a. General Overview
   b. What Are Retiree Benefits
   c. Who Is Not Protected
   d. Negotiating Parties
      (1) Benefits Covered by Collective Bargaining Agreement
      (2) Benefits Not Covered by Collective Bargaining Agreement
      (3) Procedures to Appoint a Committee of Retired Employees
   e. Requirements to Modify a Retiree Benefits Plan
   f. Procedures After Proposal Submitted
   g. Claims for Retiree Benefit Payments
      (1) Claims for Retiree Benefits for Cases Pending On June 16, 1988
      (2) Claims for Retiree Benefits for Cases Filed On or After June 16, 1988
   h. Chapter 11 Plan and Continuing Jurisdiction of the Court
   i. Pension Plans

K. Creditors' Surprise Weapons—The Debtor's Petition, Schedules of Assets and Liabilities, Statement of Financial Affairs, and Other Documents
   1. Generally
      11 USC §§301-302, 521
      FRBP 1002, 1005, 1007-1009
   2. Verified Documents
   3. Significance of Petition—Official Bankruptcy Forms 1, 2
   4. Significance of Statement of Financial Affairs—Official Bankruptcy Form 7
   5. Significance of Schedules of Assets—Official Bankruptcy Form 6

L. Bankruptcy Crimes and Penalties
   1. Fraudulent Conduct
      18 USC §§151-152, 1961(D) et seq
   2. Fraudulent Fee Arrangements
      18 USC §§155, 1961(D) et seq.
   3. Breach of Fiduciary Duty by Trustee, Examiner, or Officer of the Court
      18 USC §§153-154, 1961(D) et seq
   4. Bankruptcy Petition Preparer's Knowing Disregard of Bankruptcy Law or Rule
      18 USC §156(a)
   5. Bankruptcy Fraud (Bankruptcy Schemes to Defraud)
      18 USC §157
   6. Procedures
      18 USC §§1961(D) et seq, 3057
   7. Statute of Limitations
      18 USC §§1961(D) et seq, 3284

Research Guide

XIV. Creditors' Rights and Powers Under Bankruptcy Law

Creditors, though disadvantaged to some degree under any bankruptcy case, are not helpless. A creditor has certain rights and powers which he may exercise under bankruptcy law and which he must exercise in certain instances or forfeit his right to any payment from the bankruptcy estate. Basically, a creditor has 12 possible rights in a bankruptcy case. These include the right to: (A) file a proof of claim; (B) file a motion for relief from the automatic stay; (C) file a motion to compel abandonment of property by the trustee or debtor-in-possession (DIP); (D) attend the meeting of creditors; (E) file a motion for Rule 2004 examination of the debtor or another entity; (F) valuation of collateral, if the claim is secured by property of the debtor or estate; (G) perfect a security interest or reclaim goods post-petition in certain instances; (H) strong representation by the unsecured creditors' committee in Chapter 9 and 11 cases; (I) file a motion to compel assumption or rejection of executory contracts; (J) File a motion to compel assumption or rejection of collective bargaining agreements and assumption or modification of retiree benefits; (K) use surprise weapons—the debtor's petition, schedules, and statements; and (L) seek enforcement of laws and penalties for bankruptcy crimes.

A. File Proof of Claim

1. What Is a Proof of Claim

A proof of claim is a written statement setting forth the creditor's claim. The proof of claim must substantially conform to Official Bankruptcy Form No. 10. A proof of claim properly and timely filed is prima facie evidence of the validity and amount of the creditor's claim(s). A trustee, debtor, or other party-in-interest (creditor, equity security holder) must thereafter file an objection and prove ground(s) for disallowance of the creditor's claim under bankruptcy law or it will be allowed by the court. *11 USC §§501, 502(a); FRBP 3001(a), (f), 3002-3007; Official Bankr Form 10.*

2. Who May Sign the Proof of Claim

Only the creditor or equity security holder or his authorized agent under a power of attorney may sign the creditor's proof of claim. *FRBP 3001(b), 3002(a); Official Bankr Forms 10, 11A, 11B.*

3. Who May File a Proof of Claim

a. Creditor or Equity Security Holder

The creditor or equity security holder who holds a claim or interest against the debtor may file a timely proof of claim. The proof of claim must include (by attachment or separate filing) an original or copy of all writing(s) upon which the creditor's claim or equity security holder's interest is based. If such writing(s) have been lost or destroyed, the proof of claim must also include a detailed written statement from the claimant stating the facts surrounding the loss or destruction. If the creditor claims a security interest, the proof of claim must also include, by attachment or separate filing, evidence that the lien has been perfected under applicable nonbankruptcy law. If the creditor is asserting a priority claim, the proof of claim must state sufficient facts, and the original or copies of all documents that show a priority claim exists. *See "Priority Claims," Chapter II; 11 USC §§501, 502(a), 503(a)-(b), 507(a); FRBP 3001(b)-(d), 3002(a).*

b. Debtor or Trustee

If a creditor or equity security holder does not file a proof of claim by the first date set for the meeting of creditors, the debtor or trustee may file a proof of claim in the creditor's name before the 30th day after such creditor's time to file expires under bankruptcy law (*see "When to File," discussed below*). The clerk must immediately mail notice of the filing to the creditor, debtor, and any trustee. If the creditor thereafter files a timely proof of claim, the creditor's claim controls. *11 USC §501(c); FRBP 3004.*

c. Guarantor, Surety, Indorser, or Codebtor

If a creditor does not file a timely proof of claim, an entity that is or may become liable to such creditor, or who has provided collateral to secure the creditor's claim against the debtor, may file a proof of claim in the creditor's name, if known, or in such entity's name if the creditor is unknown, before the 30th day after the creditor's time to file expires under bankruptcy law (*see "When to File," discussed below*). If the creditor thereafter files a proof of claim allowed by the court, such creditor's claim will control. *11 USC §501(b); FRBP 3005(a).*

d. Involuntary Gap Creditor

A creditor whose claim arose in the ordinary course of the debtor's business or financial affairs, after the involuntary petition was filed but before the earlier date of the order for relief or appointment of a trustee, may file a proof of claim by the date set by the court or local bankruptcy rules. Such creditor's claim is treated as if it arose pre-petition and may be allowed as a second priority claim. *See "When to File," discussed below; 11 USC §§501(d), 502(f), 507(a)(2); FRBP 3002-3003; "Priority Claims," Chapter II.*

e. Creditor with Rejected Executory Contract

A creditor whose claim arose because the trustee or debtor rejected an executory contract or unexpired lease post-petition may file a proof of claim by the date set by the court or local bankruptcy rules. This creditor's claim is also treated as if it arose pre-petition if the contract or lease was not previously assumed in the bankruptcy case. If the contract or lease was assumed and thereafter rejected, the creditor may assert a first priority claim for administrative expenses. *See NLRB v Bildisco & Bildisco, 465 US 513 (1984). 11 USC §§365(g), 501(d), 502(g); FRBP 3002(c)(4), 3003(c)(3); see "Assumption or Rejection of Executory Contracts and Unexpired Leases" discussed below; Local Bankruptcy Rules.*

f. Creditor from Whom Property Is Recovered Under an Avoidable Transfer

A transferee from whom property or its value is recoverable under one of the trustee's or debtor's super-avoiding powers may file a proof of claim against the estate to the extent of any value given to the debtor or improvements made to the property if the transferee turns over the property or its value to the trustee or debtor. In the case of property recovered under a fraudulent transfer action, the good-faith transferee who gave less than reasonably equivalent value may file a proof of claim asserting a lien on the recovered property to the extent of any value given to the debtor in the exchange. A good-faith purchaser of real property under an avoidable post-petition transfer action will have a lien on the recovered property to the extent of any present value given in the exchange, unless the purchaser had knowledge of the bankruptcy petition, or the trustee or debtor filed a copy or notice of the petition in the deed records or real estate records of each county where the land is located before such purchaser perfected his interests in the property under applicable nonbankruptcy law. Finally, any good-faith transferee of property recovered under an avoidable transfer action may assert a lien on the recovered property to secure the lesser of: (1) the cost of improvements made to the property after the transfer (physical additions, changes, tax payments, satisfaction of an equal or senior lien) after deducting any profits received; and (2) any appreciation in value to the property as a result of such improvements. Even if the transferee of recovered property is not able to establish a lien on the recovered property, he will at least have an unsecured claim against the estate for any value given in good faith to the debtor in the avoidable transfer. The transferee must file a timely proof of claim by the date set by the court or local bankruptcy rules and attach the original or copies of all relevant documents. Such transferee's claim is then treated as if it arose pre-petition. *11 USC §§501(d), 502(d), (h), 548(c), 549(c), 550(d); FRBP 3001(a)-(c), 3002-3003; see Chapters XII and XIII; "When to File," discussed below.*

g. Post-Petition Creditor with a Tax or Consumer Debt Claim Under Chapter 13

A creditor whose claim arises post-petition in a Chapter 13 case for taxes or a consumer debt for necessary property or services to enable the debtor to perform under the plan may file a timely proof of claim. The claim will be treated as if it arose pre-petition. The proof of claim must be filed by the date for filing other pre-petition claims or by any later date set by the court or local bankruptcy rules. All documents supporting the claim should be attached or separately filed. However, the claim for a necessary consumer debt will be disallowed by the court if the creditor knew, or should have known, that prior approval of the standing trustee was practical but was not obtained by either the debtor or creditor. *See "When to File," and "Allowance of Certain Post-Petition Claims," discussed below; "Priority Claims," Chapter II; 11 USC §§501-502, 1305(a)(2), (b)-(c); FRBP 3001-3007.*

h. Post-Petition Creditor Under Chapter 11 Case

A creditor with a post-petition claim that arises before confirmation of a Chapter 11 plan must file a proof of claim by the date set by the court or local bankruptcy rules or by any court-authorized extension of such date. Such claim may be allowed as a first priority administrative claim. The creditor should assert all facts and attach the original or copies of all documents with the proof of claim showing an administrative claim. *11 USC §§503(b), 507(a)(1), 1141(d)(1)(A); FRBP 3001(b)-(c), 3002(a), 3003(c); see "Priority Claims," Chapter II; "Allowance of Certain Post-Petition Claims," discussed below.*

4. Where to File

A proof of claim must be filed with the bankruptcy clerk where the debtor's bankruptcy case is pending. *FRBP 3002(b), 5005(a).*

5. When to File

a. Chapter 7, 12, and 13 Cases

(1) Creditor

A proof of claim must be filed by a creditor who is not a governmental unit in a Chapter 7, 12, or 13 case before the 90th day after the first date set for the meeting of creditors. The claim of a governmental unit must be filed before the 180th day after a voluntary petition is filed or an order for relief is entered in an involuntary case, unless the Federal Rules of Bankruptcy Procedure provide a later date. A governmental unit includes the United States, a state, commonwealth, district, territory, municipality, or any department, agency, or instrumentality of such entities. *11 USC §§101(27), 102(6), 502(b)(9); FRBP 3002(c), 9006(b)(3).*

(2) Another Entity

A debtor, trustee, guarantor, surety, or codebtor who wishes to file a proof of claim on behalf of the creditor in a Chapter 7, 12, or 13 case must do so before the 30th day after expiration of the time for the creditor to file (before the 119th day after the first date set for the meeting of creditors), unless the court extends the time. *FRBP 3002(c), 3004, 3005(a), 9006(b).*

b. Chapter 9 and 11 Cases

(1) Creditor

A proof of claim is generally deemed filed by a creditor or equity security holder if the claim or interest is included in the Chapter 9 debtor's list of creditors or Chapter 11 debtor's schedules of liabilities or list of equity security holders. However, the creditor or equity security holder is required to file a proof of claim in a Chapter 9 or 11 case if any one of four situations exists: (a) the debtor listed the claim as disputed, contingent, or unliquidated; (b) the debtor failed to list the claim and the creditor or equity security holder had notice or actual knowledge of the debtor's case in time to file a proof of claim; (c) the creditor or equity security holder disputes the amount listed by the debtor; or (d) the creditor or equity security holder wishes to file a proof of claim for any other reason, including the possible conversion of the Chapter 11 debtor's case to Chapter 7. (However, the court will set new time periods to file proofs of claims in a converted case). *11 USC §§103(a), (e)-(f), 501(a), 502(a), 521(1), 523(a)(3), 901, 924-925, 944(c), 1111(a); FRBP 1007(a)-(b), (e), 2002(a)(5), (8), (f)(2)-(3), 3001, 3002(a), 3003(c); see "Notice of When to File a Proof of Claim," discussed below; "Exceptions to Discharge," Chapter III.*

A required proof of claim must be filed in a Chapter 9 or 11 case by the date fixed by the court in the notice of approval of disclosure statement or other notice mailed by the debtor, clerk, or other court-appointed person or by the date fixed by local bankruptcy rules. However, a governmental unit (the United States, state, territory, district, commonwealth, municipality, or any agency or instrumentality of such entities) must have at least 179 days to file a proof of claim after a voluntary petition is filed or entry of an order for relief in an involuntary case. *11 USC §§101(27), 102(6), 502(b)(9); FRBP 3003(a), (c)(3), 3017(a), (d); see Local Bankruptcy Rules.*

(2) Another Entity

A debtor, trustee, guarantor, surety, or codebtor who wishes to file a proof of claim on behalf of the creditor in a Chapter 9 or 11 case must do so before the 30th day after expiration of the date set by the court for the creditor to file, unless the court extends the time. *FRBP 3002(c), 3003(c)(3), 3004, 3005(a), 9006(b).*

c. Notice of When to File a Proof of Claim

(1) Chapters 7, 12, and 13

(a) Generally

The clerk or other court-authorized person must give notice of the last date to file a proof of claim under chapter 7, 12, or 13. The notice will be mailed to the debtor, any trustee, all committee(s), creditors, indenture trustees, equity security holders, and any other entity required by court order or local bankruptcy rules. *FRBP 2002(f)(3), (i), 3002; see Local Bankruptcy Rules.*

(b) Rejected Executory Contracts

The court or local bankruptcy rules will set a date for filing proofs of claims arising from the post-petition rejection of executory contracts or unexpired leases by the trustee or debtor. Notice of such date must be mailed by the clerk or other court-appointed person to the debtor, trustee, all creditors, committee(s), indenture trustees, equity security holders, and any other entity required by court order or local bankruptcy rules. *FRBP 2002(f)(3), (i), 3002(c)(4); see Local Bankruptcy Rules; "Assumption or Rejection of Executory Contracts and Unexpired Leases" discussed below.*

(c) Judgment Avoiding Security Interest

If the judgment of any court avoids a security interest, the creditor may file an unsecured proof of claim before the 30th day after the judgment becomes final. A judgment becomes final if no timely appeal is taken or if a final appeal has been heard and determined. *FRBP 3002(c)(3), advisory committee's note, citing In re Tapp, 61 F Supp 594 (WD Ky 1945).*

(2) Chapters 9 and 11

(a) Generally

The schedules of liabilities and list of equity security holders filed by the Chapter 11 debtor and list of creditors filed by the Chapter 9 debtor constitute prima facie evidence of the validity and amount of the creditor's claim or equity security holder's interest. A proof of claim or interest is deemed filed for such entities with three exceptions, in which case a proof of claim must be timely filed.

(i) The creditor's claim or equity security holder's interest is listed by the debtor as disputed, contingent, or unliquidated.

(ii) The creditor or equity security holder disputes the amount listed by the debtor. In such situation, the creditor or equity security holder must file a proof of claim timely and properly or he will be bound by the amount listed by the debtor.

(iii) The claim of the creditor or equity security holder is not included in the debtor's list or schedules, and the creditor or equity security holder had notice or actual knowledge of the debtor's case in time to file a proof of claim.

If any of the above exceptions apply, the creditor or equity security holder must file a proof of claim timely and properly by the date or extension of time fixed by the court, or he will not be allowed to vote or share in distribution under the plan. *11 USC §§103(a), (e)-(f), 501, 502(a), 521(1), 901, 924-925, 1111(a), 1126(a); FRBP 1007(a)(1), (3), (b)-(c), (e), 3003(a)-(b), 3017, 3021, 9006(b).*

(b) If Filing a Claim Required

If filing a proof of claim is required in a Chapter 9 or 11 case, the debtor, clerk, or other court-authorized person must give at least 20 days' notice of the date fixed by the court or local bankruptcy rules to file proofs of claims under Chapter 9 or 11. This notice is usually included in the notice of approval of the disclosure statement with date of the confirmation hearing. The notice must be mailed to the debtor, any trustee, all committee(s), creditors, equity security holders, indenture trustees, to the SEC in Washington, D.C., and District Director of the IRS where the Chapter 11 case is pending, and to any other entity required by court order or local bankruptcy rules. *FRBP 2002(a)(8), (i)-(j), 3003(c), 3017(d); Official Bankr Form 13; see Local Bankruptcy Rules.*

(3) Converted Case

The clerk of the court must mail notice of the conversion of a case to the debtor, any trustee, the U.S. trustee, all committee(s), creditors, indenture trustees, equity security holders and, in a Chapter 11 case, to the SEC in Washington, D.C. and District Director of the IRS where the case is pending. The notice will include new date(s) to file proofs of claims in the converted case. However, a proof of claim filed in a superseded Chapter 11, 12, or 13 case which is converted to Chapter 7 is deemed filed in the converted Chapter 7 case. *FRBP 1019(3), 2002(f)(2), (3), 3002(a); see "Procedure Eight—Conversion," Chapter IV; "Procedure Five—Conversion from Chapter 13," Chapter V.*

6. Why File

a. Chapter 7, 12, or 13

A creditor or equity security holder who wants to receive any payment of his pre-petition claim from the trustee or under a plan must file a timely proof of claim or interest in a Chapter 7, 12, or 13 case. *11 USC §§501, 502(a), 726, 1225(a)(4)-(5), 1325(a)(4)-(5); FRBP 3002(c), 3009; see "When to File," discussed above.*

b. Chapters 9 and 11

A creditor or equity security holder who is required to file a proof of claim or interest must file the claim timely or forfeit his right to vote and receive payments under a plan. *11 USC §§501, 502(a), 901, 924-925, 1111(a), 1126(a); FRBP 1007(a)(1), (3), (b)-(c), (e), 2002(a)(8), 3003(a)-(b), 3021.*

7. Legal Effect of Filing

A proof of claim properly and timely filed is deemed allowed unless a party-in-interest files an objection. A timely filed proof of claim supersedes any amount listed by the debtor under his schedules or list of creditors and is prima facie evidence of the validity and amount of the creditor's claim. *11 USC §§502(a), 521(1), 924-925, 1111(a); FRBP 3001(f), 3003(c)(4); see "Objection to Claims," discussed below.*

8. Contingent Claims

If a creditor's claim is contingent or unliquidated, such claim may be estimated on the proof of claim if waiting until the claim was liquidated would unduly delay administration of the bankruptcy case and distribution to creditors. Similarly, a right to payment or specific performance based on an equitable remedy under applicable nonbankruptcy law may be estimated on the proof of claim for purposes of distribution and administration of the case. *11 USC §502(c); HR Rep No 595, 95th Cong, 1st Sess 354 (1977); S Rep No 989, 95th Cong, 2d Sess 65 (1978); FRBP 3001(f).*

9. Objection to Claims

a. Who May Object

Any party-in-interest, including the debtor, any trustee, creditor, or creditor of a general partner in a partnership debtor's Chapter 7 case may file an objection to a proof of claim. *11 USC §502(a)-(b); FRBP 3007.*

b. How to Object

A party-in-interest who objects to allowance of a proof of claim or interest must file a written objection with the court. Just an objection to allowance of a claim or interest does not commence an adversary proceeding. No filing fee is required. The objecting party must mail or personally deliver a copy of the objection with at least 30 days prior notice of the hearing date to the claimant (creditor or equity security holder whose proof of claim is opposed), debtor, any trustee, all committee(s), and any other entity as required by court order or local bankruptcy rules. However, an objection which is joined with a demand for recovery of money or property or to avoid a lien generally does commence an adversary proceeding. The objection is then an adversary complaint which requires a $120 filing fee and service of the objection with a summons by first-class mail or in any other manner allowed for service of process in federal district court. If a creditor files the complaint (objection), a $120 filing fee is required upon filing. If the trustee or Chapter 11 or 12 DIP files the complaint, the $120 filing fee is only required from any estate which may exist. If the U.S. trustee files the complaint other than as a trustee in a case or the debtor files the complaint, no filing fee is required. *28 USC §1930(b), Judicial Conference Schedule of Fees (6); 11 USC §502(a)-(b); FRBP 3007, 7001 et seq, 9014; Procedural Bankr Forms B 250A, B, C.*

c. Grounds for Disallowance of Claim

Section 502(b) of the Bankruptcy Code includes eleven grounds for the court to disallow a claim or interest against the estate. The party objecting to a proof of claim or interest has the burden of proving one or more of the following grounds:

(1) The claim is unenforceable against the debtor and his property under any agreement or applicable law.

However, contingent, unliquidated, and unmatured claims may be estimated and allowed, except for unmatured interest payments. *11 USC §502(b)(1), (c).*

(2) The claim is for unmatured interest.

A claim for post-petition interest not yet due and payable is unmatured and disallowed. Similarly, any portion of prepaid interest that represents an original discounting of a claim is unmatured if the interest has not been earned by the date the petition is filed. Determining whether interest is matured or unmatured is not based on any ipso facto or bankruptcy clause contained in a pre-petition agreement. Under bankruptcy law, interest generally stops accruing on the date the petition is filed, unless the creditor's claim is secured by property whose value is greater than the allowed amount of such claim. For most claims, though, the bankruptcy petition operates as an acceleration of the principal amount owed by the debtor. *11 USC §§502(b)(2), 506(b); HR Rep No 595, 95th Cong, 1st Sess 352-54 (1977); S Rep No 989, 95th Cong, 2d Sess 62-65 (1978).*

(3) The claim is a tax claim assessed against property of the estate and such claim is greater than the value of the estate's interest in the property. *11 USC §502(b)(3).*

(4) The claim is for the debtor's attorney's fees or an insider's fees which are more than the value of services provided by such entity to the debtor or estate. *11 USC §§329(b), 502(b)(4); FRBP 2016-2017, 3007, 9014.*

(5) The claim is for alimony, maintenance, or support payments owed to the debtor's spouse, ex-spouse, or child which have not matured on the date the petition is filed.

Such payments are nondischargeable under any individual debtor's bankruptcy case and must be paid by the debtor. Further, the automatic stay does not prohibit actions to collect such payments under applicable nonbankruptcy law from property that is not part of the estate (wages, salary, or earnings of an individual Chapter 7 or 11 debtor; exempt property if such property may be reached to enforce alimony, support, or maintenance payments under applicable nonbankruptcy law). *11 USC §§362(b)(2), 502(b)(5), 523(a)(5), 541(a)(6), 1141(d)(2), 1207(a), 1228(a)-(b), 1306(a), 1328(a)-(b).*

(6) The claim is for rental payments owed to a lessor under a terminated real estate lease which is greater than the amount allowed under the Bankruptcy Code.

The Code allows a lessor who suffers damages from termination of an unexpired lease to receive only:

(a) The greater amount, without acceleration, of:

(i) one year's remaining rent, or

(ii) 15 per cent of the next three years' remaining rent, beginning on the earlier date that the bankruptcy petition was filed or the leased property was repossessed or surrendered; plus

(b) The outstanding, unpaid rent owed to the lessor, without acceleration, on the earlier date that the petition was filed or the leased property was repossessed or surrendered. *11 USC §502(b)(6).*

Claims resulting from the post-petition rejection of an unexpired lease which was not previously assumed by the debtor or trustee are also allowed in amounts outlined above, and treated as if such claims arose pre-petition. *11 USC §§365(g), 502(g), 901, 1123(b)(2), 1222(b)(6), 1322(b)(7); see "Assumption or Rejection of Executory Contracts and Unexpired Leases," discussed below.*

(7) The claim is for an employee's damages (lost wages or commissions) under a terminated executory employment contract and such claim is greater than the amount allowed under the Bankruptcy Code.

The Code allows an employee who suffers damages from a terminated employment contract to receive only:

(a) The contractual amount of the employment compensation, without acceleration, for one year after the earlier date that the bankruptcy petition was filed or the employee's services were terminated voluntarily or involuntarily; plus

(b) The amount of any outstanding, unpaid compensation owed to the employee, without acceleration, on the earlier date that the petition was filed or the employee's services were terminated voluntarily or involuntarily. *11 USC §502(b)(7).*

Claims resulting from the post-petition rejection of an executory employment contract which was not previously assumed in the bankruptcy case are also allowed in amounts outlined above and treated like pre-petition claims. *11 USC §§365(g), 502(g), 901, 1123(b)(2),*

1222(b)(6), 1322(b)(7); see "Assumption or Rejection of Executory Contracts and Unexpired Leases," "Collective Bargaining Agreements," and "Retiree Benefits," discussed below.

(8) The claim is for an employment tax resulting from a reduction in the amount of an applicable tax credit available to the debtor because of late payment of an employment tax owed on wages, salaries, or commissions earned from the debtor.

These claims generally relate to a federal tax credit for state unemployment insurance taxes which is disallowed if the state tax is paid late. Bankruptcy law disallows the federal claim for the tax just as if the tax credit had been allowed in full on the federal tax return. *11 USC §502(b)(8); HR Rep No 595, 95th Cong, 1st Sess 352-54 (1977); S Rep No 989, 95th Cong, 2d Sess 62-65 (1978); see The Federal Unemployment Tax Act (FUTA), 26 USC §3302.*

(9) The claim is for damages, costs, or expenditures from an entity that failed to turn over property (or its value) recoverable by the trustee or debtor exercising his super-avoiding powers or from an entity that failed to turn over to the trustee property of the estate or debtor that was in such entity's possession or control on the date the petition was filed. *11 USC §§502(d), 542-550; see Chapters XII and XIII; "Stage Four—Turn Over Property to the Estate," Chapter II.*

(10) The claim is for reimbursement or contribution from an entity who is a codebtor, surety, or guarantor or who secured a claim against the debtor to the extent that:

(a) The claim of the underlying creditor is disallowed by the court; or

(b) The entity's claim for reimbursement or contribution is *contingent* at the time of the court's determination (the codebtor has not yet paid the claim or the lien given by such entity to secure a claim against the debtor has not been enforced by foreclosure or otherwise). However, a claim for reimbursement or contribution that becomes fixed post-petition may be allowed. Such claim is treated like a pre-petition claim. *11 USC §502(e)(2);* or

(c) Such entity has paid the claim of the debtor and has also filed a proof of claim asserting the rights of the creditor through subrogation. Such entity's proof of claim asserting subrogated rights will be allowed unless otherwise disallowed on one of the grounds listed above, avoided under the trustee's or debtor's super-avoiding powers, or subordinated by the court. *See Chapters XII and XIII; "Sub-*

ordination of Claims," discussed below; 11 USC §§502(b), (e)(1), 509(a), 510.

(11) The Proof of Claim Was Not Timely Filed Under the Bankruptcy Code or Federal Rules of Bankruptcy Procedure

The Bankruptcy Code permits only a Chapter 7 trustee to distribute the bankruptcy estate in a Chapter 7 case to creditors who filed a proof of claim tardily (generally 90 days or more after the first date set for the Chapter 7 meeting of creditors for a nongovernmental entity) if (a) the creditor filed a proof of claim before the trustee began to distribute the estate, or (b) the creditor did not have notice or actual knowledge of the case in time to file a proof of claim timely but filed the proof of claim in time to permit the trustee to pay the claim. *11 USC §§103(a), 502(b)(9), 726(a)(1-3); FRBP 3002(c).*

A governmental unit has until the later of the end of 179 days after the voluntary petition is filed or the order for relief is entered in an involuntary case, or the date fixed by the court under the Federal Rules of Bankruptcy Procedure to file a timely proof of claim. The term governmental unit includes the United States, a state, territory, district, commonwealth, municipality, or any agency or instrumentality of such entities. *11 USC §§101(27), 102(6), 103(a), 502(b)(9); FRBP 3001-3003.*

d. Notice and Hearing

The court must hold a hearing on an objection to allowance of a claim. The party filing the objection must mail or personally deliver a notice of the hearing date with copy of the objection to the claimant (creditor or equity security holder), debtor, any trustee, committee(s), and any other entity required by court order or local bankruptcy rules. The notice and objection must be served at least 30 days before the hearing date. *See "How to Object," discussed above; 11 USC §502(a)-(b); FRBP 3007, 9014.*

10. Subordination of Claims

a. Generally

A subordination agreement enforceable under applicable nonbankruptcy law is also enforceable under a debtor's bankruptcy case. However, under a Chapter 9 or 11 plan, a class of creditors that is the beneficiary (senior creditor(s) with a superior legal right) under the subordination agreement may vote to accept a plan that waives their rights under the agreement. Thus, a senior class of creditors may voluntarily elect to give up their rights to a junior class (the subordinated creditors under the agreement) in the interests of confirmation of a plan and rehabilitation of the debtor. A class of creditors accepts a plan if at least two-thirds in dollar amount and more than 50 per cent of the number of the good-faith voting members of the class vote to accept the plan. *See "Procedure Seven—Confirmation of a Plan of Reorganization," Chapter IV; 11 USC §§103(a), (e), 510(a), 901, 943(b)(1), 1123(b)(1), (5), 1129, 1141(a); HR Rep No 595, 95th Cong, 1st Sess 359 (1977); S Rep No 989, 95th Cong, 2d Sess 74 (1978); FRBP 3017(d), 3018, 3020; Official Bankr Forms 14, 15.*

A Chapter 12 or 13 plan may also establish a class of beneficiaries whose superior legal rights under an enforceable subordination agreement are waived in favor of the subordinated creditors. However, the senior creditor-beneficiaries must agree to such terms. There is no formal voting under Chapters 12 and 13. But any creditor may file an objection to confirmation of the plan which will generally be heard at the confirmation hearing. The court cannot confirm a Chapter 12 or 13 plan over the objection of a bona fide beneficiary of an enforceable subordination agreement who does not voluntarily agree to waive his rights in favor of a subordinated creditor, unless principles of equitable subordination apply. Under such principles, if the creditor-beneficiary of an otherwise enforceable subordination agreement has acted unfairly or unjustly, the court may subordinate his rights as the court deems just and equitable. *See "Equitable Subordination," discussed below; 11 USC §§103(a), 105(a), 510(a), 1222(b)(1)-(2), (4), (11), 1224-1225, 1227, 1322(b)(1)-(2), (4), (10), 1324-1325, 1327; FRBP 3015, 3020; "Procedure Four—Confirmation of Chapter 13 Plan," Chapter V.*

b. Subordinated Claims Under Bankruptcy Law

(1) Claims of Stockholders

The claims of stockholders and equity security holders for damages, rescission, or reimbursement relating to the purchase or sale of the stock or ownership share of the debtor or its affiliate are subordinated under bankruptcy law to the claims of general unsecured creditors. Thus, unsecured creditors must receive distribution of the estate in full satisfaction of their allowed claims before stockholders may retain any ownership or be paid by a trustee or under a plan. *11 USC §§103(a), (e), 510(b); HR Rep No 595, 95th Cong, 1st Sess 359 (1977); S Rep No 989, 95th Cong, 2d Sess 74 (1978).*

(2) Claims of Guarantors, Sureties, and Codebtors

Claims of a guarantor, surety, or codebtor are subordinated to the claims of the insured creditor until such creditor is fully paid under the debtor's bankruptcy case or under applicable nonbankruptcy law. The subordinated claim may be entitled to subrogation, contribution, or reimbursement through the debtor's estate after the insured creditor is paid. *11 USC*

§§502(e)(1)-(2), 509(a)-(c); 124 Cong Rec H11,095 (daily ed Sept 28, 1978); 124 Cong Rec S 17,411-12 (Oct 6, 1978).

c. Equitable Subordination

(1) Grounds for Equitable Subordination

The court may partially or totally subordinate one allowed claim to another allowed claim, or one allowed equity security interest to another allowed equity security interest, under principles of equitable subordination. Such principles are based on existing case law developed by the courts. Generally, a claim is subordinated only if: (a) the claimholder is guilty of *inequitable* (unfair or unjust) conduct; (b) the claim is for a penalty; (c) the claim is for damages arising from the purchase or sale of stock of the debtor or its affiliate; or (d) the claim is asserted by a guarantor, surety, or codebtor and the insured creditor has not yet been fully paid. *11 USC §§509(c), 510(c), 724, 726(a)(4); 124 Cong Rec H11,095 (daily ed Sept 28, 1978); 124 Cong Rec S 17,412 (Oct 6, 1978).*

(2) Procedures

A party-in-interest (creditor, trustee, or debtor) may file a request to subordinate an allowed claim or interest other than through a Chapter 9, 11, 12, or 13 plan. Such request is an adversary complaint that commences an adversary proceeding. A $120 filing fee is required if a creditor files the request. If a trustee or Chapter 11 or 12 DIP files the request, the filing fee is only payable from any estate that may exist. If a Chapter 9 or 13 debtor files the request, no filing fee is required. A copy of the request (complaint) must be served with a summons on the claimant whose claim or interest is to be subordinated by first-class mail or any other manner allowed for service of process in federal district court. A copy of the request should also be mailed to the debtor (if another entity filed the request), any trustee, all committee(s), and to any other party-in-interest required by court order or local bankruptcy rules. *11 USC §1930(b), Judicial Conference Schedule of Fees (6); FRBP 7001(8), 7004 et seq.*

Subordination of an allowed claim or interest under a Chapter 9, 11, 12, or 13 plan does not commence an adversary proceeding and no filing fee is required. Notice of the plan's terms of subordination and an opportunity for filing objections and a hearing at the confirmation of the plan are afforded to the party whose claim or interest is sought to be subordinated under a Chapter 9, 11, 12, or 13 plan. *See "Procedure Seven—Confirmation of a Plan of Reorganization," Chapter IV; "Procedure Four—Confirmation of Chapter 13 Plan," Chapter V; 11 USC §§103(a), (e), 510, 901, 943(b)(1), 1123(b)(1), (5), 1128-*

1129, 1222(b)(1)-(2), (4), (11), 1224-1225, 1322(b)(1)-(2), (4), (10), 1324-1325; FRBP 2002(a)(9), (b), 3015, 3020, 7001(8), advisory committee's note.

11. Reconsideration of Claims

a. Which Claims

Any claim that has been allowed or disallowed may be reconsidered by the court for cause. *11 USC §502(j); FRBP 3008.*

b. Procedures

Any party-in-interest (debtor, trustee, or creditor) may file a motion for reconsideration of claim, stating the grounds for the court's reconsideration. The motion does not commence an adversary proceeding and no filing fee is required. A copy of the motion must be served on the claimant, debtor, trustee, all committee(s), the SEC in Washington, D.C., and District Director of the IRS where the case is pending in a Chapter 11 case, and any other entity required by court order or local bankruptcy rules. Service may be obtained by first-class mail or any other manner allowed for service of a summons and complaint in federal district court. No response to the motion is required, unless the court or local bankruptcy rules direct otherwise. *FRBP 3008, 7004, 9014; see Local Bankruptcy Rules.*

A party-in-interest may file a motion for reconsideration of claim even after the debtor's case has been closed. The motion for reconsideration must be filed with a motion to reopen the case. The party filing the motion to reopen must pay the same filing fee required to file an original petition under the particular debtor's case. *11 USC §502(j); 28 USC §1930(a), Judicial Conference Schedule of Fees "Language to Clarify Reopened Cases"; FRBP 3008; advisory committee's note, 9013-9014.*

c. Notice and Hearing

The court must hold a hearing on any motion for reconsideration of claim, unless local bankruptcy rules permit otherwise. Notice of the hearing date must be mailed by the clerk or other court-appointed person as directed by court order or local bankruptcy rules. *11 USC §102(1)(A)-(B); FRBP 3008, 9007; see Local Bankruptcy Rules.*

d. Court Decision

On reconsideration, the court may allow or disallow any previously determined claim. If the court disallows a previously allowed claim, the trustee or DIP may file an adversary complaint to recover any excess payment or property previously transferred to the creditor. The trustee or DIP must serve a copy of the complaint with a summons on the defendant-creditor by first-class mail or any other manner allowed for service of process in federal district court. A copy of the complaint should also be mailed or delivered to the debtor (or any trustee) and to any committee. A $120 filing fee will only be required from the estate, to the extent any estate remains or is realized from the recovery. *11 USC §502(j); 28 USC §1930(b); Judicial Conference Schedule of Fees (6); FRBP 3008, 7001(1) et seq; Procedural Bankr Forms B 250A, B, C.*

If the court allows a previously disallowed claim, disbursements already made to other creditors of the same class whose claims are not reconsidered will not be affected. However, such other creditors of the same class may not receive any additional payments or disbursements from the estate until the creditor whose claim has been reconsidered and allowed receives payments of the same proportionate value as payments already received by other creditors in his class. *11 USC §502(j); FRBP 3008.*

12. Allowance of Certain Post-Petition Claims

The following seven types of post-petition claims may be allowed by the court if a required proof of claim is timely filed. With the exception of first priority claims, such claims are treated as if they arose prepetition:

a. First priority claims for administrative expenses that represent the actual, necessary costs and expenses of preserving the estate and any other claim entitled to first priority under bankruptcy law. The creditor must file a motion for allowance of first priority administrative expenses and file a timely proof of claim that asserts sufficient facts and includes the original or copies of all relevant documents showing a first priority claim. *11 USC §§503(a)-(b), 507(a)(1); FRBP 3001(b)-(d), 3002(a); see "Priority Claims," Chapter II; "When to File," discussed above;*

b. Claims of gap creditors arising after an involuntary petition is filed but before the earlier date of the order for relief or appointment of a trustee. However, such claims must have arisen in the ordinary course of the debtor's business or financial affairs (utility, trade, or other regular payments). Such claims may be allowed as second priority claims if a proof of claim is properly and timely filed. *11 USC §§501(d), 502(f), 507(a)(2); FRBP 3001(b)-(d), 3002(a), 3003(c); see "Priority Claims," Chapter II; "When to File," discussed above;*

c. Claims arising from the debtor's or trustee's rejection of an executory contract or unexpired lease. *See NLRB v Bildisco & Bildisco, 465 US 513 (1984); 11 USC §§365(g), 501(d), 502(g); "Rights of the Non-bankruptcy Party After Rejection," discussed below; "When to File," discussed above;*

d. Claims arising from property recovered by the exercise of the super-avoiding powers of the trustee or debtor. However, the transferee must have turned over the recovered property or its value to the estate for such claim to be allowed by the court. *11*

USC §§501(d), 502(d), (h), 550, 551; see Chapters XII and XIII; "When to File," discussed above;

e. Claims arising in a Chapter 13 case for post-petition taxes or for necessary consumer goods or services provided to enable the debtor to perform under a plan if prior approval of the standing trustee either was obtained or could not practically have been obtained by the debtor or creditor. *11 USC §§503(b), 507(a)(1), 1305; see "Priority Claims," Chapter II; "When to File," discussed above;*

f. Claims arising in a Chapter 11 case post-petition but before confirmation of a Chapter 11 plan. Such claims may also be allowed as first priority claims. *11 USC §§503(b), 507(a)-(b), 1141(d)(1)(A); see "When to File," discussed above;* and

g. Seventh priority tax claims that are assessable after the petition is filed. *11 USC §§501(d), 502(i), 507(a)(7)(A)(iii); see "Priority Claims," Chapter II; "When to File," discussed above.*

13. Withdrawal of Claims

a. As a Matter of Right

A creditor may withdraw a proof of claim by filing a notice of withdrawal of claim with the bankruptcy clerk. No hearing is required unless one or more of the following four situations has occurred:

(1) An objection was previously filed to such creditor's proof of claim;

(2) An adversary complaint was filed against such creditor after he filed a proof of claim;

(3) Such creditor voted for or against a plan; or

(4) Such creditor has significantly participated in the case by voting for election of a trustee or receiving disbursements from the estate. *11 USC §§702, 726, 1129, 1141-1142, 1226, 1326; FRBP 3006, advisory Committee's note, 3022, 9014.*

The creditor should mail or personally deliver a copy of the notice of withdrawal of claim to the debtor, any trustee, committee(s), and any other entity required by the court order or local bankruptcy rules. *FRBP 3006, 5005(a), 9007, 9013-9014; see Local Bankruptcy Rules.*

b. Notice and Hearing Required

If any of the above four situations exist, the creditor may withdraw his claim only by order of the court after notice and hearing. Notice of the hearing date must be mailed or delivered to the debtor, any trustee, unsecured creditors' committee(s), and any other entity as required by court order or local bankruptcy rules. The court or local bankruptcy rules will determine who serves notice of the hearing date. *11 USC §102(1)(A)-(B); FRBP 3006, 9007, 9013-9014; see Local Bankruptcy Rules.*

c. Order of the Court

If a hearing is required on a notice of withdrawal of claim, the order of the court must contain terms and conditions which the court deems just and proper under the circumstances of the case. An order authorizing withdrawal of a claim also constitutes a withdrawal of such creditor's vote under a plan, unless otherwise stated in the order. *11 USC §105(a); FRBP 3006.*

B. Motion for Relief from Automatic Stay

The automatic stay is a powerful shield to protect the debtor, his property, and property of the estate from creditors once any petition is filed. But a motion for relief from the stay can also be a powerful tool for creditors, co-owners, or any entity that has any interest in, or rights to, property of the debtor or the estate. *11 USC §§361-364, 521(1), 541; FRBP 4001, 9013-9014.*

1. Generally

Any party-in-interest (creditor, co-owner, or committee) may file a motion for relief from the automatic stay. The court may lift, modify, terminate, or conditionally continue the automatic stay upon the debtor's providing adequate protection. *11 USC §§361-364.*

a. Purpose for the Motion

The purpose for filing a motion for relief from the automatic stay is to acquire rights to property of the debtor or estate before the debtor's case is closed or dismissed, the debtor is discharged, the debtor's plan is confirmed, or the property is no longer part of the estate. The automatic stay protecting property of the estate terminates when the property ceases to be part of the estate because of sale or abandonment by the trustee, exemption by the debtor, or dismissal of the debtor's case by the court. However, the automatic stay protecting the debtor and his (exempt) property terminates on the earliest date that the debtor's case is closed or dismissed or the debtor receives or is denied a discharge. *11 USC §§349(a), (b)(3), 362(c), 522(b), (d), 554; HR Rep No 595, 95th Cong, 1st Sess 343-44 (1977).*

b. Grounds for Lifting or Modifying the Automatic Stay

There are three main grounds for lifting or modifying the stay: for cause; the debtor's lack of equity and need for the property at issue; or the debtor is a single asset real estate debtor who has failed to comply with the 90-day post-petition requirements of the Bankruptcy Code.

(1) For Cause

This first ground for lifting the stay is broad and may include any reason the court approves. The Code specifically includes, but is not limited to, "lack of adequate protection" of the interest of the movant in property of the estate or debtor. The *interest* that is alleged not to be adequately protected could be a lienhold, property, or co-ownership interest. The debtor, trustee, or committee opposing the motion for relief has the burden of proving there is adequate protection. *11 USC §362(d)(1), (g)(2); FRBP 4001.*

Causes other than lack of adequate protection which could provide grounds for the court's lifting the stay include:

(a) Comity or the desire of the bankruptcy court to have an adversary proceeding continued in another court of competent jurisdiction. *See 28 USC §1334(b), (c)(1)-(2); "Abstention of Federal District Court in a Bankruptcy Proceeding," Chapter IX;*

(b) Lack of connection or interference with the bankruptcy case. Divorce and child custody proceedings, probate proceedings in which the debtor is the executor or administrator, proceedings in which the debtor is a fiduciary, and proceedings involving the debtor's post-petition activities generally should not be stayed. Such proceedings do not offend the purpose of the automatic stay, which is to protect the debtor from his pre-petition creditors and to allow the orderly distribution of the debtor's assets. The debtor, trustee, or creditors' committee opposing the motion has the burden of proving that the proceeding at issue is *related to* (affects the administration of) the bankruptcy case and should be stayed. *11 USC §362(g); 124 Cong Rec H11,093 (daily ed Sept 28, 1978); S17,409 (Oct 4, 1978); HR Rep No 595, 95th Cong, 1st Sess, 343-44 (1977); S Rep No 989, 95th Cong, 2d Sess 52-53 (1978);*

(c) The interests of justice warrant the court's lifting the automatic stay to permit an adversary proceeding to continue or to be filed in another court of competent jurisdiction. *11 USC §§105(a), 362(d)(1); 28 USC §1334(b), (c)(1); or*

(d) There is an adversary proceeding pending in a state court with competent jurisdiction involving an action that could not have been filed in a federal district court if the debtor had not filed a bankruptcy petition. *28 USC §1334(c)(1)-(2); see "Abstention of Federal District Court in a Bankruptcy Proceeding," Chapter IX.*

(2) Lack of Equity and Need

A second ground for lifting the stay is that the debtor does not have equity in the property at issue and such property is not necessary for the debtor's effective reorganization (rehabilitation). This second ground is a two-pronged test. If alleged, the party filing the motion has the burden of proving there is no equity; the debtor, trustee, or creditors' committee opposing the motion has the burden of proving the property is needed for the debtor's successful reorganization. The term *reorganization* is not limited to Chapter 11 cases. The term generally means the debtor's rehabilitation under any bankruptcy case. But in a Chapter 11 case, the debtor must prove that there is a "reasonable possibility of a successful reorganization within a reasonable time" for the stay to be continued. *See United Savings Association v Timbers of Inwood Forest Associates, 484 US 365 (1988); 11 USC §§103(a), 362(d)(1)-(2), (g).*

(3) Single Asset Real Estate Debtor

The third ground for the court to grant a motion for relief and lift or modify the automatic stay is that the debtor is a single asset real estate debtor (usually a Chapter 11 debtor) and by the end of the 90th day after the order for relief is entered, the debtor has either: (a) failed to file a plan of reorganization that reflects a reasonable possibility of confirmation by the court within a reasonable time; or (b) failed to begin making monthly payments to each secured creditor with a lien against the real estate equal to the current fair market rate of interest on the value of each creditor's lienhold interest in the land. Creditors with a judgment lien (obtained by judgment, levy, sequestration, or other legal or equitable process) or an unmatured statutory lien on the real estate are excluded from the 90-day mandates and remain subject to the automatic stay of the Bankruptcy Code unless one of the other two grounds for lifting the stay is proven. The bankruptcy court may extend the 90-day post-petition period for the single asset real estate debtor for cause, but a motion and court order must be entered before the end of the 90-day period. *HR 5116, Pub L No 103-394, §218, amending and adding 11 USC §101(51B) and 362(d)(3)(A)(B).*

A *single asset real estate debtor* is a legal term of art defined by the Bankruptcy Code as a debtor who has real property, other than residential realty with fewer than four residential units, that: (a) constitutes a single property or project; (b) generates substantially all the debtor's gross income; (c) provides no other substantial business conducted by the debtor except the business of operating the realty and activities incidental to such business operations; and (d) has a maximum of $4 million noncontingent, liquidated secured debt(s). *HR 5116, Pub L No 103-394, §218(a), amending and adding 11 USC §101(51B).*

c. Adequate Protection Requirement

Adequate protection may be provided by the debtor or trustee to the party seeking relief from the automatic stay in any manner the court approves. The Code lists three examples.

(1) Periodic cash payments may be given by the debtor or trustee to the extent continuation of the stay reduces the value of the party's interest in the property at issue. The interest protected could be a lienhold, ownership, or other property interest. If the property will depreciate at a relatively fixed rate, periodic payments equal to the amount of depreciation should provide adequate protection. *See United Savings Association v Timbers of Inwood Forest Associates, 484 US 365 (1988).*

(2) Replacement or additional liens may adequately protect the party from any decrease in value to the party's interest in property if the stay is continued. This method of providing adequate protection affords the protected party an alternative method of realizing the value of his original property interest (lienhold or co-ownership); or

(3) Any other relief or remedy approved by the court that will give the party-in-interest the "indubitable equivalent" of his interest in property, except giving a first priority claim for an administrative expense. The court may not grant the party-in-interest a first priority claim for administrative expenses as adequate protection for continuing the stay. Some other form of adequate protection must be provided. But the court is given latitude to formulate protection appropriate to the circumstances of the case. Adequate protection might be provided by the debtor's or trustee's obtaining a guarantee or letter of credit from a third party to compensate the party-in-interest for any loss incurred from continuation of the stay. *11 USC §361(1)-(3); HR Rep No 595, 95th Cong, 1st Sess, 338-40 (1977); S Rep No 989, 95th Cong, 2d Sess, 49, 53-54 (1978).*

The Code does not specify how the value of the party's interest in property should be determined. Bankruptcy law allows great latitude for courts to use a "forced liquidation value" (Chapter 7) or "full going concern value" or other value (Chapter 11, 12, or 13), depending upon the particular facts and circumstances of each case. *11 USC §361; S Rep No 989, 95th Cong, 2d Sess 49, 53-54 (1978); see "Valuation of Collateral," discussed below.*

d. Adequate Protection of Cash Collateral Requirement

The trustee, DIP, or Chapter 13 debtor engaged in business must obtain authorization to use *cash collateral* (cash, negotiable instruments, documents of title, or securities in which the estate and a nonbankruptcy party have an interest; or proceeds and products of collateral covered by a pre-petition security agreement). The debtor or trustee must obtain either the consent of the nonbankruptcy party or a court order before using cash collateral post-petition. The debtor or trustee must provide adequate protection to the nonbankruptcy party against any reduction in the value of cash collateral from its post-petition use. *See "Adequate Protection Requirement," discussed above; "Use, Sale, or Lease of Estate's Property," Chapter VIII; 11 USC §§102(1)(A)-(B), 361, 362(d)(1), (e), 363(a), (c), 552(b); FRBP 4001, 9007, 9013-9014.*

e. Procedures

A motion for relief from the stay does not commence an adversary proceeding. However, the party-in-interest must pay a $60 filing fee and serve a copy of the motion on the debtor, any trustee, all committee(s), and any other entity required by court order or local bankruptcy rules. If there is no unsecured creditors' committee in a Chapter 9 or 11 case, then service must be obtained on each creditor included in the debtor's list of 20 largest unsecured creditors filed with the clerk. Service of the motion may be by first-class mail or any other method allowed for service of a summons and complaint under the Federal Rules of Civil Procedure. *28 USC §1930(b), Judicial Conference Schedule of Fees (21); FRBP 1007(d), 4001(a), 7004, 9013-9014.*

The Code and FRBP do not require the debtor or trustee to file an answer or response to the motion for relief. However, local bankruptcy rules may require a timely response on penalty of default and lifting of the stay. *See Local Bankruptcy Rules; 11 USC §362(d)-(f); FRBP 4001, 9014.*

f. Notice and Hearing

Notice of the motion for relief is provided by the party-in-interest's serving a copy of the motion on the debtor, any trustee, committee(s), and all other entities directed by the court or local bankruptcy rules. But it is the debtor, trustee, or other party-in-interest (committee) who wants to retain the property that has the responsibility for obtaining a hearing and order continuing the stay before the 30th day after the motion has been filed, or the stay will be lifted by operation of bankruptcy law without need for a court order. Further, local bankruptcy rules may require the debtor, trustee, or committee opposing the motion to file and serve a timely response or the stay will be lifted. *11 USC §362(e); FRBP 4001; see Local Bankruptcy Rules.*

Once a motion for relief from the automatic stay has been filed, two hatchet rules govern the contested proceeding.

(1) First 30-Day Hatchet Rule

The automatic stay terminates automatically on the 30th day after the motion for relief has been filed for the party filing the motion, unless before the 30th day and after notice, the court has held a hearing and denied the motion or ordered the automatic stay continued. Again, it is the debtor, trustee, or other party opposing the motion who must obtain at least a preliminary hearing before the 30th day after the motion is filed. If the initial hearing was a preliminary hearing, the court may continue the stay only if the court finds there is a "reasonable likelihood" that the debtor or trustee will prevail at the conclusion of the final hearing. *11 USC §362(e); see Local Bankruptcy Rules to determine if a response to the motion for relief is required.*

(2) Second 30-Day Hatchet Rule

If the initial hearing was a preliminary hearing and the court finds that there is a "reasonable likelihood" the debtor or trustee will prevail at a final hearing and orders the stay continued, the final hearing must be concluded no later than the 30th day after conclusion of the preliminary hearing, or the automatic stay terminates for the moving party. However, this 30-day period may be extended by: (a) consent of all the parties-in-interest; or (b) the bankruptcy court, for a specific time, if the court finds compelling circumstances exist for the extension of time. The party opposing the motion for relief should obtain a court order extending the 30-day period before such period expires. *11 USC §§105(a), 362(e), FRBP 4001, see "Motion for Relief from Automatic Stay," above.*

Thus, if a creditor files a motion for relief from the stay on August 1, the debtor, trustee, or committee opposing the motion must obtain a hearing and court order denying the motion or continuing the stay before August 31, or the stay terminates automatically (first 30-day hatchet rule). The debtor or trustee may also have to file and serve a timely response to the motion under local bankruptcy rules. If the initial hearing is a preliminary hearing which concludes on August 30, a final hearing must be concluded no later than September 29 (second 30-day hatchet rule), unless the parties consent to, or the court orders an extension of, the (second) 30-day period. If a debtor fails to observe either of the two 30-day hatchet rules or local bankruptcy rules requiring a timely response to the motion, the stay terminates for the party filing the motion. However, the court has the power to reinstate the stay if, in the exercise of the court's equitable powers, the court deems such an order necessary or appropriate to carry out the provisions of the Code. But reinstatement of the stay is at the discretion of the court. *11 USC §§105(a), (c), 362(d)(3), (e); FRBP 4001(a)(1)-(3), 9007, 9013-9014; see In re Kleinsasser, 4 CBC2d 1185 (Bankr DSD 1981); In re Walker, 3 Bankr 213 (Bankr WD Va 1980).*

The clerk, debtor, or other court-appointed person must give notice of the date of any preliminary or final hearing to the debtor, the party who filed the motion, any trustee, all committee(s), to the 20 largest unsecured creditors if there is no unsecured creditors' committee in a Chapter 9 or 11 case, and to any other entity as required by court order or local bankruptcy rules. *11 USC §§102(1)(A)-(B), 362(d)-(e); FRBP 1007(d), 4001, 9007, 9013-9014.*

g. Ex Parte Relief

The court may grant relief from the automatic stay without either prior notice to the debtor or trustee or a hearing, if ex parte relief is necessary to prevent irreparable damage to the value of a party's interest in property. The party seeking ex parte relief from the stay must strictly comply with the following procedures:

(1) File an affidavit or verified motion for relief stating specific facts which clearly show that the party-in-interest will suffer immediate and irreparable injury, loss, or damage before the debtor or trustee opposing the motion, or his attorney, can be heard;

(2) The movant's attorney must file a written certificate stating the efforts made to give notice of the motion for relief to the debtor and any trustee, why such efforts have failed, and why further efforts to give notice should not be required;

(3) The party must immediately give oral notice of any order granting ex parte relief from the stay to the debtor and any trustee and to their respective attorneys; and

(4) The party must immediately mail or otherwise transmit a copy of the order granting ex parte relief from the stay to the debtor, any trustee, and to their respective attorneys. *FRBP 4001(a)(2).*

The debtor or trustee may thereafter file a motion to reinstate the stay. A hearing on the motion to reinstate may be held if the party who obtained the ex parte order has had at least two days' prior notice, unless the court reduces such time. In any event, the court must hold an immediate hearing on a motion to reinstate. *11 USC §§102(1)(A)-(B), 362(a), (f); FRBP 4001(a)(2).*

h. Settlement Agreement

The party-in-interest and debtor or trustee may reach a settlement agreement prior to a court hearing on a motion for relief and file an agreement in settlement of motion for relief. *FRBP 4001(d), 5005(a).*

(1) Procedures for Settlement Agreement

(a) Motion for Relief

The motion for relief itself may contain sufficient provisions of the settlement agreement to inform parties-in-

interest of its terms. If properly served, the motion alone may be sufficient to afford reasonable notice and opportunity for hearing required by bankruptcy law. However, the settlement agreement should also be filed either separately or with the motion for relief. A copy of the motion and agreement must also be served on the US trustee. *11 USC §§102(1)(A)-(B), 362(d); FRBP 4001(a), (d), 5005(a), 9007, 9013, 9014, 9034; see "Motion for Relief from Automatic Stay—Procedures," discussed above.*

(b) Motion for Approval

If the motion for relief does not contain sufficient information about the settlement agreement, or was not properly served are all required entities, either the debtor or trustee or the party-in-interest must file a motion for approval of settlement agreement with the agreement attached or separately filed. A copy of the motion for approval and the settlement agreement must be mailed or delivered to the debtor, any trustee, the U.S. trustee, all committee(s), and to any other entity required by court order or local bankruptcy rules. If no unsecured creditors' committee has been appointed in a Chapter 9 or 11 case, then service must be obtained on each creditor included in the debtor's list of 20 largest unsecured creditors filed with the clerk. *FRBP 1007(d), 4001(d), 5005(a), 9013-9014, 9034.*

(c) Objections

The clerk or other court-authorized person must mail notice of the motion for approval of settlement agreement and the last date to file objections to the motion or agreement to the same entities required to receive a copy of the motion and agreement discussed above. Unless the court or local bankruptcy rules require otherwise, any objection must be filed before the 15th day after the notice of the date to file objections is mailed. *FRBP 4001(d)(2), 5005(a), 9013-9014, 9034; see Local Bankruptcy Rules.*

(d) Hearing on Settlement Agreement and Order

(i) When Hearing Is Not Required

The court may determine that a hearing on the settlement agreement is not required if no objection to the motion for approval is timely filed or if the motion for relief from the stay provided sufficient notice of the terms of the agreement and an opportunity for hearing and no objection was timely filed. The court may then enter an order approving or disapproving the settlement agreement. *11 USC §§102(1)(A)-(B), 362(d)-(e); FRBP 4001(d)(3)-(4).*

(ii) When Hearing Is Required

If an objection is timely filed or if the court determines that a hearing on the settlement agreement is needed even in the absence of an objection, a hearing must be held. A minimum of five days' prior notice must be given to any objector, the party filing the motion for relief, the debtor, any trustee, the U.S. trustee, all committee(s), and to any other entity as required by court order or local bankruptcy rules. If there is no unsecured creditors' committee in a Chapter 9 or 11 case, notice of the hearing on the settlement agreement must be given to all creditors listed on the debtor's list of 20 largest unsecured creditors. Service of the notice of the hearing date may be obtained on such parties by first-class mail or any manner allowed for service of process in federal district court. *FRBP 1007(d), 4001(d)(3), 5005(a), 9013-9014, 9034; see Local Bankruptcy Rules.*

i. Creditor's Super First Priority Claim

The secured creditor with a lien on property used, sold, or leased post-petition by the debtor or trustee will have a super first priority claim against the estate if:

(1) The debtor or trustee attempted to provide adequate protection for the collateral;

(2) The adequate protection provided was not sufficient;

(3) There was a reduction in value to the collateral from the post-petition use, sale, or lease, or continuation of the automatic stay; and

(4) The post-petition use, sale, or lease of such property, or continuation of the automatic stay, benefited or helped preserve or maintain the estate. *11 USC §§361, 362(d), 363(a), (c)-(e), 364, 503(a), (b)(1), 507(a)(1), (b).*

A super first priority claim is entitled to payment from the estate before payments to any other unsecured creditors. Thus, a super first priority claimholder must be paid even before first priority claims for administrative expenses. The creditor should file a timely proof of claim asserting facts showing a super first priority claim and attach all relevant documents, including all related court order(s). *See "File Proof of Claim—When to File," discussed above; "Priority Claims," Chapter II; 11 USC §§103(a), (e), 502, 521(1), 901, 924-925, 1111(a); FRBP 2002(a)(8), (f)(3), (i)-(j), 3001-3005.*

2. Motion to Lift Codebtor Stay

Under Chapters 12 and 13, a creditor may file a motion for relief from the codebtor stay. The creditor must allege and prove that one or more of the six requirements for continuation of the codebtor stay has not been met (See *"Automatic Plus Codebtor Stay,"* *Chapter V*). The motion for relief must be served on the debtor, standing trustee, codebtor, and any other entity required by court order or local bankruptcy rules. Service of the motion may be obtained by first-class mail or any other manner provided for service of process in federal district court. If the motion alleges that the debtor's plan fails to provide for 100 per cent payment of the creditor's pre-petition claim with pre-petition interest rate, the codebtor stay automatically terminates for this creditor on the 20th day after the motion is filed, unless before such 20th day the debtor or codebtor files and serves on the creditor a written objection to the motion. A copy of the objection should also be mailed or personally delivered to the standing trustee and to any other entity required by court order or local bankruptcy rules. *11 USC §§1201, 1301; see "Automatic Plus Codebtor Stay," Chapter V; FRBP 9007, 9014; Local Bankruptcy Rules.*

The codebtor stay does not prevent a creditor from preserving his substantive rights against the codebtor under nonbankruptcy law. Thus, the creditor may present a negotiable instrument and give any notice of dishonor required by such instrument. *11 USC §§1201(b), 1301(b); S Rep No 989, 95th Cong 2d Sess 139 (1978).*

3. Relief from Stay Against a Chapter 11 Air Carrier or Water Carrier Debtor

a. Overview

Chapter 11 modifies and overrides the general automatic stay provisions of the Code for certain creditors. The bankruptcy court has limited power to stop lessors, conditional vendors, and lienholders of certain United States vessels, or of aircraft or their equipment or parts, from taking possession of such property in the case of a Chapter 11 air carrier or water carrier debtor. *11 USC §1110.*

b. Who May File a Motion for Relief

Three creditors are given special treatment under this modified Chapter 11 stay:

(1) Secured creditors with a lien on documented vessels of the United States, as defined under 46 USC §30101(1), or on aircraft, or their equipment or parts, as defined under 49 USC §40102. However, a purchase money security interest is required of creditors with a lien on such vessels or aircraft, their equipment or parts, if such collateral was in service on or before October 22, 1994;

(2) Lessors of such vessels or aircraft, or their equipment or parts. For such property in service on or before October 22, 1994,

the term *lease* includes any written agreement or substantially contemporaneous writing in which the lessor and debtor-lessee have expressed that the transaction is to be treated as a lease for federal income tax purposes; and

(3) Conditional vendors of such vessels, or of aircraft or their equipment or parts. *11 USC §1110(a) (c).*

c. Who Must Be the Debtor

The debtor must be either:

(1) A citizen of the United States that holds an air carrier operating certificate issued by the Secretary of Transportation under Chapter 447 of Title 49, United States Code, for aircraft with a capability of carrying ten or more individuals or 6,000 pounds or more of cargo; or

(2) A water carrier that holds a certificate of public convenience and necessity or a permit issued by the Interstate Commerce Commission.

d. Rights of the Creditor or Lessor

The secured creditor, lessor, or conditional vendor may take possession of such vessels, or of aircraft or their equipment or parts, in which such entities have an interest, unless the DIP or trustee, if one has been appointed:

(1) Agrees, before the 60th day after the voluntary petition is filed or order for relief is entered in an involuntary case, to honor and perform all obligations under pre-petition contract(s) as such obligations become due post-petition. However, all terms of the agreement to perform post-petition obligations are subject to court approval; and

(2) Cures all pre-petition defaults before the end of the 60th day after the voluntary petition is filed or entry of the order for relief in an involuntary case, other than a default defined under a pre-petition bankruptcy clause as the debtor's insolvency, bankruptcy, or the appointment of a bankruptcy trustee or a custodian to take possession of the debtor's property; and

(3) Cures all post-petition defaults before the later of: (a) the 30th day after the date of the default, or (b) the end of the 60th day after the voluntary petition is filed or an order for relief is entered in an involuntary case. *11 USC §§301, 303, 362(d)(1), 365(b)(2), 1110(a)(1)-(2); FRBP 4001, 9014.*

e. Agreement Between Debtor and Creditor or Lessor

The purchase-money equipment secured creditor, lessor, or conditional vendor may enter into a post-petition agreement with the DIP or trustee, if one has been appointed, to extend the 60-day hatchet period. This agreement, like all post-petition agreements involving property of the debtor or estate, is subject to court approval. *11 USC §§102(1)(A)-(B), 362(d)(1), 1110; FRBP 4001(a), (d), 9014, 9034. See "Motion for Relief from Automatic Stay—Procedures for Settlement Agreement," discussed above.*

C. Compelled Abandonment of Property

1. Generally

A trustee or Chapter 11 or 12 DIP may voluntarily abandon property of the bankruptcy estate if such property is burdensome and of inconsequential value and benefit to the estate. Abandoned property generally includes collateral that has little or no equity for the estate; rolling stock (trucks, trailers) or other collateral for which there is no insurance and little, if any, equity; or property of immeasurable value. Abandoned property is not part of the estate or subject to the automatic stay unless it is thereafter claimed as exempt by the debtor. *11 USC §§102(5), 103(a), 362(c)(1), 521(1), 522(b), (d), (l), 554(a); FRBP 1007(b)-(c), 4003, 6007(a); Official Bankr Form 6, Schedule C; see "Stage Five—Exemptions Claimed by the Debtor," Chapter II.*

2. Motion to Compel Abandonment

A party-in-interest may file a motion to compel the trustee or DIP to abandon property of the estate that is burdensome and of inconsequential value and benefit to the estate. *11 USC §§102(5), 554(b); FRBP 6007(b), 9013-9014.*

3. Procedures

a. Notice of Voluntary Abandonment by Trustee or DIP

If the trustee or DIP wishes to abandon property voluntarily, he must file and mail a notice of abandonment to all creditors, the U.S. trustee, indenture trustees, all committee(s), the debtor if a trustee is abandoning property, and to any other entity required by court order or local bankruptcy rules. Generally, no hearing will be held unless a party-in-interest files and serves an objection to the notice of abandonment before the 15th day after the notice was mailed, or by any other date set by the court or local bankruptcy rules. *11 USC §102(1)(A)-(B), 103(a), 554(a); FRBP 6007(a), (c), 9013-9014.*

b. Notice of Compelled Abandonment

A motion to compel abandonment filed by a party-in-interest does not commence an adversary proceeding. However, a $60 filing fee must be paid when the motion is filed. The party-in-interest must serve a copy of the motion by first-class mail or any other manner allowed for service of process in federal district court on the debtor, any trustee, the U.S. trustee, all committee(s), and to such other entities required by court order or local bankruptcy rules. *11 USC §§102(1)(A)-(B), 103(a), 554(b); FRBP 6007(b), 9007, 9013-9014; 28 USC §1930(b), Judicial Conference Schedule of Fees (21).*

c. **Hearing**

The court must hold a hearing on the trustee's or DIP's notice of abandonment if a party-in-interest files a timely written objection. The court must also hold a hearing if a party-in-interest files a motion to compel abandonment by the trustee or DIP, unless the court or local bankruptcy rules direct otherwise. Notice of the hearing date must be mailed to the debtor, any trustee, the U.S. trustee, and to such other entities as required by court order or local bankruptcy rules. *11 USC §102(1)(A)-(B); FRBP 6007(c), 9007, 9013-9014; see Local Bankruptcy Rules.*

d. **Burden of Proof**

If a hearing is held, the trustee or DIP in a voluntary abandonment, or the party-in-interest in a compelled abandonment, has the burden of proving the property to be abandoned is:

(1) **Burdensome to the estate; and**

(2) **Of inconsequential value and benefit to the estate.** *11 USC §§102(5), 103(a), 554(a)-(b); FRBP 6007.*

4. **Abandonment to Debtor**

Property listed under the debtor's schedules of assets which has not been administered (disbursed, sold, or leased) by the end of the bankruptcy case is automatically deemed abandoned to the debtor and fully administered, unless the court orders otherwise. No further notice, hearing, or order is necessary, unless the court or local bankruptcy rules direct otherwise. *11 USC §§350(a), 521(1), 554(c); HR Rep No 595, 95th Cong, 1st Sess 377 (1977); S Rep No 989, 95th Cong, 2d Sess 92 (1978); Official Bankr Form 6, Schedules A-C, G.*

D. Meeting of Creditors

1. What It Is

A meeting of creditors is an examination of the debtor under oath about any matter dealing with the administration of the bankruptcy case, the estate, or the debtor's discharge. In a Chapter 7 or 11 case, an election of a trustee may also occur at the meeting of creditors. *11 USC §§341, 343, 702, 705; FRBP 2003(b)(1), (3), (c); see "Attend Meeting of Creditors," Chapter III; "Priority Claims" and "Stage Seven—Distribution of the Estate," Chapter II; "Selection of Chapter 11 Trustee," Chapter IV.*

2. When It Occurs

Unless the court orders otherwise, a meeting of creditors in a Chapter 7 or 11 case must generally occur not less than 20 or more than 40 days after the voluntary petition is filed or order for relief is entered in an involuntary case. No meeting of creditors is held in a Chapter 9 case. The meeting of creditors generally occurs not less than 20 or more than 35 days after the petition is filed under Chapter 12 cases. In a Chapter 13 case, the meeting of creditors must generally occur not less than 20 or more than 50 days after the petition is filed, thereby enabling courts to hold the confirmation hearing and meeting of creditors on the same day. If there is a motion to dismiss or the petition is appealed, the court may set a later date for the meeting of creditors. *11 USC §§103(a), (e), 341-343, 901; FRBP 2002(a)(1), 2003(a).*

3. Where It Is Held

The meeting of creditors may be held at a regular place (in the building) where the bankruptcy court holds hearings or the U.S. trustee may designate another place in the same federal judicial district for the meeting of creditors in the interests and convenience of the parties-in-interest who will attend. If the place designated is not regularly staffed by the U.S. trustee, the meeting of creditors may be held not more than 60 days after the order for relief. *FRBP 2003(a), 9006(b)(2).*

4. Notice of the Meeting

The clerk or other court-authorized person must give at lesat 20 days' notice by mail of the meeting of creditors. The notice must be mailed to the debtor, any trustee, all committee(s), creditors, equity security holders, indenture trustees, and to any other entity required by court order or local bankruptcy rules. In a Chapter 11 case, the notice must also be mailed to the SEC in Washington, DC, and to the District Director of the IRS where the debtor's case is pending. If the debtor's case has a large number of creditors and parties-in-interest, the court may order notice by publication in addition to, or in place of, notice by mail. *FRBP 2002(a)(1), (i)-(j), (l).*

5. Who Attends

a. Who Must Attend

The debtor must appear at the meeting of creditors and answer questions under oath on penalty of perjury. Failure to answer truthfully at the meeting of creditors may be a bankruptcy crime, punishable by a fine for as much as $5,000 and/or imprisonment for as long as five years. *11 USC §343; 18 USC §152; FRBP 2003(b)(1); see "Bankruptcy Crimes and Penalties," discussed below.*

A debtor may refuse to answer a question at the meeting of creditors and seek immunity against self-incrimination in any subsequent criminal proceeding. If the privilege against self-incrimination is invoked, the debtor must request the United States attorney for the federal judicial district where the case is pending to seek an immunity order from the federal district court. However, any immunity so provided will be "use" immunity, not "transactional" or blanket immunity. *11 USC §344; pt V, tit 18; HR Rep No 595, 95th Cong, 1st Sess 322-23 (1977).*

If the debtor is not granted immunity, he may continue to refuse to answer questions at the meeting of creditors (or to testify at any hearing) and assert the privilege against self-incrimination. If the debtor is granted immunity but continues to refuse to answer any material question approved by the court at a meeting of creditors (or to testify at a hearing), his refusal may be grounds for denial of discharge under Chapters 7 and 11. *11 USC §§103(a), 344, 727(a)(6), 1141(d)(3); FRBP 2003, 4004; HR Rep No 595, 95th Cong, 1st Sess 332-33 (1977); S Rep No 989, 95th Cong, 2d Sess 43-44 (1978); see "Denial of Discharge," Chapter III; "Procedure Ten—Discharge," Chapter IV.*

b. Who May Attend

All creditors, equity security holders, any appointed trustee or examiner, the U.S. trustee, and all parties-in-interest may attend the meeting of creditors and examine the debtor under oath. The U.S. trustee or his delegate may administer the oath to the debtor. *11 USC §343; FRBP 2003(b)(1), (c).*

c. Who Must Not Attend

The bankruptcy judge must not preside at or attend any meeting of creditors. *11 USC §341(c).*

6. Who Presides

In Alabama and North Carolina, which are not part of the U.S. trustee system, a bankruptcy administrator or his delegate presides at the meeting of creditors. In all other regions, the U.S. trustee or his delegate will preside at the meeting of creditors. The presiding officer has the authority to administer the oath to the debtor. The presiding officer must prepare minutes of the meeting. The examination of the debtor under oath must be recorded verbatim by electronic sound recording equipment or other means of recording. The U.S. trustee must preserve and hold the record of the meeting of creditors available to the public for two years after the conclusion of the meeting of creditors. A certified copy of the transcript of the record may be obtained at the request and expense of any entity. The presiding officer must also transmit to the court the name and address of any person elected Chapter 7 trustee or member of the Chapter 7 creditors' committee. The presiding officer may adjourn the meeting of creditors and continue it by announcing at the meeting the date and time for the next (continued) meeting. No further notice of any continued meeting need be given. The U.S. trustee may call a special meeting of creditors if requested by a party-in-interest or on the U.S. trustee's own initiative. *11 USC §343; FRBP 2003(c)-(f).*

7. Final Meeting and Account

The U.S. trustee may call a final meeting of creditors. In any case where the net proceeds realized by the estate exceed $1,500 and a final meeting of creditors is called, the clerk of the court must mail to all creditors a notice of the date of the final meeting with: (a) a summary of the trustee's or debtor-in-possession's final account, and (b) a statement of the amount of allowed claims. The trustee or DIP must attend this final meeting and report on the administration of the case, if so requested. *FRBP 2002(f)(8), (i), (k), 2003(g); 11 USC §§341, 343.*

E. Rule 2004 Examination

1. Who May Be Examined

The court may order the examination of any entity, including the debtor, under FRBP 2004. If the debtor is to be examined, the party-in-interest must show cause why a Rule 2004 examination is required in addition to the meeting of creditors. *FRBP 2004(a)-(b), (d), 4002(1).*

2. Procedures

a. Motion

The party-in-interest must file a motion for Rule 2004 examination with the bankruptcy clerk. The motion must state the entity to be examined and the grounds for such examination, particularly if the debtor is to be examined. The party-in-interest must serve a copy of the motion on the entity to be examined by first-class mail or any other method allowed for service of process in federal district court. A copy of the motion must also be mailed to the debtor (if another entity is to be examined), any trustee, all committee(s), and to any other entity required by court order or local bankruptcy rules. *FRBP 2004(a), (d), 5005(a), 7004, 9007, 9013-9014; see Local Bankruptcy Rules.*

b. Notice and Hearing

If the motion for Rule 2004 examination is opposed, the court must hold a hearing on the motion with notice of the hearing date mailed to such entities as required by the court and local bankruptcy rules. *11 USC §102(1)(A)-(B); FRBP 2004, 9007, 9013-9014; see Local Bankruptcy Rules.*

3. Scope of Examination

a. Generally

A Rule 2004 examination, like the meeting of creditors, may only relate to matters affecting the administration of the estate and the financial condition and discharge of the debtor, including the acts, conduct, assets, and liabilities of the debtor; possible preferential or fraudulent transfers; or any other matter dealing with the estate or the debtor's discharge. *FRBP 2004(b).*

b. Chapters 11, 12, or 13

In addition to matters concerning the estate, the debtor, and his discharge, the Rule 2004 examination under a Chapter 11 (non-railroad debtor), 12, or 13 case may include the: (1) operation of the debtor's business, (2) desirability of continuing the debtor's business, (3) source of payments or property necessary to consummate a plan and the legal consideration given or offered in return for such payments, and (4) any other matter relevant to the bankruptcy case or plan. *FRBP 2004(b).*

4. Where Held

The Rule 2004 examination may be held within or beyond the federal judicial district where the debtor's bankruptcy case is pending. The party-in-interest must show cause why the examination should be held if the debtor is to be examined. The court may impose any terms regarding the time and place for the examination necessary to protect the debtor, estate, or parties-in-interest. *11 USC §105(a): FRBP 2004(d).*

5. Compelling Attendance at the Rule 2004 Examination

a. Generally

Attendance of the entity to be examined and production of documents may be compelled by subpoena or subpoena duces tecum in the same manner for compelling attendance of witnesses at a hearing or trial in federal district court. If the entity fails to obey the subpoena without a showing of adequate excuse, he may be held in contempt of court. *FRBP 2004(e), 2005, 4002(1), 9016, 9020; FRCP 45.*

b. Mileage

(1) Entity Other Than the Debtor

The party-in-interest who wishes to examine an entity who is not the debtor must give such entity the lawful mileage (25&edit; per mile) and witness fee ($40 per day) required for compelling one day's attendance of a witness in federal district court. If the mileage and witness fee are not provided, the entity is not required to attend the Rule 2004 examination. *FRBP 2004(e).*

(2) The Debtor

If the debtor is to be examined at a place more than 100 miles from his residence, the party-in-interest must provide the debtor with the same mileage allowed to a witness. However, the debtor's mileage is computed for the lesser of any distance which is more than 100 miles from either: (a) the debtor's residence on the date the original petition is filed; or (b) the debtor's residence on the date of the examination. *FRBP 2004(e).*

F. Valuation of Collateral

1. Generally

Under bankruptcy law, a secured creditor is secured to the lesser of the value of the collateral or the allowed amount of the creditor's claim. A creditor whose collateral is worth more than his allowed claim is oversecured; a creditor whose allowed claim is greater than the value of his collateral is underscured. But *valuation of collateral* for bankruptcy purposes is a fluid, not fixed, concept. Valuation must be determined on a case-by-case basis, with consideration given to: (a) the purpose for the valuation, and (b) the use or disposition of the collateral proposed by the debtor or trustee. *11 USC §§501, 502(a), 506(a); FRBP 3012; S Rep No 989, 95th Cong, 2d Sess 68 (1978); HR Rep No 595, 95th Cong, 1st Sess 356 (1977); see Dewsnup v Timm, 502 US 410, 112 S Ct 773 (1992).*

2. When Valuation Occurs

Depending on the particular bankruptcy case, valuation of collateral may occur at one or more of seven possible times during a bankruptcy proceeding

a. Date Petition Filed

Valuation of collateral must occur on the date a voluntary petition is filed. The petition requires at least an estimation of the value of the debtor's assets. Adequate protection of a secured creditor's interest in property (collateral) necessarily means protecting the creditor against any post-petition reduction in the value of the collateral from the date the bankruptcy petition is filed. *11 USC §§301-302, 362(d)(1), 506(a); Official Bankr Form 1.*

The value used for collateral on the date the petition is filed will depend on the particular bankruptcy chapter selected by the debtor. A Chapter 7 petition will generally include liquidation (foreclosure or forced sale) values. A Chapter 9, 11, 12, or 13 petition should include greater values, ranging from liquidation to ongoing concern or fair market values. But the value of collateral (assets) indicated on the petition is not binding for purposes of valuation of collateral at any later date during the bankruptcy case. *11 USC §§506(a), 701 et seq, 901 et seq, 1101 et seq, 1201 et seq, 1301 et seq; FRBP 3012, 4001; HR Rep No 595, 95th Cong, 1st Sess, 356 (1977); S Rep No 989, 95th Cong, 2d Sess 68 (1978).*

b. Date Schedules of Assets and Liabilities Filed

The debtor must file his schedules of assets and liabilities either with the petition or before the 15th day thereafter, unless the court extends the time. The schedules of assets and liabilities must include at least an estimated value of the collateral. This may be the same value indicated on the petition or a different value. Again, the value of collateral listed on the schedules is not controlling for a later purpose. *11 USC §§506(a), 521(1); FRBP 1007(b)-(c); HR Rep No 595, 95th Cong, 1st Sess 356 (1977); S Rep No 989, 95th Cong, 2d Sess 68 (1978); Official Bankr Form 6, Schedules A-D.*

c. Relief from Automatic Stay

A secured creditor may file a motion for relief from the automatic stay for cause, including lack of adequate protection for collateral. Adequate protection is intended to prevent post-petition reduction in value of the secured creditor's interest in collateral. Any hearing on the motion may be combined with a valuation hearing to determine the value of collateral and the necessity and amount of adequate protection required. The debtor or trustee may provide adequate protection by periodic cash payments, an additional or replacement lien on property to compensate for any loss in value of collateral, or by any other means allowed by the court except providing the secured creditor with a first priority claim for administrative expenses. To the extent the amount of adequate protection provided is insufficient and the creditor's collateral decreases in value during continuation of the automatic stay, the secured creditor is entitled to an (unsecured) super first priority administrative claim. This super first priority administrative claim must be paid before any other priority claims, including any first priority administrative claims. Several valuation hearings may be requested and required on the issue of adequate protection of collateral during the bankruptcy case. Valuation of collateral on the petition and schedules would not necessarily be binding on valuation for purposes of determining adequate protection under a motion for relief from the stay. *11 USC §§361, 362(d)(1), 503(a), 506(a), 507(a)(1), (b); FRBP 3012, 4001, 9013-9014; see United Savings Associate v Timbers of Inwood Forest Associates, Ltd, 484 US 365 (1988); "Stage Two Automatic Stay Invoked," Chapter II and "Motion for Relief from Automatic Stay," discussed above; "Priority Claims," Chapter II.*

d. Use, Sale, or Lease of Property

A secured creditor is entitled to adequate protection of any collateral which the debtor or trustee proposes to use, sell, or lease even in the ordinary course of business. The creditor may file a motion for adequate protection. A hearing must be held on the creditor's motion which may be combined with a valuation hearing. Once again, prior valuation(s) of collateral are not necessarily binding. To the extent any adequate protection provided by the debtor or trustee proves insufficient and the debtor or trustee is allowed to use, sell, or lease the collateral to benefit the estate, the secured creditor is entitled to a super first priority administrative claim which must be paid before any other priority claims, including other first priority administrative claims. *11 USC §§362(d), 363(d)-(e), 503(a)-(b), 506(a), 507(b); FRBP 3012, 6004, 9013-9014; HR Rep No 595, 95th Cong, 1st Sess 356 (1977); S Rep No 989, 95th Cong, 2d Sess 68 (1978); see Chapter VIII; "Priority Claims," Chapter II.*

e. Post-Petition Credit Secured by Senior or Equal Lien

If the court allows the debtor or trustee to obtain post-petition credit secured by a senior or equal lien on property of the estate already encumbered, each pre-petition secured creditor whose lienhold position is subordinated or shared is entitled to adequate protection against any loss in value as the result of the adjustment of its lienhold position. A hearing on post-petition secured credit may be combined with a hearing on valuation of collateral. If such adequate protection provides insufficient while post-petition secured credit was obtained to benefit the estate, the pre-petition secured creditor is entitled to a super first priority administrative claim with priority over all priority claims, including first priority administrative claims. *11 USC §§364(d)(1)-(2), 503(a)-(b), 506(a), 507(a)(1), (b); FRBP 4001(c)-(d), 9014; Chapter VIII; "Priority Claims," Chapter II.*

f. Redemption of Collateral

An individual Chapter 7 debtor may redeem (buy back) tangible, personal, consumer property securing a dischargeable consumer debt, if the property is claimed as exempt by the debtor or abandoned by the trustee. The debtor must pay the creditor cash for the lesser of the allowed amount of the creditor's claim or the market value of the collateral. A hearing on valuation of collateral may be combined with a hearing on redemption and the discharge hearing. *11 USC §§506(a), 524(d), 722; FRBP 3012, 6008, 9014; HR Rep No 595, 95th Cong, 1st Sess 356 (1977); S Rep No 989, 95th Cong, 2d Sess 68 (1978); see "Redemption of Property," Chapter III.*

g. Confirmation of a Chapter 9, 11, 12, or 13 Plan

Under a Chapter 9, 11, 12, or 13 plan, a secured creditor must either receive the collateral or retain his lien on collateral (or its proceeds) and receive the lesser of the value of the collateral or the allowed amount of the claim, with interest, over the term of the plan, unless the secured creditor agrees otherwise. Under Chapters 9 and 11, the secured creditor may alternatively receive the "indubitable equivalent" of the allowed amount of the secured claim. Valuations are determined by the court as of the effective date of the plan to allow for the *present value* (deferred use) of money. Any prior valuation of collateral which occurred during the case is not necessarily binding on the creditor, debtor, any appointed trustee, or court. A hearing on valuation of collateral may be combined with the confirmation hearing. *11 USC §§103(a), (e)-(f), 506(a), 901, 1129(b)(2)(A), 1225(a)(5), 1325(a)(5); FRBP 2002(a)(9), (b), 3012, 3015-3017, 3020; see "Procedure Seven—Confirmation of a Plan of Reorganization," Chapter IV; "Valuation of Collateral," discussed below.*

Under Chapters 9 and 11, valuation of collateral may also be important in determining whether a secured creditor's claim is impaired for the purpose of voting under the plan. If a Chapter 9 or 11 plan has any class of impaired claims, at least one of such impaired classes of creditors must vote to accept the plan, without counting the vote of any insider, or it may not be confirmed. If a class of claims is not impaired, such class is conclusively deemed to accept the plan without voting. *11 USC §§101(a), (e)-(f), 901, 1124, 1126(f), 1129(a)(10); see "Impaired Classes of Creditors" and "Procedure Seven—Confirmation of a Plan of Reorganization," Chapter IV.*

3. Valuation Hearing

The secured creditor (debtor or an appointed trustee) may file a motion for valuation of collateral at any time during a bankruptcy case. A copy of the motion must be served by first-class mail or any other method allowed for service of process in federal district court on the debtor, any trustee or standing trustee, all committee(s), and any other entity required by court order or local bankruptcy rules. The motion does not commence an adversary proceeding and no filing fee is required, unless the basis, extent, validity, or priority of the lien is at issue. If the basis, extent, validity, or priority of the lien is an issue raised by the creditor, the motion will commence an adversary proceeding. The creditor must then pay a $120 filing fee and serve a copy of the motion with a summons on the debtor by first-class mail or any other manner allowed for service of process in federal district court. If a trustee or DIP files such motion, the filing fee will only be payable from any estate that may exist. No filing fee is required if a Chapter 7 or 13 debtor files such motion. *11 USC §§323(a), 506(a), 701-702, 1101(1), 1102-1104, 1107, 1202(b)(3), 1302(b)(2); 28 USC §1930(b); Judicial Conference Schedule of Fees (6); FRBP 3012, advisory committee's note; FRBP 7001(2), 7004 et seq, 9013-9014; Procedural Bankr Forms B 250A, B, C.*

The court must hold a hearing on a motion for valuation of collateral. The clerk, creditor filing the motion, or other court-authorized person must mail notice of the hearing date to the debtor, any trustee or standing trustee, all committee(s), and to any other person required by court order or local bankruptcy rules. *11 USC §§102(1)(A)-(B), 506(a); FRBP 3012, 9007, 9013-9014.*

G. Right to Perfect a Security Interest or Reclaim Property Post-Petition

A creditor may exercise a right available under applicable nonbankruptcy law to perfect a purchase-money security interest that relates back to an earlier date. This right may be exercised even though the debtor has filed a bankruptcy petition. *See "Restrictions on Trustee's Super-Avoiding Powers," Chapter XII; 11 USC §§362(b)(3), 546(b).*

A creditor may also exercise a nonbankruptcy right to reclaim goods sold to the debtor in the ordinary course of the seller's business if the debtor received such goods while insolvent. The creditor must file a motion for relief from automatic stay with a written demand for reclamation and serve both on the debtor before the tenth day after the debtor received the goods. Service may be obtained by first-class mail or any other manner allowed for service of process in federal district court. A $60 filing fee is required. The court may not deny the creditor's right to reclaim goods post-petition unless the court grants the creditor a first priority administrative claim or a lien to secure the creditor's allowed claim. *See "Restrictions on Trustee's Super-Avoiding Powers," Chapter XII; 11 USC §546(c); 28 USC §1930(b), Judicial Conference Schedule of Fees (21); FRBP 4001, 7004, 9013-9014.*

H. Creditors' Committee(s)

The unsecured creditors' committee is a fiduciary body which can wield much power under Chapters 9 and 11 cases. The committee has the statutory right to investigate the debtor, consult with the debtor on his business and financial affairs, and participate in the *formulation* (writing) of the plan. The committee may also seek appointment of a trustee or examiner if the debtor has grossly mismanaged his financial affairs or misrepresented to the committee under a Chapter 11 case. *See "Procedure Three—Selection of Unsecured Creditors' Committee," Chapter IV; 11 USC §§103(a), (e)-(f), 901, 1102-1103.*

I. Assumption or Rejection of Executory Contracts and Unexpired Leases

1. Generally

Executory contracts, where one or more parties must perform obligations in the future, and unexpired leases receive special treatment under bankruptcy law. As a general rule, the trustee or Chapter 9, 11, 12, or 13 debtor has the right, subject to the requirements of bankruptcy law and court approval, to reject, assume, or assign an executory contract or unexpired lease. This right exists even if the pre-petition contract contains an ipso facto or bankruptcy clause which states that the nonbankruptcy party may terminate the agreement in the event of the debtor's bankruptcy, insolvency, or other specified financial condition. Subject to court approval, the trustee or debtor may reject, assume, or assign an executory contract or unexpired lease directly or as part of a plan. The nonbankruptcy party to the executory contract or unexpired lease may not thereafter terminate or modify the contract or lease because it was assumed or assigned under a bankruptcy case. *11 USC §§365(b)(2), (e)(1), (f)(3), 901, 1101(1), 1123(b)(2), 1129(a)(13), 1222(b)(6), 1322(b)(7); FRBP 6006.*

2. Restrictions on Trustee's Powers—What Contracts and Leases Cannot Be Assumed or Assigned

The trustee or Chapter 9, 11, 12, or 13 debtor may not assume or assign an executory contract or unexpired lease if:

a. Applicable nonbankruptcy law (other than an ipso facto or bankruptcy clause in the contract or lease) excuses the nonbankruptcy party from accepting or rendering performance with regard to any other entity except the debtor, and the nonbankruptcy party opposes the assumption or assignment. *11 USC §365(c)(1)(A);*

b. The executory contract is to extend a loan, debt financing, or other financial arrangement for the debtor's benefit, or to issue a security of the debtor. This restriction is intended to prevent forcing the nonbankruptcy party to make new loans or new advances of money or other property. The trustee or debtor may use and pay for property already advanced under the contract. But executory contracts for loan commitments and letters of credit may not be assumed or assigned. *11 USC §365(c)(2); HR Rep No 595, 95th Cong, 1st Sess 348 (1977); S Rep No 989, 95th Cong, 2d Sess 59 (1978);*

c. The unexpired lease is for nonresidential (commercial) real property and the lease was terminated prepetition under applicable nonbankruptcy law. *11 USC §365(c)(3);*

d. The unexpired lease is for nonresidential real estate in which the debtor is an affected air-carrier-lessee of an aircraft terminal or gate where:

   (1) the debtor has entered into more than one of such unexpired leases at the airport, and

   (2) the trustee or debtor either does not assume all of the leases or does not assume and assign all such leases to the same person.

   However, the airport operator may sign a written consent waiving this all-or-nothing requirement. An *affected air carrier* is an air carrier, as defined under the Federal Aviation Act of 1958, who leases or otherwise holds at least 65 per cent of the number of aircraft gates at an airport which is a large air traffic hub (defined by FAA Report "FAA-AP 92-1") and which had all of its remaining gates leased or under contract on September 3, 1992. *See FAA Report, FAA-AP 92-1, Feb 1992, defining "Large Airport Traffic Hub"; Rail Safety Enforcement and Review Act, §19, Pub L No 102-365, 106 Stat 972 (1992), amending and adding 11 USC §365(c)(4), (p), effective for cases pending during the 12-month period beginning Sept 3, 1992;* or

e. The unexpired lease is for nonresidential real estate in which the debtor is an affected air-carrier-lessee of an aircraft terminal or gate and a termination event has occurred. Such lease may be assumed but not assigned. A *termination event* occurs if:

   (1) the debtor-air-carrier files a voluntary Chapter 7 petition;

   (2) the debtor-air-carrier's bankruptcy case is converted to Chapter 7; or

   (3) the automatic stay in the debtor-air-carrier's case is lifted with regard to essential aircraft or its parts (as defined under §101 of the Federal Aviation Act of 1958, 49 USC §1301) needed for the debtor's successful reorganization.

   See Rail Safety Enforcement and Review Act, §19, Pub L No 102-365, 106 Stat 972 (1992), amending 11 USC §365(d)(f), and adding §365(d)(6), effective for cases pending during the 12-month period beginning Sept 3, 1992.

3. When the Trustee or Debtor Must Assume or Reject

a. Residential Real Estate and Personal Property

(1) Chapter 7 Case

If the Chapter 7 trustee does not assume or reject an executory contract or unexpired lease of the debtor's residential real property or personal property before the 60th day after the voluntary Chapter 7 petition is filed or the order for relief in an involuntary case, or by any extension of time that the court may grant, the contract or lease is deemed rejected. The trustee must file a motion to extend time before the 60th day and show just cause for an extension of the 60-day period. *11 USC §365(d)(1); FRBP 6006, 9006(b), 9014; see "Procedures to Assume, Assign, or Reject an Executory Contract or Unexpired Lease," discussed below.*

(2) Chapters 9, 11, 12, and 13 Cases

The trustee or debtor may assume or reject an executory contract or unexpired lease of residential real property or personal property any time before the plan is confirmed, unless the court orders otherwise. The debtor may assume or reject directly or through a plan for confirmation by the court. However, a nonbankruptcy party to the executory contract or unexpired lease of residential real estate or personal property may file a motion to compel the trustee or debtor to assume or reject the contract or lease by a specified date. *See "Procedures to Assume, Assign, or Reject an Executory Contract or Unexpired Lease," discussed below; 11 USC §365(d)(2); FRBP 6006, 9013-9014.*

b. Performance of Post-Petition Obligations Under Commercial Leases of Personal Property

Until a commercial lease of personal property is assumed or rejected in a Chapters 11 case or the court orders otherwise, the trustee or debtor-in-possession (DIP) must perform all post-petition obligations of the debtor-lessee under the unexpired lease that first arise 60 days or more after the voluntary petition is filed or order for relief is entered in an involuntary Chapter 11 case. However, the trustee or DIP does not have to perform obligations under an ipso facto or bankruptcy clause of the lease relating to the debtor's insolvency, bankruptcy, financial condition, or satisfaction of a penalty provision relating to the debtor's default on a non-monetary obligation. The lessor's acceptance of the debtor's post-petition obligations is not a waiver of the lessor's rights under the lease or bankruptcy law, including the right to object to the trustee's or debtor's assumption of the lease. *11 USC §365(b)(2)(d)(10).*

If the equities of the case so warrant, the court may order that the trustee or DIP is excused from performance of post-petition obligations until the lease is assumed. Before making such a decision, the court must give notice and opportunity for a hearing to the lessor, debtor, creditors' committee, and all other parties-in-interest required by court order or local bankruptcy rules. *11 USC §§102(1)(A-B), 103(a), 365(b)(d)(10), (f); FRBP 6006.*

c. Nonresidential (Commercial) Real Property

(1) If the debtor is the lessee of an unexpired lease of nonresidential real estate, the trustee or Chapter 9, 11, 12, or 13 debtor must assume or reject the lease before the 60th day after the order for relief under Chapter 7, 9, 11, 12, or 13 or the lease is deemed rejected and the trustee or debtor must immediately surrender the property to the lessor. The trustee or debtor may obtain an order extending such 60-day period, for cause, by filing a motion to extend time before the 60th day after the order for relief. Grounds for such extension of time should be clearly stated in the motion. *11 USC §365(d)(4); FRBP 6006, 9006(b), 9013-9014.*

(2) The Bankruptcy Code does not set a specific time limit for the trustee or debtor to assume or reject an executory contract or an unexpired lease of nonresidential real property where the debtor is the lessor. In Chapter 9, 11, 12, or 13 cases, the debtor may assume or reject such property under a plan for confirmation by the court. However, the nonbankruptcy party to the executory contract or unexpired lease may file a motion to compel the Chapter 7 trustee or proponent of a Chapter 9, 11, 12, or 13 plan to assume or reject by a specified date. *11 USC §§103(a), (e), 365(d), 901, 1123(b)(2), 1222(b)(6), 1322(b)(7); FRBP 6006(b), 9013-9014; see "Procedures to Assume, Assign, or Reject an Executory Contract or Unexpired Lease," discussed below.*

(3) Performance of Post-Petition Obligations

Until the lease is assumed or rejected, the trustee or debtor must perform all post-petition obligations of the debtor as lessee under an unexpired lease of nonresidential real property (except obligations under an ipso facto or bankruptcy clause of the lease relating to the debtor's insolvency, bankruptcy, financial condition, or obligations to satisfy a penalty provision relating to the debtor's failure to perform a nonmonetary obligation). The court may extend the time for performing post-petition obligations until the 60th day after the order for relief if a timely motion to extend time to perform obligations is filed by the trustee or debtor before the 60th day. After this date, all post-petition obligations must be timely performed. Failure to honor post-petition rental payments or other obligations may create a first priority administrative claim against the estate if the lease is assumed or may be grounds for the court to: (a) deny the trustee's or debtor's assumption of the lease, or (b) dismiss the debtor's case. The lessor's acceptance of the debtor's post-petition obligations is not a waiver of any right to object to assumption or of any other right of the lessor under the lease or Bankruptcy Code. *11 USC §§103(a), (e), 365(d)(3), (g), 502(g), 503(b)(1), 507(a)(1), 901, 930, 1112(b), 1208(b), 1307(c); see NLRB v Bildisco & Bildisco, 465 US 513 (1984).*

d. Nonresidential Real Property Involving Airport Leases

Congress has limited the rights of a debtor who is an affected air-carrier-lessee under an unexpired lease of nonresidential real estate to assume or assign the lease of an aircraft terminal or gate. The occurrence of a termination event prevents assignment and, in certain instances, triggers an automatic or deemed rejection of the lease. *See Rail Safety Enforcement and Review Act, §19, Pub L No 102-365, 106 Stat 972 (1992), amending and adding 11 USC §365(c)(4), (d)(5)-(9), (f)(1), (p).*

(1) Who Is an Affected Air-Carrier-Lessee

To be an affected air-carrier-lessee, three requirements must be met:

(a) The bankruptcy debtor must be an air carrier as defined under §101(3), Federal Aviation Act of 1958, 49 United States Code;

(b) The debtor-air-carrier must have leased at least 65 per cent of the number of the aircraft gates at an airport that is a large air traffic hub as defined by the Federal Aviation Administration's Report "FAA-AP 92-1," February 1992; and

(c) All of such airport's remaining gates must have been either leased or under contract on September 3, 1992. *See Rail Safety Enforcement and Review Act, §19, Pub L No 102-365, 106 Stat 972 (1992), adding 11 USC §365(p).*

(2) When a Termination Event Occurs

A termination event occurs with regard to a debtor who is an affected air-carrier-lessee of an aircraft terminal or gate if:

(a) The debtor-air-carrier files a voluntary Chapter 7 petition; or

(b) The debtor-air-carrier's bankruptcy case is converted to Chapter 7; or

(c) The automatic stay is lifted with regard to certain essential aircraft, aircraft engines, propellers, appliances, or spare parts as defined by §101, Federal Aviation Act of 1958, 49 USC §1301 *et seq.*

If the court finds that any of such property is not necessary to the debtor's effective reorganization, lifting of the automatic stay is not a termination event. *See "Relief from Stay Against a Chapter 11 Air Carrier or Water Carrier Debtor," discussed above; Rail Safety Enforcement and Review Act, §19, Pub L No 102-365, 106 Stat 972 (1992), amending and adding 11 USC §365(d)(6).*

(3) Effect of a Termination Event

The occurrence of a termination event for a debtor who is an affected air-carrier-lessee will:

(a) Prevent assignment of the unexpired lease of an aircraft terminal or gate by the debtor or any appointed trustee; and

(b) Trigger an automatic or deemed rejection of such lease, at the option of the airport operator, on the fifth day after the termination event occurs unless:

(i) The debtor or trustee assumed the unexpired lease before the termination event occurred; or

(ii) The court orders the trustee or debtor to assume the unexpired lease before the fifth day after the termination event occurs; or

(iii) The airport operator under the unexpired lease chooses, at its option, not to have the lease deemed rejected; or

(iv) The airport operator has not first waived its right to file a proof of claim or otherwise assert any damages against the estate or debtor resulting from a deemed rejection of the lease. *See Rail Safety Enforcement and Review Act, §19, Pub L No 102-365, 106 Stat 972 (1992), amending and adding 11 USC §365(d)(5)-(6), (f)(1).*

If the lease is deemed rejected, the debtor-air-carrier must immediately surrender possession of the premises to the airport operator. However, the airport operator must provide the debtor-air-carrier adequate opportunity to remove any fixtures and equipment installed by the debtor. *See Rail Safety Enforcement and Review Act, Pub L No 102-365, 106 Stat 972 (1992), amending and adding 11 USC §365(d) (5)-(6).*

(4) If No Termination Event Occurs

If a termination event does not occur, the trustee or debtor-air-carrier-lessee (DIP) must assume the unexpired lease of an aircraft terminal or gate before the 60th day after the date of filing a voluntary Chapter 11 petition or the order for relief in an involuntary Chapter 11 case, or such lease is deemed rejected. However, the trustee or DIP may file a motion to extend time to assume or reject the unexpired lease before the 60th day, showing cause for the court to extend the 60-day period. The court must then consider all relevant facts, including whether granting an extension will result in substantial harm to either the airport operator under the unexpired lease or to airline passengers. Factors relevant to determining *substantial harm* include:

(a) The level of actual use of the aircraft terminals and gates at issue;

(b) The public interest in the actual use of such terminals or gates;

(c) The effect of the court's decision to extend or reduce the time for assumption or rejection of the lease on the debtor's ability to successfully reorganize;

(d) The existence of any competing demands to use the terminals or gates; and

(e) Whether the trustee or DIP is capable of continuing to perform all post-petition obligations under the unexpired lease of aircraft terminals or gates until the lease is assumed or rejected.

The trustee or debtor must begin performing such post-petition obligations no later than the 60th day after a voluntary petition is filed or the order for relief in an involuntary Chapter 11 case. All unpaid post-petition obligations of the trustee or debtor may give rise to a first priority claim for administrative expenses by the lessor if the lease is assumed. *11 USC §§365(d)(3)-(4), (g), 502(g), 503(b), 507(a)(1); see NLRB v Bildisco & Bildisco, 465 US 513 (1984); Rail Safety Enforcement and Review Act, §19, Pub L No 102-365, 106 Stat 972 (1992), amending and adding 11 USC §365(d)(7)-(9); "Nonresidential (Commercial) Real Property—Performance of Post-Petition Obligations," discussed above.*

The trustee or DIP has the burden of proving cause exists for extending the 60-day period to assume or reject the unexpired lease. The trustee or debtor may seek more than one extension of time, if cause is shown. However, the lessor or any other party-in-interest (creditor, creditors' committee, or U.S. trustee) may file a motion to reduce such time at any stage of the debtor-air-carrier's bankruptcy case. *See Rail Safety Enforcement and Review Act, §19, Pub L No 102-365, 106 Stat 972 (1992), amending and adding 11 USC §365(d)(5)-(9)(P).*

d. FDIC/RTC and Other Government Commitments of Chapter 11 Debtor

(1) Automatic Assumption

In a Chapter 11 case, the DIP or trustee is deemed to have assumed any commitment made by the debtor to maintain the capital of an insured depository institution. The commitment must be to a federal depository institution's regulatory agency or to such agency's predecessor. Thus, in the usual Chapter 11 case, a DIP or proponent of a plan has until confirmation of the plan to decide to assume or reject an executory contract that does not involve commercial real estate. However, if the executory contract involves the debtor's commitment to maintain the capital of an insured depository institution to any of the above governmental entities, the Chapter 11 debtor or trustee is forced by operation of bankruptcy law to assume such commitments. This forced assumption presumably occurs as of the date of filing a voluntary petition or order for relief in an involuntary Chapter 11 case. *11 USC §365(o).*

(2) Immediate Cure of Deficits

The Chapter 11 debtor with a capital-maintenance commitment to the above governmental entities must immediately cure any (pre- or post-petition) deficit under such commitment. *11 USC §365(o).*

(a) Post-Petition Breach of Commitment

A claim for a post-petition breach of the debtor's commitment to maintain the capital of an insured depository institution to any of the above governmental entities may be entitled to first priority status. Since the obligations are deemed to be assumed by the debtor post-petition, they become administrative expenses which must be timely paid according to the terms of the pre-petition commitment agreement. The governmental entity may file a motion for allowance of administrative expenses for any unpaid post-petition claim. A timely proof of claim should also be filed in the debtor's Chapter 11 case by the date set by the court. Notice of the date to file proofs of claims must be mailed by the clerk or other court-authorized person to the debtor, any trustee, all creditors, committee(s), indenture trustees, to the SEC in Washington, D.C., the District Director of the IRS where the Chapter 11 case is pending, and to any other entity required by court order or local bankruptcy rules. Such notice may be included in the notice of approval of disclosure statement. However, a minimum of 20 days' notice by mail must be given of the date to file proofs of claims in the Chapter 11 case. *See NLRB v Bildisco & Bildisco, 465 US 513 (1984); 11 USC §§103(a), 365(g), (o), 502(g), 503(b)(1), 507(a)(1); FRBP 2002(a)(8), (b), (f)(3), (i)-(j), 3002(c), 3003(c), 3017(d); "File Proof of Claim—When to File," discussed above; "Procedure Seven—Confirmation of a Plan of Reorganization," Chapter IV.*

(b) Unpaid Pre-Petition Commitment Payments

(i) Eighth Priority Claim

Any pre-petition deficit in a capital-maintenance commitment which remains unpaid by a Chapter 7, 12, or 13 debtor may give rise to an eighth priority claim of the governmental institution, if allowed by the court. *See "Priority Claims," Chapter II; 11 USC §§365(o), 507(a)(8).*

(ii) Nondischargeable Debts

The malicious or reckless failure of an individual debtor to fulfill any commitment to a federal depository institution's regulatory agency to maintain the capital of an insured depository institution is a nondischargeable debt under Chapters 7, 11, and 12, and under a Chapter 13 hardship discharge. Further, a debt evidenced by a final court order, consent decree, or settlement agreement between an individual debtor and a federal depository institution's regulatory agency concerning the debtor's fraud or defalcation while a fiduciary to any depository institution or insured credit union is also nondischargeable under Chapters 7, 11, and 12, and under a Chapter 13 hardship discharge. *See "Exceptions to Discharge," Chapter III. 11 USC §§103(a), 523(a)(11)-(12), 1141(d)(2), 1228(a)(2), 1328(b)-(c).*

(3) Capital-Maintenance Commitment Not Extended

The Bankruptcy Code's protection of capital-maintenance commitments for federal insured depository institutions does not extend any commitment that would otherwise be terminated by any act of the FDIC, RTC, Director of the Office of Thrift Supervision, Comptroller of the Currency, or Board of

Governors of the Federal Reserve System. *11 USC §§365(o), 523(a)(12).*

4. Requirements to Assume or Assign

The trustee or Chapter 9, 11, 12, or 13 debtor may assume or assign an executory contract or unexpired lease as part of the administration of the debtor's case or under a plan. However, strict requirements must be followed.

a. Assumption

The court must approve any assumption, assignment, or rejection of an executory contract or unexpired lease (*see "Procedures to Assume, Assign, or Reject an Executory Contract or Unexpired Lease," discussed below*). However, if there has been any default by the trustee or debtor under an executory contract or unexpired lease, such contract or lease may not be assumed unless the trustee or debtor meets the following requirements at the time of assumption. The trustee or debtor must:

(1) **Cure all pre- and/or post-petition default(s), or provide adequate assurance that such default(s) will be promptly cured.**

However, defaults relating to a penalty provision from the debtor's failure to perform a nonmonetary obligation or to an ipso facto or bankruptcy clause concerning the debtor's insolvency, financial condition, or bankruptcy do not have to be cured;

(2) **Compensate the nonbankruptcy party for any actual monetary damages resulting from all such default(s) or provide adequate assurance that the nonbankruptcy party will be promptly compensated; and**

(3) **Provide adequate assurance of future performance under the contract or lease.**

The trustee or debtor must show good cause for any post-petition defaults in payments or other obligations under an unexpired lease or executory contract and show why such defaults will not continue to occur in the future. *11 USC §365(b)(1)-(3).*

If the trustee or debtor assumes an unexpired lease of real property in a shopping center, adequate assurance of future performance must include five requirements:

(a) Adequate assurance of the source of future rent and any other consideration required by the unexpired lease;

(b) Adequate assurance that any percentage rent due under the lease will not substantially decline after the lease is assumed or assigned;

(c) Adequate assurance that the assumption or assignment of the lease will be conditioned upon all provisions of the lease remaining in effect (including the use, radius, location, or any right of exclusivity);

(d) Adequate assurance that assumption or assignment of the lease will not breach any provision of another lease, financing agreement, or master agreement relating to the shopping center; and

(e) Adequate assurance that assumption or assignment of the lease will not disrupt any tenant mix or balance in the shopping center. *11 USC §365(b)(1), (3), (f)(2)(B).*

b. Assignment

The trustee or debtor may assign an executory contract or unexpired lease only if:

(1) The trustee or debtor first assumes the contract or lease, which requires curing all default(s), compensating for actual monetary losses from such default(s), and adequate assurance of future performance. *See discussion above;*

(2) The assignee provides adequate assurance of future performance of the contract or lease which is to be assigned, even if there was no default by the debtor under such contract or lease. If an unexpired lease of real property in a shopping center is assigned, adequate assurance of future performance must include the five requirements for assumption of such a lease outlined above plus adequate assurance that the financial condition and operating performance of the assignee and any of its guarantors are similar to the financial condition and operating performance of the debtor and any of his guarantors that existed when the debtor first became the lessee; and

(3) If the assignee will be the lessee, the lessor may demand that such assignee must pay substantially the same deposit or other security required for performance under the assigned lease which the lessor would have required under an original lease to a similar tenant. *11 USC §365(b)(3), (f)(1)-(2), (l).*

c. Payment for Lessor's Services and Supplies Before Assumption and Assignment

If the debtor-lessee has defaulted under an unexpired lease which is to be assumed or assigned (except defaults under a penalty provision relating to the debtor's nonperformance of a nonmonetary obligation or defaults under an ipso facto or bankruptcy clause relating to the debtor's insolvency, bankruptcy, or financial condition), the nonbankruptcy lessor does not have to provide postpetition services or supplies incidental to the lease before it is assumed unless the lessor is fully compensated under the existing terms of the lease for all services or supplies furnished before assumption. *11 USC §365(b)(2), (4).*

5. Procedures to Assume, Assign, or Reject an Executory Contract or Unexpired Lease

a. Generally

The trustee or Chapter 9, 11, 12, or 13 debtor must assume, assign, or reject an executory contract or unexpired lease within any time periods required by the Code (*see "When the Trustee or Debtor Must Assume or Reject,"* discussed above). If assumption, assignment, or rejection occurs under a Chapter 9, 11, 12, or 13 plan, no formal procedures are required beyond compliance with requirements for confirmation of the plan. *See "Requirements for Confirmation" of a Chapter [9, 11, or 13] Plan, Chapters IV, V, and VII; "Chapter 12 Plan of Adjustment," Chapter VI; FRBP 6006(a).*

The Chapter 7 trustee, and the Chapter 9, 11, 12, or 13 debtor who wishes to assume, assign, or reject an executory contract or unexpired lease that is not part of a plan must file a motion to assume, assign, or reject. The motion must be served on all parties to the executory contract or unexpired lease, any trustee, committee(s), and on such other entities as required by court order or local bankruptcy rules. The motion may be served by first-class mail or any other manner allowed for service of a summons and complaint in federal district court. The motion does not commence an adversary proceeding and no filing fee is required. No response or answer to the motion is required unless a court order or local bankruptcy rules state otherwise. *11 USC §365; FRBP 6006(a), 9014; see Local Bankruptcy Rules.*

b. Compelled Proceeding

A nonbankruptcy party to an executory contract or unexpired lease may file a motion to compel the trustee or debtor to assume, assign, or reject an executory contract or unexpired lease. The motion must be served by first-class mail or any other manner allowed for service of process in federal district court on the debtor, any trustee, all committee(s), and all other entities required by court order or local bankruptcy rules. No filing fee is required. No response or answer is required by the trustee or debtor, unless a court order or local bankruptcy rules state otherwise. *11 USC §365(d)(2); FRBP 6006(b), 7004, 9013-9014.*

c. Notice and Hearing

The court must hold a hearing if either the trustee or debtor files a motion to assume, assign, or reject other than as part of a plan or if a nonbankruptcy party to an executory contract or unexpired lease files a motion to compel assumption, assignment, or rejection. Prior notice of the hearing date must be mailed to all parties to the contract or lease, the debtor, any trustee, all committee(s), the U.S. trustee (except under Chapter 9), and to all other entities as required by court order or local bankruptcy rules. *11 USC §102(1)(A)-(B); FRBP 6006(c), 9007, 9014.*

6. Rights of the Nonbankruptcy Party After Rejection

a. Generally

If a trustee or debtor rejects an executory contract or unexpired lease that has not been assumed, the nonbankruptcy party is treated as having a pre-petition claim that arose immediately before the petition was filed, even though the rejection occurred post-petition. The nonbankruptcy party must file a proof of claim by the date set by the court. The clerk or other court-authorized person must mail notice of such date to the debtor, any trustee, all creditors, indenture trustees, and to any entity required by court order or local bankruptcy rules. Under bankruptcy law, a nonbankruptcy purchaser of real property or a timeshare interest who treates a rejected executory contract or timeshare plan as terminated and does not occupy the premises has a lien on the debtor's interest in such property to recover any portion of the purchase price paid (*see* discussion below). *11 USC §§348(d), 365(g)(1), (j), 501, 502(g); FRBP 2002(a)(8), (f)(3), (i)-(j), 3001(c)-(d), 3002(c)(4), 3003(c)(3); see "File Proof of Claim," discussed above.*

If an executory contract or unexpired lease is assumed and thereafter rejected, and the case is converted to Chapter 7, the debtor must file a schedule of unpaid debts listing the claim of the nonbankruptcy party to the rejected contract or lease. Such claim may be treated like a post-petition administrative claim entitled to first priority status. The nonbankruptcy party should file a motion for allowance of administrative expenses. He should also file a timely proof of claim before the 90th day after the first date set for the meeting of creditors under the converted Chapter 7 case, or by any other date fixed by the court or local bankruptcy rules. The clerk of the court must mail notice of the conversion of the case and date to file proofs of claims in the converted case. Such notice must be sent to the debtor, all creditors, any trustee, the U.S. trustee, all committee(s), indenture trustees, and any other entity required by court order or local bankruptcy rules. *11 USC §§103(a), 307, 365(g), 502(2); FRBP 1019(1)-(5), 2002(a)(8), (f)(2)-(3), (i), (k), 3002(c)(4), 9034; see NLRB v Bildisco & Bildisco, 465 US 513 (1984).*

An executory contract or unexpired lease assumed before a case is converted to Chapter 7 that is subsequently rejected is deemed rejected under the superseded (Chapter 11, 12, or 13) case immediately before the date of conversion. It does not matter if the rejection occurred after the date of conversion. Thus, any first priority claim which the nonbankruptcy party may assert may also be deemed to have arisen under the superseded Chapter 11, 12, or 13 case. And first priority claims which arise under a superseded case are subordinated to and receive payment after first priority claims that arise in the converted Chapter 7 case. *See NLRB v Bildisco & Bildisco, 465 US 513 (1984); 11 USC §§365(g)(2)(B), (i), 502(g), 503(b)(1), 507(a)(1), 726(b); FRBP 2002(f)(2)-(3), 3001-3002; "File Proof of Claim," discussed above.*

b. Rejection of an Unexpired Lease of Land by Debtor-Lessor

If the trustee or debtor rejects an unexpired lease of land where the debtor is the lessor, the nonbankruptcy lessee (including any assignee, mortgagee, or successor-in-interest permitted under the lease) who is in possession of the property has two options.

(1) Option 1

The nonbankruptcy lessee may treat the lease as terminated and vacate the premises, if the rejection would constitute a breach permitting termination under the terms of the lease, any agreement by the lessee, or applicable nonbankruptcy law. The lessee may then file a timely proof of claim by the date set by the court, claiming any damages resulting from the debtor's breach (rejection) of the lease. Such damage claims will be treated as if they arose pre-petition. *See "File Proof of Claim—When to File," discussed above; 11 USC §§365(g)-(h)(1), 502(g); FRBP 2002(a)(8), (f)(3), (i)-(j), 3001, 3002(a), (c)(4).*

(2) Option 2

The lessee may remain in possession of the premises, even after the lease is rejected, and exercise all rights for the remaining term of the lease plus any renewal or extension period provided by the lease and enforceable under applicable nonbankruptcy law. Such rights include those relating to the amount and time of rental and other payments and to the use, possession, quiet enjoyment, subletting, assignment, or hypothecation of the lease. The lessee may also offset or deduct from the remaining rental payments any damages suffered if the debtor fails to perform his obligations as lessor after the date of rejection. But the lessee may not file a proof of claim and has no further legal rights against the estate for any damages suffered after rejection of the lease if the lessee elects to remain in possession and offset damages. The lessee in possession of property should file a motion for relief from the automatic stay asserting his right, under the Bankruptcy Code, to a post-petition setoff of rental payments owed to the debtor against any post-petition damages from the rejection. *11 USC §§362(a)(3), (d)(1), 365(g), (h)(1)-(2), 502(g), 549,*

553; FRBP 4001, 9014; see "Avoidable Unauthorized Post-Petition Transfers," and "Avoidable Setoffs," Chapter XII.

Any provision in a lease of real property in a shopping center relating to radius, location, use, exclusivity, or tenant mix or balance may be enforced under applicable nonbankruptcy law if the lessee elects to remain in possession of the property. The trustee's or debtor's rejection of the lease will not affect the enforceability of such provisions. *11 USC §365(h)(1)(C).*

c. Rejection of Executory Contract for Sale of Land or Timeshare Interest by Debtor-Seller

(1) Purchaser in Possession

If the trustee or debtor rejects an executory contract for the sale of real property or a timeshare interest under a timeshare plan after the purchaser is in possession, the purchaser has two options.

(a) Option 1

The purchaser may treat the sale of land or timeshare interest as terminated and vacate the premises. The purchaser will then have a lien on the debtor's interest in the real estate to secure payment from the estate of any purchase price paid to the debtor before the date of rejection. The purchaser must file a timely proof of claim with the original or a copy of the sales contract and all other documents relating to the sale of land or timeshare interest. The court will set the date to file such claims. The clerk of the court must mail notice of the date to file proofs of claims to the debtor, any trustee, all committee(s), indenture trustees, to the SEC in Washington, D.C., and District Director of the IRS where a Chapter 11 case is pending, and to all other entities required by court order or local bankruptcy rules. Such claim will be treated as if it arose pre-petition. *See "File Proof of Claim," discussed above. 11 USC §§365(g), (h)(1), (i)(1), (j), 501, 502(g); FRBP 2002(a)(8), (f)(3), (i)-(j), 3001(c), 3002(c)(4), 3003(c).*

(b) Option 2

The purchaser may remain in possession of the realty and continue to make all payments due under the rejected contract or timeshare plan. However, the purchaser may offset or deduct from future payments any post-petition damages suffered if the debtor fails to perform contractual obligations after the date of rejection. But the purchaser may not file a proof of claim seeking any recovery for damages or any other claims against the estate if he elects to remain in possession and offset damages. The trustee or debtor must deliver title to the premises to the nonbankruptcy party according to the terms of the sales contract or timeshare plan. The purchaser in possession of property should also file a motion for relief from the automatic stay asserting his bankruptcy law right to a post-petition setoff of future payments against damages suffered from the rejection. *11 USC §§362(a)(3), (d)(1), 365(g), (h)(1)-(2), 502(g), 549, 553; FRBP 4001, 9014; see "Motion for Relief from Automatic Stay," discussed above; "Avoidable Unauthorized Post-Petition Transfers," and "Avoidable Setoffs," Chapter XII.*

(2) Purchaser Not in Possession

If the trustee or debtor rejects an executory contract for the sale of real property or a timeshare interest and the purchaser is not in possession, the purchaser has a claim against the estate for any damages suffered and will have a lien on the debtor's interest in the realty for the amount of the purchase price paid before the date of rejection. The purchaser must file a timely proof of claim by the date set by the court and attach the original or copies of all relevant documents. *11 USC §§365(g), (j), 501, 502(g); FRBP 2002(a)(8), (f)(3), (i), 3001(c), 3002(c)(4), 3003(c).*

d. Claims of Nonbankruptcy Lessor Under Rejected Lease

If the debtor as lessee rejects an unexpired lease that was never assumed in the case, the nonbankruptcy lessor may file a timely proof of claim by the date set by the court claiming any damages suffered by the breach (rejection) of lease. Such damage claims are treated as if they arose pre-petition. However, the amount of the lessor's unsecured claims is limited to:

(1) The rent stated under the lease for the greater amount of one year's rent or 15 per cent of the next three year's remaining term under the lease, without acceleration, beginning on the earlier date that the petition was filed or the leased premises were surrendered by the debtor or repossessed by the lessor; plus

(2) The amount of unpaid rent, without acceleration, owed to the lessor on the earlier date that the petition was filed or the leased premises were surrendered or repossessed. *11 USC §§365(g), 502(b)(6), (g); FRBP 3001, 3002(c)(4), 3003(c).*

e. Rights to Intellectual Property of Licensee Under Rejected License Agreement

(1) Before Rejection

The trustee or debtor may reject an executory contract in which the debtor is the licensor of rights to intellectual property. But before rejection and on written request of the licensee, the trustee or debtor must:

(a) (i) Fully perform under the contract or any supplementary agreement; or

(ii) Provide the licensee with the intellectual property, including any right to embodiment of such property to the extent protected by applicable nonbankruptcy law; and

(b) Not interfere with the rights of the licensee to intellectual property (including any embodiment of such property) as provided under the contract or any supplementary agreement, including the right to obtain the intellectual property or its embodiment from another entity. *11 USC §365(n)(4).*

(2) After Rejection

After the trustee or debtor rejects an executory contract where the debtor is the licensor of rights to intellectual property, the licensee then has two options.

(a) Option 1

The licensee may treat the license agreement as terminated if rejection by the debtor or trustee would give the licensee the right to treat the agreement as terminated under applicable nonbankruptcy law, the terms of the license agreement itself, or any other agreement between the licensee and another entity. The licensee may file a timely proof of claim for any damages suffered as a result of the rejection, including claims for any pre- or post-petition payments made under the agreement before rejection. The clerk must mail notice of the date set by the court to file such proofs of claims to the debtor, any trustee, all creditors, indenture trustees, committee(s), to the SEC in Washington, DC, and the District Director of the IRS where the case is pending in a Chapter 11 case, and to any other entity required by court order or local bankruptcy rules. The damage claims of the licensee will be treated as if they arose pre-petition. *11 USC §§365(g), (n)(1)(A), 502(g); FRBP 2002(a)(8), (f)(3), (i)-(j), 3001(c), 3002(c)(4), 3003(c)(3).*

(b) Option 2

The licensee may retain its rights to intellectual property under the executory contract and any supplementary agreement to such contract, even though the contract was rejected by the trustee or debtor. Such rights include the right to enforce any exclusivity provision and any embodiment of intellectual property to the extent such rights existed pre-petition and are protected under applicable nonbankruptcy law. Upon written request from the licensee, the trustee must provide the licensee with any intellectual property, including any right to embodiment of such intellectual property protected by applicable nonbankruptcy law, to the extent required by the contract and any supplementary agreement. The trustee must not interfere with any contractual rights of the licensee to the intellectual property or its embodiment, including the right to obtain the intellectual property or its embodiment from another entity. However, the licensee's rights do not include any other right to specific performance that may be contained under the contract or any supplementary agreement. The licensee may exercise its rights for the remaining term of the pre-petition contract plus any extension allowed the licensee under applicable nonbankruptcy law. But the licensee must continue to make all royalty payments owed under the contract during such period (including any allowed extension) to the trustee, debtor, or any entity provided under a confirmed plan, depending on the particular bankruptcy case. *11 USC §365(n)(1)(A)-(B), (2)(A)-(B), (3)(A)-(B).*

Under Option 2, the licensee who elects to retain its rights to intellectual property under a rejected executory contract is deemed to have waived:

(i) Any right of setoff of a claim held against the debtor against a debt (royalty payments) owed to the debtor, whether such setoff rights would otherwise be allowed under bankruptcy or applicable nonbankruptcy law. *See "Avoidable Setoffs," Chapter XII;* and

(ii) Any first priority claim against the estate for administrative expenses which might otherwise be allowable under bankruptcy law from the licensee's continued performance under the agreement. The licensee may file a proof of claim asserting a general unsecured claim against the estate for any damages arising under the rejected contract. The original or a copy of the contract and all other relevant documents must be filed with the proof of claim. The clerk of the court must give notice of the date set by the court to file a proof of claim arising from rejection of the executory contract. Such notice must be mailed to the debtor, any trustee, all creditors, indenture trustees, committee(s), the SEC in

Washington, DC, and District Director of the IRS where the case is pending in a Chapter 11 case, and to any other entity required by court order or local bankruptcy rules. Such damage claims will be treated as if they arose pre-petition. *11 USC §§365(g)(1), (n)(1)(B), (2)(C), 501, 502(g), 503(b), 507(a)(1); FRBP 2002(a)(8), (f)(3), (i)-(j), 3001(c), 3002(c)(4), 3003(c).*

7. Legal Effect of Assumption, Assignment, or Rejection

a. Assumption

Unless the nonbankruptcy party agrees otherwise, a court-approved assumption of an executory contract or unexpired lease imposes the same pre-petition terms and obligations on the trustee, debtor, or proponent of a Chapter 9, 11, 12 or 13 plan. The obligations became first-priority administrative claims. The nonbankruptcy party to the assumed contract or lease may not terminate or modify the contract or lease because of its assumption (or assignment), even if the terms of the contract, lease, or applicable nonbankruptcy law state otherwise. *11 USC §365(a), (b)(1), (e)(1), (f)(1)-(3), 503(b), 507(a)(1); see NLRB v Bildisco & Bildisco, 465 US 513 (1984).*

b. Assignment

If the court authorizes assignment of an executory contract or unexpired lease, the trustee or debtor and the estate are relieved of all further liability under the contract or lease after the date of the assignment. If the assignee thereafter breaches the contract or lease, the nonbankruptcy party does not have any claim against the trustee, debtor, or estate. *11 USC §365(k).*

The nonbankruptcy party to the assigned contract or lease may not terminate or modify the contract or lease because of the assignment, even if the terms of such contract, lease, or applicable nonbankruptcy law state otherwise. *11 USC §365(f)(3).*

c. Rejection

Rejection of an executory contract or unexpired lease gives the nonbankruptcy party a claim against the estate, unless a nonbankruptcy purchaser or lessee elects to remain in possession of the debtor's real estate and exercise his setoff rights (*see discussion above*). The nonbankruptcy party may file a proof of claim by the date set by the court for filing claims arising from a rejection of an executory contract or unexpired lease. The clerk must mail notice of such date fixed by the court to the debtor, any trustee, all creditors, indenture trustees, committee(s), to the SEC in Washington, D.C., and District Director of the IRS where a Chapter 11 case is pending, and to any other entity required by court order or local bankruptcy rules. If the contract or lease was not previously assumed in the bankruptcy case, the claims of the nonbankruptcy party will be treated as if they arose pre-petition. *11 USC §§365(g), (h)(1)-(2), (i)(1)-(2), 502(g); FRBP 2002(a)(8), (f)(3), (i)-(j), 3001(c), 3002(a), (c)(4), 3003(c); see "Rights of the Nonbankruptcy Party After Rejection," discussed above.*

J. Assumption or Rejection of Collective Bargaining Agreements and Assumption or Modification of Retiree Benefits Under Chapter 11

Collective bargaining agreements and benefits to retired employees receive special protection under Chapter 11. Effective July 10, 1984, collective bargaining agreements may be assumed or rejected by the DIP or an appointed trustee if allowed by the court after good-faith negotiations fail. Effective June 16, 1988, programs providing benefits to retired employees and their spouses and dependents may be assumed or modified (reduced but not rejected) under bankruptcy law if there is mutual agreement for modification between the respective authorized representatives for the estate (DIP or trustee) and the retired employees; or if good-faith negotiations between such representatives fail and the court allows modifications. The DIP or trustee must follow strict procedures unique to Chapter 11 cases. General rules governing assumption or rejection of executory contracts under other bankruptcy cases do not apply. *11 USC §§1113-1114; see Pub L No 98-353, 98 Stat 333; and The Retiree Benefits Bankruptcy Protection Act of 1988, Pub L No 100-334, 102 Stat 610.*

1. Collective Bargaining Agreements

a. General Overview

The Chapter 11 DIP or trustee, if one has been appointed, may assume, modify, or reject a collective bargaining agreement. Rejection is permitted only if the court finds that: (1) good-faith negotiations between the DIP or trustee and employees' authorized representative failed because the employees' representative, without good cause, refused to accept the DIP's or trustee's proposal for necessary modifications; and (2) the "balance of the equities" of the case favors such rejection. Unilateral modification or rejection of a collective bargaining agreement by the DIP or trustee before negotiations is not allowed. *11 USC §1113(a)-(c), (f).*

b. Requirements to Modify or Reject a Collective Bargaining Agreement

The DIP or trustee must meet five requirements to modify or reject a collective bargaining agreement and proceed in the following order.

(1) Submit Written Proposal

The DIP or trustee must first submit a post-petition proposal of necessary modifications to the authorized representative of the employees covered by the collective bargaining agreement. The proposal must be based upon the most complete and reliable information then available to the parties. The proposal must include only those modifications to employee benefits and protections that: (a) are "necessary to permit the reorganization of the debtor" and (b) assure that all creditors, affected parties, and the debtor will be "treated fairly and equitably." The proposal must be served by first-class mail or any other method allowed for service of process in federal district court on the employees' authorized representative, any trustee (if the debtor submitted the proposal), the U.S. trustee, all committee(s), and all other entities required by court order or local bankruptcy rules. *11 USC §§103(a), 307, 1109(b), 1113(a), (b)(1)(A), (f); FRBP 6006(a), 7004, 9007, 9013-9014, 9034.*

(2) Provide Relevant Information

The DIP or trustee must then provide sufficient, relevant information to enable the employees' authorized representative to evaluate the proposal, subject to any protective orders of the court necessary to prevent unfair disclosure of information and protect the debtor's competitive position in the industry. *11 USC §1113(b)(1)(B), (d)(3); see "Interim Measures—Protective Orders," discussed below.*

(3) Good-Faith Negotiations

The DIP or trustee and the employees' authorized representative must meet at reasonable times to negotiate in good faith to reach mutually satisfactory modifications to the collective bargaining agreement. Good-faith negotiations must continue between such representatives from the date the proposal is submitted until the date of the hearing on any application to reject collective bargaining agreement (*see discussion below*). *11 USC §1113(b)(2), (d)(1).*

(4) If Negotiations Fail, File Application to Modify or Reject Collective Bargaining Agreement

If good-faith efforts to negotiate modifications to the collective bargaining agreement appear unproductive or fruitless, the DIP or trustee may then file an application to modify or reject collective bargaining agreement, with a copy of the proposal attached. However, negotiations between the DIP or trustee and employees' authorized representative must nevertheless continue in good faith until the day the hearing on the application begins. *11 USC §1113(a), (b)(2), (d), (1); see "Procedures After Proposal Submitted," discussed below.*

(5) Obtain Court Approval

The DIP or trustee must obtain court approval of the application to modify or reject collective bargaining agreement. The court must approve an application to reject collective bargaining agreement only if the court, after notice and hearing, makes three determinations:

(a) The DIP or trustee submitted the required proposal of necessary modifications and all relevant information to the employees' authorized representative before filing, and the hearing on, the application to reject the collective bargaining agreement;

(b) The employees' authorized representative refused to accept the proposal without good cause; and

(c) The balance of the equities clearly favors rejection of the collective bargaining agreement. *11 USC §§102(1)(A)-(B), 105(a), 1113(c), (f); FRBP 6006(a), 9007, 9013-9014.*

c. Procedures After Proposal Submitted

(1) File Application to Reject

After the DIP or trustee has submitted the proposal of necessary modifications with relevant information to enable the employees' authorized representative to evaluate the proposal and good-faith negotiations have begun, the DIP or trustee may then file an application to modify or reject collective bargaining agreement. A copy of the proposal should be attached to the application. A copy of the application must be served by first-class mail or any other manner allowed for service of process in federal district court on the authorized representative of employees covered by the collective bargaining agreement, any trustee (if the debtor filed the application), all committee(s), the U.S. trustee, and any other entity required by court order or local bankruptcy rules. The application, like a motion, does not commence an adversary proceeding and no filing fee is required. No answer or response to the application is required, unless directed otherwise by court order or local bankruptcy rules. *11 USC §§103(a), 307, 1109(b), 1113(b), (d)(1); FRBP 6006, 7004, 9013-9014, 9034.*

(2) Hearing

The court must set a hearing when the DIP or trustee files an application to modify or reject collective bargaining agreement. The hearing on an application to reject must be held no later than the 14th day after the date the application is filed, unless the court extends the time. The court may initially extend the hearing date to begin no more than 7 days thereafter (on the 21st day after the application was filed), if the interests of justice and the circumstances of the case so warrant. The court may thereafter only extend the hearing date for additional periods agreed to by the DIP or trustee and the employees' authorized representative. All interested and affected parties may appear and be heard at the hearing. *11 USC §§102(1)(A)-(B), 103(a), 307, 1109(b), 1113(d)(1).*

(3) Notice of Hearing

The clerk, DIP or trustee, or other court-authorized person must give at least ten days' notice of the hearing date on the application to reject. The notice must provide adequate information about the proposed application and be mailed to the debtor, any trustee, the employees' authorized representative, the U.S. trustee, all committee(s), and to such other entities as required by court order or local bankruptcy rules. Notice may also be given by publication. *11 USC §§102(1)(A)-(B), 103(a), 307, 1109(b), 1113(d)(1); FRBP 2002(l), 6006(c), 9007-9008, 9014, 9034.*

(4) Court's Decision

(a) Timely Ruling

The court must rule on the DIP's or trustee's application to reject before the 30th day after the date the hearing begins; or by such additional date agreed to by the DIP or trustee and employees' authorized representative, if the interests of justice so warrant. *11 USC §1113(d)(2).*

(b) No Ruling By the Court

If the court fails to rule on the application to reject before the 30th day after the hearing begins or by such extended date agreed to by the DIP or trustee and employees' authorized representative, the DIP or trustee may terminate or alter any provision of the collective bargaining agreement without court order until the court renders a decision on the application. *11 USC §1113(d)(2).*

(5) Interim Measures

The court may authorize interim measures for the DIP or trustee in the form of protective order(s) and/or an order authorizing interim changes to the collective bargaining agreement, pending a ruling on the application to reject collective bargaining agreement.

(a) Protective Order(s)

The court may issue protective order(s) necessary to prevent disclosure of relevant information conveyed to the employees' authorized representative for evaluation of the proposal of necessary modifications, if disclosure of such information would compromise the debtor's position in the industry with regard to its competitors. However, the court must consider the needs of the employees' representative for information to evaluate the proposal and the application, as well as the needs of the debtor for protection of its competitive status in the industry. *11 USC §§105(a), 1113(d)(3).*

(b) Interim Changes to Collective Bargaining Agreement

Before the court reaches a final decision on the application to reject and while the collective bargaining agreement is still in effect, the court may authorize the DIP or trustee to implement interim changes to the terms, conditions, wages, benefits, or work rules of the collective bargaining agreement. Interim changes may only be authorized if the DIP or trustee proves that:

(i) The collective bargaining agreement continues in effect; and

(ii) Interim changes are essential to the continuation of the debtor's business and necessary to avoid irreparable damage to the estate. *11 USC §§102(5), 1113(e).*

(c) Procedures to Obtain Interim Measures

(i) Motion for Protective Order

The DIP or trustee must file a motion for protective order and state facts showing grounds for such order (protection of the debtor's competitive position in the industry). The DIP or trustee must serve a copy of the motion by first-class mail or any other method allowed for service of process in federal district court on the employees' authorized representative, any trustee (if the DIP filed the motion), the U.S. trustee, all committee(s), and all other entities required by court order or local bankruptcy rules. *11 USC §105(a), 307, 1109(b), 1113(d)(3); FRBP 7004, 9007, 9013-9014, 9034.*

(ii) Motion for Order Authorizing Interim Changes

The DIP or trustee must file a motion for order authorizing interim changes in the collective bargaining agreement pending final decision of the court on the application to reject. The motion should state facts showing the grounds for such order (the collective bargaining agreement remains in effect and interim changes are essential to the continuation of the debtor's business and to avoid irreparable harm to the estate). A copy of the motion should be served on the same entities required to receive a copy of a motion for protective order discussed above. Service may be obtained by first-class mail or any other manner allowed for service of process in federal district court. No response is required to the motion, unless required by court order or local bankruptcy rules. *11 USC §§103(a), 307, 1109(b), 1113(e); FRBP 7004, 9007, 9013-9014.*

(iii) Notice and Hearing

The court must hold a hearing on any motion for interim measures. The clerk, the DIP or trustee, or other court-appointed person must mail notice of the hearing date to the debtor, any trustee, the U.S. trustee, all committee(s), the employees' authorized representative, and to such other entities required by court order or local bankruptcy rules. Notice may also be given by publication. *11 USC §§102(1)(A)-(B), 103(a), 307, 1109(b), 1113(d)(3), (e); FRBP 2002(1), 9007-9008, 9014, 9034.*

The court must set a hearing on the motion for order authorizing interim changes according to the needs of the DIP or trustee. If the court grants the motion, the interim changes do not render an application to reject moot. *11 USC §§102(1)(A)-(B), 105(a), 1113(e); FRBP 6006, 9007, 9014.*

d. Rights of Rejected Employees

(1) Generally

Rejection of an executory contract constitutes a breach of the contract. An employee adversely affected by the rejection of a collective bargaining agreement (executory contract) will have an unsecured claim against the estate. If the agreement was rejected without having been assumed previously in the Chapter 11 case, the claim may be treated like a pre-petition claim that arose immediately before the Chapter 11 petition was filed, even though the rejection occurred post-petition. However, if the claim is for damages from termination of an employment contract, the amount of damages that may be recovered in the debtor's case is limited to a maximum of one year's compensation at the rate provided in the rejected employment agreement, without acceleration, beginning on the earlier date that the petition was filed or the employee's services terminated, plus any compensation owed to such employee on the earlier of such dates. Some or all the employee's claims may be entitled to third and/or fourth priority status (*see "Priority Claims," Chapter II*). The employee must file a timely proof of claim by the date fixed by the court. The clerk of the court must mail notice of such date to the debtor, any trustee, all creditors, committee(s), to the employees' authorized representative, to all parties affected by the rejected collective bargaining agreement, to the SEC in Washington, D.C., the District Director of the IRS where the case is pending, and to any other entity required by court order or local bankruptcy rules. Such notice may be given in the notice of approval of disclosure statement setting the dates for filing objections to the Chapter 11 plan, voting, and the confirmation hearing. Notice may also be given by publication. *See NLRB v Bildisco & Bildisco, 465 US 513 (1984); 11 USC §§103(a), 365(g)(1), 502(b)(7), (g), 507(a)(3), (4), 1113; FRBP 2002(a)(8), (b), (f)(3), (i)-(l), 3001, 3002(b), (c)(4), 3003(c)(3), 3017(d), 6006, 9007, 9008; "Priority Claims," Chapter II; "Procedure Seven—Confirmation of a Plan of Reorganization," Chapter IV; "File Proof of Claim," discussed above.*

(2) Rejection After Assumption

If a collective bargaining agreement is assumed by the DIP or trustee, expenses and obligations incurred under the assumed agreement may be treated like first priority administrative expenses. If an employee is not timely paid or the assumed collective bargaining agreement is thereafter rejected, an employee adversely affected may file a motion for allowance of administrative expenses. The employee should also file a timely proof of claim asserting a first priority status by the date set by the court. The clerk or other court-authorized person must mail notice of such date to the debtor, any trustee, all creditors, committee(s), to the employees' authorized representative, to all parties affected by the rejected collective bargaining agreement, to the SEC in Washington, D.C., the District Director of the IRS where the case is pending, and to any other entity required by court order or local bankruptcy rules. *See NLRB v Bildisco & Bildisco, 465 US 513 (1984); In re Roth American, Inc, 975 F2d 949 (3d Cir 1992); In re Moline Corp, 144 Bankr 75, 27 CBC2d 1423 (Bankr ND Ill 1992); 11 USC §§103(a), 365(g)(2)-(3), 503(b)(1), 507(a)(1), 1113; FRBP 2002(a)(8), (b), (f)(3), (i)-(l), 3001, 3002(b), (c)(4), 3003(c)(3), 3017(d), 9007-9008; "Priority Claims," Chapter II; "Procedure Seven—Confirmation of a Plan of Reorganization," Chapter IV; "File Proof of Claims," discussed above.*

If an assumed collective bargaining agreement is rejected and the debtor's Chapter 11 case is converted to Chapter 7, the collective bargaining agreement is deemed to be rejected immediately before conversion under the superseded Chapter 11 case, even though the agreement may actually be rejected under the converted Chapter 7 case. Thus, an employee adversely affected by the rejection will have a first priority claim which may also be deemed to arise under the superseded Chapter 11 case. And all first priority claims in a superseded case are subordinated to and receive payment after first priority claims that arise in a converted Chapter 7 case. *11 USC §§103(a), 365(g)(2)(B), (i), 502(g), 503(b)(1), 507(a)(1), 726(b), 1113; FRBP 1019, 2002(a)(5), (f)(2)-(3), (i), (k), 3001, 3002(c)(4); see "File Proof of Claim," discussed above; "Procedure Eight—Conversion," Chapter IV; NLRB v Bildisco & Bildisco, 465 US 513 (1984).*

e. Chapter 11 Plan and Continuing Jurisdiction of the Court

The terms of any mutual agreement between the DIP or trustee and employees' authorized representative to assume or modify a collective bargaining agreement, or of any court order authorizing rejection of such agreement, should be included in the Chapter 11 plan. The court retains jurisdiction over all orders affecting a collective bargaining agreement even post-confirmation. *11 USC §§1113(d)(2), (e), 1123(a)(2)-(4), (b)(2), 1129(a)(1)-(2), (9)(A)-(B), 1142; FRBP 3020(d), 6006.*

2. Retiree Benefits

a. General Overview

The Chapter 11 DIP, or trustee if one has been appointed, may assume or modify (but not completely reject) a retiree benefits plan whether such plan is or is not covered by a collective bargaining agreement. The DIP or trustee must follow strict procedures designed to protect the health, medical, life, and disability insurance coverage of union or nonunion retirees and their spouses and dependents. However, such procedures do not apply to any retiree and his spouse and dependents if the retiree's gross income was $250,000 or more during the immediate 12-month pre-petition period, unless the retiree proves to the court that he is unable to obtain comparable health, medical, life, and disability insurance coverage for himself and his spouse and dependents as provided by the debtor on the day before the petition was filed. *11 USC §1114(f)-(g), (k)-(l).*

The DIP or trustee must enter into good-faith negotiations with the retirees' authorized representative and strictly comply with similar provisions governing modification and rejection of collective bargaining agreements. But unlike other collective bargaining agreement provisions, the DIP or trustee may reduce, but not completely reject, benefits to retired employees under Title 11. Benefits may be reduced or modified only if the DIP or trustee and the retirees' authorized representative mutually agree or if the court authorizes such modification after the DIP or trustee has strictly complied with required procedures. The DIP or trustee must continue to pay retiree benefits post-petition. The Code permits multiple modifications to a retiree benefits plan during the course of a Chapter 11 proceeding. *11 USC §1114(e)(1)(A)-(B), (g); 134 Cong Rec H3,486-3491 (daily ed May 23, 1988).*

b. What Are Retiree Benefits

Retiree benefits are payments established or maintained by the debtor pre-petition to any entity to provide or reimburse payments for medical, surgical, hospital care, sickness, accident, disability, or death benefits for retired employees and their spouses and dependents. Such payments could be provided under any plan, fund, or program, including through the purchase of insurance, which was partially or totally established pre-petition. *11 USC §1114(a).*

c. Who Is Not Protected

A retiree, including his spouse and dependents, whose gross income was $250,000 or more for the immediate 12 months pre-petition is not included in Chapter 11 protections for retirees, unless such retiree proves to the court that he cannot obtain comparable health, medical, life, and disability coverage for himself and his spouse and dependents as provided by the debtor-employer immediately before filing the petition. *11 USC §1114(l).*

d. Negotiating Parties

The DIP or trustee must negotiate with the authorized representative for persons receiving retiree benefits. The retirees' authorized representative may be a labor organization or committee of retired employees appointed by the court. *11 USC §1114(b)-(d).*

(1) Benefits Covered by Collective Bargaining Agreement

If the retiree benefits are covered by a collective bargaining agreement, a labor organization which is a signatory to the agreement must be the authorized representative of the retirees, unless the labor organization chooses not to serve or the court determines that a different representative is appropriate. If the court so determines or the labor organization elects not to serve, the court must appoint a committee of retired employees to be the retirees' authorized representative, after motion of any party-in-interest and hearing. *11 USC §102(1)(A)-(B), 1114(c)(1)-(2), (d); see "Procedures to Appoint a Committee of Retired Employees," discussed below.*

(2) Benefits Not Covered by Collective Bargaining Agreement

If the retiree benefits are not covered by a collective bargaining agreement, the court must appoint a committee of retired employees to be the authorized representative, after motion of any party-in-interest and hearing. Retirees receiving benefits other than through a collective bargaining agreement are usually nonunion employees. *11 USC §1114(d); see "Procedures to Appoint a Committee of Retired Employees," discussed below.*

(3) Procedures to Appoint a Committee of Retired Employees

(a) Motion

The party-in-interest (labor organization, debtor, trustee, employee, or retiree) must file a motion to appoint a committee of retired employees and serve a copy of the motion by first-class mail or any other method allowed for service of process in federal district court on the debtor, any authorized representative of a labor organization involved in the case, any trustee, all committee(s), and to such other entities required by court order or local bankruptcy rules. The motion must state the ground(s) for appointment of such committee (the labor organization elects not to serve; a representative other than the labor organization is in the best interests of retired employees; or retiree benefits are not covered by a collective bargaining agreement). The court must hold a hearing on the motion. The movant or other court-authorized person must mail notice of the hearing date to the same entities required to receive copy of the motion. *11 USC §§102(1)(A)-(B), 1114(c)-(d); FRBP 7004, 9007, 9013-9014.*

(b) Committee's Powers

A committee of retired employees appointed by the court has all the powers and rights of a Chapter 11 unsecured creditors' committee, including the right to investigate the financial affairs of the DIP and participate in the formulation (writing) of a plan. The plan must provide for continuation of retiree benefits after confirmation at levels agreed to by the DIP or trustee and the retirees' authorized representative or required by court order. If the court permits, the committee of retired employees may have the power to enforce the rights of retirees with regard to such benefits. *See "Procedure Three—Selection of Unsecured Creditors' Committee," Chapter IV; 11 USC §§1114(b)(2), (c)-(d), 1129(a)(13).*

e. Requirements to Modify a Retiree Benefits Plan

(1) Generally

The DIP or trustee must continue making payments under a retiree benefits plan even after the Chapter 11 petition is filed and before confirmation of a plan of reorganization. The retiree benefits plan may only be modified: (a) by mutual agreement of the DIP or trustee and the retirees' authorized representative; or (b) by court order, after filing of an application to modify retiree benefits, notice, hearing, and a finding that the DIP or trustee strictly complied with all Chapter 11 requirements. The modifications, whether by mutual agreement or court order, must be included under a Chapter 11 plan for confirmation (approval) by the court. *11 USC §§1114(e)(1)(A)-(B), (2), 1129(a)(13).*

(2) Requirements if no Mutual Agreement

If the DIP or trustee and the retirees' authorized representative do not agree to terms to modify a retiree benefits plan, the DIP or trustee must meet the following five requirements and in the following order to modify such a plan.

(a) Submit Proposal

The DIP or trustee must first submit to the retirees' authorized representative a proposal for necessary modifications to the pre-petition retiree benefits plan necessary to permit the debtor to reorganize and to assure that all creditors, affected parties, and the debtor are treated fairly and equitably. The proposal must be submitted before the DIP or trustee files an application to modify retiree benefits with the court. The proposal must be served by first-class mail or any other method allowed for service of process in federal district court on the retirees' authorized representative, any trustee, the U.S. trustee, all committee(s), and all other entities required by court order or local bankruptcy rules. *11 USC §§103(a), 307, 1109(b), 1114(f)(1)(A)-(B); FRBP 7004, 9007, 9013-9014, 9034.*

(b) Provide Relevant Information

The DIP or trustee must then provide the retirees' authorized representative with necessary, relevant information to evaluate the proposal for necessary modifications, subject to any protective order of the court preventing disclosure of information which could injure the debtor's competitive position in the industry. *11 USC §1114(f)(1)(B), (k)(3); see "Interim Measures," discussed below.*

(c) Good-Faith Negotiations

The DIP or trustee and the retirees' authorized representative must negotiate in good faith to reach mutually satisfactory modifications (increases or reductions) to the retiree benefits. Negotiations must occur at reasonable times during the period beginning on the date the DIP or trustee submits the proposal for necessary modifications and ending no earlier than the date of the hearing on any application to modify retiree benefits. *11 USC §1114(f)(1)-(2)(k)(1).*

(d) If Negoiations Fail, File Application to Modify Retiree Benefits

If good-faith negotiations to reach an agreement on the proposal for necessary modifications fail or appear fruitless, the DIP or trustee may then file an application to modify retiree benefits with a copy of the proposal attached. However, negotiations between the DIP or trustee and retirees' authorized representative must continue in good faith after the application is filed until the hearing date on the application. *11 USC §1114(e)(1), (f)(2), (k)(1).*

(e) Obtain Court Approval

The court must approve the DIP's or trustee's application to modify retiree benefits only if the court, after notice and hearing, makes five determinations:

(i) The DIP or trustee submitted the required proposal for necessary modifications to the retirees' authorized representative;

(ii) The retirees' authorized representative refused to accept the proposal without good cause;

(iii) Modification of retiree benefits is necessary to permit the debtor to reorganize and to assure fair and equitable treatment of all creditors, affected parties, and the debtor;

(iv) Modification of retiree benefits is clearly favored by the balance of the equities; and

(v) The DIP's or trustee's application does not contain a reduced or lower level of retiree benefits payments than the level contained in the proposal. *11 USC §§102(1)(A)-(B), 1114(g); FRBP 6006(a), 9007, 9013-9014.*

f. Procedures After Proposal Submitted

(1) File Application

After submitting the proposal for necessary modifications and relevant information to the retirees' authorized representative, the DIP or trustee may then file an application to modify retiree benefits. A copy of the proposal should be attached to the application. A copy of the application must be served by first-class mail or any other method allowed for service of process in federal district court on the retirees' authorized representative, any trustee (if the debtor filed the application), the U.S. trustee, all committee(s), and all other entities required by court order or local bankruptcy rules. The application does not commence an adversary proceeding and no filing fee is required. No response or answer is required unless directed otherwise by court order or local bankruptcy rules. *11 USC §§103(a), 307, 1109(b), 1114(f)(1); FRBP 6006(a), 7004, 9013-9014, 9034.*

(2) Hearing

The court must set a hearing date when the application to modify retiree benefits is filed. The hearing must be held no later than the 14th day after the application is filed, unless the court extends the time. The court may initially extend the date for the hearing to begin no more than 7 days thereafter (on the 21st day after the DIP or trustee filed the application) if the interests of justice and circumstances of the case so warrant. The court may further extend the hearing date only for periods agreed to by the DIP or trustee and the retirees' authorized representative. All interested parties may appear and be heard at the hearing. *11 USC §§102(1)(A)-(B), 103(a), 307, 1109(b), 1114(k)(1).*

(3) Notice of Hearing

The DIP or trustee, clerk, or other court-authorized person must mail notice of the hearing date on the application to modify retiree benefits at least ten days before such hearing. Notice must be given to the debtor, any trustee, the U.S. trustee, the retirees' authorized representative, all committee(s), and all other entities required by court order or local bankruptcy rules. Notice may also be given by publication. *11 USC §§102(1)(A)-(B), 103(a), 307, 1109(b), 1114(k)(1); FRBP 2002(l), 6006(c), 9007-9008, 9014, 9034.*

(4) Court's Decision

(a) Timely Ruling

The court must rule on the DIP's application to modify retiree benefits before the 90th day after the hearing on the application begins, unless the court extends such time upon agreement of the DIP or trustee and the retirees' authorized representative and the interests of justice so warrant. *11 USC §1114(k)(2).*

(b) No Court Ruling

If the court fails to render a decision before the 90th day after the hearing on the application begins, or by the later date agreed to by the DIP or trustee and the retirees' authorized representative, the DIP or trustee may implement all modifications proposed in the application without a court order until the court does rule. *11 USC §1114(k)(2).*

(5) Interim Measures

The court may authorize interim measures in the form of protective order(s) and/or an order authorizing interim modifications pending its ruling on the application to modify retiree benefits.

(a) Protective Order(s)

The court may issue protective order(s) necessary to prevent the disclosure of information required to be submitted to the retirees' authorized representative for evaluating the proposal and application, if disclosure of such information would injure the debtor's position in the industry with regard to its competitors. The DIP or trustee must file a motion for protective order stating the grounds for such order (necessary to protect the debtor's competitive position in the industry). A copy of the motion must be served by first-class mail or any other method allowed for service of process in federal district court on the retirees' authorized representative, any trustee (if the debtor filed the motion), the U.S. trustee, all committee(s), and on such other entities required by court order or local bankruptcy rules. A protective order must also be consistent with the needs of the retirees' authorized representative for relevant information. *11 USC §§103(a), 307, 1109(b), 1114(k)(3); FRBP 7004, 9013-9014, 9034.*

(b) Interim Modifications

Before a final order on the application to modify retiree benefits is issued, the court may authorize the DIP or trustee to implement interim changes. The DIP or trustee must file a motion to implement interim changes and serve a copy of the motion by first-class mail on the retirees' authorized representative, any trustee, the U.S. trustee, all committee(s), and on such other entities as directed by court order or local bankruptcy rules. *11 USC §§103(a), 307, 1109(b), 1114(h)(1); FRBP 7004, 9007, 9013-9014, 9034.*

(c) Notice and Hearing

The court must hold a hearing on any motion for interim measures. The DIP or trustee, clerk, or other court-authorized person must mail notice of the hearing date to the debtor, the retirees' authorized representative, any appointed trustee, the U.S. trustee, all committee(s), and to any other entity required by court order or local bankruptcy rules. Notice may also be given by publication. *11 USC §§102(1)(A)-(B), 103(a), 307, 1109(b), 1114(h), (k)(3); FRBP 2002(l), 6006, 9007-9008, 9034.*

Hearing on the motion to implement interim changes must be scheduled according to the needs of the DIP or trustee. During the hearing the DIP or trustee must prove that:

(i) Interim changes (usually reductions) in payments of retiree benefits are essential to the continuation of the debtor's business; and

(ii) Interim changes in payments are necessary to avoid irreparable damage to the estate. If the court authorizes interim changes, the application to modify retiree benefits does not become moot. *11 USC §§102(5), 105(a), 1114(h)(1)-(3).*

(6) After the Court's Initial Decision

Either the retirees' authorized representative or the DIP or trustee may file subsequent applications to modify retiree benefits at any time after the court enters an order approving the initial modifications (by mutual agreement or application). *11 USC §1114(g); 134 Cong Rec H3,486-3,491 (daily ed May 23, 1988).*

(a) Application of Retirees' Authorized Representative

The retirees' authorized representative may file an application to increase retiree benefits even if the court has approved a DIP's or trustee's prior application to modify (reduce) retiree benefits. All subsequent applications to modify (decrease or increase) retiree benefits are subject to the same procedures and requirements as the initial application. The retirees' authorized representative must submit a proposal for necessary modifications to the DIP or trustee and follow the procedures outlined above. The court must grant the representative's application if increased benefits would: (i) permit the debtor to reorganize; (ii) assure that all creditors, the debtor, and all affected parties are treated fairly and equitably; and (iii) be clearly favored by the balance of the equities. Thus, if the debtor's financial condition improves post-petition, an increase in retiree benefits may be warranted after a reduction has been authorized by the court. *134 Cong Rec H3,486-3,491 (daily ed May 23, 1988); 11 USC §§102(1)(A)-(B), 1114(g); FRBP 9007, 9013-9014.*

(b) Application of DIP or Trustee

The DIP or trustee may also file more than one application to reduce or modify retiree benefit payments. Subsequent application(s) will be subject to the same procedures and requirements as the initial application to modify retiree benefits discussed above. If the debtor's financial condition deteriorates post-petition, further reduction in benefits may be warranted. *11 USC §1114(g); 134 Cong Rec H3,486-3,491 (daily ed May 23, 1988).*

g. Claims for Retiree Benefit Payments

(1) Claims for Retiree Benefits for Cases Pending On June 16, 1988

(a) Reversible Pre-Petition Claims (Applicable to Chapter 11 Cases Pending June 16, 1988)

The DIP or trustee must pay the full amount of all reversible pre-petition claims paid by a third-party administrator or other person for the benefit of a retired employee under any retiree benefits program. A *reversible claim* frequently arises under a contract between a self-insured employer (the debtor) and a third-party administrator. The administrator arranges for medical or other health-care benefits for retired employees, pays for the benefits, and then bills the employer for the cost plus an administrative fee. If the debtor-employer fails to pay such pre-petition amounts to the administrator, under some contracts the administrator may reverse the claim to the health-care provider, who in turn reverses the claim to the retired worker. Thus, the retired worker and not the debtor-employer is ultimately billed for health-care benefits. It is such reversal of claims and inequity to retired workers that is not allowed under Chapter 11 cases pending on July 16, 1988. *Section 608(b)(1) of second Title VI, Joint Resolution Making Continuing Appropriations for the Fiscal Year 1987, and Other Purposes, Pub L No 99-591 (1986), effective as to Chapter 11 cases pending on June 16, 1988, as amended and made permanent by The Retiree Benefits Bankruptcy Protection Act of 1988, Pub L No 100-334, 102 Stat 610, effective June 16, 1988; 134 Cong Rec H3,486-3,491 (daily ed May 23, 1988).*

If the third-party administrator or other person proves to the court that a pre-petition contract right to reverse a claim exists, the DIP (employer) or trustee, if one has been appointed in the Chapter 11 case, must pay the full amount of claims owed to such administrator or other person for health-care benefits provided to a retired employee. The pre-petition allowed claims of such third parties are treated like first priority administrative claims which must be paid immediately, without waiting for confirmation of a Chapter 11 plan, unless the third-party administrator or other person with a reversible claim agrees otherwise. *See §608(b)(1) of second Title VI, Joint Resolution Making Continuing Appropriations for the Fiscal Year 1987, and Other Purposes, Pub L No 99-591 (1986), effective as to Chapter 11 cases pending June 16, 1988, as amended and made permanent by The Retiree Benefits Bankruptcy Protection Act of 1988, Pub L No 100-334, 102 Stat 610, effective June 16, 1988; 134 Cong Rec H3,486-91 (daily ed May 23, 1988); 11 USC §§503(b), 507(a)(1), 1114(a), 1129(a)(9)(A); "Requirements for Confirmation of a Chapter 11 Plan," Chapter IV; "Priority Claims," Chapter II.*

(b) General Unsecured Pre-Petition Claims

A third-party administrator or other person who does not have a reversible claim has an unsecured pre-petition claim for health-care benefits provided to a retired worker. Such claims may be third or fourth priority claims. The third-party administrator or other claimholder must file a timely proof of claim with the original or a copy of all relevant contracts and documents. *See §608(b)(1) of second Title VI, "Joint Resolution Making Continuing Appropriations for the Fiscal Year 1987, and Other Purposes," Pub L No 99-591 (1986), effective as to Chapter 11 cases pending June 16, 1988, as amended and made permanent by The Retiree Benefits Bankruptcy Protection Act of 1988, Pub L No 100-334, 102 Stat 610, effective June 16, 1988; 134 Cong Rec H3,486-91 (daily ed May 23, 1988); 11 USC §§501, 502, 507(a)(3)-(4), 521(1); FRBP 3001(c), 3003(b)(1)-(2), (c)(2)-(3); "Priority Claims," Chapter II; "File Proof of Claims," discussed above.*

An allowed unsecured claim for retiree benefits, whether held by a third-party administrator whose claim is not reversible, a health-care provider, or retired employee, is not limited in amount under Chapter 11, because it arises under a terminated employment contract. *See "File Proof of Claim," discussed above; 11 USC §§502(b)(7), 507(a)(3)-(4), 1114(a)(j); §608(a)(5), (b)(1) of second Title VI, Joint Resolution Making Continuing Appropriations for Fiscal Year 1987, and for Other Purposes, Pub L No 99-591 (1986), effective as to Chapter 11 cases pending on June 16, 1988, as amended and made permanent by The Retiree Benefits Bankruptcy Protection Act of 1988, Pub L No 100-334, 102 Stat 610 effective June 16, 1988; "Priority Claims," Chapter II.*

(2) Claims for Retiree Benefits for Cases Filed On or After June 16, 1988

The DIP or trustee must continue making payments for retiree benefits post-petition even before confirmation of a plan and before a court order approving any *modifications* (increase or reduction) of such benefits. All post-petition payments of retiree benefits required before the effective date of a confirmed plan are allowed first priority claims for administrative expenses. Retiree benefit payments actually paid by the DIP or trustee between the dates that the petition is filed and the confirmed plan becomes effective may not be deducted from or offset against any allowed pre-petition or post-petition claims for unpaid retiree benefits or from future payments due under a court order or plan. And no retiree benefits claim may be limited in amount under Chapter 11 because it arises from termination of an employment contract. *11 USC §§503(b), 507(a)(1), 1114(e)(1)-(2), (i)-(j).*

h. Chapter 11 Plan and Continuing Jurisdiction of the Court

A Chapter 11 plan must provide for continued retiree benefit payments after the plan's effective date, either at the pre-petition level or at the modified level agreed to by the DIP or trustee and retirees' authorized representative or authorized by court order approving an application for modification. The court must deny confirmation of a plan that fails to include such provision. The court has continuing jurisdiction after confirmation to enforce retiree benefit payments required under a confirmed plan. *11 USC §§1114, 1129(a)(1), (13), 1142; FRBP 3020(d).*

i. Pension Plans

Provisions under the Employee Retirement Income Security Act (ERISA) permit the distress termination of pension plans under Chapter 11 cases. Effective with the 1987 Amendments to ERISA, *distress termination* of a pension plan under Chapter 11 is only permitted if the bankruptcy or other court with appropriate jurisdiction determines that the debtor-employer will not be able to pay all of its debts under a confirmed Chapter 11 plan and will not be able to continue in business outside of Chapter 11 unless the pension plan is terminated. *See Pub L No 100-203, Omnibus Budget Reconciliation Act of 1987, Dec 22, 1987, amending "Employment Retirement Income Security Act," 29 United States Code; Pension Benefits Guaranty Corp v LTV, 496 US 633 (1990).*

K. Creditors' Surprise Weapons-the Debtor's Petition, Schedules of Assets and Liabilities, Statement of Financial Affairs, and Other Documents

1. Generally

The bankruptcy petition, schedules of assets and liabilities, and statement of financial affairs contain significant information and are potential tools for creditors' use in the debtor's bankruptcy case. Data included or omitted from these required documents can provide strategy for creditors throughout the course of the bankruptcy proceeding. *11 USC §521; 28 USC §1746; FRBP 1007-1008; Official Bankr Forms 1, 2, 6, 7, 8.*

2. Verified Documents

The following bankruptcy documents must be filed and either verified or contain an unsworn declaration which has the same legal force and effect as a verification (fine and/or imprisonment for perjury):

a. **Petitions (filed by all debtors).** *Official Bankr Forms 1, 2;*

b. **Schedules of assets and liabilities (filed by all except Chapter 9 debtors).** *Official Bankr Form 6;*

c. **Statement of financial affairs (filed by all except Chapter 9 debtors).** *Official Bankr Form 7;*

d. **Statement of intent (filed by individual Chapter 7 debtor only);**

e. **List of creditors holding 20 largest unsecured claims (filed by Chapter 9 and 11 debtors).** *See Official Bankr Form 4; Official Bankr Form 8 (should be verified); 11 USC §521; 28 USC §1746; FRBP 1007-1008; "Procedure Two—Debtor's Duties," Chapter III.*

It is a bankruptcy crime for the debtor to knowingly and fraudulently make a false statement or verification on any of the above documents. The punishment for the debtor in certain situations may be a fine for as much as $500,000 and/or imprisonment for as long as five years. *18 USC §§152, 3571; see "Bankruptcy Crimes and Penalties," discussed below.*

3. Significance of Petition—Official Bankruptcy Forms 1, 2

The petition reveals the following information for use in a bankruptcy case.

a. Venue

Did the debtor file his petition in the proper place, considering the debtor's residence, principal place of business, or assets during the immediate 180-day pre-petition period? The debtor may file a petition in the federal judicial district where his domicile, residence, principal place of business, or principal assets in the United States have been located for the greater part of the immediate 180-day pre-petition period or where a bankruptcy case concerning an affiliate, general partner, or partnership is pending. If venue is improper and the debtor filed the petition in the wrong judicial district, the creditor may file a motion to transfer venue. *See Chapter X; 28 USC §§1408, 1412; FRBP 1014.*

b. Dismissal—The 180-Day Rule

The debtor's present case may be dismissed if the debtor had a prior bankruptcy case dismissed at any time within the immediate

180-day pre-petition period because the debtor voluntarily requested dismissal after a motion for relief from the automatic stay was filed or if the court dismissed the case because the debtor willfully failed to appear before the court and prosecute his case or obey a court order. The debtor's present name and all other names used by the debtor during the preceding six years, including trade names, may provide information relevant to the 180-day rule. *See "Who May Be a Debtor," Chapter II; 11 USC §109(g).*

The debtor's case may also be dismissed if the petition was filed under the wrong bankruptcy chapter. *See "Who May Be a Debtor," Chapter II; 11 USC §109(a)-(f).*

c. Denial of Chapter 7 Discharge

A Chapter 7 debtor may be denied a discharge if he knowingly and fraudulently presented a false oath or verification regarding any information on the petition. *See "Procedure Seven—Discharge of the Debtor," Chapter III; 11 USC §727(a)(4)(A).*

A Chapter 7 debtor may also be denied a discharge if he was granted a discharge under a prior Chapter 7 or 11 case which was filed during the immediate six years before filing his present petition. Similarly, a Chapter 7 debtor may be denied a discharge if he received a discharge under a Chapter 12 or 13 case which was filed during the immediate six-year pre-petition period and the debtor failed to pay 100 per cent of his unsecured debt or 70 per cent of such debt under a prior plan that was proposed in good faith and was the debtor's best efforts. The debtor's present name and all other names used by the debtor during the preceding six years indicated on the petition aid in determining whether the debtor received a prior discharge within the relevant six-year pre-petition period. *See "Procedure Seven—Discharge of the Debtor," Chapter III; 11 USC §727(a)(8)-(9).*

d. Bankruptcy Crime

Knowingly and fraudulently making a false oath on a petition may also result in the debtor's being fined as much as $500,000 and/or imprisoned for as long as five years. *See "Bankruptcy Crimes and Penalties," discussed below; 18 USC §§152, 3571.*

e. Type of Debt

The petition reveals whether the debtor's principal obligations are consumer or business debts. *Official Bankr Form 1; see also Schedules Of Liabilities, Official Bankr Form 6, Schedules D-H.*

4. Significance of Statement of Financial Affairs—Official Bankruptcy Form 7

The debtor's statement of financial affairs serves eight main purposes.

a. Grounds for Denial of Chapter 7 Discharge

The following constitute grounds for denial of a Chapter 7 discharge of the debtor.

(1) Has the debtor concealed property with the intent to delay, hinder, or defraud any creditor or bankruptcy trustee? *Questions 6-7, 10-12, 17-21, Official Bankr Form 7; 11 USC §727(a)(2).*

(2) Has the debtor, without justification, concealed, falsified, destroyed, or failed to keep or preserve records? *Questions 17-18, Official Bankr Form 7; 11 USC §727(a)(3).*

(3) Has the debtor knowingly and fraudulently withheld recorded information from the trustee or other officer of the estate? *Questions 17-18, Official Bankr Form 7; 11 USC §727(a)(4)(D).*

(4) Can the debtor satisfactorily explain the failure to pay his debts because of a loss of assets? *Questions 8, 11, 17, 18, Official Bankr Form 7; 11 USC §727(a)(5).*

(5) Did the debtor knowingly and fraudulently make any false statements on the statement of financial affairs? *Official Bankr Form 7; 11 USC §727(a)(4)(A).*

b. Determine Size of Bankruptcy Estate

Questions 1, 2, 4a, 6b, 9, 11-14, 16-18 of the statement of financial affairs, Official Bankruptcy Form 7, seek to determine the size of the bankruptcy estate. Similarly, questions on the statement of financial affairs directed at avoidable preferential or fraudulent transfers, setoffs, and turnover of property, discussed below, seek to determine if property may be recovered to increase the size of the estate. *11 USC §§541, 542-543, 547-551; see Chapter XII; Official Bankr Form 6, Schedules A-C, G, I, (Schedules of Assets and Liabilities), discussed below; Official Bankr Form 7.*

c. Determine Avoidable Fraudulent Transfers

Questions 3, 4, 5, 6a, 7, 9, 10, 11,12, 16, 19a, 20, and 21 of the statement of financial affairs are directed to determine if any avoidable fraudulent transfers were made by the debtor on or within one year before filing the present petition. *See Chapter XII; 11 USC §548; Official Bankr Form 7.*

d. Determine Avoidable Preferential Transfers

Questions 3a, 4, 5, 6a, 7, 9, 10, 12, 16, 19a, 20, and 21 also seek to determine if an avoidable preferential transfer was made to an entity on or within 90 days before the debtor filed his petition or to an insider between 90 days and one year before filing the petition. *See Chapter XII; 11 USC §547; Official Bankr Form 7.*

e. Determine Avoidable Setoffs

Question 13 seeks to determine if an avoidable setoff occurred on or within the immediate 90-day pre-petition period. *See Chapter XII; 11 USC §553(b); Official Bankr Form 7.*

f. Determine Need for Turnover Order

Question 6 seeks to determine if a custodian or other nonbankruptcy, court-appointed official holds property of the debtor which should be turned over to the trustee or debtor. *See "Nine Stages of Every Voluntary Bankruptcy Case," Chapter II; 11 USC §§541-543; Official Bankr Form 7.*

g. Determine if Sufficient Funds to Implement a Plan

Question 1 seeks to determine if the debtor will have sufficient funds to implement a Chapter 11, 12, or 13 plan. *See also Official Bankr Form 6, Schedule of Current Income and Expenditures, Schedules I, J, discussed below; Official Bankr Form 7.*

h. Bankruptcy Crimes

The statement of financial affairs may also determine if the debtor committed a bankruptcy crime by knowingly and fraudulently:

(1) Presenting false information or making a false verification. *Official Bankr Form 7. 18 USC §§152, 3571; 11 USC §521(1); FRBP 1007-1008;*

(2) Transferring or concealing property. *Questions 10-12, 17-21, Statement of Financial Affairs, Official Bankr Form 7. 18 USC §152;* or

(3) Concealing, destroying, or falsifying recorded information, including books, records or other documents or papers. *Questions 17-18, Statement of Financial Affairs, Official Bankr Form 7. 18 USC §152; see "Bankruptcy Crimes and Penalties," discussed below.*

5. Significance of Schedules of Assets—Official Bankruptcy Form 6

Schedules A, B, C, G, and I of the schedules of assets, Official Bankruptcy Form 6, seek to determine the size of the bankruptcy estate. *11 USC §541; see "Stage Three—Creation of a Bankruptcy Estate," Chapter II.*

L. Bankruptcy Crimes and Penalties

1. Fraudulent Conduct

Title 18, United States Code, imposes penalties of a fine and/or imprisonment for fraudulent conduct relating to a bankruptcy case. In many instances, conduct that would be grounds for denial of discharge of a Chapter 7 debtor are also criminal violations. Any entity, whether the debtor, a creditor, equity security holder, or other party-in-interest, in certain situations may be fined as much as $5,000 and/or imprisoned for as long as five years for perjury or making a false oath or account in a bankruptcy case. *18 USC §§151-152, 3571; 11 USC §727; FRBP 4004-4006, 7001; see "Denial of Discharge," Chapter III.*

An entity (debtor, trustee, creditor, attorney) commits criminal bankruptcy fraud by any of the following acts:

a. **Knowingly and fraudulently concealing property of the estate from a trustee, marshall, U.S. trustee, creditors, or any officer of the bankruptcy court after a petition is filed.** *18 USC §§152, 1961(D) et seq; 11 USC §§547-548, 727(a)(2)(B), (3)-(4)(D);*

b. **Knowingly and fraudulently transferring or concealing any property of the debtor or any other person pre-petition, with the intent to defeat the provisions of the bankruptcy code.** *18 USC §§152, 1961(D) et seq; 11 USC §727(a)(2)(A);*

c. **Knowingly and fraudulently making a false oath, account, declaration, certificate, verification, or any false statement under penalty of perjury in a bankruptcy case.**

   The bankruptcy petition, statement of financial affairs, schedules of assets and liabilities, and the meeting of creditors are instances where the debtor and/or his attorney are required by Title 11 (Bankruptcy Code) and Title 18 to make accurate, truthful statements about property of the debtor, the estate, and the debtor's financial condition, on penalty of perjury, fine and/or imprisonment. *18 USC §§152, 3571, 1961(D) et seq; 11 USC §727(a)(4); see Official Bankr Forms 1, 2, 4, 6, 7;*

d. **Knowingly and fraudulently filing a false proof of claim against the estate, whether acting in a personal capacity or as an agent, proxy, or attorney.**

   Objections to a creditor's proof of claim under Title 11 may also present grounds for imposing criminal sanctions against a creditor, equity security holder, or representative of such parties-in-interest. *See "File Proof of Claim," discussed above; 18 USC §§152, 3571, 1961(D) et seq; 11 USC §§501-502, 727(a)(4)(B); FRBP 3001-3005; Official Bankr Form 10; "Who May File a Proof of Claim," discussed above;*

e. **Knowingly and fraudulently receiving any material amount of property from a debtor after the petition is filed, with the intent to violate the Bankruptcy Code.**

   Unauthorized post-petition transfers of property may prove costly to the debtor and the transferee or recipient of the property. *See "Avoidable Unauthorized Post-Petition Transfers," and "Avoidable Setoffs," Chapter XII; 18 USC §§152, 1961(D) et seq; 11 USC §§549, 553, 727(a)(2)(B), (4)(C);*

f. **Knowingly and fraudulently offering to give, giving, receiving, or attempting to obtain any money, property, compensation, reward, advantage, or the promise of such reward(s), for acting or forbearing to act in any bankruptcy case.**

Any deal or agreement with a bankruptcy debtor that is not in the usual course of the debtor's legitimate business or financial affairs or that is not authorized by the court may be a violation of Title 11 and Title 18 for the debtor and the nonbankruptcy party. *18 USC §§152, 1961(D) et seq; 11 USC §§547-549, 727(a)(4)(C);*

g. **Knowingly and fraudulently concealing, falsifying, destroying, or making a false entry in any type of document (schedules, statements, books, documents, records, papers) relating to the debtor's property or financial affairs, either pre- or post-petition.** *18 USC §§152, 1961(D) et seq; 11 USC §727(a)(3);* or

h. **Knowingly and fraudulently withholding any recorded information (books, documents, records, papers) relating to the debtor's property or financial affairs from a trustee, marshall, custodian, the U.S. trustee, or officer of the court after the petition is filed.** *18 USC §§152, 1961(D) et seq; 11 USC §727(a)(4)(D).*

2. Fraudulent Fee Arrangements

Any party-in-interest (debtor, creditor, trustee, or representative of any such party) who knowingly and fraudulently enters into any agreement, whether express or implied, with another party-in-interest or his attorney to fix any fees or other compensation to be paid from the estate for services rendered in a bankruptcy case may be fined as much as $5,000 and/or imprisoned for as long as one year. *18 USC §§155, 1961(D) et seq; 11 USC §§326-331, 504; FRBP 2014, 2016-2017; see "Requirements of Debtor's Attorney," Chapter II.*

All fee arrangements involving a bankruptcy debtor, committee, or trustee and any attorney or agent of the debtor, committee, or trustee must be disclosed to and approved by the bankruptcy court. Failure to disclose and obtain court approval may be violations of Title 11 and Title 18. *11 USC §§327-331, 1129(a)(1), (4), 1225(a)(1), (3), 1325(a)(1), (3); 18 USC §§155, 1961(D) et seq; FRBP 2014, 2016-2017.*

3. Breach of Fiduciary Duty by Trustee, Examiner, or Officer of the Court

a. Embezzlement or Misappropriation

Any trustee, examiner, marshall, custodian, or other officer of the bankruptcy court who knowingly and fraudulently misappropriates, embezzles, spends, or transfers property or documents of the estate in such person's control may be fined as much as $5,000 and/or imprisoned for as long as five years. The criminal sanctions apply to any agent, employee, or other person who misappropriates while engaged by such officer of the court to perform a service for the bankruptcy estate. *18 USC §§153, 1961(D) et seq.*

b. Self-Serving or Conflict of Interest

A bankruptcy trustee, examiner, custodian, or other officer of the court may be fined as much as $500 and must forfeit his position for:

(1) Knowingly purchasing, either directly or indirectly, any property of the estate in his bankruptcy case; or

(2) Knowingly refusing any party-in-interest, including the U.S. trustee, a reasonable opportunity to inspect any document or account in his control relating to the estate in his bankruptcy case, if permitting such inspection was directed by the court. *18 USC §§154, 1961(D) et seq.*

4. Bankruptcy Petition Preparer's Knowing Disregard of Bankruptcy Law or Rule

A bankruptcy petition preparer whose knowing attempt to disregard the requirements of the Bankruptcy Code or federal rules of bankruptcy procedure results in the dismissal of a bankruptcy case or related proceeding may be fined and/or imprisoned. A *bankruptcy petition preparer* is any person other than an attorney or employee of an attorney who prepares for compensation any document for filing in a bankruptcy case in the federal district or bankruptcy court. *HR 1116, Pub L No 103-394, §312, amending and adding 18 USC §156(a).*

5. Bankruptcy Fraud (Bankruptcy Schemes to Defraud)

Any person involved in a *scheme to defraud* in a bankruptcy case may be fined and/or imprisoned for as long as five years. A person commits bankruptcy fraud: (a) by devising or intending to devise a scheme or artifice to defraud in a bankruptcy case; and (b) in order to execute or conceal, or in attempting to execute or conceal, such scheme or artifice: (i) files a bankruptcy petition; (ii) files any document in a bankruptcy proceeding; or (iii) makes a false or fraudulent representation, claim, or promise pre- or post-petition with regard to an actual bankruptcy proceeding or to a bankruptcy proceeding falsely asserted to be pending in a bankruptcy case. *HR 1116, Pub L No 103-394, §312(a), amending and adding 18 USC §157.*

A bankruptcy scheme to defraud by filing a petition or making a false representation regarding a bankruptcy proceeding is not a racketeering activity under the Racketeer Influenced and Corrupt Organizations (RICO) Act, 18 USC §1961(1)(D). However, a bankruptcy scheme to conceal, withhold, transfer, or destroy property or documents in a bankruptcy case is a racketeering activity under the RICO Act.

6. Procedures

Any person with reasonable grounds to believe a bankruptcy crime has been committed should report such information to any judge or trustee (including U.S. trustee). If the judge or trustee determines that reasonable grounds in fact indicate that a violation of Title 18 occurred or an investigation of a debtor's bankruptcy case should be conducted, the judge or trustee must report all relevant facts and circumstances to the appropriate United States attorney for the federal judicial district where the case is pending. The United States attorney must then investigate all facts and report back to the judge. If probable cause appears to indicate a criminal offense occurred, the United States attorney must "without delay" either present the matter to the grand jury or, if he determines that the "ends of public justice" do not warrant further "investigation" or "prosecution," report the facts to the Attorney General for his direction. *18 USC §§1961(D) et seq, 3057.*

7. Statute of Limitations

Concealing assets of the debtor in a bankruptcy case is a continuing offense until the date the debtor is granted or denied a discharge. The statute of limitations for such offense commences when the court's order granting or denying a discharge becomes final (the order is affirmed on any appeal). *18 USC §§1961(D) et seq, 3284.*

Research Guide

Anderson, *Chapter 11: Reorganizations* chs 10, 11 (Shepard's/McGraw-Hill 1983)

Anderson & Morris, *Chapter 12: Farm Reorganizations* chs 6, 7 (Shepard's/McGraw-Hill 1987)

Drake, *Bankruptcy Practice for the General Practitioner* ch 7 (Shepard's/McGraw-Hill 2d ed 1990)

Drake & Morris, *Chapter 13: Practice and Procedure* chs 8, 9 (Shepard's/McGraw-Hill 1983)

Jaroslavsky, *Practical Bankruptcy Procedure* chs 11, 12 (Shepard's/McGraw-Hill 1993)

Murphy, *Creditor's Rights in Bankruptcy* ch 4 (Shepard's/McGraw-Hill 2d 1988)

Pollard & Burton, *Guide to Effective Bankruptcy Litigation* chs 14, 16 (Shepard's/McGraw-Hill 1988)

Official Federal Bankruptcy Forms

Form 1	Voluntary Petition
Form 2	Declaration Under Penalty of Perjury on Behalf of a Corporation or Partnership
Form 4	List of Creditors Holding 20 Largest Unsecured Claims
Form 5	Involuntary Petition
Form 6	Schedules
Form 7	Statement of Financial Affairs
Form 8	Chapter 7 Individual Debtor's Statement of Intention
Form 9	Notice of Commencement of Case under the Bankruptcy Code, Meeting of Creditors, and Fixing of Dates
Form 10	Proof of Claim
Form 15	Order Confirming Plan
Form 16A	Caption
Form 16B	Caption (Short Title)
Form 16C	Caption of Adversary Proceeding
Form 18	Discharge

Procedural Forms

Form No. B250A	Summons in an Adversary Proceeding
Form No. 250B	Summons and Notice of Pretrial Conference in an Adversary Proceeding
Form No. 250C	Summons and Notice of Trial in an Adversary Proceeding

COMMITTEE NOTE

The form has been amended to require a debtor not represented by an attorney to provide a telephone number so that court personnel, the trustee, other parties in the case, and their attorneys can contact the debtor concerning matters in the case.

B1
(Rev. 5/92)

FORM 1. VOLUNTARY PETITION

United States Bankruptcy Court

________________ District of ________________

VOLUNTARY PETITION

IN RE (Name of debtor—If individual, enter: Last, First, Middle)

NAME OF JOINT DEBTOR (Spouse) (Last, First, Middle)

ALL OTHER NAMES used by the debtor in the last 6 years
(Include married, maiden, and trade names.)

ALL OTHER NAMES used by the joint debtor in the last 6 years
(Include married, maiden, and trade names.)

SOC. SEC./TAX I.D. NO. (If more than one, state all.)

SOC. SEC./TAX I.D. NO. (If more than one, state all.)

STREET ADDRESS OF DEBTOR (No. and street, city, state, and zip code)

COUNTY OF RESIDENCE OR PRINCIPAL PLACE OF BUSINESS

STREET ADDRESS OF JOINT DEBTOR (No. and street, city, state, and zip code)

COUNTY OF RESIDENCE OR PRINCIPAL PLACE OF BUSINESS

MAILING ADDRESS OF DEBTOR (If different from street address)

MAILING ADDRESS OF JOINT DEBTOR (If different from street address)

LOCATION OF PRINCIPAL ASSETS OF BUSINESS DEBTOR
(If different from addresses listed above)

VENUE (Check one box)

- ☐ Debtor has been domiciled or has had a residence, principal place of business, or principal assets in this District for 180 days immediately preceding the date of this petition or for a longer part of such 180 days than in any other District.
- ☐ There is a bankruptcy case concerning debtor's affiliate, general partner, or partnership pending in this District.

INFORMATION REGARDING DEBTOR (Check applicable boxes)

TYPE OF DEBTOR

- ☐ Individual
- ☐ Joint (Husband & Wife)
- ☐ Partnership
- ☐ Other: ____________
- ☐ Corporation Publicly Held
- ☐ Corporation Not Publicly Held
- ☐ Municipality

NATURE OF DEBT

- ☐ Non-Business/Consumer
- ☐ Business—Complete A & B below

A. TYPE OF BUSINESS (Check one box)

- ☐ Farming
- ☐ Professional
- ☐ Retail/Wholesale
- ☐ Railroad
- ☐ Transportation
- ☐ Manufacturing/Mining
- ☐ Stockbroker
- ☐ Commodity Broker
- ☐ Construction
- ☐ Real Estate
- ☐ Other Business

B. BRIEFLY DESCRIBE NATURE OF BUSINESS

CHAPTER OR SECTION OF BANKRUPTCY CODE UNDER WHICH THE PETITION IS FILED (Check one box)

- ☐ Chapter 7
- ☐ Chapter 9
- ☐ Chapter 11
- ☐ Chapter 12
- ☐ Chapter 13
- ☐ Sec. 304—Case Ancillary to Foreign Proceeding

FILING FEE (Check one box)

- ☐ Filing fee attached
- ☐ Filing fee to be paid in installments. (Applicable to individuals only.) Must attach signed application for the court's consideration certifying that the debtor is unable to pay fee except in installments. Rule 1006(b); see Official Form No. 3.

NAME AND ADDRESS OF LAW FIRM OR ATTORNEY

Telephone No.

NAME(S) OF ATTORNEY(S) DESIGNATED TO REPRESENT THE DEBTOR
(Print or Type Names)

☐ Debtor is not represented by an attorney. Telephone No. of Debtor not represented by an attorney: (   )

STATISTICAL/ADMINISTRATIVE INFORMATION (28 U.S.C. § 604)
(Estimates only) (Check applicable boxes)

- ☐ Debtor estimates that funds will be available for distribution to unsecured creditors.
- ☐ Debtor estimates that, after any exempt property is excluded and administrative expenses paid, there will be no funds available for distribution to unsecured creditors.

THIS SPACE FOR COURT USE ONLY

ESTIMATED NUMBER OF CREDITORS

1-15	16-49	50-99	100-199	200-999	1000-over
☐	☐	☐	☐	☐	☐

ESTIMATED ASSETS (in thousands of dollars)

Under 50	50-99	100-499	500-999	1000-9999	10,000-99,000	100,000-over
☐	☐	☐	☐	☐	☐	☐

ESTIMATED LIABILITIES (in thousands of dollars)

Under 50	50-99	100-499	500-999	1000-9999	10,000-99,000	100,000-over
☐	☐	☐	☐	☐	☐	☐

EST. NO. OF EMPLOYEES—CH. 11 & 12 ONLY

0	1-19	20-99	100-999	1000-over
☐	☐	☐	☐	☐

EST. NO. OF EQUITY SECURITY HOLDERS—CH. 11 & 12 ONLY

0	1-19	20-99	100-499	500-Over
☐	☐	☐	☐	☐

Name of Debtor ______________________

Case No. ______________________
(Court use only)

FILING OF PLAN

For Chapter 9, 11, 12 and 13 cases only. Check appropriate box.

☐ A copy of debtor's proposed plan dated ______________ is attached.

☐ Debtor intends to file a plan within the time allowed by statute, rule, or order of the court.

PRIOR BANKRUPTCY CASE FILED WITHIN LAST 6 YEARS (If more than one, attach additional sheet)

Location Where Filed	Case Number	Date Filed

PENDING BANKRUPTCY CASE FILED BY ANY SPOUSE, PARTNER, OR AFFILIATE OF THIS DEBTOR (If more than one, attach additional sheet.)

Name of Debtor	Case Number	Date
Relationship	District	Judge

REQUEST FOR RELIEF

Debtor requests relief in accordance with the chapter of title 11, United States Code, specified in this petition.

SIGNATURES

ATTORNEY

X ______________________ ______________
Signature Date

INDIVIDUAL/JOINT DEBTOR(S)

I declare under penalty of perjury that the information provided in this petition is true and correct.

X ______________________
Signature of Debtor

____
Date

X ______________________
Signature of Joint Debtor

____
Date

CORPORATE OR PARTNERSHIP DEBTOR

I declare under penalty of perjury that the information provided in this petition is true and correct, and that the filing of this petition on behalf of the debtor has been authorized.

X ______________________
Signature of Authorized Individual

____
Print or Type Name of Authorized Individual

____
Title of Individual Authorized by Debtor to File this Petition

____
Date

EXHIBIT "A" (To be completed if debtor is a corporation requesting relief under chapter 11.)

☐ Exhibit "A" is attached and made a part of this petition.

TO BE COMPLETED BY INDIVIDUAL CHAPTER 7 DEBTOR WITH PRIMARILY CONSUMER DEBTS (See P.L. 98-353 § 322)

I am aware that I may proceed under chapter 7, 11, or 12, or 13 of title 11, United States Code, understand the relief available under each such chapter, and choose to proceed under chapter 7 of such title.

If I am represented by an attorney, exhibit 'B' has been completed.

X ______________________ ______________
Signature of Debtor Date

X ______________________ ______________
Signature of Joint Debtor Date

EXHIBIT "B" (To be completed by attorney for individual chapter 7 debtor(s) with primarily consumer debts.)

I, the attorney for the debtor(s) named in the foregoing petition, declare that I have informed the debtor(s) that (he, she, or they) may proceed under chapter 7, 11, 12, or 13 of title 11, United States Code, and have explained the relief available under each such chapter.

X ______________________ ______________
Signature of Attorney Date

Form 1

Exhibit "A"

[If debtor is a corporation filing under chapter 11 of the Code, this Exhibit "A" shall be completed and attached to the petition.]

[Caption as in Form 16B]

Exhibit "A" to Voluntary Petition

1. Debtor's employer identification number is _______________.

2. If any of debtor's securities are registered under section 12 of the Securities and Exchange Act of 1934, the SEC file number is _______________.

3. The following financial data is the latest available information and refers to debtor's condition on _______________.

a. Total assets $ _______________

b. Total liabilities $ _______________

		Approximate number of holders
Fixed, liquidated secured debt	$ ________	________
Contingent secured debt	$ ________	________
Disputed secured claims	$ ________	________
Unliquidated secured debt	$ ________	________

		Approximate number of holders
Fixed, liquidated unsecured debt	$ ________	________
Contingent unsecured debt	$ ________	________
Disputed unsecured claims	$ ________	________
Unliquidated unsecured debt	$ ________	________

Number of shares of preferred stock	________	________
Number of shares of common stock	________	________

Form 1

Exhibit "A" continued

Comments, if any: ____
____
____
____

4. Brief description of debtor's business: ____________________________
____
____

5. List the name of any person who directly or indirectly owns, controls, or holds, with power to vote, 20% or more of the voting securities of debtor: ______________________
____
____
____

6. List the names of all corporations 20% or more of the outstanding voting securities of which are directly or indirectly owned, controlled, or held, with power to vote, by debtor: ________
____
____
____

(Added Aug. 1, 1991.)

NOTES OF ADVISORY COMMITTEE ON RULES

Form 1, the Voluntary Petition, is to be used to commence a voluntary case under chapter 7, 11, 12, or 13 of the Bankruptcy Code. A chapter 9 petition requires other allegations, (see § 109(c) of the Code), but this form may be adapted for such use. The form also may be adapted for use in filing a petition ancillary to a foreign proceeding under § 304 of the Code.

The form departs from the traditional format of a captioned pleading. All of the elements of the caption prescribed in Rule 1005 have been retained. Their placement on the page, however, has been changed to make the form compatible with electronic data processing by the clerk. The form of the caption of the case for use in other documents, formerly incorporated in Official Form No. 1, has been made a separate Form 16A.

All names used by the debtor, including trade names, names used in doing business, married names, and maiden names should be furnished in the spaces provided. If there is not sufficient room for all such names on the form itself, the list should be continued on an additional sheet attached to the petition. A complete list will enable creditors to identify the debtor properly when they receive notices and orders.

Redesign of this form into a box format also is intended to provide the court, the United States trustee, and other interested parties with as much information as possible during the 15-day period provided by Rule 1007(c), when schedules and statements may not have been filed. The box format separates into categories the data provided by the debtor, and enables the form to be used by all voluntary debtors in all chapters.

For the first time, the form requires both a street address and any separate mailing address, as well as any separate addresses used by a joint debtor. Disclosure of prior bankruptcies is new to the petition but formerly was required in the statement of financial affairs; its inclusion in the petition is intended to alert the trustee to cases in which an objection to discharge pursuant to § 727(a)(8) or (a)(9) or a motion to dismiss under § 109(g) may be appropriate. The information about pending related cases, also new to the petition, signals the clerk to assign the case to the judge to whom any related case has been assigned.

Rule 1008 requires all petitions to be verified or contain an unsworn declaration as provided in 28 U.S.C. § 1746. The unsworn declaration on page two of the petition conforms with 28 U.S.C. § 1746, which permits the declaration to be made in the manner indicated with the same force and effect as a sworn statement. The form may be adapted for use outside the United States by adding the words "under the laws of the United States" after the word "perjury."

Exhibit "A," to be attached to the petition of a corporate debtor, is for the purpose of supplying the Securities and Exchange Commission with information it needs at the beginning stages of a chapter 11 case in order to determine how actively to monitor the proceedings. Exhibit "B" was added by § 322 of Pub. L. No. 98-353, the Bankruptcy Amendments and Federal Judgeship Act of 1984. The references to chapters 11 and 12 of the Code found in Exhibit "B" and its related allegations were added by § 283(aa) of the 1986 amendments, (Pub. L. No. 99-554). This exhibit has been included in the form of the petition.

The form effects a merger of the petition and the bankruptcy cover sheet to assist the clerk in providing the statistical information required by the Director of the Administrative Office of the United States Courts pursuant to the Congressional reporting mandates of 28 U.S.C. § 604. The Director is authorized to change the particulars of the statistical portion of the form as needed in the performance of these statutory duties.

Form 2

Form 2. DECLARATION UNDER PENALTY OF PERJURY ON BEHALF OF A CORPORATION OR PARTNERSHIP

I, [the president *or* other officer *or* an authorized agent of the corporation] [*or* a member *or* an authorized agent of the partnership] named as the debtor in this case, declare under penalty of perjury that I have read the foregoing [list *or* schedule *or* amendment *or* other document (describe)] and that it is true and correct to the best of my information and belief.

Date __________________________

Signature __________________________________

____

(Print Name and Title)

(Added Aug. 1, 1991.)

NOTES OF ADVISORY COMMITTEE ON RULES

This form is derived from former Official Form No. 4.

Rule 1008 requires that all petitions, lists, schedules, statements, and amendments thereto be verified or contain an unsworn declaration conforming with 28 U.S.C. § 1746. This form or adaptations of the form have been incorporated into the official forms of the petitions, schedules, and statement of financial affairs. See Official Forms 1, 5, 6, and 7. The form has been amended for use in connection with other papers required by these rules to be verified or contain an unsworn declaration.

COMMITTEE NOTE

The form has been amended to delete reference to the specific subsection of 11 U.S.C. §101 in connection with the definition of the term "insider." Section 101 of the Bankruptcy Code contains numerous definitions, and statutory amendments from time to time have resulted in the renumbering of many of its subsections. The more general reference will avoid the necessity to amend the form further in the event of future amendments to §101.

Form 4. LIST OF CREDITORS HOLDING 20 LARGEST UNSECURED CLAIMS

[Caption as in Form 16B]

LIST OF CREDITORS HOLDING 20 LARGEST UNSECURED CLAIMS

Following is the list of the debtor's creditors holding the 20 largest unsecured claims. The list is prepared in accordance with Fed. R. Bankr. P. 1007(d) for filing in this chapter 11 [*or* chapter 9] case. The list does not include (1) persons who come within the definition of "insider" set forth in 11 U.S.C. § 101, or (2) secured creditors unless the value of the collateral is such that the unsecured deficiency places the creditor among the holders of the 20 largest unsecured claims.

(1)	(2)	(3)	(4)	(5)
Name of creditor and complete mailing address including zip code	*Name, telephone number and complete mailing address, including zip code, of employee, agent, or department of creditor familiar with claim who may be contacted*	*Nature of claim (trade debt, bank loan, government contract, etc.)*	*Indicate if claim is contingent, unliquidated, disputed or subject to setoff*	*Amount of claim [if secured also state value of security]*

Date: ______________

____
Debtor

[Declaration as in Form 2]

Form 5

FORM 5. INVOLUNTARY PETITION

United States Bankruptcy Court
District of ____________

INVOLUNTARY PETITION

IN RE (Name of debtor - If individual: Last, First, Middle)

ALL OTHER NAMES used by debtor in the last 6 years (Include married, maiden, and trade names.)

SOC SEC./TAX I.D. NO. (If more than one, state all)

STREET ADDRESS OF DEBTOR (No. and street, city, state, and zip code)

MAILING ADDRESS OF DEBTOR (If different from street address)

COUNTY OF RESIDENCE OR PRINCIPAL PLACE OF BUSINESS

LOCATION OF PRINCIPAL ASSETS OF BUSINESS DEBTOR (If different from previously listed addresses)

CHAPTER OF BANKRUPTCY CODE UNDER WHICH PETITION IS FILED

☐ Chapter 7 ☐ Chapter 11

INFORMATION REGARDING DEBTOR (Check applicable boxes)

Petitioners believe
☐ Debts are primarily consumer debts
☐ Debts are primarily business debts (Complete sections A and B)

TYPE OF DEBTOR
☐ Individual
☐ Partnership
☐ Other
☐ Corporation Publicly Held
☐ Corporation Not Publicly Held

A. TYPE OF BUSINESS (Check one)
☐ Professional
☐ Retail/Wholesale
☐ Railroad
☐ Transportation
☐ Manufacturing/ Mining
☐ Stockbroker
☐ Commodity Broker
☐ Construction
☐ Real Estate
☐ Other

B. BRIEFLY DESCRIBE NATURE OF BUSINESS

VENUE

☐ Debtor has been domiciled or has had a residence, principal place of business, or principal assets in the District for 180 days immediately preceding the date of this petition or for a longer part of such 180 days than in any other District.

☐ A bankruptcy case concerning debtor's affiliate, general partner or partnership is pending in this District.

PENDING BANKRUPTCY CASE FILED BY OR AGAINST ANY PARTNER OR AFFILIATE OF THIS DEBTOR (Report information for any additional cases on attached sheets.)

Name of Debtor	Case Number	Date
Relationship	District	Judge

ALLEGATIONS
(Check applicable boxes)

1. ☐ Petitioner(s) are eligible to file this petition pursuant to 11 U.S.C. §303(b).
2. ☐ The debtor is a person against whom an order for relief may be entered under title 11 of the United States Code.

3.a. ☐ The debtor is generally not paying such debtor's debts as they become due, unless such debts are the subject of a bona fide dispute;

or

b. ☐ Within 120 days preceding the filing of this petition, a custodian, other than a trustee, receiver, or agent appointed or authorized to take charge of less than substantially all of the property of the debtor for the purpose of enforcing a lien against such property, was appointed or took possession.

COURT USE ONLY

Form 5

FORM 5 Involuntary Petition

Name of Debtor ______

Case No. ______ (Court use only)

TRANSFER OF CLAIM

☐ Check this box if there has been a transfer of any claim against the debtor by or to any petitioner. Attach all documents evidencing the transfer and any statements that are required under Bankruptcy Rule 1003(a).

REQUEST FOR RELIEF

Petitioner(s) request that an order for relief be entered against the debtor under the chapter of title 11, United States Code, specified in this petition.

Petitioner(s) declare under penalty of perjury that the foregoing is true and correct according to the best of their knowledge, information, and belief.

X ______ Signature of Petitioner or Representative (State title)	X ______ Signature of Attorney
______ Name of Petitioner	______ Name of Attorney Firm (If any)
Name & Mailing Address of Individual Signing in Representative Capacity ______	______ Address
	______ Telephone No.
X ______ Signature of Petitioner or Representative (State title)	X ______ Signature of Attorney
______ Name of Petitioner	______ Name of Attorney Firm (If any)
Name & Mailing Address of Individual Signing in Representative Capacity ______	______ Address
	______ Telephone No.
X ______ Signature of Petitioner or Representative (State title)	X ______ Signature of Attorney
______ Name of Petitioner	______ Name of Attorney Firm (If any)
Name & Mailing Address of Individual Signing in Representative Capacity ______	______ Address
	______ Telephone No.

PETITIONING CREDITORS

Name and Address of Petitioner	Nature of Claim	Amount of Claim
Name and Address of Petitioner	Nature of Claim	Amount of Claim
Name and Address of Petitioner	Nature of Claim	Amount of Claim
Note: If there are more than three petitioners, attach additional sheets with the statement under penalty of perjury, petitioner(s) signatures under the statement and the name(s) of attorney(s) and petitioning creditor information in the format above.		Total Amount of Petitioners' Claims

____ continuation sheets attached

(Added Aug. 1, 1991.)

Form 5

NOTES OF ADVISORY COMMITTEE ON RULES

This form has been redesigned in a box format similar to that of Form 1. See Advisory Committee Note to Form 1.

The allegations required under § 303 are grouped together, and a separate section has been provided for additional allegations based upon the prohibitions and requirements set forth in Rule 1003(a) concerning transfer of claims by petitioning creditors. Petitioners may wish to supplement the allegations set forth in the form with a further statement of facts. Additional information concerning any allegation can be requested by the debtor as part of the discovery process.

Each petitioning creditor, by signing on the line provided, signs both the petition and the unsworn declaration which 28 U.S.C. § 1746 permits instead of verification. The addresses as well as the names of individuals signing the petition in a representative capacity are required, together with disclosure of which petitioner is represented by each signatory.

This form is intended to be used in every involuntary case, including that of a partnership. The separate form for a petition by a partner has been abrogated. Pursuant to § 303(b)(3)(A) of the Code, a petition by fewer than all of the general partners seeking an order for relief with respect to the partnership is treated as an involuntary petition. Such a petition is adversarial in character because not all of the partners are joining in the petition.

Section 303(b)(3)(B) permits a petition against the partnership if relief has been ordered under the Code with respect to all of the general partners. In that event, the petition may be filed by a general partner, a trustee of a general partner's estate, or a creditor of the partnership. This form may be adapted for use in that type of case.

28 U.S.C. § 1408(1) specifies the proper venue alternatives for all persons, including partnerships, as domicile, residence, principal place of business, or location of principal assets. Venue also may be based on a pending case commenced by an affiliate, general partner, or partnership pursuant to 28 U.S.C. § 1408(2). Both options are set forth in the block labeled "Venue."

28 U.S.C. § 1746 permits the unsworn declaration instead of a verification. See Committee Note to Form 2.

COMMITTEE NOTE

Schedule E (Creditors Holding Unsecured Priority Claims) has been changed to conform to the statutory amendment that added subsection (a)(8) to §507 of the Code. Pub. L. No. 101-647, (Crime Control Act of 1990), added the new subsection, which had the effect of creating an eighth priority for claims of certain governmental units based on commitments to maintain the capital of an insured depository institution.

Form 6

FORM 6. SCHEDULES

Summary of Schedules

Schedule A - Real Property

Schedule B - Personal Property

Schedule C - Property Claimed as Exempt

Schedule D - Creditors Holding Secured Claims

Schedule E - Creditors Holding Unsecured Priority Claims

Schedule F - Creditors Holding Unsecured Nonpriority Claims

Schedule G - Executory Contracts and Unexpired Leases

Schedule H - Codebtors

Schedule I - Current Income of Individual Debtor(s)

Schedule J - Current Expenditures of Individual Debtor(s)

Unsworn Declaration under Penalty of Perjury

GENERAL INSTRUCTIONS: The first page of the debtor's schedules and the first page of any amendments thereto must contain a caption as in Form 16B. Subsequent pages should be identified with the debtor's name and case number. If the schedules are filed with the petition, the case number should be left blank.

Schedules D, E, and F have been designed for the listing of each claim only once. Even when a claim is secured only in part or entitled to priority only in part, it still should be listed only once. A claim which is secured in whole or in part should be listed on Schedule D only, and a claim which is entitled to priority in whole or in part should be listed on Schedule E only. Do not list the same claim twice. If a creditor has more than one claim, such as claims arising from separate transactions, each claim should be scheduled separately.

Review the specific instructions for each schedule before completing the schedule.

Form 6

United States Bankruptcy Court

______________________ District of ______________________

In re ______________________________, Case No. ______________________
Debtor (If known)

SUMMARY OF SCHEDULES

Indicate as to each schedule whether that schedule is attached and state the number of pages in each. Report the totals from Schedules A, B, D, E, F, I, and J in the boxes provided. Add the amounts from Schedules A and B to determine the total amount of the debtor's assets. Add the amounts from Schedules D, E, and F to determine the total amount of the debtor's liabilities.

NAME OF SCHEDULE	ATTACHED (YES/NO)	NO. OF SHEETS	AMOUNTS SCHEDULED: ASSETS	LIABILITIES	OTHER
A - Real Property			$		
B - Personal Property			$		
C - Property Claimed As Exempt					
D - Creditor Holding Secured Claims				$	
E - Creditors Holding Unsecured Priority Claims				$	
F - Creditors Holding Unsecured Nonpriority Claims				$	
G - Executory Contracts and Unexpired Leases					
H - Codebtors					
I - Current Income of Individual Debtor(s)					$
J - Current Expenditures of Individual Debtor(s)					$
Total Number of Sheets of ALL Schedules ►					
Total Assets ►			$		
Total Liabilities ►				$	

Form 6

In re ______________________________, Case No. ______________________
Debtor (If known)

SCHEDULE A - REAL PROPERTY

Except as directed below, list all real property in which the debtor has any legal, equitable, or future interest, including all property owned as a co-tenant, community property, or in which the debtor has a life estate. Include any property in which the debtor holds rights and powers exercisable for the debtor's own benefit. If the debtor is married, state whether husband, wife, or both own the property by placing an "H," "W," "J," or "C" in the column labeled "Husband, Wife, Joint, or Community." If the debtor holds no interest in real property, write "None" under "Description and Location of Property."

Do not include interests in executory contracts and unexpired leases on this schedule. List them in Schedule G - Executory Contracts and Unexpired Leases.

If an entity claims to have a lien or hold a secured interest in any property, state the amount of the secured claim. See Schedule D. If no entity claims to hold a secured interest in the property, write "None" in the column labeled "Amount of Secured Claim."

If the debtor is an individual or if a joint petition is filed, state the amount of any exemption claimed in the property only in Schedule C - Property Claimed as Exempt.

DESCRIPTION AND LOCATION OF PROPERTY	NATURE OF DEBTOR'S INTEREST IN PROPERTY	HUSBAND, WIFE, JOINT OR COMMUNITY	CURRENT MARKET VALUE OF DEBTOR'S INTEREST IN PROPERTY WITHOUT DEDUCTING ANY SECURED CLAIM OR EXEMPTION	AMOUNT OF SECURED CLAIM
		Total ►	$	

(Report also on Summary of Schedules.)

Form 6

In re ______________________________________, Case No. __________________________
Debtor (If known)

SCHEDULE B - PERSONAL PROPERTY

Except as directed below, list all personal property of the debtor of whatever kind. If the debtor has no property in one or more of the categories, place an "X" in the appropriate position in the column labeled "None." If additional space is needed in any category, attach a separate sheet properly identified with the case name, case number, and the number of the category. If the debtor is married, state whether husband, wife, or both own the property by placing an "H," "W," "J," or "C" in the column labeled "Husband, Wife, Joint, or Community." If the debtor is an individual or a joint petition is filed, state the amount of any exemptions claimed only in Schedule C - Property Claimed as Exempt.

Do not list interests in executory contracts and unexpired leases on this schedule. List them in Schedule G - Executory Contracts and Unexpired Leases.

If the property is being held for the debtor by someone else, state that person's name and address under "Description and Location of Property."

TYPE OF PROPERTY	NONE	DESCRIPTION AND LOCATION OF PROPERTY	HUSBAND, WIFE, JOINT OR COMMUNITY	CURRENT MARKET VALUE OF DEBTOR'S INTEREST IN PROPERTY, WITHOUT DEDUCTING ANY SECURED CLAIM OR EXEMPTION
1. Cash on hand.				
2. Checking, savings or other financial accounts, certificates of deposit, or shares in banks, savings and loan, thrift, building and loan, and homestead associations, or credit unions, brokerage houses, or cooperatives.				
3. Security deposits with public utilities, telephone companies, landlords, and others.				
4. Household goods and furnishings, including audio, video, and computer equipment.				
5. Books, pictures and other art objects, antiques, stamp, coin, record, tape, compact disc, and other collections or collectibles.				
6. Wearing apparel.				
7. Furs and jewelry.				
8. Firearms and sports, photographic, and other hobby equipment.				
9. Interests in insurance policies. Name insurance company of each policy and itemize surrender or refund value of each.				
10. Annuities. Itemize and name each issuer.				

Form 6

In re ______________________________ , Debtor   Case No. ______________ (If known)

SCHEDULE B - PERSONAL PROPERTY

(Continuation Sheet)

TYPE OF PROPERTY	NONE	DESCRIPTION AND LOCATION OF PROPERTY	HUSBAND, WIFE, JOINT OR COMMUNITY	CURRENT MARKET VALUE OF DEBTOR'S INTEREST IN PROPERTY, WITHOUT DEDUCTING ANY SECURED CLAIM OR EXEMPTION
11. Interests in IRA, ERISA, Keogh, or other pension or profit sharing plans. Itemize.				
12. Stock and interests in incorporated and unincorporated businesses. Itemize.				
13. Interests in partnerships or joint ventures. Itemize.				
14. Government and corporate bonds and other negotiable and non-negotiable instruments.				
15. Accounts receivable.				
16. Alimony, maintenance, support, and property settlements to which the debtor is or may be entitled. Give particulars.				
17. Other liquidated debts owing debtor including tax refunds. Give particulars.				
18. Equitable or future interests, life estates, and rights or powers exercisable for the benefit of the debtor other than those listed in Schedule of Real Property.				
19. Contingent and noncontingent interests in estate of a decedent, death benefit plan, life insurance policy, or trust.				
20. Other contingent and unliquidated claims of every nature, including tax refunds, counterclaims of the debtor, and rights to setoff claims. Give estimated value of each.				
21. Patents, copyrights, and other intellectual property. Give particulars.				
22. Licenses, franchises, and other general intangibles. Give particulars.				

Form 6

In re ______________________, Case No. ______________________
Debtor (If known)

SCHEDULE B - PERSONAL PROPERTY

(Continuation Sheet)

TYPE OF PROPERTY	NONE	DESCRIPTION AND LOCATION OF PROPERTY	HUSBAND, WIFE, JOINT OR COMMUNITY	CURRENT MARKET VALUE OF DEBTOR'S INTEREST IN PROPERTY, WITH-OUT DEDUCTING ANY SECURED CLAIM OR EXEMPTION
23. Automobiles, trucks, trailers, and other vehicles and accessories.				
24. Boats, motors, and accessories.				
25. Aircraft and accessories.				
26. Office equipment, furnishings, and supplies.				
27. Machinery, fixtures, equipment and supplies used in business.				
28. Inventory.				
29. Animals.				
30. Crops - growing or harvested. Give particulars.				
31. Farming equipment and implements.				
32. Farm supplies, chemicals, and feed.				
33. Other personal property of any kind not already listed. Itemize.				

___ continuation sheets attached Total ➡ $

(Include amounts from any continuation sheets attached. Report total also on Summary of Schedules.)

Form 6

In re ______________________________, Case No. ______________________
Debtor (If known)

SCHEDULE C - PROPERTY CLAIMED AS EXEMPT

Debtor elects the exemption to which debtor is entitled under

(Check one box)

☐ 11 U.S.C. § 522(b)(1) Exemptions provided in 11 U.S.C. § 522(d). Note: These exemptions are available only in certain states.

☐ 11 U.S.C. § 522(b)(2) Exemptions available under applicable nonbankruptcy federal laws, state or local law where the debtor's domicile has been located for the 180 days immediately preceding the filing of the petition, or for a longer portion of the 180-day period than in any other place, and the debtor's interest as a tenant by the entirety or joint tenant to the extent the interest is exempt from process under applicable nonbankruptcy law.

DESCRIPTION OF PROPERTY	SPECIFY LAW PROVIDING EACH EXEMPTION	VALUE OF CLAIMED EXEMPTION	CURRENT MARKET VALUE OF PROPERTY WITHOUT DEDUCTING EXEMPTIONS

Form 6

In re ______________________________. Debtor

Case No. ______________________ (If known)

SCHEDULE D - CREDITORS HOLDING SECURED CLAIMS

State the name, mailing address, including zip code, and account number, if any, of all entities holding claims secured by property of the debtor as of the date of filing of the petition. List creditors holding all types of secured interests such as judgment liens, garnishments, statutory liens, mortgages, deeds of trust, and other security interests. List creditors in alphabetical order to the extent practicable. If all secured creditors will not fit on this page, use the continuation sheet provided.

If any entity other than a spouse in a joint case may be jointly liable on a claim, place an "X" in the column labeled "Codebtor," include the entity on the appropriate schedule of creditors, and complete Schedule H - Codebtors. If a joint petition is filed, state whether husband, wife, both of them, or the marital community may be liable on each claim by placing an "H," "W," "J," or "C" in the column labeled "Husband, Wife, Joint, or Community."

If the claim is contingent, place an "X" in the column labeled "Contingent." If the claim is unliquidated, place an "X" in the column labeled "Unliquidated." If the claim is disputed, place an "X" in the column labeled "Disputed." (You may need to place an "X" in more than one of these three columns.)

Report the total of all claims listed on this schedule in the box labeled "Total" on the last sheet of the completed schedule. Report this total also on the Summary of Schedules.

☐ Check this box if debtor has no creditors holding secured claims to report on this Schedule D.

CREDITOR'S NAME AND MAILING ADDRESS INCLUDING ZIP CODE	CODEBTOR	HUSBAND, WIFE, JOINT OR COMMUNITY	DATE CLAIM WAS INCURRED, NATURE OF LIEN, AND DESCRIPTION AND MARKET VALUE OF PROPERTY SUBJECT TO LIEN	CONTINGENT	UNLIQUIDATED	DISPUTED	AMOUNT OF CLAIM WITHOUT DEDUCTING VALUE OF COLLATERAL	UNSECURED PORTION, IF ANY
ACCOUNT NO.								
			Value $					
ACCOUNT NO.								
			Value $					
ACCOUNT NO.								
			Value $					
ACCOUNT NO.								
			Value $					

____ Continuation sheets attached

Subtotal ➡ $
(Total of this page)

Total ➡ $
(Use only on last page)

(Report total also on Summary of Schedules)

Form 6

In re ______________________________, Case No. ______________
Debtor (If known)

SCHEDULE D - CREDITORS HOLDING SECURED CLAIMS

(Continuation Sheet)

CREDITOR'S NAME AND MAILING ADDRESS INCLUDING ZIP CODE	CODEBTOR	HUSBAND, WIFE, JOINT OR COMMUNITY	DATE CLAIM WAS INCURRED, NATURE OF LIEN, AND DESCRIPTION AND MARKET VALUE OF PROPERTY SUBJECT TO LIEN	CONTINGENT	UNLIQUIDATED	DISPUTED	AMOUNT OF CLAIM WITHOUT DEDUCTING VALUE OF COLLATERAL	UNSECURED PORTION, IF ANY
ACCOUNT NO.			VALUE $					
ACCOUNT NO.			VALUE $					
ACCOUNT NO.			VALUE $					
ACCOUNT NO.			VALUE $					
ACCOUNT NO.			VALUE $					

Sheet no. ____ of ____ continuation sheets attached to Schedule of Creditors Holding Secured Claims

Subtotal ▶ $
(Total of this page)
Total ▶ $
(Use only on last page)
(Report total also on Summary of Schedules)

B6E
(Rev. 5/92)

In re ______________________________, Case No. ____________________
Debtor (If known)

SCHEDULE E—CREDITORS HOLDING UNSECURED PRIORITY CLAIMS

A complete list of claims entitled to priority, listed separately by type of priority, is to be set forth on the sheets provided. Only holders of unsecured claims entitled to priority should be listed in this schedule. In the boxes provided on the attached sheets, state the name and mailing address, including zip code, and account number, if any, of all entities holding priority claims against the debtor or the property of the debtor, as of the date of the filing of the petition.

If any entity other than a spouse in a joint case may be jointly liable on a claim, place an "X" in the column labeled "Codebtor," include the entity on the appropriate schedule of creditors, and complete Schedule H—Codebtors. If a joint petition is filed, state whether husband, wife, both of them, or the marital community may be liable on each claim by placing an "H," "W," "J," or "C" in the column labeled "Husband, Wife, Joint or Community."

If the claim is contingent, place an "X" in the column labeled "Contingent." If the claim is unliquidated, place an "X" in the column labeled "Unliquidated." If the claim is disputed, place an "X" in the column labeled "Disputed." (You may need to place an "X" in more than one of these three columns.)

Report the total of claims listed on each sheet in the box labeled "Subtotal" on each sheet. Report the total of all claims listed on this Schedule E in the box labeled "Total" on the last sheet of the completed schedule. Repeat this total also on the Summary of Schedules.

☐ Check this box if debtor has no creditors holding unsecured priority claims to report on this Schedule E.

TYPES OF PRIORITY CLAIMS (Check the appropriate box(es) below if claims in that category are listed on the attached sheets)

☐ **Extensions of credit in an involuntary case**

Claims arising in the ordinary course of the debtor's business or financial affairs after the commencement of the case but before the earlier of the appointment of a trustee or the order for relief. 11 U.S.C. § 507(a)(2).

☐ **Wages, salaries, and commissions**

Wages, salaries, and commissions, including vacation, severance, and sick leave pay owing to employees, up to a maximum of $2000 per employee, earned within 90 days immediately preceding the filing of the original petition, or the cessation of business, whichever occured first, to the extent provided in 11 U.S.C. § 507(a)(3).

☐ **Contributions to employee benefit plans**

Money owed to employee benefit plans for services rendered within 180 days immediately preceding the filing of the original petition, or the cessation of business, whichever occurred first, to the extent provided in 11 U.S.C. § 507(a)(4).

☐ **Certain farmers and fishermen**

Claims of certain farmers and fishermen, up to a maximum of $2000 per farmer or fisherman, against the debtor, as provided in 11 U.S.C. § 507(a)(5).

☐ **Deposits by individuals**

Claims of individuals up to a maximum of $900 for deposits for the purchase, lease, or rental of property or services for personal, family, or household use, that were not delivered or provided. 11 U.S.C. § 507(a)(6).

☐ **Taxes and Certain Other Debts Owed to Governmental Units**

Taxes, customs duties, and penalties owing to federal, state, and local governmental units as set forth in 11 U.S.C. §507(a)(7).

☐ **Commitments to Maintain the Capital of an Insured Depository Institution**

Claims based on commitments to the FDIC, RTC, Director of the Office of Thrift Supervision, Comptroller of the Currency, or Board of Governors of the Federal Reserve System, or their predecessors or successors, to maintain the capital of an insured depository institution. 11 U.S.C. § 507(a)(8).

_______ continuation sheets attached

Form 6

In re ______________________________________. Case No. ____________________
Debtor (If known)

SCHEDULE E - CREDITORS, HOLDING UNSECURED PRIORITY CLAIMS

(Continuation Sheet)

TYPE OF PRIORITY ____________________

CREDITOR'S NAME AND MAILING ADDRESS INCLUDING ZIP CODE	CODEBTOR	HUSBAND, WIFE, JOINT OR COMMUNITY	DATE CLAIM WAS INCURRED AND CONSIDERATION FOR CLAIM	CONTINGENT	UNLIQUIDATED	DISPUTED	TOTAL AMOUNT OF CLAIM	AMOUNT ENTITLED TO PRIORITY
ACCOUNT NO.								
ACCOUNT NO.								
ACCOUNT NO.								
ACCOUNT NO.								
ACCOUNT NO.								

Sheet no. ____ of ____ sheets attached to Schedule of Creditors Holding Unsecured Priority Claims

Subtotal ▶ $
(Total of this page)

Total ▶ $
(Use only on last page of the completed Schedule E)

(Report total also on Summary of Schedules)

Form 6

In re ______________________________, Debtor

Case No. ______________________ (If Known)

SCHEDULE F - CREDITORS HOLDING UNSECURED NONPRIORITY CLAIMS

State the name, mailing address, including zip code, and account number, if any, of all entities holding unsecured claims without priority against the debtor or the property of the debtor, as of the date of filing of the petition. Do not include claims listed in Schedules D and E. If all creditors will not fit on this page, use the continuation sheet provided.

If any entity other than a spouse in a joint case may be jointly liable on a claim, place an "X" in the column labeled "Codebtor," include the entity on the appropriate schedule of creditors, and complete Schedule H - Codebtors. If a joint petition is filed, state whether husband, wife, both of them, or the marital community may be liable on each claim by placing an "H," "W," "J," or "C" in the column labeled "Husband, Wife, Joint, or Community."

If the claim is contingent, place an "X" in the column labeled "Contingent." If the claim is unliquidated, place an "X" in the column labeled "Unliquidated." If the claim is disputed, place an "X" in the column labeled "Disputed." (You may need to place an "X" in more than one of these three columns.)

Report total of all claims listed on this schedule in the box labeled "Total" on the last sheet of the completed schedule. Report this total also on the Summary of Schedules.

☐ Check this box if debtor has no creditors holding unsecured non priority claims to report on this Schedule F.

CREDITOR'S NAME AND MAILING ADDRESS INCLUDING ZIP CODE	CODEBTOR	HUSBAND, WIFE, JOINT OR COMMUNITY	DATE CLAIM WAS INCURRED AND CONSIDERATION FOR CLAIM, IF CLAIM IS SUBJECT TO SETOFF, SO STATE	CONTINGENT	UNLIQUIDATED	DISPUTED	AMOUNT OF CLAIM
ACCOUNT NO.							
ACCOUNT NO.							
ACCOUNT NO.							
ACCOUNT NO.							

____ continuation sheets attached

Subtotal ➔ $

Total ➔ $

(Report total also on Summary of Schedules)

Form 6

In re ______________________________________, Case No. ____________________
Debtor (If known)

SCHEDULE F - CREDITORS HOLDING UNSECURED NONPRIORITY CLAIMS

(Continuation Sheet)

CREDITOR'S NAME AND MAILING ADDRESS INCLUDING ZIP CODE	CODEBTOR	HUSBAND, WIFE, JOINT OR COMMUNITY	DATE CLAIM WAS INCURRED AND CONSIDERATION FOR CLAIM. IF CLAIM IS SUBJECT TO SETOFF, SO STATE	CONTINGENT	UNLIQUIDATED	DISPUTED	AMOUNT OF CLAIM
ACCOUNT NO.							
ACCOUNT NO.							
ACCOUNT NO.							
ACCOUNT NO.							
ACCOUNT NO.							

Sheet no. ____ of ____ sheets attached to Schedule of Creditors Holding Unsecured Nonpriority Claims

Subtotal → $
(Total of this page)
Total → $
(Use only on last page of the completed Schedule F)
(Report total also on Summary of Schedules)

Form 6

In re ______________________________, Debtor   Case No. ______________ (If Known)

SCHEDULE G - EXECUTORY CONTRACTS AND UNEXPIRED LEASES

Describe all executory contracts of any nature and all unexpired leases of real or personal property. Include any timeshare interests.

State nature of debtor's interest in contract, i.e., "Purchaser," "Agent," etc. State whether debtor is the lessor or lessee of a lease.

Provide the names and complete mailing addresses of all other parties to each lease or contract described.

NOTE: A party listed on this schedule will not receive notice of the filing of this case unless the party is also scheduled in the appropriate schedule of creditors.

☐ Check this box if debtor has no executory contracts or unexpired leases.

NAME AND MAILING ADDRESS, INCLUDING ZIP CODE, OF OTHER PARTIES TO LEASE OR CONTRACT	DESCRIPTION OF CONTRACT OR LEASE AND NATURE OF DEBTOR'S INTEREST. STATE WHETHER LEASE IS FOR NONRESIDENTIAL REAL PROPERTY. STATE CONTRACT NUMBER OF ANY GOVERNMENT CONTRACT

Form 6

In re ______________________________, Case No. ______________________
Debtor (If known)

SCHEDULE H - CODEBTORS

Provide the information requested concerning any person or entity, other than a spouse in a joint case, that is also liable on any debts listed by debtor in the schedules of creditors. Include all guarantors and co-signers. In community property states, a married debtor not filing a joint case should report the name and address of the nondebtor spouse on this schedule. Include all names used by the nondebtor spouse during the six years immediately preceding the commencement of this case.

☐ Check this box if debtor has no codebtors.

NAME AND ADDRESS OF CODEBTOR	NAME AND ADDRESS OF CREDITOR

Form 6

In re ______________________________, Debtor

Case No. ______________________ (If known)

SCHEDULE I - CURRENT INCOME OF INDIVIDUAL DEBTOR(S)

The column labeled "Spouse" must be completed in all cases filed by joint debtors and by a married debtor in a chapter 12 or 13 case whether or not a joint petition is filed, unless the spouses are separated and a joint petition is not filed.

Debtor's Marital Status:	DEPENDENTS OF DEBTOR AND SPOUSE		
	NAMES	AGE	RELATIONSHIP

EMPLOYMENT:	DEBTOR	SPOUSE
Occupation		
Name of Employer		
How long employed		
Address of Employer		

Income: (Estimate of average monthly income)	DEBTOR	SPOUSE
Current monthly gross wages, salary, and commissions (pro rate if not paid monthly.)	$	$
Estimated monthly overtime	$	$
SUBTOTAL	$	$
LESS PAYROLL DEDUCTIONS		
a. Payroll taxes and social security	$	$
b. Insurance	$	$
c. Union dues	$	$
d. Other (Specify ______________________)	$	$
SUBTOTAL OF PAYROLL DEDUCTIONS	$	$
TOTAL NET MONTHLY TAKE HOME PAY	$	$
Regular income from operation of business or profession or farm (attach detailed statement)	$	$
Income from real property	$	$
Interest and dividends	$	$
Alimony, maintenance or support payments payable to the debtor for the debtor's use or that of dependents listed above.	$	$
Social security or other government assistance (Specify) ______________________	$	$
Pension or retirement income	$	$
Other monthly income	$	$
(Specify) ______________________	$	$
______________________	$	$
TOTAL MONTHLY INCOME	$	$

TOTAL COMBINED MONTHLY INCOME $______________ (Report also on Summary of Schedules)

Describe any increase or decrease of more than 10% in any of the above categories anticipated to occur within the year following the filing of this document:

Form 6

In re ______________________________, Case No. ______________________
Debtor (If known)

SCHEDULE J - CURRENT EXPENDITURES OF INDIVIDUAL DEBTOR(S)

Complete this schedule by estimating the average monthly expenses of the debtor and the debtor's family. Pro rate any payments made bi-weekly, quarterly, semi-annually, or annually to show monthly rate.

☐ Check this box if a joint petition is filed and debtor's spouse maintains a separate household. Complete a separate schedule of expenditures labeled "Spouse."

Rent or home mortgage payment (include lot rented for mobile home) $ ________
Are real estate taxes included? Yes ________ No ________
Is property insurance included? Yes ________ No ________
Utilities Electricity and heating fuel $ ________
Water and sewer $ ________
Telephone $ ________
Other ________________________ $ ________
Home Maintenance (Repairs and upkeep) $ ________
Food $ ________
Clothing $ ________
Laundry and dry cleaning $ ________
Medical and dental expenses $ ________
Transportation (not including car payments) $ ________
Recreation, clubs and entertainment, newspapers, magazines, etc. $ ________
Charitable contributions $ ________
Insurance (not deducted from wages or included in home mortgage payments)
Homeowner's or renter's $ ________
Life $ ________
Health $ ________
Auto $ ________
Other ________________________ $ ________
Taxes (not deducted from wages or included in home mortgage payments)
(Specify) ________________________ $ ________
Installment payments (In chapter 12 and 13 cases, do not list payments to be included in the plan)
Auto $ ________
Other ________________________ $ ________
Other ________________________ $ ________
Alimony, maintenance, and support paid to others $ ________
Payments for support of additional dependents not living at your home $ ________
Regular expenses from operation of business, profession, or farm (attach detailed statement) $ ________
Other ________________________ $ ________

TOTAL MONTHLY EXPENSES (Report also on Summary of Schedules) $ ________

[FOR CHAPTER 12 AND 13 DEBTORS ONLY]
Provide the information requested below, including whether plan payments are to be made bi-weekly, monthly, annually, or at some other regular interval.

A. Total projected monthly income $ ________
B. Total projected monthly expenses $ ________
C. Excess income (A minus B) $ ________
D. Total amount to be paid into plan each ________________ $ ________
(interval)

Form 6

In re ______________________________, Case No. ______________________
Debtor (If known)

DECLARATION CONCERNING DEBTOR'S SCHEDULES

DECLARATION UNDER PENALTY OF PERJURY BY INDIVIDUAL DEBTOR

I declare under penalty of perjury that I have read the foregoing summary and schedules, consisting of ____________ sheets, (Total shown on summary page plus 1) and that they are true and correct to the best of my knowledge, information, and belief.

Date ______________________ Signature ______________________
Debtor

Date ______________________ Signature ______________________
(Joint Debtor, if any)

[If joint case, both spouses must sign.]

DECLARATION UNDER PENALTY OF PERJURY ON BEHALF OF CORPORATION OR PARTNERSHIP

I, the ______________________ [the president or other officer or an authorized agent of the corporation or a member or an authorized agent of the partnership] of the ______________________ [corporation or partnership] named as debtor in this case, declare under penalty of perjury that I have read the foregoing summary and schedules, consisting of ____________ sheets, and that they are true and correct to the best of my knowledge, information, and belief. (Total shown on summary page plus 1)

Date ______________________ Signature ______________________

[Print or type name of individual signing on behalf of debtor]

[An individual signing on behalf of a partnership or corporation must indicate position or relationship to debtor.]

Penalty for making a false statement or concealing property. Fine of up to $500,000 or imprisonment for up to 5 years or both. 18 U.S.C. §§ 152 and 3571.

(Added Aug. 1, 1991.)

Notes of Advisory Committee on Rules

These schedules shall be used to comply with § 521(1) of the Code and Rule 1007(b). Schedules A, B, D, E, and F constitute the schedule of assets and liabilities. Schedules I and J constitute a schedule of current income and current expenditures for individual and joint debtors. Two new schedules have been created, Schedule G—Executory Contracts and Unexpired Leases, and Schedule H—Codebtors.

The order of the schedules has been arranged with the summary sheet in front and with the schedules of assets appearing first, followed by the schedules of liabilities. This structure corresponds to the customary pattern by which trustees and creditors review these documents and to the format of the accounting profession for balance sheets.

The schedules require a complete listing of assets and liabilities but leave many of the details to investigation by the trustee. Instructions in the former schedules to provide details concerning "written instruments" relating to the debtor's property or debts have been deleted. Section 521(3) of the Code requires the debtor to cooperate with the trustee, who can administer the estate more effectively by requesting any documents from the debtor rather than relying on descriptions in the schedules which may prove to be inaccurate.

Leasehold interests in both real and personal property are to be reported in Schedule G—Executory Contracts and Unexpired Leases. This information should not be repeated in the schedules of assets.

Generally in these schedules, a creditor's claim will be listed only once, even if the claim is secured only in part, or is entitled only in part to priority under § 507(a) of the Code, with the remainder of the claim to be treated as a general unsecured claim. For example, a partially secured creditor whose claim is reported in Schedule D—Creditors Holding Secured Claims will be listed together with the value of the property securing the claim and a notation of the amount of any unsecured portion of the claim. Information concerning the unsecured portion should not be repeated in Schedule F—Creditors Holding Nonpriority Unsecured Claims. Any resulting overstatement of the amounts owed on secured and priority claims as reported on the summary sheet is offset by a corresponding understatement of the amount owed on unsecured claims.

If a debtor has no property or no creditors in a particular category, an affirmative statement to that effect is required. Married debtors should indicate whether property is jointly or separately owned and whether spouses are jointly or separately liable for debts, using the columns provided in the schedules.

Former "Schedule B-3. Property not otherwise scheduled," has been deleted and its two questions moved. Schedule B—Personal Property now includes at item 33, "Other personal property of any kind not already listed." The only other question on former Schedule B-3 concerned assignments for the benefit of creditors; it has been moved to the Statement of Financial Affairs.

Schedule A—Real Property. Instructions at the top of the form indicate the scope of the interests in property to be reported on the schedule. Leasehold interests of the debtor are not reported here but on the Schedule of Executory Contracts and Unexpired Leases. The trustee will request copies of deeds or other instruments necessary to the administration of the estate.

Schedule B—Personal Property. This schedule is to be used for reporting all of the debtor's interests in personal property except leases and executory contracts, which are to be listed on the Schedule of Executory Contracts and Unexpired Leases. Several new categories of property have been added to the schedule, i.e., aircraft, and interests in IRA, ERISA, Keogh, or other pension or profit-sharing plans. To minimize the potential for concealment of assets, the debtor must declare whether the debtor has any property in each category on the schedule. The trustee can request copies of any documents concerning the debtor's property necessary to the administration of the estate.

Schedule C—Property Claimed as Exempt. The form of the schedule has been modified to eliminate duplication of information provided elsewhere. The location of property, for example, which formerly was required here, is disclosed in the schedules of real and personal property. The requirement that the debtor state the present use of the property also has been eliminated as best left to inquiry by the trustee. Exemptions in some states are granted by constitutional provisions; accordingly, the requirement that the debtor state the "statute" creating an exemption has been changed to request a statement of the relevant "law."

This schedule adds a new requirement that the debtor state the market value of the property in addition to the amount claimed as exempt.

Schedule D—Creditors Holding Secured Claims. Schedules D, E, and F have been redesigned with address boxes sized to match the number of characters which can be accommodated on the computerized noticing systems used by the courts. The size also closely approximates that of standard mailing labels. Space is designated at the top of the box for the debtor's account number with the creditor. The design of the form is intended to reduce the volume of misdirected creditor mail.

The form requires the debtor to state affirmatively that a claim is disputed, unliquidated, or contingent. The existence of any type of codebtor is to be disclosed, but details are to be provided in Schedule H, as they are not needed here. Duplication of information also has been kept to a minimum by deleting requests that the debtor indicate on this schedule whether a debt has been reduced to judgment and the date on which a creditor repossessed any collateral. Requests for details concerning negotiable instruments and the consideration for a claim, formerly part of the schedule, are left to the trustee's inquiries.

Schedule E—Creditors Holding Unsecured Priority Claims. The schedule lists all of the types of claims entitled to priority and requires the debtor to indicate the existence of claims in each category. Continuation sheets are provided. The type of priority claim is to be noted at the top of the continuation sheet, and each type must be reported on a separate sheet. This schedule also requires the debtor to indicate the existence of any codebtors. As in Schedule D—Creditors Holding Secured Claims, requests for information concerning judgments and negotiable instruments have been deleted.

Schedule F—Creditors Holding Unsecured Nonpriority Claims. This schedule has been revised generally in conformity with the other schedules of creditors. If a claim is subject to setoff, the debtor is required to so state.

Schedule G—Executory Contracts and Unexpired Leases. Rule 1007(b) requires the debtor to file a schedule of executory contracts and unexpired leases, unless the court orders otherwise. All unexpired leases of either real or personal property are to be reported on this schedule. The schedule also requires the debtor to disclose specific information to assist the trustee in identifying leases which must be assumed within 60 days after the order for relief or be deemed rejected under § 365(d) of the Code.

Schedule H—Schedule of Codebtors. This schedule is designed to provide the trustee and creditors with information about codebtors of all types other than spouses in joint cases. The completed schedule provides information concerning non-debtor parties, such as guarantors and non-debtor spouses having an interest in property as tenants by the entirety. In chapter 12 and chapter 13 cases, the completed schedule also indicates those persons who may be entitled to certain protections from creditor action under §§ 1201 and 1301 of the Code.

Schedule I—Schedule of Current Income of Individual Debtor(s) and Schedule J—Schedule of Current Expenditures of Individual Debtor(s). Former Official Form No. 6A has been divided into a schedule of current income and a separate schedule of current expenditures. The language is substantially the same as in former Official Form No. 6A. In light of the abrogation of Official Form No. 10, the Chapter 13 Statement, style changes have been made so that these schedules can be used by individual and joint debtors in all chapters.

COMMITTEE NOTE

The form has been amended in two ways. In the second paragraph of the instructions, the third sentence has been deleted to clarify that only a debtor that is or has been in business as defined in the form should answer Questions 16-21. In addition, administrative proceedings have been added to the types of legal actions to be disclosed in Question 4.a.

FORM 7. STATEMENT OF FINANCIAL AFFAIRS

UNITED STATES BANKRUPTCY COURT

____________________ DISTRICT OF ____________________

In re ____________________, Case No. ________________
(Name) (If known)
Debtor

STATEMENT OF FINANCIAL AFFAIRS

This statement is to be completed by every debtor. Spouses filing a joint petition may file a single statement on which the information for both spouses is combined. If the case is filed under chapter 12 or chapter 13, a married debtor must furnish information for both spouses whether or not a joint petition is filed, unless the spouses are separated and a joint petition is not filed. An individual debtor engaged in business as a sole proprietor, partner, family farmer, or self-employed professional, should provide the information requested on this statement concerning all such activities as well as the individual's personal affairs.

Questions 1-15 are to be completed by all debtors. Debtors that are or have been in business, as defined below, also must complete Questions 16-21. **If the answer to any question is "None," or the question is not applicable, mark the box labeled "None."** If additional space is needed for the answer to any question, use and attach a separate sheet properly identified with the case name, case number (if known), and the number of the question.

DEFINITIONS

"In business." A debtor is "in business" for the purpose of this form if the debtor is a corporation or partnership. An individual debtor is "in business" for the purpose of this form if the debtor is or has been, within the two years immediately preceding the filing of this bankruptcy case, any of the following: an officer, director, managing executive, or person in control of a corporation; a partner, other than a limited partner, of a partnership; a sole proprietor or self-employed.

"Insider." The term "insider" includes but is not limited to: relatives of the debtor; general partners of the debtor and their relatives; corporations of which the debtor is an officer, director, or person in control; officers, directors, and any person in control of a corporate debtor and their relatives; affiliates of the debtor and insiders of such affiliates; any managing agent of the debtor. 11 U.S.C. §101(30).

---

1. Income from employment or operation of business

None ☐

State the gross amount of income the debtor has received from employment, trade, or profession, or from operation of the debtor's business from the beginning of this calendar year to the date this case was commenced. State also the gross amounts received during the two years immediately preceding this calendar year. (A debtor that maintains, or has maintained, financial records on the basis of a fiscal rather than a calendar year may report fiscal year income. Identify the beginning and ending dates of the debtor's fiscal year.) If a joint petition is filed, state income for each spouse separately. (Married debtors filing under chapter 12 or chapter 13 must state income of both spouses whether or not a joint petition is filed, unless the spouses are separated and a joint petition is not filed.)

AMOUNT SOURCE (if more than one)

B7
(Rev. 12/92)

2. Income other than from employment or operation of business

None ☐ State the amount of income received by the debtor other than from employment, trade, profession, or operation of the debtor's business during the two years immediately preceding the commencement of this case. Give particulars. If a joint petition is filed, state income for each spouse separately. (Married debtors filing under chapter 12 or chapter 13 must state income for each spouse whether or not a joint petition is filed, unless the spouses are separated and a joint petition is not filed.)

AMOUNT	SOURCE

---

3. Payments to creditors

None ☐ a. List all payments on loans, installment purchases of goods or services, and other debts, aggregating more than $600 to any creditor, made within **90 days** immediately preceding the commencement of this case. (Married debtors filing under chapter 12 or chapter 13 must include payments by either or both spouses whether or not a joint petition is filed, unless the spouses are separated and a joint petition is not filed.)

NAME AND ADDRESS OF CREDITOR	DATES OF PAYMENTS	AMOUNT PAID	AMOUNT STILL OWING

None ☐ b. List all payments made within one year immediately preceding the commencement of this case to or for the benefit of creditors who are or were insiders. (Married debtors filing under chapter 12 or chapter 13 must include payments by either or both spouses whether or not a joint petition is filed, unless the spouses are separated and a joint petition is not filed.)

NAME AND ADDRESS OF CREDITOR AND RELATIONSHIP TO DEBTOR	DATE OF PAYMENT	AMOUNT PAID	AMOUNT STILL OWING

---

4. Suits and administrative proceedings, executions, garnishments and attachments

None ☐ a. List all suits and administrative proceedings to which the debtor is or was a party within one year immediately preceding the filing of this bankruptcy case. (Married debtors filing under chapter 12 or chapter 13 must include information concerning either or both spouses whether or not a joint petition is filed, unless the spouses are separated and a joint petition is not filed.)

CAPTION OF SUIT AND CASE NUMBER	NATURE OF PROCEEDING	COURT OR AGENCY AND LOCATION	STATUS OR DISPOSITION

None ☐ b. Describe all property that has been attached, garnished or seized under any legal or equitable process within one year immediately preceding the commencement of this case. (Married debtors filing under chapter 12 or chapter 13 must include information concerning property of either or both spouses whether or not a joint petition is filed, unless the spouses are separated and a joint petition is not filed.)

NAME AND ADDRESS OF PERSON FOR WHOSE BENEFIT PROPERTY WAS SEIZED	DATE OF SEIZURE	DESCRIPTION AND VALUE OF PROPERTY

5. **Repossessions, foreclosures and returns**

None ☐ List all property that has been repossessed by a creditor, sold at a foreclosure sale, transferred through a deed in lieu of foreclosure or returned to the seller, within one year immediately preceding the commencement of this case. (Married debtors filing under chapter 12 or chapter 13 must include information concerning property of either or both spouses whether or not a joint petition is filed, unless the spouses are separated and a joint petition is not filed.)

NAME AND ADDRESS OF CREDITOR OR SELLER	DATE OF REPOSSESSION, FORECLOSURE SALE, TRANSFER OR RETURN	DESCRIPTION AND VALUE OF PROPERTY

6. **Assignments and receiverships**

None ☐ a. Describe any assignment of property for the benefit of creditors made within 120 days immediately preceding the commencement of this case. (Married debtors filing under chapter 12 or chapter 13 must include any assignment by either or both spouses whether or not a joint petition is filed, unless the spouses are separated and a joint petition is not filed.)

NAME AND ADDRESS OF ASSIGNEE	DATE OF ASSIGNMENT	TERMS OF ASSIGNMENT OR SETTLEMENT

None ☐ b. List all property which has been in the hands of a custodian, receiver, or court-appointed official within one year immediately preceding the commencement of this case. (Married debtors filing under chapter 12 or chapter 13 must include information concerning property of either or both spouses whether or not a joint petition is filed, unless the spouses are separated and a joint petition is not filed.)

NAME AND ADDRESS OF CUSTODIAN	NAME AND LOCATION OF COURT CASE TITLE & NUMBER	DATE OF ORDER	DESCRIPTION AND VALUE OF PROPERTY

7. Gifts

None ☐ List all gifts or charitable contributions made within one year immediately preceding the commencement of this case except ordinary and usual gifts to family members aggregating less than $200 in value per individual family member and charitable contributions aggregating less than $100 per recipient. (Married debtors filing under chapter 12 or chapter 13 must include gifts or contributions by either or both spouses whether or not a joint petition is filed, unless the spouses are separated and a joint petition is not filed.)

NAME AND ADDRESS OF PERSON OR ORGANIZATION	RELATIONSHIP TO DEBTOR, IF ANY	DATE OF GIFT	DESCRIPTION AND VALUE OF GIFT

8. Losses

None ☐ List all losses from fire, theft, other casualty or gambling within one year immediately preceding the commencement of this case or since the commencement of this case. (Married debtors filing under chapter 12 or chapter 13 must include losses by either or both spouses whether or not a joint petition is filed, unless the spouses are separated and a joint petition is not filed.)

DESCRIPTION AND VALUE OF PROPERTY	DESCRIPTION OF CIRCUMSTANCES AND, IF LOSS WAS COVERED IN WHOLE OR IN PART BY INSURANCE, GIVE PARTICULARS	DATE OF LOSS

9. **Payments related to debt counseling or bankruptcy**

None ☐ List all payments made or property transferred by or on behalf of the debtor to any persons, including attorneys, for consultation concerning debt consolidation, relief under the bankruptcy law or preparation of a petition in bankruptcy within one year immediately preceding the commencement of this case.

NAME AND ADDRESS OF PAYEE	DATE OF PAYMENT, NAME OF PAYOR IF OTHER THAN DEBTOR	AMOUNT OF MONEY OR DESCRIPTION AND VALUE OF PROPERTY

10. Other transfers

None ☐ a. List all other property, other than property transferred in the ordinary course of the business or financial affairs of the debtor, transferred either absolutely or as security within one year immediately preceding the commencement of this case. (Married debtors filing under chapter 12 or chapter 13 must include transfers by either or both spouses whether or not a joint petition is filed, unless the spouses are separated and a joint petition is not filed.)

NAME AND ADDRESS OF TRANSFEREE, RELATIONSHIP TO DEBTOR	DATE	DESCRIBE PROPERTY TRANSFERRED AND VALUE RECEIVED

---

11. Closed financial accounts

None ☐ List all financial accounts and instruments held in the name of the debtor or for the benefit of the debtor which were closed, sold, or otherwise transferred within one year immediately preceding the commencement of this case. Include checking, savings, or other financial accounts, certificates of deposit, or other instruments; shares and share accounts held in banks, credit unions, pension funds, cooperatives, associations, brokerage houses and other financial institutions. (Married debtors filing under chapter 12 or chapter 13 must include information concerning accounts or instruments held by or for either or both spouses whether or not a joint petition is filed, unless the spouses are separated and a joint petition is not filed.)

NAME AND ADDRESS OF INSTITUTION	TYPE AND NUMBER OF ACCOUNT AND AMOUNT OF FINAL BALANCE	AMOUNT AND DATE OF SALE OR CLOSING

12. Safe deposit boxes

None ☐ List each safe deposit or other box or depository in which the debtor has or had securities, cash, or other valuables within one year immediately preceding the commencement of this case. (Married debtors filing under chapter 12 or chapter 13 must include boxes or depositories of either or both spouses whether or not a joint petition is filed, unless the spouses are separated and a joint petition is not filed.)

NAME AND ADDRESS OF BANK OR OTHER DEPOSITORY	NAMES AND ADDRESSES OF THOSE WITH ACCESS TO BOX OR DEPOSITORY	DESCRIPTION OF CONTENTS	DATE OF TRANSFER OR SURRENDER, IF ANY

13. Setoffs

None ☐ List all setoffs made by any creditor, including a bank, against a debt or deposit of the debtor within 90 days preceding the commencement of this case. (Married debtors filing under chapter 12 or chapter 13 must include information concerning either or both spouses whether or not a joint petition is filed, unless the spouses are separated and a joint petition is not filed.)

NAME AND ADDRESS OF CREDITOR	DATE OF SETOFF	AMOUNT OF SETOFF

14. Property held for another person

None ☐ List all property owned by another person that the debtor holds or controls.

NAME AND ADDRESS OF OWNER	DESCRIPTION AND VALUE OF PROPERTY	LOCATION OF PROPERTY

15. Prior address of debtor

None ☐ If the debtor has moved within the two years immediately preceding the commencement of this case, list all premises which the debtor occupied during that period and vacated prior to the commencement of this case. If a joint petition is filed, report also any separate address of either spouse.

ADDRESS	NAME USED	DATES OF OCCUPANCY

The following questions are to be completed by every debtor that is a corporation or partnership and by any individual debtor who is or has been, within the two years immediately preceding the commencement of this case, any of the following: an officer, director, managing executive, or owner of more than 5 percent of the voting securities of a corporation; a partner, other than a limited partner, of a partnership; a sole proprietor or otherwise self-employed.

(An individual or joint debtor should complete this portion of the statement only if the debtor is or has been in business, as defined above, within the two years immediately preceding the commencement of this case.)

16. **Nature, location and name of business**

None ☐ a. If the debtor is an individual, list the names and addresses of all businesses in which the debtor was an officer, director, partner, or managing executive of a corporation, partnership, sole proprietorship, or was a self-employed professional within the two years immediately preceding the commencement of this case, or in which the debtor owned 5 percent or more of the voting or equity securities within the two years immediately preceding the commencement of this case.

b. If the debtor is a partnership, list the names and addresses of all businesses in which the debtor was a partner or owned 5 percent or more of the voting securities, within the two years immediately preceding the commencement of this case.

c. If the debtor is a corporation, list the names and addresses of all businesses in which the debtor was a partner or owned 5 percent or more of the voting securities within the two years immediately preceding the commencement of this case.

NAME	ADDRESS	NATURE OF BUSINESS	BEGINNING AND ENDING DATES OF OPERATION

---

17. **Books, records and financial statements**

None ☐ **a. List all bookkeepers and accountants who within the six years immediately preceding the filing of this bankruptcy case kept or supervised the keeping of books of account and records of the debtor.**

NAME AND ADDRESS	DATES SERVICES RENDERED

None ☐ **b. List all firms or individuals who within the two years immediately preceding the filing of this bankruptcy case have audited the books of account and records, or prepared a financial statement of the debtor.**

NAME	ADDRESS	DATES SERVICES RENDERED

None ☐ c. List all firms or individuals who at the time of the commencement of this case were in possession of the books of account and records of the debtor. If any of the books of account and records are not available, explain.

NAME ADDRESS

None ☐ d. List all financial institutions, creditors and other parties, including mercantile and trade agencies, to whom a financial statement was issued within the two years immediately preceding the commencement of this case by the debtor.

NAME AND ADDRESS DATE ISSUED

---

18. Inventories

None ☐ a. List the dates of the last two inventories taken of your property, the name of the person who supervised the taking of each inventory, and the dollar amount and basis of each inventory.

DATE OF INVENTORY	INVENTORY SUPERVISOR	DOLLAR AMOUNT OF INVENTORY (Specify cost, market or other basis)

None ☐ b. List the name and address of the person having possession of the records of each of the two inventories reported in a., above.

DATE OF INVENTORY	NAME AND ADDRESSES OF CUSTODIAN OF INVENTORY RECORDS

---

19. Current Partners, Officers, Directors and Shareholders

None ☐ a. If the debtor is a partnership, list the nature and percentage of partnership interest of each member of the partnership.

NAME AND ADDRESS	NATURE OF INTEREST	PERCENTAGE OF INTEREST

None ☐ b. If the debtor is a corporation, list all officers and directors of the corporation, and each stockholder who directly or indirectly owns, controls, or holds 5 percent or more of the voting securities of the corporation.

NAME AND ADDRESS	TITLE	NATURE AND PERCENTAGE OF STOCK OWNERSHIP

20. Former partners, officers, directors and shareholders

None ☐ a. If the debtor is a partnership, list each member who withdrew from the partnership within one year immediately preceding the commencement of this case.

NAME	ADDRESS	DATE OF WITHDRAWAL

None ☐ b. If the debtor is a corporation, list all officers, or directors whose relationship with the corporation terminated within one year immediately preceding the commencement of this case.

NAME AND ADDRESS	TITLE	DATE OF TERMINATION

21. Withdrawals from a partnership or distributions by a corporation

None ☐ If the debtor is a partnership or corporation, list all withdrawals or distributions credited or given to an insider, including compensation in any form, bonuses, loans, stock redemptions, options exercised and any other perquisite during one year immediately preceding the commencement of this case.

NAME & ADDRESS OF RECIPIENT, RELATIONSHIP TO DEBTOR	DATE AND PURPOSE OF WITHDRAWAL	AMOUNT OF MONEY OR DESCRIPTION AND VALUE OF PROPERTY

* * * * * * *

[If completed by an individual or individual and spouse]

I declare under penalty of perjury that I have read the answers contained in the foregoing statement of financial affairs and any attachments thereto and that they are true and correct.

Date ____________________ Signature of Debtor ____________________

Date ____________________ Signature of Joint Debtor (if any) ____________________

• • • • • •

[If completed on behalf of a partnership or corporation]

I, declare under penalty of perjury that I have read the answers contained in the foregoing statement of financial affairs and any attachments thereto and that they are true and correct to the best of my knowledge, information and belief.

Date ____________________ Signature ____________________

Print Name and Title

[An individual signing on behalf of a partnership or corporation must indicate position or relationship to debtor.]

____ continuation sheets attached

Penalty for making a false statement: Fine of up to $500,000 or imprisonment for up to 5 years, or both. 18 U.S.C. § 152 and 3571

Form 8

Form 8. CHAPTER 7 INDIVIDUAL DEBTOR'S STATEMENT OF INTENTION

[Caption as in Form 16B]

CHAPTER 7 INDIVIDUAL DEBTOR'S STATEMENT OF INTENTION

1. I, the debtor, have filed a schedule of assets and liabilities which includes consumer debts secured by property of the estate.

2. My intention with respect to the property of the estate which secures those consumer debts is as follows:

a. *Property to Be Surrendered.*

	Description of Property	Creditor's name
1.		
2.		
3.		

b. *Property to Be Retained. [Check applicable statement of debtor's intention concerning reaffirmation, redemption, or lien avoidance.]*

	Description of property	Creditor's name	Debt will be reaffirmed pursuant to § 524(c)	Property is claimed as exempt and will be redeemed pursuant to § 722	Lien will be avoided pursuant to § 522(f) and property will be claimed as exempt
1.					
2.					
3.					
4.					
5.					

3. I understand that § 521(2)(B) of the Bankruptcy Code requires that I perform the above stated intention within 45 days of the filing of this statement with the court, or within such additional time as the court, for cause, within such 45-day period fixes.

Date: ____________________

____
Signature of Debtor

(Added Aug. 1, 1991.)

NOTES OF ADVISORY COMMITTEE ON RULES

This form is derived from former Official Form No. 8A. Rule 1007(b)(2) requires the debtor to serve a copy of this statement on the trustee and all creditors named in the statement. In a joint case, if the property and debts of both debtors are the same, the form may be adapted for joint use. If joint debtors have separate debts, however, each debtor must use a separate form.

COMMITTEE NOTE

The title page of the form has been amended to conform to the headings used on Forms 9A-9I. Alternate versions of Form 9E and Form 9F have been added for the convenience of districts that routinely set a deadline for filing claims in a chapter 11 case. When a creditor receives the alternate form in a case, the box labeled "Filing Claims" will contain information about the bar date as follows: "Deadline for filing a claim: __(date)__." If no deadline is set in a particular case, either the court will use Form 9E or Form 9F, as appropriate, or the alternate form will be used with the following sentence appearing in the box labeled "Filing Claims": "When the court sets a deadline for filing claims, creditors will be notified."

Form 9. NOTICE OF COMMENCEMENT OF CASE UNDER THE BANKRUPTCY CODE, MEETING OF CREDITORS, AND FIXING OF DATES

9A.........Chapter 7, Individual/Joint, No-Asset Case

9B.........Chapter 7, Corporation/Partnership, No-Asset Case

9C.........Chapter 7, Individual/Joint, Asset Case

9D.........Chapter 7, Corporation/Partnership, Asset Case

9E.........Chapter 11, Individual/Joint Case

9E (Alt.)..Chapter 11, Individual/Joint Case

9F.........Chapter 11, Corporation/Partnership Case

9F (Alt.)..Chapter 11, Corporation/Partnership Case

9G.........Chapter 12, Individual/Joint Case

9H.........Chapter 12, Corporation/Partnership Case

9I.........Chapter 13, Individual/Joint Case

FORM B9E (Alt.)
(Rev. 5/92)

United States Bankruptcy Court

Case Number

____________________ District of ____________________

NOTICE OF COMMENCEMENT OF CASE UNDER CHAPTER 11 OF THE BANKRUPTCY CODE, MEETING OF CREDITORS, AND FIXING OF DATES

(Individual or Joint Debtor Case)

In re (Name of Debtor)	Address of Debtor	Soc. Sec./Tax Id. Nos.
	Date Filed (or Converted)	
Addressee:	Address of the Clerk of the Bankruptcy Court	
Name and Address of Attorney for Debtor	Name and Address of Trustee	
Telephone Number	Telephone Number	

This is a converted case originally filed under chapter ______ on ________________

FILING CLAIMS

DATE, TIME, AND LOCATION OF MEETING OF CREDITORS

DISCHARGE OF DEBTS

____________________ is the Deadline to File a Complaint to Determine Dischargeability of Certain Types of Debts.

COMMENCEMENT OF CASE. A petition for reorganization under chapter 11 of the Bankruptcy Code has been filed in this court by or against the person or persons named above as the debtor, and an order for relief has been entered. You will not receive notice of all documents filed in this case. All documents filed with the court, including lists of the debtor's property, debts, and property claimed as exempt are available for inspection at the office of the clerk of the bankruptcy court.

CREDITORS MAY NOT TAKE CERTAIN ACTIONS. A creditor is anyone to whom the debtor owes money or property. Under the Bankruptcy Code, the debtor is granted certain protection against creditors. Common examples of prohibited actions by creditors are contacting the debtor to demand repayment, taking action against the debtor to collect money owed to creditors or to take property of the debtor, and starting or continuing foreclosure actions, repossessions, or wage deductions. If unauthorized actions are taken by a creditor against a debtor, the court may penalize that creditor. A creditor who is considering taking action against the debtor or the property of the debtor should review § 362 of the Bankruptcy Code and may wish to seek legal advice. The staff of the clerk of the bankruptcy court is not permitted to give legal advice.

MEETING OF CREDITORS. The debtor (both husband and wife in a joint case) is required to appear at the meeting of creditors on the date and at the place set forth above for the purpose of being examined under oath. Attendance by creditors at the meeting is welcomed, but not required. At the meeting, the creditors may examine the debtor and transact such other business as may properly come before the meeting. The meeting may be continued or adjourned from time to time by notice at the meeting, without further written notice to creditors.

EXEMPT PROPERTY. Under state and federal law, the debtor is permitted to keep certain money or property as exempt. If a creditor believes that an exemption of money or property is not authorized by law, the creditor may file an objection. An objection must be filed not later than 30 days after the conclusion of the meeting of creditors.

DISCHARGE OF DEBTS. The debtor may seek a discharge of debts. A discharge means that certain debts are made unenforceable against the debtor personally. Creditors whose claims against the debtor are discharged may never take action against the debtor to collect the discharged debts. If a creditor believes that the debtor should not receive a discharge under § 1141(d)(3)(C) of the Bankruptcy Code, timely action must be taken in the bankruptcy court in accordance with Bankruptcy Rule 4004(a). If a creditor believes that a debt owed to the creditor is not dischargeable under § 523(a)(2), (4), or (6) of the Bankruptcy Code, timely action must be taken in the bankruptcy court by the deadline set forth above in the box labeled "Discharge of Debts." Creditors considering taking such action may wish to seek legal advice.

PROOF OF CLAIM. Schedules of creditors have been or will be filed pursuant to Bankruptcy Rule 1007. Any creditor holding a scheduled claim which is not listed as disputed, contingent, or unliquidated as to amount may, but is not required to, file a proof of claim in this case. Creditors whose claims are not scheduled or whose claims are listed as disputed, contingent, or unliquidated as to amount and who desire to participate in the case or share in any distribution must file their proofs of claim. A creditor who desires to rely on the schedules of creditors has the responsibility for determining that the claim is listed accurately. The place to file a proof of claim, either in person or by mail, is the office of the clerk of the bankruptcy court. Proof of claim forms are available in the clerk's office of any bankruptcy court.

PURPOSE OF CHAPTER 11 FILING. Chapter 11 of the Bankruptcy Code enables a debtor to reorganize pursuant to a plan. A plan is not effective unless approved by the court at a confirmation hearing. Creditors will be given notice concerning any plan, or in the event the case is dismissed or converted to another chapter of the Bankruptcy Code. The debtor will remain in possession of its property and will continue to operate any business unless a trustee is appointed.

For the Court: ____________________ Clerk of the Bankruptcy Court __________ Date

FORM B9F (Alt.)
(Rev. 5/92)

United States Bankruptcy Court

Case Number

_______________ District of _______________

NOTICE OF COMMENCEMENT OF CASE UNDER CHAPTER 11 OF THE BANKRUPTCY CODE, MEETING OF CREDITORS, AND FIXING OF DATES

(Corporation/Partnership Case)

In re (Name of Debtor)	Address of Debtor	Soc. Sec./Tax Id. Nos.
	Date Filed or Converted	
Addressee:	Address of the Clerk of the Bankruptcy Court	

☐ Corporation ☐ Partnership

Name and Address of Attorney for Debtor	Name and Address of Trustee
Telephone Number	Telephone Number

This is a converted case originally filed under chapter _______ on _______________

FILING CLAIMS

DATE, TIME, AND LOCATION OF MEETING OF CREDITORS

COMMENCEMENT OF CASE. A petition for reorganization under chapter 11 of the Bankruptcy Code has been filed in this court by or against the debtor named above, and an order for relief has been entered. You will not receive notice of all documents filed in this case. All documents filed with the court, including lists of the debtor's property and debts, are available for inspection at the office of the clerk of the bankruptcy court.

CREDITORS MAY NOT TAKE CERTAIN ACTIONS. A creditor is anyone to whom the debtor owes money or property. Under the Bankruptcy Code, the debtor is granted certain protection against creditors. Common examples of prohibited actions by creditors are contacting the debtor to demand repayment, taking action against the debtor to collect money owed to creditors or to take property of the debtor, and starting or continuing foreclosure actions, or repossessions. If unauthorized actions are taken by a creditor against a debtor, the court may penalize that creditor. A creditor who is considering taking action against the debtor or the property of the debtor should review § 362 of the Bankruptcy Code and may wish to seek legal advice. If the debtor is a partnership, remedies otherwise available against general partners are not necessarily affected by the filing of this partnership case. The staff of the clerk of the bankruptcy court is not permitted to give legal advice.

MEETING OF CREDITORS. The debtor's representative, as specified in Bankruptcy Rule 9001(5) is required to appear at the meeting of creditors on the date and at the place set forth above for the purpose of being examined under oath. Attendance by creditors at the meeting is welcomed, but not required. At the meeting, the creditors may examine the debtor and transact such other business as may properly come before the meeting. The meeting may be continued or adjourned from time to time by notice at the meeting, without further written notice to creditors.

PROOF OF CLAIM. Schedules of creditors have been or will be filed pursuant to Bankruptcy Rule 1007. Any creditor holding a scheduled claim which is not listed as disputed, contingent, or unliquidated as to amount may, but is not required to, file a proof of claim in this case. Creditors whose claims are not scheduled or whose claims are listed as disputed, contingent, or unliquidated as to amount and who desire to participate in the case or share in any distribution must file their proofs of claim. A creditor who desires to rely on the schedule of creditors has the responsibility for determining that the claim is listed accurately. The place to file a proof of claim, either in person or by mail, is the office of the clerk of the bankruptcy court. Proof of claim forms are available in the clerk's office of any bankruptcy court.

PURPOSE OF CHAPTER 11 FILING. Chapter 11 of the Bankruptcy Code enables a debtor to reorganize pursuant to a plan. A plan is not effective unless approved by the court at a confirmation hearing. Creditors will be given notice concerning any plan, or in the event the case is dismissed or converted to another chapter of the Bankruptcy Code. The debtor will remain in possession of its property and will continue to operate any business unless a trustee is appointed.

For the Court: ______________________________ ______________
Clerk of the Bankruptcy Court Date

COMMITTEE NOTE

The form has been amended to accommodate inclusion of the priority afforded in §507(a)(8) of the Code, which was added by Pub. L. No. 101-647, (Crime Control Act of 1990), and to avoid the necessity of further amendment to the form if other priorities are added to §507(a) in the future. In addition, sections 4 and 5 of the form have been amended to clarify that only prepetition arrearages and charges are to be included in the amount of the claim.

United States Bankruptcy Court
_______________ District of _______________

PROOF OF CLAIM

In re (Name of Debtor)

Case Number

NOTE: This form should not be used to make a claim for an administrative expense arising after the commencement of the case. A "request" for payment of an administrative expense may be filed pursuant to 11 U.S.C. § 503.

Name of Creditor
(The person or other entity to whom the debtor owes money or property)

Name and Address Where Notices Should be Sent

Telephone No.

☐ Check box if you are aware that anyone else has filed a proof of claim relating to your claim. Attach copy of statement giving particulars.

☐ Check box if you have never received any notices from the bankruptcy court in this case.

☐ Check box if the address differs from the address on the envelope sent to you by the court.

THIS SPACE IS FOR COURT USE ONLY

ACCOUNT OR OTHER NUMBER BY WHICH CREDITOR IDENTIFIES DEBTOR:

Check here if this claim ☐ replaces ☐ amends a previously filed claim, dated: __________

1. BASIS FOR CLAIM
   - ☐ Goods sold
   - ☐ Services performed
   - ☐ Money loaned
   - ☐ Personal injury/wrongful death
   - ☐ Taxes
   - ☐ Other (Describe briefly)
   - ☐ Retiree benefits as defined in 11 U.S.C. § 1114(a)
   - ☐ Wages, salaries, and compensation (Fill out below)
     Your social security number __________
     Unpaid compensation for services performed
     from __________ (date) to __________ (date)

2. DATE DEBT WAS INCURRED

3. IF COURT JUDGMENT, DATE OBTAINED:

4. CLASSIFICATION OF CLAIM. Under the Bankruptcy Code all claims are classified as one or more of the following: (1) Unsecured nonpriority, (2) Unsecured Priority, (3) Secured. It is possible for part of a claim to be in one category and part in another.
CHECK THE APPROPRIATE BOX OR BOXES that best describe your claim and STATE THE AMOUNT OF THE CLAIM AT TIME CASE FILED.

☐ SECURED CLAIM $ __________
Attach evidence of perfection of security interest
Brief Description of Collateral:
☐ Real Estate ☐ Motor Vehicle ☐ Other (Describe briefly)

Amount of arrearage and other charges at time case filed included in secured claim above, if any $ __________

☐ UNSECURED NONPRIORITY CLAIM $ __________
A claim is unsecured if there is no collateral or lien on property of the debtor securing the claim or to the extent that the value of such property is less than the amount of the claim.

☐ UNSECURED PRIORITY CLAIM $ __________
Specify the priority of the claim.
- ☐ Wages, salaries, or commissions (up to $2000), earned not more than 90 days before filing of the bankruptcy petition or cessation of the debtor's business, whichever is earlier—11 U.S.C. § 507(a)(3)
- ☐ Contributions to an employee benefit plan—11 U.S.C. § 507(a)(4)
- ☐ Up to $900 of deposits toward purchase, lease, or rental of property or services for personal, family, or household use—11 U.S.C. § 507(a)(6)
- ☐ Taxes or penalties of governmental units—11 U.S.C. § 507(a)(7)
- ☐ Other—Specify applicable paragraph of 11 U.S.C. § 507(a) __________

5. TOTAL AMOUNT OF CLAIM AT TIME CASE FILED: $ __________ (Unsecured) $ __________ (Secured) $ __________ (Priority) $ __________ (Total)

☐ Check this box if claim includes charges in addition to the principal amount of the claim. Attach itemized statement of all additional charges.

6. CREDITS AND SETOFFS: The amount of all payments on this claim has been credited and deducted for the purpose of making this proof of claim. In filing this claim, claimant has deducted all amounts that claimant owes to debtor.

7. SUPPORTING DOCUMENTS: *Attach copies of supporting documents*, such as promissory notes, purchase orders, invoices, itemized statements of running accounts, contracts, court judgments, or evidence of security interests. If the documents are not available, explain. If the documents are voluminous, attach a summary.

8. TIME-STAMPED COPY: To receive an acknowledgement of the filing of your claim, enclose a stamped, self-addressed envelope and copy of this proof of claim.

THIS SPACE IS FOR COURT USE ONLY

Date	Sign and print the name and title, if any, of the creditor or other person authorized to file this claim (attach copy of power of attorney, if any)

Penalty for presenting fraudulent claim: Fine of up to $500,000 or imprisonment for up to 5 years, or both. 18 U.S.C. §§ 152 and 3571.

Form 10

Rule 2002(g) requires the clerk to update the mailing list in the case by substituting the address provided by a creditor on a proof of claim, if that address is different from the one supplied by the debtor. The form contains checkboxes to assist the clerk in performing this duty. The form also alerts the trustee when the claim is an amendment to or replacement for an earlier claim.

Form 15. ORDER CONFIRMING PLAN

[Caption as in Form 16A]

ORDER CONFIRMING PLAN

The plan under chapter 11 of the Bankruptcy Code filed by ____________________, on ______________ [*if applicable*, as modified by a modification filed on ______________,] or a summary thereof, having been transmitted to creditors and equity security holders; and

It having been determined after hearing on notice that the requirements for confirmation set forth in 11 U.S.C. § 1129(a) [*or, if appropriate*, 11 U.S.C. § 1129(b)] have been satisfied;

IT IS ORDERED that:

The plan filed by ______________________________, on ______________, *[If appropriate, include dates and any other pertinent details of modifications to the plan]* is confirmed. A copy of the confirmed plan is attached.

Dated: ______________________

BY THE COURT

____
United States Bankruptcy Judge.

(Added Aug. 1, 1991.)

NOTES OF ADVISORY COMMITTEE ON RULES

This form is derived from former Official Form No. 31. The form has been simplified to avoid the necessity of repeating the statutory requirements of 11 U.S.C. § 1129(a). In the case of an individual chapter 11 debtor, Form 18 may be adapted for use together with this form.

Form 16A

Form 16A. CAPTION (FULL)

UNITED STATES BANKRUPTCY COURT
____________________ DISTRICT OF ____________________

In re ____,)
[Set forth here all names including married,)
maiden, and trade names used by debtor within)
last 6 years.])
Debtor) Case No. ______________
)
) Chapter ______________
)
Social Security No(s). ____________________ and all)
Employer's Tax Identification Nos. *[if any]* __________)
____________________)

[Designation of Character of Paper]

(Added Aug. 1, 1991.)

Notes of Advisory Committee on Rules

This form has been transferred from former Official Form No. 1, which included the form of caption for the case. Rule 9004(b) requires a caption to set forth the title of the case. Rule 1005 provides that the title of the case shall include the debtor's name, all other names used by the debtor within six years before the commencement of the case, and the debtor's social security and tax identification numbers. This form of caption is prescribed for use on the petition, the notice of the meeting of creditors, the order of discharge, and the documents relating to a chapter 11 plan, (Official Forms 1, 9, 12, 13, 14, 15, and 18). See Rule 2002(m). In the petition (Official Form 1), and the notice of the meeting of creditors, (Official Form 9), the information required by Rule 1005 appears in a block format. A notation of the chapter of the Bankruptcy Code under which the case is proceeding has been added to the form.

Form 16B. CAPTION (SHORT TITLE)

UNITED STATES BANKRUPTCY COURT
____________________ DISTRICT OF ____________________

In re ______________________________,
Debtor

Case No. ____________________

Chapter ____________________

[Designation of Character of Paper]

(Added Aug. 1, 1991.)

Notes of Advisory Committee on Rules

This form of caption is prescribed for general use in filing papers in a case under the Bankruptcy Code. Rule 9004(b) requires a caption to set forth the title of the case, and Rule 1005 specifies that the title must include all names used by the debtor within six years before the commencement of the case and the debtor's social security and tax identification numbers. This information is necessary in the petition, the notice of the meeting of creditors, the order of discharge, and the documents relating to the plan in a chapter 11 case. See Rule 2002(m) and Official Form 16A. In other notices, motions, applications, and papers filed in a case, however, a short title containing simply the name of the debtor or joint debtors may be used. Additional names, such as any under which the debtor has engaged in business, may be included in the short title as needed.

Form 16C

Form 16C. CAPTION OF ADVERSARY PROCEEDING

UNITED STATES BANKRUPTCY COURT
________________ DISTRICT OF ________________

In re ________________, *Debtor*	Case No. __________
________________, *Plaintiff*	Chapter __________
v.	
________________, *Defendant*	Adv. Proc. No. __________

COMPLAINT [*or* other Designation]

(Added Aug. 1, 1991.)

NOTES OF ADVISORY COMMITTEE ON RULES

This form previously was numbered Official Form No. 34. A notation of the chapter of the Bankruptcy Code under which the case is proceeding has been added to the form. Rule 7010 refers to this form as providing the caption of a pleading in an adversary proceeding.

Form 18

Form 18. DISCHARGE OF DEBTOR

[Caption as in Form 16A]

DISCHARGE OF DEBTOR

It appearing that a petition commencing a case under title 11, United States Code, was filed by or against the person named above on ____________________, and that an order for relief was entered under chapter 7, and that no complaint objecting to the discharge of the debtor was filed within the time fixed by the court [*or* that a complaint objecting to discharge of the debtor was filed and, after due notice and hearing, was not sustained];

IT IS ORDERED that

1. The above-named debtor is released from all dischargeable debts.

2. Any judgment heretofore or hereafter obtained in any court other than this court is null and void as a determination of the personal liability of the debtor with respect to any of the following:

(a) debts dischargeable under 11 U.S.C. § 523;

(b) unless heretofore or hereafter determined by order of this court to be nondischargeable, debts alleged to be excepted from discharge under clauses (2), (4) and (6) of 11 U.S.C. § 523(a);

(c) debts determined by this court to be discharged.

3. All creditors whose debts are discharged by this order and all creditors whose judgments are declared null and void by paragraph 2 above are enjoined from instituting or continuing any action or employing any process or engaging in any act to collect such debts as personal liabilities of the above-named debtor.

Dated: ____________________

BY THE COURT

____

United States Bankruptcy Judge.

(Added Aug. 1, 1991.)

NOTES OF ADVISORY COMMITTEE ON RULES

This form previously was numbered Official Form No. 27. The form has been revised to accommodate cases commenced by the filing of either a voluntary or an involuntary petition.

Form No. B 250A

SUMMONS IN AN ADVERSARY PROCEEDING

United States Bankruptcy Court

_____________ **District of** _____________

In re

Bankruptcy Case No.

Debtor

Plaintiff

Adversary Proceeding No.

Defendant

SUMMONS IN AN ADVERSARY PROCEEDING

YOU ARE SUMMONED and required to submit a motion or answer to the complaint which is attached to this summons to the clerk of the bankruptcy court within 30 days after the date of issuance of this summons, except that the United States and its offices and agencies shall submit a motion or answer to the complaint within 35 days.

Address of Clerk

At the same time, you must also serve a copy of the motion or answer upon the plaintiff's attorney.

Name and Address of Plaintiff's Attorney

If you make a motion, your time to answer is governed by Bankruptcy Rule 7012.

IF YOU FAIL TO RESPOND TO THIS SUMMONS, YOUR FAILURE WILL BE DEEMED TO BE YOUR CONSENT TO ENTRY OF A JUDGMENT BY THE BANKRUPTCY COURT AND JUDGMENT BY DEFAULT MAY BE TAKEN AGAINST YOU FOR THE RELIEF DEMANDED IN THE COMPLAINT.

____

Clerk of the Bankruptcy Court

_____________________ By: _____________________

Date *Deputy Clerk*

CERTIFICATE OF SERVICE

Form B 250A **PROCEDURAL FORMS**

I, ______________________, certify that I am, and at all times
(name)
during the service of process was, not less than 18 years of age and not a party to the matter concerning which service of process was made. I further certify that the service of this summons and a copy of the complaint was made ____________ by:
(date)

☐ Mail Service: Regular, first class United States mail, postage fully pre-paid, addressed to:

☐ Personal Service: By leaving the process with defendant or with an officer or agent of defendant at:

☐ Residence Service: By leaving the process with the following adult at:

☐ Publication: The defendant was served as follows: [Describe briefly]

☐ State Law: The defendant was served pursuant to the laws of the State of ______________, as follows: [Describe briefly]
(name of state)

Under penalty of perjury, I declare that the foregoing is true and correct.

______________________ ______________________________
Date *Signature*

Print Name		
Business Address		
City	State	Zip

Form No. B 250B

SUMMONS AND NOTICE OF PRETRIAL CONFERENCE IN AN ADVERSARY PROCEEDING

United States Bankruptcy Court

__________ **District of** __________

In re

Bankruptcy Case No.

Debtor

Plaintiff

Adversary Proceeding No.

Defendant

SUMMONS AND NOTICE OF PRETRIAL CONFERENCE IN AN ADVERSARY PROCEEDING

YOU ARE SUMMONED and required to submit a motion or answer to the complaint which is attached to this summons to the clerk of the bankruptcy court within 30 days after the date of issuance of this summons, except that the United States and its offices and agencies shall submit a motion or answer to the complaint within 35 days.

Address of Clerk

At the same time, you must also serve a copy of the motion or answer upon the plaintiff's attorney.

Name and Address of Plaintiff's Attorney

If you make a motion, your time to answer is governed by Bankruptcy Rule 7012.

YOU ARE NOTIFIED that a pretrial conference of the proceeding commenced by the filing of the complaint will be held at the following time and place.

Address	Room
	Date and Time

IF YOU FAIL TO RESPOND TO THIS SUMMONS, YOUR FAILURE WILL BE DEEMED TO BE YOUR CONSENT TO ENTRY OF A JUDGMENT BY THE BANKRUPTCY COURT AND JUDGMENT BY DEFAULT MAY BE TAKEN AGAINST YOU FOR THE RELIEF DEMANDED IN THE COMPLAINT.

____
Clerk of the Bankruptcy Court

__________________ By: ____________________________
Date *Deputy Clerk*

CERTIFICATE OF SERVICE

I, ________________________ (name), certify that I am, and at all times during the service of process was, not less than 18 years of age and not a party to the matter concerning which service of process was made. I further certify that the service of this summons and a copy of the complaint was made __________ (date) by:

☐ Mail Service: Regular, first class United States mail, postage fully pre-paid, addressed to:

☐ Personal Service: By leaving the process with defendant or with an officer or agent of defendant at:

☐ Residence Service: By leaving the process with the following adult at:

☐ Publication: The defendant was served as follows: [Describe briefly]

☐ State Law: The defendant was served pursuant to the laws of the State of __________________ (name of state), as follows: [Describe briefly]

Under penalty of perjury, I declare that the foregoing is true and correct.

Date	*Signature*

Print Name		
Business Address		
City	State	Zip

Form No. B 250C

SUMMONS AND NOTICE OF TRIAL IN AN ADVERSARY PROCEEDING

United States Bankruptcy Court

________ District of ________

In re	Bankruptcy Case No.
Debtor	
Plaintiff	Adversary Proceeding No.
Defendant	

SUMMONS AND NOTICE OF TRIAL IN AN ADVERSARY PROCEEDING

YOU ARE SUMMONED and required to submit a motion or answer to the complaint which is attached to this summons to the clerk of the bankruptcy court within 30 days after the date of issuance of this summons, except that the United States and its offices and agencies shall submit a motion or answer to the complaint within 35 days.

Address of Clerk

At the same time, you must also serve a copy of the motion or answer upon the plaintiff's attorney.

Name and Address of Plaintiff's Attorney

If you make a motion, your time to answer is governed by Bankruptcy Rule 7012.

YOU ARE NOTIFIED that a trial of the proceeding commenced by the filing of the complaint will be held at the following time and place.

Address	Room
	Date and Time

IF YOU FAIL TO RESPOND TO THIS SUMMONS, YOUR FAILURE WILL BE DEEMED TO BE YOUR CONSENT TO ENTRY OF A JUDGMENT BY THE BANKRUPTCY COURT AND JUDGMENT BY DEFAULT MAY BE TAKEN AGAINST YOU FOR THE RELIEF DEMANDED IN THE COMPLAINT.

____
Clerk of the Bankruptcy Court

________________ By: ________________________
Date *Deputy Clerk*

CERTIFICATE OF SERVICE

I, ____________________ (name), certify that I am, and at all times during the service of process was, not less than 18 years of age and not a party to the matter concerning which service of process was made. I further certify that the service of this summons and a copy of the complaint was made __________ (date) by:

☐ Mail Service: Regular, first class United States mail, postage fully pre-paid, addressed to:

☐ Personal Service: By leaving the process with defendant or with an officer or agent of defendant at:

☐ Residence Service: By leaving the process with the following adult at:

☐ Publication: The defendant was served as follows: [Describe briefly]

☐ State Law: The defendant was served pursuant to the laws of the State of ________________ (name of state), as follows: [Describe briefly]

Under penalty of perjury, I declare that the foregoing is true and correct.

____________________ Date

____________________ Signature

Print Name		
Business Address		
City	State	Zip

Glossary

Glossary
11 USC §101 et seq
UCC §§2-105, 3-104, 8-102, 9-105, 9-106, 9-109
FRBP 7001, 7004, 9001-9002

Glossary

1. **Account:** any right to payment for goods sold or leased or for services rendered which is not evidenced by an instrument or chattel paper. *UCC §9-106.*
2. **Action:** adversary complaint, contested petition, or proceeding to determine any contested matter. *FRBP 7001, 9002(1), 9014.*
3. **Adequate Protection:** bankruptcy term of art whereby the debtor or trustee provides protection against a decrease in value of an entity's interest in property of the debtor or estate. *11 USC §§361-364; FRBP 4001, 9014.*
4. **Adversary Complaint:** lawsuit filed in the bankruptcy court; equivalent of a complaint filed in federal district court or petition filed in state court; action that commences an adversary proceeding. *FRBP 7001 et seq.*
5. **Affiliate:** entity that directly or indirectly owns or controls or has the power to vote at least 20 per cent of the outstanding voting stock or securities of a bankruptcy debtor; a corporation 20 per cent or more of the stock or securities of which is directly or indirectly owned or controlled by the debtor or by an entity that directly or indirectly owns or controls or has the power to vote at least 20 per cent of the outstanding voting stock of the debtor; a person whose business is operated under a lease or operating agreement with a bankruptcy debtor or substantially all of whose property is operated under an operating agreement with the debtor; an entity that operates the debtor's business or substantially

all of the debtor's property under a lease or operating agreement. However, an affiliate does not include an entity that holds stock or securities of the debtor in an agency or fiduciary capacity if such entity does not have the sole discretionary power to vote the stock or securities or if such entity holds the stock or securities solely as collateral, unless the power to vote the securities has been exercised by such entity. *11 USC §101(2).*

6. **Allowed Claim:** claim of a creditor allowed by the bankruptcy court for sharing in distribution of the estate. *11 USC §§501-502, 541.*

7. **Bankruptcy Case:** case or proceeding under Title 11, United States Code (Bankruptcy Code), commenced by filing a bankruptcy petition. *11 USC §§301-304.*

8. **Bankruptcy Code:** Title 11, United States Code, effective Oct 1, 1979, as amended.

9. **Chattel:** personal property; tangible property, other than real property, that is capable of being moved; or goods.

10. **Chattel Paper:** writing(s) which evidence both a monetary obligation and a security interest in or lease of specific goods; group of writings which evidences both a security agreement or lease and instrument(s). However, chattel paper does not include a charter or contract involving the use or hire of a vessel. *UCC §9-105(1)(b).*

11. **Claim:** right to payment; equitable remedy for breach of performance that creates a right to payment of any kind—liquidated or unliquidated, contingent or noncontingent, secured or unsecured, disputed or undisputed. *11 USC §101(5).*

12. **Clerk:** bankruptcy clerk if one has been appointed in the federal judicial district or federal district court officer or clerk responsible for bankruptcy records in the federal judicial district. *FRBP 9001(3), 9002(3).*

13. **Collateral:** secured property; property subject to a lien or security interest, including accounts and chattel paper which have been sold. *UCC §9-105(1)(c).*

14. **Commodity Broker:** a futures commission merchant, foreign futures commission merchant, clearing organization, leverage transaction merchant, or commodity options dealer. *11 USC §101(6).*

15. **Community Claim:** claim in a bankruptcy case against the debtor and his spouse. *11 USC §§101(7), 541(a)(2).*

16. **Confirmation:** court approval. *11 USC §§901, 944, 1129, 1225, 1325.*

17. **Consumer Debt:** debt incurred by an individual primarily for personal, family, or household purposes. *11 USC §101(8).*

18. **Consumer Property:** property purchased by an individual primarily for personal, family, or household purposes.

19. **Contested Matter:** A motion or request filed with the bankruptcy court which is opposed by the party (debtor, trustee, creditors' committee)

against whom relief is sought; litigation to resolve an actual dispute, other than an adversary proceeding, before the bankruptcy court. *FRBP 9014, advisory committee's note.*

20. **Contingent:** dependent upon a future or subsequent event.
21. **Court:** bankruptcy court unless indicated otherwise. *See FRBP 9001(4), 9002(4).*
22. **Creditor:** entity that holds a claim against the bankruptcy debtor. *11 USC §101(10).*
23. **Debt:** liability or obligation owed by the bankruptcy debtor on a claim. *11 USC §101(12).*
24. **Debtor:** entity against whom a claim is held; bankruptcy debtor, including a person or municipality unless indicated otherwise. *11 USC §101(13).*
25. **Debtor-In-Possession (DIP):** Chapter 11 or 12 bankruptcy debtor. *11 USC §§1101(1), 1203.*
26. **Discharge:** release of the debtor from personal liability for a debt. *11 USC §§524, 727, 944(b), 1141(d), 1228, 1328.*
27. **Effective Date:** the date a statute or section of such statute becomes operative, governing law; the date a Chapter 9, 11, 12, or 13 plan becomes effective by its terms and provisions which have been confirmed (approved) by the court. *11 USC §§901, 943, 1129, 1225, 1325.*
28. **Enactment Date:** the date the United States President signs legislation passed by both Houses of Congress.
29. **Entity:** person, estate, trust, governmental unit, and the U.S. trustee. *11 USC §101(15).*
30. **Equipment:** goods used or bought for use primarily in business, including farming or a profession that are not inventory or farm products. *UCC §9-109(2).*
31. **Equity:** difference between the market value of the property subject to a lien or security interest and the amount of the debt owed to the secured creditor.
32. **Equity Security:** share in a corporation, whether transferable or denominated as "stock" or other similar security; a limited partner's interest in a limited partnership; or a warrant or right to purchase, sell, or subscribe to such share, security, or interest in a corporation or limited partnership. However, the term does not include a right to convert such share, security, or interest. *11 USC §101(16).*
33. **Equity Security Holder:** entity that holds an equity security of the debtor. *11 USC §101(17).*
34. **Estate:** bankruptcy estate, unless indicated otherwise, which includes all the presently owned property of the debtor and interests of the debtor in such property on the date the petition is filed, regardless of where the property may be located, and certain property acquired postpetition. *11 USC §§541, 1207, 1306.*

35. **Exempt Property:** property of the debtor that is not subject to the claims of unsecured creditors. *11 USC §522(b), (d).*

36. **Farming Operation:** includes any type of farming; ranching; production or raising of crops, poultry, livestock or their products in an unmanufactured state; and tillage of the soil. *11 USC §101(21).*

37. **Farmout Agreement:** written agreement under which an owner of a right to drill, produce, or operate liquid or gaseous hydrocarbons on property agrees or has agreed to transfer all or part of his right to another entity, and as consideration for the transfer, such entity, directly or through its agents or assigns, agrees to develop or produce liquid or gaseous hydrocarbons on the subject property by performing drilling, reworking, recompleting, testing, or similar operations. *Pub L No 102-486 (1992), amending and adding 11 USC §101(21A), effective Oct 24, 1992.*

38. **Financial Institution:** commercial or savings bank, industrial savings bank, savings and loan association, or trust company; a "customer" when a financial institution is acting as the customer's agent or custodian under a securities contract. *11 USC §101(22).*

39. **Forward Contract:** contract for the purchase, sale, or transfer of a commodity, as defined under the Commodity Exchange Act, 7 USC §1 *et seq,* or any similar good, article, service, right, or interest which is or becomes the subject of dealing in the forward contract trade. *11 USC §101(26).*

40. **Fraudulent Transfer:** voluntary or involuntary transfer of property by the debtor to prevent creditors from receiving payment or for which the debtor did not receive reasonably equivalent legal consideration (value) in the exchange. *11 USC §548.*

41. **Goods:** includes all things movable at the time of identification of a contract for sale or time a security interest attaches, including the unborn young of animals, growing crops, or standing timber to be cut, but excluding money, investment securities, documents, and things in action. *UCC §2-105(1).*

42. **Governmental Unit:** the United States, any department, agency or instrumentality of the United States, a state, commonwealth, district, territory, municipality, foreign state, foreign or domestic government. The term does not include the U.S. trustee while serving as trustee under any bankruptcy case. *11 USC §101(27).*

43. **Ground:** legal basis for a cause of action or lawsuit; a count.

44. **Health-Care Provider:** person who directly provides health care or administers a facility in which health care is provided. The term includes a physician, dentist, nurse, podiatrist, optometrist, physician assistant, or ancillary personnel employed under the supervisor of a physician, hospital, alcohol and drug abuse treatment facility, outpatient facility, or health maintenance organization. *§608(b)(2) of second Title VI, Joint Resolution Making Continuing Appropriations for Fiscal Year 1987 and for Other Purposes, Pub L No 99-591 (1986), as amended and made permanent by the*

Retiree Benefits Bankruptcy Protection Act of 1988, Pub L No 100-334, 102 Stat 610 (1988); see 11 USC §1114.

45. **His:** generic term which includes "his," "her," or "its."

46. **Indenture:** a mortgage, deed of trust, or indenture under which there is an outstanding security, other than a voting trust certificate, that constitutes either a claim against the debtor, a claim secured by a lien on any of the debtor's property, or an equity security of the debtor. *11 USC §101(28).*

47. **Indenture Trustee:** trustee under an indenture. *11 USC §101(29).*

48. **Individual:** natural person, not a partnership or corporation.

49. **Insider:** includes a relative, partnership, or general partner of an individual debtor; a shareholder, member of the board of directors, officer, or control person of a corporate debtor; a general partner, relative of a general partner, or person in control of a partnership debtor; or an elected official or relative of such official of a municipal debtor. *11 USC §101(31).*

50. **Insolvent:** financial condition of an entity whose aggregate debts exceed the fair value of such entity's property, excluding property fraudulently transferred or claimed as exempt; financial condition of a municipality which is unable to pay or generally is not paying its debts as they become due, unless such debts are subject to a bona fide dispute; financial condition of a partnership whose aggregate debts exceed the aggregate fair value of its property and the sum of the excess value of each general partner's nonpartnership property, excluding property fraudulently transferred or claimed as exempt. *11 USC §101(32).*

51. **Instrument:** a negotiable instrument or certificated security or any other writing which evidences a right to payment of money and is not a security agreement or lease and which is transferred by delivery with any necessary endorsement or assignment in the ordinary course of business. *UCC §§3-104, 8-102, 9-105(1)(i).*

52. **Intellectual Property:** includes patent application; trade secret; invention process, design, or plant protected under Title 35, United States Code; plant variety; work of authorship (copyright) protected under Title 17, United States Code; and mask work protected under Title 17, Chapter 9, United States Code. *11 USC §101(56) [sic].*

53. **Inventory:** goods held for sale or lease or to be furnished under contracts of service; raw materials; work in progress; or materials used or consumed in a business. *UCC §9-109(4).*

54. **Judgment:** appealable order of the court. *FRBP 9001(7), 9002(5).*

55. **Judicial Lien:** lien obtained by judgment, levy, sequestration, or other legal or equitable process or proceeding. *11 USC §101(36).*

56. **Jurisdiction:** power or authority of the court to hear a case, proceeding, or contested matter and render a valid judgment. *28 USC §§151, 157, 1334.*

57. **Lien:** charge against or interest in property to secure payment of a debt or performance of an obligation. *11 USC §101(37).*

58. **Liquidated:** reduced to cash or its equivalent or to a dollar amount.

59. **Liquidated Claim:** claim reduced or capable of being reduced to a dollar amount by reference to a simple agreement or by computation. *See In re Robertson, 143 Bankr 76 (Bankr ND Tex 1992); In re Sylvester, 19 Bankr 671 (BAP 9th Cir 1982).*

60. **Margin Payment:** for purposes of Title 11, United States Code, a payment or deposit of cash, security, or other property commonly known in the forward contract trade as original margin, initial margin, maintenance margin, or variation margin. The term also includes mark-to-market payments or variation payments. 11 USC §101(38).

61. **Meeting of Creditors:** meeting between the debtor and creditors in a Chapter 7, 11, 12, or 13 case, at which the U.S. trustee or his designee presides and the debtor is examined under oath about the administration of the bankruptcy case and the bankruptcy estate. 11 USC §§341, 343; FRBP 2003.

62. **Municipality:** political subdivision, public agency, or instrumentality of a state. *11 USC §101(40).*

63. **Noncontingent:** not subject to or triggered by any future or subsequent event. *See In re Robertson, 143 Bankr 76 (Bankr ND Tex 1992).*

64. **Order for Relief:** the filing of a voluntary petition; an order of the bankruptcy court declaring a debtor to be a bankruptcy debtor after an involuntary petition is filed under Title 11, United States Code. *11 USC §§301-303.*

65. **Party-In-Interest:** an entity that has an interest in the debtor or the bankruptcy estate and standing to appear and be heard before the bankruptcy court, generally including the debtor, creditor, trustee, U.S. trustee, as well as any authorized representative of such persons. *11 USC §§307, 1109; 18 USC §155.*

66. **Person:** individual, partnership, or corporation, but generally not a governmental unit. *11 USC §101(41).*

67. **Personal Jurisdiction:** power or authority of the court to force a defendant or party-in-interest to appear and defend himself.

68. **Personal Property:** goods, chattel, or tangible movable property.

69. **Petition:** bankruptcy petition which commences a voluntary or involuntary bankruptcy case under Title 11, United States Code. *11 USC §§101(42), 301-304.*

70. **Post-Petition:** occurring after a voluntary or involuntary bankruptcy petition is filed.

71. **Preferential Transfer:** voluntary or involuntary transfer of property by the debtor, generally on or within 90 days before a bankruptcy petition is filed, or between 90 days and one year pre-petition if to an insider,

and which favors one or more creditors to the disadvantage of other unsecured creditors. *11 USC §547.*

72. **Pre-Petition:** occurring before a voluntary or involuntary bankruptcy petition is filed.

73. **Presumption:** reasonable inference which the law requires be accepted as true based upon the actual existence of certain facts; may be rebuttable or irrebuttable.

74. **Priority Claim:** claim entitled to first payment or satisfaction before other claims are paid; claim of an unsecured creditor entitled to first payment from the debtor's bankruptcy estate before payments to general unsecured creditors. *11 USC §§503(a)-(b), 507.*

75. **Proceeding:** bankruptcy case; hearing before the bankruptcy or federal district court concerning a contested or uncontested issue in a bankruptcy case. *FRBP 9013-9014.*

76. **Pro-Rata:** same percentage of payment received by each member of a particular category or class of creditors.

77. **Purchaser:** the buyer or transferee of a voluntary transfer. The term includes an initial transferee and any immediate or mediate (subsequent) transferee of the initial transferee. *11 USC §§101(43), 550.*

78. **Reaffirmation of Debt:** agreement approved by the court and entered into by the debtor and creditor before the debtor is granted a discharge, whereby the debtor agrees to remain personally liable for a debt that would otherwise be dischargeable under the Bankruptcy Code. *11 USC §524(c)-(d).*

79. **Real Property:** land or real estate, together with all improvements or property thereon which cannot be removed without causing damage to the land.

80. **Redemption of Property:** procedure by which an individual debtor redeems or buys back tangible, personal, exempt or abandoned consumer property which secures a consumer debt, otherwise dischargeable under the Bankruptcy Code, by paying to the secured creditor the lesser of the fair market value of the collateral or the amount of the allowed claim owed to the creditor. *11 USC §§523, 722.*

81. **Request:** motion for relief sought in a bankruptcy case, which may be contested or uncontested. *FRBP 9013-9014.*

82. **Repo Participant:** entity who had an outstanding repurchase agreement with the debtor on or during the immediate 90 days before the debtor's bankruptcy petition was filed. *11 USC §101(46).*

83. **Repurchase Agreement [and Reverse Repurchase Agreement]:**agreement providing for the transfer of certificates of deposit, eligible bankers' acceptances, or securities with a simultaneous agreement by the transferee to transfer to the transferor, at a definite date not exceeding one year after such transfer or on demand, such certificates of deposits, acceptances, or securities which are the direct obliga-

tion of, or fully guaranteed (principal and interest) by, the United States or any agency of the United States against the transfer of funds by the transferee. *11 USC §101(47).*

84. **Secured Claim:** claim secured by a lien or charge against property of the debtor or estate to secure payment of a debt or performance of an obligation; amount of a creditor's debt owed to the debtor subject to a setoff against a creditor's claim held against the debtor. *11 USC §101(37), (50)-(51), 506(a).*

85. **Secured Creditor:** creditor who holds a lien against property of the debtor or estate or whose claim is subject to a setoff. *11 USC §§101(5), (10), (37), (50)-(51), 506(a), 553.*

86. **Security:** includes note, stock, treasury stock, bond, debenture, certificate of deposits, voting trust security, pre-organization certificate or subscription, transferable share, interest of a limited partner in a limited partnership, but does not include check, currency, draft, bill of exchange, bank letter of credit, commodities future contract, forward contract, or option, warrant, or right to subscribe or purchase a commodity or commodities futures contract. *11 USC §101(49).*

87. **Security Agreement:** agreement that creates or provides for a security interest. *11 USC §101(50).*

88. **Security Interest:** lien created by an agreement entered into by the debtor and secured creditor. *11 USC §101(51).*

89. **Serve:** manner prescribed by law by which a motion, request, or other document filed in court is made available for receipt by the other parties. *FRBP 7004-7005.*

90. **Service of Process:** manner prescribed by law by which a lawsuit (complaint, adversary complaint) with a summons are made available for receipt by the defendant. *FRBP 7004.*

91. **Settlement Payment:** for purposes of Title 11, United States Code, a preliminary, partial, interim, final, or net settlement payment; settlement payment on account; or other similar payment commonly used in the forward contract trade. *11 USC §101(39).*

92. **Setoff:** procedure by which a creditor may offset a claim against the debtor against an obligation owed to the debtor. Thus, a creditor with a $100 allowed claim against the debtor and who owes the debtor $25 may be allowed to setoff the two amounts for net allowed claim of $75. *11 USC §§362(a)(7), 506(a), 553.*

93. **Standing Trustee:** individual appointed by the U.S. trustee under 28 USC §586(b), subject to approval of the United States Attorney General, to serve as a trustee under Chapter 12 or 13 cases. *Id.*

94. **State:** includes the District of Columbia and Puerto Rico, except for purposes of defining a Chapter 9 debtor. *11 USC §101(52).*

95. **Statutory Lien:** lien arising solely by force of a statute, or lien for distress of rent, whether statutory or not; but does not include a judicial

lien, even if such lien is provided by, dependant on, or made fully effective by, a statute. *11 USC §101(53).*

96. **Stockbroker:** includes a person dealing in transactions in securities for another's account or with members of the general public from or for such person's own account. *11 USC §101(54) [sic].*

97. **Subject Matter Jurisdiction:** power or authority of the court to hear a particular subject matter and render a valid judgment. *11 USC §§151, 157, 1334.*

98. **Swap Agreement:** includes a rate swap agreement, basis swap, forward rate agreement, commodity swap, interest rate option, forward foreign exchange agreement, rate cap agreement, rate floor agreement, rate collar agreement, currency swap agreement, cross-currency rate swap agreement, currency option, as well as any combination of or master agreement for such agreements. *11 USC §101(55) [sic].*

99. **Swap Participant:** entity that has an outstanding, pre-petition swap agreement with the debtor. *11 USC §101(56) [sic].*

100. **Timeshare Interest:** the interest purchased under a timeshare plan. *11 USC §101(57) [sic].*

101. **Timeshare Plan:** includes a membership agreement, tenancy-in-common, sale, lease, deed, license, rental agreement, right-to-use agreement, or any other means, except an exchange program, by which a purchaser, in exchange for legal consideration, buys an interest in or right to use improved or unimproved accommodations, facilities, or recreational sites for a specified time less than a full year during any given year, and which extends for more than three years. The years do not have to be consecutive. *11 USC §101(57) [sic].*

102. **Transfer:** includes every mode of disposing of or parting with property or an interest in property of the debtor, including retention of title as a security interest and foreclosure of the debtor's equity of redemption. The transfer may be voluntary or involuntary, direct or indirect, absolute or conditional. *11 USC §101(54) [sic].*

103. **Title 11, United States Code:** the Bankruptcy Code, as amended.

104. **Trustee:** officer of the court and representative of the bankruptcy estate, including a Chapter 9 debtor and Chapter 11 or 12 debtor-in-possession. *11 USC §§322-323, 902(5), 1101(1), 1203; FRBP 9001(10).*

105. **United States Trustee:** Individual appointed by the U.S. Attorney General to serve in each of 21 regions comprised of federal judicial districts, for a term of 5 years and thereafter until a successor is appointed and qualifies. The term includes an assistant U.S. trustee appointed by the Attorney General and any designee selected by the U.S. trustee. *11 USC §307; 28 USC §§581-582; FRBP 9001(11).*

106. **Unliquidated:** not reduced or capable of being reduced to a dollar amount by reference to an agreement of simple contract.

107. **Unsecured Claim:** claim that is not secured by a lien. *11 USC §101(5), (37), (50)-(51).*

108. **Unsecured Creditor:** a creditor who does not hold a lien against, or security interest in, property of the debtor or bankruptcy estate or whose claim is not subject to a setoff. *11 USC §§506(a), 553.*

109. **Venue:** the place or locality where a lawsuit or bankruptcy case may lawfully be filed. *28 USC §§1408-1410, 1412.*

110. **Void:** a legal nullity; never existed in the eyes of the law.

111. **Voidable:** valid, legal, and existing until declared void by a court of law.

Cases

B

C

D

V

W

Statutes

Federal Rules of Bankruptcy Procedure

Index

A

E

G

H

I

J

O

P

R

T

U

V

W